KARST LANDFORMS

KARST LANDFORMS

Marjorie M. Sweeting

Macmillan

First published 1972 by
THE MACMILLAN PRESS LTD
London and Basingstoke
Associated companies in New York Toronto
Dublin Melbourne Johannesburg and Madras

SBN 333 01165 1

Phototypeset by Oliver Burridge Filmsetting Ltd.,
Crawley, Sussex
and printed in Great Britain by
Compton Printing Ltd.
Aylesbury, Bucks.

To my research students from Oxford and Cambridge

Contents

Preface   ix

Acknowledgements   x

List of Photographs   xi

List of Figures   xiii

List of Tables   xvi

1   INTRODUCTION   1

2   KARST LIMESTONES   10

3   THE SOLUTION OF LIMESTONES   24

4   THE LANDFORMS. ENCLOSED HOLLOWS OF MODERATE DIMENSIONS: DOLINES   44

5   THE SUPERFICIAL FEATURES OF LIMESTONES: KARREN OR LAPIÉS   74

6   KARST VALLEYS   103

7   WATER SINKS AND WATER SWALLOWS   122

8   CAVES   129

9   CAVE DEPOSITS   173

10 POLJES   192

11 KARST SPRINGS   208

12 KARST WATER AND KARST WATER TRACING   218

13 KARST HYDROLOGY   235

14 TYPES OF KARST   252

15 TROPICAL KARST   270

16 OTHER TYPES OF KARST   297

17 THE EFFECT OF THE CYCLIC CONCEPT UPON THE KNOWLEDGE OF
    KARST LANDFORMS   309

18 THE AIMS AND APPLICATIONS OF KARST LANDFORM STUDY   315

    SELECTED GLOSSARY   332

    Index of Authors   353

    Index   356

Preface

To write a book dealing with such a rapidly advancing field as karst morphology is never satisfactory, but a review of the present state of karst studies has long been necessary. Any book attempting to survey the whole field of karst landforms is bound to be unequal in its treatment of the different facets of the subject. This work therefore deals with those aspects which I have personally found interesting or have had the opportunity to work upon. I am very conscious of the many aspects of karst morphology which are dealt with inadequately or not at all.

The work on which this book is based began when I was a research student, later Research Fellow, at Newnham College, Cambridge, during which time I had the opportunity to study karst landforms in the British Isles and Europe. I have since then been fortunate enough to work in many of the world's karst areas, work which has been done in collaboration with many organisations, particularly the Geological Survey Department of Jamaica, the U.S. Geological Survey in Puerto Rico, the Departments of Geography of the Australian National University of Canberra and of Guelph and McMaster Universities in Ontario, and the Food and Agriculture Organisation of the United Nations. I am indebted not only to these organisations for their assistance, but also to the kind hospitality of many people in Jugoslavia and others interested in karst studies throughout the world. The work has also been facilitated by generous grants from many bodies but especially from the Leverhulme Trust, the Royal Society and the Royal Geographical Society and from Oxford University.

The present time is one of great advances in geomorphology. I therefore regard this work as bridging two phases in the development of the subject; it links the historical and classical phases to the modern ideas of landform analysis and Karst hydrology. The inclusion of much material on the historical development of Karst studies was felt to be justified by the fact that much of the literature is virtually unknown to English readers. There is furthermore an enormous literature on Karst landforms, on the chemistry of waters, and on carbonate rocks, of which only a minute selection is given in this book. Though the countries of Southern and Central Europe led the way in the beginnings of Karst studies, much significant work is now being done in Great Britain and North America.

This book has been written while I have been a Fellow of St Hugh's College and a member of the Oxford School of Geography, in a number of periods of sabbatical leave. I have drawn freely upon the work of my former research students, from both Oxford and Cambridge; for this reason and because the future of karst studies lies in their hands, this book is for them.

Mr Kenneth Addison of St Peter's College has given me great assistance with the compilation of the bibliography. My father (G. S. Sweeting of the Imperial College) has assisted with the proof-reading. I am also grateful to Miss Mary Potter of Oxford for substantial help in the preparation of the diagrams.

M. M. SWEETING

Oxford

January 1972

ix

Acknowledgements

The author and publisher wish to thank and acknowledge the help given by the following in connection with the photographs listed below:

Audiovisual Services Dept., University of Guelph, Canada Nos. 4(*a*), 5, 6, 7(*a*), 9(*b*), 16(*b*), 19(*a*), 23, 24, 25, 26, 28, 38, 40(*a*), 40(*b*), 49(*a*), 51, 54, 57
D. C. Ford Nos. 9(*a*), 30, 31, 32, 33(*a*), 33(*b*), 34, 35, 36, 37(*a*), 37(*b*), 39, 45, 46
Jamaica Geological Survey No. 47(*b*)
W. Monroe Nos. 7(*b*), 15(*b*), 48(*a*), 49(*b*), 50

List of Photographs

1(*a*) Micrite 17
1(*b*) Sparry limestone 17
1(*c*) Biomicrite 17
2(*a*) Algal reef limestone 21
2(*b*) Jointing in Carboniferous
Limestone 22
3(*a*) Development of joints 23
3(*b*) Curved jointing in
Carboniferous Limestone 23
4(*a*) Dolines, Montenegro 48
4(*b*) The doline of the Atiyo shi
dai, Japan 48
5 Kotlici, snow dolines,
Julian Alps 51
6 Solution subsidence 62
7(*a*) Collapse doline, Slovenia 65
7(*b*) Tres Pueblos sink 67
8 Cockpits, Brit. Honduras 69
9(*a*) Rillenkarren, Canadian
Rockies 78
9(*b*) Rillenkarren, E. Transvaal 79
10(*a*) Variations of rillenkarren:
'cockling' or 'crinkling' 81
10(*b*) Rillenkarren and rainpits 81
11 Trittkarren, Co. Clare,
Ireland 82
12 Rinnenkarren and rundkarren,
Westmorland 83
13(*a*) Spitzkarren and solution
basins, N.W. Australia 84
13(*b*) Solution basins,
N.W. Yorkshire 85
14 Kluftkarren, N.W. Yorkshire 86
15(*a*) Bogaz, N.W. Australia 88
15(*b*) Zanjon in Puerto Rico 89
16(*a*) Rundkarren, N.W. Yorkshire 90
16(*b*) Rundkarren, New Zealand 91
17 Karrenfussnäpfe, N.W. Yorks. 92

18 Hohlkarren, N.W. Yorkshire 93
19(*a*) Soil-covered karren, S. Africa 94
19(*b*) Soil-covered karren,
West Virginia, U.S.A. 94
20(*a*) Freshly exposed limestone
pavement 95
20(*b*) Limestone pavement after
exposure for about ten years 95
21 Limestone pavement,
N.W. Yorks. 97
22 Glacial erratic block on
limestone pavement 99
23 Allogenic valley, Jugoslavia 104
24 Dry river bed, N.W. Yorkshire 105
25 Tufa deposition 110
26 Disappearing river, Yorks. 113
27 Recess of the Brooking Spring,
N.W. Australia 115
28 Dry valley, Tasmania 118
29(*a*) River disappearing into cave 123
29(*b*) Stream disappearing into joint
fissures 124
30 Cave with bedded plane-type
roof 135
31 Cave breakdown 136
32 Joint-determined passage 137
33(*a*) Phreatic tube 142
33(*b*) Phreatic solution features 143
34 Scallops on cave wall 145
35 Features formed by vadose
flow 147
36 Ice crystals in cave 175
37(*a*) Stalactites in cave 178
37(*b*) Stalactites formed under a
glacier 178
38 Stalagmite 182
39 Moon milk 190
40(*a*) Flooded polje, Jugoslavia 196

40(*b*)	Corrosion surface, S. France	197
41	Malham Tarn area, N.W. Yorkshire	204
42	Spring in West Virginia, U.S.A.	210
43	Dinaric holokarst	257
44	Fluviokarst, W. Virginia	260
45	Emerging schichttreppenkarst	264
46	Periglacial karst	268
47	Air views of the Cockpit Country, Jamaica	271
48(*a*)	Karst types in Puerto Rico: doline karst and	277
48(*b*)	Lares limestone karst	277
49(*a*)	Asymmetric kegelkarst and	279
49(*b*)	Solution holes, Puerto Rico	279
50	Tower karst, Puerto Rico	281
51	Air view of karst with mogotes, Puerto Rico	282
52	Foot caves, N.W. Australia	285
53	Pediment surface on limestone, N.W. Australia	286
54	Development of tower karst, N.W. Australia	292
55	Tufa barrier, N.W. Australia	293
56	Fossil karst, Poland	304
57	Pseudo-karst, N. Bohemia	307

List of Figures

1	Karstlands in Jugoslavia	2
2	Main areas of karst landforms	7
3	Main constituents of limestones	16
4	Textural characteristics of carbonate rocks	16
5	Differential solubility of limestones in N.W. Yorkshire	18
6	Properties of CO_2 (and H_2CO_3), HCO_3^- and CO_3^{--} in solution at different pH values	25
7	Solution of limestone	27
8(a)	Relationship between the calcium content of saturated solutions at different temperatures and the pH	28
8(b)	Saturation of water samples with respect to calcium carbonate	29
9	Solution of calcium in karst waters, N.W. Yorkshire	29
10	Calcium carbonate solubilities at 10°C	31
11	Calcium carbonate content of karst waters in the Peak district	33
12	Variations in calcium content of the Malham waters	33
13(a)	Difference in calcium carbonate content as a function of stream discharge	35
13(b)	Calcium carbonate content of the major Mendip risings	36
13(c)	Variations in calcium carbonate concentrations at East Mendip risings	36
14(a)	Storm variations in discharge, limestone removal, and calcium carbonate concentration	37

14(b)	Discharge and limestone removal	37
15	Calcium carbonate values in the Mendips	38
16(a)	Doline formation	46
16(b)	Types of doline	46
17	Doline	47
18	Dolines in the Mendips	49
19	Variations in doline formation	49
20	Formation of asymmetrical dolines	50
21	Zonation of vegetation in a large doline	52
22	Dolines in Indiana	52
23	Limestone plateau, Ingleborough	54
24	Factors affecting karst depressions	55/56
25	Uvala	57
26	Karstic features, Malham Tarn district	58
27	Stages in the development of shake-holes	60
28	Shake-hole development	61
29	Solution Subsidences, S. Wales	63
30	Formation of collapse hollows, S. Africa	64
31	The Škocjanske Caves	64
32	Collapse depressions, Ireland	66
33	Limestone, Puerto Rico	68
34	Section of central Cockpit Country, Jamaica	70
35	Stylised cross-section, Cockpit Country	71
36	Typical uvala	73
37(a)	Rillenkarren	80
37(b)	Trittkarren	81

38	Development of grikes	87
39	Surface features of the limestones, Sarawak	88
40	Surveyed clint on Twisleton Scar	90
41	Karrenfussnäpfe	91
42	A method of determining the relative ages of runnels and grikes	92
43	Hohlkarre	93
44	Limestone pavement in Chapel-le-Dale	96
45	Superficial limestone deposits	98
46	The effects of dip and slope on pavement form	99
47	Pavement types in Chapel-le-Dale and Twisleton Dale	101
48	Geomorphological features of the Ingleborough district	106
49	The Plitvice lakes	109
50	Blind valleys	111
51	Gouffre de Roc de Corn	112
52	Feizor Nick	114
53(a)	Dry valley system, Derbyshire	116
53(b)	Dry valley system of the Avon basin, Wiltshire	117
54	Trow Gill	118
55	Box valley network near Geikie Gorge, N.W. Australia	119
56	Profile of the Greta valley	119
57	Buchan Caves country, Aust.	126
58	Swallow holes and springs, north-central Jamaica	128
59	Mixture corrosion	132
60	Cross-section of Yorkshire stream passage	134
61	Buchan-type cave	136
62	Forms of vertical features in caves, Ireland	137
63(a)	Dachstein Mammuth Cave	138
63(b)	Suggested tectonic development of the Dachstein caverns	139
64(a)	Passages formed by forced flow	141
64(b)	Passages formed by free flow	141
65	Bore passages	141
66(a)	Typical roof cavities	143
66(b)	Suggested formation of some cave roof features	143
67	Network cave pattern	144
68	Scallop formation	144
69	Cave passages in Slovenia	145
70	The Postojna Cave, Jugoslavia	146
71	The development of the Mendip Caves	150
72	Demänová Caves, Czechoslovakia	152
73	Formation of vertical shafts	154
74	Carlsbad Caverns	160
75	The Predjama Cave	162
76	Tunnel Cave, W. Kimberley, W.A.	164
77	Cross-section through the formations near Mammoth Cave	165
78	Gaping Gill cavern system	167
79(a)	Shafts under different conditions of precipitation	169
79(b)	Development of shafts	169
80	Gouffre Grotte Berger	170
81	Cave collapse, Golconda Caverns	171
82	Formation of subterranean ice in the absence of air circulation	175
83	Stalactite growth	177
84	Crystal structure of a stalactite	179
85	Schematic vertical section of a stalagmite	182
86	Old Napier Downs Cave	187
87	Livno Polje	193
88	Cerkniško Polje	195
89	Underground drainage connections of the Cerkniško Polje	195
90	Evolution of corrosion planes	198
91	Map of the closed basins of the Parnassos–Ghiona area, Greece	201

92	Karst landforms, north-central Jamaica	203
93	Physical map of the Carran depression	205
94	The drainage of Leck and Casterton Fells	209
95(*a*)	Vauclusian spring	212
95(*b*)	Intermittent spring	212
96	Argostoli	215
97(*a*)	Distribution of solution through a limestone mass	220
97(*b*)	Solutional transport of $CaCo_3$	220
98	Models of limestone waters	224
99	Solution patterns	225
100	Swallet input and rising output discharge	227
101	Map of the vicinity of Caveside, Tasmania	229
102	Results of *Lycopodium* spore tests in the Dachsteingebiet	230
103	Flood-pulse characteristics	232
104	Flood-pulse experiment Black River, Jamaica	233
105	Theories of karst waters	236
106	Patterns of groundwater flow in limestone	238
107	Imotski Polje	241
108	Regime of the Poljes in the Ljubljanica area	242
109(*a*)	Mendip hydrology	245
109(*b*)	Limestone hydrology, Blackdown, Mendips	245
110	Extent and morphological types of the Dinaric karst	256
111	Fluviokarst, Franconian Jura	260
112	Schichttreppenkarst	265
113	The Triglav Pothole, Slovenian Alps	266
114	Tropical karst	272
115	Formation of the Goenoeng Sewoe kegelkarst	275
116	Longitudinal section of a glade	280
117(*a*)	Towers and 'flats' in Sarawak	283
117(*b*)	Cave formation by stream erosion	283
118	Cliff-foot caves, Sarawak	284
119	Cliff-foot caves, W. Kimberley, W.A.	285
120	Pediment profiles	287
121	Cross-section of tower karst	288
122	Distribution of tower karst in southern China and North Vietnam	289
123	Joint-controlled karst	292
124	Fossil tower karst	304
125	Karst cycle	310
126(*a*)	Some karst features in the Ingleborough district	316
126(*b*)	Swallet relationships in the Ingleborough district	317
127	Lilaia spring group, Greece	321/322

List of Tables

I(a) Selected analyses of carbonate rocks 11

I(b) Physical properties of selected carbonate rocks 11

II Classification of rocks intermediate in composition between pure limestones and dolomites 12

III Inorganic constituents of marine invertebrates 14

IV The variety of textures of limestone 19

V The solubility (in water deprived of CO_2) of $CaCO_3$ and $MgCO_3$ 24

VI The solubility of CO_2 in pure water 24

VII The solubility of $CaCO_3$ at 25°C under different CO_2 pressures 24

VIII The solubility of $CaCO_3$ at various temperatures for two important CO_2 pressures 25

IX The solubility of dolomite, calcite and magnesite 28

X Corbel's figures for the amount of limestone lost by solution in karst regions 41

XI Limestone corrosion in different areas 42

XII Table of simple karren types 75

XIII Stalactite drips 180

XIV Characteristics of Carboniferous Limestone and Millstone Grit waters 219

XV Calcium and magnesium content of waters from various sites in the Yorkshire dales 223

XVI Correlation matrix of calcium carbonate observations at six sampling stations in the Malham area 226

1 Introduction

THE STUDY of karst landforms is a branch of geomorphology, the study of the landscape features of the earth's surface and the processes by which these landforms are formed. The essential characteristic of areas of karst landforms is the presence of vertical and underground drainage. All karst regions are areas of massive limestones. Of all the commonly occurring rocks, limestone is the only one which is slightly soluble in ordinary atmospheric water and in the acidulated water associated with vegetation. As a result of the solution of the rock, drainage in limestones sinks into the ground and does not become integrated into surface rivers, whereas in non-karst areas the surface water becomes organised and systematised into valleys to form a connected network. The surface and underground relief features in limestones are shaped in a vertical sense. The parts of the surface where the water sinks into the ground become isolated from one another, so that the relief forms appear unconnected and disparate; hollows or pits are formed where the drainage sinks into the ground, giving the landscape a pitted character. Organised river valleys developed on other rocks become replaced by a series of disconnected and enclosed hollows, forming a landscape that has until quite recently been regarded as of a chaotic or disorderly nature. [1]. Earlier writers on karst areas distinguished between the so-called normal landscape (or tallandschaft) and the corrosion landscape (or korrosionlandschaft) of limestones, which distinction was made by Grund [2]. Jovan Cvijič, the first to write a comprehensive treatise on karst landforms, used the terms *wannenlandschaft* (pitted relief) and *blättersteppige* (blistered relief) to describe the landscape [3], while A. Penck frequently referred to the *unruhigen* (disordered) nature of the relief [4]. Today, as a result of detailed work in karst areas, we are beginning to find karst relief less disordered.

Thus the landforms of limestone areas and the processes which give rise to them are so distinctive that they are now known universally as *karst landforms* and *karst processes*. The word *karst* is the German form of the Slovene word *kras* and the Italian word *carso*. The word itself is probably of pre-Indo-European origin and originally denoted bare, stony ground. Kras when spelt with a capital denotes in Slovenian the region between the Gulf of Trieste in the west, the flysch (non-limestone) valley of the Vipava in the north, the basin of the Pivka in the east, and the valley of the Notranjska Reka in the southeast. When the area of Kras was first described in modern times, it formed the barest and most stony region of the routeway from Central Europe to the Mediterranean. In this once deforested region, karst landforms are clearly visible and are its main characteristic, and in this way the word kras or karst became common in the geomorphological literature. In Slovenia, the most characteristic part of the Kras is usually regarded as the Notranjski Kras (Inner Carniola karst), the area which includes the Postojna caves, the Cerkniško polje and the Rakov Škocjan. But the whole region of the Slovene karst between Trieste and Ljubljana is now considered the *Classical Karst* area and has been the focus of much attention by scientists from about

1

1850. The karst areas of Jugoslavia to the south of the Slovene karst, i.e. those along and inland from the Adriatic coast as far as the Albanian frontier, are collectively known as the Dinaric karst, but are not part of the Classical Karst. As a result of reafforestation, the original Classical Karst is now covered with forests and much less bare than many other areas of the Dinaric karst. Karstlands cover 25 per cent of all Jugoslavia, and in Slovenia 35 per cent of the total area, about 20,250 km² [5]. The distribution of karstlands in Jugoslavia is shown in the map, Fig. 1.

The actual extensive use of the word karst dates from the systematic surveys of Istria and Carniola by the Austrians during the late 1840s; in these works the word is used in a regional sense only. Later, the word came to be used in a generic sense, as a type area for caves and limestone studies [6]. The mid-nineteenth century in particular saw, as in so many aspects of the geological and geographical sciences, the beginnings of the branch of natural history with which we are dealing. Thus in this period we have the first real description of the caves of the Classical Karst and the first Cave Society

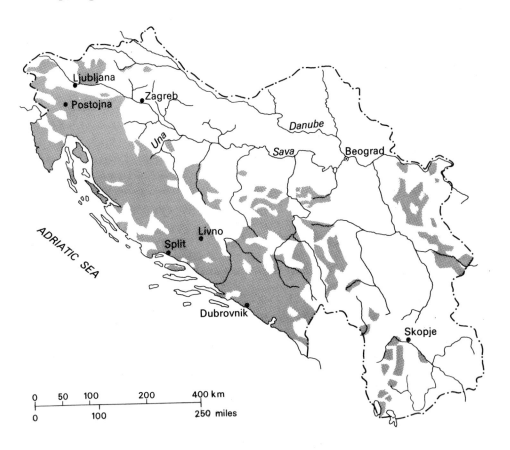

Fig. 1　Karst lands in Jugoslavia (from Ref. 131)

formed in Vienna in 1879, the first attempts to describe and account for the 'swallow holes' of the chalk country of southern England [7], and the first descriptions and exploration of the Yorkshire caves [8]. Both Tietze [9] and Mojsisovics [10] in 1880 were able to publish work which had titles of *Zur Geologie der Karsterscheinung*, and Reyer in 1881 also wrote on *Studien über Karstrelief* [11]. Among the many works published during the nineteenth century on the caves and waters of the Classical Karst region, the most important is that of Schmidl on the *Grotten und Höhlen von Adelsberg, Planina und Laas* [13] in 1854. It was therefore not surprising that Cvijič, the Serbian geographer, with a great love of the karst and trained under A. Penck in Vienna, should in 1893 produce *Das Karstphänomen,* a work that marks the beginning of karst studies proper [3]. Cvijič was not only the first to discuss the dominance of solution in the process of landform development; he was also the first to give clear simple definitions of karst landforms, such as dolines, karren, poljes. A study of Cvijič's work is therefore essential for any student of karst morphology.

From this it is apparent that karst studies are essentially a central and south-east European science and, though much of the literature is written in either French or German, a considerable part of it is in the Slav languages, Slovene, Serbo-Croat and Czech. Thus as far as the British and Americans are concerned the subject is to some extent an exotic one. However, France has about one-fifth of her area covered by limestones, and the French have always been active in karst studies. This activity dates in part from the visit of E. Martel to the classical karstlands in 1879. Martel, who lived from 1859 to 1938, wrote many books on the caves and underground waters of France and elsewhere. These include, in particular, the *Nouveau Traité des Eaux Souterraines* [13], *Les Abîmes* [14], and *Irlande et Cavernes Anglaises* [15]; in 1895 he was the first to descend into the greatest English cave, Gaping Gill. Also, Fournier contributed some very important studies of the hydrology and caves of the Jura [16].

In addition to the word karst, other words of a Slovene or Serbo-Croatian origin have become part of geomorphological literature; these words include *doline, polje* and *jama,* whose definitions will be discussed later. From the word karst many derivations are now widely used, notably *karstic,* an adjective frequently applied to landscapes which possess some or all of the landforms to be discussed in this book; *karstification,* a word used to describe the processes by which limestones are dissolved and vertical and underground drainage established; *karstified,* a term frequently applied to landscapes which have been subjected to karst processes in either the past or present geological periods; and *karstland,* an area of the world's surface possessing karst landforms.

A characteristic of karst regions is that each local area has its own names and terms for the various karst phenomena. Caves, sinking streams and large springs have different names according to the language and patois of the district in which they occur. Though this is a difficulty common to all landform studies, it is particularly difficult in karst landforms, because of the abundance of the terms. As in other branches of landform study, words have been taken from local languages and invested with a precise scientific meaning which they did not have originally. As Lehmann has said, 'La terminologie karstique s'est développée suivant les formes des paysages du karst et de ses régions voisins' [17]. Because of this difficulty, a glossary of the most widely used names for

Karst landforms is provided at the end of this book. It is of interest that the Commission Française des Phénomeènes Karstiques (Comité National de Géographie) has recently produced a *Vocabulaire français des phénomènes karstiques,* which gives a clear statement of the French equivalents of the terms used in the study of karst landforms [18]. Lexicons of speleological and karst terms in five languages have also appeared in the publications of the International Congress of Speleology [19]. An International Conference on Karst terminology took place in 1971, and the last few years have seen the appearance of many glossaries of Karst terminology. The most notable of these are those published for the United States Geological Survey by Watson H. Monroe [480] and for the F.A.O. by David Burdon.

The sinking of water and its circulation underground is the essence of the karst process. This process is dominated by a chemical (solutional) activity, and true karst landforms result largely from the action of one erosive process, namely solution. Such landforms are as distinctive as those formed by other erosive agents, such as rivers, glaciers and the sea, but in some respects more difficult and more subtle to analyse. This is due first to the fact that solutional processes, though sensitive and persistent, are slow and imperceptible and, compared with rivers, glaciers and waves, do not appear to alter the landscape within a short time; secondly, to the apparent unconnectedness and lack of relationship of the landforms; thirdly, to the absence of water on the surface and the frequently rocky and desolate nature of the terrain; fourthly, to the fact that a substantial proportion of karst landforms are underground, i.e. caves, and are therefore difficult and often impossible to explore; and fifthly, there is not necessarily any clear relationship between the landforms which occur at the surface and those which occur underground. Karst areas must always be investigated three-dimensionally, and any work on karst landforms must include a discussion of caves.

However, because karst processes are almost entirely of one kind, chemical, and because predominantly only one major rock group is involved, the problems concerned with these landforms should in many ways be simpler than those in areas involving several kinds of denudation agents and more than one major rock type. Furthermore, the introduction of more sophisticated chemical techniques and the advances in the study of carbonate rocks in the last few years have given a much better idea of the rates of solution of limestones; until these techniques were available, karst morphology developed more slowly than other branches of the science but is now developing rapidly. Rates of solution are much affected by climate and vegetation, particularly rainfall, and karst landforms are sensitive to climatic variations and climatic change. This makes the study of the landforms important from the point of view both of the morphological effects of climatic change, and of elucidating climatic changes from a consideration of the landforms themselves, both on the surface and underground.

In a true karst landscape no water exists on the surface, all is circulating through fissures underground. Roglič, a great purist, remarks, 'Neither river can exist nor can a soil mantle be formed, or slope washing and erosion take place' [20]. Depressions and cavities, which in other rock types become gradually filled in, in karst areas are gradually widened and enlarged by solution, and the rock waste is carried away. 'The karst underground is a scene of complex and powerful processes which widen the fissures and reduce the limestone mass. While impermeable rocks are altered by slope wash and erosion, soluble rock undergoes a complex process of circulation through fissures and destruction of the rocky mass' [20]. It will be realised therefore that not only are the landforms distinctive but also the hydrological, geochemical and geomechanical phenomena of karstlands.

Despite the great development of vertical drainage, karstlands are also characterised by the widespread development of horizontally planed areas (Ebenheiten); these have been called by Roglič 'rim-corrosional widenings' and are particularly associated with solution at the zone of contact of the limestones and non-karstic rocks. Ebenheiten are characteristic of many karst areas, and such wide corrosional plains form distinctly flatter areas than those occurring in fluvially eroded areas [5].

Karst processes are at their maximum in areas of strong compact limestones, possessing well-defined joints, and where the rainfall is sufficiently high to give rise to much underground water. Not every limestone outcrop gives rise to karst landforms, pure soft limestones often having only a few aspects of a true karstland. While this book deals with the many factors giving rise to karst landforms, a brief mention of the three chief factors is now appropriate.

The first and main condition is the outcrop at the surface of a pure massive limestone, which may be well bedded or compact, and possessing well-defined joints, fissures and cracks, along which water can penetrate. Recent work has shown that limestones are very varied in texture and lithology and not all massive limestones are equally soluble or give rise to solutional features to the same extent. In order to develop karst landforms the limestone must possess some strength, so that hollows caused by solution do not immediately collapse. The Cretaceous chalk in England is an example of limestone without sufficient strength to give rise to karst landforms. The density and hardness of some well-known karst limestones and of some non-karstified limestones are given in Table I, p. 11

It is probable that the crushing strength (or compressibility) and hardness, in addition to purity, are the most important geomorphological qualities of karst limestones. The texture (whether crystalline or micritic) and the porosity of the limestones, though highly significant, are of less importance. Dolomites and dolomitic limestones occasionally give rise to true karst landscapes, and can possess many aspects of karstification. Moreover, with impure limestones residual material collects on the surface; this restricts and impedes the development of the underground drainage and the widening of the fissures and causes fluviokarstic relief. Thus the ideal kind of limestone for karst development is one which is pure, hard and compact, with well-developed fissures along which solution takes place, while the rock itself is impermeable.

Clearly the limestones must be exposed at the surface, and the thicker the limestones the greater the depth to which underground waters can circulate. This is why the great thickness (over 13,000 ft, 4,000 m) of pure compact limestones in the Dinaric karst has given rise to deep fissure circulation. Karst landforms can, however, be formed in any kind of structure, in both flat-lying beds and in highly folded and contorted beds; highly folded and fissured conditions favour the greater development of underground water circulation, and might be regarded by many Central European geomorphologists as a prerequisite for karst formation.

The second main requirement for the development of karst landforms is a climate with an adequate rainfall. Without water, solution of the limestone cannot take place, and in arid climates karst landforms do not develop or are atrophied. Thus in tropical desert areas and in the high-latitude polar deserts, karst processes are at a minimum, and karst landforms are poorly developed, even where there are thousands of feet of typical karst limestones. Karst landforms tend to be absent if the rainfall is much below about 10–12 in. (250–300 mm) per year. They reach their maximum development in areas of heavy rainfall or of snowfall, and in regions with strongly marked seasons of heavy rainfall and drought.

Thirdly, since the essential characteristic of karstlands is the vertical and underground circulation of drainage, this is assisted by a relatively large development of available relief, and karstlands tend to be relatively high above sea-level. Because of this and the fact that the Classical and Dinaric karsts are both hilly and mountainous in character, there is a tendency to associate karstlands with mountainous lands only. To some extent karst and mountains have become synonymous, the significance of the karstic component being so great that 'uninformed persons and strangers often identify the notions of karst and mountain' [5]. Although this is to a certain extent unavoidable, the presence of hills and mountains is not essential for the development of karstland, the purity and massiveness of the limestone and the fissure circulation being more fundamental. There are many karstlands of relatively low relief, for instance in central Kentucky, in Florida and central Ireland and the Limestone Ranges of the Fitzroy area of north-west Australia, though these areas do not usually have landforms as spectacular as the areas of higher karst relief.

This book is concerned essentially with the landforms of massive limestones formed predominantly by solutional and associated mechanisms. The landforms on relatively impure and less massive limestones and those formed in association with other agents of denudation will be referred to only briefly; this includes the fluviokarstic landforms of areas of the Chalk and the Cotswolds of southern and central England, and the only partially karstified landforms of the Permian (dolomitic) limestones of northern England. The many associated subjects, such as sedimentary geology, hydrology and speleology, will be considered only in relation to the landforms.

Karst landforms are widely distributed over the earth's surface. This is because limestone is an abundantly occurring sediment and the study of karst landforms is in part a study of limestones and various aspects of their sedimentation and erosion. Approximately 75 per cent of the total land area of the earth is directly underlain by sedimentary rocks, and carbonate rocks (limestones and dolomites) constitute about 15 per cent of all sedimentary deposits [21]. These carbonate rocks are widely distributed both in place and in geological time, ranging from the Pre-Cambrian to Recent, and they are divisible into several hundred different types. Hence it is not surprising that a large number of areas which are underlain by limestones of the types discussed are in topographical situations and climatic regimes giving rise to karst landscapes. The world map, Fig. 2, shows a generalised distribution of the main karstlands of the world.

Limestones occur in all systems of the geological column, though they are more important and more widespread in the Mesozoic and Cainozoic rocks than in the Pre-Cambrian and Palaeozoic rocks. This means that limestones are usually rather rare in the ancient shield areas and much more abundant in the Tertiary folded

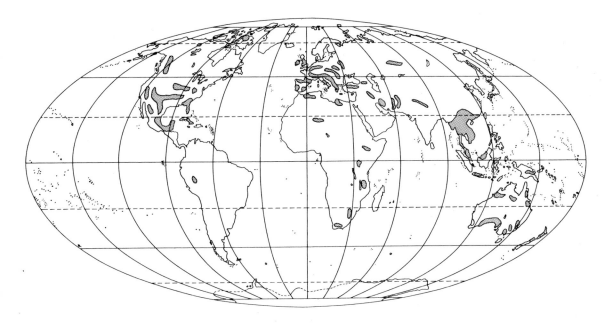

Fig. 2 The main areas of karst landforms as known at present

mountain belts. Karst landforms may occur in any exposures of these limestones, but, as we have already indicated, the occurrence of a limestone does not necessarily imply the presence of karst landforms or the existence of a vertical underground drainage system. In the British Isles, for instance, limestones occur in almost every system of the geological column, but it is only the limestones of Carboniferous age that show any marked degree of karstification; the other main limestone series, the Devonian and Jurassic limestones and the Chalk, show some aspects of karstification (particularly in their hydrological behaviour), but are essentially fluviokarstic. Even the areas on the Carboniferous Limestones are relatively small and karst landforms are only developed on a small scale in Britain. The best areas are in the Ingleborough district of north-west Yorkshire, the Peak District of Derbyshire and in the Mendips. Some of the finest karst areas in the British Isles are in Ireland, where much of the central plain and some of the surrounding uplands are formed of Carboniferous Limestones, and where but for the interference caused by glacial deposits underground drainage would be even more developed.

Outside the British Isles, on the continent of Europe, Devonian and Carboniferous Limestones form important karst areas, e.g. in the Dinant district of the Ardennes. Limestones of Cambro-Silurian age give rise to important cave areas in northern Norway, and in the island of Gotland in the Baltic there is a karst region on the Silurian (Gotlandian) limestones. In the Hercynian areas karstification may occur in limestones of varying ages – in the Devonian (Moravia); in the Triassic and Jurassic (the Swabian and Franconian Jura); and in the Jurassic and Cretaceous (Massif Central of France).

But it is in the areas of Alpine folding in Europe that karstlands are particularly developed, occurring on limestones of ages varying from the Permian to the Tertiary. The sediments associated with deposition on the Alpine foreland and in the former sea of Tethys, now folded and uplifted, form the high Calcareous Alps in the Northern Alps, and the predominantly limestone mountains of the southern Alpine zone to which the Classical and Dinaric karstlands belong. The Mediterranean region is particularly famous for its karstlands. Karst areas occur in many areas of the U.S.S.R., in central European Russia on Permian limestones, in the Caucasus on Mesozoic and Tertiary limestones and in Siberia near Lake Baikal on Palaeozoic limestones.

Both the Alpine–Himalayan fold-mountain belt and the Circum–Pacific belt have some prominent limestone areas, both flat-bedded and folded. One of the world's most extensive karst regions lies within the folded mountain belt of south-east Asia, in South China, Vietnam and Malaya. In both the East and the West Indian islands perfectly developed karstlands occur. In the Americas, limestones occur in both the Rockies and the Andes and there are extensive tracts in Central America. Some of the most interesting karst landforms of North America occur on flat-lying limestones in Indiana and Kentucky and in Florida. In the Arctic regions thick deposits of limestones are important, as in the Carbo-Permian in Spitsbergen and in the Siluro-Devonian limestones of Somerset Island in the northern Canadian archipelago. Important karst regions occur in Australia, as in the Nullarbor Plain in the South and in the Limestone Ranges of the north-west. Karsts are relatively rare in Central and Southern Africa, but there are significant, though scattered, examples, as

in the dolomites of the western and northern Transvaal and the limestones of Tanga in Tanzania. Finally, there are many interesting karst phenomena associated with modern coral limestones and coral reefs. From all these examples it can be seen that the study of karst landforms is a world-wide one.

Besides giving rise to such distinctive relief forms, areas of massive limestones are frequently regions of difficulty. This is due first to the lack of surface drainage, all the water even in heavy-rainfall areas circulating underground; secondly, to the apparently disordered distribution of the enclosed hollows and the highly irregular relief; and thirdly to the lack of soil, since solution of a massive limestone yields relatively little insoluble residual material; limestones even in well-vegetated areas usually have thin and easily erodible soils, and tend to be rocky and stony. The development of such lands in the modern economic sense demands much technical expertise, as the general absence of flat land and of surface water means that ordinary agricultural practices cannot be applied.

The hydrology of limestone areas is quite different from that of other rock types and needs special consideration; this has been illustrated by the work of the hydrology branch of the Food and Agriculture Organisation of UNESCO. The building of reservoirs in karst terrains has hitherto been regarded as impossible because of the cavernous nature of the limestones, but many of the difficulties are now being overcome in Jugoslavia. Areas of irregular and chaotic relief make road and rail construction difficult and karst areas have until now tended to be isolated and undeveloped. Thus we have Sawkins's description of the Cockpit Country in central Jamaica: 'The rough and uneven surface of the country . . . renders it quite impassable; high peaks, steep hills, ravines, gullies, sink holes, etc., present so many obstacles that this portion of the parish has well earned the appellation of "terra incognita'" [22].

None the less, they have a more positive side. Limestones provide a valuable source of lime, particularly in regions of high rainfall where the soils tend to be leached. Alluvial pockets in limestone areas, especially in tropical regions, have formed good agricultural soils; this was as true for the ancient Maya cultivators on the limestones of Yucatán and British Honduras as it is today for the Indian cultivators in middle America. The quarrying of limestones both for building stone and for lime is an important extractive industry. Although the surface is waterless, underground water from limestone regions tends to emerge at their contact with other rocks in the form of large springs. These form important sources of domestic and industrial water, as seen in the spring of the Axe at Wookey Hole in the Mendips, and at Ombla near Dubrovnik.

Because of their peculiarities, karstlands have always been associated with much folklore, particularly in western Europe. In the British Isles caves and hollows in limestones are often known as Hell's Hole, or Fairy Holes, as for example in Ireland. The large springs have also always attracted attention, and in addition to forming the nuclei of settlements have frequently been invested with religious significance, as for example at Wells in the Mendips, Holywell in North Wales, and at Delphi in Greece; in fact a map of the settlements in ancient Greece would largely be a map of the main karst springs. Limestones also form a large percentage of the Biblical lands of the Near East, particularly in the hills of Judaea where they produce a 'land of fountains and depths that spring out of valleys and hills' (Deut., viii.7).

2 Karst Limestones

1. CHEMICAL COMPOSITION

It is important before discussing the landforms of karst regions to consider the karst limestones themselves. The term is ambiguous, as limestones are a complex polygenetic group of rocks and many different types exist; it is applied to any rock which contains more than 50 per cent carbonate. Limestones can consist of carbonate in the form of calcite, aragonite, magnesium-calcium or dolomite. Most karst limestones consist of calcite, and rocks that are normally called limestones consist of 90 per cent or more of calcite, as can be seen from Table I. Some karst areas are, however, developed on dolomitic or magnesium limestones.

Calcite, $CaCO_3$, exists in nature in three crystalline polymorphs–calcite, vaterite and aragonite – as well as in an amorphous form. Vaterite is a very unstable hexagonal form of calcite ($U—CaCO_3$) and changes to calcite in a few days. Aragonite crystallises in an orthorhombic, often acicular, form and has a specific gravity of 2·9. It has a denser molecular packing than that of calcite, but is nevertheless more soluble. Aragonite is precipitated in sea-water by organisms under warm conditions and when the sea is highly supersaturated with $CaCO_3$. Ordinary aragonite is deposited in shallow waters in restricted bays, banks and lagoons of tropical and subtropical regions such as exist in the Bahamas today. During deposition it is penetrated by an immense number of fine pores which in the living animals are filled with horny animal matter. This material later decays and the existence of the small pores makes aragonite more soluble. Furthermore, aragonite is unstable and normally changes into calcite in the course of time with an accompanying 8 per cent increase of volume. The effect of this transformation causes a recrystallisation or conversion to a mosaic of calcite and a loss of much or all of the original internal structure of the aragonite. Only small amounts of magnesium are present in aragonite (approximately 1–2 per cent) as it has a different crystal form from magnesium carbonate. Aragonite changes to low magnesium calcite (i.e. calcite with a relatively low percentage of magnesium, 1–2 per cent) by polymorphic inversion or by solution and reprecipitation [24]; Bathurst also believes that solution reprecipitation processes are likely to be the dominant mechanics of the changes. Roques has said that the crystalline form of $CaCO_3$ is governed by the rapidity of loss of CO_2 from solution [25].

Calcite is rhombohedral in form and has a specific gravity of 2·72. At present calcite deposition occurs mainly in deep sea conditions and in middle and low latitudes. Sediments with more than 30 per cent of $CaCO_3$ cover nearly half of the deep sea floor and most calcite is of pelagic origin. The average rate of the deposition of pelagic calcareous deposits is probably greater than 1 cm per 1,000 years. The rate of deposition of calcite in colder seas is less rapid because of the difficulty of organic precipitation of $CaCO_3$ in cold subsurface waters. Bathurst in fact claims that 'the only $CaCO_3$ known to be precipitated from sea water is aragonite, whereas calcite cement is formed from fresh water' [24]. Calcite is closely associated with $MgCO_3$, with which

TABLE I(a)

SELECTED ANALYSES OF CARBONATE ROCKS

	(1)	(2)	(3)	(4)
CaO	42·61	42·92	54·84	54·54
MgO	7·90	0·42	0·26	0·59
CO_2	41·58	35·36	43·26	42·90
SiO_2	5·19	1·36	1·14	0·70
Al_2O_3	0·81	0·18 ⎫	0·41	0·68
Fe_2O_3 ⎫	0·54	0·20 ⎭		0·08
FeO ⎭				
	Composite analysis of 345 lists	Medway (White Chalk)	N. Wales (Carboniferous Limestone)	Salem Limestone (Mississippian) Indiana, U.S.A.

	(5)	(6)			(7)	
CaO	53·80	$CaCO_3$	98·62	CaO	55·16	
MgO	0·56	$MgCO_3$	0·27	MgO	0·20	
CO_2	42·69	ScO_2	0·60	CO_2	43·74 ⎫	
SiO_2	1·15	Fe_2O_3	0·21	SiO_2	0·23 ⎭	
Na_2O	0·07	Al_2O_3				
Fe_2O_3	0·26					
Al_2O_3	0·45					
	Bavaria (Solenhofen limestone)	Buxton, N. Derbyshire		Bermuda (Recent Coral)		

(From Clarke [23] p. 564.)

TABLE I(b)

PHYSICAL PROPERTIES OF SELECTED CARBONATE ROCKS

	App. Sp. Gravity	App. Porosity	Compressive Strength (1,000 lb/in²)	M. Rup. (1,000 lb/in²)
Limestone fossiliferous (Indiana)	2·37	11	10·9	1·6
Coarse white limestone (Alabama)	2·83	0·9	24·0	
Chalky limestone (South Dakota)	1·81	8·3	3·7	0·6
Limestone (Ohio)	2·69	0·7	28·5	2·9
Limestone metamorphic (California)	2·80		15·3	0·6
Dolomitic limestone (Ohio)	2·5	6·4	13	17
Limestone (Oklahoma)	2·67	1·2	18·9	2·0
Limestone (Ohio)	2·6	2·7	8·0	13·0
Chalky limestone (South Dakota)	1·71	26·0	2·4	0·3
Dolomite (Ohio)	2·6	3·4	23·0	19·0
Marble	2·87	0·6	30·8	2·8

M. Rup = Modulus of rupture
(From Chilingar et al. [35] vol. 9B, pp. 362–3.)

it is partly isomorphous. In deep water environments, only low magnesium calcite is formed. High magnesium calcite (with a magnesium content of from 10 to 15 per cent) is normally deposited in calcite shells. Like aragonite, it is unstable and usually is converted to low magnesium calcite by leaching of the magnesium or by microscale solution [24].

Rock-building organisms have both calcite and aragonite in their skeletons. For instance, calcareous algae may deposit either aragonite or calcite. *Halimeda* is aragonite, while *Lithothamnion* is calcitic. Most corals consist chiefly of aragonite. In fossil reefs the original aragonite has been converted to a mosaic of calcite, with the consequent destruction of the original structural details. Echinoderm plates are composed of large single crystals of calcite. In the Foraminifera, some tests are composed of calcite, others of aragonite; in the older rocks the aragonite has been converted into calcite. The factors responsible for the differences in the deposition of calcite and aragonite by organisms have been discussed by Lowenstam [26]. Both minerals are also deposited as lime mud, as a chemical or biochemical precipitate. Some of the standard tests for differentiating aragonite from calcite are given by Warwick [27].

With the passage of time, the aragonite is dissolved and converted to calcite, and high magnesium calcite is changed to low magnesium calcite; therefore the most commonly occurring mineral in limestones is low magnesium calcite, $CaCO_3$ with 1–4 per cent magnesium, which has increased through geological time [28]. The ratio Ca/Mg has augmented from the Palaeozoic to the Quaternary; the modern magnesium content has dropped to 1/25 of its Proterozoic value, whereas the Ca content has risen 40 per cent in the same period [29]. Modern carbonates laid down in warm shallow waters consist for the most part of the metastable mineral (aragonite and high magnesium calcite); ancient carbonates consist of dolomite and low magnesium calcite. Generally when the natural aragonite and/or the metastable calcite are exposed to rainwater they rapidly invert to the stable forms. Occasionally dolomite replaces the aragonite or high magnesium calcite in quite modern deposits [30].

Dolomites are those varieties of limestones containing more than 50 per cent carbonate, of which more than half is dolomite, $MgCO_3 . CaCO_3$. In chemical composition dolomites resemble limestones except that MgO is a large and important constituent. Rocks intermediate between limestone (*sensu stricto*) and dolomite have been variously named, Table II. The origin

TABLE II

CLASSIFICATION OF ROCKS INTERMEDIATE IN COMPOSITION BETWEEN PURE LIMESTONE AND DOLOMITES

	Content %	
	Calcite	Dolomite
Limestone	>95	<5
Magnesium limestone	90–95	5–10
Dolomite limestone	50–90	10–50
Calcitic dolomite	10–50	50–90
Dolomite	<10	>90

(From Chilingar *et al.* [35] vol. 9A, chap. 4.)

of dolomites is not satisfactorily understood and, though it is now known that there are certain areas of the world where dolomite precipitation may be actually taking place [28], most dolomite appears to be a post-depositional product and shows replacement relations with calcite. Dolomite may occur as isolated rhombs transecting the primary structures of the rock, but in dolomites proper the entire rock is a mosaic. In calcareous marine shells the magnesium content and the Mg/Ca ratio vary according to the temperature of the environment; the higher the temperature the greater the proportion of $MgCO_3$ in the shell skeleton [29]. Chave concluded that the shells of more simple organisms contained a higher proportion of Mg. The maximum amount of $MgCO_3$ in inorganically precipitated carbonate is approximately 4 per cent, whereas in organically formed carbonates it is about 30 per cent.

The carbonate rocks therefore consist essentially of two stable minerals, calcite and dolomite. We do not yet understand fully the physical and chemical changes accompanying the recrystallisation of the unconsolidated metastable carbonate minerals to stable carbonate minerals. The metastable minerals are generally absent in Pliocene and older carbonate rocks, which must mean that if the Pliocene and older limestones were formed originally of metastable carbonate minerals, then virtually all limestones have undergone recrystallisation.

Some of these recrystallisation changes are diagenetic, i.e. involving only the rearrangement of the materials already present. The two most important alterations are those which convert the original carbonate, the vaterite or aragonite, to calcite, and those which lead to the formation of dolomite. Both these processes lead to a loss of textural detail; for instance, aragonite shells lose their internal structure and are converted to a coarse calcite mosaic with only faint relics of their original form. This kind of recrystallisation is controlled by the original composition of the rock, i.e. only those materials which were aragonite are recrystallised – the calcite parts are unaffected. There is also a non-selective recrystallisation which is not controlled by

the original composition; this gives rise to patches of coarsely crystalline calcite. Another great change in limestones is brought about by solution, which may remove as much as 40 per cent of the original material. The primary textures and structures are therefore greatly altered. Selective solution may remove fossils and leave voids [28]. Some of the problems and questions raised by cementation and lithification of carbonates have been reviewed by Bathurst (481).

There are therefore three distinctive sedimentary aspects of the carbonate rocks. First, their intrabasinal origin; most carbonate sediment has been formed at or very close to the point of final deposition, the best examples of in-place deposition of carbonate rocks being those of true coral reefs. Secondly, most carbonates are highly dependent upon some type of organic activity. Organisms exert a stronger influence on the early post-depositional history of carbonate than on most other sediments. The interpretation of the size, shape and sorting of the grains in carbonate rocks is therefore much more difficult than in sandstones, for instance. There is also a wide range in specific gravity of the organic carbonate materials, and this is complicated by voids caused by solution. Thirdly, the carbonate rocks are in a class by themselves in their proneness to alterations and post-depositional modification. The processes of recrystallisation, replacement, cementation, neomorphism (= lithification) and solution create distinctive and complex changes, which have a profound bearing on the behaviour of the carbonate rocks. This shows why problems associated with the study of limestones are quite different from any other rock type.

2. CLASSIFICATION

Limestones are partly detrital, partly chemical, partly organic and partly metasomatic. There is no single or best classification, and classifications involve both genetic and textural differences. Limestones may be divided into two main groups on genetic grounds, *autochthonous* (autogenic) and *allochthonous* (allogenic). Autochthonous limestones have formed *in situ* by an accumulation of organic structures; they have not been subject to current transport and redeposition and grew in place by biological and biochemical action. Allochthonous limestones consist of detritus, broken pieces of reef rock, fragments of shells, muds, etc., of either a chemical or a biochemical origin; all these materials are current-sorted and are deposited like a normal clastic rock.

Autochthonous limestones include those formed by corals, lime-secreting algae and foraminifera. The calcareous algae are the most important rock builders at the present time and were also important in the Pre-Cambrian and other periods of geological time. Table III shows the range of the important constituents in the shells of the different groups of organisms. The shells of many molluscs are partly calcite and partly aragonite; almost all sea-water forms consist of both calcite and aragonite; freshwater forms are mostly calcite. The most interesting autochthonous limestones are possibly reef limestones – formed by masses of coral reefs in many parts of the world, and occurring in every part of the geological column since the Ordovician. Coral reefs include colonies of coral plastered over each other, usually with little or no stratification. Coral reefs have been defined

TABLE III

INORGANIC CONSTITUENTS OF MARINE INVERTEBRATES

Class	$CaCO_3$ %	$MgCO_3$ %	CaP_2O_3 %
Foraminifera	77·0 to 90·1	1·8 to 11·2 (av. 8·2)	
Calcareous sponges	71·0 to 85·0	4·6 to 14·1	? to 10·0
Corals			
Madreporaria	97·6 to 99·7	0·1 to 0·8	
Aleyonaria	73·0 to 98·9	0·3 to 15·7 (av. 11·1)	
Echinoderms			
Crinoids	83·1 to 91·5	7·9 to 13·7	
Echinoids	77·9 to 91·7	6·0 to 13·8	
Brachiopods	88·6 to 98·6	0·5 to 8·6	
Crustaceans	28·6 to 82·6	3·6 to 16·0	6·6 to 49·6
Molluscs			
Pelecypods	98·6 to 99·8	0 to 1·0	
Gastropods	96·6 to 99·0	0 to 1·8	
Cephalopods	93·8 to 99·5	0·2 to 6·0	
Algae (calc.)	73·6 to 88·1	10·9 to 25·2 (av. 17·4)	

(From Pettijohn [28] p. 385.)

as wave-resistant structures, and are often referred to as bioherms. The term bioherm has been defined by Cumings and Shrock as '. . . any dome-like, mound-like . . . or otherwise circumscribed mass; built exclusively or mainly by secreting organisms and enclosed in a normal rock of different lithological character' [30]. Bioherms may be composed not only of coral colonies but also of algal colonies, stromatoporoid colonies and crinoid or brachiopod remains. They may be merely small mounds a few inches across or very large structures several thousand feet wide and one or two hundred feet thick. Bioherms are important to the karst morphologist because they usually consist of a massive central mound of uneven and unbedded limestone, which is frequently dolomitic; this core is surrounded by well-bedded strata which lap against and grade into the core and commonly show steep dips away from the core. A description of the reef facies of the Devonian rocks of the Limestone Ranges in the Fitzroy district of Western Australia has been given by the writer and J. N. Jennings [31]. Both in this district and in other limestone areas, such as the Carlsbad Cavern area of southern New Mexico and the Dinantian limestones of Derbyshire, an understanding of the limestone facies of the reefs is essential to a full comprehension of the landforms of the area.

Allochthonous limestones are formed of fragments which have been deposited mechanically. They are frequently classified according to their dominant grain size, namely:

calcarenites: 1/16–2 mm in diameter
calcirudites: over 2 mm in diameter
calcilutites: very fine-grained.

The carbonate debris consists of fossil materials, pebbles, grains, pellets and granules of calcilutites and of oolites.* The

normal cement of calcarenites is calcite, appearing as a coarsely crystalline mosaic between the grains. By decrease in grain size, calcarenites grade into carbonate silts and mudstones. Calcilutites are often very fine-grained and dense. They are partly the finer product of marine attrition, but some calcareous muds are chemical or biochemical precipitates. In tranquil waters aragonite may be precipitated as minute acicular crystals. The origin of fine-grained and dense structureless limestones is not certain. In north-west Yorkshire well-marked bands of dense fine-grained limestones occur within the Carboniferous sequence; these are known as porcellanites or china stones [33]. Chalk, whose density is 1·5, is an example of a fine-grained carbonate rock; it consists of the tests of microorganisms (both foraminifera and planktonic algae) composed of clear calcite and set in a structureless matrix of fine-grained carbonate. Chalk is a porous and friable limestone and is believed to be an almost unaltered deposit; it has thus failed to become a dense hard rock and because of this does not give rise to typical karst landforms. As indicated above the problem is 'how to cement a carbonate mud while it is still largely uncompacted.' [481]

Of more importance to the study of karst landforms are the recent attempts to classify limestones from a textural point of view [34]. These classifications have come about as a result of advances in oil geology, because limestones frequently form important reservoir rocks. Folk recognises a

*Oolites are small spherical or subspherical accretionary bodies 0·25–2·00 mm in diameter. Within any given rock they are highly uniform, both in size and shape. In calcareous oolites, aragonite or calcite fibres radiate from a centre (see Pettijohn [28], p. 95). Illing says of the calcareous oolites of the Bahamas that their 'accretion depends fundamentally on the movement of grains under the impetus of marine currents' [32].

division of limestones based on groups of textural types [34]. The major constituents in limestones from the textural aspect are:

(1) The distinct carbonate aggregates (grains, pellets, skeletal debris, etc.) called by Folk *allochems*.

(2) *Microcrystalline ooze* (micrite); this type of calcite forms grains from 1 to 4 microns in diameter, and in hand specimens is dull and opaque. Microcrystalline carbonate ooze is considered to be formed largely by rapid chemical or biochemical precipitation in sea water and settling to the bottom.

(3) *Sparry calcite cement,* which forms grains or crystals 10 microns or more in diameter and can be distinguished from microcrystalline calcite by its clarity and coarser crystal size. However, because of diagenetic alteration of the original limestone textures, even this classification is 'very difficult to follow' – and 'Folk's concepts should be considered with care' [35]. Grain growth and recrystallisation may form a sparry limestone from one that originally was not a sparite – a process known as neomorphism [35].

A useful division of the main limestone types can none the less be made. Thus Type 1 includes the *sparry allochemical* limestones or *sparites*. These consist chiefly of the allochems cemented by sparry calcite cement, with all the interstitial pores filled by sparry calcite. Type 2, the *microcrystalline rocks* or *micrites*. These consist

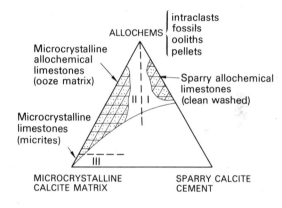

Fig. 3 The main constituents of limestones (ignoring recrystallisation) (from Folk, 1959 [34])

MICRITES   BIOMICRITES   SPARRY LIMESTONES

	A. Sporadic	B. Packed	a	b
1–10% calcite	10–20% calcite	20–50% calcite	50–75% calcite	Over 75% calcite
Dense groundmass (cement) with occasional dust-like particles and micro. fragments of fossils	Dense to dusty groundmass (cement) with small and shred-like flakes of calcite; and with small and occasional determinate fossils, all dispersed and scattered through matrix	Fine grained ground-mass (cement) made up of closely packed particles and angular fragments of calcite with fossils, occas, oolites (Oomicrites)	Medium to coarse-grained groundmass. Well formed crystal plates of calcite. Also fragmental, and granules, of calcite as a cement. Fossils common	Course-grained groundmass, with large plates and mosaic-forms of calcite. Numerous fossils can occur and these are often preserved in cryst. calcite. Cement very sparry with little pore-space

Fig. 4 A divisional scheme for the textural characters of carbonate rocks (modified from Folk, 1959 [34])

almost entirely of microcrystalline ooze with little or no allochemical material. Type 3, the *microcrystalline allochemical rocks*. These contain allochems but their matrix is largely microcrystalline ooze and sparry calcite is subordinate; this type includes the *biomicrites* and *biosparites* (Fig. 3).

The interest to the karst morphologist of this classification is the effects these textures have upon the porosity and openness of the limestones. The water-holding capacity of a rock is governed by its porosity. Thus a porous limestone is one which contains interstices or pore spaces through which water can pass freely and unhindered. The perviousness of a rock is not dependent entirely upon the total pore space, but on the size of the pore spaces and their continuity with one another. Micrites have a very low porosity, estimated at about 2 per cent or less, with a dense compact ground mass or cement made up of microscopic calcite particles and clay paste carbonate, Photo 1. Sparites have an estimated porosity of about 5–8 per cent; in these rocks crystalline calcite reaches over 90 per cent in amount and occurs as large united plates and mosaic aggregates, tending to restrict the pore space, Photo 1. Those rocks in the middle of Folk's textural groups (Fig. 4), for example the biosparites and the bio-

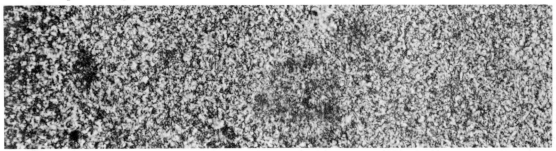

1(*a*) *above* Micrite. Porcellanous band, Gaping Gill Hole, Yorkshire (× 800) 1(*b*) *below left* Sparry limestone, N.W. Yorkshire (× 70) 1(*c*) *below right* Biomicrite, N.W. Yorkshire (× 30)

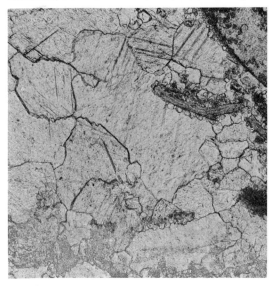

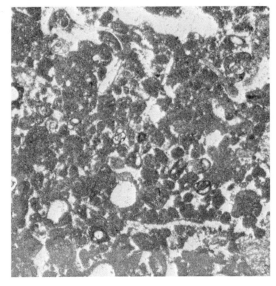

micrites, tend to have a higher porosity, of about 15–25 per cent. The ground-mass is mainly composed of finely granular and fragmental matter which allows many interstices to occur. More water is able to pass through biomicrites and biosparites, so that these rocks are all the time in contact with greater amounts of groundwater; they should therefore be relatively more soluble than the micrites or sparites where water is not able to enter so easily. In a study of solution of limestones in north-west Yorkshire, some of the evidence suggests that such a differential solubility exists; water draining from or in contact with biomicrites possesses higher calcium values in parts per million than the more highly crystalline sparry rocks under similar conditions. The results of these experiments are plotted in Fig. 5.

A similar conclusion is given by Schoeller in his consideration of the waters in limestones. He divides limestones into three groups: *compact,* with little pore space; *fine-grained,* also with feeble pore space; and *porous* limestones with variable interstices and with a high porosity [36]. However, water circulates in limestones not only through pore spaces, but also by means of cracks and fissures, so that a highly fissured rock may be relatively more soluble than a less fissured one, irrespective of the type of pore space. Porosity in limestones is also affected by the presence of *stylolites,* irregular structures usually parallel to the bedding and along which solution has taken place. Porosity tends to increase upward and downward away from the stylolite, as if calcium carbonate had moved outward from the stylolitic seam

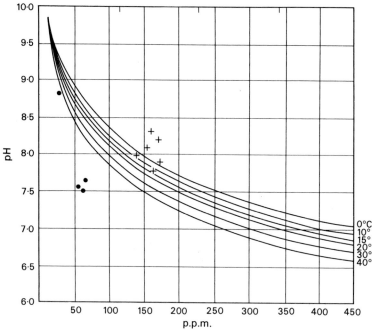

N.W. YORKSHIRE

● Sparry limestones   + Biomicrites
   W. part   E. part

Fig. 5 Differential solubility of limestones in north-west Yorkshire

Note. These results are plotted on the curves of Trombe, which have been shown recently by Picknett to be slightly in error. This error does not affect the fundamental argument.

TABLE IV

THE VARIETY OF TEXTURES OF SOME LIMESTONES

	Locality	Formation and Age	Description
(1)	Fitzroy Limestone Ranges, N.W. Australia	Napier Calcarenite (Devonian)	Foraminiferal limestone, sparry, 70 per cent calcite.
(2)	Buchan Caves, Victoria, Australia	Buchan Caves Limestone (Devonian)	Medium-textured; calcite in fresh and mosaic forms, set in a matrix of disseminated granular calcite; a biomicrite, 50 per cent sparry calcite.
(3)	Mole Creek, Tasmania	Gordon Limestone (Ordovician)	Medium-textured, with interlocking fragments of calcite and quartz, in a very finely divided mixed cement. A siliceous limestone with 55 per cent sparry calcite.
(4)	Brucebyen, central Westspitsbergen	Permian	A fine-textured limestone, with a ground mass of calcareous mud and patchy calcite. A biomicrite with 40–50 per cent sparry calcite.
(5)	Jamaica, Cockpit Country, northern side	White Limestone (Eocene)	Fine- to medium-textured, fresh calcite in the ground-mass, with no mud or paste. A sparry limestone with 80 per cent sparry calcite.
(6)	Kent, northern Jamaica	Montpelier Limestone Series (Eocene to mid-Miocene)	A fossiliferous micrite, with 5–10 per cent sparry calcite. Largely composed of a compact muddy ground-mass with minute grains of calcite.
(7)	Mountain Pine Ridge, south of Georgeville, British Honduras	Eocene	A packed biomictite with 30–40 per cent sparry calcite. A compact, finely granular ground-mass with irregularly shaped calcite.
(8)	Near Roaring Creek, British Honduras	Cretaceous	A micrite with up to 10 per cent sparry calcite. A clayey ground-mass with only occasional small fragments of calcite.
(9)	Causse Méjean, central France	Calcaire en plaquettes (Sequanian)	A fossiliferous micrite with 5 per cent sparry calcite. A close-grained, dense-textured rock–calcareous paste with dust-like particles of calcite.

[481]. Variations in the porosity of the Niagaran Dolomites in relation to stylolites have been demonstrated by Pluhar & Ford [482] [483].

In the course of investigations into karst landforms, the textures of many karst limestones have been examined, and some comments on these are included now. In general, since limestones are particularly susceptible to alteration, older limestones tend to be more crystalline and sparry. In north-west Yorkshire, of over 100 samples of Carboniferous Limestone that have been examined, over 75 per cent were sparry limestones and the other 25 per cent were biomicrites. The average amount of calcite present in the sparry limestones is estimated to be about 73 per cent. In the Carboniferous Limestones sampled from the Burren region of County Clare, Ireland, about 95 per cent were sparry limestones with the average amount of calcite about 84 per cent. Thus the limestones of the Burren region are much more fresh and clean with a higher percentage of sparry calcite than those in Yorkshire. In the Classical and Dinaric karst areas of Jugoslavia, a series of limestones were collected on a traverse from Ljubljana to Montenegro. These rocks were extremely compact, structureless, and hard and dense in character. They contained much less sparry calcite than the British Carboniferous Limestones, on an average about 35 per cent; about 80 per cent of the rocks were biomicrites in which the allochems occur in a fine- to medium-grained matrix; sparry limestones with a very high percentage of sparry calcite, such as occurs in western Ireland, were extremely rare. The ground-mass of the Jugoslav limestones does, however, show evidence of strain and stress in the form of cracks, which are filled with secondary calcite, and ramifying like mud cracks [37].

Table IV gives some idea of the great variety and textures of karst limestones.

Though dolomites closely resemble limestones in many aspects, there are also many differences. Since dolomitisation involves large-scale recrystallisation, it generally destroys the original structures of the limestone. The textures of dolomites are usually granular and they are normally more even and not so fine-grained as limestones; to the naked eye they often have a saccharoidal (sugary) texture. Powers has discussed the effects of dolomitisation on porosity and permeability [38]. Within the range of 5–75 per cent dolomitisation, as dolomitisation increases, permeability decreases; above about 77 per cent dolomitisation, however, 'the dolomite network begins to open up and an open network of dolomite crystals form and inter-crystalline porosity develops and reaches a maximum where the rock is 80 per cent dolomite' [38]. After this point, either solution vugs may become so important that the porosity is greatly increased, or more dolomite may be added, in which case the porosity and the permeability of the dolomite is decreased. Powers's general summary suggests that in any given textual group the porosity and

permeability (a) progressively decrease as dolomite increases from 10 to 80 per cent, (b) increase where dolomite forms 80–90 per cent of the rock, and (c) again decrease as dolomite exceeds 90 per cent. Chilingar also states that the replacement of calcite by dolomite gives an increase in porosity of about 12–13 per cent [35].

Dolomitic limestones forming the core of coral reefs may be very porous. This is because the dolomites though well cemented have many voids, some of which may have been original voids in the reef. The high porosity of the reef rock originally favours dolomitisation. In the Limestone Ranges in the Fitzroy District of Western Australia, the rocks of the barrier reef facies normally weather more rapidly than either the forereef or the backreef facies and are from 50 ft (15 m) to 100 ft (30 m) lower in height. This lower resistance is believed to be due to the presence of more primary voids in the rocks, which has promoted the movement of the solvent ground waters [31]. In the Carlsbad area of southern New Mexico, in the Guadalupe Permian Reef complex, the barrier reef rocks are also full of voids and appear to be more susceptible to weathering [39].

Dolomite is closely associated with limestone in the field, with which it may be interbedded. The distribution of dolomite is frequently controlled by faults or folds; this can be seen in the Grands Causses of France and along some of the faults in north-west Yorkshire. In the field dolomite is often a yellowish-buff-coloured rock.

Though karst limestones consist mainly of carbonates of calcium and magnesium, other slight impurities may be highly significant in their weathering. The presence of quartz or other (*secondary* silica) grains in general tends to make the limestones more resistant to solution; this can be seen in the sedimentation of the limestones

2(*a*) Massively bedded algal reef limestones (Devonian) near Barnet Spring, Limestone Ranges, N.W. Australia

surrounding Ingleborough mountain in Yorkshire, where small quartz crystals are common along the bedding planes at the base of massive beds [40]. The presence of any sulphide minerals, particularly pyrite [40], in the limestones or in beds associated with them tends to make the limestones rather more soluble; this is because sulphuric acid may be produced by oxidation of the sulphides, and the calcium is converted to form the sulphate, gypsum. Limestones made more soluble in this way have been described from the Mammoth Cave area in the U.S.A. by White [41].

3. FISSURES AND JOINTS

In addition to stylolitic seams karst limestones are characterised by cracks and fissures and this feature is quite as important as that of their composition and texture. Limestone is normally a fissured rock, and in many limestones where the crystals of calcite are closely interlocking, and the rock is of low porosity, the fissures are the main means by which water passes through them. All writers on the origin of caves and hollows in limestones have stressed the importance of fissures, particularly Martel [13, 14, 15].

The main lines of weakness in limestones are normally along the bedding planes and along the joint planes, but in many rocks there exist other lines of fracture which have been called diaclases, and which are equally fundamental to the development of karst landforms. In limestones of barrier reef facies, where the rock is frequently compact and unbedded, they may be traversed by vertical joints only, and bedding planes are absent, Photo 2 (*a*). Extremely compact and vertically jointed limestones are characteristic of the Cretaceous limestones in the Dinaric karst. Massive undivided cliffs are therefore important in the landscapes.

The manner in which the carbonates are deposited is of great importance to the later development of the bedding planes. The compaction of the sediments under great loads causes a decrease in the porosity and the permeability, fine-grained limestones in particular suffering enormous losses of porosity and moisture content [42]. Limestones may vary in any one sequence both in texture and in type of bedding. In the Carboniferous Limestones of the Burren of County Clare, the sequence is composed of a fairly uniform series of massive sparry limestones laid down in a shelf sea. [43]. In north-west Yorkshire, limestones of a roughly similar age have also been laid down on a shelf area, but the sequence shows much more vertical variation, and is made up of an alternating, not necessarily cyclic, series of beds consisting of massive sparites, biomicrites, true micrites, shaley and ferruginous mudstone layers [37, 40].

2(*b*) Jointing in different beds in the Great Scar Limestone, Scar Close, N.W. Yorkshire

Bedding planes, both in the Burren and in north-west Yorkshire, Photo 2 (*b*), are former erosion surfaces, and today form the lines of weakness in the limestones for the entry of karst waters; the relative importance of vertical variation in the two sequences has affected the development of the landforms [44].

Joints and fractures (diaclases) are as important as bedding planes to the development of karst relief. Wager showed how the pattern of the jointing of the Carboniferous Limestones (Great Scar Limestone) of north-west Yorkshire is related to the tectonics of the Askrigg Block [45]. However, more detailed work shows that each bed is affected by the jointing in a distinct way, which has been proved by a study of the jointing of the Carboniferous Limestones in north-west Yorkshire recently made by Doughty [46]. Jointing is much less frequent in the more massive beds of sparry limestones, being about $\frac{1}{2}$ to 1 metre apart; in one area in Chapel-le-Dale, there is an area of over 100 yd^2 (100 m^2) without any joint or fissure at all and in this area the major joints are on an average about 1–2 m apart. In the biomicrites and in the micrites, joints tend to be much closer, about $\frac{1}{4}$–$\frac{1}{2}$ m apart; the appearance of a weathered face rock is much more blocky and cuboidal compared with a castellated appearance in the more massive sections. Photo 2 (*b*) shows the jointing in different beds on Scar Close, Chapel-le-Dale. Hence, though the pattern and direction of faults

and joints may be determined by the tectonics, their incidence and spacing are dependent upon the texture and density of limestone [47]. A similar difference in the frequency of jointing was noted in the Limestone Ranges in the Fitzroy District of north-west Australia; in the Barrier Reef facies joints are rare; in the forereef facies, deep joint planes are important; in the less massive, backreef facies, jointing is frequent and shallower, and the bedding planes tend to be more conspicuous [31].

Normally one set of joints tends to be dominant – the master joints; these are crossed, usually at between 70°–90°, by another set to form conjugate joints. The master joints tend to be long and straight and may be of greater importance in the development of karst landforms and in the flow of underground water [48]. There are often other subordinate lines of jointings, illustrated in Yorkshire by the line of the valley of Clapdale on the slopes of Ingleborough, which runs NE–SW, whereas the major lines of jointing in the immediate vicinity are NNW–SSE and ENE–WSW. Joints may also be triangular or wedge-shaped, giving rise to weathered diamond- and triangular-shaped rock fragments, Photo 3 (*a*); or they may be curvilinear as on Borrins Moor Rocks near Alum Pot Hole in Yorkshire, Photo 3 (*b*), or as in the Carboniferous Limestones of the Gort lowland in County Clare. The weathering of biohermal and reef-like mounds may occasionally give rise to areas of spherical

3(*a*) Development of two sets of joints, Carboniferous Limestone, Newbiggin Crags, Westmorland

jointing, as has been described in the Gort lowland; curved jointing also occurs in the weathered bioherms in the Devonian limestones of the Limestone Ranges of the Fitzroy area.

In addition to bedding planes and joints, there are other small fractures and cracks in limestones, often called diaclases, which are neither faults nor joints. Many are associated with folding and faulting of the limestones. In Yorkshire, it is well known that the frequency of such fractures in the limestones increases in the vicinity of the main faults of the area. The highly jointed and fractured cliffs of Gordale Scar and of others like Tow Scar, near Ingleton, were referred to by Kendall and Wroot, the fracturing being spoken of as similar to the 'cleat' in coal seams [49]. In areas of recently folded limestones, as in the Alps and in the Jugoslav karst, fractures and diaclases are extremely important features.

Karst limestones are also cut by fault lines, which may cut across several beds. Faults are extremely important from the point of view of guiding the direction of and focusing the solution of the rock and are therefore of profound importance in the development of karst landforms. This was recognised by Martel in his early work in the Causses and Alps of France [14], and emphasised by Simpson in his work on the Craven faults and the Yorkshire potholes [50]. In studies of tropical limestone landforms, Lehmann has referred to *gerichteter* (or oriented or directed) karst, and Pannakoek has also stressed the importance of faulting in the delineation of tropical karst landforms [51].

Thus lines of weakness of all kinds, from small cracks and laminae to fault lines of considerable throw, are of great importance in facilitating the entry of water into limestones and hence in the development of karst landforms.

3(*b*) Curved jointing, Carboniferous Limestone near Alum Pot Hole, N.W. Yorkshire

3 The Solution of Limestones

1. THE SOLUTION OF CALCIUM AND MAGNESIUM CARBONATES

One of the most important processes in the formation of karst landforms is the solution, caused predominantly by atmospheric and vegetational waters, of the limestones we have just described. The literature dealing both with the solubility of calcium and magnesium carbonates and with carbon dioxide in water is large, though it is only recently, and particularly in France, that work has been applied directly to the problem of karst landforms.

Calcium carbonate, in the form of either aragonite or calcite (or amorphous), is slightly soluble in pure water, as Table V shows.

Other workers give accordant results. Thus Hutchinson [52] gives 12·7 mg $CaCO_3$ per litre, and Pia in 1933 gave about 12 mg per litre calcite in CO_2-free water and about 14 mg aragonite per litre, both at a temperature of 20°C [53]. It is not possible, however, to define a true solubility of calcite in the absence of CO_2, because the formation of CO_3 ions implies a certain concentration of free CO_2 in solution. Aragonite, though more soluble than calcite, is slower in attaining equilibrium [54].

TABLE V
THE SOLUBILITY (IN WATER DEPRIVED OF CO_2) OF $CaCO_3$ AND $MgCO_3$

25°C	Calcite	Aragonite	Amorphous	$MgCO_3$
	$1,433 \times 10^{-2}$	$1,528 \times 10^{-2}$	$1,445 \times 10^{-2}$	$94 \times 117 \cdot 6 \times 10^{-2}$

(From Schoeller (1962) [36] p. 265.)

TABLE VI
THE SOLUBILITY OF CO_2 IN PURE WATER

Temperature   0·030 per cent of CO_2

°C	Wet atmosphere containing 0·030 per cent of CO_2 per unit volume of the dry components at sea-level
0	1·00
1	0·96
5	0·83
10	0·70
15	0·59
20	0·51
25	0·44
30	0·38

(From Hutchinson [52] p. 654.)

TABLE VII
THE SOLUBILITY OF $CaCO_3$ AT 25°C UNDER DIFFERENT CO_2 PRESSURES

CO_2 vol. % 10^{-2} atmos.	Solubility mg/kg		
	$CaCO_3$	Ca	HCO_3^-
0·01	35	14	43
0·03	52	21	63
0·04	57	23	70
0·06	65	26	79
0·08	72	29	87
0·10	78	31	95
0·20	99	40	121
0·25	106	42	129
0·30	113	45	138

(From Hutchinson [52] p. 662.)

Carbon dioxide is very soluble in pure water, as seen from Table VI, which gives accepted values for the solubility of CO_2 within the normal temperature range [52]. The variation of solubility with pressure obeys Henry's Law, which means that the solubility of CO_2 increases with a decrease in temperature and an increase in pressure. Thus, all things being equal, CO_2 is more soluble at lower than at higher temperatures.

The solubility of calcium carbonate is given by the general equation:

$$CaCO_3 + CO_2 + H_2O \rightleftarrows Ca(HCO_3)_2$$

Variations in the CO_2 pressure are extremely important in the mechanism of the solution of limestones, and the solubility of $CaCO_3$ under various pressures of CO_2 is given in Table VII, and at various temperatures for two important CO_2 pressures in Table VIII.

TABLE VIII

THE SOLUBILITY OF $CaCO_3$ AT VARIOUS
TEMPERATURES FOR TWO IMPORTANT
CO_2 PRESSURES

Temp. °C	0·033 %	0·44 %
0	96	106
5	86	94
10	75	83
15	67	74
20	59	65
25	54	59
29	49	54

(From Hutchinson [52] p. 663.)

The suite of equations which register the formation of calcium bicarbonate can be written as follows:

(1) Equilibrium of hydration:
$$CO_2 + HO_2 \rightleftarrows H_2CO_3$$
(2) Dissociation of carbonic acid:
$$H_2CO_3 \rightleftarrows H^+ + HCO_3$$
(3) Combination of hydrogen and carbonic ions:
$$HCO_3 \rightleftarrows H^+ + CO_3{}^-$$
(4) Dissociation of the carbonate mineral:
$$Ca^{++} + CO_3{}^{--} \rightleftarrows CaCO_3$$
(5) Ionic dissociation of the water:
$$H_2O \rightleftarrows H^+ + OH^-$$

All these reactions are reversible. The variations in the solubility of $CaCO_3$ form a series of reactions, variations in the rate of one affecting the rate of the others. The interrelationship of these reactions is perhaps best shown by Roques's diagram, Formula 1 [55]. Roques' views of the reaction kinetics of the system $CO_2-H_2O-CaCO_3$ on the basis of Mass-Transfer theory is given in his article [484].

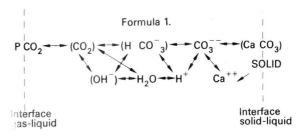

Formula 1.

The CO_2 dissolved in water and which regulates the equilibrium of the $CaCO_3$ is called the CO_2 of equilibrium. If the pressure of the CO_2 dissolved in water is lower than the pressure of the free gaseous CO_2, the solution is not in equilibrium and $CaCO_3$ is precipitated. If the pressure of the dissolved CO_2 is greater than that of the free CO_2, the water will attack and dissolve the limestone. This surplus CO_2 is sometimes called aggressive CO_2. The pH

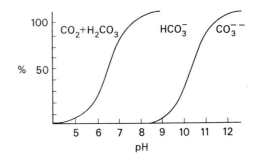

Fig. 6 Properties of CO_2 (and H_2CO_3), HCO_3^- and $CO_3{}^{--}$ in solution at different pH values (Buch) (from Hutchinson [52])

corresponds to the equilibrium CO_2 and is called the pH of equilibrium. Below pH 5, only total free CO_2 is of any quantitative importance; between pH 7 and pH 9 the bicarbonate is the most significant; and above 9·5 carbonate begins to be important, as given in Fig. 6 [52]. In most cases, i.e. where the pH is below 8·3 or 8·4, it is theoretically possible to determine the free CO_2. However, carbon dioxide is notoriously difficult to work with because of its continuous variations, and its determination in a limestone environment (either surface or underground) can be almost impossible. Smith and Mead found in the Mendips that attempts to calculate the amount of aggressive carbon dioxide were very difficult [56]. Jennings and Sweeting also tried to estimate the free CO_2 in cave waters at Wee Jasper in New South Wales, but found that because of the continually changing CO_2 pressure the results were not reliable. Older views used to consider the carbon dioxide present in an aqueous solution of $Ca(HCO_3)_2$ as being in a number of different states [57]. These include the CO_2 of the bicarbonates, and also the free CO_2, Formula 2.

Formula 2

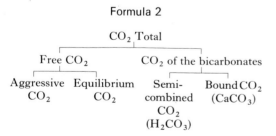

In the past few years European investigators have developed field apparatus which measure CO_2 (gas) both in free air and in soil air. Some results which seem to be reliable are described by Ek and others [485] [486].

The facility or power of water to dissolve the calcium carbonate is known as the aggressivity of the water [58]. This can be measured by considering the free CO_2 or by measuring the concentration of the H^+ ions in the water, expressed as the pH. Trombe discusses the experimental work of Tillmans, and gives the equivalents of $CaCO_3$ in solution for given amounts of the different kinds of CO_2 [57]. Precipitation of $CaCO_3$ is brought about (1) by diminution in the amount of CO_2 present, (2) by evaporation of H_2O and (3) by bacterial or organic action. In temperate and many other areas the first is the most important cause; in the tropics, the second is often more important. Bacterial and organic action in precipitating $CaCO_3$ may locally be the cause of large deposits of reprecipitated $CaCO_3$.

Bögli was the first to discuss and relate the different phases in the solution of calcium carbonate to stages in the solution of limestones [59]. He describes the solution of limestone as the result of four phases, Fig. 7. In the *first* phase, the calcium carbonate is dissociated and the Ca and carbonate ions are lost into the water, as in equation 4, p. 25. In the *second* and *third* phases, the H^+ ions in the water react with the carbonate ions; in these phases, also, a part of the dissolved CO_2 reacts with the water to form carbonic acid as in equation 1. The dissociation of this carbonic acid, as in equation 2, releases hydrogen ions which become associated with the carbonate ions from the first phase (equation 3). This removes the CO_3 from the solution equilibrium and the replacement of these carbonate ions involves further solution of the limestone. Also in the third phase physically dissolved CO_2 becomes chemically dissolved to form carbonic acid. The total quantity of limestone dissolved in the second and third phases is controlled by the original CO_2 content of the water.

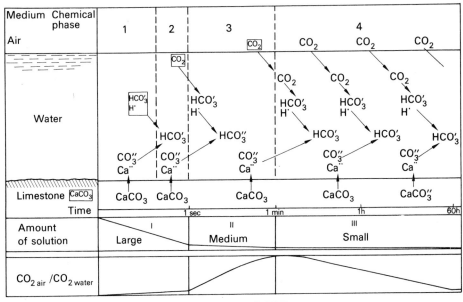

Fig. 7 Scheme of solution of limestone (after Bögli [59])

Eventually, the water will become saturated with the amount of CaCO₃ which is in equilibrium with the hydrogen ion activity of the water. In the *fourth* phase, there is a diffusion of atmospheric carbon dioxide into the water. This phase will prevent the water from becoming saturated with calcium carbonate; as long as CO_2 diffuses into the water, more limestone can be dissolved, and this will go on until an equilibrium between dissolved and un-dissolved limestone is reached. Any change in the controlling factors may cause either further solution or precipitation of the calcium carbonate. Pressure of CO_2 varies from one part of the soil environment, or of an underground water system, to another; where the CO_2 pressure rises there will be further solution of the limestone, where the CO_2 pressure is lower, calcium carbonate will be precipitated.

Bögli also examined the rate at which limestone passes into solution in relation to the four phases of the solution process [59]. He claims that solution during the first two phases is rapid. From Fig. 7 it will be seen that more limestone passes into solution in the first second of a fixed set of conditions than it does in all the rest of the time during which those conditions remain constant. Nearly all the limestone which can in fact be taken up is dissolved during the first minute, but the time taken to reach equilibrium may be as much as from twenty-four to sixty hours. Roques also discusses the response times of the various interactions. (See article referred to above).

In 1952 Trombe produced tables giving the relationship between the calcium content of saturated solutions at different temperatures and the pH [57]. Though Trombe's figures are not entirely accurate according to modern data, they are still a very useful guide to the aggressivity or otherwise of limestone waters. Picknett and others consider Trombe's figures to be too

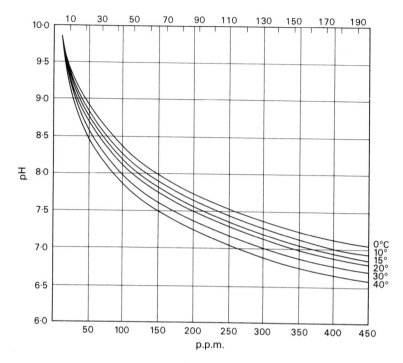

Fig. 8(*a*) Relationship between the calcium content of saturated solutions at different temperatures and the pH (from Trombe [57])

More sophisticated work by Picknett and others suggests that these curves should be replaced by those in Fig. 8(*b*).

high by 0·1 to 0·5 units, and recommend the use of a saturometer [60]. Trombe's curves have been used by many workers on karst waters, including both Corbel [61] and Gerstenhauer [62] (see Fig. 8).

The solution reactions for magnesium carbonates and for dolomites resemble those for calcium carbonates. $MgCO_3$, magnesite, and $MgCO_3:3H_2O$, nesquehonite, are the most important magnesium carbonates. Magnesite is hardly ever found as separate crystals but is present in many organic limestones and magnesian limestones in solid solution with calcite; it thus occurs in carbonate rocks as part of crystals consisting largely of calcium carbonate. Some confusion exists in the literature about the solubility of magnesium carbonates, but the figures given by both Schoeller (Table IX) and by Chilingar show that magnesium carbonate is more soluble than calcium carbonate at all temperatures and all CO_2 pressures.

The solution rate of dolomite, $CaCO_3.MgCO_3$ is not well understood but it seems that the double carbonate is less soluble

TABLE IX

THE SOLUBILITY OF DOLOMITE, CALCITE AND MAGNESITE

Temp.	$p\,CO_2$ in atmos.	Dolomite	Calcite	Magnesite ($MgCO_3$)
0	1	10·74	15·08	22·52
25	1	6·49	9·0	16·50
25	1	6·08	6·09	15·59
25	0·0012	1·42	0·81	1·65

Millimoles of $(HCO_3)_2$ in 1 kg soil
(From Schoeller (1962) [36] p. 283.)

Fig. 8(b) Saturation of water
samples from St. Dunstan's Well
with respect to calcium carbonate
(based on curves developed by
Picknett [60] from work by Drew
[70])

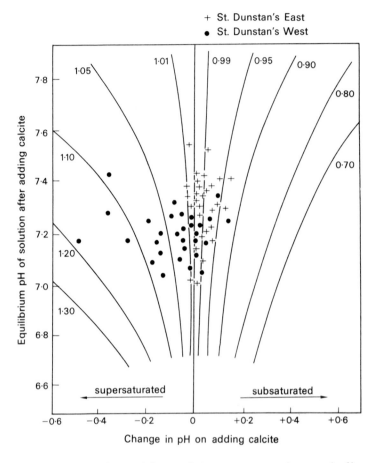

Fig. 9 Solution of calcium in karst
waters, north-west Yorkshire

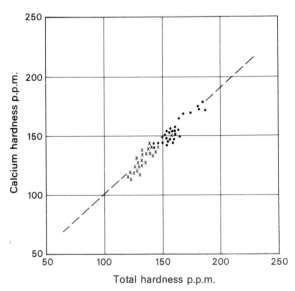

than either calcite or magnesite, as indicated above. This is confirmed by
Gerstenhauer and Pfeiffer [63] and Preisnitz [64]. Frequently the double carbonate
molecules of dolomite go into solution as
units, i.e. congruently, as is indicated by
the solution of calcium and magnesium in
karst waters in north-west Yorkshire, Fig.
9, and in the Durness area of Sutherland.
So far field observations, as opposed to
laboratory conditions, suggest that, whatever the proportion of magnesium to
calcium carbonate in the original limestones,
the solubility of magnesium to calcium
carbonate is always congruent provided
there has been sufficient time to reach
equilibrium. Under some conditions more
of the magnesium is dissolved than of the

calcite, the indications being that where there is rapid movement of water or rapid wetting of a rock surface the solubility of dolomite is not congruent, and that more magnesium goes into solution than calcite.

As is well known, the precipitation of calcium carbonate is much more readily brought about than that of magnesium carbonate, magnesium tending to remain in solution for a long time after the conditions of CO_2 partial pressure and temperature which influenced its solution have changed. This is the typical situation in a cave where the loss of CO_2 from the water to the cave atmosphere results in the formation of stalagmites and stalactites of calcium carbonate, but not magnesium carbonate. Evaporation from rivers and pools also increases the proportion of magnesium. Douglas has given a good review of some of the problems presented by magnesium solubility in karst waters [65], and aspects of carbonate precipitation are also discussed by Roques.

In most of the work on karst landforms we are dealing with the fresh waters of the surface, rivers and lakes with ionic strength of the order 0·01. But in coastal regions there is evidence of solution of the limestone by sea water. The extent to which sea water, whose ionic strength is 0·7, is an effective solvent of limestones is still not known; in a symposium on the 'Regional Aspects of Carbonate Deposition', it was said that it 'has not yet been demonstrated beyond all reasonable doubt that surface sea water . . . is an effective solvent of limestone' [66]. Garrels and Christ discuss the chemical interactions that take place in sea water, where 'large percentages of carbonate, bicarbonate and sulphate can be considered to form ion pairs with cations', and speak of the 'relatively high solubility of the alkaline earths . . .' [67]. Sea organisms, algae and animals, certainly help by

both respiration of CO_2 and other action to cause corrosion of the limestones with which they come into contact. Experiments by both Kaye [68] and Guilcher [69] have shown that there is a marked diurnal variation in the CO_2 content of coastal sea waters and in the pH of pools in the intertidal zone. During the night, plants increase the CO_2 content of waters by respiration; in the daytime, they reduce the CO_2 by photosynthesis. Hence there is a low pH in the waters in the pools during the night and a high pH in the day; in Puget Sound, pools in the intertidal zone had a pH of 7·43 in the early morning, and of 8·80 in the afternoon; increased solution of the limestones will therefore take place during the night. No similar studies on the variation of CO_2 content of inland surface waters in well-vegetated karst areas have been reported, though the work of Drew has shown that fluctuations in pH values occur over short periods in the Mendips [70].

Calcium and magnesium are important constituents of all natural waters, the percentage proportions of cations in average river water being as follows: calcium 63·5, magnesium 17·4, sodium 15·7 and potassium 3·4 [70]. In inland waters the most commonly occurring anion is bicarbonate. In passing from the source of a river towards the sea, the waters tend to become calcium-enriched.

Since the introduction of the Schwarzenbach method, the determination of the calcium and magnesium content of natural water is easy. Many complexometric methods now exist, but one of the most accurate is by titrations with E.D.T.A., a full acount of which is given by Schwarzenbach [71], and details of the procedure are given in Smith and Mead [72]. The estimated accuracy of each titration is of the order of 3 ppm and may be as close as 1 ppm. Water hardness tablets are now also on the market and these are particularly useful for reconnaissance work and when it is impossible to obtain facilities for laboratory titration. The most important of these tablets are those known as Palintest, made in England, and those called Durognost, produced in Germany. A discussion of the relative merits of these as indicators of calcium and magnesium hardness has been dealt with by Douglas [73]; the average accuracy of the tablets is about 5-9 ppm. More recently Bray has discussed new techniques of complexometric titrimetric analysis for the direct determination of calcium and magnesium in waters containing both substances [487]. Many experiments have also been carried out on the electrical conductance of cave waters, and this method promises to be of great use in karst water studies [487], [488]. The terms alkalinity, carbonate alkalinity and alkaline reserve, etc., and the question of hardness in natural waters, are discussed by Hutchinson [52]. The term total hardness is usually used for the combined Ca and Mg hardness, while calcium hardness and magnesium hardness are used for the $CaCO_3$ and $MgCO_3$ content respectively.

2. FACTORS AFFECTING THE SOLUBILITY OF LIMESTONES

We can now discuss the factors which contribute to the solubility of karst limestones. As we have seen, the solubility of calcium carbonate in pure water is only of the order of 12–14 ppm, and the main factor in the solution is the variations in the CO_2 pressure. Carbon dioxide by itself is more soluble in waters of lower temperatures than in waters at higher temperatures, hence – other things being equal – more

calcium carbonate should be dissolved in cooler climates. CO_2 is a feeble constituent of the atmosphere, being only about 0·033 per cent by volume (or 0·00033 atmos. pressure), though Kreutz gives a figure of 0·044 per cent for 1939–1941 [52]. The percentage of CO_2 in the atmosphere varies slightly with latitude and more significantly with altitude; in the higher parts of the Andes or Himalayas pressures of 0·00020 at heights of 4,000 m to 5,000 m might be expected [52]. This fact could be of great importance in the solubility of limestones at high altitudes.

Two types of solubility are concerned with CO_2. First, *anaerobic solubility*, where the water comes into an initial equilibrium with the air but where the carbon dioxide is cut off when calcium carbonate solution takes place; the carbonate solubility is then only 14 ppm. Second, the more usual in nature, *equilibrium solubility*, where the water is in contact with a continuous supply of air during the calcium carbonate solution process; the carbonate solubility at 10°C is then 74 ppm [72] (see Table VII, p. 24, and Fig. 10).

However, karst waters contain much more than 74 ppm of calcium and magnesium, frequently as much as 300–400 ppm. Since CO_2 pressure is probably the

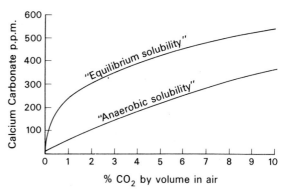

Fig. 10 Calcium carbonate solubilities at 10°C (from Smith & Mead [56])

most important factor in the solution process, environments where the CO_2 is increased should therefore first be examined. One type of variation in the amount of CO_2 and acidity of water reaching the limestones is the variation in the acidity of rain water. The pH of rain water varies over the world from about pH 4·0 to 7·1, with averages about 5 to 5·5 [74]. Douglas, in his study of the pH values of rain water, states that there is no special basis for the supposed greater acidity of the rainfall in tropical areas, and says the 'contrast between inland and coastal areas is probably greater than the overall contrast between tropical and temperate areas' [75]. However, atmospheric pollution is an important source of the acidity of rainfall. In west Yorkshire, it has been shown that the rain water and snowfall is distinctly more acid when the wind is from the south-east and east than when the wind is from west or north-west (pH 4·0 as against 6·6); this is due to the proximity of the manufacturing industrial area to the south-east [76]. In coastal localities, as the effects of sea spray, the water contains more chlorides and sulphates and is distinctly more acid. However, the role of CO_2 in rain water has probably been overrated.

The most important environment for the increase in CO_2 pressure is in the soil. The pressure of CO_2 in the soil is many times greater than that of the CO_2 in the atmosphere and according to Birot may be as much as 100 times that of the atmosphere in cracks in the bedrock [77]. Adams and Swinnerton drew attention to the fact that, since the CO_2 content of the soil air was much greater than that of the atmosphere itself, this higher CO_2 content might be responsible for the large quantities of $CaCO_3$ carried off in solution from limestone areas [78]. The increase in CO_2 pressure is clearly related to vegetational

and microbiological activity, and Schoeller maintained that there was an increase in carbon dioxide in underground waters of areas with a greater biotic activity [36]. However, biological activity within the soil shows, in temperate areas at least, a seasonal rhythm and is greatest in spring and summer. Yet, as Smith and Mead found in the Mendips, the karst waters do not always show any seasonal variation in the recorded amounts of dissolved calcium carbonate, since many spring waters have about 235 ppm calcium regardless of season [72]. Pitty has, however, claimed that variations in the calcium carbonate content of the solute of sites in Poole's Cavern in the Peak District of Derbyshire result from a dominance of organic carbon dioxide, particularly produced by root activity, in the limestone solution; 'carbon dioxide, therefore, explains the high mean hardness and the fluctuations in part, even if other modifications mark the rhythm of the main factor' [79] (Fig. 11). There is also other evidence to show that calcium carbonate values in karst waters rise during seasons of greater biological activity, for instance in the readings for north-west Yorkshire in the Malham Tarn group of waters. The waters of Malham Tarn are of especial interest, since it will be seen that the waters issuing from the tarn itself show a decrease and not an increase during the summer months; this is due to the activity of calcareous algae and other lime-secreting plants which live in the tarn waters and which are particularly biologically active during the summer and secrete the lime, Fig. 12. Similarly in the Mellte river of South Wales, Groom and Williams found distinctly greater values of calcium in summer than in winter [80]; and Stellmack and White obtained the same kind of pattern for the solution of limestone in Virginia [81]. Gams has done the most

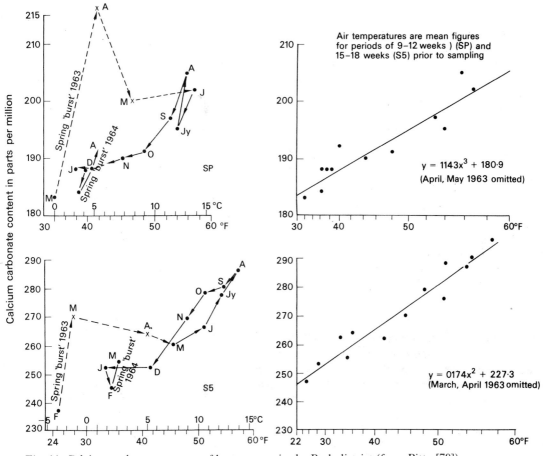

Fig. 11 Calcium carbonate content of karst waters in the Peak district (from Pitty [79])

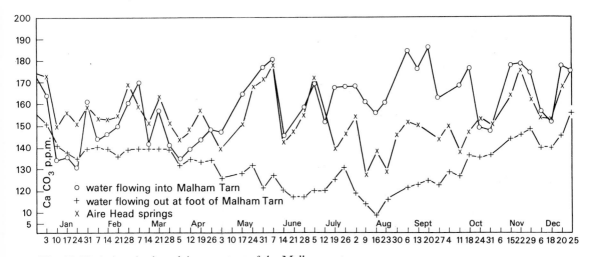

Fig. 12 Variations in the calcium content of the Malham waters

thorough work on this problem in Slovenia and shows that in the Postojna cave area the total hardness fluctuates much more under woodland (beech or pine) than under meadow (33–35 per cent fluctuation as against 10 per cent). The waters are hardest in the autumn and less in winter and spring [82].

Organic acids increase the acidity of the soil water though the exact amount is not really known. Acids such as formic, tannic, oxalic, lactic, acetic, etc., result from the growth of plants and from the decomposition of vegetable matter; the extent to which these acids are efficient solvents of limestones has not yet been satisfactorily proved. Experiments were tried by Aub in Jamaica, but were inconclusive. Fetzer showed that humic acids were not a solvent of limestones [83]. Organisms in direct contact with the limestone, particularly in forest environments, also produce carbon dioxide and humic acids; root hairs produce chelating acids which dissolve calcium carbonate in the soil. Weathering and attack on limestones also occurs through epilithic and endolithic lichens and algae, as has been demonstrated by Jones on the Carboniferous Limestones of north-west Yorkshire [84]. Such organisms also help to produce mechanical disintegration of the rock [85]. In intertidal zones along the coast, marine plants and animals are particularly important in the dissolution of limestones. Along the coast of the Burren of west County Clare, for instance, small hollows (100 mm × 50 mm approximately) formed by the action of living echinoderms are common in the Carboniferous Limestones. The rate of lowering of these limestones by organic solution has never been measured but is probably quite considerable. The CO_2 produced by algae is probably also significant, particularly during the night, and will assist in the dissolution of limestones.

Another environment in which the CO_2 pressure is increased is in snow banks. We have already seen that CO_2 is more soluble in cold water than in warmer water. The daily freezing and thawing of the snow surface leads to a greater concentration of CO_2 in the air contained within the snow banks; since CO_2 is heavier than air it tends to remain towards the base of the snow bank, and rain and meltwater passing through the snow become highly charged with CO_2. Williams discussed the air highly charged with CO_2 and its effects on solution hollows under snow banks in 1949 [86]. Solution by highly charged water draining from snow banks is also important. Even in north-west Yorkshire, the pH of snow after some hours becomes quite low, about 4·0 [86]. Although snow may become heavily charged with CO_2, it is still uncertain whether glaciers and glacier ice also become important reservoirs for CO_2. Corbel, particularly from work in Norway, believes that meltwaters from glaciers contain considerable quantities of CO_2 [87]. But some recent work of Ek on glacial meltwaters in the Marmolada area in the Dolomites shows that the waters issuing from the glaciers are poor in CO_2, only very slightly aggressive and capable of dissolving relatively little limestone [88]. Gams had also found low carbonate hardness (about 16 ppm) in waters from the Triglav glacier at 2,380 m altitude [89] in Slovenia. But some recent work has shown that waters emerging from glacial snouts tend to deposit calcium carbonate. Both in the Rocky Mountains of Canada (Mt. Castleguard area) and in the Zugspitz in the Bavarian Alps, small stalactitic deposits are associated with receding glaciers. Such deposits are soon dissolved by atmospheric waters [489]. Thus the question of the aggressivity of water issuing from glaciers is still an open one.

Another source of CO_2 which is of

significance both on the surface and underground is that produced by the mixing of waters saturated with $CaCO_3$. This was first discussed by Bögli in 1964, and called by him *Mischungskorrosion* (mixture corrosion or mélange des eaux) [90]. If two waters both saturated with $CaCO_3$ yet containing different concentrations of $CaCO_3$ mix, active CO_2 is released. This is because the mixed waters require less total CO_2 for equilibrium than the sum of the CO_2 required for the equilibrium in the two individual solutions. The CO_2 released is therefore available for the further solution of the limestone. This point is discussed further in Chapter 9, p. 177.

We must also discuss the factors which assist the solution of the calcium carbonate and the rock itself. One of the most important of these is the temperature, a rise in which accelerates the rate of solution and so to some extent negates the effect of the greater solubility of CO_2 in waters of low temperatures. Bögli has said that 'The velocity of solution in the Tropics may increase up to 400 per cent as compared with that in Alpine or Arctic climates' [91]. The degree of turbulence or agitation of the water also speeds up the solution process, as the products of the reactions are removed from the solid–liquid interface; 'the greater the velocity of solvent flow past the crystal face, the thinner the diffusion layer; and the thinner the diffusion layer, the faster the solution rate for a given set of conditions'[92]. Weyl also has showed that greater turbulence causes more rapid solution, and that stagnant water becomes supersaturated [93]. In the same way, large drops of water or thin sheets of water falling on to the rock dissolve calcium carbonate more rapidly, as the ratio of surface rock to the volume of water is large. This can be confirmed by the very high calcium values for waters collected as they fall upon bare rock, particularly in the tropics; in British Honduras, for instance, water collected from an inclined surface of limestone during a heavy rainstorm, and having only flowed over the rock for a few seconds, gave a value of 367 ppm [94]. This kind of experiment supports Bögli's theory of the way in which limestone is dissolved (see above, p. 26).

The volume of water which falls or passes through a given area of volume of limestone is clearly of importance to the total amount of solution of the rock. In the Mendips, in G.B. cave, the $CaCO_3$ content varies inversely with the stream discharge [79], Fig. 13(a), (b) and (c). This is also true for the waters of north-west Yorkshire, low water conditions giving average values of 180 ppm $CaCO_3$ and flood conditions giving 60–80 ppm $CaCO_3$ for the same spring. More limestone in total amount is dissolved however under flood conditions, despite the lower concentrations of $CaCO_3$ in ppm in the water, Fig. 14(a) and (b). This was stressed by Groom and Williams in their study of the Mellte river in South

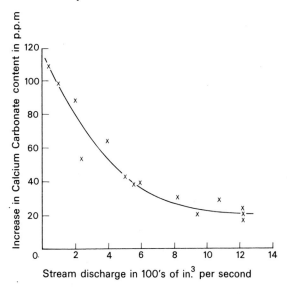

Fig. 13(a) Difference in calcium carbonate content as a function of stream discharge (from Smith & Mead [56])

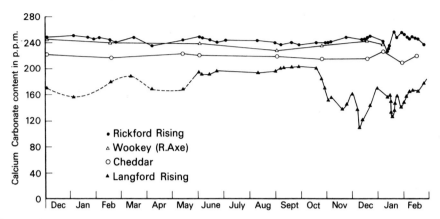

Fig. 13(*b*) Calcium carbonate content of the major Mendip risings (from Smith & Mead [56])

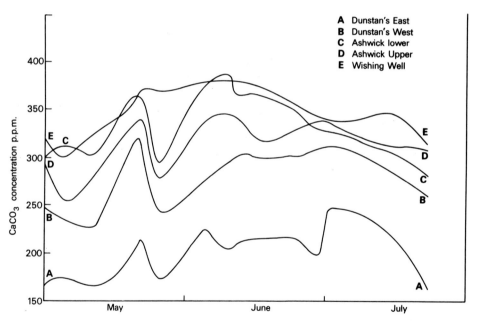

Fig. 13(*c*) Variations in calcium carbonate concentrations at East Mendip risings, May–August 1965 (from Drew [70])

Wales, where it was found that 'the total amount of solutional activity through the year is very much greater under run-off conditions than under ground-water conditions' [80]. Hence in general the more water available the more limestone will be dissolved. In dry climates, as in polar and tropical deserts, limestone corrosion will be at a minimum, and in very wet regions both temperate and tropical, corrosion will be greatest.

It might also be expected that the *length of time* that the CO_2-charged water is in contact with the limestone would affect the

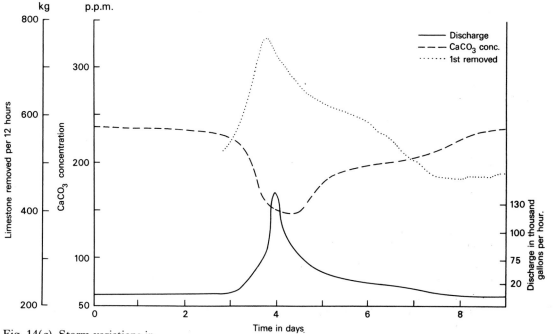

Fig. 14(a) Storm variations in discharge, limestone removal, calcium carbonate concentration at St. Dunstan's Well (from Drew [70])

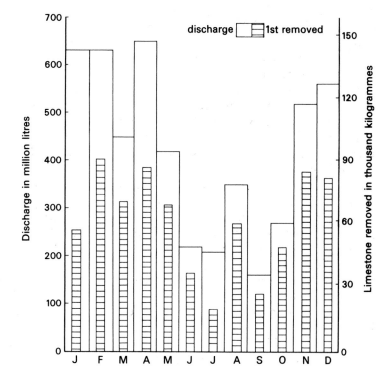

Fig. 14(b) Discharge and limestone removal at St. Dunstan's Well 1966 (from Drew [70])

Fig. 15 Calcium carbonate values, G. B. Cave, Mendips (from Smith & Mead [72])

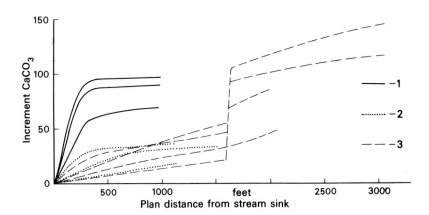

amount of solution accomplished. This was suggested by the results of Smith and Mead in G.B. cave, where water dripping from the roof at a depth of about 120 ft (38 m) had a calcium value of 120 ppm, but drips from the deepest part of the cave, 440 ft (130 m) below the surface, had a calcium value of 240 ppm; the water that had percolated through the greater thickness of limestone had the higher value [72]. Smith and Mead were of the opinion that the speed of limestone solution suggested by Bögli is too rapid, and that 'the time necessary for the water flowing in joints and fissures to reach equilibrium with the dissolved carbon dioxide should be thought of in terms of days rather than hours' [72]. Pitty's results tend to this conclusion too [79]; also he has tried to show that it is possible to deduce from the calcium content of a karst water the length of time it has been in contact with the limestone – the greater the calcium content, the older the water. While this conclusion may be correct for the waters with which Pitty is dealing, it certainly does not apply to all karst waters, relatively 'new' karst waters being found to contain much more $CaCO_3$ than waters known to be of a great age. Other results also go against Pitty's conclusion, such as the high values of calcium near the surface

discussed by P. Williams in western Ireland, where water samples from Coole showed a total hardness of 300 ppm acquired in the first 25 ft of vertical percolation [95]. In Slovenia, Gams is of the opinion that the bulk of corrosion in the limestone occurs in the uppermost 10 m of the percolation zone [96]. In Yorkshire high values of $CaCO_3$ are found shortly after the waters reach the outcrop of the limestones, and these often do not seem to vary with increasing length of time in contact with the rock. It is far more likely in fact that several cycles of solution and precipitation occur during the passage of waters through limestones (Fig. 15).

The solution of limestones is further affected by chemical impurities and variations. We have already shown that the carbonate minerals themselves have differential solubilities. Picknett has examined the effect of magnesium carbonate upon the solubility of calcite. He says 'it appears that traces of magnesium in solution increase the amount of calcite which can dissolve for a given carbon dioxide concentration. It is only when large amounts of magnesium are present that the expected happens, and the solubility of the calcite is reduced' [60]. Chilingar claims that calcite is selectively leached out of limestones and that the speed of leaching of limestones is about five times greater than that of dolomite [35, 97]; he also says that rocks which have a relatively high percentage of $MgCO_3$ give rise to a preponderance of Ca in the resulting solutions, despite the greater solubility of the $MgCO_3$. In the initial stages, the magnesium goes into solution faster than the $CaCO_3$; but as time of solution proceeds, the Ca/Mg ratio is greatly increased [35, 97].

The effects of other impurities have long been known to influence the solubility of limestones, as shown by Cosyns's work in Belgium [98]. Recently Terjesen and others have indicated that small traces of heavy metals such as lead, scandium, copper and manganese have an inhibiting effect upon the solution of calcite [99]. For instance, in the experiments by Terjesen, the effective solubility of calcite was reduced to one-half by a scandium concentration of only 0·2 per cent of the calcium concentration. Grains of quartz also occur in many limestones; in north-west Yorkshire it can be shown that beds containing these grains are more resistant to solution [76]. On the other hand, the presence of lead or iron sulphides which commonly occur in association with limestones will increase their solution. This is due to the oxidation of the sulphides to sulphuric acid. Sodium and potassium are also considered to increase the solubility of calcite. Salts formed by the association of alkali cations with anions like Cl^- and $SO4^{--}$ will also increase the solubility.

In addition there is the texture and structure of the limestones themselves to be considered. As we have already seen, karst limestones are very variable in texture. Two points are important; first, the pore space or porosity of the rock which determines the amount of water the rock can take up; secondly, the ease with which water can pass through the rock. Both are important

from the point of view of solubility. Generally the more porous limestones are the more soluble, because more water containing carbon dioxide is able to permeate the rock. This is illustrated by the fact that the average calcium hardness values for the chalk of southern England is about 260–280 ppm, whereas the average calcium hardness value for the older, less porous limestones is usually much less. However, ease of penetration of the water is also important, either by joints or diaclases; this is because if the water becomes too slow-moving the equilibrium with the carbonate and the CO_2 is reached and no further solution takes place. Karst limestones consisting of a high percentage of sparry calcite tend to be more resistant to solution except along the joint or fissure planes. The interlocking crystals make the rock very tight and impermeable, and permeability is only of the order of 2–3 per cent. Micritic and lime-mud limestones are also very dense and have a low porosity, also of about 3–5 per cent. Limestones in the middle of the textural spectrum of Folk appear to have greater porosities. From field experiments in north-west Yorkshire, some differential solution of the different kinds of limestones has been proved; limestones with a greater percentage of sparry calcite appear to be somewhat less soluble under similar conditions of temperature and time than those limestones with a smaller percentage of sparry calcite and a greater amount of lime-mud, Fig. 5. Chilingar in writing of magnesium limestones says that there is a greater tendency for water to enlarge the pre-existing cracks and fractures than to increase the porosity. He also says that water moves more easily through carbonate rocks that have a diverse rather than a preferred orientation of the constituent grains or through those that have a high porosity [35, 97]. Verstappen in his study of the morphology of the Star Mountains in New Guinea also drew attention to the importance of porosity and any water-holding capacity, and noted that these differed widely for the limestones of the area with which he was dealing. It has also been found experimentally by Williams that limestones that are crushed and pulverised are more soluble than those which are more bulky [100]; this point has also been made by Preisnitz [64]. Limestones with roughened surfaces are also more soluble than those with smoothed surfaces [63]. Factors affecting limestone solubility are discussed by Douglas [104]. The field experiments of the writer have been corroborated by Rauch & White in Ordovician Limestones in Pennsylvania, and by Gerstenhauer & Pfeiffer [63, 491].

3. ESTIMATES OF THE RATE OF LIMESTONE SOLUTION

Thus the factors that influence the solution of karst limestones are very varied. There have been many attempts to estimate the loss of limestone by solution and the rate of lowering of limestone areas. Goodchild in 1890, by observation on local monuments and tombstones, for example, in northern England, calculated that the rate of weathering of the limestones was about 1 in. in 500 years (about 50 mm per 1,000 years). Kilroe, in the Shannon basin in Ireland, calculated that the Carboniferous Limestones were being dissolved away at the rate of 1 ft in 1,200 years or about 250 mm in 1,000 years [101]. In the U.S.A., Ewing in 1885 calculated the corrosion of limestone in a river basin in Centre County, Pennsylvania, to be about 1 ft in 9,000 years (about 34 mm per 1,000 years) [102].

Today, a widely used formula for estimating limestone loss from an area by solution is that devised by Corbel [61]. This formula has since been modified by Williams [103]. Corbel's formula is simple:

$$4ET(N)/100 = X$$

where E = run-off in decimetres, T = average $CaCO_3$ content of the water in ppm, and X = the value of the limestone solution in cubic metres per year per square kilometre or in millimetres/1,000 years (mm/1,000 years); $1/N$ = the proportion of limestone in the basin, as a fraction of the total area of the basin. Corbel assumed that limestones have an average density of 2·5. However, as Williams has pointed out, limestones may vary in density from 2·72 for the Carboniferous Limestones in County Clare to less than 2·0 for more porous chalky limestones [103]. Corbel also included only calcium hardness in T, but magnesium hardness is often present in large quantities, and T should always represent total hardness [103]. Further, colloidal calcium is not allowed for in Corbel's formula, although it is difficult to estimate the effects of colloidal calcium on the result. Moreover, the usefulness of the formula depends upon the accuracy of the determination of the value of E, the run-off, or water surplus, i.e. the percentage of precipitation which remains after losses through evaporation and transpiration. The measurement of relative quantities of surface run-off and infiltration, particularly in a limestone area, are difficult. Furthermore, though measurements of precipitation may be available, measured values for evapotranspiration are rare.

Williams's modified formula if flow-gauge records are available is as follows:

$$X = FQTn/10^{12}AD$$

where

X = the equivalent thickness of limestone removed, in mm, over a
a specified period

Q = the discharge over the period

T = the mean total hardness of the
water, in ppm (or mg/l) over the
period

A = the area of the river basin in square
kilometres

D = the density of the limestone (or
dolomite)

$\dfrac{1}{n}$ = the area of limestone, as a fraction
of the total area of the basin

f = a conversion factor; 28·3 if Q is in
cubic feet, but 1,000 if Q is in cubic
metres (fQ is equivalent to discharge in litres).

If it is preferred to calculate the value of
corrosion in $m^3/yr/km^2$, as in Corbel's
formula, then

$$X = fQTn/10^9AD.$$

Where no discharge records are available,
then the formula is as follows:

$$X = ETn/10D$$

where

X = the value of the limestone removed
in solution in mm/1,000 years or in
$m^3/yr/km^2$

E = mean water surplus per annum in
decimetres

T = mean total hardness in ppm (or
mg/l)

D = the density of the limestone (or
dolomite)

$\dfrac{1}{n}$ = the fraction of the basin occupied
by limestone.

Williams, both in his paper on the 'Speed
of limestone solution in County Clare' and
in his thesis, discusses fully the difficulties
of these formulae [103].

Corbel used his original simple formula
to deduce the amount of limestone lost by
solution in karst regions. His figures in 1959
were based on random 'spot' observations
in a number of areas. The main features of
his results were the high rates of corrosion
of limestones in Alpine and snowy Arctic
regions compared with relatively low rates
for warmer humid areas, as shown by the
figures in Table X.

Subsequent work has shown that the
apparent correlations of high corrosion

TABLE X

CORBEL'S FIGURES FOR THE AMOUNT OF LIMESTONE LOST BY SOLUTION
IN KARST REGIONS

Location	Limestone	Rate of corrosion in mm/1,000 years
Spitsbergen	Permo-Carboniferous	27
Svartisen, N. Norway	Ordovician-Silurian	400
Alaska (S.E.)	Unspecified	770
Mendip Hills	Carboniferous	40
Sligo, W. Ireland	Carboniferous	40
Florida, U.S.A.	Upper Tertiary	5
Colombia	Unspecified	10

(From *Ann. Géog.*, 1959.)

values with low temperatures are far too simple and that the factors affecting the solution of limestones are more complex than Corbel originally supposed. Thus in 1964 it was shown both that in a small area like that of Britain there were great variations in the hardness of karst waters, and also that hardness values from different areas of the world did not directly reflect a climatic or temperature variation. More recent work, by Pitty [79] in the Peak District of Derbyshire and by Gams [105] in Slovenia, also suggests that 'at the present state of knowledge no exact valuation of the influence of climate on corrosion (of limestones) is possible'. The necessity for prolonged series of observations has been illustrated by Douglas [104].

However, in selected karst areas where observations of hardness values of the waters have been taken over a period of time, and where the other values discussed in connection with Corbel's modified formula are known, an approximate estimate of the amount of limestone corrosion can be made. Figures are given in Table XI.

One of the most interesting aspects of these calculations, which are based on a fair number of experiments, is how closely they approximate to the older estimates of limestone denudation. As a result of this modern work there is now a much greater interest in the solution geochemistry of limestone waters and in the development of limestone aquifers [492].

The figures given in Table XI are estimates for the total overall dissolution of limestone in an area. But it is quite obvious that, because of the pitted nature of the relief, the dissolution of limestone is by no means uniform, and that certain parts are more affected by the solution than others. Differential solution takes place and the actual overall lowering must be lower than that given in the calculations. Locally accentuated or accelerated solution which produces the pits or hollows has been called by Gams *accelerated corrosion* [106]. By accelerated corrosion, Gams implies a corrosion intensity which exceeds the mean intensity in the neighbourhood, and it is this which produces the depression forms so characteristic of the karst landscapes. He lists the conditions which favour accelerated corrosion; they are due partly to physiographic factors and are as follows:

(*a*) *Where impermeable rocks adjoin limestones.* In these localities streams from non-karstic areas have aggressive waters and will cause above-average dissolution of the

TABLE XI

LIMESTONE CORROSION IN DIFFERENT AREAS

Author	Locality	Rate of denudation in mm/1,000 years
V. Williams	S. Wales	18
P. W. Williams	Co. Clare, Ireland	55
Sweeting	N.W. Yorkshire	49–50
Gams	Slovenia	77–80
Pigott	Derbyshire	55–100
Bögli	Glattalp, Lucerne	15·1
Bingelli	S. Alps	250–333
Perrin	E. Anglia (Chalk)	25
Versey	White Limestones, Jamaica	72
Pitty	Peak District, Derbyshire	75–83

limestone. This is particularly so if the streams come off siliceous rocks. Two areas where this can be seen are the Shenandoah Valley, Virginia, described by Hack, and the Castleton area in Derbyshire where streams come off the gritstones of Rushup Edge [107]. Different types of depression are caused by this type of accelerated corrosion.

(*b*) *Alluvial corrosion.* Intense corrosion takes place by water which percolates through alluvium and morainic sands and gravels. Such waters always have a very high degree of hardness, which Gams believes is due to their percolation through soils rich in CO_2.

(*c*) *Corrosion by mixture corrosion*, which occurs when two waters of different hardness meet, either on the surface or underground. Bögli applies this only to underground (cave) corrosion, but 'there seems to be no reason to deny its activity in surface streams and rivers'.

(*d*) At the margins of *snow fields and icefields*. As has already been shown, snow meltwater is probably able to dissolve more limestone than rain water, and where such meltwater comes into contact with limestones accelerated corrosion takes place.

(*e*) Accelerated corrosion caused by water passing *from bare karst to vegetated karst*. This is caused by the addition of CO_2 from the soil and vegetation. Work in the Julian Alps on a limestone scree showed a hardness increase of about 6–10 ppm where the bare slope passed from one covered with soil. The past and present variations in the tree line are also relevant to the concept of accelerated corrosion [108].

Work on the denudation of limestone areas using many of the methods described in this chapter is now well established. An attempt to standardise the methods on a world-wide basis is the object of a recently established commission on Karst Denudation, a commission of the International Speleological Union [493].

4 The Landforms. Enclosed Hollows of Moderate Dimensions: Dolines

WE ARE now in a position to discuss the main groups of karst landforms. As in other branches of landform study, classification is difficult because of their transitional nature, but five main groups can be recognised. These are:

(1) Closed depressions of moderate dimensions – dolines of various types – and often regarded as the essential unit of karst relief.

(2) Superficial landforms (small-scale features) produced by solution of the surface of the rock.

(3) Landforms of limestone areas formed by normal or fluvial erosion.

(4) Underground landforms – caves and cave deposits.

(5) Closed depressions of large dimensions; these are of complex polygenetic origin.

The landforms will be discussed in the order given, dolines being considered before the smaller superficial landforms because of their greater importance. Thus in many karst areas there are from 100–200 dolines per square kilometre. Gams calculates that dolines occupy 24 per cent of the whole of the karst area in Jugoslavia. His figures for the different republics in Jugoslavia are: Montenegro, dolines make up 64 per cent of the total land surface; in Bosnia-Hercegovina, 45 per cent; in Slovenia, 33–35 per cent; and in Serbia, the least karstic area, 8–9 per cent [494].

1. CLOSED DEPRESSIONS OF MODERATE DIMENSIONS. DOLINES

Dolines are closed hollows of small or moderate dimensions; they can be cone- or bowl-shaped, with rocky or vegetated sides and of a circular or elliptical plan. The diameter is usually greater than the depth, and average dolines vary in size from about 2–100 m deep and from 10–1,000 m in diameter. They can occur isolated or in groups in close proximity to one another. The pitted relief of karst areas is caused by the presence of innumerable dolines, and they are usually regarded as the fundamental unit of karst relief, because they replace the valleys of a fluvial terrain.

The term doline (or dolina) was first used by Austrian geologists in the middle of the nineteenth century, when they were studying the Classical Karst area; the name doline means in Serbo-Croat a valley or hollow (not necessarily a closed hollow). The name was given because in the Classical Karst only such closed hollows (and no valleys) occurred. Cvijič in his work in 1893 also used the term doline. Thus over the years the doline has been loosely used for the small depressions in limestone areas. One of the main problems in karst terminology is the various names given in the different Slav languages to similar landforms. Thus a closed depression in Serbo-Croat is called a 'do' or 'dolac', while in Slovenian this is used for a short dry valley. In a discussion held by the Slovenian

Geological and Geographical Society in 1962 on karst terminology, it was proposed that the word *vrtaca* be used instead of 'doline' or 'dolina' even though vrtaca is a word only in popular use in Slovenia and not used generally in the Dinaric karst. Thus the terms *skledasta vrtaca* (dish-shaped hollow), *lijakasta vrtaca* (funnel-shaped hollow), and *kalali lokva vrtaca* (waterlogged hollow) were proposed. Gams also suggested other terms, such as *kraska* (i.e. karst) *dolina*; *koliesvka*, for bigger depressions with steep and rocky slopes; and *kukava* for depressions with less inclined slopes and alluvial covered bottoms. One of the figures given in this discussion illustrated the different types of small depressions existing in the Slovenian karst [109].

Because of the confusion caused by this discussion, Williams in 1964 proposed that the term doline be discontinued and that it be replaced by 'enclosed hollow of moderate dimensions' [95]. However, it seems that use of the word doline is now too entrenched in the literature of English, French and German geomorphologists for it to be abandoned in favour of the longer term 'enclosed hollow' or the more difficult and less known 'vrtaca'. Thus in this book the word doline will continue to be used.

Cvijič devoted about half of his *Das Karstphänomen* to a study of dolines. He defined them as follows: 'Die Doline ist eine Wanne von kleinem, rundlichem Umfang und nicht allzu bedeutender Tiefe, welche im Kalkstein eingesenkt ist; ihr Durchmesser variiert meist innerhalb Grenzen von zehn bis tausend Metern, ihre Tiefe bewegt sich zwischen zwei und hundert Metern. . . . Wir fassen also mit dem Namen Doline alle kleinen trichter-förmigen Einsenkungen zusammen, welche den Karstgebieten ihren eigenthümlichen landschaftlichen Charakter verleihen.' [3].

Cvijič distinguished three main morphological types of doline:

(1) *Bowl-shaped dolines* (dolines en auge), which are of feeble depth compared with their breadth. The ratio of the diameter to the depth is approximately 10:1 and the angle of the slope is approximately $10°-12°$. The bases are flat-bottomed, covered with soil and frequently marshy.

(2) *Funnel-shaped dolines* (dolines en entonnoir), where the diameter is two or three times the depth, and the slopes of the sides, either of soil or of rock, are inclined at $30°-40°$. The funnel-shaped doline has a narrow base.

(3) *Well-shaped dolines* (dolines en fenêtre). The diameter is usually less than the depth and their sides, usually of rock, are abrupt or vertical slopes closing directly to the base of the doline.

According to Cvijič, the bowl-shaped doline is the most frequently occurring, being four times as common as the funnel type in Montenegro and in Hercegovina and more than six to ten times as common in Carniola and Istria. Type 3, the deep-well type, is the least frequent. All these types develop in the limestones and are not dependent upon a cover of drift or other rock.

Since Cvijič's work there have been many studies of dolines and many attempts at classification. Though all hollows in limestones result to some extent from solution, this is not always the predominant mechanism giving rise to the hollows. An important article on dolines appeared in 1941 by Cramer, who suggested a classification and a transition series of dolines. Fig. 16(*a*) is taken from that article [110].

Thus, though there are many different types of doline, they can be placed essentially in one of the following groups: normal solutional dolines; alluvial dolines; solution subsidences; collapse dolines, Fig. 16(*b*). In

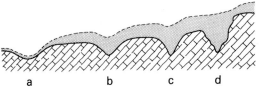

Fig. 16(*a*) Doline formation under different amounts of cover rocks (after Cramer [110])

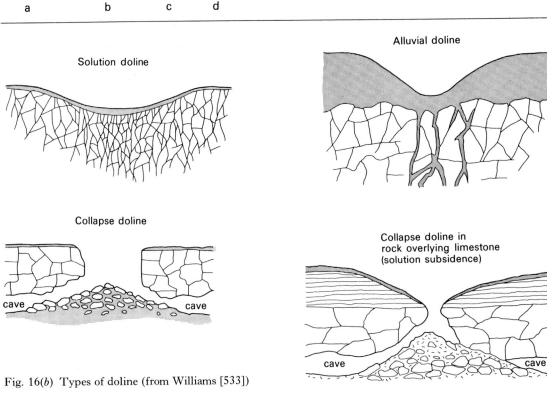

Solution doline

Alluvial doline

Collapse doline

cave   cave

Collapse doline in
rock overlying limestone
(solution subsidence)

cave   cave

Fig. 16(*b*) Types of doline (from Williams [533])

the humid tropics, the characteristic rounded doline form is replaced by a less regular, star-shaped hollow, sometimes known as a 'cockpit'.

(A) THE NORMAL SOLUTIONAL DOLINE

For a long time in the nineteenth century there was considerable controversy in the Classical and Dinaric karsts about the origin of dolines, as to whether they had been formed predominantly by solutional action or by collapse of the rock [111].

Cvijič was insistent that, though many dolines might be formed in other ways, the most characteristic dolines had been formed by solution.

Water infiltrates into the joints and fissures in the rock and solution takes place along them. Fig. 17 is from Cvijič's original work, and from Kunsky's more recent work on the karst of Moravia [112]. As a result of the enlargement of the fissures by dissolution, a settling and lowering of the surface takes place, which is represented on the surface by a closed depression. This is

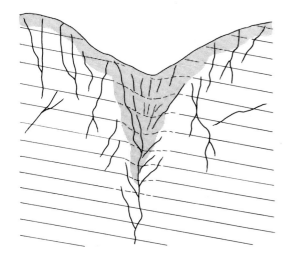

Fig. 17 Doline (after Cvijič [3])

the beginning of the normal doline. Into this depression, residual clay and alluvial material collect and these further assist the solution of the rock. Solution along one more or less vertical fissure may produce a circular doline, solution along several fissures may produce a less regular feature. As the dolines enlarge and in times of high intensity rainfall, their slopes are subject to slope wash and fluvial action.

Many proofs of this mode of formation can be seen in road and railway cuttings in the Classical Karst, where it can be shown that there is no dislocation or derangement of the limestone and hence no collapse. Towards the base of the hollow the limestone is decomposed and there is a mixture of blocks and residual soils. It will be seen that the process which has formed the dolines is like that which formed the pipes and swallow holes in the chalk of southern England, described by Prestwich [7], and the 'orgues géologiques' of Picardy. Photos 4(*a*) and 4(*b*) show the development of dolines in different areas, from initiation, in Montenegro, to a well-developed form in Japan.

In recent years some interesting studies of dolines have been made, which throw light upon the factors which govern their formation and distribution. In Britain two areas for the development of dolines are in the Mendips and in the Peak District of Derbyshire. In the Mendips it seems now established that the greatest number of the surface depressions (of those that are natural and not mining hollows) are of solutional origin, and that the suggestion of Coleman and Balchin that they are collapse features is not correct [113]. Ford and others have made detailed studies of the depressions of Mendip. Ford mapped 566 karstic depressions within the 14 sq. miles (36 sq. km) of limestone drained by the Ebor and Cheddar basins, and showed that the area provides three contrasted environments, viz. narrow valley floors, comparatively steep side slopes, and flatter interfluves. Of all the depressions, 80·5 per cent occur within the narrow valley floors; they are aligned down the valley floors and usually centrally located. The greatest number of depressions occur near to the contact of the Carboniferous Limestone with the underlying shales, where it is as high as 196 per sq. mile (70 per sq. km). The frequency of the depressions was found to be inversely proportional to the gradient, and they do not occur when the gradient increases to about 225 ft per mile (43 m/km). 13 per cent of all depressions are found on the steep side slopes; these are normally aligned straight down the slope and are close together, suggesting that they have developed in a shallow first- or second-order channel that has subsequently become disused. The remaining 6·5 per cent of all the depressions occur on the interfluves, and these tend to occur in isolation. According to Ford, the depressions show little relationship to the courses of known caves and the caves are at great

4(*a*) Dolines, near Cetinje, Montenegro

4(*b*) Doline of the Atiye shi dai, Japan *(see
'Speleology in Japan', by Takahashi and Kawano,
Bull. Nat. Speleol. Soc. 21 (2), 1959) (from
Prof. Takahashi, Okayama, Japan)*

depth and have not collapsed through to
the surface. Thus Ford concludes that 'the
depressions are the product of the infall of
pipe walls, weakened by a solutional attack
directed downwards from the surface. . . .
The valley floor site is preferred because of
the greater concentration of solvent water
there. On the valley floor, the occurrence or
non-occurrence of a depression is determined by the velocity of the overground
flow. Only when this falls below an un-
determined critical value do significant
quantities of water escape from the surface
channel into the many available fractures
and commence the process of depression
formation' [114] (see Fig. 18). He also says
that, where there has been much infall or
collapse of the enlarged and eroded pipe
walls associated with the depressions, they
are similar to the dolines percées of de
Martonne [1]. Ford concluded that it could
not be shown decisively whether the
depressions are forming under the present
climate, though evidence from the caves
suggests that at present there is much
groundwater solution, which would in

general indicate that the depressions were
deepening today. During Wurmian times,
when there was permafrost in the area, it is
possible that the depressions did not
deepen [114].

Some of the most interesting studies of
dolines came from the French regional
monographs of the 1930s and 1940s. In
particular one should mention the work of
Marres on *Les Grands Causses* [115],
Chabot on the *Plateaux du Jura Central*
[116], and Clozier on *Les Causses du
Quercy* [117]. On the Grands Causses,
dolines are known locally as *sotchs* and are
the equivalent of the dolines of the karst.
The sotchs are both circular and elongated,
their diameters and depths variable and
their topographic situations diverse. They
are particularly numerous in the dry
valleys, where their formation depends
upon the disorganisation of the original
surface drainage and valley slope, Fig.
19 [115]. Where for instance the valley is
sinuous, sotchs occur on the upstream side
of the meander. They also occur on slopes
and on cols where, as has been shown by

Fig. 19 Variations in doline formation
(from Marres [115])

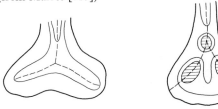

(a) Transformation of valley heads by development
of dolines (scale 1 : 55,000)

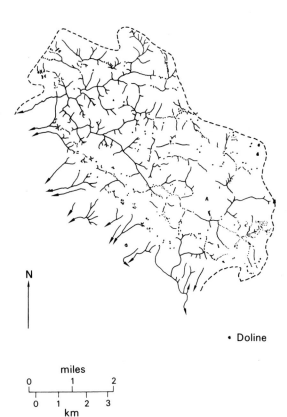

• Doline

miles

0   1   2

0   1   2   3
km

Fig. 18 Distribution of dolines in the Central
Mendips (after Ford [114])

(b) Dry valleys disrupted by doline formation, East
of Mas Saint-Chély, Causse Méjean. Dolines are
shown shaded. Scale 1:65,000 (from the Carte
d'État-Major)

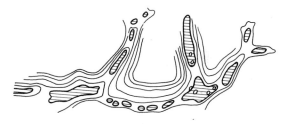

A   B

Section

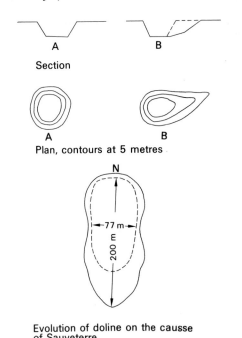

A   B

Plan, contours at 5 metres

N

←77 m→

E

200 m

Evolution of doline on the causse
of Sauveterre

(c) Evolution of doline forms

Ford in the Mendips, stream flow slackens
and water gathers. All obstacles which
retard stream flow favour the action of
corrosion and hence the formation of
sotchs. Sotchs on the cols are often quite
large, because snow lasts longer there and
accomplishes much solution. Sotchs are
also frequent on the high edges or 'corniches' of the Causses overlooking the
deeply cut allogenic valleys, in which
position they are particularly numerous and
deep; this is due to the deepening of the
drainage of the nearby surface valleys, and
partly to the increased rainfall along the
Corniche of the Causses. Marres believed

in 1935 that, though some of the dolines were probably deepening at present, many of them originated during the colder and more snowy phases of the Quaternary, and the larger ones might even have formed in the warm phases of the Pliocene. Such views have been substantiated by more recent work in the Causses, particularly by Enjalbert [495] who also shows that dolines in the Causses are filled with frost and other peri-glacial deposits.

The importance of the lithology and structure of the limestones is clearly seen in the sotchs of the Causses. In the homogeneous and dense micritic limestones like those of the Calcaire en Plaquettes (Sequanian), the sotchs are formed by solution only. They are circular, of modest diameter (about 50 m average), and of rather feeble depth, about 5 m. But much of the Grands Causses are made up of dolomitic limestone and in this rock the sotchs are deeper, more elongated and possess steep, often cliff-like, side walls. The dolomitic limestones are more heterogeneous in composition, yield to differential solution and tend to crumble and collapse. Where the limestones dip, the sotchs are asymmetrical, the up-dip side being relatively gentle, the down-dip side steeper, Fig. 20. However, such asymmetry can also result from climatic factors, the steepest sides being those exposed to the most humid winds.

Marres shows how the sotchs in the Causses enlarge and deepen when they become a local centre for drainage; they

become elongated and coalesce. In the dolomitic rocks the coalescence of sotchs is particularly rapid, and it is here also that incision (or emboîtement) of the sotchs takes place [115].

In the Causses of Quercy, Clozier shows that there too the dolines (here called cloups) are essentially forms of differential dissolution, and that their shapes reflect the nature of the limestones. Two main types of cloups occur in Quercy: (a) cloups in the form of a *baquet*, with steep sides and flat floor, and (b) cloups in the form of a *cuvette*, with more gently sloping sides. These types are related to the different limestones, the first being associated with compact Bajocian and Callovian limestones, the second with the Calcaire en Plaquettes. The cloups occur in all types of morphological positions but are unequally distributed over the area; thus in some parts there is 'une topographie chénillée avec des dolines protéiformes', whereas in other parts the dolines are small and undeveloped or non-existent [117].

Permeability and porosity of the limestones affect doline formation. Corrosion is likewise influenced by the distribution of soil layers and other non-limestone sediments. Morawetz has discussed how corrosion is 'delayed by sediment layers or spots of soil', a statement not entirely corroborated by other work [496]. Thus in recent French work on dolines in the Karsts of Provence it has been stated by Nicod [497] that on bare limestone surfaces dolines do not develop and that a cover of vegetation or soil is necessary. Dolines develop where diaclases exist in the rock, and where snow or vegetal cover assist the solution. Factors which are not favourable for doline formation include limestones with very frequent diaclases, intense periglacial action and the dispersal of the vegetal cover. Because of recent reduction in vegetation Nicod con-

Fig. 20 Formation of asymmetrical dolines

cludes that present day conditions are not favourable (in Provence) to doline formation [497] [498].

In his work on the Jura, Chabot discusses the distribution of dolines. He says that they are found in nearly all the different types of limestone. He notes a good correlation between their occurrence and the dry valleys, and states in his comments on the localisation of dolines: 'Nous pourrons donc retenir que si la corrosion reste bien l'agent essentiel dans leur formation, le ruissellement garde toute son importance dans leur localisation. C'est lui qui amène les eaux atmosphériques à pied d'œuvre, et dans les régions où il est intense, les dolines s'organisent sous son influence' [116]. He states that frequently dolines are aligned following the directions of the major joints or small faults. Furthermore they are often asymmetric. This is due, first, to the original slope of the ground, the uphill slope being steeper than the slope downhill; secondly to the dip of the limestone beds; and thirdly to the influence of slopes facing south or north (adret or ubac), the steeper slope facing towards the north or east, the gentler slope facing the south and west, which is explained by the action of snow and snow-melt being more corrosive on the south-facing than on the north-facing side. Similar asymmetry can be seen in dolines in the Santa Rosa Limestone (Permian) near Vaughan in New Mexico, U.S.A., at 6,000 ft, where the steeper slopes face westwards, the direction of the Pacific snowfall.

In Alpine areas snow is an important factor in doline formation. Any hollow or intersection of joints where snow is able to lie becomes deepened during the winter months. In the limestone massif of the Vercors in south-eastern France, Corbel attributes the fine doline development to the solution caused by a heavy snow-

fall [118]. In the higher parts of the Julian Alps, steep-sided rocky *kotlici* (or kettles) are dolines formed solely from the solution caused by small snow banks, Photo 5 [108]. Many other localities have good examples of dolines formed largely by the solutional action of snowfall; these include the Western and Central Atlas in Morocco, where Martin has described uplifted blocks of limestone as being 'criblés de petites cuvettes karstiques'. These small dolines are usually not more than 50 m in diameter, and about 5 m deep; they occur at high altitudes, particularly at above 1,900 m, and like those described in the Jura they are of asymmetric form, the easterly-facing sides being steeper than the other sides. Similar dolines can be described from the limestone

5 Kotlici, snow dolines, Julian Alps, near Triglav summit

mountains in the Lebanon where winter snowfall is again important. Dolines formed by the solutional action of snow were called *Schneedolinen* by Cvijič [3].*

Vegetation, particularly trees, also assist doline formation, and in the Jura there is a good correlation between the occurrence of trees and the development of the dolines [116]. The mechanical and chemical action of the roots of trees, the accumulation of organic debris and the increased growth of fungi and other plants in the forest environment all mean that the CO_2 of the soil is greatly enriched in the neighbourhood of trees. In the Alps this is particularly important and dolines tend to cease their development altogether at the tree line; the forested zones in the Alps are also the doline zones [119]. In deep dolines in forested areas, there is an inversion of temperature, the cold air accumulating at the base; as a result there is a zonation of the vegetation similar to that found on a mountain, only in the reverse way, the warmth-loving plants being at the top of the doline and the colder-climate plants at the bottom; Fig. 21 shows the zonation of vegetation in a large doline in the Triestine karst [120].

In America, Malott has described dolines 'with gentle soil-covered sides and flattish bottoms . . . largely developed by solution under a soil mantle . . .' [121]. These are particularly well developed in the south Indiana karst and in Central Kentucky, on a belt of limestones of Mississippian age. Such dolines are known as *sink holes* in America, and in the Lost River sink-hole plain, south-west of Orleans, in Orange County, 1,022 sink holes were counted in one square mile. 'It is not unlikely that the

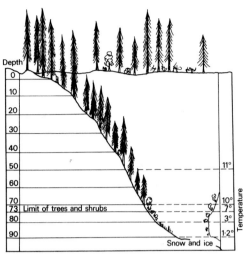

Fig. 21 Zonation of vegetation in a large doline (after Gèze [120])

whole karst region . . . has a total number in excess of 300,000 sink holes. . . . The vast majority of them are more or less symmetrical depressions from 10 to 30 ft in depth' (Fig. 22) [121]. This very fine doline Karst has recently received much attention from Quinlan and White [500], [501].

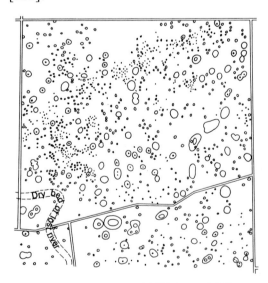

Fig. 22 Plane table map of 1022 located doline depressions in one square mile of the Lost River doline plain south-west of Orleans, Orange Co., Indiana (from Malott [121])

*Cramer in 1941 distinguished between dolines in areas where there was a long snow cover during the year from those where the snow cover was relatively short [110].

Dolines formed from solution by snow banks tend to be steep-sided and rocky and are associated with little alluvial or soil material, whereas those formed under a vegetation cover have gentler, i.e. 'older' slopes, and are much encumbered with soil and debris. Thus it is possible to differentiate between dolines formed in the two distinct ways [108]. Slovenian work on the high Julian Alps is particularly perceptive in this respect. Movements of the tree line and deforestation will clearly affect the nature of doline development.

In the Dinaric karst, S. M. Milojevič has stressed the importance of brachyclases (diaclases). Dolines originate at the points where brachyclases converge and their rate of deepening depends upon the size of the brachyclases, and the rate of accumulation of debris. The sides of an evolving and developing doline will converge towards its base, whereas a doline which is not developing will have a more rounded base. Thus Milojevič thought the most important morphological aspect of a doline was not the relationship between the depth and the diameter as stressed by Cvijič but the nature of the contact between the base and its slope. 'Well'-shaped dolines with steep-walled sides (œil or oko) tend to be almost entirely of a solutional origin, with little modification by stream action or wash slopes; funnel-shaped dolines and 'doline plates' are much more modified by the mechanical action of slope wash [122].

In any study of dolines the conditions of their bases are of importance. They may consist of bare limestone as in snow dolines, but they more frequently contain either residual or transported material. If the material is truly residual there will be stratification and no essential difference between its lower and upper parts. Fragments of the undissolved limestone bedrock will be scattered throughout. In the Classical Karst area such residual material is known as the terra rossa and varies in thickness from a few centimetres to about one metre and sometimes as much as four metres. The deposit is thickest at the base of the dolines. However, as dolines enlarge, superficial streams drain into them and bring in alluvial material which may show stratification. In areas which have been glaciated the dolines may contain glacial deposits, and in central Europe many dolines contain periglacial and loess deposits. Examination of the deposits on the floors of dolines can therefore yield interesting results. Transported sediment can also help to date the main period of formation of the doline.

As would be expected, solution doline development is much controlled by structural lines in the limestones. This view was demonstrated statistically by Matchinski in 1964, and recently in 1968 [123]. From a study of dolines in the Causses and Jura he showed that their distribution and alignment were strongly controlled by tectonic lines, both Amorican and Alpine. However, Morawetz in a study of the karst of Istria claimed that dolines are distributed along the dry valleys rather than along the structural features of the rock, joints, strike, etc., and that their positions are determined by local, rather more indefinable features, such as the distribution of soil or residual deposits [124]. In north-west Yorkshire both the structural factors and the distribution of glacial drift deposits are important in controlling their position, Fig. 23. Morawetz says that in Istria as many as 400 small dolines occur to a square kilometre, and that the largest are from 500–700 m in diameter. From a study of the $CaCO_3$ content of the waters and the present-day solution rates, he concludes that a doline of about 50 m in diameter and 15 m deep would have taken no more than 14,000 years to form and that the largest dolines of about

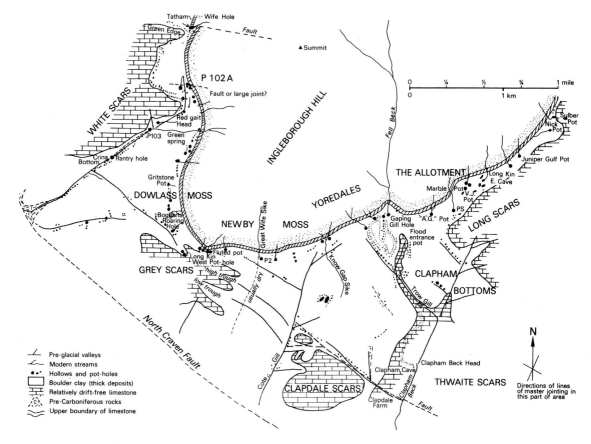

Fig. 23 Limestone plateau, southern slopes of Ingleborough, showing dolines and hollows of various types

500 m diameter and 120 m deep would be between 500,000 and 2 million years old. Thus the smallest dolines have been formed since and during the Wurmian and the larger ones may date from the end of the Pliocene [124]. However such generalisations are not always valid, and it is difficult to say that there is any distinct relationship between age and the size of development of dolines. Morawetz asks why are dolines of similar altitudes and formed in the same rock, 'at one time small, the other time far larger' [499]. For this reason morphometric analysis may throw light on doline development.

Lavalle has made one of the few morphometric studies of dolines to date, though since he does not differentiate between one type of karst depression and another the study is not as helpful as it might be [125]. However, he makes some useful comments on the interrelationships between orientation and elongation of karst depressions in south-central Kentucky. He found that structurally aligned depressions are more common in those areas where (1) the limestones have a low insoluble residue content, (2) where the available relief (hydraulic gradient) is high, (3) where a high proportion of the surface run-off is concentrated on the subterranean drainage system, and (4) in those areas nearest to major karst spring heads. The same factors also give rise to the most elongated depressions, Fig. 24. In a further statistical article in 1968, he stresses the influence of the joints and permeability of the limestones.

The formation of solutional dolines is

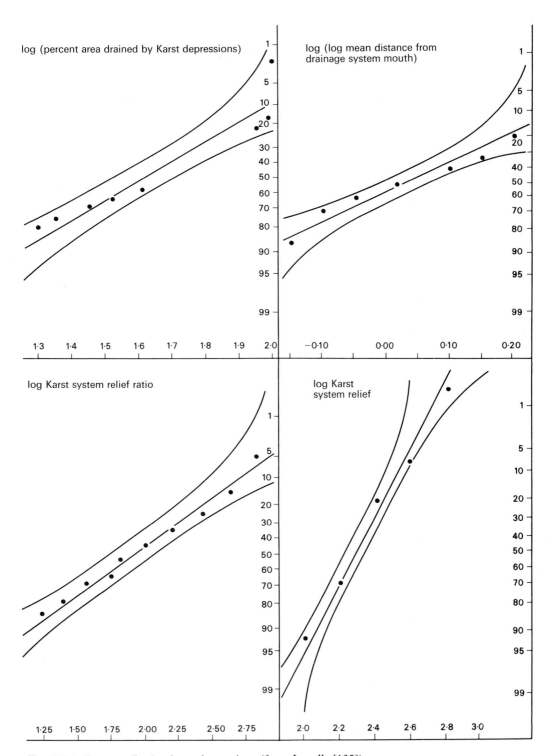

Fig. 24(a) Factors affecting karst depressions (from Lavalle [125])

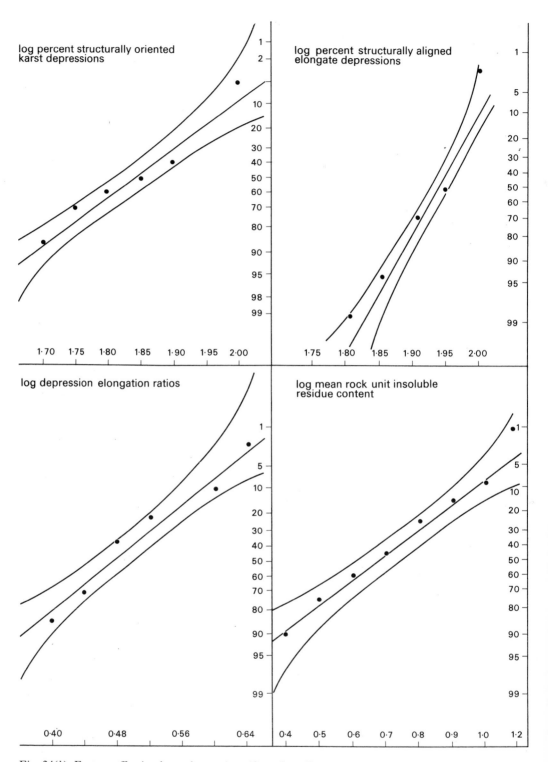

Fig. 24(*b*) Factors affecting karst depressions (from Lavalle

related essentially to the ponding of water on the limestone surface and the ease with which water can disappear into the rock. They are therefore more important in areas where the surface is planed or only slightly inclined or undulating; where slopes are steep, water flows more quickly away and the initial solution needed to start the formation of the doline does not take place. Furthermore, certain lithological and climatic conditions are of importance. First, limestones that are impermeable between the cracks and joints are much more likely to absorb water selectively than porous limestones which absorb water more uniformly at their surface. Well-jointed dense or sparry limestones, for instance, are more likely to give rise to doline development than less jointed porous chalky limestones where the solution is less selective and more overall, and accelerated corrosion does not take place. Secondly, in arid and semi-arid regions, rainfall comes in intense showers and run-off is particularly rapid; under these circumstances surface water does not have the time to percolate and penetrate into the limestones and doline formation is less likely. In more semi-arid areas, like the Limestone Ranges in the Fitzroy area in north-west Australia and in the Carlsbad area of New Mexico, both areas of fine karst limestones, there is scarcely any doline development. At Carlsbad flash floods have given rise to steep 'normal' valleys and in the Fitzroy area the limestone has been drained by sheet flooding and has been finely pedimented; hence in both these regions the statement that the doline is the essential unit of karst relief is erroneous [31].

There is also a time element in their formation and dolines evolve or become bigger; as they grow they sometimes coalesce and such coalescent dolines are known as *uvalas*. Uvalas are hollows with undulating floors made up of more than one doline, Fig. 25. They are of irregular shape, frequently being about 500–1,000 m in diameter and as much as 100–200 m deep. Cvijič gives an example of coalescent dolines (Doppeldolinen or Zwillingsdoline) in Ingriste in eastern Serbia. Uvalas occur in the Mendips and in the Craven district of Yorkshire. North of Malham Tarn House in Yorkshire, they are an important feature of the landscape despite the fact that solutional dolines of the type we have been describing are rare in this area. Uvalas between Malham Tarn and Arncliffe are shown in the map, Fig. 26; the deepest is on Clapham High Mark and is about 200 acres in extent and over 100 ft (30 m) deep. The map shows their general alignment in a NW–SE direction along small fault lines and they are also formed in the floors of dry valleys. They are roughly circular and contain deposits of boulder clay; at the bottom they are frequently marshy with alluvium, deposits which so far have not been investigated. Dowkabottom on

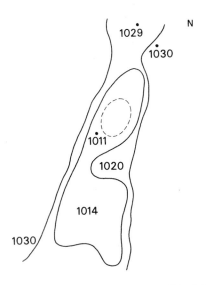

Fig. 25 Compound doline (uvala), Vallée de la Bégude (Méjean). Scale 1:50,000, heights in metres (from Marres [115])

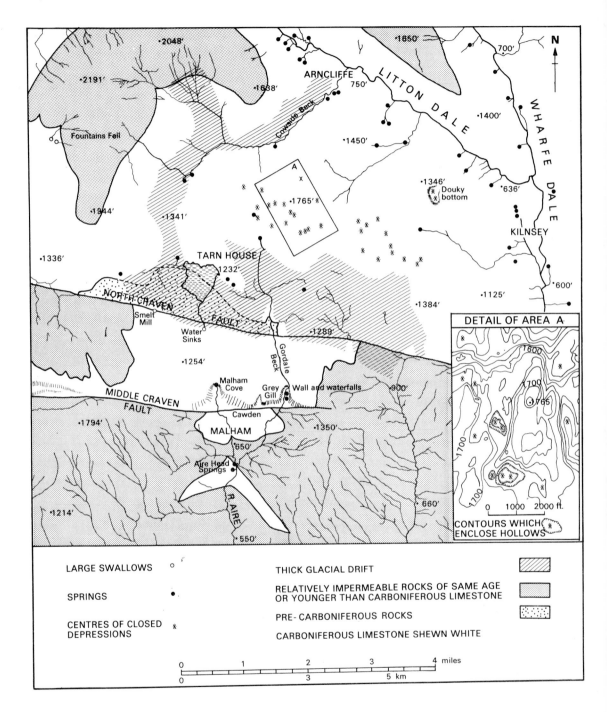

Fig. 26 Some karstic features of the Malham Tarn district (from Moisley [171]). (Based on the Ordnance Survey map by permission of the Controller, H.M. Stationery Office—*Crown copyright reserved*)

Hawkeswick Clowder between Kilnsey and Arncliffe is another good example which is over 200 m in diameter; in the base of this hollow is an opening which is the collapsed roof of a cave.

In the Slovenian discussion in 1962, several different types of uvala were recognised:

Elongated uvalas or *dols*
Uvalas composed of a number of adjoining basins (or *vrtačasta uvala*)
Periodically inundated uvalas
Waterlogged uvalas.

Some areas, such as north-west Yorkshire and the Burren of County Clare, have few solutional dolines at the present time and this is probably due to the severity of recent glacial erosion. Where such glacial action has not occurred, as in the Mendips and to a certain extent in South Wales, dolines have had the time to form. Dolines are best seen in the unglaciated parts of southern and central Europe, and particularly in the Classical and Dinaric karst and in the limestone areas of Greece, as on the slopes of Parnassus. In these areas the high mountainous limestone tracts consist almost entirely of one doline after another, with intervening conical hills; in these regions also the largest dolines have had the time to develop and deepen. The photograph of the Cetinje area in Montenegro and of the Atiyo shi dai in Japan illustrate the classical doline landscape, Photo 4. However, though dolines evolve and take time to develop, they are not now considered part of a cyclic development as was once thought by Clozier in 1940 [117]. He commented: 'Dans la famille des formes karstiques les dolines sont les dernières à se manifester. . . . Les cloups n'apparaissent donc qu'à un certain stade de l'évolution karstique ou dans certaines conditions d'érosion karstique.'

(B) ALLUVIAL DOLINES

The second main type is the alluvial doline. Where limestones are covered with alluvium or other superficial deposits, hollows develop whose slopes are formed of these overlying rocks. Solution of the limestone takes place beneath the cover rocks and enlarges cracks and joints; the superficial material subsides into the enlarged joints leaving crater-like hollows on the surface. They are therefore subsidence cones. Cvijič quotes a locality in Serbia, in western Kucaj, as having excellent examples, where yellow clay up to 6 m thick covering the limestones is peppered with funnel-shaped hollows up to 10 m in diameter [3]. As would be expected with such loose alluvial material, the slopes are always changing, particularly as the joints in the rock below are continually enlarged by solution. Hence the sides of alluvial dolines tend to be unstable and full of small landslips and broken slopes and are constantly changing in shape. Clayey material may collect in the hollow and a small marsh may accumulate. There are also differences in the vegetation between those alluvial dolines which are subject to change and those which have become stabilised. Newly formed hollows with freshly steepened slopes frequently develop inside older hollows; they may also occur in association with much larger ordinary solution dolines.

Alluvial dolines are abundant in limestone areas where there are superficial deposits of any kind. They occur in Britain in north-west Yorkshire where they are formed in association with a cover of glacial drift. In the north of England these dolines are known as *shake-holes*.* Shake-holes

*Shake-hole, or shack-hole: originally a mining term – 'a hollow in the ground, resembling a funnel, which receives the surface water'. (W. Carr, *The Dialect of Craven in the West Riding of Yorkshire*, 1824.) 'A hollow in the ground where water has undermined the supporting rock which has fallen in.' (J. Lucas, *Studies in Nidderdale*, 1881, p. 276.)

form where glacial and alluvial drift has
fallen into enlarged and widened joints in
the limestones. They are usually funnel-
shaped and in their simplest form the sides
and base are entirely in the drift cover and
the limestone below does not appear.
Average shake-holes may be about 3 m deep
and from 8 to 11 m in diameter. Their size
and depth depend upon four main factors:
(1) the width and depth of the joints in the
underlying limestone; (2) the thickness of
the overlying drift deposits; (3) the amount
of surface drainage entering the hole; (4)
the general slope of the land. Clayton in
1966 gives a series of diagrams, Fig. 27,
illustrating the stages in the development
of shake-holes [126]. He also says: 'Although the concentration of aggressive
water in these holes has intensified the
solution of the underlying limestone, and
individual blocks may have shifted position,
there is rarely any sign of widespread
collapse. The initiation and growth of the
hollows can be traced from the development
of their sides and active development is
shown by tears in the vegetation mantling
their inner slopes. . . . Size is no criterion
of age since it is principally a function of the
depth of material over the limestone.
Similarly the frequency of these shake holes
seems to be primarily a function of the
depth of the overburden . . .' (p. 371) . . .
'they increase in frequency up to a thickness
of 6–8 ft and then decline steadily in
frequency (although increasing in individual
size) until with more than 30–40 ft of
overburden they are rare'.

In stable shake-holes the slope of the
sides is about 30°–40°, but where the overlying material is slipping into the limestone,
slopes may be as much as 60°–70°. Surface
water usually drains away rapidly at their
base, indicating the loose and unconsolidated nature of the drift cover. In time fine
sand and mud accumulate at the bottom

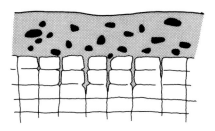

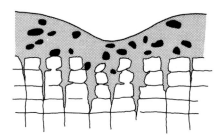

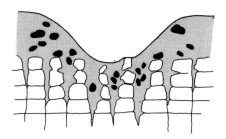

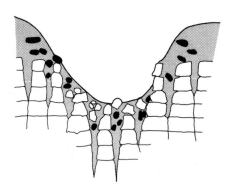

Fig. 27 Stages in the development of shake-holes
(from Clayton [126])

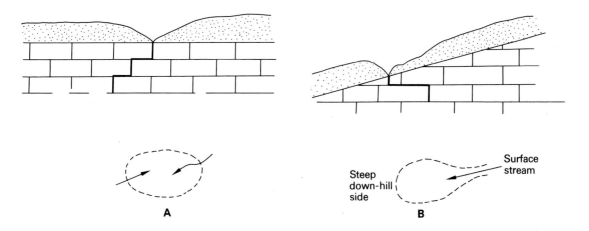

Fig. 28 Sketch to illustrate shake-hole development on horizontal parts of a plateau A and on inclined surfaces B

and drainage is impeded, so that a marsh or a pond is formed; when this occurs the vegetation changes. Many examples of shake-holes with small ponds may be seen on Leck Fell and on the slopes of Ingleborough. Shake-holes which have developed in peat-covered drift deposits tend to be rather more basin- or saucer-like in shape. Where the drift-covered slopes are less than 5° shake-holes remain generally circular, symmetrical and fairly stable. On slopes that are steeper than 5°, shake-holes tend to become elongated and less symmetrical; slumping is more active on the uphill side, which becomes less steep, the downhill side remaining quite steep, as much as 50°–70°, Fig. 28. Small surface streams enter from the uphill side and disappear into the drift or into fissures and caves exposed at the downhill end. Elongated shake-holes may be up to 30 m long, a good example being Ash Tree shake-hole on Leck Fell, which is 10 m deep and over 30 m long.

Factors affecting the distribution of shake-holes are well shown in the Ingleborough district. They are found on and along the margins of mounds of glacial drifts, as near Gaping Gill Hole; they are also aligned along major joints and faults. Both these points are illustrated in Fig. 23.

Shake-holes rarely occur singly. Frequently they occur in series separated from one another by low cols or bridges a few metres wide; slipping and slumping recurs more at the cols, which become narrower, and eventually a series of shake-holes coalesce to form one elongated hollow. An example is seen at Blea Dubs at the southern end of Gragareth, north-west of Ingleton.

Shake-holes also occur in north-west Yorkshire where the Carboniferous Limestone is overlain by thin deposits of Yoredale Shales or where shales overlie the Yoredale limestones. Thus they occur in a shale cover overlying the Main Limestone (Yoredale) on Ingleborough and were mentioned by Thomas West in 1793 as occurring 'not only all over the base of Ingleborough, but particularly in a row near the summit'.

Because of the huge amounts of glacial drift and alluvium and because the limestones had become scoured by ice erosion,

Cvijič (and also de Martonne) was of the opinion that alluvial dolines were characteristic of the karsts of north-west Europe, and that the rocky solutional dolines were typical of the Classical and Dinaric karsts [3].

(c) SOLUTION SUBSIDENCE

As already indicated, enclosed hollows can also form on the beds overlying limestone when these are not merely alluvium or glacial drift. If limestones are succeeded by shales or sandstones, there are occasions when fissures in the limestones are enlarged; subsidence of the overlying beds into the fissures then gives rise to crater-like dolines in the overlying rocks (a process sometimes known as *suffosion*). The hollows are analogous to alluvial dolines, though the American term *solution subsidence* is perhaps a better name. Such dolines are formed on the surface of the impermeable rocks which then simulates a karst relief. Such a simulated karst relief is known as a covered karst (*unterirdische Karst* or *karst couvert*) [127].

Where the rock covering the limestone is of clay or fine-grained material, the subsidence of this into the joints and cracks of the underlying limestone is slow and smooth, and hollows with gentle slopes in the cover rocks are formed. Where the overlying rocks are strong, as for instance sandstones, the subsidence is more uneven and the hollows more irregular. In the northern part of the South Wales coalfield the Pennant sandstone of Millstone Grit age lies upon the Carboniferous Limestone. Here large hollows are found on the Pennant sandstone where it overlies the limestone, and are the result of the subsidence of the sandstone into enlarged joints and cavities in the limestone below. These solution subsidences are crater-like, often almost circular, and with near-vertical, joint-faced walls, and a ratio of diameter to depth of 6:1. They are particularly numerous where the Pennant Grit is about 150–200 ft thick, when 20–30 hollows per acre have been counted [128], but they occur even where the Grit cover is as much as 450–500 ft thick. Thomas considers that solution of the underlying limestone has

6 Solution subsidence, Santa Rosa, New Mexico, U.S.A. In sandstones overlying carbonate and gypsum beds

caused the undermining and subsequent collapse *en bloc* of large masses of the Grit beds and that the size of some of those masses suggests that 'large caverns or halls forming segments of major cave systems in which the connecting links are relatively narrow passageways with more stable roofs, have been involved' (Fig. 29) [128]. The recent discoveries of large cave systems in this part of South Wales supports this view.

Similar subsidence hollows occur in the Santa Rosa Sandstone which overlies Permian limestones and gypsum beds in the upper Pecos river area of New Mexico. Underground drainage is active within the limestones and there is much solution, particularly in the vicinity of the Pecos river, where subsidence of blocks of the sandstones is especially common. Such hollows have steep-cliffed walls of sand-

stone dipping at all angles. Where they are at the level of the Pecos river they are steep-sided and may contain lakes, whereas away from the river they become degraded and lose their steep sides. Thus a sequence of subsidence can be traced, the newest near the present level of the Pecos river, the oldest on the surrounding plateau; three main types are discernible and these are related to a sequence of river terraces of the Pecos river, Photo 6.

Features formed by solution subsidence have also been described by Dicken from the Dripping Springs escarpment area in Kentucky, where sandstones overlie the Mississippian limestones [129]. Solution subsidences formed by catastrophic collapse have been studied in the Far West Rand in the Transvaal by Brink and Partridge [130], who discuss the causes of

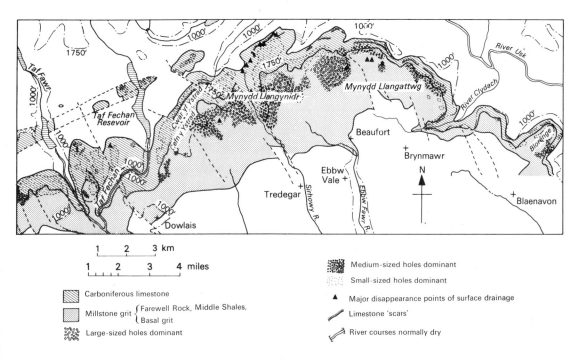

Fig. 29 Dolines on the Carboniferous Limestone and solution subsidences on Millstone Grit outcrops on the northern rim of the S. Wales coalfield (from Thomas [128])

the sudden collapse of the overlying material (Fig. 30).

(D) COLLAPSE DOLINES

In this type of small closed depression the walls are abrupt and cliff-like and are formed by large-scale collapse of the rock. They are called *Einsturzdolinen* by Cvijič,

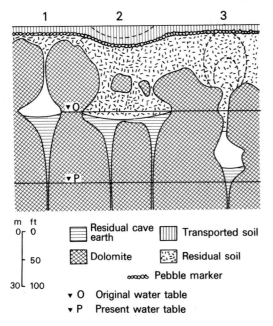

Fig. 30 Formation of collapse hollows in the Far West Rand area, Transvaal (after Brink & Partridge [130])

and are the *dolines d'effondnement* of the French. Collapse of limestones is a fairly frequent phenomenon, despite the fact that it is not often actually recorded. The most characteristic collapse dolines have steep-cliffed sides, an oval or irregularly shaped near-circular form. Though they are usually relatively shallow they have a high depth : diameter ratio. The base is also filled with a chaos of collapsed limestone blocks. They occur as the result of the breakdown of cavern roofs relatively near to the surface or by the collapse of blocks in the neighbourhood of a large karst spring.

Cvijič recognised two types of dolines associated with caves. First he found that some dolines lead into short 'blind-ended' cave passages eroded along joints and cracks. This type has a funnel-like opening and leads to a closed or little developed cave, which is sometimes horizontal, but more often is in the form of a vertical chimney. He quoted the jama (cave) of Prevala, near Škocjan, as an example and the Aven de la Bresse in the Causse Noir, in France.

Secondly, he recognised two types of dolines associated with underground river systems. The first type he called the *Macocha* type, named after the Macocha doline in the Devonian Limestones of Moravia; this he regarded as a simple form,

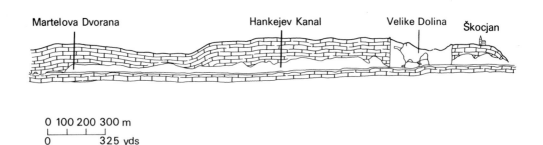

Fig. 31 The Škocjanske caves (from Gams in [131])

7(*a*) Collapse
doline, Škocjan,
Slovenia

where the roof of an underground river has fallen in and exposed the course of the subterranean river. Steep-sided, cliff-like walls and cones of debris of fallen limestone blocks characterise this type. The second type in this group he called the *Trebič* type, which is also associated with an underground river system, but the connection is not so direct and many passages and caverns intervene between the surface doline and the underground river passage.

Some of the most splendid collapse dolines in the world are to be seen in the Classical Karst in Slovenia where they are associated with the large caves. The collapse dolines of Škocjan, Photo 7(*a*), the Rak valley and of Otok, near Postojna, are world-famous. At Škocjan they have been caused by falling in of the roofs of caves connected with the underground river Notranjska Reka (or the upper Timavo), and the largest, the Velika dolina, is 164 m deep and about 500 m in diameter, Fig. 31. They occur in thick and dense micritic Cretaceous limestones (Senonian), which are highly fractured; the limestones are folded in the Dinaric trend (NW.–SE.), and where the collapses have occurred there are faults both parallel to and across the folding. Because the dolines are deep and the walls cliff-like, the air at the base is usually cooler than the air of the surrounding plateau;

there is therefore an inversion of temperature and an interesting cold flora is found at the base of the dolines, including *Silene saxifraga*, *Primula auricula* and *Aconitum paniculatum*, L. [131]. It was because of these impressive collapse dolines of the Classical Karst that both Schmidl and Tietze were so convinced that all enclosed hollows in the karst were formed by collapse [12]. In Slovenia such collapse dolines are sometimes called *kolisevke* and occasionally *udova doline*. In Serbia they are known as *vigledi* (literally, light holes). Other well-known collapse hollows include the Macocha, the one cited by Cvijič, a collapse hole associated with the Punkva caves in Moravia, and there is also the Gouffre de Padirac, made famous by Martel, and formed by the collapse of the cave connected with the Padirac river in the Causses of Quercy.

In north-west Yorkshire, Douk Cave hollow (Chapel-le-Dale), Gavel Pot Hole on Leck Fell, and Hull Pot on the slopes of Pen-y-ghent are all good examples. Gavel Pot hole is about 60 m long, 30 m wide and about 40 m deep, and Hull Pot is 100 m long, 20 m deep and 10 m wide; recent falls of the limestones along shaley or ferruginous mudstone bands have contributed to their enlargement.

In the Carboniferous Limestones of

County Clare, Williams has made a study of some collapsed depressions in the Gort lowland. He says: 'The majority of the small closed depressions of the Gort Lowland can probably be ascribed to collapse. The surface of the plain is always within 50 ft of the level of the ground water, and an active water circulation at a shallow depth promotes the caving-in of passage roofs. Some collapse depressions obviously lie above the route of underground rivers, for example the Punchbowl ... south of the town of Gort. Other depressions mark the course of former subterranean waterways, for example, the Pollonora Holes, 2·5 miles north of Gort. The cluster of ten collapse depressions within two miles south-west of Kinvarra probably also marks a former underground water network' [95]. Williams's diagrams of those depressions from the Gort lowland are shown in Fig. 32. In the higher areas of the Burren to the west, where the water-table is lower relative to

the limestone surface, collapse features are not so important but some roofs of the bigger cave chambers have fallen in, as at Poulelva and Pollbinn [95, 502].

An interesting series of collapse dolines occur in association with well-defined water-conduits and caves near Itea, in the Parnassus area of Greece [132]. Jennings has also described an Australian example from the Punchbowl–Signature cave system at Wee Jasper, New South Wales [133]. In the Nullarbor Plain in South Australia collapse dolines also form 'oblong or circular enclosed depressions surrounded on all or most sides by vertical cliffs or steep broken rock slopes. . . . Chowilla Landslip is one of the largest collapse dolines, about 90 ft deep and roughly elliptical in plan approximately 150 ft by 200 ft' [133]. In the West Indies, Dunn's Hole is described, from the Dry Harbour Mountains of central Jamaica [134] and the Tres Pueblos hole, Photo 7(b), from the Rio Camuy district in

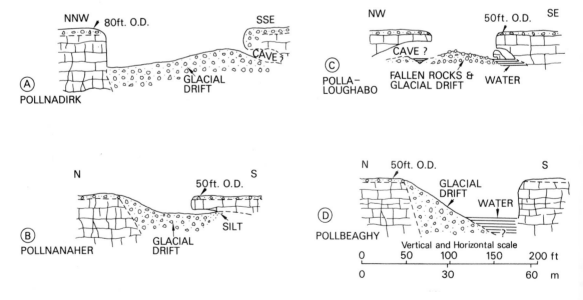

Fig. 32 Collapse depressions, Gort lowland, Co. Clare (after Williams [95])

7(*b*) Tres Pueblos sink – aerial view from north. The sink is about 150 m wide and 120 m deep from top of wall at left side of photograph to Rio Camuy below. This is a collapse doline (*Photo taken by W. H. Monroe*)

Puerto Rico. The Tres Pueblos hole is in plan 'crudely square and about 150 m in diameter. Measured from the top of its nearly vertical wall at its lowest point to the Rio Camuy . . . Tres Pueblos is 90 m deep. The underground river enters along the south-east side at an altitude of 184 m and leaves at an altitude of 179 m' [135]. In Yucatán, the well-like cenotes are also regarded as collapse dolines, though their extreme regularity of form and occurrence makes this explanation questionable [136].

As the sides of collapse dolines weather and slump inwards, it is difficult to differentiate them from normal solution dolines. A suggested scheme of development of a collapsed hollow and its gradual infilling has been given by Balchin and Coleman [113]; they, however, regarded all the depressions on the Mendip Hills as due to a collapse origin, a view which is now considered untenable [114]. Excavation at the base of the dolines helps to reveal the main mode of origin, and the presence of many separate and large blocks of limestone in the base of the hollow may mean that collapse has occurred.

Collapse dolines usually result from the falling-in of the roofs of particularly big cave chambers, rather than from the systematic collapse of a long winding cave system; thus the winding shape of Cheddar Gorge is not characteristic of a collapsed cavern [114].

Collapse dolines are more common in areas where underground drainage is well established and usually in wetter karstlands rather than drier ones. They are also important in regions with well-marked variations of seasonal rainfall as in the Classical Karst. In the humid tropics, variations in rainfall from wet to dry season, and the consequent variations in the volume of underground water, mean that cave roofs are subjected to enormous differences in hydraulic pressure and collapse is therefore more likely. In western temperate oceanic areas where the seasonal variations in the rainfall are not so great, the actual conditions which 'trigger off' the final collapse of a cave roof have never been properly studied. In 1950, the writer suggested that in north-west Yorkshire some of the collapse dolines of that area might have been caused by a rapid lowering of the water-level in the caves caused by a sudden rejuvenation – in this case caused by movement along the South Craven Fault [137]. An explanation also involving a fall in the water-level in limestones and the draining of underground caverns has recently been put forward by Brink and Partridge for the collapse solution subsidences already referred to in the Western Rand mining region near Johannesburg in South Africa [130]. In the area studied by these two authors there has been an artificial lowering and withdrawal of the water-level in the lime-

stone as a result of drainage for mining [130].
Such conclusions are supported by Lavalle's
statistical survey: his evidence shows that
collapse depressions are deeper and more
numerous near the mouth of subterranean
drainage networks [125]. Collapse of cavern
roofs might also take place during frosty

and cold phases of climate, especially since
well-jointed limestones are particularly
affected by frost action. Thus in many
Mediterranean and central European areas
the cold phases of the Pleistocene may well
have been important for the formation of
collapse dolines. In the Adloun cave near

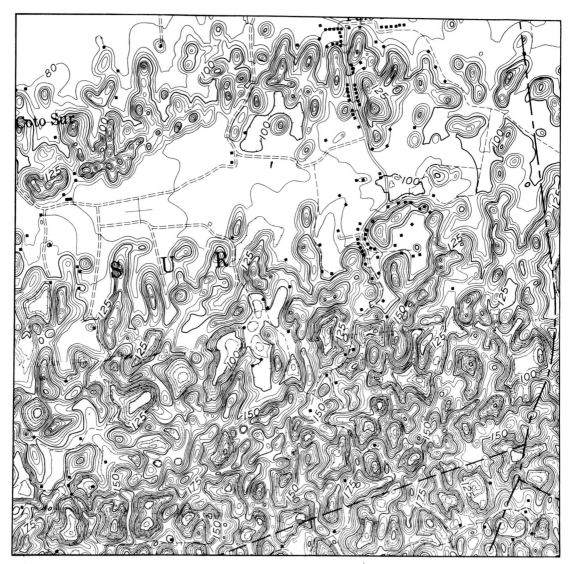

Fig. 33 Limestone country south-east of Manati, north coast of Puerto Rico (scale 6 cm = 1 km)
(U.S. Geological Survey)

8 Irregular karst hollows (cockpits), S.W. of Belize, British Honduras

Sidon in the Lebanon, both frost and lowering of the water-table may have been important. In this cave there has been collapse of the archaeological layers since man's occupation; the relationship of the layers to the raised beach and other deposits suggests that collapse may have taken place during a late phase of the Wurmian glaciation, during which time frost action was probably important; a rapid lowering of the sea level is also believed to have taken place [138].

In addition to these climatic factors, collapse dolines are more important in regions where the limestones are of a type that fracture easily, such as micrites and porcellanites; and also where the limestones have been subjected to much tectonic stress. In the Classical Karst, all factors, both climatic and geological, are important and explain the great development in that area of collapse dolines.

2. ENCLOSED HOLLOWS IN TROPICAL AREAS

In the tropics normal more or less circular solutional dolines are replaced by irregular star-shaped hollows. On a map of dolines in temperate areas the contours of the dolines are more or less rounded, either in the shape of a funnel or basin or of a steep-sided collapse feature. A map of a tropical limestone area, Fig. 33, shows several series of rounded contours, but each rounded feature is in fact a hill; between the regularly spaced hills, the depressions are angular and sinuous, star-shaped and irregular. As H. Lehmann has said, 'La reproduction cartographique d'un paysage karstique dans les zones tropicales nous donne donc l'impression du paysage karstique à dolines classique, mais inversé; au lieu des dolines rondes qui caracterisent le karst des zones tempérées, ce sont les cones, les pitons calcaires arrondis qui attirent notre attention dans le karst tropical' [17].

The irregular depressions in tropical areas are now often known as cockpits, after the name given to them in Jamaica. The intervening regular hills are known as *cones* or *kegel(n)*, and the assemblage is known usually as cockpit or kegelkarst [139]. The purpose of this section is to describe the small enclosed depressions in tropical limestone areas rather than to discuss the assemblage of tropical karst landforms (see Chapter 15).

Early European travellers and geologists commented upon the strange hollows of the tropical limestone lands [22]. Sawkins in his *Report on the Geology of Jamaica* in 1869 accounted for the Jamaica cockpits (Photo 8) as collapse features. 'The waters sinking through the cavernous structure of the limestones forced their way through and removed the subadjacent beds of shale and sand, thus forming cavities below the limestone which being unsupported gave way and originated the "Cockpit" depressions' [22]. However, both Danes and Grund believed they had originated similarly to solutional dolines and the cockpit landscape was in an advanced stage of the karst cycle. Modern work on these depressions dates from H. Lehmann's work in Java in 1936, and his work in the West Indies since 1950 [140–2]. In his early work he was still influenced by the cyclic scheme of karst evolution, and his idea of the development of the cockpits is given on p. 33 of his *Morphologische Studien auf Java*.

In 1955 the writer made a survey of the Cockpit Country of Jamaica, and a traverse made across it gives a good idea of the general succession of these depressions, Fig. 34. Some of the description of the cockpits given by the writer at that time is given below.

In this area the average depth of the cockpits is between 300 ft and 400 ft . . . the bases of the cockpits consist frequently of a puddled muddy area, containing yellow or brownish residual clay; in wet seasons this area may contain a pond forming a small perched water-table. The slopes of the cockpits are usually between 30°–40° and are made up of chemically weathered and honey-combed blocks and scree; where the White Limestones are exposed, the sides are steeper and can be cliff-like. . . . The cockpits and the cone-like hills are conspicuously arranged in lines following the trend of the joint and fault patterns in the White Limestones. . . . Normally the cockpits and conical hills are more or less symmetrical, but sometimes the slopes

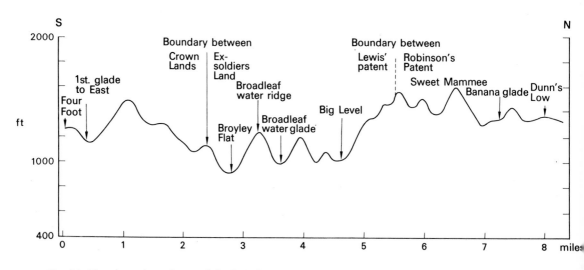

Fig. 34 Sketch section of central Cockpit Country (Sweeting in Geological Survey of Jamaica, *Report* No. 3, 1956)

on one side of a cockpit are steeper than those on the other [134].

The writer concluded that, because of their ubiquitous distribution and even scatter, the cockpits were largely the result of solution working downwards from the surface. However, Versey in 1959 put forward some pertinent ideas about the origin of the cockpits and particularly about the ways in which small doline-like depressions could be transformed into more steep-sided and irregular depressions. Thus he writes:

> Solution, while initiating the underground drainage and the surface features has thereafter a subordinate role, the main erosive work being done mechanically by the sheer strength of the underground waters and the abrasive action of their suspended sediment. These undermine the land by enlarging the cave systems and prepare the way for the collapse of the roof . . . it is doubtful whether the rainfall into a particular cockpit is sufficient to excavate it to such a magnitude. . . . It is much more plausible that the perpetuation of the physiographic character of the Cockpit Country is due to the hydraulic and abrasive action of flood waters in the underground drainage system. During the rainy season many of the cockpits become flooded by springs of turbid water boiling up in them, these issuing from the sink holes which at other times drain the valleys. . . . The amount of water flowing beneath the Cockpit boundary during and immediately after the rainy season is certainly over 10 times greater than the dry-weather flow. [143]

In much more recent work Aub gives a precise account of cockpits in the forested Pedro river area of Central Jamaica, and a detailed cross-section shows the main elements in their relief, Fig. 35. This

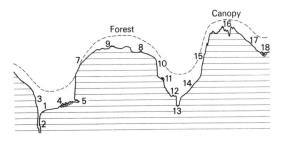

Fig. 35 Stylised cross-section, Cockpit Country, showing the main elements of the relief (from Aub [111])

1. Glade floor with soil and projecting rock.
2. Joint-guided sinkhole.
3. Cliff over sinkhole, with gentle solution scallops.
4. Scree slope.
5. Outcrop of a bed of impure limestone, associated with undercut cliffs. Many major cliffs do not have such undercuts, and the soft limestone is absent.
6. High cliff with scalloped or slightly pitted face.
7. Very steep but even slope, with honeycombed rock and loose fragments. The vegetation is thin and poorly rooted.
8. Rounded hill summit with projecting rocks and some loose fragments. There is a semi-continuous soil cover. Such summit surfaces are not necessarily horizontal.
9. Large rock remnants completely dissected into pinnacle-and-cleft 'castles'. They stand in isolation or in groups on the summit surfaces, and may reach 10 m in height.
10. Cliff without undercut base, rising from a hard limestone bench. Such cliffs are not visible on the air-photographs.
11. A 'staircase' slope consisting of steps up to 3 m high and ledges up to 5 m wide. Many of the ledges are undercut, and the slopes are strewn with large limestone blocks.
12. Cockpit floor with some soil and boulders.
13. Well-shaped sinkhole with rubble floor and solid limestone walls, indicating that the cockpit is not a collapse feature.
14. Exposed cockpit floor with some joint solution and abundant rubble. Frequently it is not possible to distinguish the solid from the broken rock.
15. 'Broken cliffs' with honeycombed walls, narrow bedding-plane ledges, and interruped by joint-plane gaps.
16. 'Pinnacle-and-cleft' topography on a hill summit, with large broken boulders. The vegetation grows out of the joint openings, forming matted bridges over other openings. The relief and vegetation are completely chaotic.
17. Small cockpit with soil-covered slopes and some surface drainage channels.
18. Impenetrable sink among boulders at the lower end of the drainage channels.

indicates that their features are much more complex than earlier descriptions had suggested and he says that his work shows that the 'processes of cockpit formation must be acting mainly at the surface', and that they are largely solutional in origin. Aub's accurate descriptions of the depressions and their slopes are now discussed [111].

Cockpits are star-shaped depressions with a slightly concave floor, which is usually covered with limestone rubble and soil. In larger cockpits there is a marked break of slope at the foot of the hill slopes, while in the smaller depressions the floor and sides grade into one another. Usually rocks protrude above the surface of the soil and the soil cover is patchy. The cockpits have no surface outlets, and must therefore have subterranean outlets, which are often near the centre. Where the floor is rocky there may be more than one swallow hole and during heavy rains it is possible to see that capture of drainage has taken place. Surface channels lead to these holes from the surrounding passes; such surface drainage is only temporary. During short periods of rain there is no run-off at all and the water disappears immediately among the joint openings, rubble and soil. In heavier rain periods, the drainage is concentrated into a limited number of vertical conduits. Over 160 swallow-holes were examined by Aub; of these about half were boulder-covered and in rubble and could not be studied further; the other half were in solid limestone. Those in the limestone were mainly vertical, parallel or laterally offset shafts, and were largely joint-guided, following the line of the jointing which guided the original depression. Aub concluded from his survey that the cockpits have solid limestone floors and that any collapse theory cannot explain the origin of the main depressions in his area. He also concluded from an examination of the groundwater

levels that the height of the cockpits was above the zone of groundwater fluctuations, so that the depressions are unlikely to have been affected by the mechanism discussed by Versey (see above, p. 71). He therefore states that the cockpits in the area he closely examined must have been largely formed by solution at the surface, aided by minor collapse.

Aub also noted aspects of the vegetation and of the rainfall. The natural vegetation is thinner on the hilltops than it is in the depressions; vegetation hides all small relief features and softens the appearance of all others. The relief is therefore greater and more rugged than the contours of the forest canopy suggest. He also kept rainfall measurements for a year. These measurements showed that there was a steady difference between the top and bottom of the depressions, and that on the average the throughfall in the depressions is 13–15 per cent higher than that on the hill summits. Hence displacement of the throughfall by the forest canopy must play an important part in increasing the throughfall in the depressions. Once therefore a depression is formed, the concentration of rainfall, dtainage, soil and vegetation ensure that the development of the depression continues. This has also been shown by Corbel [504] who has attempted to estimate the present day solution of the limestone. His figures show a much higher figure for superficial dissolution in the cockpits.

In addition to the star-shaped cockpits, more elongate depressions occur known as *glades* in Jamaica. Glades are also surrounded by steep slopes. The floor consists of a series of small basins separated by divides much lower than the passes leading out of the glade. In general, cockpits and glades tend to merge into one another. The hydrological conditions in the deeper basins of the glades resemble those of the cockpits, but the shallower basins of the glades are usually soil-covered and have no visible drainage outlets. The *glades* are thus roughly similar to *uvalas*. One of the most often-quoted glades is Barbacue Bottom in the Jamaican Cockpit Country, but many others can be found. They are almost always elongate, aligned along the lines of major joints and of faults [134]. (Fig. 36.)

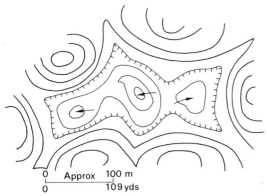

Fig. 36 Uvala south of Chanal, Northern Chiapas, Mexico (field sketch by A. Gerstenhauer)

Doline- and cockpit-like hollows have also been discussed in south-east Asia [144] and in tropical New Guinea [145]. It is clear from these discussions that enclosed hollows in tropical areas take many forms. Some writers like Kossack assert that there is no translation from dolines to cockpits [146], while others tend to agree with Grund and Danes that cockpits are only old-age dolines. The French National Committee in their *Vocabulaire* refer to the cockpit as 'seulement un doline' (p. 31). In this connection it is useful to call attention to the nature of tropical rainfall. As we have already shown, the rate of surface run-off is an important factor in the formation of normal solutional dolines, dolines being less important in areas of rapid run-off. In tropical areas rainfall is more intensive and water runs off more rapidly and is not so quickly absorbed into joints and cracks in the rock; instead therefore of the slow percolation along a joint or fissure as in a temperate area, runnels flow on the surface for longer distances and erosion and solution caused by the convergence of many such runnels give rise to a star-shaped hollow. This conclusion is confirmed by the morphometric work of Williams on tropical Karst hollows in New Guinea [505]. In this work, Williams has used well-known procedures of fluvial morphometry, justified 'because of the manifestly fluvial nature of the dissection within the Karstic basins examined, even though the fluvial process is intermittent, largely corrosional and centripetally directed'. When the swallow holes 'are centrally placed, the radiating centripetal stream channels mould the internal contours into a star shape. The star shape, sometimes considered a special attribute of humid, tropical Karst depressions, is dependent on fluvial processes for its creation'.

5 The Superficial Features of Limestones: Karren or Lapiés

SMALL-SCALE solutional and other weathering features are common on karst limestones, and there exists a large literature on them and many local names. The most widely used names for them are *karren* or *schratten* or *lapiés*, terms in use in the Alps where these solutional features are particularly well developed. The name karren was originally used to describe solution runnels cut into limestones, but it is now used for the whole complex of micro-forms that occur on outcrops of karst limestones.

Karren range from a few millimetres or centimetres in size to about one or two metres, though they occasionally attain 15-20 m in length. Their most important characteristic is the small-scale chiselling of the rock which becomes etched into definite patterns. They are of great variety and it is only in the last few years that any significant advances have been made in the study of them.

The first modern reference to karren was in a short paper by Heim in 1878, 'Über die Karrenfelder', who realised that karren were essentially formed by the chemical action of water, particularly snow melt, on bare limestone surfaces, and that they were not formed by glacial abrasion or mechanical action [147]. He also saw that they were related to the snow line. Heim studied the karren of the Glattalp, near Schwyz, an area still being closely studied by Bögli today. Cvijič in his work in 1893 gave only a page or two to skrape or skripovi as they are known in Serbo-Croat, and considered that they were adequately known. But in his later works, he gave more emphasis to

the study of karren, both in his paper on their suggested mode of evolution in 1924, and in the posthumous work on *La Géographie des Terrains Calcaires* [148].

This was largely because between 1893 and Cvijič's later work a number of descriptive works on karren in different parts of Europe were produced. Many of these referred to the high Alpine areas like that of E. Chaix on the Désert de Platé in Savoie [149]. Probably the most significant work of this period was that by Eckert on the 'Gottesackerplateau, ein Karrenfeld im Allgäu' in 1902 [150]. This paper is one of the most thorough ever to be written on karren, and indeed in the whole of karst morphology; it recognised many different kinds of karren and realised the importance of soil and vegetation in their formation, though it attempted no experimental work. Lindner in 1930 made a beginning in the use of new techniques in the study of karren and tried to relate the chemical composition of carbonate rocks in the Alps with the altitudinal distribution of karren [151]. But the most important advances have been made since 1960 by the work of Bögli [59] in Switzerland, of Bauer [152] in Austria and of Miötke in the Pyrenees [503]. As a result of their work we are able to make some association between the types of karren and their mode of origin.

In the strictest sense karren refer to solutional holes and runnels formed directly on bare limestones and to the solutional features of limestones formed under a moss or vegetational cover. They can also be divided into single forms and complex groups. Furthermore, though they are the result of solution on the surface of the rock, solution features formed in past climatic phases may also be present. The factors which give rise to present-day solution features will be discussed first; this will be followed by a description of the main karren types and their distribution. The chief types of karren are tabulated in Table XII.

The main factors affecting the formation of karren are as follows:

(a) The nature of the chemical reaction involving the limestone, carbon dioxide and water.

(b) The amount and distribution of and nature of the precipitation, whether in the form of rain or snow.

(c) The nature and texture of the limestone.

(d) The slope or dip of the limestones and their structures.

(e) The nature (or absence) of the vegetation cover, soil, peat, etc.

(f) Past climatic phases, since many of the present small-scale features on karst limestones are related to former climatic phases.

TABLE XII

TABLE OF SIMPLE KARREN TYPES

Type	Average size	Free or covered	Horizontal or inclined surfaces	Sharp or smoothed crests
Rillenkarren	1–2 cm deep up to 50 cm long	Free	Inclined	Sharp
Trittkarren	3–50 cm high 20–100 cm wide	Free	Horizontal	Sharp
Rinnenkarren	50 cm deep up to 20 cm long	Free and half-free half-free	Inclined	Sharp crests, sometimes slightly rounded bases
Spitzkarren	50 cm wide 50 cm deep	Free	Inclined crests and roof-like surfaces	Sharp
Meanderkarren	50 cm deep up to 20 cm long	Free and half-free	Only slightly inclined	Sharp crests, slightly rounded bases
Rundkarren	12–50 cm deep up to 15 cm long	Covered	Inclined	Smoothed
Solution Basins (Kamenitzas)	few cm to over 3 metres diam. up to 50 cm deep	Both free and covered according to type	Horizontal	Sides { fretted when free karren smoothed when covered karren
Kluftkarren	Few cm to 4 m deep up to 4 m wide	Both free and covered	Development along joints and diaclases	Bases normally smoothed Sides { sharp when free smoothed when covered Bases normally smoothed
Hohlkarren (or Mohrkarren)	60 cm–1 m deep 50 cm wide	Covered – formed under peat	Inclined or slightly inclined	Smoothed sides and bases
Deckenkarren	Normally a few mm or cm deep	Covered – formed by direct action of plants	Both inclined and horizontal	Smoothed but can be sharp

(A) THE NATURE OF THE CHEMICAL
REACTION

Workers in the Alps have always been
interested in the chemical reactions between
rain and peaty waters and the different
kinds of limestone. From Bögli's work on
the solution of limestones, it will be
remembered that he claims that the
chemistry of solution of $CaCO_3$ is in four
phases (see p. 27, Fig. 7), and that the
maximum amount of solution is accomplished during the first few seconds that
water charged with carbon dioxide comes
into contact with the limestones. He further
claims that each of the solutional phases is
associated with a distinctive type of solution
rate of the rock and that different types of
solution give rise to different morphological
types of karren. Thus rillen-, rinnen-, tritt-
and spitzkarren are formed by solution
during phases 1 and 2 and are the result of
the quicker phases of solution; they are
known as free karren. Hohl-, rund-, and
mohrkarren and kamenitzas are formed
during the slower chemical reactions, particularly under the influence of biological
CO_2 resulting from solution by long-
standing water on the rock or from a peat
or vegetation cover. They are known as
half-free (halbfreie) and covered karren.
Free karren formed by rapidly flowing
water over the bare rock tend to be sharply
and finely cut and rough to the touch.
Karren formed under a peat or vegetation
cover or formed slowly under a water cover
tend to be smoothed and rounded. The
sharply cut karren are also formed more
quickly and are therefore younger features
than the rounded and smoothed ones.

(B) THE AMOUNT AND DISTRIBUTION
AND THE NATURE OF THE
PRECIPITATION

Since karren are formed by surface solution
of the limestone, the nature and amount of
the precipitation is of fundamental importance. The speed and type of chemical
reaction is partly conditioned by the nature
and type of the rainfall.

All types of karren are particularly well
developed in the mountain areas of southern
and Alpine Europe. In the Alps it was first
thought that karren were caused by glacial
action, because they are formed by the
large quantities of snow and meltwater
associated with a retreating glacier. A heavy
rainfall in addition to the meltwater assists
the formation of karren. In the Alps too, the
heavy snowfall is of importance as we have
seen that snow can be highly charged with
CO_2. In the limestone massif of the Vercors
and other parts of the calcareous Alps, the
writer has seen long rinnenkarren in
association with snow banks and snow
runnels. In Mediterranean Europe, the
intensive winter showers of that region
cause much runnelling of the bare limestone surfaces, and along the Adriatic coast
rillenkarren are particularly in evidence. In
Great Britain, however, bare rock surfaces
do not normally show any of the karren
associated with the more rapid solution
phases. Indeed the only part of the British
Isles where anything resembling freely
formed karren can be found is along the
western side of the Burren in County Clare,
Western Ireland; in this locality the rainfall
intensity is possibly heavier than in any
other part of the British Isles, due to its
position along the Atlantic seaboard where
strong westerly gales drive the rain on to the
coastal limestones. In other parts of the
British Isles the generally gentle drizzling
rainfall, characteristic of much of our

highlands, seems to be unable to produce free karren as they are developed in the Alps. In addition to the low intensity of rainfall it is possible that the absence of a markedly cold winter (such as occurs in the Alps) allows vegetation, particularly lichens (both epilithic and endolithic) to thrive on the limestones in Britain all the year and so reduce the effectiveness of free solution by rainwater. Miötke's work stresses the importance of drizzle upon limestone dissolution.

In tropical areas, where rainfalls of great intensity are much more frequent, the effects of rain-beat and heavy falls are much more evident, though these occur only where the limestone is sufficiently bare for the rain to fall directly upon it. Karren are important in tropical savannah, semiarid and monsoonal areas where there is a dry season, and where the vegetation dies down. Thus large solutional flutings have been described by Balázs [153] from south China and by Jennings and Sweeting [31] from north-west Australia. Such flutings tend to subdivide into 'successive sectors the one above the other by small rain pits, tiny hemispherical hollows, about 5 mm to 20 mm deep'. Rain-pitting of this type is quite different from anything seen in the Alps or the Mediterranean karst areas.

In dry climates, there are fewer solutional features on the limestone surface. In the tropical and polar arid climates, they are much smaller than those described from the Alps and Mediterranean. In desert areas, channelling caused by water flow and normally associated with karren is absent, and the limestone surfaces are roughly etched and pitted with tiny holes.

The type of water flow down a limestone cliff or face is also of importance. In Sarawak, Wilford and Wall have shown that runnels of water with a pulsating flow have probably produced a scalloped form of karren, on a limestone face [154]. In caves it is known that uneven solution of the rock can produce flutes or scallops; such pitting or scalloping is partly related to the petrographic nature of the limestone but is also related to the size of the pulses or eddies of the water flow. - small trickles of water giving rise to small scallops (1–2 cm long), larger flows producing scallops and pits from $\frac{1}{2}$–1 m long [155]. Such features can be seen on limestone walls in Britain.

(C) THE NATURE OF THE LIMESTONES

Though karren develop on limestones of all ages, not all beds develop them equally well. The *Schrattenkalk* (Triassic age) of the Alps was so named because of the rich development of schratten (karren) that characterised its outcrop. Beds that are dolomitised are usually poor in karren. However, relatively little is known about the different types of limestone and their reaction to the different phases of solution. We do not yet know whether dense micrites, for example, are likely to be more or less runnelled by karren than biomicrites or sparry limestones, under similar conditions. The rate of solution of a limestone surface depends largely upon the extent to which water can enter into the pore spaces of the rock, but this rate may not be related to the landforms produced. Karren are rare, for instance, on porous limestones like chalk; and Eckert noticed that a dense arrangement of crystals of calcite impeded solution [150]. In north-west Yorkshire the presence of quartz grains, as we have seen, tends to make the beds more resistant to solution; beds on Scar Close, which appear to have a great many silica grains in them, certainly possess fewer karren [76]. In the limestones of the Fitzroy area, it was found

9(a) Rillenkarren, Castleguard, Canadian Rockies (*Photo by D. C. Ford*)

however, the effects of micro-organisms and other types of biological weathering tend to reduce the limestone surface more uniformly.

The nature of the bedding of the limestones is also significant. Limestones that are thinly – or flaky – bedded are less important for karren formation and are more susceptible to frost-weathering.

(D) THE STRUCTURE AND DISPOSITION OF THE LIMESTONES

The dip or slope of the limestones affects the nature of the karren which develop upon them. Rillenkarren are particularly well developed on relatively steep limestone faces, preferably between 60° and 80°. Rinnenkarren are probably more characteristic of moderate slopes. Meanderkarren form on moderately gentle slopes where channels of water are able to meander on the limestone surface. All three types are rare on horizontal surfaces when they become irregular and are made up of a network of small channels. Trittkarren, however, tend to be formed on more gentle slopes, from 10°–15°. On flat surfaces solution basins or kamenitzas are the most likely types of karren.

The length of the karren will also depend upon the length of the exposed surface of the limestone; where undisturbed dip slopes occur, karren up to 15–20 m long may be found.

The frequency of joints and fissures in the limestones will also affect karren development. Karren can be formed along joints (kluftkarren), and hence a highly jointed limestone has a greater potential for the development of kluftkarren (though not all joints may be opened up by solution). Limestones that are very highly fractured tend to have rather few karren.

that the deep karren with rain pits already described tended to occur on the forereef limestones, whereas the true reef limestones were characterised by a much more smooth type of weathering. In general, very sparry limestones possess fewer karren than biosparites or micrites. One of the few studies of rock characteristics (porosity in particular) in relation to karren formation is that done by Pluhar & Ford [483].

Little is known also about the actual weathering of limestones. Finer-grained limestones, such as micrites, tend to produce a grey or white patina on the weathering surface, similar to that produced in flints. For example, in Yorkshire the fine mudstone beds, the *Porcellanous* bands first discussed by Garwood and Goodyear [156], can easily be recognised in the field by their white weathered surfaces. Again in the Classical Karst area the micrites weather with a grey or white patina, a very different kind of surface from that found on limestones which have a much more varied textural composition. Micrites also seem to break with a conchoidal fracture, and have many brachyclases. When limestones are freshly exposed to atmospheric attack, calcite shells and veins appear the most resistant to solution, probably because of the densely packed calcite crystals of which they are composed. As weathering proceeds,

9(*b*) Rillenkarren, Wolkberg, East Transvaal

(E) THE PRESENCE OF A VEGETATION
COVER

If vegetation or peat is in contact with the limestone, the type of reaction between the water with its organic CO_2 and the rock is of the slower type discussed by Bögli [59]. Consequently all karren formed by solution under a vegetation cover are of the rounded varieties, and rund- (round) karren are the most numerous. Hohlkarren and boden- karren are also formed under a peat or humus cover. The presence of rundkarren in an area now without vegetation is an indication of a recent change in vegetation cover. Frequently rillen- and rundkarren occur in the same area, indicating that the limestone has been affected both by solution in free air solution and under vegetation. The direct action of plant roots and soil upon the limestone must also be considered.

(F) PAST CLIMATIC PHASES

The final factor important in the formation of karren is an assessment of former climatic phases. This is because frequently superficial features on limestones are the result of more than one climatic phase. One of the more obvious examples of this is the limestone pavements of north-west York- shire. Glaciation scoured the Carboniferous Limestones in this area leaving glaciated surfaces; in the post-glacial period solution

has opened up many joints into kluftkarren and cut up the pavements by rundkarren, a type of solutional activity very different from the process which formed the lime- stone pavements themselves.

Having discussed the main factors in karren formation, we can now consider the chief karren types.

1. RILLENKARREN

These were the first type of karren to be described and are abundant in the Alps and in the Dinaric Karst. They are finely chiselled runnels or grooves with rounded troughs and sharp fine ridges; they are usually about 1 to 2 cm deep, 1–2 cm wide and usually less than 50 cm long. They normally occur in groups on roof-like pro- jections of limestone, being most perfectly developed along and near the crest of the 'roof' where the water is mostly highly charged with CO_2 and grading into un- grooved rock below, Photo 9(*a*) and (*b*). They occur most freely on slopes of from 40°–80° [152]. In the Alps they do not occur at the highest levels close to the snow line because of the frost action which would destroy them. They form the most quickly of all karren and appear on rocks that have been exposed to rain or meltwater for only a few years, or even months. In their most perfect form they occur like flutes on a Doric column [150], Fig. 37(a). In the Dinaric karst, along the Adriatic coast, the rillenkarren are rather differently developed from those in the Alps and tend to be wider and longer. They have been described from

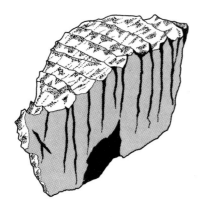

Fig. 37(a) Rillenkarren (drawn from an actual example from the Glattalp by M. E. Potter)

all well-known limestone localities in the Mediterranean (Greece, Italy, Spain, Portugal, etc.) [1]. In the southern hemisphere rillenkarren can be seen on limestones in New South Wales at Bungonia, and in Devonian limestones at Buchan in Victoria (Australia); both these localities have climates which allow the rock to be bare for a good part of the year and to be exposed to a fairly intensive rain-beat in the winter.

In the Jura and Causses of France, however, rillenkarren are only poorly developed; this is partly due to the more humid climate and the presence of more vegetation and micro-organisms which obliterate any

rillenkarren which form. In western oceanic climates rillenkarren rarely form, though occasionally rain-beat gives rise to irregular cockled and crinkled surfaces; these can be seen on rock faces and erratic blocks in north-west Yorkshire which are exposed to the south-west winds, Photo 10(a) [76].

In tropical areas, where the limestone is not obscured by vegetation, rillenkarren are conspicuous. They are then usually much longer than those in the Alps; they have been described from the Melinau region of Sarawak by Wilford and Wall [154], who speak of vertical surfaces free of vegetation on which 'vertical grooves are separated by knife sharp ridges, comparable to the rillenkarren of Bögli' [59]. In the Fitzroy district rillenkarren are 2–3 cm deep and 5–6 cm wide, 'separated by razor-sharp, hollow ground partitions' [31]. In Puerto Rico, rillenkarren are absent on the northern side of the island, owing to dense vegetation cover, but on the drier southern side, where there is less vegetation, rillenkarren are well developed, Photo 10(b).

In arid or semi-arid climates, where the rainfall is less than about 10 in. (250 mm), rillenkarren are very fine and small, Photo 10(b). Rills about 1 m in diameter and a few cm long occur; they too have rounded troughs and sharply crested ridges. Laudermilk and Woodford, who discussed these rills on inclined surfaces in the desert areas of California, were of the opinion that in their formation there was 'no possible source of acid except from the atmosphere itself' [157]. Such rilled limestones can also be seen on the Kaibab Limestones at the top of the Grand Canyon in Arizona. They are also found in cold deserts where the solution is assisted by snowfall; excellent examples can be seen on the limestones of Permian age in central Bünsow Land, Vestspitsbergen.

Rillenkarren do not occur on limestones

10(a) *left* Variations of rillenkarren: 'cockling' or 'crinkling' on erratic block, N.W. Yorkshire

10(b) *right* Rillenkarren and rainpits, Emmanuel Range, N.W. Australia

where solution brings about the disintegration of the rock, as often occurs with dolomites or with soft limestones which break down easily. However, rillenkarren can be found on the Transvaal Dolomites in South Africa, in the neighbourhood of Wolkberg, Photo 9(b).

Rillenkarren are formed rapidly, possibly in many cases in the space of a few months or years. In many Mediterranean areas, deforestation and soil erosion in historic times has caused the exposure of much 'new' rock, which is now covered with rillenkarren. These are an indication of the amount of solution which has taken place since the deforestation and also of the extent of the removal of the soil.

2. TRITTKARREN

These occur on flat surfaces and also result from the first two phases in the solution of the rock. Trittkarren form steps, with a flat tread and steep back-slope or riser, Fig. 37(b) and Photo 11; they look rather like a series of small biscuits cutting into the limestone. The back-slope may be from about 3 cm to 50 mm high, while the tread may be from about 20 cm to one metre long. The flow of water over the limestone in the formation of trittkarren is shown in Fig.

37(b). They often occur in conjunction with rillenkarren, the rills forming on the steeper slopes, the trittkarren forming on the gentler slopes. They are well developed in the Alps, notably on the Glattalp, at over 2,000 m, where they have been studied by Bögli and where snowfall on gentle slopes may be an important factor in their formation [59].

In the British Isles, the only place where I have seen trittkarren is along the coast of the Burren in County Clare. These occur on smoothed and bare glaciated surfaces of

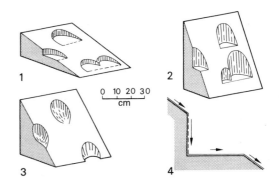

Fig. 37(b) Trittkarren (from Bauer [152])
1 and 2. Solutional forms on gently and steeply inclined rock surfaces.
3. Trichterkarren (funnel-karren).
4. Diagram of water flow. It is believed that the lower layer of water is highly alkaline and the upper layer aggressive.

11 Trittkarren, west coast of the Burren, Co. Clare, Ireland

sparry Carboniferous Limestones. Heavy showers with large raindrops beat upon these surfaces and may be the explanation of the occurrence of trittkarren in this locality. Under these conditions two water layers develop and solution is mainly horizontal.

3. RINNENKARREN

These are believed by Bögli to be formed in the third reaction phase by water in sufficiently large flows to produce deeper and wider runnels. This water is also of mixed origin, both from the falling rain and from water already flowing down the surface of the rock; it also flows in definite channels. Rinnenkarren are bigger than rillenkarren, being up to about 40 cm deep and about 40-50 cm wide, and may be some metres long, sometimes up to 15-20 m. Though the troughs are generally rounded, the limestone is frequently roughened and pitted and scalloped; the crests between are sharp. When the crests are peaked they are called *spitzkarren*.

Rinnenkarren occur in both the Alps and in the Dinaric karst in similar environments to rillenkarren. They are also characteristic of steep slopes. On less steep slopes the water flow forms a wandering channel over the rock surface giving rise to meandering solutional channels sometimes known as *meanderkarren* [59]. Bögli gives examples of meanderkarren caused by the solution from channels of melting snow in the Muotatal area of Switzerland. Smaller rinnenkarren caused by the flow of rainwater are sometimes known as regenrinnenkarren.

In Lapland, snow and glacial meltwater flowing in runnels over Palaeozoic limestones has given rise to conspicuous rinnenkarren which have been described by Corbel from Jordbrudalen and Krokvatn in Norwegian Lapland as *roches peignées* [87]; they are from 5-20 cm deep and about 20 cm wide. They are also well developed in the high-altitude karsts of the Slovenian Alps, and have been studied by Kunaver [108]; there they are called *zlebiči* when small and *skraplje* when large. Rinnenkarren also occur in caves with large deposits of ice. Thus in the Eisriesenwelt cave in the Salzburg area, rinnenkarren have been formed by the solution of glacial meltwaters during the summer half year; these rinnenkarren resemble those formed in exterior limestone environments.

Rinnenkarren also occur in the tropics. In Sarawak 'The most common type of groove on steep limestone surfaces has an essentially vertical axis . . . the limestone surfaces between the grooves approach knife-edge forms, particularly where vegetation is sparse or absent' [154]. In the Fitzroy area rinnenkarren up to 50 cm wide and 50 cm deep are often found accompanied by bigger solutional gullies up to one or two metres deep; these run in unbroken series down nearly vertical walls, particularly in the limestones of the barrier and algal reef facies, and are over 50 m long; on less steep surfaces, spitzkarren are important.

No true rinnenkarren occur in Britain, but forms transitional from rundkarren to rinnenkarren are found on the dip slopes of the Carboniferous Limestone blocks surrounding the Lake District, Photo 12. They occur as sub-parallel series of long runnels on the dip slopes and are well developed at Warton Crag, at Hampsfell near Grange and at Hutton Roof Crag where they are on limestones dipping at from $30°–50°$ and are from 10–12 m long. These runnels were originally rounded and developed under a vegetation cover, but have been sharpened by exposure to atmospheric solution. This change from rundkarren to rinnenkarren therefore indicates a change in the vegetation cover of the limestones [76].

12 Rinnenkarren and rundkarren, Hutton Roof Crag Westmorland

4. SOLUTION BASINS OR KAMENITZAS

Where rock surfaces are more or less horizontal, water collects in pools and basins, and as a result of solution by stagnant water such basins become enlarged. Solution basins or pans, known as kamenitzas in the Dinaric karst, are important in all types of climate.

They vary in size from a few centimetres to over three metres in diameter and from a few millimetres to over 50 cm deep. They are usually round or oval in shape; their sides tend to be steep or vertical, while the bottoms are flat and there is normally a sharp junction between the base and the sides. The sides are usually irregularly and sharply fretted with pits and ridges, indicating some solution by free-flowing and moving water; the sides may sometimes overhang. The bottoms are normally smooth and even in dry climates dust or soil accumulates in them; further accumulation of algal spores and peaty dust gives rise to organic CO_2 which increases the acidity of the water in the pan. Solution of the rock at the base of the pan takes place according to phase 4 because of the presence of the organic CO_2 and the base remains smooth and not jagged, in comparison with the sides. Solution pans are frequently aligned in groups along joints or fissures – like beads on a string.

Zotov described solution pits from limestones in New Zealand which were from

13(a) Spitzkarren and solution basins, Napier range, N.W. Australia

10–20 cm in diameter and whose maximum depth was 30 cm [158]. Small solution basins are common in dry climates. In the Permian limestones of Bünsow Land, central Vestspitsbergen, solution basins are only a few millimetres wide and deep; in this Arctic climate they may probably be regarded as the work solely of snow (and rain) without the intervention here of any organic CO_2. The pans are probably smaller in this type of climate than in any other. Jennings found solution pans in the Nullarbor Plain – about 1–2 ft across and $1\frac{1}{2}$–2 in. deep and round or oval in shape. Udden gives a good description of 'etched potholes' or tinajitas, solution pans in the Comanchean Limestone in Texas; he says that they tend to be more numerous on hills and ridges, 'evidently for the reason that in such situations the growth of the algae is favoured by intense and strong sunshine' [159]. He also gives a good description of the presence of bubbling CO_2 in the pools. Solution pans of this type are also referred to by Smith and Albritton [160].

Solution pans are common in the Fitzroy Limestone Ranges, where the 'flat bottoms are usually coated with a thin film of loam or clay' and dried algal remains are often found in them. The sides are covered by flutings and are undercut, steepened and reduced into knife-edged ridges and flutings. The effect of the solution taking place in the solution pans is to operate in vertical and horizontal directions, and to eliminate intermediate slopes [31], Photo 13(a) [76].

In wetter climates and more vegetated areas, much litter and humus accumulate in the basins and they can then enlarge rapidly. In north-west England, many such hollows cut into the bare limestone surfaces and vary in size from a few millimetres to about 60 cm in diameter; they also have fretted sides and smooth bases. Algae and mosses accumulate in these hollows, which eventually become filled with a black peaty humic soil,* and in wet climates like that in northern England, Photo 13(b), they frequently overflow. Measurements taken in both Tasmania and in north-west England indicate the increased solution and calcium content of the water in the pans after the water has lain on the surface for some considerable time. These show the effectiveness of the water in the pans as a solvent of the rock. The water takes up more $CaCO_3$ near or at the base of the pool than in the upper layers, the pH of the water reflecting this to some extent, being 6·5–7·0 in the

*An analysis of this black peaty soil is given in *The Weathering of Limestones*, p. 200. Sweeting [76].

13(b) Solution basins with peaty soil, N.W. Yorkshire

surface layers and 7·6–7·9 or 8·0 at the base. However, if CO_2 is being given off by organisms in the pools, the pH can be much lower, about 5·0–5·5. In northern England, experiments have shown that solution pans up to 3–5 cm deep can be formed in a few years (less than ten years) [76].

In the Clare–Galway area, Williams has described small depressions which are colonised 'by mosses (e.g. *Tortella tortuosa, Otenidium molluscum, Encalypta streptocarpa* and *Grimmia aspocarpa*), but are often water-filled and support blue-green algae. . . . The bottoms of the rock pools are roughly flat and are covered with a layer of organic and mineral waste. In this area in both summer and winter, pH determinations always show a fall to slight alkalinity or neutrality within the mud, despite a greater alkalinity in the water above' [95]. In Clare very high alkalinities are met with in pool water (up to 10·2) which are difficult to explain. The presence of the algae and other organisms plays an important part in determining the reaction of the pool water; during the day the algae abstract CO_2 from the water and precipitate $CaCO_3$, but at night their respiration reverses the reaction and solution takes place. Williams also notes the flatness of the bottom of the rock pools and says 'since pH is lowest in the sludge at the bottom of the pool, vertical

enlargement would be expected to be greater'. His explanation of 'this apparent contradiction is as follows. On the sheltered bed of the pool, beneath the blanket of sediment, the solvent at the water/rock interface is normally saturated because there is little water circulation. Solution is therefore kept to a minimum. But at the edges of the pool, evaporation, rain and wind encourage water movement, and corrosion is therefore more effective' [95]. This is in keeping with the findings of Weyl [93].

In tropical areas there are fewer developments of such surface pans owing to the effects of vegetation, though there is much solution caused by plant roots, etc., which will be discussed below. But on some surface outcrops of limestones solution cups have been described, as for instance those discussed by Wilford and Wall in Sarawak [154]. They describe circular to subcircular cavities from 0·25 to 6 in. in diameter which 'vary from shallow forms where the limestone surface is almost horizontal, to almost hemispherical forms on steeper slopes. . . . A large number of the cups have coalesced into composite forms, and, where this process has been intense, only a skeletal honeycomb of the original limestone remains. Most cups have smooth, flat to gently rounded bases. The shallow

14 Kluftkarren (grike), N.W. Yorkshire

cups on horizontal surfaces generally contain water and some rotting organic matter' [154].

5. KLUFTKARREN

The greatest amount of solution in compact limestones takes place along lines of weakness in the rock, i.e. along either bedding planes or joints or other kinds of fissures. Where such fissures are vertical or highly inclined, deep solution along them may take place into the limestone and kluftkarren are formed. Bögli classifies kluftkarren as formed by *ablaufwasser* (gutter or ditch water), and not essentially formed by solution from vegetation. Kluftkarren are cleft-like ruts, cut into the rock, normally caused by solution along joints, diaclases or brachyclases. In England,

particularly in northern England, such wide and opened joints are known as grikes, a word first used in scientific literature in 1897 [161]. Such widened joints are also a feature of the limestone areas in Counties Clare and Galway in Ireland.

The direction and frequency of grikes in the Carboniferous Limestones of Yorkshire and of Clare–Galway depend upon the variations in the frequency, direction and nature of the jointing. Some joints are vertical, others are oblique. Where joints are arranged in wedge-form or diamond patterns or where they are curvilinear, the grikes are similarly disposed [162]; Williams describes some enlarged curvilinear jointing from the Gort lowland. In Yorkshire, grikes vary from about 15 cm to about 60 cm, narrowing downwards towards their base; and from about 0·5 m to 3 m deep, sometimes as much as 5 m, Photo 14. In the Clare–Galway area the grikes tend to be both slightly narrower, averaging about 24 cm wide, and also shallower, about 1 m deep; however, the joints and grikes are more conspicuously exposed and run for longer distances in Clare than they do in Yorkshire. The walls of the grikes are often smoothed, but if they have been exposed to the atmosphere for some time they may be fretted [162]; further the grike walls are frequently fluted or runnelled by rinnen- or rundkarren, which bite deeply into the rock on either side of the enlarged joint. Where two or more joints intersect, additional solution may take place and well-like rounded hollows up to over 5 m deep may form. These are called *karrenrohren* or *lapiés wells* in the Alps [150], and have been called centripetal drainage pits by Jones in Yorkshire [84]. Similar features have been described in the Niagaran dolomites of Ontario [483].

Not every joint or diaclase is enlarged by solution. Where the joints are cemented by calcite veins they may not be enlarged and the frequency of the kluftkarren is reduced; this is believed to be the case on Scar Close on the north-west of Ingleborough, where grikes are few. It has been shown by Doughty and the writer that the joint frequency in the Yorkshire Carboniferous Limestone is variable, hence the opportunity for joint enlargement is also variable [46]. Williams is of the opinion that the selective solutional weathering of joints takes place under subaerial conditions; he claims that joints in limestones permanently covered by water (either by lakes or by the sea) are not enlarged, but that the moment the limestone becomes exposed to the action of vegetation the joints become deepened and enlarged into grikes [162]. Williams's conception of the development of grikes as a result of progressive exposure to vegetation is given in Fig. 38. The effects of a drift cover on limestones upon the enlargement of joints depends essentially upon the thickness of the cover; where it is fairly thick, over 2 m, they are not enlarged, and a sequence of the progressive development of joints away from a boulder clay cover is shown by Williams, Fig. 38; where, however, the drift cover is thin, of a metre or less, acid waters may percolate through to the limestones and the joints

may be actively enlarged beneath the cover, as has been shown by Jones [84]. At the famous locality of Norber in north-west Yorkshire, joints protected by the erratic blocks are not widened, whereas the unprotected have been widened into grikes [76].

Kluftkarren similar to the grikes of northern England and western Ireland occur commonly in the Alps and have been discussed by Eckert [150] and Bögli [59]. In the Glattalp area Bögli states that they are of largely interglacial age (pre-Wurmian). In Yorkshire and western Ireland, the evidence from their relationship to erratic blocks suggests that enlargement of joints into grikes has taken place during postglacial time [162]. Widened joints are uncommon features in areas outside the glaciated areas in Britain, such as in the Mendips; in Derbyshire, grikes occur beneath turf in some localities, and Pigott is of the opinion that in this area joint enlargement was of pre-Wurmian age [163]. Kluftkarren are abundant in recently glaciated limestones, hence meltwaters may have also helped in their formation.

In Indiana and Missouri and other areas of the centre of the U.S.A., deepened and widened joints are common in the Mississippian and Pennsylvanian limestones and here always develop under a soil cover; they are sometimes known in the U.S. as *cutters*. The jointing in the Salem Limestone, for instance in Indiana, is particularly prominent, and has been widened by solution into deep kluftkarren, with residual limestone masses or pinnacles left between. Fellows states that 'Cutters and pinnacles form at the bedrock–regolith contact'. They are due to solution by 'slow lateral movement of water, charged with hydrogen ions "moving" through regolith on a gradient related to the slope of the bedrock surface'. The cutters become exposed at the surface by accelerated erosion and by removal of the

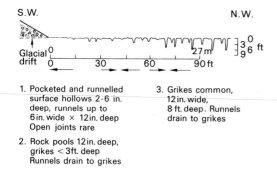

1. Pocketed and runnelled surface hollows 2-6 in. deep, runnels up to 6 in. wide × 12 in. deep Open joints rare

2. Rock pools 12 in. deep, grikes < 3 ft. deep Runnels drain to grikes

3. Grikes common, 12 in. wide, 8 ft. deep. Runnels drain to grikes

Fig. 38 Development of grikes (from Williams [162])

karst subsequently suggests that 'des processes mécaniques (destruction et dénudation) coopèrent aussi à la formation du bogaz' [122].

Corridor features of this type are quite common. Widened joints occur in the Fitzroy area of the Limestone Ranges in north-west Australia [31]. These are more often of the scale of bogaz rather than kluftkarren, being from 5 m wide to over 30 m deep, Photo 15(a); circular pits (lapiés wells or karrenrohren) also occur, and are from 0·5 m to 4 m in diameter and up to 5 m deep. They have flat floors of rock debris and sometimes have nearly vertical walls, but at other times the walls overhang a cave-like widening of the fissure at the base. In Brazil, Tricart and da Silva thought that tree roots were important in promoting solution in the formation of widened joints [165]. In Sarawak, Wilford and Wall remark that the surfaces of most hills are commonly traversed by joint-guided linear and angular meandering corridors from 2–5 ft (1–2 m) wide and from 6–20 ft (2–7 m) deep, most of which are partly filled with limestone debris, Fig. 39. These corridor

regolith. In the more arid areas of Texas, joints in the Stockton Plateau limestones of L. Cretaceous age show a pronounced solution-widening. The widened joint openings are as much as a foot across (30 cm); others are only about 1 in. (2–3 cm). In this area soil and moisture are trapped in the widened joints and support a relatively dense vegetation which forms long narrow bands. Seen from the air these bands are conspicuous as thin, dark, evenly spaced parallel lines [164].

Kluftkarren occur in the Classical and Dinaric karsts and were discussed by Cvijič [3]. He also mentions much wider fissures which he believed to have been formed by the enlargement of kluftkarren, and which he called *bogaz* or *strugas*. Bogaz are corridor-like features from 2 to 4 m wide and stretching for some tens of metres. They are from 1 to 5 m deep. Cvijič believed that kluftkarren could become enlarged by solution *only* into bogaz. But work in the

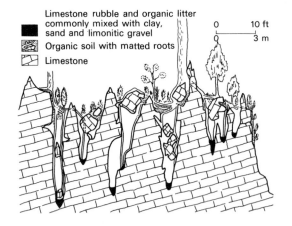

Fig. 39 Surface features of the limestones in Sarawak (after Wilford & Wall [154])

15(b) Zanjon at Torrecillar, between Ciales and Morovis, Puerto Rico (*photo by W. H. Monroe*)

walls are usually smooth and in places are undercut [154].

Similar corridor features, also joint-controlled, have been discussed by Monroe from limestones in Puerto Rico, Photo 15(b). These are known as zanjones (singular zanjon) which form parallel trenches as long as 100 m with vertical sides ranging in width from a few cm to about 3 m, in depth from about 1 to 4 m. One is described from the Florida area: 'this zanjon, most of which is impassable because of heavy jungle growth, is 1½ to 3 m wide, 3 to 4 m deep, and at least 50 m long. The walls are nearly vertical and fairly straight, and the tops of the ridges on each side of the trench are nearly flat. The floor is covered with forest litter and irregular blocks of limestone which appear to have fallen from the walls' [166]. In another area the zanjones are from 30 cm to 1 m wide and 2 to 3 m deep; they form a series of parallel trenches separated by ridges less than a metre wide. In the Morovis area the zanjones are restricted to places where the Lares limestone consists of beds of limestone from 10 to 30 cm thick. Where the thinly-bedded limestone changes to more massive limestones the zanjones disappear. They are related in some way to jointing, for they occur in preferred directions and seem to represent a persistent deepening and widening of joint cracks by action of acidic waters derived largely from decay of forest vegetation. As in Yorkshire, the sets of parallel joints form more readily in the thinner-bedded limestones and extend less far into massive-bedded limestone. Widening of the zanjones seems to take place by spalling off of limestone from the sides.

Thus kluftkarren are normally enlarged joints, but other cracks and fissures can also be enlarged. They range from the simple widening of joints like the grikes of northern England to the more complex corridor landforms like the bogaz and zanjones and often replace dolines.

6. RUNDKARREN

Rundkarren are formed under a vegetation or humus cover. They are grooves or channels cut into the limestone and are similar in size to rinnenkarren, about 12 cm to 50 cm wide and about 12–50 cm deep and of varying length, from a few centi-

16(*a*) Rundkarren near Alum Pot Hole, N.W. Yorkshire

metres to over 10 m. Their troughs, crests and sides are always smooth, a contrast with the sharp, crinkly and finely etched surfaces caused by the free flow of water over the rock; they result from solution in phase 4. Bauer shows in his article in 1962 [152], the transition from rinnenkarren to rundkarren as the result of the development of a peat cover on the limestone.

Rundkarren are basically drainage features, and even though they are developed under a peat or vegetation cover they are normally related to the slope and dip of the rock. They may occur singly or in integrated networks and their distribution resembles that of rinnenkarren. On horizontal surfaces they are short (1–2 m long) and may form a dendritic pattern; on

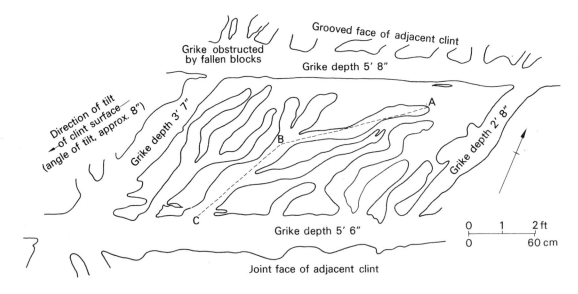

Fig. 40 Surveyed clint on Twisleton Scar showing rundkarren

16(b) Rundkarren, Takaka, New Zealand

inclined surfaces longer sub-parallel rundkarren occur.

On the horizontally bedded limestones of north-west Yorkshire rundkarren are common, where they appear as grooves or furrows in the limestone pavements [76]. Such furrows begin on the upslope side of a limestone block; they cross the block in the direction of the steepest slope and drain into widened joints (grikes) on the downslope side. The long profile of these rundkarren is undulating with reversed slopes, unlike a profile formed by freely flowing water [84]. The smoothed sides are sometimes undercut by increased solution at the base. In Yorkshire the rundkarren are often widest and deepest a short distance above the point where they discharge into the joints, leaving wedge-shaped or triangular facets between each furrow, Fig. 40 and Photo 16(a). Many joint-guided blocks are cut by series of several short subparallel rundkarren which leave wedge-shaped remnants of the rock between them. Forms similar to these have been studied in the Alps by Bauer and Haserodt who call them *karrenfussnäpfe* [167]. Karrenfussnäpfe are explained as due to solution by water issuing from dead ice or peat-covered

morainic deposits in the manner shown in Fig. 41. This kind of karren can often be seen on Twisleton Scar, Photo 17, near Ingleton and on the pavements on the sides of Ingleborough, and their relationship to the morainic deposits is similar to those studied by Haserodt.

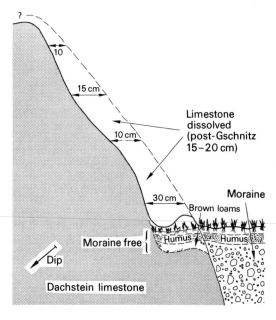

Fig. 41 Karrenfussnäpfe (after Haserodt [167])

Yorkshire and in County Clare where both widened joints and rundkarren are rare. This is due to the outcrop of massive sparry limestones which are particularly resistant to solution. Jones has also shown the importance of lichens in the formation of the Yorkshire rundkarren [84].

Rundkarren have long been recognised in the Alps and in the karsts of Slovenia and of the Dinaric coasts. In the Julian Alps rundkarren occur alongside recently formed rillen- and rinnenkarren in areas where peat and humus have formed on the limestones. They were also described by Chaix in the Désert de Platé [149]. In areas outside

Rundkarren are well developed on the inclined dip-slopes of the Carboniferous Limestones in the area surrounding Morecambe Bay, and on Hutton Roof Crag, near Kirkby Lonsdale, are as much as 13 m long. The limiting factor to their length is the occurrence of widened cross-joints, into which their drainage discharges. As pointed out by Williams the interrelationships between rundkarren and the widened joints (grikes, kluftkarren) throws light upon the relative ages of both features. Thus, where long rundkarren have been dismembered by widened joints, the rundkarren are older than the widening of the joints; other shorter rundkarren may postdate the joint enlargement. These relationships are seen on Hutton Roof Crag [162] (Fig. 42).

Both Jones and Williams imply that where there are many widened joints there are fewer rundkarren, and that where there are few joints rundkarren are more numerous [84]. This is to a certain extent true, but there are certain areas of limestone in both

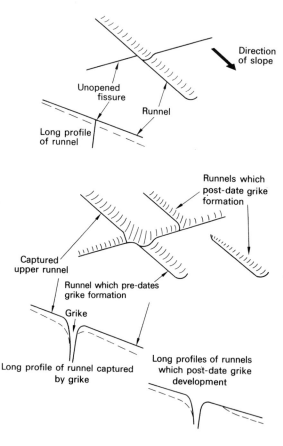

Fig. 42 A method of determining the relative ages of runnels and grikes (after Williams [162])

Europe, rundkarren are found in many places and on many different kinds of limestones. In New Zealand, some very good examples can be seen near Takaka in the north of South Island, in limestones of Ordovician age now emerging from a bracken and scrub cover, Photo 16(b). In the Gordon Limestones of Tasmania, also under a bracken and forest cover, some narrow rundkarren can be found.

Rundkarren are obviously important in the wet damp tropics where there is much vegetation and forest litter. Tropical rundkarren tend to be larger than those in cooler climates, being from 30 cm to over 2 m wide, and of the same depth, and of several metres long (up to 39–50 m), like long flutings. They were described by Jones and Scrivenor [168] from Malaya in what they termed 'trough and pinnacle country', and by Jennings and Sweeting [31] from the Fitzroy area of Australia; in the latter area long flutings of the rundkarren type cut across several beds of the forereef and algal limestones. Tropical rundkarren tend to be sharper and to have more pinnacle-like crests than those in cooler regions.

18 Hohlkarren, Harry Hallam's Moss, N.W. Yorkshire.

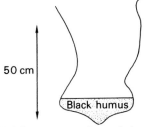

50 cm

Black humus

Fig. 43 Hohlkarre—transformed rinnenkarre. Diagrammatic section of an example in the Hagengebirge, Berchtesgadener Alpen (from Haserodt [167])

7. HOHLKARREN

Hohlkarren are karren formed under a peat or humus cover. They are rounded and smoothed like rundkarren, but tend to have broader troughs and crests. Humus gathers in the base of the trough, where the solution is of phase 4 type. Hohlkarren, Photo 18, have wider troughs and more undercut sides, compared with rundkarren. Fig. 43 (from Haserodt) gives some idea of their size and shape, about 60 cm–1 m deep and about 50 cm wide. Hohlkarren occur in the western slopes of Ingleborough, near Harry Hallam's Moss and Scar Close, where peaty waters draining on to the Carboniferous Limestone have cut channels into the rock from 50 cm to nearly a metre deep and several metres long. These channels are probably of postglacial age, and indicate the rapid rate of solution of the limestone during this time, under favourable conditions.

19(*a*) Deckenkarren, known locally as Mekondo. Makapan, Transvaal

8. KARREN FORMED BY ROOTS AND SOIL (DECKENKARREN) AND THE DIRECT ACTION OF PLANTS

In addition to the rounded karren formed by humus and litter (vegetable) accumulation, roots may cause solution of the rock. In particular, roots penetrate along joints, and root grooves are common on joint faces, particularly in the humid tropics. In Sarawak hemispherical such grooves have been described, mostly from 0·1 to 0·5 in. in diameter and occupied by the actual roots filling the grooves. They can also be seen on the White limestones in Jamaica, where the limestones are also weathered into pits and honeycombed by penetrating roots. In fact, in tropical forest conditions the effects of root solution may give the limestone surface a somewhat rough pitted surface beneath the soil rather than a smoothed one. However, subsoil weathering normally gives a smoothed rock. In Puerto Rico and in Jamaica, where the surface soil is stripped from the rock, smoothed undulating surfaces, often full of holes, are revealed. This occurs both along bedding planes and along joints. Solution at the bedrock contact is particularly important if the residuum of soil is highly permeable. Lateral movement of water occurs within the regolith and is determined by the slope of the bedrock and by the position of the joints and depressions in the limestone. Water also moves laterally in the subsurface in the Burlington Limestone (Missouri). Isolated depressions in the bedrock are also enlarged and deepened by solution, eventually giving rise to a doline type of depression. In Jamaica, joints enlarged by solution frequently contain bauxite, and in the Parnassus area of Greece residual deposits of bauxite occur over a smoothed limestone surface. Smoothed surfaces of limestone developed beneath a soil or bauxite cover are sometimes called deckenkarren, Photo 19. Deckenkarren are common in limestones which are overlain by sandstones, examples

19(*b*) Weathered limestone under soil, West Virginia, U.S.A.

20(*a*) *left* Glaciated limestone pavement, Newbiggin Crags, Westmorland

20(*b*) *right* Glaciated limestone pavement after exposure to weathering for ten years, Long Kin East Cove, N.W. Yorkshire

being in South Wales where the Pennant Grit overlies the Carboniferous Limestone, and in the Mitchell Plain in southern Indiana.

Mosses, lichens and other plants growing on limestones cause the development of fine pits and holes. Solution caused by lichen hyphae gives rise to hollows 0·1 mm to 1·0 mm deep; such hollows provide an entry for raindrops and thus more solution of the rock takes place.

The effects of lichen colonisation upon the limestones in Yorkshire have been discussed by Jones. He describes the new appearance given to the surface of the rock as the lichens become established, the 'smoothness of contour giving way to rugged, even careous weathering'. . . . 'At many places lichen colonisation may be seen to be progressive . . . the surface near to the drift is entirely free from lichens, except for a few round spots, and fossil fragments in the rock lie proud of the surface through differential solubility. The contours are smooth. A small distance away from the boundary the area covered by lichen exceeds that of the bare limestone, the individual colonies have coalesced but the contours are still smooth. Farther still from the boundary, is an entire lichen cover with secondary lichens now replacing the early established ones. The surface of the rock is no longer smoothly contoured but irregularly and minutely eroded' [84]. Both epilithic and endolithic lichens colonise the limestones. Other aspects of the biological weathering of limestones have been discussed by Smyk and Drzal [169]. Lichenometry has not yet been applied to the colonisation of limestones to any extent.

9. LIMESTONE PAVEMENTS

Limestone pavements form a complex group of karren phenomena, and result from the glaciation of a limestone surface followed by solution. Glaciation scours and abrades limestones; glaciated rock surfaces on limestones are common but striae normally are quickly removed by solution. On the slopes of Ingleborough, striae freshly exposed by removal of ground moraine disappeared as a result of weathering after about ten years [76] (Photo 20).

Glaciated rock pavements are important features in the surface morphology of limestone areas in north-western and Alpine Europe. They are strictly glaciokarstic landforms.

Limestone pavements in the British Isles were first studied by the Geological Survey in the latter half of the nineteenth century, both F. J. Foot working in Clare (1863) and J. R. Dakyns in Yorkshire referring to them; also both Boyd Dawkins in *Cave Hunting* (1874), and L. C. Miall in Whitaker's *History of Craven* (1873), described the pavements in Yorkshire. Dawkins seems to have been the first to use the term *limestone pavement*. References to the peculiar solutional forms of the pavements

of Ingleborough are numerous. One of them is that of Thomas West in 1774, who says of one area: 'It consists of a large plain of naked limestone rock, a little inclined to the horizon, which has evidently once been one continued calcareous mass, in a state of softness, like that of mud at the bottom of a pond. It is now deeply rent with a number of fissures of six, eight or ten inches wide just in the form of those which take place in clay or mud, which is dried in the sun.'

Williams has defined a limestone pavement as 'a roughly horizontal exposure of limestone bedrock, the surface of which is (*a*) approximately parallel to its bedding, (*b*) is divided into a geometrical pattern of blocks by the intersections of widened

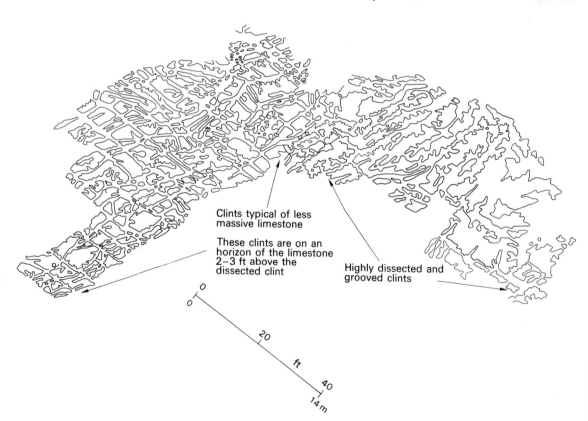

Fig. 44 Limestone pavement on Twisleton Scars (from a survey made by M. M. Sweeting [76])

21 Limestone pavement, Twisleton Scars, N.W. Yorkshire

fissures' [162]. In Yorkshire, the widened fissures are the *grikes* (or kluftkarren) and the residual blocks are *clints* (or flachkarren), but are sometimes known as *helks*. Locally the total expanse of limestone pavements were once called *clowders* or *scales*, but these two terms, though surviving on the 6-in. O.S. map, are now rarely used. Limestone pavements resemble an Alpine *karrenfeld* or a *champs de lapiés*.

The most widespread limestone pavements in the British Isles occur in the Clare–Galway area, where on both the Burren Hills and on the Gort Lowland they are particularly well developed. Both in Clare and in Yorkshire the pavements are on more or less horizontal strata, but inclined pavements are also common in Britain and occur on the fault blocks surrounding the Lake District, notably on Hampsfell and on Newbiggin Crags; pavements are also found in North Wales and in a much more weathered form on the limestones of the north crop of the South Wales Coalfield where they have been described by Thomas [506]. They do not occur in either the Mendips or in Derbyshire, consistent with the idea that limestone pavements are landforms dependent upon glacial action during the most recent glaciation.

In both Yorkshire and Clare, the sedi-

mentation in a shelf sea gave rise to limestones with relatively rapid vertical but little lateral variation. Weathering during the Tertiary period, followed by glacial scour upon these limestones, has produced the 'step and stair' relief referred to by Goodchild in 1875 [170]. In recent years much attention has been given to the limestone pavements, particularly by Moisley [171], Jones [84] and Williams [162].

Limestone pavements consist of a number of separate blocks called *clints*. Each clint has its own dip or slope which may or may not be the same as the local bedding or the regional dip of the limestone; the surface of the block may be flat and unindented or may be dissected by rundkarren according to the lithology of the limestone. Deep clefts (grikes) separate the clints. The morphology of the clints is varied and this is illustrated in a surveyed portion of a limestone pavement in Fig. 44 and in Photo 21. Pigott regards the intensity of glacial scour as being one of the main causes of their variation, the result of the degree of truncation of the original bedrock by glacial erosion, as shown in Fig. 45 and Photo 22. While to a certain extent the most impressive stretches of limestone pavement occur in areas where glacial scour is known to have been particularly effective, detailed work

shows that this cannot be the only explanation for the immense variation in pavement
morphology. First, there is much evidence
for postglacial solution, as shown in the
development of rundkarren and in the
enlargement of the grikes; secondly, the
limestones themselves show varying resistance to the agents of erosion and weathering.
Some of the factors affecting pavement
formation will now be discussed.

Firstly, one of the most important factors
affecting the morphology of limestone
pavements is the degree of jointing. In
Yorkshire the clints are generally rectangular (or parallelogram-shaped) because of
the occurrence of two sets of master
joints [45]. Thus a typical clint block is
about 1 m by 2 m (4 ft by 6 ft). Near fault
lines the frequency of the jointing increases

where the pavement becomes reduced to
knife-like clints about 30–50 cm wide
separated by grikes of about the same width.
In north-west England at Newbiggin Crags
in Westmorland, diagonal jointing and
wedge-shaped pavement blocks occur. In
the Durness limestones in northern Scotland, there is a high frequency of jointing
and the clints in this area are small and
undeveloped.

Secondly, the relationship between the
dip of the rock and the topographic surface
to pavement formation has been discussed
by Williams [162], and is summed up in
Fig. 46. He makes three points: (1) that
pavements are best developed where both
the bedding and the land surface are more
or less horizontal; (2) that stepped or
terraced pavements occur when horizontal

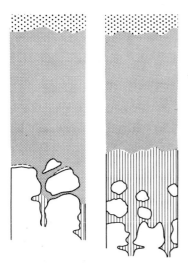

Profiles of superficial deposits on the limestone of
Derbyshire. Dots represent mixture of loess and solution
residue, vertical hatching represents yellow clay; the thin
layer of uncontaminated residue in contact with the
limestone is indicated by a broken line.

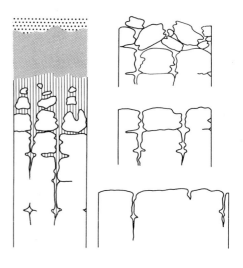

Three types of limestone pavement (right) which would
be derived from a deeply weathered limestone profile
(left) by planing down to three different levels.

Fig. 45 Limestone surfaces in Derbyshire (from Pigott [163])

22 Glacial erratic block on limestone pavement, Twisleton, N.W. Yorkshire

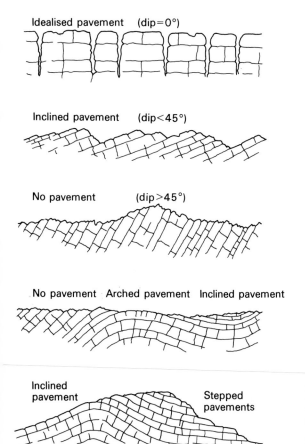

Idealised pavement (dip=0°)

Inclined pavement (dip<45°)

No pavement (dip>45°)

No pavement Arched pavement Inclined pavement

Inclined pavement Stepped pavements

Fig. 46 The effects of dip and slope on pavement form (after Williams [162])

strata outcrop down a hillside such as at Twisleton Dale, near Ingleton, and at Glencolumkille in Clare; (3) that inclined pavements occur where the dip of the beds coincides with the hillside slope provided the beds are not dipping much above 45°. Above about 45° pavement formation is impossible and this partly explains the poor development of pavement forms in South Wales. At Hutton Roof Crag and in the Gort Lowland a scarp and vale topography has been formed on limestones dipping at between 25° and 50°, with inclined and furrowed pavements on the dip slopes.

Thirdly, the strength of the limestone beds is important in the formation of pavements. Where the beds are weak, pavements do not occur, as for instance in the Permian limestones of northern England which, although glaciated, do not show glacial bedrock pavements. In both Yorkshire and in Clare, where the beds are thin or pseudo-brecciated, any bedrock pavements that have been formed by glaciation have been largely destroyed by later mechanical, particularly frost, weathering, which appears to affect more readily the thinly bedded limestones. Some beds on the other hand seem particularly strong and able to support extensive pavements and to be relatively resistant to both chemical solution and to mechanical action. On these beds are pavements, over 80–100 m^2 in extent without interruptions of jointing or where the joints for some reason do not become enlarged; such beds tend also to be less dissected by rundkarren and solution hollows.

Schwarzacher has already shown that the Carboniferous Limestones in Yorkshire possess distinct vertical variations, and that the sequence is divided by master bedding planes into lithological units; beds in the vicinity of the master bedding planes tend to have a relatively high quartz content and to be more resistant to solution [40]. Doughty also divided the Carboniferous Limestones into a series of units and showed that the upper beds of each unit possess a lower frequency of jointing and are more massively bedded. He implied that such upper beds would be those on which pavement formation would be most likely to occur [46]. This work is confirmed by the writer who has shown that the beds with the lower frequency of jointing are those that have a high percentage of sparry calcite, while those beds in which the jointing is much more frequent are of a more biomicritic type [172]. The sparry limestone beds are also thicker-bedded and, because of their lower porosity, more resistant to solution, all factors combining to make them much more resistant and more likely pavement formers than the other beds. Williams, in his survey in Glencolumkille in County Clare, showed that there was a relationship between the heights of the cliff formed by the bed and its thickness, but concluded that there was 'no evidence . . . to show why particular beds were preferentially selected for pavement development' [162]. However, he mentions the work of M. J. Clarke who has studied the limestones of west Clare and whose

observations are similar to those of Doughty; Clarke found that the purity of the beds increases upwards in each cycle 'until the pavement bearing bed is reached. The pavement bed is the most resistant to erosion because it is pure and compact' [173]. The limestones of Clare and Galway are in general more sparry than those of north-west Yorkshire [37]. This may explain the more ubiquitous development of pavements in Clare and their better development and why Williams could say 'Pavements are extremely common, particularly on the Visean Limestones, west of Gort, and while not every bed supports a pavement, most are probably capable of doing so' [162]. The distribution of pavement types in Chapel-le-Dale, Yorkshire, is shown in Fig. 47.

On beds that do not support pavements, mechanical weathering may be important; pseudo-brecciated beds in north-west England, as at Arnside Knott, for instance, weather in a rough knobbly fashion instead of supporting pavements.

On the Continent, the works of Eckert and E. Chaix described limestone pavements from the French and Swiss Alps. In speaking of the Désert de Platé and other 'déserts' of Haute Savoie, Chaix refers to the residual blocks between the widened fissures as *dalles*; these are equivalent to clints. He also uses the word *trottoir* (pavement), but not precisely in the sense in which the term is used in English [149]. In recent years Bögli has worked on the glaciated limestones at the head of Muotatal, central Switzerland, where there exists a terraced and stepped relief (like Yorkshire and Clare), a karst 'en banquettes structurales'. Bögli has called this type of glacially formed relief *schichttreppenkarst*, which he classifies as belonging to a group of complex karren [90]. Limestone pavements occur in northern Norway adjacent to the Svartisen

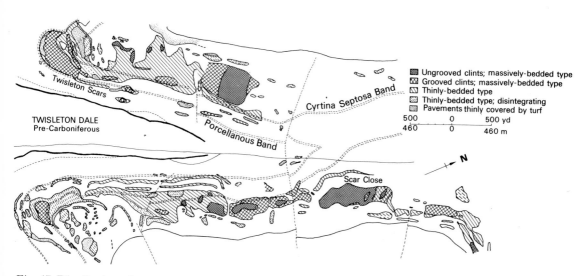

Fig. 47 Distribution of pavement types in Chapel-le-Dale and Twisleton Dale (from Sweeting [76])

ice cap. In the Causses of southern France only occasional patches of pavement occur at the highest levels where it is possible some glaciation or snow solution has taken place. Pavements occur in the Julian (Slovenian) Alps and in the Triglav area, where there is ample evidence of glaciation and where they have been studied by Kunaver [108]. They do not occur in the Classical Karst area which was not glaciated; they are also absent in the Dinaric karst except on the highest summits, such as Biokovu in the Velebit mountains [174].

Summing up, it is difficult to see what agent other than ice could produce such flat scoured and smoothed surfaces on limestones. Marine and lacustrine erosion can form horizontal limestone platforms, but they are not so flat or table-like as for instance the limestone surfaces below the lakes in western Ireland. Where soil-covered limestones have become exposed, the bared limestone surface tends to be formed of rocky stones, as can be seen in parts of the Classical Karst today, or in the soil-eroded limestone areas of Greece and the Lebanon. Furthermore, in northern England, if the beds now forming the limestone pavements are removed, the surface becomes grass-covered and the pavements are not renewed; this suggests that limestone pavements are relict landforms formed under different climatic conditions from those which exist today in Britain [76]. However, the pavements have been subject to many vegetational changes, which have caused their partial dissolution but not their destruction.

10. MARINE KARREN (LAPIÉS LITTORAUX OR SEEKARREN)

These are solution features produced on limestones by the action of seawater and marine organisms. They are some of the most neglected features of limestones and will only be briefly referred to here. Some of the most important work in this field has been done by Guilcher [69]; in the British Isles, some work has been done by Common [175].

In the British Isles, solution by salt-water spray gives rise to fretted and roughened pits and hollows, separated by sharp pinnacles. There is a sequence of forms from low tide to above high-tide mark. Where the rock is more continuously under the influence of salt-water solution, it is cockled and fretted with small pits and pinnacles, and though elongated hollows develop along joints, in general the joints are not widened, as in grikes. The roughened surface of the rock becomes smoother towards high-tide level and rounded hollows and widened joints become more prominent, particularly when vegetation is able to colonise the limestone. This kind of transition can be well seen on the coasts of the Aran islands, along the western coast of the Burren in County Clare, and also at Worms Head on the Gower peninsula in South Wales and in the Devonian Limestones at Brixham. Along the coast of Clare and elsewhere, echinoderms cause some solution of the rock, but no quantitative work has yet been undertaken on this point [176].

Guilcher and others claim that marine karren reflect temperature differences and that coastal solutional features on limestones differ in cool temperate, Mediterranean and tropical regions [69]. The hollows in coastal limestones in temperate regions tend to be small, only a few centimetres across, whereas in warmer seas the inter-tidal zone is characterised by wide and flat solution pans more than a metre in diameter. These large and shallow solution pans are known as *vasques* and have been described from coastal limestones in Morocco and some Pacific islands. In tropical and Mediter-

ranean seas also, coastal limestones tend to become undercut by solution about mean tide level, forming overhanging 'visors'. The extent to which visors are the result of climatic and temperature differences rather than tidal and sea-level influences is difficult to say; there is still some controversy on their mode of origin. In general, the weathering of coastal limestones by sea water appears greater in tropical than in temperate regions. But so far no quantitative work has yet been done, and the actual chemical processes involved in the reactions between the sea water and limestones are not well known. The work by de Vaumas [507] on the dune limestone coastal features of the eastern Mediterranean is likewise descriptive.

Many beaches consist of calcareous sand, as for instance the 'machair' in north-west Scotland. In warm climates, cementation of calcareous sand gives rise to beach rock, on which a great deal has been written. Some of the problems associated with the origin of beach rock concern those connected with the origin of karst landforms [177]. In general, however, since the action of sea water upon limestones tends to be solutional rather than attritional, limestone coasts usually have little debris, except where rivers enter the sea. The coasts of karst areas consist normally of pinnacled and pitted limestones, with very little sand, but with solutionally rounded pebbles and rocks at and below the mean water-level. The coast of the Dinaric karst between Rjeka and Dubrovnik illustrates many of these features and has been discussed by Milejović [178]; other examples of limestone coasts are seen in the Lebanon, in the coast of Galway Bay and the Burren of western Ireland and in the coasts of Puerto Rico.

6 Karst Valleys

IF IT IS accepted that karst landforms are those formed only as a result of vertical and underground drainage, then strictly valleys in limestones are not karst landforms. Valleys are essentially the result of water flowing over the surface of an area, and are formed by fluvial processes. Roglič in fact goes so far as to say that use of the term karst valley is both misleading and illogical. 'Water in the karst sinks in and the features are shaped in a vertical sense, and they are therefore isolated from each other. In this way the "pit country" (the Wannenlandschaft) is formed. More regular features of river erosion and slope washing do not belong to typical karst scenery. Impermeable rocks have essentially different water circulations, which produce the corresponding differences between river erosion and the karst process' [179]. This view will be regarded by many as very pedantic, but since many valleys in karst areas are now considered to have been formed after the main phase of karstification there is some justification for it.

Cvijič in 1893 said that 'owing to the permeability of limestone, running water disappears in karst country, normal valleys are rare or completely missing, and their place is taken by blind valleys and other different "basin forms" (Wannenformen)'. However, in his later works he says 'The flow of water over the surface is not entirely missing from karst country' and continued to use the term 'karst valley' [179].

Karst valleys are the most important of the landforms occurring in the karst which are not produced by true karst processes. They can be divided into the following groups: allogenic or through valleys, formed by rivers which rise on the impermeable rocks surrounding the limestone area; blind valleys (together with half-blind valleys); pocket valleys (or reculées); and dry valleys including those formed in limestones during conditions of glaciation or of permafrost.

1. ALLOGENIC VALLEYS

These form some of the most scenic features of karst areas. The most typical are narrow and steep-sided. 'Allogenic valleys are always canyon-like; the purer the limestone, the more strongly developed is the canyon. This rule is valid for the rivers of the Dinaric karst, the river valleys consisting of widenings in the impermeable rock and of canyons in the limestones' [179]. The river waters tend to be clear since the load is mostly solutional and there is little attritional debris; they also tend to be of a vivid emerald-green colour due to the presence of calcareous algae.

Early workers in the Karst realised that river erosion in limestone was only possible in canyons cut by rivers rising in areas outside the limestones and bringing in rock waste and water from impermeable areas. Only the largest rivers and bodies of water rising outside the karst will survive with sufficient volume to traverse the limestone area. Thus in the Dinaric karst there are only four normal valleys which cross it, those of the Zrmanja, the Krka, the Cetina and the Neretva [180] (Photo 23). Cvijič said of the Tara and Piva canyons in Montenegro: 'These rivers, as mighty water courses, enter the waterless karst

23 Allogenic valley, Krka, Šibenik, Jugoslavia

plateaus around Durmitor, which are built up of almost horizontal limestone layers. Only these rivers have been able to resist the intensive karst process. The other rivers, poor in water, have succumbed to this process, and their valleys have become blind valleys. The canyon rivers, rich in water, have deepened their beds down vertically, and the slopes of their valleys have risen canyon-like above them'. The allogenic Tara Canyon has been discussed by Nicod [181]. Grund in 1903 [182] was the first person to use the term kalkklamm (limestone gorge) for such steep-sided limestone gorges. They are absent only in areas of extremely deep karst. In western Europe there are numerous allogenic rivers. Some of the best known occur in the Causses of France, where streams rising on the impermeable rocks have cut through the limestones and isolated them into blocks. The Tarn gorge is probably the most famous. The Tarn flows for several miles through the limestones of the Grands Causses. At Ste-Énimie, the gorge is only 2 km wide but it is over 300 m (1,000 ft) deep; its walls are generally cliff-like, though the presence of less pure marly layers in the limestones gives rise to gentler ledges or 'terrasses' [115]. It is now believed that the main phase of karstification in the Causses preceded the cutting of the gorges [495, p. 301]. Other limestone gorges include those of the and Lesse in Belgium; the Punkva in Moravia; the Verdon in Provence; the

Bienne in the Jura; and the Litany in the Lebanon. In Britain the most characteristic are the Dove and Manifold valleys which cut through the Carboniferous Limestones of Derbyshire, both having risen on the shales and grits of the surrounding area. In north-west Yorkshire, the Ribble and Wharfe are also allogenic, though these have been considerably modified by glaciation and glacial deposits, Fig. 48 and Photo 24.

Allogenic limestone gorges are common in the humid tropics and are generally wider and less canyon-like than those in temperate areas; this is usually regarded as due to the larger quantities of debris affecting limestones in tropical areas, with consequent increase in abrasion. Examples occur in the Rio Cobre gorge in Jamaica; in the karst rivers in Malaya; in the Geikie Gorge of the Fitzroy river in north-west Australia; in the short north-flowing rivers of Puerto Rico, the Rio Grande de Arecibo, and the Rio Grande de Manati; and in the Sibun river, south of Belize in British Honduras.

The shapes of allogenic gorges depend partly upon the nature of the limestones through which the rivers traverse. They are more steep-sided in thicker-bedded limestones; in dolomites, valley walls frequently weather particularly in peri-glacial conditions into tower or ruin-like masses, such as at Montpellier-le-Vieux in the Causse Noir and in Derbyshire at Tissington Spires. There are few studies of allogenic

24 Dry bed of Skirfare river, north-west Yorkshire, with relatively low frequency of jointing

river valleys in limestone areas partly due to their steepness and inaccessibility. The Verdon, Tarn and Dordogne in France are much frequented, but there is little known about the actual morphology of the cliffed valley sides, the distribution of pebbles and alluvium, or the distribution of shallows and deeps in the beds of the rivers. It is known that limestone pebbles often show a greater degree of flattening than pebbles of other rock types; thus pebbles taken from the Skirfare in north-west Yorkshire have an index of flattening of 2·22, compared with 1·5 an average for non-limestone streams. Though limestone gorges usually contain little alluvium, river terraces can be sometimes important, as in the Buchan river in southern Victoria, Australia, and in the Dordogne in the Causses of Gramat in France [183].

Abrasion and solution are both active in allogenic gorges, and the limestone bedrock is finely potholed; this can be seen in many rivers in northern England where they cross outcrops of the Carboniferous Limestones, as in the Lune near Kirkby Lonsdale and the upper Wharfe in Langstrothdale. The potholes tend to develop on riverside benches formed on massive sparry limestone beds, the more flaggy beds seemingly not being strong enough to develop potholes of any size. The potholes are asym-

metric, with the steeper side facing downstream and the more gentle side facing upstream; they tend to be deeper than potholes in other rock types, probably due to increased solution. Solution is often helped by the presence of freshwater algae which colour and smooth the rock surface.

Differential solution along joints and bedding planes is also important. Where joints are strongly marked the rivers may be confined between vertical joint walls, as at Ease Gill Kirk in Westmorland, where the river flows in a canyon not more than a metre wide in places. The differential solution along bedding planes is well shown at Howstean Gorge in Nidderdale, not far from Pateley Bridge. On dipping beds, the effects of abrasion and solution give rise to waterfalls, the dip of the bedding planes being important in influencing the direction of the stream, as in the Dee in Dentdale. In some tributaries of the Wharfe, Hodgson concludes from a detailed study of both the stream courses and the original depositional features of the limestones (mounds, etc.) that many of the minor trends of the modern streams are influenced by such original features, and not by the present regional dip of the limestones [184].

Collapse of limestone blocks enlarges the valleys which can be shown to form quickly despite the hardness of the rocks

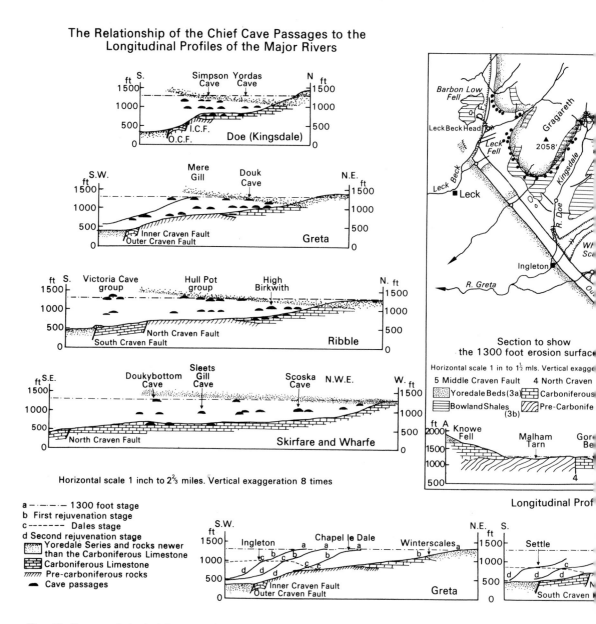

Fig. 48 Geomorphological features of the Ingleborough district (*Geogr.J.*, Jan.–Mar. 1950)

[183]. The extent of the collapse of limestone in the formation of such allogenic valleys has not yet been properly established. Certain sections of such valleys are probably due to large-scale collapse, as in the Tarn at the Pas de Soucy. Corbel has in fact suggested that the whole of the Tarn in its gorge section through the Grands Causses has been formed by the unroofing of a series of caverns, but this seems unlikely [185].

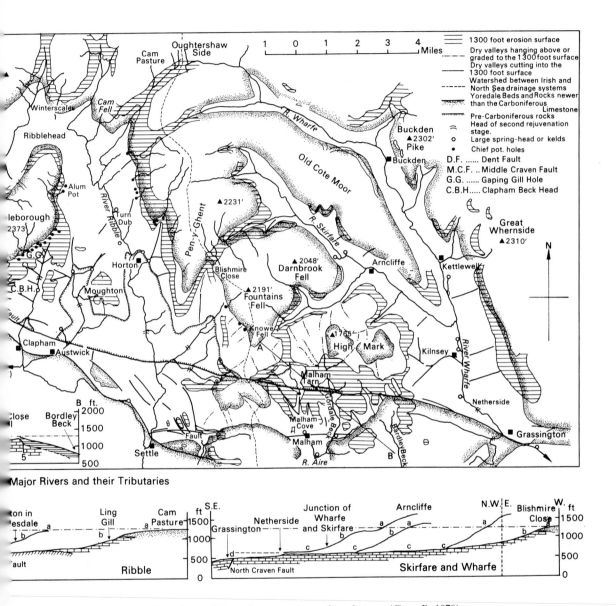

Major Rivers and their Tributaries

Note. Recent work by Waltham gives a different interpretation to these features (*Geogr.J.*, 1970)

However, collapse on a local scale may give rise to small steep-sided valleys, of which the Rakov Škocjan (the Rak valley) in Slovenia is one of the most famous [185] (Fig. 31). Cvijič also described some gorge-like valleys in eastern Serbia which had probably been formed by the collapse of cavern roofs[148]. In Yorkshire the southern end of Gordale Beck shows some signs of collapse, but if it has occurred it has formed only a small part of the valley [186]. Short steep-sided valleys caused by collapse of an underground cavern and exposing the river to the surface are called *karst windows* [148]. Moussa has recently called attention to an example in southern Puerto Rico [508].

Solution along the joints and bedding planes causes their enlargement and eventually water from the allogenic streams disappears underground. Hence allogenic valleys are dry for part of the year, one of the most notable being the Tarn at the Pas de Soucy; in Britain, the Manifold in Derbyshire is a good example. Such dry river beds are full of irregular limestone blocks, and frequently of pebbles showing preferred orientations. Enlarged joints and bedding planes swallowing up water from the river bed have been described by Warwick for the Lesse and Meuse valleys [187]. They can be seen also in the Mellte in South Wales and in the Skirfare in Yorkshire.

A combination of collapse and of widening of joints by solution leaves sections of the limestone in the form of natural bridges or arches, unusual scenic features which have attracted much attention. In Yorkshire, there is a small arch in Gordale Beck and also one in Browside Gill in Ribblesdale; both these have had a relatively simple history. The Natural Bridge in Virginia which has been explained by Lobeck has had a more complex origin [188].

Allogenic valleys may be transformed by the large-scale deposition of calcium carbonate. Tufa and travertine deposits are common in some valleys – the cause being either an extensive loss of CO_2 or the action of algae mosses, and other lime-secreting plants. In the tropics, in addition to these two factors, evaporation of water is important. Tufa is an irregular deposit of amorphous $CaCO_3$ often formed around plant roots and leaves; it is not necessarily

laminated, though many tufa deposits are finely laminated, as at Gordale Scar in Yorkshire. It is usually relatively soft and light, full of holes left by the decay of the plant roots around which it originally formed. Travertine is normally formed of crystalline $CaCO_3$ and is a layered deposit; it is harder than tufa, and tends to form sheets rather than irregular deposits. The terms are used to some extent interchangeably.

In Britain tufa deposition is frequently associated with waterfalls in allogenic valleys as at Gordale Scar where the river falls over 250 ft (80 m) just north of the line of the Middle Craven fault. Falling water loses a certain amount of its CO_2 and oxygen; the pH of the water varies throughout the fall, being low at the top (5·0–5·5), highest in the middle (6·5–7·5) and rather low again at the base, having absorbed more air in the lower part [76]. Quite often the tufa is deposited in the form of a triangular or 'beehive' shape, each falling stream of water being associated with a separate 'beehive'. However, tufa deposits are not only found in waterfalls and many occur in layers in lake-like extensions in floors of the valleys. Thus in Britain the upper parts of Gordale Beck and Clapham Beck in Yorkshire have several feet of tufa within their valleys. In Derbyshire, valleys like Lathkilldale have substantial tufa deposits; and in the Mendips where springs emerge at Cheddar, there is also tufa. 'Petrifying' springs which coat objects left in them with tufa are well known at Matlock in the Derwent valley in Derbyshire. Relatively little work has been done on tufa deposits in Britain, though Sinker discusses some of the flora associated with them in the Malham area [189].

In warmer regions, where there is both more CO_2 in the karst water and also more evaporation, deposition of tufa and traver-

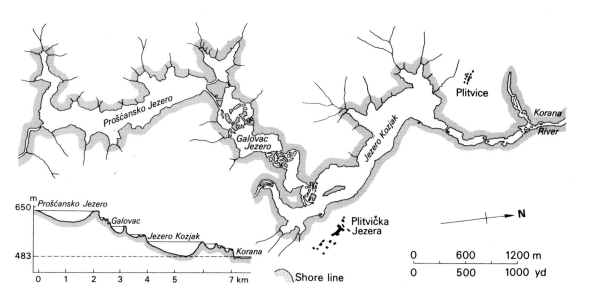

Fig. 49 The Plitvice lakes, Jugoslavia

tine can reach substantial proportions. Gregory was the first person to call attention to the deposits of tufa in allogenic valleys in Serbia. He noted that as a consequence of tufa deposition many water-falls became higher and more extensive with time rather than decreasing as is more usual with waterfalls, and he called them 'constructive waterfalls' [190]. Not only are the waterfalls built outwards, but they may reach right across the valley and form barriers behind which large lakes may be dammed. One of the best-known series of tufa barriers and the lakes dammed up by them can be seen at Plitvice in Bosnia, Jugoslavia, on the Korana river. Sixteen major lakes and many minor ones have been formed in this valley by the building of tufa dams, and there are over a hundred water-falls. The lakes form two series, stretching over 8 km in distance and about 134 m in height. The upper series is known as the *Gornja Jezera,* and consists of fourteen lakes; these are in a part of the valley cut into dolomitic limestones and where the

slopes are wooded and relatively gentle. The lower series is the *Donja Jezera* and is the better known. The lower lakes are situated in a part of the valley cut into pure limestones and are surrounded by high valley walls containing caves; tufa cascades and beehives are numerous in this section and the water in the lakes has the peculiar emerald or turquoise colour for which the Plitvice lakes are famous. The map, Fig. 49, shows the Plitvice lakes, the largest of which is 46 m deep and 82 ha in area. They have been studied by Pevalek [191] and by Roglič [192]. Pevalek concludes that the barriers have been built up by the lime-secreting action of two plants in particular, the moss, *Bryum pseudotriquetrum,* and the algae, *Cratoneuron commutatum.* Roglič has said that the activity of these plants occurs particularly where the valleys cross dolo-mites, and claims that the deposits which have formed the barriers to the Plitvice lakes are of postglacial age [192]. The colour of the waters is due both to the accumulation of algae and also to plankton.

25 Falls of the Krka, Šibenik, Jugoslavia, showing tufa deposition

Tufa cascades and barriers also occur on the Krka river, near Šibenik [193] (Photo 25).

In tropical areas, tufa and travertine deposits have also been recorded. In semi-arid regions like the Carlsbad area of New Mexico and in the Limestone Ranges in north-west Australia, the occurrence of tufa deposits in dry valleys probably indicates a change from a wetter to a drier climate. This point of view has also been advanced by Marker in a study of tufa deposits in valleys in the north eastern Transvaal [509], and also discussed by her in the *Zeitschrift für Geomorphologie* (1971).

2. BLIND VALLEYS

Solution of the limestones in the bed and banks of a river enlarges joints and bedding planes, which in time will absorb all water from the stream and the river will dry up. In highly jointed limestones, rivers of quite large volume can be absorbed, and in areas of deep and well-developed karst all drainage coming on to the limestones from the impermeable rocks is absorbed almost immediately into the limestones. However, some rivers traverse the limestones for some distance before their waters sink into the rock. River valleys, closed at their lower ends by disappearing streams, are known as *blind valleys* (blinde Täler, vallées fermées, vallées aveugles). In a true blind valley all the water disappears into the limestones more or less at one locality, all the year. Cvijič recognised also *half-blind* valley (halbblind or demi-fermée), in which water is normally absorbed at one point of disappearance but under flood or high-water conditions it flows beyond the usual point of disappearance into a lower part of the valley beyond; there are thus two parts to a half-blind valley, the upper part which usually stops at the water swallow, and the lower part in which water flows only during periods of high water or floods.*

A blind valley begins as a normal fluvial valley eroded into the impermeable rocks

*Cvijič divided blind valleys into primary and secondary. *Primary* blind valleys are where 'a river from impermeable rock enters strongly porous jointed limestone, its water disappears in the limestone fissures and in time big sinkholes are formed there'. *Secondary* blind valleys are where if 'through the formation of sinkholes in a bed of a normal karst river, its valley becomes blind'. This statement gives an idea of Cvijič's equivocation on the whole subject of valleys (J. Roglič, *Erdkunde*, 1964).

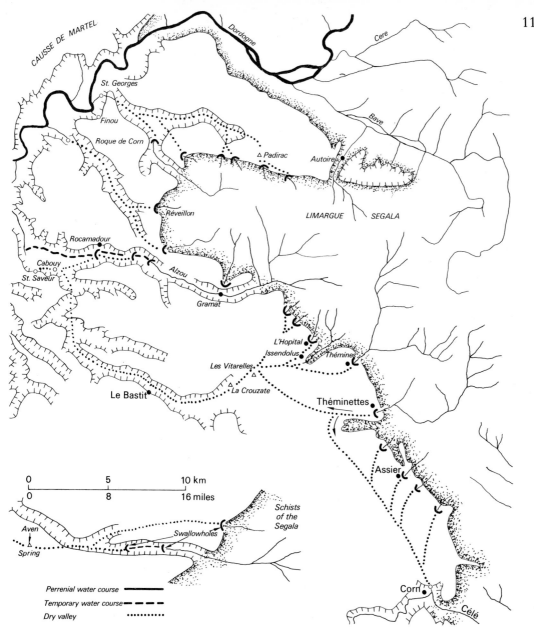

Fig. 50(a) Blind valleys on the Causse of Gramat (from Clozier [117])

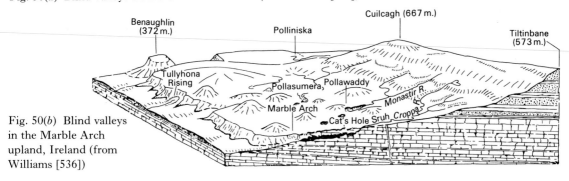

Fig. 50(b) Blind valleys in the Marble Arch upland, Ireland (from Williams [536])

above the limestones: as it passes on to the limestones its water becomes swallowed up by holes in the rock and the river permanently disappears. Normal fluvial abrasion, in addition to solution, takes place on the limestones above the disappearance, but only weathering and solution occur below it, the blind valley is therefore at a much lower level than the area which lies downstream; frequently the termination of a blind valley is marked by a limestone cliff, often with a cave at its base into which the river disappears. The height of this cliff gives some indication of the age of the disappearance of the river and of the blind valley; in general the higher the cliff, the older the point of disappearance. The most favourable conditions for the formation of blind valleys are hilly areas of heavy rainfall with well-developed streams on impermeable rocks upstream of the areas of massive limestone; such conditions are seen in the Classical Karst, in the Moravian karst, in the Causses of France, in West Virginia, and in the centre of Jamaica, all areas where particularly good blind valleys can be seen. They are also well developed in the Marble Arch area of Ireland, as instanced by the Monastir Sink. (Fig. 50(a) and (b).)

In Istria, large streams rise on impermeable flysch deposits and become blind valleys as they flow on to the karst limestones. Two of the more spectacular are the Pazinski Potok (the Foiba valley), which is terminated by an abrupt cliff over 80 m high at Pazin, and the Notranjska Reka, a river flowing along the strike of the flysch, and is engulfed at Škocjan, where the cliffs of the limestone are in places over 300 m high. In France, the Cazelle river is engulfed at the Roc de Corn on the Causse of Gramat, after 3 km flow across the Causse; the difference in height between the 'live' valley and the 'dead' valley is 38 m, Fig. 51. Another excellent example is the disappearance of

the Bonheur river in the Causse of Camprieu, shortly after it leaves the granite and impermeable rocks of the Aigoual massif. In Jamaica, good blind valleys occur along the southern margin of the Cockpit Country and the Dry Harbour mountains, some of the best examples being the Cave River valley and the Quashies river. The cliffed termination of these rivers is sometimes sub-circular or armchair-like in form.

In Britain blind valleys are on a much smaller scale, Photo 26. This is due not only to our much smaller and less developed limestone areas, but also to the effects of glaciation. Blind valleys are best developed in Britain outside the glacial limits, such as in the Mendips, where a good example is the valley terminated by Eastwater Swallet, where the terminal cliff is 80 ft (24 m) high. In northern Britain, in particular, the effect of glaciations has meant that drainage has only recently become re-established and the points of disappearance of water are now being re-formed; there is therefore normally no real cliff termination to the blind valley, and the 'live' valley is not much incised below the 'dead' valley. Examples of these occur around the northern part of Ingleborough, on Park Fell. In Derbyshire, the absence of glaciation in the last glacial phase has meant that blind valleys are more developed than in Yorkshire [194], as at Perryfoot, near Castleton [195]. Malott has

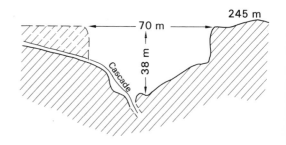

Fig. 51 Gouffre de Roc de Corn (from Clozier [117])

discussed examples of blind valleys in the karst of Indiana in the central U.S.A. For instance, near Needmore in Lawrence County 'a small stream enters a swallow hole in a valley cut 60 ft lower than its former surface course' [196]. Blind valleys are also particularly well developed in the Moravian karst. According to Kunsky, 'The present blind valleys are secondary . . . developed from the original normal karst valleys. A swallow hole was formed, grew larger as the surface water drained into it, and due to its deepening, one of its walls became the blind close wall' [197].

Many examples of half-blind valleys can also be found. Kunsky regards the valley of the Sloup Brook in Moravia as a type example [197]. In Indiana, Malott discusses the Lost River in the following way: 'Lost River after gathering its waters from 53 sq. miles of non-karst upland, sinks in a number of channel swallow holes. . . . In times of heavy rainfall the swollen stream discharges across the sink hole plain in a meandering storm water channel more than 20 miles in length. Such a stream channel normally dry, but kept open, is called in Indiana, a *dry bed*.' It is in fact a good example of a half-blind valley [196]. In Britain, because of the recently established surface channels in the glaciated limestone areas, half-blind valleys are numerous. The Water Sinks valley at Malham Tarn is one example; another is the Crina Bottom valley on the southern slopes of Ingleborough, where there is a series of swallow holes below the normal disappearance of the stream which absorb the overflow in flood conditions.

Gams noted that blind valleys are a focus for accelerated corrosion in karst areas. He also made the point that the shape of blind valleys was often related to the total hardness of the streams flowing on to the limestones [198]. Streams with low initial

26 Gingling Hole, Fountains Fell, Yorkshire. A blind valley

hardness give rise to wider valleys on the limestones because they can take up more calcium carbonate. Streams with high initial hardness flow in valleys which become narrower because they are not able to take up more calcium carbonate; they tend to abrade with sand and gravel rather than corrode.

3. POCKET VALLEYS (VALLÉES EN CUL DE SAC, RECULÉES, OR SACKTÄLER)

Blind valleys occur in the upper part of limestone areas where water enters the rock. Pocket valleys are the reverse of blind valleys, occurring in association with the large springs which resurge at the foot of a limestone massif. They consist of flat-bottomed, often U-shaped, valleys with steep walls, and a steep, abrupt cliff at their head. The headward cliff is frequently cirque-like and a spring normally issues from its foot. Because of their distinctive

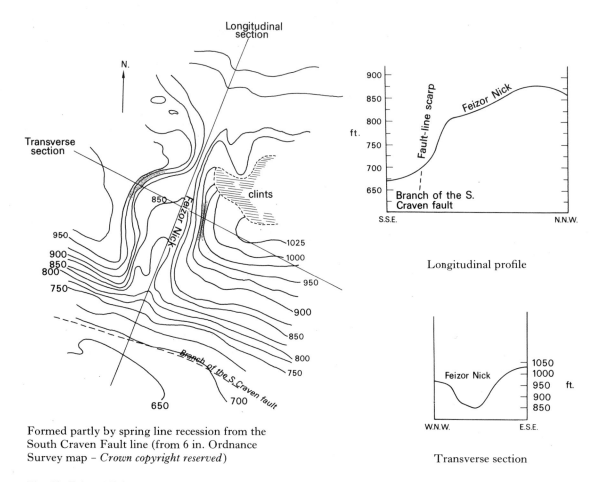

Formed partly by spring line recession from the
South Craven Fault line (from 6 in. Ordnance
Survey map – *Crown copyright reserved*)

Longitudinal profile

Transverse section

Fig. 52 Feizor Nick

shape they are also known as *bouts du monde*
or *fin du monde* or, in the Jura, as *reculées*.
There is no local term in English, though
the term *coombe* in the chalk areas is sometimes used in a similar sense to that of
reculée.

On the lower side of a limestone mass,
where it rests on the impermeable rocks
below, springs emerge frequently from
caves at the foot of cliffs. Because of the
general resistance of limestone to fluvial
degradation and slope washing, it often
forms upstanding ground, or edges. In the
Causses of France, the upstanding edges

are frequently referred to as the *couronne*
des Causses or *corniche* du Causses [115].
The springs which issue at the foot of such
upstanding masses cut back by a combination of spring sapping, cavern collapse and
river erosion. In time the steep edges of the
limestone masses are indented and pocket
valleys are formed, Fig. 52.

One of the best-known pocket valleys in
Britain is Malham Cove in north-west
Yorkshire. Here structure has assisted the
perching of the limestone area. The cove
forms a recess in the Middle Craven Fault
Scarp, of over 600 m; the surrounding

27 Recess of the Brooking Spring, Limestone Ranges, N.W. Australia

valley walls of limestone are about 100 m high and the cliff from which the river Aire emerges as a spring is over 120 m high [186]. The river Axe in the Mendips also issues from a pocket valley at Wookey Hole.

Some of the best examples of pocket valleys occur in the western edge of the Jura in the Arbois and Salins region, where they are up to 8 km long and 1,000 m wide, and often 350–400 m deep. The high upstanding edges or *corniches* of the Causses have many pocket valleys, two of the most notable being the 'bout du monde' of the river Hérault and the reculée of the Sorpt which extends for over 2 km parallel to the fault of Chastaux in the Causse Martel. In the Classical Karst the source of the river Ljubljanica is 'encased by the vertical walls of the high karstic plateaux' [193]. In southeast Australia one of the most impressive is at Bungonia where a steep reculée is cut back into the crest of the Great Dividing Range.

The springs which emerge at the head of the pocket valleys are often clear and free from coarse debris; they meander across flat alluviated floors, Photo 27. The cliffs at the head of the valley are kept fresh by the continuous activity of the issuing springs. In tropical areas, springs emerging into pocket valleys tend to have more alluvium, as can be seen at Windsor on the north side of the Cockpit Country in Jamaica.

In areas where the limestones form the lower ground, pocket valleys are less spectacular; they are thus less in evidence in Derbyshire and the Gort-Clare lowland than they are in north-west Yorkshire and the Marble Arch area, where the limestones are perched. They are however characteristic of almost all karstlands.

4. DRY VALLEYS (VALLÉES SÈCHES OR VALLÉES MORTES; TROCKENE TÄLER)

Dry valleys are those without, or with only a temporary, watercourse. They are probably the most numerous of valley forms in karst areas and in many ways the most difficult to account for, similar dry valley forms probably being originated in many different ways. Clozier has said that 'les vallées mortes sont . . . les fidèles témoins de l'évolution fluviale' [117]. Roglič says 'The term "dry valley" comprises the most undefined features'. As a result of the study of dry valleys in limestone areas in western Europe and central Europe, it is clear that many of them may fall into systems related to a past drainage network superimposed upon and later let down on to the limestone beds. This is very well shown in the map of the Derbyshire dry valleys reproduced in

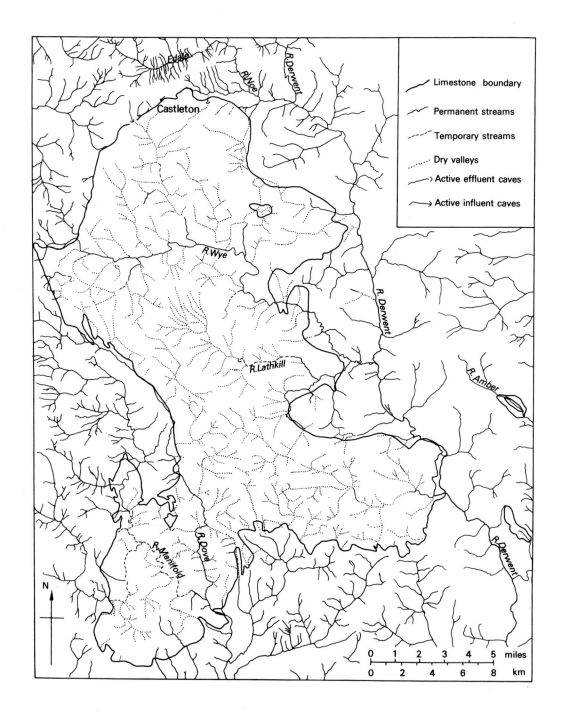

Fig. 53(a) Dry valley system of the Carboniferous Limestones in Derbyshire (from Warwick [199])

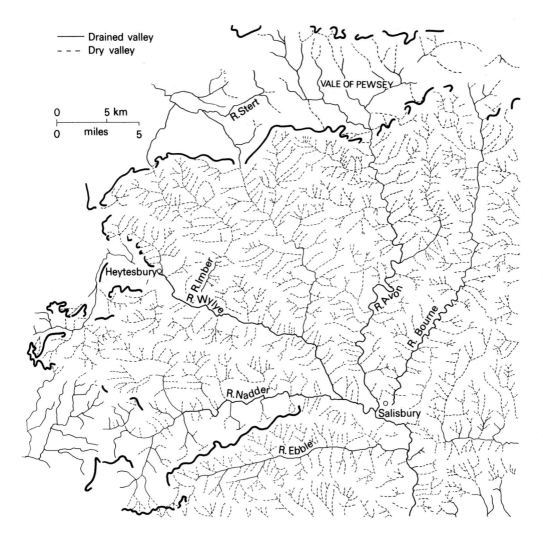

Fig. 53(*b*) Dry valley system of the Avon basin on the Chalk, Wiltshire (from Pinchemel [201])

Warwick in 1964, Fig. 53(*a*) [199]. It was probably this kind of observation that caused A. Penck to believe, in his proposed cycle of erosion, that there was a period of river erosion on the limestone which preceded the development of the karst processes. Roglič has said that this idea was put forward without 'any justification, facts being fitted into this scheme' [179]. How-

ever, there is no doubt that a network of fluvial valleys has existed on some limestones; a lowering of the water level, or a change in climate as for instance in the chalk of England and of Picardy, are accepted modes of formation of dry valleys [200, 201] (Fig. 53(*b*)).

Dry valleys in limestones tend to be steep-sided, with well-jointed rock sides

28 Dry valley near
Marakoopa, Mole
Creek, Tasmania

and steep scree slopes, Photo 28. The floors may be either flat and rather U-shaped, as in the Watlowes valley above Malham Cove, or more V-shaped as in dry valleys in Derbyshire. The shapes vary with the types of limestone and with the origin of the valley, in addition to modifications caused by glacial and periglacial action. In well-jointed massive limestones they are steeper-sided than in more thinly-bedded rocks; older valleys tend to have gentler-sloping sides than those more recently formed. In the Causses of Quercy, Clozier recognises two morphological forms, collinos (coul-lino), wide, gently sloping dry valleys of Pliocene age, and steep-sided, ravine-like gorges, combes, cut out during the Quaternary [117]. The situation of embayed or encased dry valleys is common in western Europe. Thus in the Mendips the dry valleys, formed under glaciation or permafrost, occur as a dendritic network of shallower valleys on the plateau, and lead into more steep and narrow valleys below. Such a dry valley network converges upon Cheddar Gorge, which has been formed by

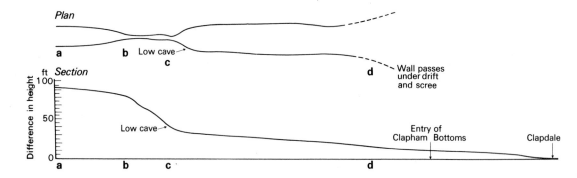

Fig. 54 Trow Gill – plan and longitudinal section

Trow Gill
(b–c) Upper gorge section, possibly interglacial or postglacial in age
(c–d) Lower section, probably a collapsed preglacial cavern
(a–b) Dry valley above Trow Gill

torrent action and is not a collapsed cavern [202]. In north-west Yorkshire an older series of wide valleys occurs, but there are in this district many dry ravines cut into the limestones which may be of glacial melt-water origin; these include Trow Gill on the slopes of Ingleborough, Fig. 54, Gurling Trough near Conistone in Wharfedale, and Ease Gill Kirk on the Yorkshire–Westmorland border.

In northern and western Europe other effects of permafrost and snow melt during the Quaternary period have to be taken into account. Disintegration of limestones by frost is particularly accelerated along fault and joint-lines. In the Grizedales area between Settle and Malham every fault line is the locus of a dry valley and their formation by frost and snow action is a possibility [126]. These dry valleys in north-west Yorkshire demonstrate again the close link between erosion and structure in limestone areas. In Derbyshire, scree deposits of periglacial origin have considerably modified the dry valleys [195].

In areas of more obvious permafrost action, valleys in the limestone areas of Bünsow Land, central Vestspitsbergen, for instance, are entirely made up of scree and may have been formed by frost and snow action and not by ordinary fluvial erosion on the limestones [203]. This means that not all valley forms on limestones are necessarily the result of fluvial erosion and slope wash.

In the humid tropics, dry valleys are less numerous, which may be due to the greater intensity of karstification. But in the semi-arid regions, we have already seen that in karst areas of high rainfall intensity valleys replace dolines as the normal unit of drainage [31]. In both the Carlsbad region of New Mexico and in the Limestone Ranges of north-west Australia, an integrated network of dry valleys characterises

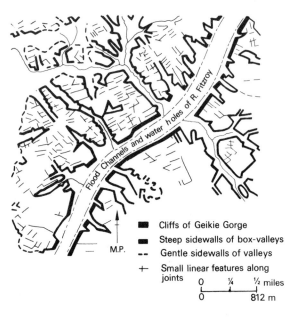

Fig. 55 An area of box-valley network near Geikie Gorge, Limestone Ranges, north-west Australia (from Jennings & Sweeting [31])

the limestone surface; such valleys take the flash floods caused by heavy rain showers, Fig. 55. Along the edge of the limestone Ranges dry valleys show an alternation of gently graded reaches with steep falls, i.e. storied valleys [31]. Similar valleys caused

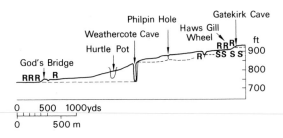

Fig. 56 Longitudinal profile of part of the River Greta, north-west Yorkshire (from Warwick [204])

Dotted lines represent probable underground water level.

S and R indicate sites of stream swallow holes and resurgences respectively.

by flash flooding are found on the steep seaward slopes of the Velebit mountains in the Dinaric karst, as for example near Karlobag, north of Zadar, and at Omiš, south of Split.

As we have seen, dry valleys are the most favoured locations for the development of dolines, because water collects into small pools and sinks into joints and fissures. Hence the profiles of dry valleys tend to be irregular and to become broken up, and show increased gradients. This is illustrated by the profiles of Borrins Wood valley near Giggleswick and Tattersalls valley near Malham. A discontinuous and disorganised valley is also illustrated by the profile of the Greta valley, Fig. 56 [204].

5. DISORGANISATION OF NORMAL VALLEYS

Normal valleys are disintegrated by the development of karst features. Continuous dissolution of the limestone and the progressive widening of fissures cause the disappearance of rivers from the lower to the upper parts of the valleys. Unlike fluvial erosion which works from the base-level upwards, karstic erosion works downwards towards its lowest point.

The upper part of a valley in a limestone terrain becomes progressively drier as fissures are widened and the river disappears into a series of swallow holes which migrate successively upstream. The best examples of this type of stream absorption in Britain are seen in Derbyshire, where the streams have not been much disturbed by recent glaciation; the successive swallow holes of the Manifold have been discussed by Warwick [205]. In Yorkshire, the re-establishment of the drainage after the glaciations is too recent to have allowed of

the development of many large postglacial swallow holes; for instance, on the slopes of Ingleborough water infiltrates into joints and cracks in the limestone above Gaping Gill during dry weather, but Gaping Gill still takes the bulk of the water in times of average and high water. The hydrology of the dry valley of Burrington Combe in the Mendips has also been discussed by Tratman [206].

The transformation of a normal valley into a dry valley by the progressive absorption of water is well described by Cvijič in his last work [148]. He shows how the lowest swallow hole will become the base level for the river flowing on the surface; how the slope on the downstream side of the swallow hole will have a reversed slope and become a barrier; and how in time a swallow hole situated higher up in the valley will enlarge, absorb the stream and the lower swallow hole will become 'dead'. This process can be repeated successively. But, there can be two different cases. In the first, the absorption of the river takes place by swallow holes which are successively higher, in the second they are successively lower. Cvijič claims that this depends upon the intensity of cutting of the stream; where cutting is feeble the swallow holes become higher, where cutting is vigorous the floor of the river is deepened and they will become lower.

In the first example, the lower underground channels may be older than the upper ones. In western Ireland, in the Burren, at Poulnagollum, the upper swallow hole and cave is younger than the lower. The reason for this is that the lower swallow hole developed before the last glaciation; during the glaciation more of the limestone became exposed as a result of glacial scour, and subsequent to this the upper swallow hole developed. In the Greta and Skirfare valleys in Yorkshire, the rivers are also being engulfed at successively higher levels.

In the second example, swallow holes develop in series one below the other; this is either due (as Cvijič supposed) to a vigorously down-cutting river or to the rapid uplift of a limestone area. In the Classical Karst, there are successive swallow holes one below the other at both Postojna and Predjama, where there are three upper-level swallow holes and a fourth level into which the rivers disappear at present. The Bonheur river near Bramabiau in the southern part of the French Causses also has a series of swallow holes at descending levels. Examples are more rare in Britain, but in the Manifold in Derbyshire swallow holes occur at successively lower levels. Frequently series of descending swallow holes can be related to a series of resurgences, also in a descending order; the resurgences at Cheddar are an example.

The effects of the progressive cutting down of the allogenic valleys, together with the karstic disorganisation discussed above, cause many tributary valleys to hang above the principal valleys. Each successive lowering of the main valley, or rejuvenation of any kind of the area, will deplete both main and side valleys and cause more and more water to disappear into holes in the limestone. While the principal valleys are able to continue downcutting, side valleys may dry up completely, and become hanging valleys. This process is similar to that described in chalk country by Fagg [200] and by Pinchemel [201]. The effect of rejuvenation upon a valley is to cause swallow holes to migrate upstream and springs to migrate downstream, the upper and lower parts of the valleys being subjected to the maximum amount of deepening. These conditions are illustrated in the Ingleborough district where, as a consequence of rejuvenations and movements along the South Craven Fault, the main allogenic valleys have been repeatedly lowered and the tributaries have become depleted of their drainage and become dry hanging valleys, Fig. 48. In Derbyshire, Warwick has described dry valleys now hanging above the Dove and Manifold rivers [194]. Such conditions are also seen in the Sloup valley in the Moravian karst [197].

However, where as in some areas, for example the Grands Causses, karstification probably preceded the formation of the valleys, it is the karst landforms which have become altered and disorganised by the fluvial activity rather than the fluvial valleys disorganised by karstification.

7 Water Sinks and Water Swallows

IN LIMESTONE areas, the total or partial absorption of a watercourse, i.e. a river or stream as distinct from infiltrating water, is known usually in England as a swallow hole (or swallet) and in America as a water or stream sink. There are many equivalent words in all the European languages. The sink or swallow of a stream denotes the disappearance of the stream at some place; swallow holes commonly occur as obvious and sometimes large openings, and therefore belong to two main groups. First, those where water disappears slowly into the valley and where there is no real topographic feature; the French call these *pertes filtrantes*. To this group also belongs the underwater or subfluvial swallow hole. Secondly, those in which the disappearance of the river is marked by a conspicuous relief feature, a large hole or holes. This second group can be further subdivided into (*a*) where the river enters a more or less horizontal cave, (*b*) where the river enters the rock by a vertical or steeply sloping shaft, and (*c*) where the river disappears into holes in alluvium or drift covering the limestones (i.e. similar to alluvial dolines).

In the discussion of the Slovenian Academy of Geology and Geography it was stated that the terms *ponor, ponikva* and *poziralnik* were all used in Slovenian for any kind of 'sinking'. But the discussion proposed that *ponor* be used for swallow holes where water disappears into horizontal caves, *poziralnik* for small caverns in the rocky bottom of an intermittent watercourse, and *ponikva* for places where water disappears down through superficial layers

of silt [207]. Cvijič used the word *ponor* for all these variations, and it is probably most helpful to use *ponor* as the equivalent of swallow hole [148].

1. SWALLOW HOLES WITH LITTLE OR NO TOPOGRAPHICAL EXPRESSION

Where a stream disappears slowly into the limestone, the bed becomes gradually drier downstream and less and less incised. There are no visible cavities, the water sinking into bedding planes and joints and into grass-covered floors as if they were a sieve. There is little, if any, reversal of gradient of the valley. Such swallow holes must be relatively new, as any stream which has been entering the limestones for any period of time would have both eroded and corroded visible holes in the rocky bed. They occur in Yorkshire where glacial drift has recently been deposited upon the limestone, and newly established rivers sink gradually into the drift. The water sink at Malham Tarn is of this type, where the river sinks into a mass of limestone boulders and grass. Clozier quotes the examples of the two swallow holes of the Issendolus in the Causses of Quercy, Fig. 50(*a*), p. 111 [117]. In times of low and average flow enlarged fissures are able to absorb all the flow; in periods of flood the river may overflow below the swallow holes. In time the fissures become more enlarged and distinct holes appear in the river bed; Warwick has described the developing swallow holes in the Manifold valley near Wetton Mill [205].

29(*a*) River disappearing into cave, West Virginia, U.S.A.

As a result of the solution of the rock in the bed of the river, swallow holes migrate upstream, those upstream replacing the ones lower down.

Underwater or subfluvial swallow holes tend to occur in newly established streams. They have been recorded by Clozier in rivers in the Causses of Gramat; Malott gives a photograph of the disappearance in a vortex of the storm waters of the Lost River [208].

2. SWALLOW HOLES WHICH FORM A RELIEF FEATURE

(A) SWALLOW HOLES ASSOCIATED WITH CAVES (PONORS [SENSU STRICTO], PERTES-GROTTES)

These are normally formed by the enlargement of bedding planes by the action of the river; but occasionally the flow of the river may be absorbed into a cave formed in a previous period of solution, i.e. the cave may be formed after or before the initiation of the surface channel. Swallow holes connected with caves tend to occur in limestones that are horizontally bedded or only gently dipping. In north-west Yorkshire they are common, many streams disappearing into bedding-plane caves on the slopes of Ingleborough and Pen-y-Ghent, as for example at Long Kin East and Borrins Moor caves on the slopes of Ingleborough and at Blishmire on the eastern slopes of Pen-y-Ghent. There are also many examples from the Burren of western Ireland, where the limestones are almost horizontal, two being the Coolagh river swallet and the Upper Poulelva cave. In the Mendips, the stronger dip of the limestones means that the water falls more rapidly through the rock, but the swallet at Swildon's Hole is of this type [209]. One of the most spectacular disappearances of a large river into a big cave is seen at Cave river in central Jamaica, in the White Limestones [210]. In the Saut de la Pucelle in the Causses of Quercy, the stream disappears into a cave without any change in velocity or flow; this is sometimes known as a perte-grotte [117].

In the Classical Karst, the disappearance of the Puika river is connected with the Postojna caves; both here and at Predjama, the present river disappears into the lowest of a series of caves which mark the former levels of the river. In Yorkshire and west Ireland, on the other hand, many of the disappearing streams have formed the bedding-plane caves which they now enter, by solution and abrasion, Photo 29(*a*). Some caves are closely related to glacial deposits

29(b) Stream disappearing into joint fissures, N.W. Yorkshire

and are of postglacial age and their size is an indication of the amount of erosion (and especially solution) which has taken place in the postglacial. At Blishmire, the cave is about 100 m long and the Callaun caves in west Ireland are over 1,000 m long [211].

(B) SWALLOW HOLES WITH VERTICAL OR STEEPLY SLOPING SHAFTS (POTHOLES)

This is the most spectacular type of swallow hole and develops where vertical joints in limestones are particularly conspicuous or where the beds are steeply dipping, Photo 29(b). They are especially important in areas where the available relief is great and where the height of the top of the limestone beds is much above that of the level of the resurgence of the water. In the karst of Croatia and Serbia, this kind of swallow hole is called a *jama*, but in Slovenia the term jama is used for a ponor-type cave (as at Predjama, above). Cvijič distinguished two types. First, the jama (or zvekara in Serbian), in the form of a narrow shaft terminating at its base with a closed cave of relatively little development. Secondly, the Trebič type, which also opens from the surface in the form of a narrow shaft, but which is related to a developed cave system. Shaft-like swallow holes tend to occur in strong and hard, particularly sparry limestones, and also in limestones which are not easily shattered or collapsed. Their shape is normally rift-like but may be roughly circular if much water-worn.

In north-west Yorkshire this type of swallow hole is called a *pothole*, a dialect word originally, but now used in other parts of Britain. It first appeared in geological literature about 1875, being employed by L. C. Miall in the 3rd edition of Whitaker's *History of Craven*. He says: 'Near Horton and Selside are many pits in the limestone, known locally as "pots"' (p. 23). The Ingleborough district in particular is famous for the development of potholes, and illustrates the conditions necessary for their formation. It possesses a massive, sparry limestone series, which though only 600 ft (200 m) thick has strong vertical jointing; it is perched high above the surrounding non-karstic rocks; it is bounded by a fault system (particularly the South Craven Fault), which has been active in relatively recent times; it has experienced recent glaciation and meltwater conditions; and it has peaty deposits and a high rainfall at the present time. In the Ingleborough area, there are two main types of vertical swallow hole which correspond broadly to those distinguished by Cvijič, viz. those with little cavern development, and those associated with a well-defined cave system. Many potholes in this area today are no longer active and only receive streams from small drainage areas and may be regarded as 'dead' potholes. They were formed in previous climatic periods.

The first type in north-west Yorkshire forms a deep and narrow shaft, caused by enlargement of a joint or small fault plane. Usually such shafts are much longer than they are wide, being as much as 20 m long, but only 1 or 2 m wide; they may vary greatly in depth from about 20 m to over 100 m. Long King West pothole on the southern slopes of Ingleborough is a good example and is 33 m long, only 1 m wide and over 100 m deep, Fig. 23. The walls of the potholes may be relatively straight and ungrooved and not greatly altered by solution and abrasion of falling waters (in some, slickensides can be seen on the walls). But frequently the falling streams have caused the formation of fluted and rounded walls and columns, about 1 m wide and $\frac{1}{2}$ m deep, like large rinnenkarren. This is seen at Pillar Pot on Newby Moss on the southern side of Ingleborough and at Bull and Cow potholes on Leck Fell; they are also seen in the potholes known as the Buttertubs in the Main Limestone (Yoredale) between Wensleydale and Swaledale [49]. The base of this type of pothole is usually filled with rounded and polished boulders through which waters coming into the shaft disappear.

The second type in north-west Yorkshire is typified by Gaping Gill hole on Ingleborough and by Rowting and Marble Steps potholes on the slopes of Gragareth. Gaping Gill receives the drainage of a part of southern and eastern Ingleborough; its shape is determined largely by the disposition of the master joints, but it has been rounded to some extent by corrosion and erosion of falling water. The mouth of the hole is 40 ft (13 m) in diameter and it is over 350 ft (120 m) deep, the waters of Fell Beck falling sheer into it by one of the highest waterfalls in Britain. There is an extensive cave system at the base of Gaping Gill [76].

There are other examples of pothole-type swallow holes in other karst areas. In the Causses of Quercy, the Gouffre de Roc de Corn is the well-known swallow hole formed in the river Cazelle; Cvijič also quotes the Gouffre of Ingriste on the Kurjac river in Serbia [148]. In Ireland, the Sligo and the Marble Arch districts (near Enniskillen) have the best-developed potholes. Shaft-like potholes connected with cave systems are also common in the Alpine limestone areas, as in the Vercors, the Dachstein-gebirge and the Julian Alps; they are also recorded in the Pyrenees [108, 119]. Both here and in the Causses of France some of the swallow holes are still active, but others no longer have streams entering them. Examples of such 'dead' potholes are Eldon Hole in Derbyshire and the pothole associated with the cave of Aven Armand in the Causse Méjean.

Enlargement of this type of swallow hole takes place by the falling away of limestone blocks, as has occurred at Bar pothole and Alum Pot, Ingleborough, or in the Abîme of Rabaoul near Padirac, France. Occasionally more widespread collapse takes place, as at Kara Jama in the Karst, where there is a debris cone 80 m high.

Vertical swallow holes are particularly influenced by faulting. For instance, there are ten pothole-type swallow holes along a few miles of the Padirac fault in the Causses of Quercy. Mere Gill and Hunt potholes in north-west Yorkshire are also formed along fault lines.

However, though structural and lithological considerations are very important, the regions with the greatest number of pothole-type swallow holes are those of both present and recent glaciation. Thus we have indicated that high Alpine and Pyrenean limestone areas are regions of extensive pothole development. Corbel has claimed that many potholes originate at the contact of or beneath the ice [119]. They

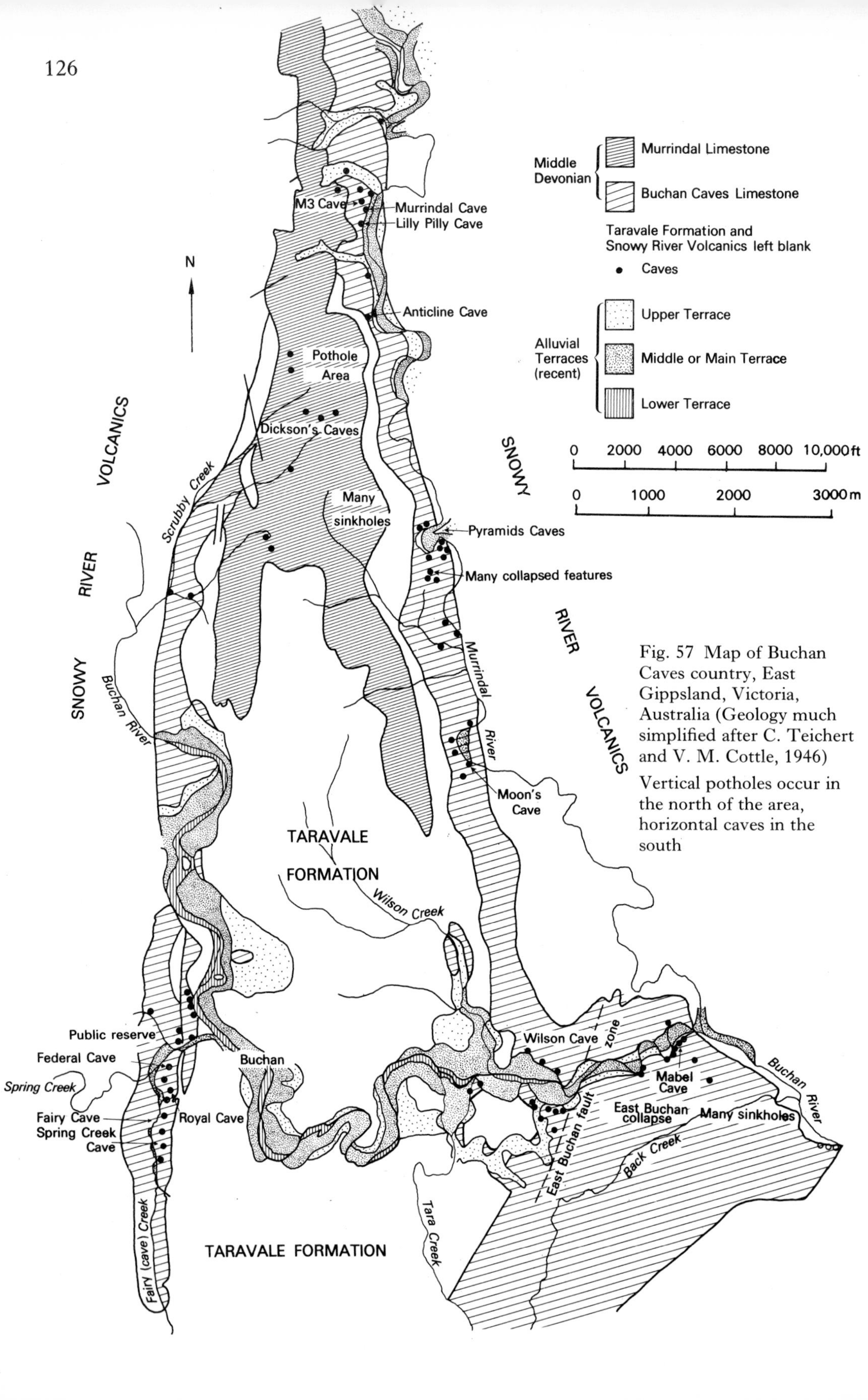

Fig. 57 Map of Buchan Caves country, East Gippsland, Victoria, Australia (Geology much simplified after C. Teichert and V. M. Cottle, 1946)

Vertical potholes occur in the north of the area, horizontal caves in the south may be seen in formation on the slopes of Triglav in the Julian Alps, where the recently explored Triglav pothole has become exposed as a result of the recession and thinning of the Triglav glacier; similarly in the Svartisen district of northern Norway, pothole-like shafts are developing alongside the Svartisen ice cap [87]. Potholes are also connected with glacial drift and on the slopes of Ingleborough it can be shown that they occur around the edges of the drift deposits and also where the drift deposits are thick. On the southern part of Ingleborough known as the Allotment, where drift is over 30 ft (10 m) thick, there are at least fifteen potholes over 300 ft (100 m) deep within a few square yards, Fig. 23. This indicates that the acid waters draining from glaciers and from the drift deposits have caused much solution as they have entered joints in the very sparry upper beds of the limestones. In the Rocky Mountains Ford and others have explored potholes beneath the Castleguard glacier in Alberta [489].

In non-glacial environments, potholes occur (though not so abundantly) where structural and lithological conditions and the relief conditions are suitable. Thus, in the Buchan area of Victoria in Australia, potholes occur in strongly jointed and perched limestones at Murrindal, Fig. 57 [183]. Aub has also described potholes at the foot of many cockpits in the White Limestones of Jamaica; these have a limited development and are of Cvijič's first type, being unconnected with cave systems [111].

In cold climates, the steep-sided shafts form reservoirs for cold air. In those which have no underground outlet and no interconnecting passages, snow and ice may remain the whole year. In Yorkshire, after a snowy winter like that of 1947, snow may remain in deep potholes all the summer.

(c) SWALLOW HOLES FORMED IN ALLUVIUM OR DRIFT

This type of swallow hole is sufficiently distinctive as a landform to be discussed separately. The stream sinks into a hole, but because of the drift or alluvial cover the swallow hole is neither of a cave nor of a pothole type. Instead the hole is usually a muddy depression in the flat floor of a valley. In the Dinaric karst it is usually known as a ponor, and is especially connected with the poljes, areas of flat, planed, often alluvium-covered limestone, which are discussed in Chapter 10. Ponors in the Livno and Gacko poljes are illustrated in Fig. 87, p. 193. They are normally about 6 to 10 m deep with muddy and stony sides and bases [214].

They occur in limestone areas with much alluvium, such as parts of the Jura, in the Mouthe–Pontarlier area in France and in the Mole Creek limestone area of Tasmania. In the latter region, the river disappears into a series of such holes which are as much as 15 m deep. In the Classical and Dinaric karsts many swallow holes of this type function during low-water conditions as true swallow holes, but during the winter, when water-levels are higher, water issues to the surface through these holes and they function as springs. They are then sometimes known as estavelles.

In tropical humid areas, because of the large amount of organic debris which accumulates on the limestones, a high percentage of the swallow holes are of this type. Thick deposits of alluvium cover the allogenic river beds and rivers of considerable volume disappear through holes in this alluvium into the limestone bedrock below. There are many examples in Jamaica and Puerto Rico; in Jamaica, at Troy, the Hectors river disappears by means of many such swallow holes, and in Lluidas Vale the

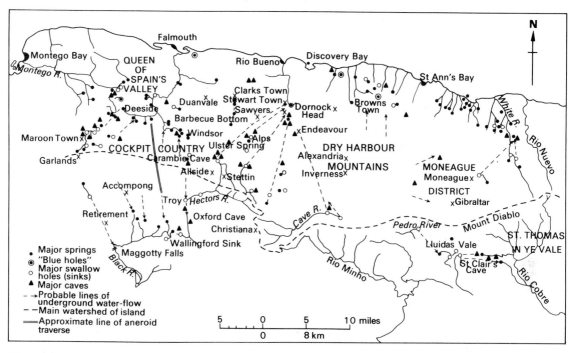

Fig. 58 Swallow holes and springs, north central Jamaica

Murmuring Brook, a tributary of the upper Rio Cobre, disappears into a fine alluvial swallow hole, Fig. 58.

Where swallow holes are not able to absorb all the stream water, lakes may be formed; swallow holes may be blocked by boulders and vegetational debris, called *swallow-hole rafts* in Indiana [208]. Sometimes the disappearing rivers divide into two branches, each branch being engulfed by a separate swallow hole. This fact was noted by Cvijič and also by Martel. Martel called attention to its occurrence in the river Ballylee, a tributary of the river Gort in western Ireland [15]. The sinking of the stream at the Smelt Mill stream sink on Malham Moor in Yorkshire also takes place by means of a bifurcation. Cvijič referred to this phenomenon as 'the dispersion and the bifurcation of karstic water courses'. He quoted the Serre in the department of Aveyron as an example; in this river, bifurcations are absorbed into different swallow holes, from which the water flows underground to different surface catchments, one branch going to the Lot, the other to the Aveyron [148]. No investigations have so far been made to explain the dividing of sinking streams, but the decline in the volume and velocity of the river flow is presumably part of the cause.

8 Caves

1. INTRODUCTION

Since the definition of karstification involves the development of underground drainage, the formation and development of underground landforms become part of any study of karstlands. Until recently underground landforms were not regarded as relevant to the study of limestone landforms, though Cvijič said 'L'étude des vallées sèches montre qu'il est impossible de comprendre bien des formes superficielles sans considérer les cavités. C'est de ce point de vue que nous abordons ici . . . l'étude des grottes' [148]. However, as Cvijič went on to say, the study of caves is in many ways a separate discipline, that of speleology, a discipline as distinct in itself as geography or geology. Despite this separation it is essential for any student of karst landforms to be thoroughly acquainted with the development and origin of caves and their main features.

The first scientific investigation of the caves of Europe took place in the eighteenth century, when Nagel descended the Macocha in Moravia in 1748. Much exploration took place in the nineteenth century; Schmidl's work on the Classical Karst and the Adelsberg Cave (Postojna) was in 1854 [12]; the first English work on caves, Boyd Dawkins's *Cave Hunting*, was in 1874 [8]. The first descent of Gaping Gill was in 1895 by E. A. Martel, who called attention to the scientific problems of caves and the applications of their study. His books, like *Nouveau Traité des Eaux Souterraines* [13], *La France Ignorée* [212], *Irlande et Cavernes Anglaises* [15], and *Les Grands Causses* [213], although written with an unrestrained enthusiasm, are in many ways years ahead of their time. Cave study developed first where the caves were both imposing and easily accessible. Thus the Classical Karst (whether it was Austrian, Italian or Jugoslav territory), the Austrian Alps and the limestone areas of France have all been centres for European cave research; all these areas today have government research stations for the study of caves.

During the nineteenth century and the early part of the twentieth, much data was accumulated on caves, but little theoretical literature emerged until about the 1930s. There then appeared two major works on caves and karst hydrology; these were Otto Lehmann's *Die Hydrographie des Karstes* [214] and W. M. Davis's long essay on the 'Origin of Limestone Caverns' [215]. The French made great advances in speleology during the 1939–45 war when they were confined to their own homeland, and as a result they emerged at the end of the war as the nation with the most advanced speleological knowledge. This was reflected in the publication of Félix Trombe's *Traité de Spéléologie* (1950), which marked a real advance in the study of caves. Meanwhile, in the U.S.A., Harlen Bretz [216] followed up Davis's work, and the National Speleological Society of America began to produce *Bulletins* with important articles on caves [217]; America now has a Cave Research Foundation. In Britain, the British Speleological Association started before the war, but the most rapid advances in cave research have been since by the Cave Research Group of Great Britain, founded in 1947; in Britain also there are many caving clubs which publish material about caves, an important one being the University of Bristol Speleological Society. In most countries of the world today, from the Soviet Union to Australia, speleological organisations exist and much valuable literature appears each year on every aspect of caves.

The first international Congress in Speleology was held in Paris in 1953, and the fourth was held in Ljubljana and the Classical Karst in 1965. In all these congresses, though much attention was paid to the biological and archaeological aspects of caves, by far the greatest attention has been given to the origin of caves and their hydrology, i.e. to those aspects which may be regarded as relevant to the study of karst landforms.

The great difficulty in the study of caves and of underground drainage is that, particularly where the limestone is thick, we can never actually see them. 'We are concerned', says Roglič, 'with subterranean forms which are not easily accessible and therefore only partly known' [218]. The underground landforms are the most essential elements of a karst area and distinguish it from areas on other rocks. In non-calcareous rocks any cavities formed by erosion become filled in; in karst areas, the fissures become clogged only temporarily, and as water percolates it deepens the depressions.

The Oxford Dictionary defines a cave as 'an underground hollow usually with an horizontal opening'. American writers are much concerned to define a cave; thus Bretz in the *Caves of Missouri* in 1956 opens his discussion with the following: 'No one will ever know how many caves Missouri has, nor is it possible that everyone will ever agree on a definition of a cave. Is a rock shelter a cave? Is a natural bridge, a cave? Is a hole that can barely be crawled into for only a few feet a cave? Is it a cave if one's

light shows an opening into which one cannot force his way?...In terms of human experience we generally think of a cave as being a natural, roofed cavity in rock which may be penetrated for an appreciable distance' [219]. However, a cave is not an object, it is a space. Hence, as is said by Curl, 'the specification of a cave involves the specification of the boundaries of a space' [220]. The minimum size of a cave is given by the limiting dimension of the human explorer, in order to distinguish the term 'cave from such contiguous spaces as inter-crystalline pores'. 'A definition is desirable in order to be specific when discussing the different kinds of natural subterranean cavities' [220]. In Britain the term cave includes usually not only horizontal cavities, but also vertical passages. In Slovenia, the term jama normally means a cave (any hollow underground space), but more usually is used for horizontal caverns. In Serbo-Croatia, a horizontal cavern is a *pecina*, a jama is used only for vertical caves. A short cavern, like an abri or shelter, is a spodmol [218].

The first problem in the origin of caves is to explain why some joints and fissures become enlarged into caves at all. This point is discussed by Howard, who says: 'If it is postulated that the principal dissolving occurs because of an original undersaturation with respect to calcite, of the groundwater entering the limestone, it is hard to imagine caves even beginning to form, for the small quantities of groundwater flowing through the joints would become almost completely saturated within the first centimetre of the joint, according to the evidence given by Weyl (1958). The first stages of joint enlargement by solution call for a different mechanism' [221]. Otto Lehmann distinguished between primary cavities (hydrographically pervious) and those cavities which are hydrographically effective in the karst process [214]. If the joints and fissures are to be hydrographically effective, they must form a network allowing the water to enter as well as flow out. The first phase is represented by the widening of the primary cavities (the Urhohlräume), which can only be carried out by corrosion.

The primary cavities are completely filled with water so that they are no longer in contact with either the cave air or the surface air. Only after there is a sufficient widening of the primary fissures can pressure and gravity flow take place. As we have seen in Chapter 3, a supply of CO_2 is necessary for the dissolution of the calcium carbonate. The sources of CO_2 for underground water are from incoming streams, from the cave air, and from organic substances. It is clear that these sources do not penetrate far into the groundwater (phreatic) zone; cave air in fact does not exist at all in the groundwater zone, either in the primary cavities or in the pressure flow, and organic CO_2 only exists where there is air to oxidise the organic substances. Thus the development of large cave systems is not easily explained by the ordinary corrosion formula, because the CO_2 is missing.

The mechanism of the enlargement of the original fissures and fractures within limestones has therefore been discussed recently to account for the presence within the limestones of large cavities, such as, e.g., one of the longest caves in the world, Hölloch, in Muotatal, Switzerland, which is over 70 km long. It has been suggested that the extra solubility needed to produce local solution of the rock could be produced either by bacterially assisted oxidation of organic matter in the groundwater or by sulphide minerals in the bedrock [221]. Pyrite is a frequent constituent of limestone shales (as in north-west Yorkshire), and such impurities might well start the solution

needed along the fracture lines (see p. 39).

However, in the last few years other mechanisms of underground solution have been suggested. One of these is that put forward by Bögli. This is of corrosion by *mélange des eaux* (*Mischungskorrosion* or *mixture corrosion*) [90]. Mixture corrosion is a process by which the mixing of two streams of water differing in the quantities of limestone that they are potentially able to dissolve results in an increase in the total amount of limestone that can be dissolved. Water in narrow and capillary fissures, and water well below the surface as it dissolves limestone, loses its corrosive power and may only regain this power if it meets a further air surface or if organic matter is introduced into the water. Mixture corrosion can provide a partial answer to this problem. In Fig. 59, if two saturated solutions, represented by the points W_1 and W_2 in the figure, mix, the resultant solution is represented by the point D, the position of the point D on the line depending on the relative volumes of the two solutions W_1 and W_2. The figure shows that the resulting solution will be capable of dissolving a further quantity of limestone (per unit volume) represented by the length of the line CD. Thus Bögli gives an example of a stream which is saturated at 273 ppm (of $Ca(HCO_3)_2$) dividing, one half going into a flooded passage and remaining unaltered, and the other half overflowing along a passage where it releases CO_2 and deposits calcium carbonate until the concentration is 125 ppm. Upon rejoining the other half of the stream, the resulting mixed water will be capable of dissolving an additional 13·5 ppm, Fig. 59. Bögli also shows how corrosion and deposition will occur in waters passing through limestones with variable soil temperatures due to seasonal variations [90]. He has also commented that (1) the higher the concentration of one of

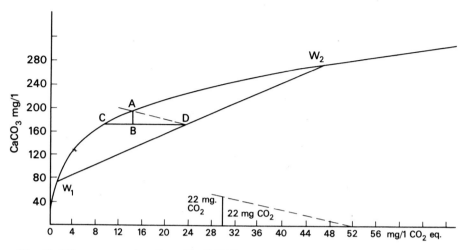

Fig. 59 Mixture corrosion (from Bögli [90])

the components due to the stability of the others, the greater is the additionally dissolved amount of $CaCO_3$; and (2) even the highest calcium carbonate concentrations display an additional corrosive activity when mixed. Hence the importance of mixture corrosion cannot be overestimated and in addition corrosion forms due both to pressure flow and to gravity flow (to be discussed below) may be influenced by it.

A further explanation of the solution of limestone at depth has been suggested by P. Renault [222]. His ideas are based on the temperature fluctuations of temperate latitudes, and only apply there. They are based on the fact that, in winter, the surface of a limestone area is cold, but that in the earth below the surface the limestone is relatively warmer. Renault suggests that as rain water strikes the cold surface it will dissolve the limestone and become saturated; later, as this saturated water penetrates downwards into the warmer zone, loss of CO_2 takes place and there is redeposition of $CaCO_3$. As the water sinks further downwards, it will therefore become aggressive and begin to dissolve more limestone; thus caves will form at depth. Renault claims that in areas

where there is no variation in the seasonal temperature of the surface, as in equatorial regions, this mechanism of deep solution and warming-up of the soil water will not occur and there will be no formation of deep caverns. It seems to be a fact that in tropical areas caves of great depth are more rare. Bögli's explanation by mixture corrosion is also to a certain extent dependent upon temperature variations within temperate climatic conditions, since in tropical and periglacial areas, for instance, the mixing of waters of widely varying temperatures is less likely to occur. Renault has postulated the existence of geochemical zones within the upper part of a Karst mass if in a temperate zone [510].

The first stages in the initiation of cave passages are of great importance, as the eventual pattern of groundwater flow through the cavern and the pattern of its development are determined to a great extent by the beginnings of solution.* The moment that cave development begins,

*See T. Atkinson, *Proc. Conference British Speleological Association* (1969).

groundwaters have a widespread mesh of minutely open, randomly distributed solutional courses to choose from, and this mesh constitutes the first phase of the cave's history.

Joints with greater hydraulic gradient along them and larger initial diameter will be enlarged more than those with lesser hydraulic gradients and smaller widths. Only a few of the numerous original limestone fractures will become enlarged into cavern passages. If available discharge is sufficient, a transition from laminar to turbulent flow in the larger of the primitive passages may occur. Mixture corrosion can take place in turbulent flow and the rate of solution is several times that occurring with laminar flow, and passages where turbulent flow can begin will be enlarged most. White and Longyear have suggested that, when the diameter of the order of 5·0 mm occurs in a groundwater circuit, turbulent flow can begin and the rate of solution is greatly increased; 5·0 mm may therefore be taken as the threshold for cave development [223]. Initial flow in limestones has been discussed by Thrailkill [224]. Ford considers that anastomosing channels form the early development of caves in rocks where the dip is gentle; in steeply dipping rocks simple, linear tubes oriented down the dip-'dip tubes'-occur. Both anastomoses and diptubes are phreatic [511].

2. THE MAIN FACTORS IN CAVE FORMATION

The most interesting aspect of caves to the geomorphologist is probably the record which they contain of types of water flow and of their conditions of formation. No two caves are alike in the way that no two surface rivers are alike; this does not mean that useful generalisation and statistical information cannot be made about caves. An experienced observer in a cave can deduce an enormous amount of information about the conditions in which the cave passage was formed. Each form in a cave passage, either erosional, corrosional or depositional, reflects an episode in its formation. Such episodes have also affected landforms on the surface, but because of weathering and denudation all traces may have been removed from the surface. Thus the great value of cave study from the morphological point of view is the preservation of phases in the denudational history of the area of which there is no trace at the surface. Glennie has said, 'A cave is a three-dimensional palimpsest inscribed with the writings of many different episodes in its history. Each episode has its characteristic style and language' [225].

The factors which influence the form of a cave passage are as follows:

The form of the primary capillary.
The petrological and chemical character of the limestones.
The structure of the limestones, such as the dip, joints and faults, etc.
The type and amount of water flow through the passages, i.e. whether the flow is forced or free (phreatic or vadose).
The regional physiography of the area.
The influence of preceding developments in the caves, i.e. the history of the cave.
The climate and past climatic variations.
The influence of cave deposits.

The most important, and certainly the most studied, of these factors are the character and structure of the limestones, the type of water flow, the physiography of the area, and the climate; these will be considered in detail. Little work has so far been done on the other aspects affecting cave formation except for Ford's work on the Mendip caves.

(A) THE CHARACTER AND STRUCTURE OF THE LIMESTONES

Except for reef limestones, limestone is normally bedded and jointed so that the lines of bedding and jointing form the primary channels along which water enters the rock. Caves frequently originate at the contact of relatively impure bands with purer bands of limestone. In north-west Yorkshire, shale bands within the Carboniferous Limestone are particularly important in the initiation of caves. The shale bands tend to retain water and may also contain some iron pyrite (which oxidises to sulphuric acid); hence limestone in contact with the shale bands tends to be dissolved more rapidly [76]. Furthermore the shale is more easily removed by washing and erosion by percolating water than more massive limestones; frequently, as in Yorkshire, shale bands occur in conjunction with particularly massive sparry limestones which form the roof of the incipient cave. A typical bedding-plane cave in Yorkshire is shown in Fig. 60 and there are many examples on the slopes

of Ingleborough. The influence of less pure rock bands was also noticed by Ford in the Mendips, as for example in the G.B. Cave, where 'The karst ground water . . . tends to penetrate bedding, in particular bedding planes that are 2–8 ft apart vertically so that the rock is quite massive in its geomorphic function; shale or cherty planes are generally favoured for penetration' [209, 226]. In St Cuthbert's Cave, swirlhole (or pothole) development is also influenced by the presence of shale bands [209, 226].*

In the caves of County Clare in western Ireland, where shale bands are rare or non-existent, the bedding planes themselves are the main points of entry for the water; chert bands also occur in Clare, but they seem to be unimportant in cave initiation. Differential solution occurs along bedding planes producing wide thin shelves, often with razor-sharp edges [227]. The bedding-plane passages have a flattened oval section, and may be as much as 30 m wide; they are usually only about a metre in height, but may be as low as about 50 cm. The roofs of the caves are often formed by the same bed over long distances and, as the direction of the cave is frequently the same as that of the dip, the roof slope is the same as the dip slope. In Clare such caves are developed very close to the surface; in the Doolin Cave, for instance, the roof is only 7 m below the surface at about 3,700 m from the entrance [227] (Photo 30).

As has been shown in Chapter 2, lime-

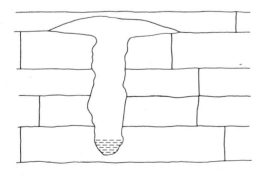

Fig. 60 Cross-section typical of Yorkshire cave stream passage (from Warwick [27])

*Thus Ford has said more recently: 'The spacing of significantly penetrated bedding-planes generally ranges from 4 to 30 ft (about 1 to 10 m). . . . Such planes almost invariably show some peculiar feature that probably accounts for their preferential selection'; and he goes on to say that the presence of a very thin shale bed is very common (*Trans. C.R.G.*, (1968), **10**(1), 11).

30 Cave with bedding plane roof, Mill Bridge Cave, Rocky Mountains, Canada (*Photo by D. C. Ford*)

stones themselves are extremely variable, both in their porosity and crystallinity, and, as we have suggested, in their susceptibility to solution. In Ogof Ffynnon Ddu in South Wales, Glennie has shown how the cave has developed essentially within one bed [225]. The degree of fissuration of the limestone and its primary permeability are also important. These characteristics influence the hydraulic conductivity in a limestone mass. In the Carlsbad Caverns in New Mexico, the caverns have a distinctly different form when they are in the ordinary bedded limestones, as compared with those parts in the reef limestones; in the reef limestones, which have a higher primary permeability, the cave walls have many more cavities and the cave itself is wider [228]. A similar contrast between caves in reef and non-reef limestones can be seen in the Devonian limestones of the Fitzroy area of north-west Australia. In the Manifold valley in Derbyshire, most of the caves are formed in the reef limestones [205]. These are but a few examples of differential cave development in limestones of different porosity and texture. Much more work is needed on this aspect of cave formation as is exemplified by the work of Rauch and White [491].

The shape of a cave passage is determined partly by the inclination of the bedding, and by the frequency and dominance of joints. In flat-lying limestones, as in County Clare, the bedding planes are often the more important and the caves are low and wide. In more steeply inclined limestones bedding-plane control may also be dominant, as in Fleming Cave in Pennsylvania (described by White) [41], and in Slovenia, as shown by Gams [229]. In Victoria, the Buchan Caves have been formed in limestones dipping as much as 40°, and here the bedding planes form the roofs, Fig. 61 [183].

It has been shown that some limestones are cut up by frequent joints or diaclases (p. 21). Caves in compact sparry and less well-jointed limestones tend to have smoother and more regular walls and are less subject to breakdown by collapse; in north-west Yorkshire and in County Clare,

31 Cave breakdown, Mill Bridge Cave, Rocky Mountains, Canada (*Photo by D. C. Ford*)

owing to the occurrence of highly sparry limestones, big cave collapses are fairly rare. Caves formed in biomicrites and in micrites tend to break down more easily because the limestone has frequent jointing, Photo 31. Examples can be seen in the caves of the Nullarbor Plain (Australia) and in caves in the Chartreuse massif in France. In the Guiers Vif cave, for instance, the highly jointed rock walls are subject to pressure release and the passages are littered with fallen blocks; the cave roofs are broadly arched, also partly the result of the spalling away of loose blocks of the rock.

Caves formed along joint planes tend to be high, narrow, winding, sometimes just vertical slits. Joint-plane caves are quite common in north-west Yorkshire, Fig. 60. ? They also occur in County Clare; ~~here~~ Tratman has noted that many of the joints are filled with calcite and he believes that this filling has been the starting-point for solution, due to the crystalline structure of the calcite which has facilitated the entry of the water [227]. Joint-plane caves may often develop into corridor-type caves, particularly if they later become occupied by a flowing stream. The shape of joint

passages depends partly upon the nature of the beds through which they cut but also upon the water flow, both in type and in volume. The influence of jointing upon the form of some Appalachian caves is discussed by White [41]. Glennie shows how in Ogof Fynnon Ddu in South Wales 'Joints are often . . . found parallel to the passage in the walls, and this is an important factor in the enlargement. . . . Blocks, forming the whole depth of a particular bed, fall outwards from the joint into the passage, thus widening it' [225, 230]. A further good example of a cave developed

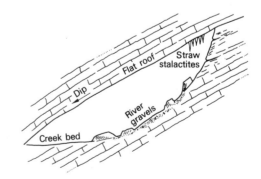

Fig. 61 Buchan type cave, showing the influence of dipping strata

along a joint network is Moking Hurth formed in a thin limestone in Teesdale [231]. However, as Glennie points out in his study of Ogof Ffynnon Ddu, joints are not always opened out and the direction of passages may be determined by other factors [225, 230].

Joint-controlled passages are usually of two main types, Photo 32. First, the purely solutional widening of joints, in which the mouldings and re-entrants reflect differential solubility of the limestone beds. This type is on the whole rare, though examples are reported by Bretz [219], and one is also given by Glennie in 1952, that of Ogof Clogwyn. Secondly and more frequently, joint-controlled passages are triangular, with the base wide and the passage narrowing upwards. This is due to solution working laterally along the bedding plane at the base of the joint: 'it is not unusual for

32 Joint-determined passage, Mill Bridge Cave, Rocky Mountains, Canada (*Photo by D. C. Ford*)

a vertical shaft to be narrow, and about the same width for some distance from the top, and then to widen out before the bottom is reached' [232]. The enlargement of joints into cave passages in the Callaun series of County Clare is discussed by Tratman, Fig. 62 [227].

Faults are even more important in cave formation, and have been much discussed in the literature from the works of Martel onwards [13]. In north-west Yorkshire, many of the vertical sections or 'pitches' in the caves occur along minor faults with but little modification, as for example in Mere Gill pothole on the north-west side of Ingleborough and in Bull pothole in Kingsdale; in fact Simpson was of the opinion that the vertical pitches in the Yorkshire

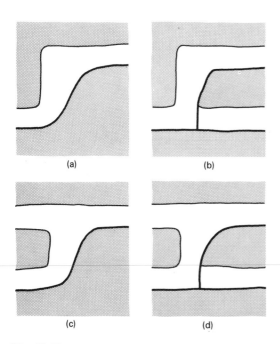

(a)

(b)

(c)

(d)

Fig. 62 Forms of vertical features in the Callaun Caves, Co. Clare (from Tratman [227])

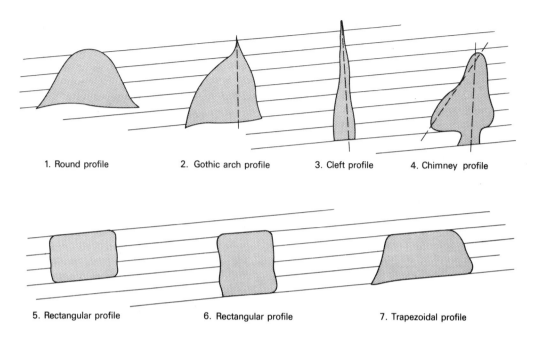

1. Round profile   2. Gothic arch profile   3. Cleft profile   4. Chimney profile

5. Rectangular profile   6. Rectangular profile   7. Trapezoidal profile

Fig. 63(a) The Dachstein Mammuth Cave – typical cross-sections

caves had resulted from jointing and faulting in the limestones accompanied by little, if any, solutional or corrosional action of water [50]. In G.B. Cave in the Mendips it has been said that 'the joints and faults are much more important' than the bedding planes in the development of the cave [233]. There are also many examples in the French Causses of caves owing their origin to fault lines, one of which is the Igue de Gavel in the department of Lot [117].

Caves are also developed along thrust faults and in the crests of anticlines, as at Buchan in Victoria, Fig. 57 [183]. In highly folded and faulted limestones, as in the Alps, the influence of tectonics on cave development is even more clearly seen. Passages in caves like the Gouffre Grotte Berger in the Vercors massif in the pre-Alps of France, and in the Mammuth Hole and Eisriesenwelt caves in the Dachstein massif, are all controlled in their development by faults, thrusts and slip-planes.

More recently Arnberger suggested that the actual origin of the Dachstein caves may in some circumstances be tectonic. He attempted to show how passages may well have been formed as a result of the sliding and slipping of the beds; the roof and floor of the cave are usually bedding planes, while the sides are usually joint or fault planes, and the cross-section is rectangular or trapezoidal (Fig. 63). Arnberger was of the opinion that these caves originated during the periods either of formation or of reactivation of the Dachstein nappe; during these periods the limestone beds were subjected to local tensions in directions generally coincident with the dip. Such bedding planes became surfaces along which slipping movement took place and cave spaces then appeared between the moved blocks. Evidence of the movement can be seen in slickensides and in the friction breccia, particularly along the vertical planes [234]. Arnberger's theory, though

A   TYPICAL SECTIONS

1. Differential movement of "bed packets"

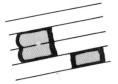

2. The resultant caverns

B   BLOCK DIAGRAMS

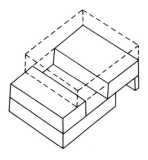

1. Simple straight caverns

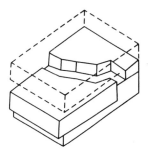

2. Sinuous development

Fig. 63(b) The suggested tectonic development of the Dachstein caverns (from Arnberger, modified by Groom & Coleman [234])

attractive is less convincing when the Mammuth Höhle passages are examined. The passages are more likely to be of phreatic origin. He further mentions the influence of the limestone spalling under pressure and maintains that rounded profiles generally occur in passages overlain by great thicknesses of rock, and in these roof spalling is a common feature. He gives as an example a part of the Schmetterlingsgang in the Mammuth Cave (Dachstein), where masses of fallen roof fragments have been detached and have left a rounded profile. Such spalling has been caused, in his opinion, by the effect of strong mountain pressure from above. This is the reverse of the idea of the release of surface pressure which has been suggested above in connec-

tion with the Guiers Vif and caves in the Classical Karst, where great volumes of water assist in the release of the surface pressure on the rock. Gams is also of the opinion that the tearing and dislocation of strata during folding is important in cave origin [229].

Greatly contorted limestones are those in which large collapse structures are normally found, particularly where, as in the Classical Karst area, large volumes of water in addition pass through the limestones. The big chambers associated with the Škocjan and Postojna caves are examples, and are characterised by extensive fallen blocks and debris.

In relatively thin limestone series the caves tend to occur at or towards the base of the outcrop of the limestones because water tends to concentrate along the contact of the limestone with the underlying impermeable bed. This is true to a certain extent of the caves in north-west Yorkshire, and is excellently illustrated by the White Scar caves, near Ingleton; however, this is not the only control in their development [235]. Structures in limestones affecting cave development are discussed in a Symposium on the Origin and Development of Caves, held by the Cave Research Group 1971 [512].

(B) THE TYPE AND AMOUNT OF WATER FLOW

The factors under this heading include some of the most important in the formation of caves, and were particularly the subject of much controversy at the end of the nineteenth and the beginning of this century. It was originally believed that caves were formed by the solutional and erosional action of underground streams behaving in a similar way to their action at the surface, i.e. free-flowing and being under no hydrostatic pressure [1]. Martel also favoured this view [13]. On this hypothesis the caves were largely the product of the present streams flowing through them. Freely flowing streams are known as *vadose* streams (eau libre). However, there are many features of caves and cave patterns to which this does not apply and which can only be explained if the passages at some stage have been completely filled with water under hydrostatic pressure. Flow under hydrostatic pressure is *phreatic* flow (or eau forcée). In general, vadose flow occurs above a water-table system, and phreatic flow below the water-table. The establishment and recognition of these two different types of water flow can be made

without reference to any detailed discussion of karst hydrology, or to the difficult question of the existence of a water-table in karst areas, both topics which will be discussed later. Between these two main types, the flow is of an intermediate character, when the water is sometimes free-flowing and at other times under pressure. This is known as paraphreatic, or epiphreatic, flow [236, 229].

The two main workers who put forward ideas on the different types of water flow as they affected caves were O. Lehmann in 1933 [214], and W. M. Davis in 1930 [215]. Lehmann's work is based on the European knowledge of the Classical and Dinaric karst, the Alps and the Causses of France; it was inductive and experimental and based on many field observations. Davis's work was a masterpiece of deduction based on observations in the Mammoth Cave area, but mostly worked out from his own developments of the idea of the erosion cycle. Written at the age of eighty, this paper is in many ways the most interesting and significant that he ever wrote; he declared he was now too old for further cave exploration and exhorted young people to look at caves in a much more discriminating light. He gives a detailed account of the types of cave passages to be expected with vadose and phreatic flow. Both Lehmann's and Davis's work was followed by many papers in both Europe and America; in 1944 Chevalier gave a succinct account of the main types of cave passages to be found in the Alps, and their association with the main types of water flow [237]. Patterns of water flow and their bearing on cave formation have been studied by Thrailkill [224].

Phreatic or forced flow. The main feature of a passage formed by phreatic flow or forced flow is a circular or elliptical form offering the least resistance to the infiltrat-

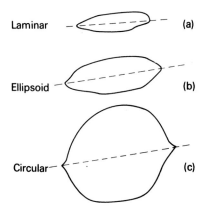

Fig. 64(a) Passages formed by forced flow along lines of stratification

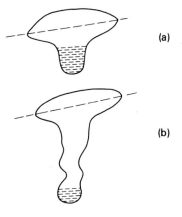

Fig. 64(b) Subsequent development of passages by free flow (from Chevalier [237])

ing waters and guided by pre-existing fissures, either bedding planes, joints or diaclases. Since the flow is under considerable hydrostatic pressure, the passage is similar in form, both at the top and bottom, and may also have an uphill gradient. The sides of the passage are also often convex. Where the rock is homogeneous there is little variation in passage width, though it may be narrower where the water moves quickly and wider where the water flows more slowly (Chevalier). Since the water is not flowing under the influence of gravity, the floors of such caves will be uneven and

often have siphons, where the roof comes down to the level of the floor, Fig. 64. In the Fontaine de la Vaucluse, the cave passage rises at least 50 m in a short horizontal distance. Ford gives a description of such a phreatic passage in St Cuthbert's Cave in the Mendips: 'the form of these passages is remarkable, being nearly a perfectly rounded tube, sometimes centred on the guiding fracture, sometimes developed directly above it. . . . Different passages vary from 0·5 to 15 ft in diameter (15 cm to 5 m). The variation is predictable and regular according to that of width–depth variation in surface channels . . . indicating adjustment to positive or negative changes in volume of flow.' The term *bore passage* is

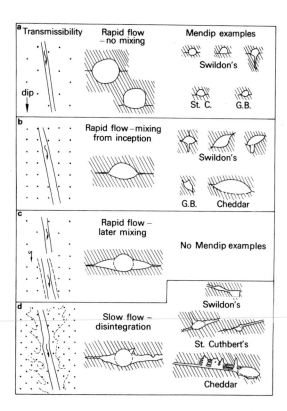

Fig. 65 Phreatic bore passages in various Mendip caves (from Ford [233])

33(a) Phreatic tube, north-east end of Perseverance Passage, Mill Bridge Cave (*Photo by D. C. Ford*)

given by Ford to these features [233]; he also calculates the total discharge for such a passage of 4 ft (1·3 m) diameter in St Cuthbert's as being 600–1,000 ft per day (0·007–0·012 ft per second), Fig 65. In addition to the tubes are joint chimneys up which the water is lifted; the tubes and chimneys constitute a 'phreatic loop', Photo 33(a).

It has been suggested that the ellipse is the stable form where turbulent flow occurs in a bedding plane in the phreatic zone [233]. However, Bögli argues that the ellipse is the product of mixture corrosion, caused by the mixing of water moving through the bedding planes (in minute channels) and of the water moving through the major conduits. The mixture corrosion thus effects a distortion of the form of the major conduits which would be circular if they were entirely produced by water fed in at the upstream ends [233]. It appears that a circular type of passage tends to form first, before there is much groundwater mixing; as the abundance of conduits increases, and hence more groundwater mixing, the elliptical form is created. Bögli describes elliptical passages existing over hundreds of metres; e.g. the elliptical passages of the Hölloch Cave are several kilometres long [238].

It is possible to discriminate between slow and deep phreatic flow, and a shallower, and probably much faster, phreatic flow. In Ogof Ffynnon Ddu discussed by Glennie, the development of the cave within a very limited set of beds indicates formation by slow phreatic flow [225, 230, 232, 239]; in flat-lying limestones, passages of this type may be very extensive. However, shallow phreatic flow seems to be particularly important in cave formation [224].*

Other cave features characteristic of phreatic flow have been described in detail, particularly by Bretz [216].

(1) The first of these is *spongework* (or honeycombing). Many cave walls and ceilings have a complicated pattern of minor cavities and separating partitions, a few cm to 0·5 m in depth. This phenomenon is explicable as the result of differential solubility of the limestones when submerged in the groundwater. The cavities indicate no differential current attack, and the ceilings have suffered as much solution as the walls.

(2) *Pockets*. These are larger than spongework and are commonly separated by stretches of unaffected wall. They are usually more deep than wide.

(3) *Bedding-* and *joint-plane anastomoses.* Anastomoses are systems of minor, curvilinear tube-like solution cavities lying in one

*This point is well shown in Tunnel Cave, S. Wales (C. L. Railton (1958) *The Survey of Tunnel Cave, S. Wales*, C.R.G. Publication No. 7).

33(b) Phreatic solution features, Mill Bridge Cave (*Photo by D. C. Ford*)

plane and making an intricate pattern with repeated intersections and crooked courses. They occur on joint and bedding planes. A good example in Tunnel Cave in South Wales is given by Glennie [225, 230, 232, 239].

(4) Joint-determined *wall and ceiling cavities*. The walls and ceilings of many cave chambers have deep and narrow vertical slots, dissolved out along a trace of a joint. Some of these cavities extend several feet up into the roof, and are due to

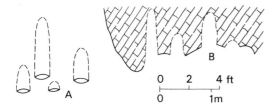

Fig. 66(a) Typical roof cavities, showing (A) shape and (B) section giving position in cave roof

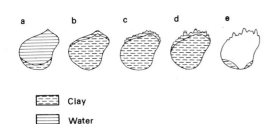

Clay

Water

Fig. 66(b) Suggested formation of some cave roof features according to Bretz

(a) Formation of cave passage beneath water-table
(b) Uplift of cave to near water-table and deposition of clay almost to roof
(c) Water moving slowly between roof and surface of clay dissolves network of small channels into roof
(d) Water circulation becomes better defined
(e) Further uplift of passage above water-table results in streams cutting down and removing much of the clay

(after Bretz [219])

differential solution along the joint. Many of these cavities have been formed by water penetrating upwards from the cave passage itself and not by descending waters; however, it is possible that sometimes cavities like these can be caused by mixture corrosion. (Fig. 66 and Photo 33(b).)

(5) The *network or maze patterns* of some caves are believed to be due to solution along controlling joints in completely saturated rock; such network patterns are seen in the Ogof Ffynnon Ddu in South Wales (Glennie, loc. cit.) and in the Mark Twain Cave described by Bretz from Missouri [219]. Much of St Cuthbert's swallet in the Mendips also shows a phreatic network, Fig. 67.

(6) *Rock pendants* which are formed of limestone, but resemble stalactites. They are probably the result of differential solution under groundwater and occur in the roofs of many caves.

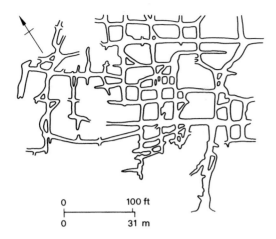

Fig. 67 Network cave pattern (from Moore & Nicholas [295])

Shallow phreatic caves are formed in a less deep zone, and tend to be formed not so far below the upper level of saturated conduits in the limestone. Inclined or vertical forced water passages will give rise to vertical or inclined tubes such as that described by Chevalier in the Trou de Glaz [240].

Associated with the regular flow in phreatic passages, there are frequently scallops (or cockles) on the walls and ceilings, particularly in the 'bore' passages. Scallops have recently been discussed at length by Curl, in an excellent paper [241]. They may be described as 'interrupted concavities', usually covering a surface in an irregular pattern which, while appearing largely random, exhibits a degree of uniformity in size, shape and spacing, Fig. 68. The ridges or crests between the concavities vary from sharp to smooth. A section taken through the crests transverse to the flow direction always shows that the downstream slope is steeper than the upstream. Scallops are therefore an indication of the former flow direction in caves which now no longer possess streams. There also occur *flutes* (as

defined by Curl), forms where the crests are nearly parallel to one another for distances greater than the distance between their crests; these are of more rare occurrence. Both scallops and flutes are similar to the wave phenomena which occur in sand ripples and water waves and can be seen frequently on melting ice and snow. They vary in size (i.e. from crest to crest), from a few millimetres to a metre; 5–10 cm is the most usual size. In Mammoth Cave, Kentucky they are commonly two metres long.

Both scallops and flutes, though they are solutional forms, are the result of the character of the water flow; the rock is of secondary importance. The distance between their crests (their period) is inversely proportional to the flow velocity. They are the consequence of the interaction of fluid flow and rate of solution of a soluble surface. The removal of the material at the surface gives rise to the concavity; this in turn establishes a new boundary for the flow, which in turn modifies the flow pattern and the rate of removal of the material. Lange [242], quoted by Curl, showed that uniform solution rate over a surface produces with time a rounding of all

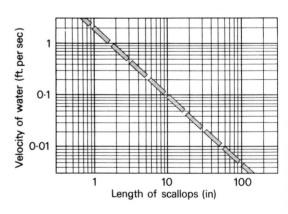

Fig. 68 Scallop formation (from Curl [241])

internal (concave) corners and a sharpening of all external convex corners; all convex surfaces will eventually form cusps. Flutes are more useful than scallops as indicators of past flow conditions in a cave, but it is possible that with 'sufficient study of scallop patterns their statistical properties may be interpreted in terms of the responsible flow conditions' [241]. Scallops can also be formed under free-flow conditions, but when they occur all over the walls and on the roofs of caves then it is assumed that they were formed when the cave was full of water or under the conditions of forced flow. There have been many passing references to scallops on cave walls, but Curl's paper is the first attempt to study them in a statistical and systematic manner. Scallops and flutes do not seem to occur if there is much sand, grit or mud in the cave waters, abrasion being destructive of solutional features.

(Photo 34.) Scallop patterns have been simulated in the laboratory by Goodchild and Ford [513].

Vadose or free flow. The moment the level of the water in the cave is lowered so that air enters into the passage and the flow is free and no longer confined, the passage shape begins to change. The original circular or elliptical passage is deepened by normal stream erosion as well as by corrosion, and the shape becomes much more rectangular. The flow is now subject to the effects of gravity, and the stream will therefore cut into the passages which originated earlier in the phreatic zone, often forming a canyon or gorge. Normal features which accompany surface streams will appear, such as meanders, cut-offs and stream potholes. The transitions from the phreatic into vadose passages in caves of the Slovenian karst are illustrated in Fig. 69, taken from Gams [229]. Vadose passages are frequently triangular with the broad base of the triangle at the bottom, due to the lateral cutting and solution of the cave stream. In addition, waterfalls from one level to another will appear, and cave passages or galleries at different levels will be formed. Vadose streams behave very much like those flowing on the surface, and the pattern of passages produced by vadose flow resembles in many ways that of a surface river system; it is branching and

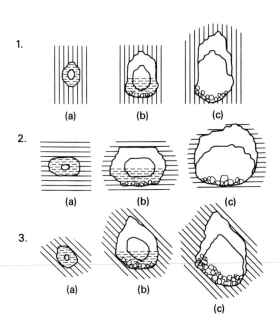

Fig. 69 Development of cave passages in Slovenia, according to the dip of the limestones (after Gams [229])

dendritic – a quite different pattern from the cave network created by phreatic flow, Fig. 70 and Photo 35.

Certain solutional features are also common to vadose caves. These include, first, horizontal grooves or niches caused by stream flow in low-roofed horizontal slots; these are common in the Missouri caves and are a feature of many of the passages in Mammoth Cave, Kentucky, and can be seen in the Bezez el Mugharet in the

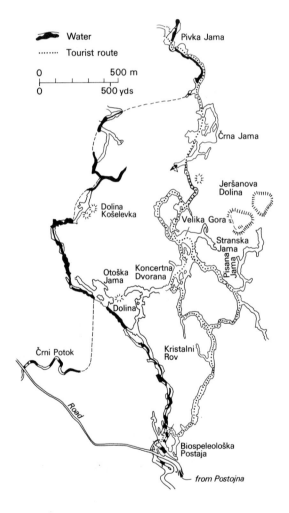

Fig. 70 The Postojna Cave, Jugoslavia (after Gams [82])

Lebanon. Secondly, vertical mouldings or groovings on steeply inclined or vertical sections of the caves; the features are not joint-controlled and are caused by descending sheets or falls of water. Such grooved surfaces are characteristic of the steep 'pitches' in the Yorkshire caves as in Rowting Pot (Kingsdale) and also of the Mammoth Cave area of Kentucky [244]. In the U.S.A. vertically grooved cavities are sometimes known as dome pits, but not all vertical cavities in vadose caves originate in the same way. Bretz also maintains that roof pendants and channels cut into cave ceilings are indicative of vadose solution.

Once some kind of flow has been established along a bedding plane, a stream channel or corridor is formed and this is often along the line of a joint. The shape of the channel, with its alternating narrow and broad sectors, depends upon many factors. Corridor caves of this type are particularly well developed in the caves of the Burren in County Clare, and many of the caves in north-west Yorkshire are typically vadose (Fig. 60). They show variations in width indicating a greater or less solution at the different stages of their formation. The factors which may give rise to such variations in solution are (a) differential solubility of the limestone beds, (b) a relatively long or short period of standstill of the stream at one particular level, (c) a decrease or increase in volume of the stream entering the cave and (d) a change in the acidity of the water entering the cave, brought about for instance by an increase or decrease in vegetation cover.

Many caves show excellent examples of vadose features. In Poulnagollum in County Clare there are two series of meanders superimposed one upon the other [245]; the upper gorge in G.B. Cave in the Mendips is a good example of a vadose passage [233]; D. St Pierre has discussed and compared

35 Features formed by vadose flow: scallops and flutes also shown (*Photo by D. C. Ford*)

phreatic and vadose passages in caves in Graatadalen in northern Norway [246]; in the United States, some of the biggest caves in Indiana and Kentucky, such as Wyandotte and Mammoth Caves, possess many miles of corridor-shaped vadose passages; recently Bleahu has discussed the types of confluences of underground streams and indicates how much can be derived from a close study of a vadose cave system [247].

Our knowledge of vadose passages is much greater than our knowledge of phreatic passages, for the main reason that vadose caves can be seen in process of formation, whereas phreatic passages cannot be seen (except very occasionally by cave divers) until the water conditions under which they were formed have changed.

It remains to discuss the forms caused by mixture corrosion and their modification of those produced by either phreatic or vadose flow. One of the difficult things to explain about some large cave passages is that they begin without any apparent entrances or exits, the water which formed them only being supplied by joints. If these joints are filled by water from varying sources, i.e. by mixing water, then it is possible that, as a result of mixture corrosion, a large cavity could be formed, sometimes without any passable entrance. Examples of this are to be found in Hölloch [238]. In addition 'sack' or bag-like passages running out from the main passage and enlarging suddenly into a circular apse have been explained by Bögli as due to mixture corrosion. They are formed by the mixture of water from the main cave with water from the side passages. Elongated or bell-shaped corrosion hollows are also formed when the joint opens out into a horizontal ceiling, and when a joint crosses a passage already filled with water. Such corrosion hollows are found in many horizontal cave roofs and are aligned along joints; they have a rounded cross-section and penetrate deeply into the roof, often for some metres [238].

Many caves show indications of phreatic, paraphreatic and vadose flow and of mixture corrosion; they have thus had alternations between phases of being wholly water-filled and phases of drained, gravitational flow. Deep phreatic caves develop predominently in steeply dipping rocks; water-table caves are common in flat-lying rocks. The greater the hydraulic conductivity, the more likely is the water-table type of cave to develop [511].

(C) THE PHYSIOGRAPHIC FACTORS AFFECTING CAVE FORMATION

In addition to the conditions of water flow and the type and structure of the limestones, there are other important factors which influence the development of caves. Perhaps the most important of these is the regional geographical and physiographical setting.

It is frequently noted that complex ramifying cave systems are more characteristic of relatively thin limestone sequences and of shallow karsts than of the deep karsts characteristic of the Dinaric area. In this respect it is useful to compare the great development of caves in Yorkshire with the deep karsts of parts of the Cockpit Country in Jamaica. The number of horizontal caves per square mile of the limestone in northwest Yorkshire compared with those in the interior of the Cockpit Country is at least about five to one.

The thickness of the limestone in the Yorkshire area is only 600 ft but in Jamaica it is over 2,000 ft. A similar contrast may be made in Derbyshire, where the number of caves around the edge of the limestone in contact with the Namurian shales is infinitely greater than the number in the more truly karstified central area of the limestone, Fig. 53(a). These points indicate that the concentration of aggressive water and therefore of accelerated corrosion is an important factor in cave development. Many of the world's biggest caves are developed at the contact of impermeable rocks with karst limestones; for instance, the Postojna Cave in Slovenia is at the contact of the Eocene flysch with the Cretaceous limestones; the Cave River Cave in Jamaica at the contact of the rocks of the central Inlier with Eocene White limestones; the Padirac Cave in Quercy at the contact of the Jurassic limestones with the Liassic clays; and the Rio Frio Cave in British Honduras at the junction of Cretaceous limestones with underlying granites.

It is difficult to know to what extent solution takes place in limestones before the non-karstic cover rocks are removed. In Indiana substantial cavern development has taken place in limestones still covered by the Dipping Springs sandstone. Here Powell describes the Ray Cave in the Solsberry Quadrangle which is developed in the Beech Creek limestone where it is overlain by sandstone [248]. The only area of considerable development of caves in Britain under an impermeable cover is in South Wales, where solutional activity in the Carboniferous Limestones has taken place beneath the cover of Millstone Grit [128]. In his explanation of Ray Cave, Powell shows how its plan is related to the exposure of the Beech Creek limestone and its contact with the overlying sandstones. The nearness of the cavern to the zone of contact suggests a connection between the amount of groundwater flow and the proximity of the outcrop. The cave contains numerous enlarged joints or domes, from 5–7 m high, which extend from the cave passages into the base of the overlying sandstone. These vertical solution features indicate that water had entered the cave from the top of the limestone from the overlying sandstone. Pohl gives a similar explanation for vertical shafts in the limestone caves of central Kentucky [244]. It is significant that such cavern development below a cap rock does not seem to take place when the beds overlying the limestones are 'tight' and impermeable, as the Namurian shales in Derbyshire and Yorkshire.

The relative height and available relief of the land itself is an important factor which affects cavern development. This importance is partly connected with the development and enlargement of the cave system. As more solution and erosion of the cave passages takes place they enlarge and the cave is therefore a continually changing feature and a continuously enlarging space. In a young or developing cave, water is subject to much capillary pressure and its height within the rock fissures will be very variable. As the fissures enlarge and the cave develops, the water is less subject to capillary action and is under less pressure;

the general 'level' which the water reaches in the cave passages will be rather less variable. Though the question of the existence of a water-table in karst terrains will be discussed later, the age and development of a cave will affect the paths water takes through the passages and, given infinite time, these paths will become flatter in an older cave than they are during the original stages of its formation. Hence cave passages in a more advanced stage will differ from those formed in the initial stages; Howard has given a theoretical scheme in the development of a major cave [221].

There is no necessary correlation between the surface relief and the morphology of the underground cave passages. In general, however, where limestones have recently been stripped of their overlying cover rocks, cave development is relatively new; the longer the limestones are exposed to denudation the bigger can the fissures become and the more evolved the cave development. Except in South Wales this is true of the karst regions of the British Isles. It is particularly well shown in the caves of County Clare. In this area Namurian shale cover has only been removed from the limestones on the slopes of Slieve Elva during the last glaciation; since then a new series of caves has been formed. Thus in some of the caves of this area, particularly Poulnagollum, there are two series of passages, an upper set with distinctly more youthful features and a lower set with older and more evolved features; the younger passages are narrow and relatively straight; the older passages wider, containing meanders and oxbows [211].

So far there have been few attempts to reconstruct the development of caves in this way. The work of Ford on the Mendip caves is important in this respect [209]. Ford attempts to trace the development of three Mendip caves, and shows how a network of phreatic tubes may be broken down and replaced by an expansion in the phreatic cave form – possibly helped by the increasing significance of mixture corrosion – as the caves developed. This expansion gave rise to large cave segments, which were later joined up into active stream passages below the confluence of the vadose stream channels. In this way a master cave develops in which 'low arches, bore passages, and bell-shaped solutional forms are mingled with gravitational trenches and walls undercut by lateral solution at floor level. . . . The thalweg of the master cave is composed of long, gentle sections of pebble and cobble shoals, interspersed with shorter, steeper trenches and sumps' (Fig. 71) [209]. The early master cave at Swildon's Hole shows that it was made up of many loops cutting across the dipping strata and by this means the principal groundwater stream made its way to the outlet spring. Later the highest parts of these loops were preferentially selected and expanded to become the accessible caves. In this way the series of loops of the selected flow path constituted a defined water-gradient or water-table, though the feature was not a plane. Thus Ford concludes, 'within considerable limitations it can be said that the large caves are accordant to a particular water-table'. However, the latter does not precede the caves in the cave zone; each cave or flow path determines its own water-table gradient. In the Mendips there are great variations in the mean water-table gradients considering the very small area involved; thus for Swildon's Hole–Cheddar outlet it is 1:80; for St Cuthbert's–Wookey Hole, 1:40; and for G.B. Cave–Cheddar, 1:19. Furthermore the cave passages need not be developed along the water-table for more than a short part of their course from sink to rising. The

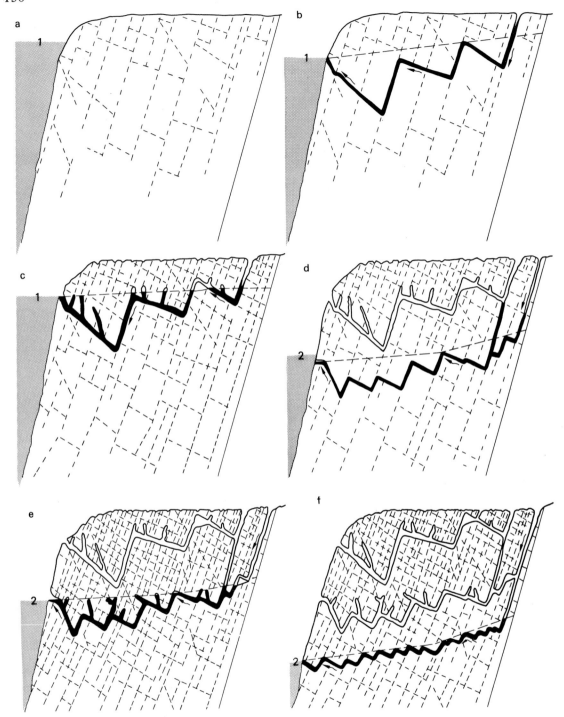

Fig. 71 The development of the Mendip caves (after Ford [209])
Only the principal flow-paths are shown:
1. Phreatic passages of the first water-table
2. Phreatic passages of the second water-table
Note the predominance of sub-water-table loops in the flow-path.

differences in the level of these caves is believed by Ford to be due to the different stages in the development of the Mendip land mass and to the situation of each cave in relation to the local base level, which is the Bristol Channel.

Howard has given a theoretical model of the development of water conduits on a dissected upland, an extremely common relief form. Water enters at the top of the limestone outcrop and issues in springs at the base [221]. He shows that in time a strong hydraulic gradient is established. Beneath most of the upland the hydraulic head will be less than that beneath the isolated entrances of underground drainage and a water-level will become graded to these longer groundwater entrances. The shallowing of the zone of groundwater movement will restrict major solution to a few cavern passages because of the selective effects of the transition to turbulent flow. The idea behind this mode of cavern formation was suggested by Swinnerton in 1932 [249] and developed by Rhoades and Sinacori in 1941 [250]. Glennie (1954) also discusses the progressive development of a cave in a limestone upland, and gives a diagram called progressive cave formation [251].

The first ideas on major drainage conduits in Britain was given by Simpson in an article in 1934 [50]. Simpson was using his own caving experience and that of Foley, who first described a 'master cave', in Lost John's Cave on Leck Fell, on the borders of Yorkshire and Lancashire, a description which still makes exciting reading [252]. Since that time other master conduits have been discovered in north-west Yorkshire, one of the most recent being the master cave in Kingsdale. It was this idea of master conduits which was used by the writer in her study of the caves of the Ingleborough area in 1950, Fig. 48 [235]. Thus it was

shown that there is a tendency for the caves to occur at fairly well-defined levels. It was suggested that the upper levels might represent former major conduits of drainage, at a time when the main valley floors were higher and less incised. Terrace benches representing stages in the down-cutting of the main valleys were tentatively correlated with the master conduits. As the valleys were rejuvenated, so the conduits became drained and became accessible caves. However, more recent work on the caves of north-west Yorkshire confirms the existence of the cave levels, but relates them both to the occurrence of shale bands and also possibly to phases in the glaciation and deglaciation of the valleys during the Quaternary [253]. It is probable also that these cave levels have been partly controlled by recent movements along the South Craven Fault, since this fault determines the level of the cave outlets, Fig. 48 [253]. Waltham has also shown, as a result of much new exploration in north-west Yorkshire, that both phreatic and vadose cave sections exist and that the relatively simple explanation put forward by the writer does not now apply. Many of the caves are said to predate the formation of the valleys, and this view completely alters the interpretation of the cave origin [514].

Connections between valley development and cave formation have been demonstrated in many areas. Studies from areas as far apart as the Demänová Caves in Slovakia [254], the Bungonia Caves in New South Wales [255], the caves in the Ourthe valley in Belgium [256], the Buchan Caves in Victoria [183], and of caves in the Appalachians [257] are sufficient to show that cave development can be closely related to stages in the denudation of the surface valley forms. Davies has also shown how in folded limestones 'cave passages cut right across the bedding planes . . . most caves in

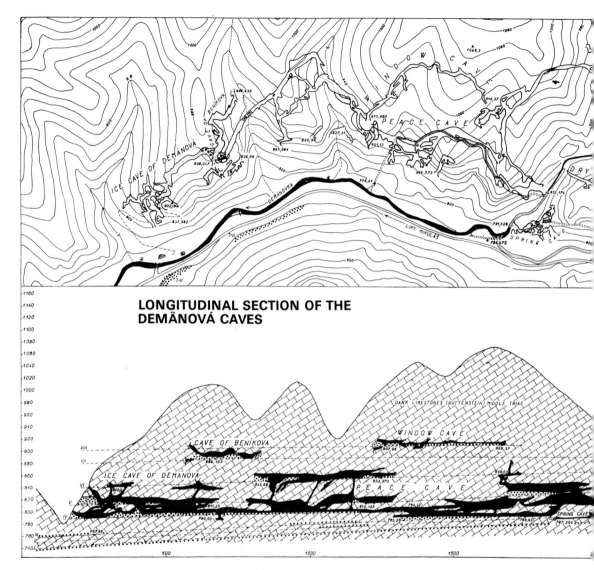

Fig. 72 Demänová caves, near Liptovsky Mikulaš, Czechoslovakia (from Droppa [254])

folded rocks are developed at a single level' [258]. In particular, the evidence from Demänová Caves, near Liptovsky Mikulaš in Czechoslovakia, seems to be conclusive (Fig. 72) [254].

In the western Carpathians, streams have originated upon the crystalline cores of the mountains, cut across the adjoining limestone areas and created there a series of almost horizontal galleries. These galleries are without doubt of fluvial origin as is shown by their oval cross-section and by the river deposits lying on their floors. A process is found to occur whereby the

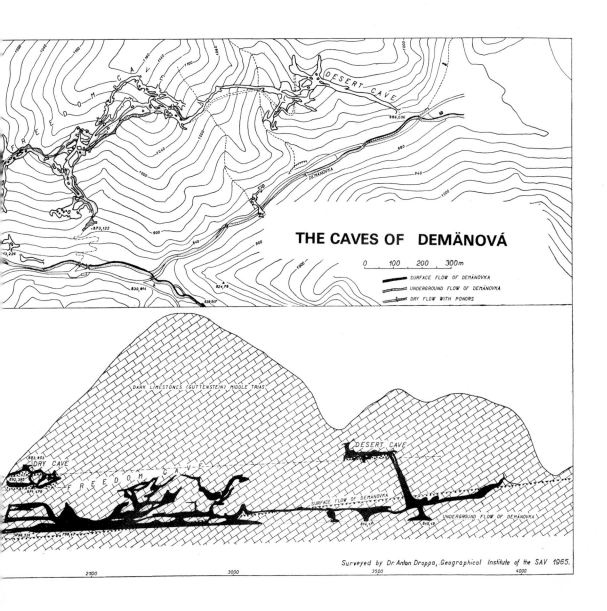

THE CAVES OF DEMÄNOVÁ

0   100   200   300m

━━━━ SURFACE FLOW OF DEMÄNOVKA

┄┄┄┄ UNDERGROUND FLOW OF DEMÄNOVKA

┄┄┄ DRY FLOW WITH PONORS

Surveyed by Dr. Anton Droppa, Geographical Institute of the SAV 1965.

underground rivers become less and less steep as they cut into the limestone, until they become stabilised in cave-levels. These levels are related to the rivers on the surface at certain stages of their development, when the underground river flows through the cave-level for its whole length with a relatively slight gradient and becomes connected with the surface river bed at the same height at the edge of the limestone massif' [254]. 'These levels were formed during the periods of tectonic calm when lateral cutting and erosion prevailed over vertical erosion' [254]. In the Demänová valley, such a sequence of horizontal cave levels is perfectly developed; two rivers have created a series of successive cave galleries, arranged storey-like one below another. The correlation of the cave levels with the development of the river terraces on the surface is suggested for the following reasons: (1) The existence of the cave galleries at levels without any relationship to the dip of the limestone beds. (2) The regularity of the longitudinal profiles of the cave galleries and the similarity to those of the surface drainage. (3) The similarity of the direction of the cave galleries and of the river beds on the surface. (4) The fluvial character of some of the cave deposits, and the fact that these deposits can be correlated from faunal remains and the degree of weathering with those in the river terraces on the surface. For instance, a study of the deposits of terrace III of the river Vah corresponds with the deposits in the gallery forming the third level of the Demänová Caves. Likewise cave-level II can be found to correspond to terrace II which is dated as of Late Riss Age [254].

Not only horizontal caves, but also vertical features, can be shown to be partly dependent upon physical factors. This is particularly so of vertical features formed by vadose streams, since vadose water will tend to form vertical caves when there is considerable available relief. Examples of this can be seen in the potholes of Ingleborough, where the perching of the limestones above the impermeable beds, brought about by rejuvenation along the Craven Fault system, enables percolating water entering at the top of the limestones to circulate freely and rapidly; marked solution features along the joints are thus formed. In the Mammoth Cave region of Kentucky, vertical features (or dome pits) are also common; it has been demonstrated by Pohl [244] and also by Merrill [259] that

the dome pits are either located near the edges of the Dripping Springs Escarpment, or along the edges of ridges within the dissected plateau, or near the margin of the capping of the sandstone at the head of the

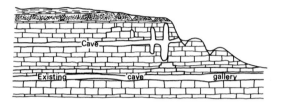

Shaft walls crumble with the approach of the valley head, but tubes still carry off surface drainage from sinkholes formed at the position of shaft collapse. Because of abundance of shafts and tubes draining into the valley, new galleries of large size are not produced.

Fig. 73 Formation of vertical shafts (from Pohl [244])

escarpment slope, Fig. 73. In areas of low available relief, as in central Ireland or Florida, dome pits are absent.

The type of non-karstic terrain adjacent to the limestones is also important. Gams has shown in a study of the Slovenian caves that the largest occur where streams entering the caves come from terrain which yields pebbles and coarse debris, compared with smaller caves whose streams come from areas which only yield clay (from the flysch) [243]. This is because river abrasion is important in addition to karstic solution in the formation of any river cave. In the caves of British Honduras, in the Mai area (Mountain Pine Ridge), water bearing quantities of sand from disintegrated granite nearby has been an important factor in their formation. Furthermore the size of the collecting basin for the drainage entering the cave will also be of significance, since more water and debris are likely to come from the larger basin. On Ingleborough the largest caves are in general associated with the largest intake streams, as, for example, Gaping Gill and Alum Pothole. The Rio Camuy Cave in Puerto Rico drains a large area of non-karstic rocks and this has helped in the enlarging of the cave. This feature has been discussed by Williams, in a paper on karst morphometry [260].

Typical situations for the formation and enlargement of caves are seen in meandering streams in allogenic valleys. On the upstream side of such meanders the current of the river impinges upon the limestones; caves are frequently found in this position in the river banks and bed, particularly if the river flows in the general direction of dip. At low water the river may disappear entirely into the rock and emerge on the downstream side of the meander, a cave being formed under the meander spur, see Fig. 57. Numerous examples of caves of this type can be found; they include the caves in the Manifold at Wetton Hill [205], and many of those in the Buchan Caves area in Victoria [183]. In Indiana, Malott discusses several such examples of the diversion of streams under meander spurs, giving rise to swallow holes which absorb the stream caves within the spurs and springs emerging on the downstream side; in the U.S.A. they are known as *subterranean cut-offs* [261]. In Indian Creek, for example, the subterranean route of the river is about $\frac{1}{4}$ mile long, but the surface meander route is more than 3 miles. If the neck of the meander becomes very small, a natural bridge may be found, as in Virginia [262].

There are thus many connections between cave development and the physiography of the karst area. Once the initial cave network has become established, the physiographic situation is of the utmost importance and will often indicate why one cave has developed and another has remained small.

(D) CLIMATIC FACTORS AND CAVE FORMATION

Climate affects cave formation in two main ways; (a) by variations in rainfall and snowfall, (b) by temperature variations.

First, cave formation is more important in wet regions than in dry ones. In arid or semi-arid areas, cave development is restricted. The existence of large caves in desert regions usually implies the occurrence of former pluvial periods; for instance, in the Hadramut in southern Arabia [263], in the Nullarbor Plain in South Australia and in the Fitzroy area in north-west Australia [264, 284] the main periods of cave development occurred during wetter climatic phases than those which exist today in these regions. Groundwater may create a phreatic network of deep caves in dry regions, but no enlargement of this network will take place unless the surface area is one of reasonable rainfall. Intense showers of rain in semi-arid climates may help to dissolve out cavities in the limestone, but in these regions the evaporation is so strong that rapid deposition of calcium carbonate takes place and the caves become blocked by stalagmite. Thus in general the largest caves occur in regions of heavy rainfall or snowfall. Regions of big caves include the Classical Karst, the limestone areas of the Alps, the Mammoth Cave district of Kentucky, and limestone areas in the Appalachians. Cave development is greater in the wet tropics than in the dry tropics; for instance, it is greater in British Honduras than in the drier country of Yucatan, and greater on the windward northern sides of Jamaica and Puerto Rico than on the drier leeward sides of those islands [94, 134, 136].

In north-west Europe the variations in rain and snowfall during the Pleistocene period are of great importance in discussing the shape and formation of caves. We have already seen that the shapes of the corridor-type caves are likely to be influenced by variations in the discharge of streams reaching the limestones, cave development being greater in wetter climatic phases than in the drier ones. Ford, for instance, has worked in detail on the cave passages in the Mendips, in particular those in St Cuthbert's Cave and in Swildon's Hole. He concludes that certain features, such as stream potholes and narrow trenches, occur systematically in certain passages and are not related to structural features in the limestone beds. He interprets stream pothole formation as having been formed during a period of large stream flow, and the trenches as being formed during periods of reduced stream flow. He recognises two successive phases of pothole and of trench formation, representing in his opinion fluctuations in the volume of the streams flowing in the passages. He claims that such fluctuations can only be ascribed to the variations in the stream flow brought about by the growth and retreat of the Pleistocene ice caps and other climatic fluctuations during the postglacial period [265]. In north-west Europe it is likely that periods of greatest volumes of water would be at the beginning of the Interglacials, and that the periods of least volume would be at the height of the Glacials [266]. Similar conclusions have been reached by Ollier and Tratman in their study of Poulnagollum Caves in County Clare, Ireland [211].

In the Alps, studies of the cave passages suggest that there also variations in their cutting and solution are dependent upon the climatic fluctuations of the Pleistocene, as in the Hölloch Cave. In the Mediterranean also, caves show alternating periods of greater and less erosion; in this area, phases of greater solution took place during the Pluvials, i.e. Glacials, and phases of less solution during the drier Interglacials. A study of a cave in the Lebanon, the Bezez

el Mugharet at Adlun, indicates that this interpretation is a correct one, for in this locality the cave contains remains of a raised beach deposit, which can be related by archaeological means to the Pleistocene sequence [138]; this cave has parts which indicate greater solution and others which show less solution.

Secondly, temperature variations affect cavern development in various ways. Since CO_2 is more soluble in colder than in warmer waters, caves in cooler climates should have longer passages. No statistical work is available on this point, but limestones associated with snowfields are sometimes very cavernous, as in northern Norway near Narvik, and in the limestone massifs of the Alps [87]. However, since caves do not form during prolonged periods of frost action, they are not usually associated with periglacial climates. This is not only due to the reduced effects on solution caused by the frozen ground, but also to the fact that limestones are very susceptible to frost shattering; caves formed in wet climates are destroyed during periglacial phases. One of the few sub-Arctic caves to be studied in detail is the small Lummelunda Grotte on the island of Gotland, Sweden [267].

Seasonal variations in temperature in mid-latitude climates may have distinctive effects upon cave-forming processes, as compared with the more uniform yearly temperatures of the tropical zones. Not only do the surface layers of the earth fluctuate widely in temperature in mid-latitudes, but there are greater opportunities for the mixing of waters of different temperatures and CO_2 content. Though there are many large caves in the tropical humid zones, so far the greatest and deepest that are known are in the mid-latitude areas. This could of course be due to lack of systematic exploration in the tropics.

These observations mean that the temperature fluctuations of the Pleistocene would of themselves have had some effect upon cave formation. During periods of intense cold it is likely that cave formation was arrested, and that many of the rock-shattered entrances and near-surface passages are the result of frost shatter during one or other of the cold phases. In the caves of south Devon near Buckfastleigh, frost shattering occurs particularly near cave entrances, and is believed to have been formed during the last period of the ice (Weichselian) in Britain. Similar frost-formed screes occur in association with caves in northern England, for instance Victoria Cave, near Settle, the result of a period of periglaciation which followed the recession of the last ice. This kind of phenomenon is particularly well known in caves in Czechoslovakia, an area which was affected by all the phases of the Pleistocene climatic changes. In periods of intense periglaciation, passages up to 10–20 m below the present surface show evidence of frost riving.

(E) OTHER FACTORS WHICH INFLUENCE THE FORMATION OF CAVES AND THE RATES OF FORMATION

One of those caused by human agency is that of deforestation, which has been referred to by Terzaghi [268]. As a result of the removal of forest vegetation, there is much less organic CO_2 in the incoming cave waters and it is likely that solution of the limestone is reduced; this reduction in CO_2 has to be set against the effects of greater run-off. Therefore the post-Neolithic changes in the plant covering of many limestone areas might well have affected the rate of development of caves in Europe.

Little work has yet been done on the actual rate of formation of caves. In north-west Europe, many caves can be shown to be of postglacial age, by their relationship to the deposits of glacial drift. The University of Bristol Speleological Society have studied the distribution of drift and its relationship to the caves in north-west Clare [211], and their results indicate that caves of 1,000 m long may well be of postglacial age. Similarly in Yorkshire, it can be shown that caves of about 1 m high by 2 m wide and up to 50 m long are also postglacial [31]; an example is Blishmire Cave on the slopes of Pen-y-Ghent. Renwick came to the same conclusion in a study of caves in Norway [269]. Vadose caves formed by free-flowing streams can therefore be formed in relatively short periods of time. Recently the University of Bristol have set up micro-erosion meters to record directly the solution of and wearing away of limestone on the actual floors of various caves in the Mendips and in County Clare. The results from these experiments should give us some more precise evidence of the rate at which caves are forming in these areas at the present time [270].

The longest surveyed cave in the world at present is Hölloch in Muotatal, Switzerland, where Bögli and his colleagues have surveyed up to 78 km (48·7 miles) of passages. In the Mammoth Cave of the U.S.A. there are 71·2 km (44·5 miles) of passages, and in the neighbouring Flint Ridge Cave, over 70 km, and in the Eisriesenwelt in Austria 42·0 km (26·3 miles). Two long caves in Britain are Agen Allwedd Cave and Dan yr Ogof, both in South Wales, which are 14·4 km (9 miles) and 11 km (7 miles) respectively. Carlsbad Cavern, which probably has the largest single individual cave room, is only 11·8 km (or 7·4 miles) long. The Grotta Gigante near Trieste has one cave room which is 60 m wide, 280 m long and 120 m high.

In a list of the deepest known caves in the

world made by T. Shaw in 1961, every cave but one of a list of fifteen belonged to areas either in or near the Alps or in the Pyrenees; the remaining one was in Algeria. The deepest cave in the world is at present considered to be the Gouffre Berger near Grenoble, France, which is *c*. 1,130 m or 3,750 ft deep and was first descended in 1956 [271]. The second deepest is the Gouffre de la Pierre St-Martin in the Basses Pyrénées, which is 800 m deep (or 2,589 ft) and the third is the Sistema della Piaggia Bella in Piedmont, *c*. 700 m (or 2,261 ft). The deepest cave in Britain is probably Pen-y-Ghent Long Churn, about 512 ft deep (160 m); the deepest in the U.S.A. is Neff's Canyon Cave, Utah, 1,186 ft (380 m); and in Mexico, the Sotano de las Golondrinas, over 1,094 ft (350 m).

3. SOME MAIN TYPES OF CAVES

From this discussion of the main factors in cave formation we can now say something about the different types of caves and to some extent their distribution. Though no two caves are alike, it is possible to generalise about the caves of particular areas. Two main generic types of cave systems can be recognised, first, those found in deep karst, where the depth and nature of the fissure circulation and steeply dipping rocks gives rise to vertical caves as in the southern part of the Dinaric karst. And secondly, those caves found in shallow karst which are chiefly horizontal channels; these are the more usual and more typical of areas of thin limestones. Alternation of limestones with other rock or with limestones of varying purity also favours the formation of horizontal caves; deep vertical caves are therefore the characteristic forms and the reflections of the deep karst, while horizon-

tal caves are more typical of shallow karst. Different cave types are also associated with specific types of karst landforms.

Since caves are characteristic of shallow karst, the number of caves in an area is not an index of karstification, as has been suggested by Curl [155], but an index of fluvial activity in a limestone terrain; Curl's attempts to devise a stochastic model of cave occurrence as an index of karst does not yet help in the understanding of karst processes. Moreover, caves though related to the fissuration of the limestones are not necessarily related to any stage in the development of a landscape, as was suggested in ideas on the cycle of erosion as developed by Cvijič [272] and Davis [215], and also by Coleman and Balchin [113]. Despite these remarks, caves are probably the most abundant of all karst landforms, there being many areas without dolines but few without caves [117].

Caves are difficult to classify. Perhaps the most satisfactory classification is that based on formation due to type of water flow – i.e. water-table, phreatic or vadose. There are also inlet and outlet caves. Inlet caves (or caves of engulfment) are those which develop where waters are engulfed into the rock by means of a swallow hole and occur normally where the impermeable rocks abut on to the limestones. They descend rapidly if the available relief is considerable. Examples are Gaping Gill Hole on the slopes of Ingleborough, Swildon's Hole in the Mendips and the Postojna Cave in the Classical Karst. Outlet caves (or caves of debouchure) are those formed where there are issuing springs (or where there have once been springs) and occur towards the base of the limestone outcrop or at the level of outlet of the karst water. These caves are often flooded and impenetrable to all except cave divers; they are usually of a much more gentle gradient than the inlet caves, though they may have reversed gradients due to pressure flow as in the Fontaine de la Vaucluse in southern France; other examples are at Wookey Hole in the southern Mendips, the Planina Cave in the Planisko Polje in the Classical Karst, and Clapham Cave in the Ingleborough district. Outlet caves sometimes have many branches, each of which forms an outlet for the discharging springs [70].

Most of the best-known caves are at present river caves or once had rivers flowing through them. This does not mean that these caves did not have a phreatic or artesian stage, but that as they have been inundated and traversed by the rivers many of the phreatic traces have been obliterated. However, there are some caves which are not related to the present rivers or the present relief, probably the most famous of which is the Carlsbad Cavern in New Mexico.

(A) PHREATIC CAVES

The *Carlsbad Caverns* occur in the Permian Capitan reef complex of the Guadalupe block, one of the most easterly ranges of the basin and range region of the U.S.A. and on the western edge of the great plains of Texas. They are in a semi-arid region, the average recorded rainfall being 15·35 in. per year. Fig. 74 is a diagram of the caverns. They occur partly in the unbedded Capitan Reef rock and partly in the inter-tonguing and interbedded rocks of the Carlsbad group. The Capitan limestone consists of thick-bedded to massive, very light grey to pinkish-grey, finely crystalline to aphanitic crystalline limestones; the Tansill formation, which is largely back-reef, consists primarily of bedded yellowish-grey dolomite or dolomitic limestone [228]. The Guadalupe escarpment rises to over 4,500 ft above sea level and the plain of the Pecos

river, which lies to the east of the escarpment, is at about 3,600 ft. The entrance to the caves is at 4,000 ft; the caves are situated very close to the southern edge of the escarpment but are unrelated to it. The total depth of the Carlsbad Caverns is over 1,100 ft, so that their lowest part is at a lower level than the nearby plain. The present caverns probably once extended to higher levels, and parts have been completely eroded from the Guadalupe ridge. The largest section of the present cave is developed at about 600–750 ft below the surface of the Guadalupe ridge. This contains the Big Room, probably the largest single cave in the world; it is over 1,500 ft (500 m) long and has a perimeter of $1\frac{1}{4}$ miles (over 2,000 m) and a floor space of 14 acres; at one place its roof is 285 ft (nearly 90 m) above the floor. Associated with the Big Room is part of the cavern used as a lunch room, which is 750 ft below the surface and which can seat a thousand people.

The caves, though below the level of the plain, are above the present groundwater level; the Pecos river, 25 miles away at the city of Carlsbad, is at least 500 ft below. The main cave consists essentially of two parts: the first part is from the natural entrance at 4,400 ft which runs westwards and downwards to 829 ft (256 m) below the surface and is known as the main corridor; this leads to the complex which includes the Queen's Chamber and the King's Palace. The second part consists of the Big Room which is basically on one level. The main corridor has some aspects of a normal epiphreatic or paraphreatic cave and is cut chiefly into the back-reef limestones; it descends steeply in the form of a tunnel cutting across the bedding and was probably formed by a large integrated sub-water-table river. According to Thrailkill [273], Carlsbad Caverns have well-developed flat bedrock floors but these are all unrelated to the bedding of the back-

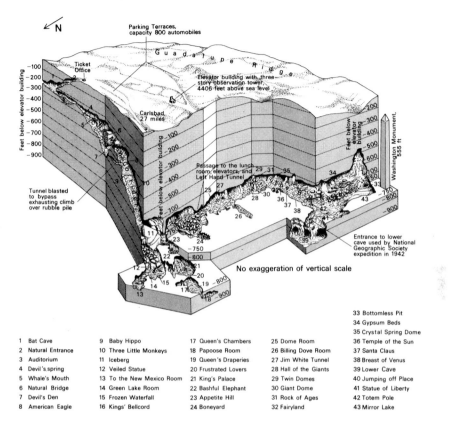

Fig. 74 Cutaway diagram of Carlsbad Caverns (Copyright National Geographic Society, reprinted from *National Geographic Magazine* and reproduced in Hayes [228])

reef beds. Collapses of the roof and walls have taken place, but the passage is mainly that of a corridor type and the bedding in the rock is clear. The Big Room, on the other hand, is cut largely into the Reef facies, where the limestone is unbedded. Where the cave is in the Reef facies its character changes completely, especially in the effects of solution of the limestone. The cave walls are smooth, and are full of voids, looking as if they had been eaten or corroded away. This is seen particularly in the part of the cave called the Bone Yard (Fig. 74), where the walls and roof have the appearance of a corroded set of bones. The plan shows the

influence of the jointing upon the solution of the rock, and the big vertical slots cut into the rock, especially on the south east side of the Big Room. There is no evidence of any integrated stream flow having existence in the Big Room; there is, however, evidence of stagnant water-levels.

Below the Big Room there is the Lower Cave which also forms an extensive series of caverns, and this part goes down to over 1,100 ft (335 m) below the surface. Here too, the contrast between the bedded back-reef facies and the unbedded reef facies is apparent in the character of the cavern, the unbedded reef limestones being extremely full of voids and holes, like a network of smoothed limestone ridges enveloping the holes.

The origin of the Carlsbad Caverns is not yet known, though it is now attracting the attention of many geologists and physiographers. Clearly much of the solution has taken place in deep groundwater and the cave is not related to a modern river in any normal sense. Thrailkill has suggested that the water that caused the solution of the caverns came from backwater flooding of the Pecos river, when for a long period relatively still water could remain in the Reef facies. There is certainly no present source of water nearby which could have caused the solution of so large a cavern. In addition to the peculiar solution of the Reef facies, Carlsbad Caverns are also interesting in that they contain gypsum, aragonite, hydromagnesite and dolomite deposits. It is possible that the occurrence of some of these minerals may have made the limestones in the neighbourhood of the caves rather more soluble.

Although Carlsbad is a gigantic spongework, there is also a development of passages at distinct levels. These have been formed by lateral solution in the paraphreatic zone, where groundwater circulation is most pronounced and organic acids most concentrated. Vadose development was inaugurated by the uplift of the Guadalupe block, and vadose streams used some of the old phreatic passageways. Some vadose features are forming today, in addition to stalactite and stalagmite. The Carlsbad Caverns are probably quite old features, but the splendid display of stalactites and stalagmites is more recent and was formed in the Pleistocene and in the last few thousand years [228].

Differential solubility of limestones by groundwater has also been noted by Jennings and the writer in caves in the Limestone Ranges of the Fitzroy area of north-west Australia [31].

Many other examples of phreatic caves exist, especially in areas of deep groundwater; many were cited by Bretz in 1941 [216]. Deal has discussed Jewel Cave in South Dakota in the following terms: 'The cave is a rigorously joint-controlled maze. . . . The passages are predominantly influenced by the set of conjugate joints trending N-S and E-W, preferential development having taken place along the E-W joints. The N 65° E joint trend is the other predominant influence. Very little passage development has occurred at right angles to the N 65° E trend' [274].

Evidence suggests that there are many large water-filled cavities at great depths in limestones, phreatic cave passages that we can never explore. However, such caves are changed by the action of free and vadose water flow into stream-type caves, with only relatively little indication of their phreatic origins. Disconnected cave chambers formed as a result of phreatic solution will be integrated into vadose passages by stream action. Thus the development of vadose or at least paraphreatic flow may be necessary before caves can develop into the features that are traditionally accessible.

(B) VADOSE AND WATER-TABLE CAVES

Many of the explored and described caves of the world are river caves. Perhaps the most famous group are those of the Postojna area in the Classical Karst. The Postojna Caves occur in folded and faulted Turonian and Senonian (Cretaceous) limestones, which alternate in this region with impermeable Eocene flysch. The main Postojna Cave occurs in the block-faulted area of Javorniki, and on the north side of the Predjama Fault which separates the Ctetaceous limestones from the flysch of

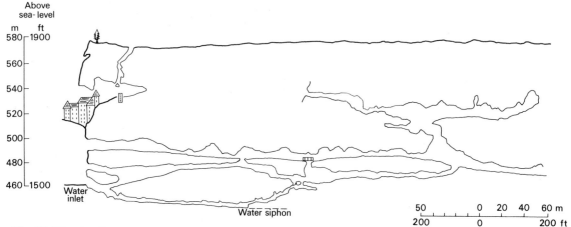

Fig. 75 The Predjama Cave (from Gams [275])

the Postojna basin. The fault block is anti-clinal, and the cave lies in the steeper south-west wing of this anticline; the anticlinal ridge trends NW.–SE. following the Dinaric trend. Most of the galleries of Postojna Cave are eroded into the upper Cretaceous (Turonian) both stratified and non-stratified limestones; parts of the present underground river Pivka are in the thick Senonian strata. The Postojna anti-cline is crossed by faults and the shape and direction of the cave passages are influenced both by these and by the strike and dip of the strata, and by the joints. An examination of the limestones in which the Postojna Cave is formed shows how different these are from those in which, for instance, the caves of either north-west Yorkshire or of Clare have been formed. Whereas in the British Carboniferous Limestones the rocks are very sparry and with a low frequency of fracture, the Cretaceous limestones in the Classical Karst are dense micrites, with a low porosity, and with a high frequency of fracture.

The Postojna Cave and its tributary caves are over 17·8 km long and with other associated caves the total length of passage is nearly 50 km, Fig. 70. The cave occurs

where the river Pivka flows off the Eocene flysch of the Postojna basin and sinks along the line of the Predjama Fault at a height of 511 m at the foot of Sovic Hill (height 674 m). The Postojna basin of 311 km^2 area (120 sq. miles) has been drained by other swallow holes which have also developed along the Predjama Fault, the Postojna Cave swallow hole (ponor) being the lowest in the basin at the present time. The river Pivka has shifted its course and its place of sinking, and in the course of this movement has given rise to many cave swallow holes, now no longer used, one of the best known being the Predjama Cave, Fig. 75. In older speleological literature only two storeys or levels of the Postojna Cave are mentioned – the tourist level at 529·5 m and the under-ground Pivka Cave at 511 m; but Gams claims that the ceiling and galleries of the cave show five development phases [275]. During these five phases the most typical cave stretches of the Postojna Cave arose. Results indicate that it has been forming since the end of the Pliocene [275].

The actual shape of the passages in Postojna are indicative of gravitational water flow; they are usually wider and higher than 10 m, and the most spacious galleries can be shown to occur where the waters have flowed for the longest periods of time, as in the parts known as the Velike and Otoska jamas (caves). The largest chamber, the Dvorana, is situated where there is a confluence of two underground rivers. Much sand and gravel is brought in by the Pivka, and the galleries are particularly wide; they are also gently graded and in 1892 a 2-km-long railway was constructed in the cave at a gradient of only 4–5 per cent. The gradient of the underground river itself is only 5–8 per cent. The Pivka, which is 26 km long, has its high waters in spring and autumn, the low water flow being about 0·06 m^3/sec, the high water flow being about 30 m^3/sec. During low water most of its water comes from the flysch, but in the high-water stages it also comes from the limestones. The present river level also flows over shingle and sand at the bottom of the cave, and this is said by Gams to be similar to that found in the main galleries in the upper levels. In times of extraordinary high waters the present swallow holes and caves at river level cannot absorb all the Pivka river and a lake extends in front of the Sovic Hill. The total hardness of the waters coming into the cave varies between 106 and 196 $CaCO_3$ per litre, and their temperature varies between 0°C and 24°C. In the first stages of the drainage of the area, waters from the Pivka basin flowed eastwards on the surface to join the Planinsko drainage and eventually to the Sava. When erosion reached the edge of the Predjama Fault, water began to percolate into the limestones, and the Predjama Cave was the first entry for the Pivka river; later, when the Pivka river shifted towards Postojna, other streams used the Predjama Caves.

From Fig. 75 it will be seen that today the Lokve river sinks at Predjama, at the foot of a limestone wall, 123 m high, which forms a fine blind valley developed along the Predjama Fault – here separating Bartonian flysch from Cretaceous limestones and Triassic dolomites. The present water-level is at 462 m, and there are at least two horizontal levels above the modern stream. The total length of the galleries in Predjama is of the order of 5,780 m, and a study of the deposits suggests that they were eroded during the upper Pliocene and lower Pleistocene.

In the neighbourhood of the Postojna and Predjama caves other equally impressive caves have been formed at the contact of the impermeable flysch and the Cretaceous limestones. The Škocjan Caves are another good example. One reason for their great development in this part of the Classical Karst is the large volumes of water carried by streams in periods of high water, volumes which were no doubt intensified during certain periods of the Pleistocene. As already mentioned, Gams also attributes the length of the caves to the fact that the rivers carry a big load of pebbles and sand; he concludes that the load of pebbles was particularly important in the formation of large connected cave rooms and of the gravitational transverse profiles. Underground rivers with a considerable pebble-bed load have a more even slope through the limestones and flow through larger and more connected caves than those rivers which carry a high percentage of their load as clay; rivers containing much fine debris are in a sense more truly karstic. These points illustrate how the development of karstic landforms differs from the so-called 'normal' and expected laws of river development. Furthermore, the limestones in the Classical Karst are highly faulted, folded and fractured, as a result of the Alpine folding movements. Thus several factors have contributed to the development of large caves in this area.

Underground river caves show great

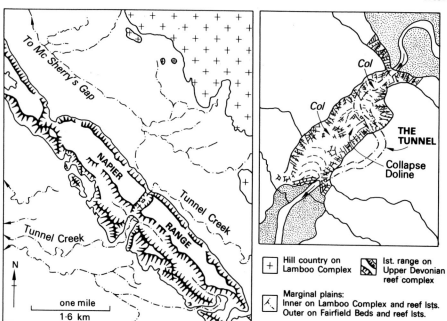

Above Location of the tunnel and its relationship to the overlying wind gap
Below The tunnel (surveyed by J. N. Jennings and M. M. Sweeting)

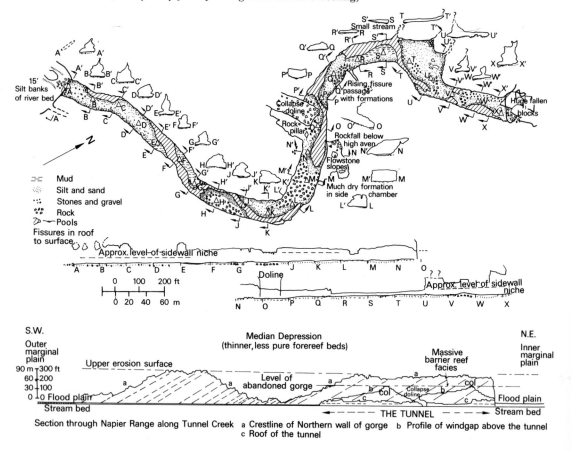

Section through Napier Range along Tunnel Creek a Crestline of Northern wall of gorge b Profile of windgap above the tunnel c Roof of the tunnel

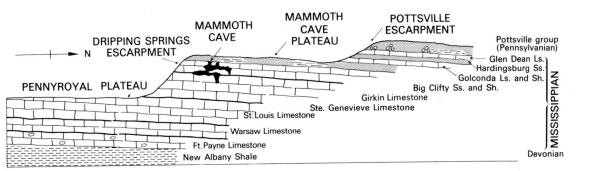

Fig. 77 A north-south cross-section through the formation in the vicinity of Mammoth Cave would pass through the rocks shown above. In the soft, soluble limestone lowlands, caves and sinkholes are developed. The highlands above the Pennyroyal Plateau, and separated from it by the Dripping Springs Escarpment, are protected from rapid erosion by the Big Clifty and Pottsville sandstones (from A. Livesey and P. McGrain, *Geology of the Mammoth Cave, National Park Area,* University of Kentucky Special Publication no. 7, 1962)

adaptations to geological structures. Thus Jennings and the writer have discussed the Tunnel Cave which cuts through a limestone ridge, 1,400 yds (1,350 m) wide, in the Limestone Ranges of the Fitzroy area in Western Australia [276]. The tunnel cave is a simple river passage, 750 yds (700 m) long, 60–70 ft (20 m) wide, and about 40–50 ft (15 m) high. In this example the river started on the surface as a meandering stream and has since substituted an underground for its surface course. In so doing the river has lengthened its course by more than a third in consequence of a closer adaptation to the geological structure, Fig. 76. This process is the reverse from those rivers which shorten their courses by subterranean cut-offs as described by Malott from Indiana [261].

Many other examples of river caves have been explored and described. They occur in association with large rivers in the Moravian and Slovakian karsts in Czechoslovakia, where caves like the Punkva and St Catherine's Caves are excellent examples [197]. On the northern side of the central

inlier in Jamaica large caves are associated with the disappearance of rivers into the White Limestones. One of the biggest of these, Cave River Cave, has recently been explored and surveyed by the Karst Hydrological Expedition to Jamaica [210]. As already mentioned, one of the longest caves in the world, Mammoth Cave, Kentucky, is also a water-table cave, Fig. 77. This with its neighbour, the Flint Ridge Cave, forms one of the longest known cave-passage complexes; there are nearly 45 miles (72 km) of surveyed passage in Mammoth Cave, and in the adjoining Flint Ridge Cave over 40 miles (64·5 km). Both phreatic and vadose features are found in this system, which was much quoted by W. M. Davis in his paper on the 'Formation of Limestone Caverns' in 1930 [215]. The visitor to the cave system today is probably most impressed by the long, elliptical and canyon-shaped passages which seem to go on for ever, and which were described by Mark Twain in *Tom Sawyer.* Thus Cleaveland Avenue in Mammoth Cave, an elliptical passage, extends for 1·5 miles with an average width of 40 ft and a height of 15 ft. From work of J. F. Quinlan, it is known that the great extent of these caves has been developed in limestone beds only 200–250 ft thick. The gradual removal of the sandstone cover enables the extensive development of underground drainage in the Mammoth Cave area [501, 511].

(C) VERTICAL CAVES

Caves are not always more or less horizontal or passage-like. Many possess deep vertical shafts, sometimes known as *domepits,* or *pitches* in northern England. The domepits are cylindrical cavities with fluted walls and occur along joints or small faults. In the caves of County Clare, the pitches are found at the same points at which the roofs of the passages descend abruptly to lower bedding planes. They are found along joints and are elliptical in plan with their major axes less than twice the length of the minor ones. They mark the points at which the initial streams in the bedding planes descended down open joints to lower bedding planes; they are thus chambers of the type that Bretz originally termed domepits [216], though they have not developed exactly as discussed by him.

Cylindrical shafts or pitches are also characteristic of the Yorkshire caves for reasons similar to those which have made the area famous for its vertical swallow holes (see p. 124). The development of the pitches has been assisted by the strong jointing and faulting in the Carboniferous Limestones, by the rapid rejuvenation of the underground drainage, and by the increased abrasion and solution caused by meltwaters in the Glacial period. The vertical shaft of Gaping Gill illustrates some of their chief features. It is over 360 ft (120 m) high and the water flowing down the shaft is probably the highest freely falling waterfall in the country. The shaft is essentially narrow and elliptical in shape with solution flutings on the walls. It leads into the Main Chamber of the cave which is the largest single cave room in the British Isles, being 500 ft (152 m) long, 90 ft (27 m) wide and 110 ft (34 m) high (Fig. 78, map). A characteristic of the Main Chamber is the large number of limestone blocks which occur particularly on its east and west sides, and which illustrate one method of cavern enlargement, viz. collapse of blocks on a large scale. The lower walls of the Main Chamber are not much fluted or smoothed by water but are rough and angular where the detached blocks have broken away. Explorers who have stayed in Gaping Gill overnight have said that it is possible in quiet conditions to hear blocks of limestone become detached and fall away. The floor of the Main Chamber is also covered with boulders and pebbles but these have been subjected to solution and corrasion by the incoming waterfalls and are therefore rounded. Under normal conditions water disappears into these boulders, but in flood conditions the floor of the chamber may become a lake, and its underground channels are not able to take away all the water. Horizontal galleries occur near the base of the vertical shaft of Gaping Gill (see Fig. 78). Large deposits of sand as in Sand Cavern, and of varved clays as in Mud Hall, are associated with these passages, which appear like overflow channels leading from the foot of the Main Chamber. Below these galleries there is another level, indicating that there were other phases of passage formation, Fig. 78 [235].

Mammoth Cave, in addition to its long simple passages, possesses conspicuous domepits developed in the limestones beneath the overlying cover of sandstones. The domepits are usually less than 50 ft

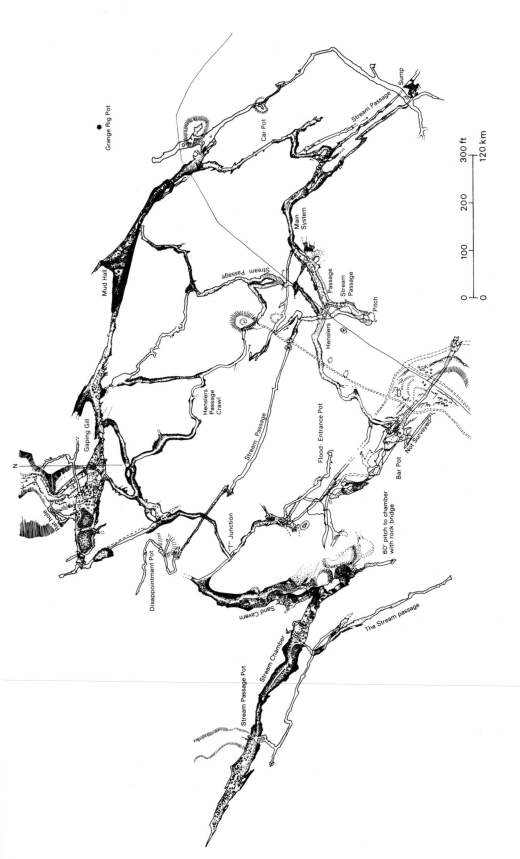

Fig. 78 Gaping Gill cavern system (Revision 1966 by B. M. Grainger and members of the Peveril Underground Survey Association and others. This survey does not include the discoveries made in 1970 and 1971 and known as *The Far Country*)

(17 m) in diameter, and are from 10–200 ft (3–60 m) high. They are restricted to the edges of the Chester cuesta and to the solution escarpment in central Kentucky, where they occur in a narrow zone, no more than 200 ft (60 m) wide; in this zone about 200 to 500 vertical shafts are found per mile of the caprock outcrop. The dome pits are believed to be initiated by the vadose solution of joints by waters percolating into the limestone from the overlying capping of sandstone. It is suggested that impure limestones or non-limestone beds, such as chert, are important in determining the top and bottom of the domepits. They are an example of sub-surface karstification or *unterirdische Karstphänomen* [127], and are related to groundwater movement along the outcrop of the sandstone caprock with the underlying limestone [244]. Solution under these circumstances is less common along the bedding planes than along the joints, where descending groundwater differentially dissolves portions of the walls of the joints. In general, the greater the rate of flow, the greater the rate of solution, therefore the joints which receive the greatest amount of water are the most likely to be enlarged. Pohl, who studied this kind of vertical feature, also showed that they could be developed independently of large cave systems [244].

Vertical features caused by the solution of limestones by seepage water below an impermeable caprock have also been discussed by Glennie [277]. Seepage water of a low pH value works downwards at cross-joints; this forms cavities with dome-shaped roofs and vertical flutings caused by films of flowing water. Drops of water fall freely from the central hole of the dome and the solution formed by their impact forms a cup- or saucer-shaped basin at the bottom. The relation between the vertical and horizontal dimensions of the cavities de-pends on the nature of the limestones and on the amount of seepage. Since joint drainage is required to keep these cavities growing, they have been called *Pohl cells* by Glennie [278], after the original work on seepage features by Pohl in 1955. The most favoured positions for the development of such Pohl cells are near escarpments and on valley sides, but never near dolines. This kind of vertical cavity is only seen when their destruction has begun and they have little surface expression. It is possible that seepage from a peat cover on a limestone would have a similar effect and also form Pohl cells. Burke has discussed solution shafts occurring beneath a caprock in South Wales; solution has taken place in the Carboniferous Limestones beneath the Millstone Grit, producing shafts up to 100 ft (30 m) deep in the limestones, Fig. 79.

The deepest vertical caves of the world occur in deep karsts, but are less accessible and less well known. In north-west Greece, a vertical cave has recently been discussed by Eyre [279]. It is called Proventina, and occurs in the Astraka massif of the Pindus mountains, and its entrance is on a plateau at a height of about 1,840 m. In this cave there exists a vertical shaft about 200 m deep with no interruptions. Eyre has described it as follows: 'I was able to observe the whole shaft clearly. It was a clean elliptical, 25 m by 33 m and about 200 m deep. It is the cleanest shaft I have ever encountered. The thin horizontal bedding had been subjected to water action and the joints had been all rounded off until the west face resembled a man-made wall' (loc. cit., p. 10).

Other examples occur in the highly folded and faulted limestones of the Alps, and are particularly developed not only where the relief and tectonics are favourable but also where large quantities of water such as meltwater have been able to enter the

x Burke & Bird 1966.

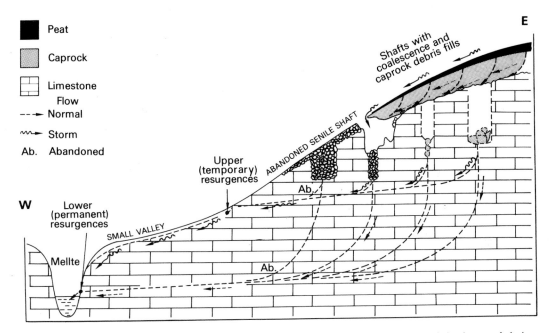

Fig. 79(a) Surface and groundwater feeds to shafts under different conditions of precipitation, and their relation to resurgences

after Burke and Bird. Nature 1966

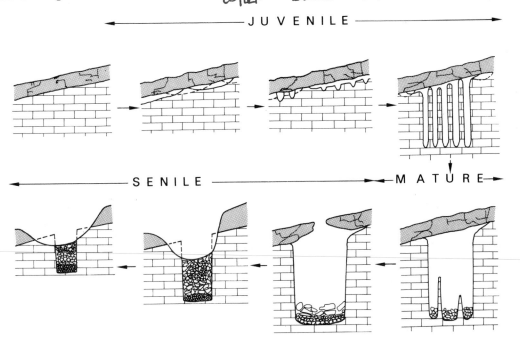

Fig. 79(b) Diagrammatic W–E sections of a typical simple shaft, illustrating successive morphological stages in the sequence of development

limestone. They therefore often occur in association with modern glaciers and near the sites of former glaciers. One of the best known associated with a modern glacier is the Triglav Cave on the slopes of Triglav Mountain in the Julian Alps. This is situated at the edge of the small Triglav glacier at a height of 2,400 m; the entry to the cave has become exposed by the retreat of the glacier since 1850, and its total depth is about 260 m [280]. A section of the deepest cave so far explored in the world, the Gouffre Grotte Berger (1,130 m deep), is given in Fig. 80. It is known that many deep vertical caves exist in folded limestones in the Rocky Mountains and in the New Guinea highlands, areas where deep karst exists, but they are so far unexplored. Ford has recently explored the Castleguard cave in the Rockies.

4. CAVE COLLAPSE AND BREAKDOWN

The great heaps of debris and limestone blocks which litter many caves suggest there may have been periods of great collapse in their history. However, records of collapses in historic times are rare. Little has been written on cavern breakdown, yet it is an important way in which many caverns have become enlarged. Gèze comments, 'Ainsi un remplissage presque uniquement formé par de grands blocs anguleux identiques à la roche environnante prouve que les effondrements autochtones ont joué le rôle essentiel à un moment où les galeries étaient déjà abandonnées par les eaux courantes' [120]. Miskovsky states that collapses are of two kinds; they are either (1) due to dissolution, i.e. to predominantly chemical reasons, or (2) to predominantly mechanical agencies, i.e. essentially frost action. When the collapse has been caused by dissolution, Miskovsky claims that the

fallen boulders should be largely rounded; where the collapse is mechanical, frost-shattered angular pebbles should be found. There are, however, many reasons why caves break down and this differentiation between dissolution and frost action is too simple [281].

We have already mentioned that many caves appear to enlarge by a process of spalling under tectonic pressure or of pressure release (p. 136). It is possible that in many seismic areas such pressure release is augmented by earth tremors and movements along existing fault lines. Many caves are known to contain stalagmites and blocks which have been moved as a result of earthquakes, as in Jamaica. However, Davies has pointed out that earthquakes are inadequate to cause great rock-falls in caverns and says that negligible rock-falls have taken place in natural caves close to the epicentres of large earthquakes [282].

He divides cavern breakdown into four main types:

(*a*) *Block breakdown*, the failure *en masse* of a cave ceiling and walls. This type of failure is usually of short horizontal, but of much vertical, extent, stretching upwards into the tension dome. Large blocks of roughly rectangular blocks in piles form where the breakdown has occurred.

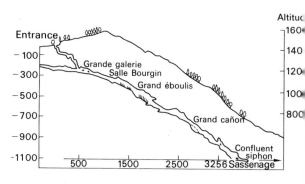

Fig. 80 A sketch section of the Gouffre Grotte Berger (from Gèze [120])

(b) *Slab breakdown*. This type of failure takes place over great horizontal distances, but is of limited vertical extent. It is caused by the breaking away of a single bed or relatively few beds in the ceiling. Thin irregular slabs are scattered over long lengths of the cave passage.

(c) *Plate breakdown*. This is caused by solution or pressure loosening thin plates of limestone a few feet across and a few inches thick.

(d) *Chip breakdown*. In this kind of failure only small fragments of the limestone fall away; the pieces are flat and crumbly, and minute layers of the rock scale off [282].

Collapse of caves most probably takes place when passages through which forced waters flow under considerable hydrostatic pressure become passages in which the water is no longer under any hydrostatic head and is flowing freely. This was suggested by the writer for certain collapses in the caves of north-west Yorkshire. The writer has also examined a cave in the Lebanon, where collapse of its floor can be shown to have taken place since the occupation of the cave by upper Palaeolithic man [283]. A study of the chronology of this cave suggests that water was withdrawn from the lower passages during a stage of the Wurmian glacial phase when the sea level in the Mediterranean would be below the present level. Under such conditions, phreatic water would have been withdrawn from the deeper parts of the cave; collapse of some of the upper galleries into the lower ones might then have taken place.

Alternating types and variations in the limestones are also conducive to collapse. One of the best examples of this kind is in Yucatán, Mexico, where the limestones alternate between soft, rather friable beds and harder porcellanous beds (which are often concretionary). Undercutting by weathering and solution of the softer beds leads to collapses of the harder beds; many of the cenotes (the steep-sided well-like caves) of Yucatán have been formed in this way. Jennings, in the Nullarbor Plain in South Australia, supposes that much of the cave formation and collapse has been due to this cause [284, 264]. Monroe, speaking of the caves of Puerto Rico, also mentions that caverns and natural bridges due to collapse are 'most common in formations characterised by alternating hard and soft layers', particularly in the Lares and Aguada limestones [285] (Fig. 81).

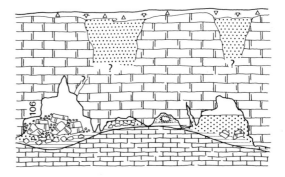

Fig. 81 Composite diagram of the Golconda Caverns and their evolution, showing floors of bedded galena-baryte-dolomite accumulates covered by roof-collapse blocks with or without inwashed sands. One cavern shows a lining of late calcite crystals. Two sand-filled solution collapse pits, which may lead to yet unproven caverns, descend from the surface. Sands and dolomitised limestone (large brick symbol) alike are overlain by boulder clay with lenses of chert gravel. Unaltered limestone below the caverns is shown by a small brick symbol (from Ford & King [398])

The influence of fault lines in assisting cave breakdown has already been referred to (p. 138). From the earliest days of cave study the association of large cave chambers with lines of tectonic weakness has been evident (as at Padirac or Škocjan). In north-west Yorkshire and in the Burren of County Clare, cave collapse tends to take place along the master joints, leaving long straight joint walls. Where the jointing is more varied, cave collapse may give rise to an irregular and hackly type of cave wall.

The influences of frost shattering on limestones have also been mentioned (p. 157). It is tempting to suggest that many of the collapse features associated with present-day caverns have resulted from periods of intense frost action during the Pleistocene. Gèze gives an example from the Dachstein massif of the Austrian Alps [120], but many others can be found in the Alpine limestone areas and in the Slovenian and Dinaric karsts. Renault claims that frost breccia is forming in the entrance to caves in the Pyrenees today at above 8,000 ft (2,500 m). In Britain, rock shattering and scree formation is not particularly active at the present time, and it is likely that broken-down material associated with the caves is a relic from the Pleistocene [286]. Frost-shattered debris is also associated with caves in the Appalachian area of North America.

Cavern breakdown is further assisted by the presence of different minerals in veins in the limestones. W. and E. White have studied cave breakdown in the Mammoth Cave and Flint Ridge systems [287]. There is much ceiling breakdown in these systems and it is attributed to the presence of sulphate minerals often in veins following fractures in the rock. As a result of aeration and the addition of oxygen into the cave, gypsum (calcium sulphate) is formed by the reaction of the sulphate minerals with the limestone. The gypsum lies along the fracture lines in the rock, it is more soluble

than the limestone, and thus breakdown occurs by solution of the gypsum. Blocks of limestone fall along the fracture lines and these blocks form piles lying beneath the ceiling; they take the shape of 'curved plates of bedrock seemingly peeled from the ceiling and thin splinters of rock removed from ceilings along bedding planes' (loc. cit., p. 25).

In the central Kentucky karst, many passages appear to be the segments of once longer passages, and in the Mammoth Cave and Flint Ridge systems there are many which were once continuous. A truncated cave passage is one which has been cut at one or both ends by collapse after the passage has been formed; a terminal break-down is a portion of the collapsed rock which collects during truncation to terminate the cave passage. It has been found in the Mammoth Cave area that massive break-downs occur where vertical drainage is most active. Vertical drainage and solution is most active where the sandstone caprock is relatively thin; where the caprock is thicker, solution of the vertical joints and the formation of vertical shafts in the limestone does not take place so readily. Thus where the caprock is thin, the edge of its outcrop with the limestones has abundant shafts and features of vertical solution; this is where most breakdown takes place. The solution weakens the rock over the cave passages in these areas, causing collapse and the segmenting of formerly continuous passages. The stages in the segmentation of cave passages by such breakdown are discussed by Brucker and many examples are given from the Mammoth Cave–Flint Ridge cave systems [288].

9 Cave Deposits

CAVE DEPOSITS are an intrinsic part of the study of caves. They can be divided into two main types: (1) *allochthonous,* or derived, which have been brought into the cave by phreatic or by vadose water. These include muds, sands and gravels etc. (2) *autochthonous,* that is, cave deposits resulting from solution of the limestone and its subsequent redeposition within the cave itself. These include the better-known stalactites and stalagmites, but also collapse material and residual clays from the dissolution of the limestones. The deposits are also essentially calcareous and non-calcareous. The study of cave deposits has been neglected in Britain, partly because they are less obvious in British caves than in other areas. Their importance results from the fact that, whereas at the surface many of these deposits would be weathered and eroded away, because of the lack of surface weathering in caves they are preserved. Hence they are of great importance in reconstructing the previous weathering phases in a cave area.

1. NON-CALCAREOUS DEPOSITS

These are usually allochthonous, brought into the cave by both phreatic, but chiefly by vadose, water. The most important non-calcareous deposit in all caves is some form of clay, which is important because of the relatively fine cracks in the limestones through which only clays can pass; also the quiet and non-turbulent waters that are found in cave lakes enable the clay to be deposited, whereas in a turbulent stream on the surface the same clay would be carried along in suspension. Usually, clays are carried far into the recesses of cave systems, whereas larger-sized gravels can only be carried into relatively large and open passages. Clays are in particular retained in cul-de-sac-like passages by very slow currents. The particles, from 2 to 20 microns in diameter, remain for a long time in suspension and are only deposited a long way from their origin. Also in the deeper caves the subterranean climate is very uniform and clays prove resistant to increased CO_2 pressure in the cave atmosphere. Many phreatic passages contain clays which have been brought in by the phreatic water; these deposits, if extensive, may be important in the location and confining of the latter paraphreatic and vadose flow. Any silting-up of the deeper cavities enhances the shallow movement of the groundwater and protects the bedrock from solutional attack [289]. The most abundant mineral in cave clays is illite, though deposits of kaolinite and occasionally sepiolite are found. The hydrates of iron are the ions to which the clays become attached; they are reddish brown when oxidised and blue or grey in the ferrous state [290].

Most clays are derived from outside the caves and from outside the limestone environment; some, however, are derived from the decalcification and ion exchange replacement of the limestones. In temperate regions, the alternations of weather conditions from summer to winter may give rise to varved clays; at the end of the summer percolating waters contain relatively little clay and only sand is deposited;

at the end of the winter, by contrast, the soil is more decalcified, and the clay is free to be moved and is deposited [281]. Many caves in fact contain varved clays, but these are more likely to have been laid down during former glacial and periglacial conditions; this is the explanation given by Miskovsky for the large deposits of clays in the caves of the Causses. Deposits of terra rossa are regarded as an indicator of former warm conditions [266, 290].

In Britain, there are excellent varved clays in Mud Hall in Gaping Gill and in the Victoria Cave near Settle, both these occurrences being the result of conditions in the Glacial period [49]. In the Mendip caves and those of the Buckfastleigh area in South Devon, there are deposits of red clays, which may be residual terra rossa deposits from the warmer climates of the Tertiary period. Warwick also has discussed laminated clays from Agen Allwedd Cave in South Wales [291].

Davis and Bretz believed that there was an epoch of deposition of fine-textured clay recorded in the life histories of many caves; according to them this epoch occurred after the original phreatic solutional episode and before the vadose solution had begun [215, 216]. The vadose water later removed the red clays, and reopened large parts of the earlier-formed caverns. However, a clay infill is probably only characteristic of caves in areas where a very old land surface has developed and where a deep mantle of insoluble residue and weathered material covers the limestone. Under these circumstances fine-textured clay in the residual soil will migrate downwards along joints and cracks with the descending waters. If the circulating water is slow, almost motionless, the clay will settle in the phreatic cavities. There are, however, many cave areas where the drainage is more vigorous and any tendency for the clay to settle is prevented, as in the Ingleborough area [219].

The other main non-calcareous deposits associated with caves are river sands and gravels laid down in terraces by vadose streams. The sands are of the dimensions of 0·3 to 1·0 mm. Larger material can only be swept into caves through large and open passages, but pebbles are quite common in both British (as in Clapham Cave, Yorkshire), and Australian caves [183]. Studies have been made on the granulometry of cave pebbles, and Siffre maintains that they are much flatter (applatis) and also more rounded than pebbles derived from non-cave environments [292]. The index of flattening of limestone pebbles taken from terraces of the river Skirfare in Littondale, north-west Yorkshire, is 2·2, while the index of flattening of pebbles taken from a cave in Littondale (Boreham Cave) is 2·9. In some caves cobble deposits are found in passages where it is difficult under present conditions to see both where they came from and how they got there. In high gradient Alpine caves sand and pebbles have been important scouring agents; in low gradient caves sediment moves more slowly. E. L. White and W. B. White have discussed the dynamics of sediment transport in caves; their article is also useful for its reference to work on the sediments of Mammoth Cave by Davies and Chao and to Swiss work on cave sediments by Schmid [515].

All these non-calcareous deposits in caves tend to become cemented by $CaCO_3$. This cementation helps to preserve the deposits, since they become harder and more indurated – hence their importance in the stratigraphic record.

Ice may be regarded as a non-calcareous deposit in caves. From the climatic point of view caves can be divided into warm and cold; ascending caves are warm caves (dynamic), descending caves are cold (static). In vertical or descending caves cold

36 Ice crystals: Ice Cave in Crow's Nest area, Alberta (*Photo by D. C. Ford*)

air accumulates and does not circulate; at high altitudes the temperature of the air in such cavities is low and accumulations of ice and snow are common. The most common ice caves are in the Alps and the Pyrenees, but they also occur in the Rockies, Photo 36. In Austria the most famous is the cave of the Eisriesenwelt, near Salzburg, which contains a glacier 100 m high, and glacial formations occur for more than 2 km of the passageway (total passageway 30 km); drips of water freeze and form ice stalagmites and these are over 6 m high. Other ice caves occur in the Slovakian mountains, where the Dobsina ice cave is the best known, and in the Pyrenees where the Marboré ice cave is famous. One of the lowest in Europe is the Grotte de la Glacière in the Jura, near Passavant, which is at 630 m. A typical section of an ice cavern is given in Fig. 82. In the Alps, caves with permanent ice are usually situated above 1,450 m.

Not a great deal of work has been done on the structure of cave ice. It is possible that much of it is fossil or relic – the relic ice never having disappeared since the Pleistocene – and the study of cave ice could be extremely valuable. Some of the problems associated with the ventilation of ice caves and their micro-climate are discussed by Wigley and Brown [516].

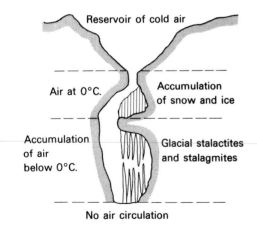

Fig. 82 Formation of subterranean ice in the absence of air circulation (from Trombe [57])

2. CALCAREOUS DEPOSITS

When speaking of calcareous deposits, one normally thinks of stalactites and stalagmites. However, the action of frost or the widespread collapse of limestones gives rise to angular blocks or limestone breccias. The accumulations of angular blocks at the entrance to a cave or within a cave are known as *cave breccias*. Frequently such blocks are created by calcium carbonate into hard deposits. Cave breccias are common at the entrance to many caves in the Mediterranean, where they are often regarded as having been formed during frosty periods [266]. Collapse of cave roofs will, moreover, give rise to angular material, and these will give rise to cave breccias inside caves. The most useful study of cave breccias has been made by Brain in relation to the Transvaal cave deposits [293]. In Britain, angular block deposits occur in caves in South Devon, where it is possible that they were formed during glacial periods [286]. As already indicated, collapse of cave roofs seems to occur in well-defined phases, hence collapse breccias in any one area may have a common history [293].

By far the most common calcareous deposits are, however, those reprecipitated from water in a variety of forms. The study of such redeposited calcium and other minerals in caves has given rise to a large amount of literature. This is particularly so in Europe where stalagmite and stalactite formations are numerous, and where there has always been a great interest in cave mineralogy and the chemistry of deposits. This section will not deal in any detail with the chemistry involved nor with the occurrence of eccentric minerals in caves, but with the significant aspects of calcite deposition as it affects the interpretation of the caves and their history as landforms. There is a good chapter on cave deposits in

British Caving by Warwick, and also in a paper on 'Cave Deposits and Palaeoclimatology', where much of the recent literature is summarised by him [27, 294]. The word *stalactite* was first applied to pendant cave deposits by the Danish naturalist Worm in 1655, though Pliny described the growth of stalactites and stalagmites in ancient Greece and Italy. They are known as *speleothems* in America (from Greek: *spelaion*, a cave, and *thema*, a deposit).

The principal mineral in calcareous deposits in caves is calcite. The calcite in stalactites and other cave deposits is the normal rhombohedral mineral in its crystalline form which is stable at ordinary temperatures. However, some cave deposits are composed of the less stable orthorhombic mineral of the same composition, aragonite; this is about 16 per cent more soluble than calcite in water at cave temperatures, and therefore tends to be dissolved in water which is slightly supersaturated with calcite. Deposition of aragonite is sometimes regarded as an indicator of warm environments, but this conclusion is not well founded [295]. Gypsum ($CaSO_4$) deposits also occur in many caves, particularly in dry passages and especially where the limestones contain shale bands which are pyritiferous; this is true of some of the caves in north-west Yorkshire, notably the Shale Cavern in Lost John's Cave and in the Gypsum Cavern of the Ease Gill series, and in caves in the Mammoth Cave area of the U.S.A. [287].

A delicate balance exists between solution and deposition by cave waters and very minor changes in conditions will shift the reaction from one to the other. Calcareous deposits are related to cave environments and can be divided into those formed (a) by dripping water, (b) by running water, (c) by seepage water, and (d) under water. Though the forms may vary within each type, those of one type never grow in another situation.

It is still commonly believed that evaporation of water is the main reason for the precipitation of $CaCO_3$. But in many caves the cave atmosphere is already too saturated, with humidity at 100 per cent, to allow a significant amount of evaporation to be the main cause of calcite deposition. As shown by Holland and others [296], deposition in caves is caused by a reduction in the CO_2 pressure, and this reduction in the CO_2 is the overriding factor in calcite deposition. Only rarely is the CO_2 pressure abnormally small, when evaporation of water or temperature changes become effective. Ordinary atmospheric air has a CO_2 partial pressure of 0.0003 atmospheres and rain water in equilibrium with it will contain $1,364 \times 10^{-5}$ mol/litre of CO_2 in solution. After the passage of this water through the soil and plant layer and between the surface of the ground and the cave, it may contain 25–90 times the amount of CO_2 normally found in the atmosphere; such percolating water may contain up to about 1.3×10^{-3} mol/litre of dissolved CO_2. So long as the cavities in the limestones are filled with water the CO_2 cannot escape. But when the water comes into contact with a cavity or cave where the CO_2 content of the cave air is similar to that of the free air, then some CO_2 is released from the percolating water. The release of this CO_2 causes the deposition of the $CaCO_3$ and the formation of stalactites, stalagmites and the other features of cave deposition [297]. The CO_2 content is therefore the dominant factor in the formation of these deposits and without the CO_2 of biological origin the precipitation of $CaCO_3$ would be much reduced. Evaporation of water may also cause the calcium bicarbonate-bearing groundwater to lose some of its CO_2, and in dry areas the loss of water by evaporation into the cave atmo-sphere may in time become a more important factor in the deposition of the calcium carbonate than the loss of CO_2. The shape of the precipitate of the minerals is influenced by internal lattice structure. Where the growth is impeded good crystal forms cannot grow.

(A) DRIPPING AND RUNNING WATER FORMS

These are the best known and include stalactites and stalagmites.

Stalactites are caused by the dripping of water from cave roofs. These and other depositional features are often formed under glaciers in limestone areas as in the

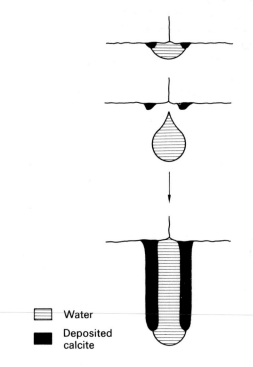

Fig. 83 Growth of a tubular stalactite. Water issues from a crack in the cave roof and loses carbon dioxide to the cave air. The first deposition occurs where the surface of the drip intersects the roof (after Moore & Nicholas [295])

straw

37(a) *above* Stalactites, Cave, Crow's Nest Area

37(b) *below* Stalactites formed under a glacier, Castleguard, Alberta (*Both photos taken by D. C. Ford*)

Castleguard area of the Rocky Mountains, Photo 37(b). Percolating water enters caves through cracks and joints in the roof and loses its excess CO_2 on mixing with the cave atmosphere. As the water drops enter the cave and the CO_2 is lost, calcite is deposited as a tiny ring where the surface of the drop is in contact with the cave roof, Fig. 83 [295]. As more drops emerge, ring upon ring of calcite is added to form a hollow cylinder, the diameter of which is the same as the diameter of the drops of water; the average size of a water drop is 5 mm. As the cylinder grows the water moves down through the central hollow and adds a small increment of length to the stalactite. In this way a straw or tubular stalactite (or fistuleuse) is formed. These vary from about 5–10 mm ($\frac{1}{4}-\frac{1}{2}$ in.) in diameter and they may be several metres long; in the Grotte de la Clamouse (Hérault) a length of 4·2 m is recorded [120], and in Boranup Cave there is a straw stalactite which is 6 mm in diameter and 6·2 m long [298]. The structure of straw stalactites is simple. They are composed of nearly pure calcite and each stalactite behaves in structure as if it were a single crystal; each time a new layer is added to the end of the tube the molecules arrange themselves in accordance with the pattern laid down during the deposition of the previous layer. If the flow of water is rapid there will not be time for the deposit of calcite to form before the drop has fallen and no stalactite will occur, but a stalagmite may form on the floor.

Straw stalactites are common in many British caves, and some good examples occur in the Ease Gill Caverns. They are particularly common in cool temperate latitudes, as in Ireland and Norway, but are less frequent in caves in Mediterranean and tropical areas. They are fragile depositional forms and are often destroyed in the exploration of newly found caves, Photo 37.

All shapes of stalactites are controlled by gravity, but many things can take place to interrupt the simple growth of a stalactite. The orifice of the tubular straw may become constricted or sealed, or the walls may be ruptured and an irregular shape formed. In time much of the precipitation takes place on the outer walls of the stalactite, forming the conical, spherical and tubular masses which are so common in caves. The deposits on the outside of the stalactites are in layers almost parallel to the surface; in cross-section these layers appear as concentric rings. These are usually incomplete and dating of the growth of stalactites by analysis of the rings has been unsuccessful, probably because the layers are not formed regularly. In tubular stalactites, the crystals have their long axes directed downwards, whereas in conical stalactites the crystals radiate perpendicularly to the axis of the stalactite [295] (Fig. 84). The way in which the crystals grow and how crystals in the most favoured direction advance the growth of the stalactite is given by Moore, loc. cit., p. 98. Not all stalactites have a central tube; many result solely from the precipitation of $CaCO_3$ from water flowing down their surfaces; this kind, though common in Britain, is particularly important in caves in central and Mediterranean Europe.

In some caves bulbous or onion-like stalactites form; these bulbous concretions are added secondarily to the original tube. Particularly good examples occur in the Buchan Caves of Buchan, in Victoria, and they are also important in many of the caves in Mediterranean climates. It is possible that the secondary bulbous accretion has

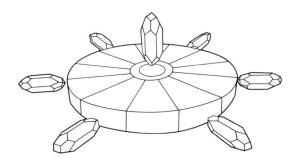

Fig. 84(a) Crystal structure of a section of a stalactite

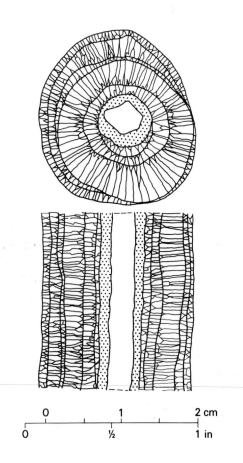

Fig. 84(b) Crystal structure of a stalactite from Cumberland Bone Cave, Maryland (from Moore & Nicholas [295])

TABLE XIII

STALACTITE DRIPS

(Wee Jasper, New South Wales)

Locality	Date	Temp. °F	pH	Total hardness (MgCO$_3$ and CaCO$_3$)	CaCO$_3$mgl	MgCO$_3$mgl
Drip from stalactite:						
Dogleg Cave	Dec 1958	67·5	7·45	231·0	220·6	10·4
Signature Cave	Dec 1958	67·5	7·39	238·0	232·0	6·0
	Mar 1959	54·0	7·5	242·0	242·0	Nil
	Nov 1959	57·0	7·8	382	327	55

been caused by a change in the climatic conditions from when the original tube was formed and may indicate a greater supply of water and of Ca(HCO$_3$)$_2$ in solution. This interpretation is given to explain bulbous stalactites occurring in the caves of Moravia, by Kunsky [299].

Stalactites also occur in the form of curtains (or draperies), long continuous sheets which hang from cave roofs. These are flowing, not dripping, water deposits. Wells says that they form either as one continuous crystalline structure or as a series of scalenohedrally terminated prismatic crystals in parallel growth [300]. They occur when a stream of water flows down an inclined roof leaving behind a sinuous trail of CaCO$_3$. This is followed by another trail and the deposit is built downwards layer by layer. Impurities in the deposits of CaCO$_3$ give rise to a banded structure in the curtains. They are made up of crystals which may be several inches long and each new layer of molecules follows the orientation of the adjoining crystals in the previous layer, similar to a conventional stalactite. The crystals may be of any size. The curtain will maintain a constant width if the crystals are all the same size and are perpendicular to the course of the water flow [298].

Some of the highest figures for calcium carbonate in parts per million in limestone waters have been obtained from the drips from stalactites. At Wee Jasper in New South Wales the writer and Jennings took samples from persistently dripping stalactites. Some of the results are given in Table XIII.

The last value of 327 ppm is the highest Jennings has recorded for a stalactite drip in Australia. He remarks that the stubbly stalagmite receiving the drip 'does not appear to be growing very actively' [301]. This may be due to the high CO$_2$ content of the cave air which prevents the escape of the CO$_2$ and therefore there is no deposition. Investigations of the amount of CaCO$_3$ in stalactite drips have also been carried out in the U.S.A. by Moore and others [295]. The pH of water dripping from stalactites was taken in both winter and in early summer (May):

	Winter	Early summer
Gage Caverns, New York	pH 7·7	pH 7·5
Breathing Cave, Virginia	pH 8·1	pH 6·5
Tumbling Rock Cave, Alabama	pH 8·2	pH 5·8

Moore attributes these differences to the greater amount of vegetation in the areas above the caves in May, when there would be more CO_2 in the groundwater. Detailed measurements also show an upward drift of pH with time, after water has issued from a stalactite. Cave pools are found to be more alkaline than water from the stalactites. This is explained by a loss of CO_2 from the dripping water. Ordinarily the solution is supersaturated before it deposits. Change in water characteristics during stalactite growth, from stalactite to water in a cave pool is given below, for Cave City Cave, California (Moore [298]).

	Stalactite	Pool
Ca	95 ppm	42 ppm
Mg	–	18 ppm
HCO_3	348	190
CO_2 (per cent)	1·8	–
pH	7·30	7·99

Observations on the pH of the waters coming into Breathing Cave, Virginia, showed that there is much more CO_2 in the cave in the summer than in the winter (0·037 per cent in January and 0·071 per cent in May). Stalactite growth may cease in areas where there is little CO_2 in the winter because of lack of growth of vegetation, and the principal lengthening may take place during the warmer months.

In the Postojna Cave, Gams has examined the calcium content of dripping water from stalactites. He found that water at the 'base' of stalactites nearest the roof contained about 200 ppm calcium, while water collected at the tips of the stalactites contained about 140 ppm. Like Moore, he finds that in winter the calcium content of the dripping waters is much less [302]. Gams says that the total hardness of stalactite drips is greatest in autumn under fir forest, followed by beech forest and pasture. He also claimed that the biggest stalactites and stalagmites occur where the percolating water is most abundant (in *150 Let Postojnske Jame*, 1818–1968, p. 103).

Czajlik, working in the Vass Imre Cave in Hungary, has measured the calcium hardness of the water inside a stalactite and also the water draining on its surface. There is a substantial difference in hardness between the two types of water, that on the inside containing about 16–25 ppm Ca and that on the outside 200–250 ppm. This difference seems to be due to the segregation of the $CaCO_3$, and this idea is confirmed by laboratory experiments. Observations over the years in the cave also suggest that the hardness of the water dripping from the same stalactite may vary by as much as 170 ppm Ca. These variations are ascribed to the coolness of the soil in winter when there is little microbiological activity and less CO_2. Czajlik also concluded that, as a result of the precipitation of $CaCO_3$, the hardness of waters standing or stagnant in a cave becomes after a period of time adjusted to about 70 ppm, which corresponds to the state of equilibrium with the air [303]. Land use seems to affect the colour of stalactites. In Aggtelek Cave, Hungary, stalactites forming below a coniferous forest cover are of a light colour, while those below cultivated land are darker and redder.

In Poole's Cavern in Derbyshire, Pitty has studied the varying seepage rates of three stalactites; he showed that, despite fluctuations in the rates of seepage, these fluctuations were not related to the variations in the $CaCO_3$ content of the stalactite drips. He concluded that in this cave the seepage was relatively slow [79].

When compared with stalagmites, stalactites are slow-growing features. In general, slow drop formation or slow drip rate, rapid loss of CO_2, and rapid evaporation favour the development of stalactites; rapid drip rate, slow loss of CO_2 and slow evaporation favour the development of stalagmites.

Stalagmites are more varied than stalactites because they are built up from the floor.

38 Stalagmite, Carlsbad Cavern, New Mexico
(*Cavern Supply Company, New Mexico*)

Franke in his work in central Europe believes he is able to form equations for the rate of growth of a stalagmite and for its cross-section, as a function of the rate of supply of solution, the CO_2 content of the solution, and the CO_2 content of the solution in equilibrium with the surrounding air [297]. There are relationships between these conditions and rate of deposition of stalagmites. The rate of growth depends on the CO_2 content of the solution and not on the amount of solution supplied; but the size of the cross-section is a measure of the water supplied. If therefore a stalagmite shows a vertical change in thickness, this may indicate a change in conditions, either locally or regionally. When for instance a stalagmite thickens vertically, this is an indication of an increase in the rate of flow; where a stalagmite shows a thinning vertically and tapers to a cone, the supply of solution has decreased [297]. Warwick, however, gives the reverse conclusion [27].

Stalagmites are usually larger than stalactites and they have no central tube. They can be extremely large, some in the Postojna Cave being over 15 m high, and one in Carlsbad Caverns, New Mexico, 17 m high. The largest in Aven Armand is 30 m high and some in Aggtelek cave in Hungary over 40 m. They are also very varied in shape. Variations in the shape and development of stalagmites result partly from the height that the drops of water

In most cases water falling from the roof or stalactite contains a high amount of $Ca(HCO_3)_2$; as the water falls evaporation takes place and the drop reaches the floor again supersaturated. When the drop reaches the ground it spreads out radially. Precipitation is greatest at the centre and decreases outwards. In this way a thin layer of calcium carbonate is precipitated in the form of a disc or plate (assiette). This is followed by other drops so that a series of dome-shaped layered hoods build up one above the other, Photo 38. Stalagmites are rounded, not pointed; the normal shape is candle-like, which is regarded as representing constant conditions of growth. The structure is shown in Fig. 85, where the centre consists of horizontal layers while at the edges these grade into thin vertical layers. Stalagmites do not grow radially, and a study of the growth of a stalagmite must be made with a longitudinal and not with a horizontal section.

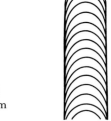

Fig. 85 Schematic vertical section of a stalagmite (from Franke 1965 [297])

have to fall before reaching the floor of the cavern. Some of the most splendid stalagmites are in fact found in very large caverns, such as those in Postojna Cave and in the celebrated 'forêt vierge' of stalagmites in Aven Armand in the Causse Méjean. Water dripping down from some of the great domes in these big caves may be somewhat less saturated than water which has percolated through to the deeply recessed cave passages. There is some slight solution as these drops hit the cave floor, but this is quickly followed by deposition and a cup-shaped stalagmite form. The stalagmites in Aven Armand are stated by Enjalbert to have been formed during the glacial period. Snowfall, highly charged with $CaCO_3$, percolated through to the roof of the Aven, and fell into the interior cavity where the very large stalagmites have been formed [495].

There is considerable variation in stalagmite shapes from the regional point of view too. Stalagmites are on the whole not well developed in north-west Europe and there are relatively few fine specimens. Some of the finest are to be seen in caves with at present rather warmer summers than our own: for example, in the caves of the Causses and Mediterranean France, in northern Tasmania, in south-east Australia (the Jenolan Caves), and in the northern Transvaal (in the Wolkberg Cave).

Stalagmites in the Postojna Cave have also been studied by Gams, where many of these are over 8 m high. Nearly all of the rainwater which percolates into the cave deposits $CaCO_3$ in some form; the hardness of the depositing water is from 178–195 ppm, while water that is aggressive may have a hardness of from about 89–125 ppm. Water which percolates through the overlying subsoil varies in hardness both according to the season and to whether the subsoil is wooded; under woods in late autumn, for instance, the water hardness may be as much as 267 ppm. Percolation of water into the Postojna Cave is both great and rapid, and calcareous formations which are caused by large amounts of percolating water are therefore characteristic of the cave – in particular stumpy stalagmites. This is in contrast to British caves, where percolation is relatively slow, and where straw stalactites and helictites (see below) are more common. Over the 150 years that the Postojna cave has been open to visitors the stalagmites have in places darkened in colour, probably in part due to the increase in CO_2 in the cave atmosphere; some re-solution is also evident. Eight stalagmites have been analysed and have been found to contain 99.1–100 per cent $CaCO_3$ (up to 0.23 per cent SiO_2); it has also been found that in one year about 0.2–2.0 kg of calcite was deposited at any one locality [275].

In the Murrindal and Buchan Caves in Australia, the limestones contain an appreciable quantity of dolomite. Stalagmites from these caves were analysed by Dr J. A. Talent and the results were as follows:

	Stalactite(A)	Stalactite(B)	Limestone
$CaCO_3$	97%	96.4%	77.4%
$MgCO_3$	1.8%	1.9%	15.4%
Dolomite	–	–	33.7%
Calcite	–	–	59.1%

This is an instance of the selective deposition of $CaCO_3$ [183].

In humid tropical areas, stalagmites are also important; they form organ-pipe-like masses aggregated into thick deposits. The immense quantities of stalagmite occurring in tropical caves suggests that they are not only formed by the loss of CO_2 from solution but also by the evaporation of water [276]. Because of the intense evaporation, stalagmites in tropical areas often appear rather dead and lifeless compared with the shining crystal growths which occur in cooler climates; this may be due to the drying out of the stalagmite during dry periods.

We know very little about the causes of variations in stalagmites, but some study has been made of the variations in their shapes. In the Aven Orgnac in the Ardèche in southern France, Gèze briefly discusses two different types – one 'en piles d'assiettes' and the other 'à grandes feuilles' [120]. In the leaf-like variety the stalagmite is made up of a vertical trunk; attached to this are leaf-like appendages made up of calcite deposits up to 3 m long and branching upwards forming a hollow between the leaf and the trunk. Frequently water accumulates in this hollow, but the main growth points of this type of stalagmite are on the tips of the 'leaves' farthest away from the main trunk. Gèze believes that the water reaches the exterior of the 'leaf' by capillarity, where the calcite crystals form. Another common form of stalagmite is the cauliflower (or choufleur) type. This gives rise to columns over 10 m high in both the Postojna Cave and the Carlsbad Caverns, Photo 38, p. 182. The plate-like forms appear to vary in size according to the height from which the water drop falls; thinner and smaller 'plates' form when the roof is very high as in Aven Armand.

The growth of stalactites and stalagmites thus depends upon a great variety of conditions. Historical records of measurements of stalactite and stalagmite growth are therefore of importance. It is certainly not possible to extrapolate from present-day observations on the rate of formation of these features or to assume that the present rate is the one at which they have always formed. On the other hand, stalactite and stalagmite growths do reflect changes in climatic conditions or changes in the rate of water seepage and flow in caves. At present

stalactites and stalagmites are growing relatively rapidly in British caves. This is confirmed by D. C. Ford in the Mendips [265]. Moreover, measurements of the Jockey Cap stalagmite in Clapham Cave, Yorkshire, showed that it increased in height and width by 7·66 mm per year from 1839 to 1873 [8], and that it has increased both in height by 2 cm and in width by over 20 cm since 1873 (measured by the author in 1965).

Stalactitic growth on concrete or mortar cemented structures exposed to the atmosphere outside caves is much more rapid than that in caves, and gives an erroneous picture of the rate of growth of cave stalactites and stalagmites. Since the dating of the growth of stalactites and stalagmites is not possible by a study of the 'rings', other attempts have been made to date them, some using radio-carbon methods. These depend on the fact that C^{14} produced in the atmosphere has a relatively short life and that it also finds its way into stalactites. Radio-carbon evidence suggests that very little dissolving of radio-carbon-free limestone takes place after the water leaves the soil zone [298].

Kunsky has described stalagmites from the Zbrasovke Cave near Hranice in Czechoslovakia (Moravia) which have resulted from the deposition from thermal mineralised waters. They are relatively small, and frequently have a small hole or pit at the top; they may be up to 2 m long [299]. In caves where water drops on to a muddy floor and there are frequent incursions of muddy waters into the cave, mud stalagmites may form. These were first described by Malott and Schrock in 1933 [304] and have been described from other caves since that time. Warwick discusses some of their occurrences in Chapter 6 of *British Caving* [27].

When the supply of supersaturated water is cut off from stalagmites, crystal growth ceases and they lose their shine and lustre. Water is also lost from the crystals which become dull and earthy in appearance. Moreover, the introduction of more aggressive water into a cave, caused for instance by increased vegetational growth or increased rainfall, may cause the stalactite and stalagmite deposits to be redissolved. Re-solution of cave deposits is relatively common. In the caves of the dolomitic limestones in the Transvaal, South Africa, for instance, many of the deposits show the effects of re-solution. In the Echo Caves and the Sterkfontein Caves, the colour and shapes of the stalactites have been completely altered by re-solution, and this phenomenon is characteristic of almost all explored caves of the Transvaal region [509].

Cave pearls. These are also formed by dripping water; they are oolitic-type formations ranging from small grains of pin head size to sometimes several inches in diameter. The smaller ones tend to be spherical, but the larger ones are less regular. Cave pearls generally have a nucleus which may be a grain of sand or the fragment of a stalactite, and surrounding this nucleus concentrated layers are deposited as in an oyster pearl. They are formed in nests or clusters below dripping water. Constant agitation and rotation seem to be necessary for the formation of large cave pearls. They can be found actively forming today, as in the Carlsbad Caverns and in Stoke Lane Slocker, and fossil cave pearls also occur, as in the caves at Makapan in the Transvaal.

(B) FLOWSTONE AND RIMSTONE DEPOSITS

These are flowing or running water forms. Water flowing down the walls of caves or over the floor gives rise to flowstone, in which the crystals are orientated perpendicular to the surface of deposition. The surface is usually smooth. The calcite is deposited where the water runs over a ledge or a projection, for this is where CO_2 is lost and deposition takes place. Flowstone is often found between lake-like extensions of water in caves; it also occurs near cave mouths where there is opportunity for the loss both of CO_2 and of water by evaporation. Flowstone is quite common in British caves; it is more common in some southern and Welsh caves than in Yorkshire caves; Gough's Cave in the Cheddar Gorge has some excellent flowstone deposits. Flowstone is particularly abundant in tropical caves owing to the greater evaporation; caves described in northern Australia and in Malaya and Borneo are good examples [276].

Flowstone formed in caves is normally crystalline and hard and when it occurs in substantial deposits is known as travertine. It is frequently layered or bedded, the inclination of the bedding depending upon the place in which the deposits accumulate. If it has been formed by the deposition from water flowing down the cave walls, the flowstone is laid down in originally inclined or vertical layers; where it is deposited from water flowing over the cave floor or from cave pools, the flowstone is laid down in horizontal layers, resembling a normal water-laid rock; flowstone of both types occurs in the Makapan Caves in the Transvaal. As we have already seen, $CaCO_3$ deposits which form from surface waters tend to be soft and non-crystalline, forming tufa (p. 108).

Flowstone deposits are normally smooth, and relatively evenly laid down, but they may be deposited unevenly, and rims or dams formed. Such barriers seem to occur where water flows over irregularities in the rock floor and where eddies and riffles provoke evaporation and loss of CO_2.

Frequently each barrier or dam encloses a small pool. These are known as rimstone pools in England and America and as gours in France. Flowstone and rimstone are related deposits, but so far the critical conditions for the formation of rimstone barriers rather than smooth flowstone have not been established. The formation of rims or dams a few centimetres high is easy to explain, but the formation of dams several metres high enclosing deep pools has so far no explanation.

In the formation of rimstone deposits, accretion of $CaCO_3$ takes place at the upper edge of the dam where the deepest discharge over the rim occurs. Generally, the wall of the dam leans upstream. Once deposition begins in a stream it seems to continue and, as Bretz remarks, 'Rimstone growth is a kind of epidemic in some cave streams'. . . . 'Little dam after little dam grows across the channel to make a stream staircase of what was at first a stream ramp. These step-like dams may succeed each other in close array. They must grow simultaneously, for each one as it grows, raises the water level above riffling depth at the site of the next dam upstream' [219]. Gèze says that they form barriers often tens of metres long and are often very undulating; they also vary in height from a few centimetres to several metres. Famous rimstones and gours occur in Padirac Cave in the Causse of Quercy, where they are in a gently sloping stream section and where the active stream is completely dammed up; 36 enclosed basins occur in 1 km of passage, one basin being 7 m deep, and the barriers vary from a few centimetres to several metres high. Martel concluded that such rimstone barriers formed only in caves where there is no torrential water action even in winter, and he regarded calm flow as essential. Warwick in a comprehensive article on rimstone pools says that when they

are formed in steeply sloping caves the dams are higher and the ratio of area of surface to the depth is much smaller; when the slope of the floor is more gentle, the pools are generally wide in proportion to their depth [305]. In the Škocjanske Cave the barriers are superimposed one below the other in a descending sequence several metres high. They are also well developed in caves in the Mole Creek area of northern Tasmania, where in Croesus Cave rimstone pools occur in nearly a mile of very gently graded passage.

In north-west Australia Jennings and the writer have discussed rimstone dams in old Napier Downs Cave, Fig. 86. 'The floor of the main cave and of the side passage inside the flowstone riser is practically horizontal and is very largely composed of flowstone. A succession of rimstone dams enclosed basins, the rims being highest at the front of the cave and the basins deepest at the rear so that the profile is a slightly descending one inwards. In May–June 1959, the forward basins were dry, some small pools survived near the right angle bend whilst further in there were larger pools. . . . The surface of the inner pools carried calcite crystals and there were accumulations of such flakes on the floor of the pools in parts. . . . The margins of the pools were crenulate through the outgrowth of flowstone at water level forming projecting ledges. No dripping was observed at the time of exploration and the decorations were somewhat dull of surface. . . . A sample of water from pools B (see Fig. 86) had 120 mg/l of calcium carbonate and 7 mg/l of magnesium carbonate in solution with a temperature of 71°F and a pH of 8·2 at the time of collection. . . . this was a saturated solution with respect to calcium carbonate as might be expected from the presence of the calcite flakes on the surface. . . . In this part of the cave the dry and wet bulb

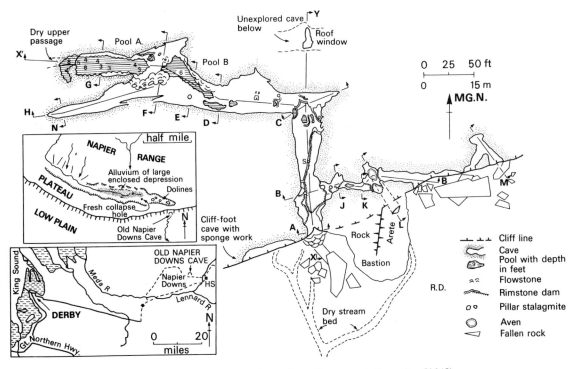

Fig. 86 Old Napier Downs Cave (from Jennings & Sweeting [301])

temperatures were 76°F and 60°F respectively, giving a relative humidity of 38 per cent. Such a low humidity would permit substantial evaporation from dripping and flowing films of water, even with little air circulation, and it is therefore possible that this process is contributing to the precipitation of calcite in this cave' [301].

Micro-gours or terraced flowstones consist of small dams about 1 cm wide and of similar height. They form quite frequently on stalagmite flows, giving rise to a series of small terraces separated by tiny pools. These can be seen in some British caves, as in Clapham Cave [253].

However, in general, rimstone barriers are not very frequent in British caves. As with other depositional features they appear to be better developed in climates with warmer summers and where evaporation and loss of CO_2 is more important. So far it

is not possible to make a generalisation about the occurrence of rimstone deposits, or to use them as an index of palaeoclimates.

(C) SEEPAGE DEPOSITS

Helictite (or anthodite) deposits formed by seeping water include some of the most beautiful and delicate ornamentation to be seen on cave walls. Among the best known are helictites, or eccentrics. These are irregular stalactites, usually small and twisting; they may be several centimetres long, but are normally about a centimetre in diameter. They were once called anemolites, because it was believed that their eccentricity was due to wind currents in the cave causing freaks of deposition. It is now known that they are due to seeping water under hydrostatic pressure issuing from a minute opening (often less than one-hundredth of an inch in diameter). The seepage is so slow that a drop of water does not form and therefore gravity does not affect the shape. 'Most of the deposition takes place right round the hole in the tip of the helictite. Each new layer is shaped like a tiny cone and each cone consists of a single crystal. Their crystal form causes the cones to be slightly distorted, so that a new one never fits perfectly on the one it covers. Hence each cone is systematically tilted, and the whole helictite assumes a twisted or spiral shape' [306]. Helictites may be thread-like (when they are only about 1 mm thick) or, more commonly, worm-like when they are thicker. Prinz published in Belgium as early as 1908 some very relevant studies on helictites [307]. Helictites are quite common in British caves, Ogof Ffynnon Ddu in South Wales having some particularly fine examples. Some of the best described have been from the cave of Moulis in the Ariège by Gèze [308]. In Moulis the helictites are formed of both calcite and aragonite. In all caves they tend to occur in the inner recesses, where percolation by water is slowest. Moore has ascribed the formation of aragonite helictites in California to the high mean annual temperature (over 16°C). But in Moulis, Gèze considers the deposition of aragonite as due simply to a current of air; he says 'le courant d'air provoquera son évaporation [of a drop of water] rapide au point que le seuil de saturation en calcite pourra être dépassé avant le début du dépôt du calcaire en solution. Lorsque celui-ci se produira, ce sera donc sous la forme d'aragonite ou d'un mélange des deux variétés' [308].

Many of the helictites in G.B. Cave in the Mendips are of aragonite. Moore considers that there are caves where aragonite helictites are still forming; these are chiefly in caves in the south of the U.S.A. In the north he claims that caves occur where the past deposits were of aragonite but they are now forming calcite, while further north still there are caves where there have never been any aragonite deposits and they are all of calcite. From this evidence, Moore suggests that there has been some form of climatic change. In his view a mean annual temperature ranging from 56–63°F may be the lowest temperature in which aragonite will be deposited in caves [309]. However, recent work suggests that deposition of aragonite is not controlled by temperature in this way.

Cave shields or palettes. The other major form caused by seeping water is cave shields or palettes. These are semicircular sheets of calcite and average about an inch in thickness and may be several feet in diameter. They are always attached by a straight edge to the cave ceiling or wall or floor and project outwards at different angles into the cave chamber. They are associated with joints or fractures in the rock wall. Each shield consists of two parallel plates separated by a fracture which is an extension of the joint in the rock wall. It is suggested that water seeps under pressure along this fracture and moves out to the rim of the shield. Here deposition occurs and the shield slowly increases in diameter. Because the water is under hydrostatic pressure, the shields can grow at any angle with the walls or floor. Some of the best known occur in Lehmanns Cave, Nevada, and they have also been reported from New St Michael's Cave, Gibraltar. Very fine examples, over 2 m in diameter occur in the Grotte de Pech-Merle, Cabrerets, in the Causses de Quercy. It is possible that shields may form only in relatively dry conditions, but so far there is not enough known about them. They have not yet been described in Britain.

Cave coral (or globulite or cave popcorn). Knobbly clusters of calcite occur on the walls of many caves. These are generally smooth individual knobs about 1 to 2 cm in diameter and stand out about 2–3 cm from the cave wall. In cross-section they show a concentric banded structure. They are usually known as cave coral and are believed to be caused by water seeping along cracks. Similar forms were described by Boyd Dawkins in a cave in Pembrokeshire [8]. In the Carlsbad Cavern in New Mexico, the walls of the Big Room and many of the stalagmites are covered with cave coral which resembles a fungus-like growth. Thrailkill has called these deposits cave popcorn [273]. Cave popcorn consists of branching fronds of nodular segments which have no tendency to orientate vertically. They have been deposited sub-aerially on the cave walls and on stalagmites by water which (1) seeps out from behind, (2) flows down from above, (3) splashes on to the walls and (4) is introduced by surface tension. Stalactites and flowstone are formed when the water is supersaturated with respect to the carbonate being deposited or where flow is rapid. But where the flow is slight, as under seepage conditions, cave coral or popcorn is formed, because the deposition is controlled principally by the escape of CO_2. The velocity of this escape is inversely related to the thickness of the water layer, hence because of their greater surface area irregular surfaces will be the site of greater deposition than smooth surfaces. Also the ends of the nodules will have a thinner film than the bases and re-entrants and therefore grow more rapidly. If ventilation is poor, a pCO_2 gradient may develop in the air near the wall and longer fronds will grow preferentially. Where evaporation is important in inducing super-saturation, a pH_2O gradient may exist with similar effect [273]. This explanation of cave coral is different from that given by Bretz in 1956, who regarded it as of subaqueous origin, and that its occurrence was indicative of the former existence of a lake or pool in the cave.

Cave flowers are also formed by seeping water. In these the material is not deposited at the free end as in helictites but at the attached end. They sprout from the walls of dry caves in a curving way like helictites; the main difference between cave flowers and helictites being that the flowers have no central canal. They are normally about 4–5 cm long, but in Mammoth Cave they are over 30 cm long. Cave flowers are usually made of gypsum, and are particularly important in Mammoth Cave and in the Grotte de la Cigalère, Ariège. They also occur in Ogof Ffynnon Ddu in South Wales.

(D) DEPOSITS FORMED IN OR UNDER WATER

Calcite rafts. As mentioned already, in very dry caves rafts of calcite crystals occur on the surface of standing pools of cave water. Such calcite rafts are usually not more than one-hundredth of an inch thick, are supported by surface tension, and are usually easily disturbed. Other *cave crystals* form under water and grow from the walls and floor. It is usually the dog-toothed calcite that predominates under these circumstances. When the pools drain away these crystals remain as witness of the former occupation of the cave by standing water. Calcite crystals have been reported from two caves in Missouri by Bretz [219]. Some of the best calcite crystals formed in pools in Britain are to be found in Reed's Cavern near Buckfastleigh in South Devon. Some very fine examples of crystals formed under water are to be found in the Black Hills area of the United States where as many as four cycles of inundation can be recognised. These have been described in

39 Moon milk (*Photo by D. C. Ford*)

detail by Deal, whose work on the Jewel Cave also discusses the nature and origin of 'boxwork', a composite deposit to be found on the cave walls and believed to result from inundation by highly mineralised waters [274].

Other deposits formed under water give rise to shelf-like features. These are flat on top conforming to the surface water level of the pool and are rounded in outline. They extend down to the bottom of the pool as inverted cones. They have been called by Bretz *lily pads*. Most of the lily pads grow under water and the top part grows at the air–water interface [219].

From this account it will be seen that the best-known cave deposits are those formed by dripping or running water. Micro-organisms can also contribute to cave deposits, particularly in the formation of *rock milk* or *moon milk,* Photo 39. Rock milk occurs as either a white paste or as a soft crumbly white powder or chalky substance. It is found on cave floors, on walls, and in fissures. It is believed that it has been formed by micro-organisms bringing about the disintegration of the limestone wall rock [310, 295]. In some caves rock milk consists entirely of microscopic grains of calcite, the calcite being in a micro-

crystalline form. In other caves the rock milk is made up of hydromagnesite, ($Mg_4(OH)_2(CO_3)_3,3H_2O$), magnesite, dolomite and other minerals containing magnesium and calcite. In the Windsor Great Cave in Jamaica, there are very fine deposits of rock milk.

It is possible that freezing of the limestone by ice may also produce a milky rock fluid because of the expelling of CO_2 as the rock is frozen; this takes place in the Eisriesenwelt and may have happened in Ogof Ffynnon Ddu.

The importance of the study of cave deposits cannot be over-estimated, and it is one which is so far in its infancy. Cave studies suggest that the phases of solution and deposition occur simultaneously throughout any one cave or in caves in the same neighbourhood. This has been shown by Ford to occur in the Mendips where successive phases of corrosion and deposition can be shown to have taken place. Thus in G.B. Cave in the Mendips, Ford has said, 'Rhythm is characteristic; successive phases of erosion, clastic deposition, stalagmite formation, then erosion again, etc., are found in each sequence. Erosion (re-excavation) and calcite re-solution mark the modern phase in every example and there is always a penultimate stalagmite phase' [233]. Such variations reflect variations in the volume of water entering the cave, the mean annual temperature of the cave air, and other changes in the external and internal cave environment. In G.B., 'the rhythmic changes of phase were evidently caused by changes in the external environment. This appears to be true in other caves also. The pattern of general frequent environmental change suggests the climatic variations of the Pleistocene' [233]. Similarly Gèze gives a scheme of successive phases of cutting and of deposition and alluviation for a cave in the Gironde [120].

On a world scale, cave deposits are already being used to identify the warm and cold, and wet and dry phases of the Pleistocene. 'On pourra admettre que les couches d'éléments grossiers correspondent à des périodes de froid, les couches à éléments fins provenant de périodes intermédiaires plus chaudes' [57]. In the Mediterranean and the Middle East, stalagmite and flowstone deposits are identified with wet conditions. The occurrence of cave breccia is believed by some to be associated with a wet and frosty climate in the Mediterranean, possibly to be correlated with the cold phases of northern Europe [266]. King has claimed that the sequence of deposits in the Makapan Caves of the Transvaal has a common history of internal deposition [311]. This has been partly borne out by the work of Brain on the cave breccias of Makapan and Sterkfontein [293]. Lund in 1885 established a sequence in Brazil remarkably like that observed in Africa by King [311]. Though correlations of cave deposits over wide areas are not yet possible, it is evident that the objective study of caves and cave deposits is of great value. This will be even more so as stalactites and stalagmites and other deposits are dated by radio-carbon and C14 techniques [540, p. 247].

10 Poljes

1. INTRODUCTION

The word polje in most of the Slav languages means a field, and is used to signify an area which can be cultivated, whether or not the area is in limestone; it refers only to a land surface which is more or less flat, alluviated and arable, and of a certain agricultural value, and not to the whole ensemble of the depression. This flat area can be formed by any process and be on any rock type. Thus we have the polje of Kossovo, for instance, in eastern Serbia, famous for its tragic battle, or the polje of Zagreb. A polje usually takes its name from a town or village which is situated in it, as Nikšić polje or Cetinje polje, or from a river which is associated with it as, for instance, the Gacka polje or the Lika polje. Because in the barren karst area any flat land is cultivable and valuable, the term polje is used by peasants in karst regions for areas of relatively flat land occurring in the depressions which have become internationally known as poljes; they are regarded as typical of the Dinaric karst. Roglič makes the point that, until the introduction of maize cultivation into the Balkans in the seventeenth century, the poljes in the Karst were not very important in the economy of the region, but with the change from a pastoral economy to one based on maize the flat cultivable land of the poljes became of much greater significance. Because poljes are not confined to karst areas, though it is true that poljes are characteristic of the karst region, Roglič says that we should not talk of *karst poljes,* but rather of *poljes in the karst.* Furthermore, poljes have been described as *open* if they are drained externally by a river, such as the polje of Bihač drained by the river Una, and the polje of Knin drained by the Krka; and as *closed* poljes if they are drained subterraneously. This is more characteristic of the karst, and is typified by the poljes of Gacka, Lika, Duvno and Imotski. Grund in 1903 proposed to reserve the term karstic polje to these closed basins. But Roglič maintains there is no essential difference between the open and closed poljes; in both cases, according to him, they are due to the presence of impermeable rock and to processes of erosion that are not karstic – a very 'purist' point of view. In this chapter the chief characteristics of poljes as landforms will be discussed. Aspects of their hydrology will be dealt with in Chapter 13.

In 1894, Cvijič described poljes in the following words: 'Eine Polje ist eine grosse, flache, breitsohlige Karstwanne, deren Gehänge sich scharf gegenüber der Sohle absetzen und welche eine ausgeprägte, mit Schichtreihen parallele Hängserstreckung zeigt. Die Poljen kommen nur in dislocierten Karstgebieten vor' [3]. Later in 1901 in his *Morphologische und glaziale Studien aus Bosnien, der Hercegovina und Montenegro. Die Karstpoljen* [312], and in his 1918 article [272], he supposed a cyclic evolution of karst landforms, from the doline through the uvala to the polje. This both perpetuated an incorrect idea of the origin of the polje and also added to the confusion of the terminology. Also, until recently, geomorphologists referred to landforms as poljes when they were not poljes in the Classical Karst sense. Thus 'polje' is yet another example of the misuse of a local word in geographical literature. Moreover, as will be seen in this chapter, the processes and the historical events which have given rise to the poljes in the Dinaric karst have taken place in few other regions of the world, so that in many ways the poljes in the Karst are unique.

2. THE POLJES OF THE CLASSICAL AND DINARIC KARST

Poljes in the Karst are large depressions, with conspicuously flat floors. They are almost always aligned in the direction of the major tectonic lines – in the Dinaric karst this is NW.–SE. They vary in size from about 2 km long to over 60 km, and most of them are oval, or longer in one direction than the other. Their floors are always planed or alluviated; the sides usually rise steeply at about 30° and the transverse profile of a polje is of a wide open U-shape. Poljes may be drained by one river, as in the Popovo polje, drained by the Trebinjčica river; or more often they are divided into several hydrological basins, as in the Livno polje which has four or five separate drainage basins (Fig. 87). Some poljes are karst depressions developed in valley systems, as in the polje of Popovo. In the Classical and Dinaric karst many poljes are flooded during the autumn and winter, and are dry during the summer; the duration and time of the flooding depends upon the climatic conditions, particularly rainfall, but also upon the degree of openness of the fissures in the limestones. According to the type of or absence of inundation, the poljes are classified as dry poljes if they are never inundated, periodically inundated or overflow poljes if they are flooded during part of the year or intermittently, and as waterlogged poljes (jezersko polje) if they are permanently inundated (from Slovenian Academy of Sciences). In general, the higher poljes are driest and the lowest are most frequently inundated. Poljes act as

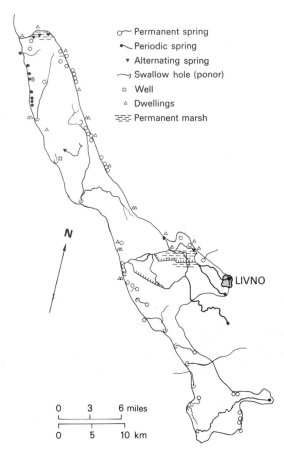

Fig. 87 Livno polje (from O. Lehmann [214])

reservoirs or catchments for non-calcareous debris in limestone areas, and normally their floors are formed of alluvium; in the high Dinaric and Apennine areas, glacial and periglacial material is also important. The floors of many poljes are formed of planed limestones, as in the higher part of Popovo polje and in the Bihač polje. Isolated residuals of limestone which rise above the floor are known as hums (hume), after the village of Hum in the Popovo polje.

The inundation of the poljes is brought about partly by the flooding of surface rivers which enter the poljes, but also of great importance are the springs which feed the poljes from underground water sources, like the Obod spring in Fatničke polje. The poljes are again drained underground through swallow holes or ponors. Where the floor is of limestone, water drains through fissures in the rock and into horizontal caves; where it is covered with drift or alluvium, alluvial dolines form by collapse of alluvium into the fissures and these absorb the overflow water from the polje. Alluvial ponors absorb water less rapidly than ponors in the bare rock; thus inundations of poljes usually last longest in those parts covered with alluvium. As would be expected, the alluvial dolines constantly change; new ones form, old ones collapse and are covered up by the alluvium. In Slovenia different names are given to the various types of ponor [207]. It will be seen that the Slovenes advise *ponor* to be used where water disappears into a horizontal cave; *poziralnik* for small caverns in the rocky bottom of an intermittent watercourse; and *ponikva* for places where water disappears down through a superficial layer of silt. During periods of inundation, ponors become springs and are therefore estavelles (see p. 214). The polje of Cerknica has twelve estavelles, one of the most important of which is Vranja jama, at the foot of the mountain of Javorniki. Normally the rate of inflow into poljes is greater than the rate of outflow. Thus, for instance, in Lasko polje during the period of inundation the water arrives at $119 \text{ m}^3/\text{sec}$, but it flows out at $17 \text{ m}^3/\text{sec}$; in the Cerknica basin the inflow is 155 m^3, but the outflow is at 85 m^3; in the Planinsko polje 79 m^3 inflow and outflow at 21 m^3. In the Popovo polje in 1893 water came in at the rate of 350 million m^3/sec, but the outflow was only at 72 m^3 [313].

In general, in the Dinaric poljes, flooding first appears on the upper north-east edge,

where the large springs occur, and the ponors are on the south-western side. The times of flooding depend upon the regime of the rainfall, the poljes in Slovenia flooding for a greater length of time and earlier in the year than those in Hercegovina and in Bosnia to the south. Thus Planinsko and Cerknica flood often at the beginning of September, as in 1965, and may extend to July and occasionally in wet years may continue throughout the year. In Cerknica, two to three days of heavy rain will fill the lake basin, about 11 km^2 in area, and water may remain for 14–21 days. Cerknica may flood for two to three years continuously, and in 1714 it remained flooded for seven years [131]. In the south of Bosnia and in Hercegovina rainfall is more abundant in December and snow is important in the high mountains in February and March. Here the flooding of the poljes starts in December and continues until May. In Hercegovina and in Dalmatia, nearer the coast, flooding starts in early October and continues until about June, as in Popovo polje. In general, as one goes towards the Adriatic coast, the flooding is due chiefly to the rains of the autumn and their duration is not only due to the lower altitude. In the extreme south of Jugoslavia, Lake Skardar is permanently inundated partly as a result of the post-glacial rise in sea-level; it is at 20 ft above sea level, 146 square miles in area and 20–25 ft deep. In the southern Balkans, particularly in southern Greece, the flooding of the poljes begins in October and attains its maximum in November and December; the inundation persists during January and February and then diminishes. Occasionally if the spring rainfall is heavy the poljes in Greece may be inundated during March and April.

Both the Cerknica and Planinsko poljes are part of the Ljubljana Basin and lie along a NW.–SE. faulted belt in which Triassic

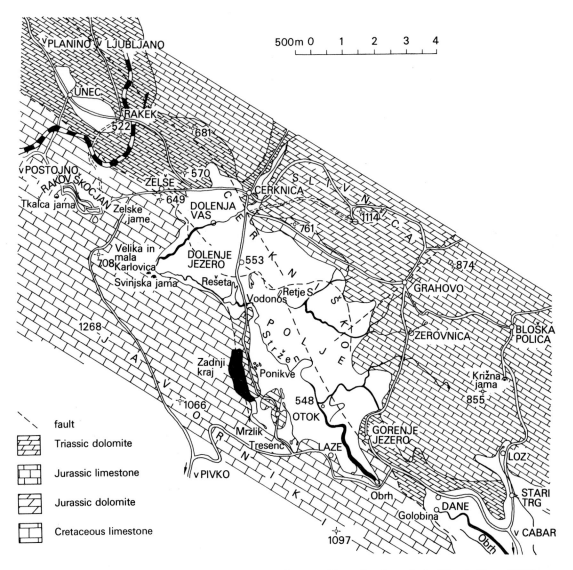

Fig. 88 Cerkniško polje (from *Guide-book of the Congress Excursion through the Dinaric Karst* [193])

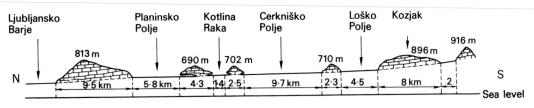

Fig. 89 Underground drainage connections of the Cerkniško polje (from Naše Jame [5])

40(*a*) Flooded polje in September, Planina, Classical Karst

and Jurassic dolomites outcrop. Cerknica (Cerkniško) polje is the largest in the Ljubljana Basin and the largest in Slovenia; it is 8 km long by about 4 km wide, Figs. 88 and 89. The floor of the polje is at 450 m and the surrounding mountains in the karst limestones rise to 1,114 m high in Slivniča and to 1,268 m in Javorniki. The affluent side of the polje is in the east and south-east where the water comes out from below Javorniki and from the Loško polje to the south-east; surface waters also come from the dolomites to the south. The ponors lie in the middle and along the western edge; the floor is lowest in the south-west. The central river bed in the polje is the Stržen, which gets most of its waters from the Obrh spring at the south-eastern end of the polje. The waters from this spring have more calcium than those which rise on the south-west edge. The bed of the Stržen is visible only in drought. The river Stržen loses its water as the ponors become more numerous towards the western edge of the polje, one of the most important groups of ponors being the *vodonos*, which are alluvial dolines. Melik is of the opinion that the deposits of the floor of the Cerknica polje show that during the Quaternary period it was a permanent lake [314]. The waters of the middle part of the polje flow off directly to the Ljubljanica springs, while the waters sinking in the west of the polje go first to Planinsko polje and thence to the Ljubljanica [131].

The largest polje in Jugoslavia is the Livno (Livanjsko) which is 70 km from NW. to SE., 10 km wide, and 405 km^2 in area; it is 750 m above the sea and about 400 m above the river Cetina to which it is connected by underground fissures. The surrounding rocks are limestones and dolomites of Jurassic and Cretaceous age, but the base of the polje is made up of Neogene and Quaternary sediments – marlstones, clays, sands and lignites. It is periodically flooded up to 5 m deep, especially in the southern part known as Busko Blato, floods being caused by waters discharged from springs along the north-western and eastern edges. The ponors are along the south-western edge, and at Caič there is a group through which drains about 400 million m^3 of water each year. There are at least three separate basins in the Livansjko polje which flood quite independently of each other with different regimes. Each basin is emptied by ponors at the foot of the western wall, the fragments of the three rivers draining obliquely across the polje [214].

40(*b*) Corrosion surface, Plan de Canjuers. A polje in Provence, Southern France

East of the Livanjsko polje is Duvno, which has been well studied by Roglič. This also follows the Dinaric trend and is at 900 m above sea level. It lies between outcrops of Cretaceous limestones, but the base is covered with river gravels, conglomerates and peat [315, 316].

Popovo is a large polje situated 25 km from the Adriatic, near Dubrovnik. It extends for over 40 km from NW. to SE. but is quite narrow, being only 1·5 km wide for much of its length. Its floor slopes gently to the north-west at about 800–700 m. Unlike many of the karst poljes, Popovo is not drained transversely but is followed throughout its length by the river Trebinjčica. Popovo polje is sinuous in form, rather like a normal valley, and has a blind ending. In the south-east, the floor consists of remarkably planed limestone beds, known as lug or sumn; this part of the polje floor is diversified by the abruptly rising hills of limestones, known as hums (hume). But in the north-west, at its narrow end, the polje is subject to flooding by the Trebinjčica river and thick deposits of alluvium have been built up. The Trebinjčica river rises in large springs and its size is such that the polje is flooded in winter to a depth of 40 m and a lake of 900 million m³ is

formed [316]. The flooding of the floor is very rapid and the valley may be covered with flood water in one or two days. The draining of the polje is also rapid; for instance in June 1951 when a lake of some km² at the north-west end disappeared in a few hours into the large alluvial ponors.

In the Nikšić, Dugo and others of the high poljes of Hercegovina and Montenegro, it has been shown that there are morainic deposits and fluvio-glacial gravels derived from the high Dinaric mountains. Moraines have been mapped and in the Nikšić polje 'one can observe the passage between the fluvio-glacial deposits and the fluvial alluvium' [316]. The moraines are disposed around the polje and the polje itself is covered with gravel and fine alluvium. In the investigations for the construction of a hydro-electric plant, nineteen profiles were made of the Nikšić polje. These have shown that the limestone floor varies at $4\frac{1}{2}$ m to 80 m below the present surface and that the polje is covered with clays, sands, gravels and conglomerates of various sizes and origins.

Although poljes are covered by some form of alluvial or drift material, many of them are remarkable for their extremely planed and horizontal limestone surfaces, which are difficult to explain by river erosion, Photo 40. This is particularly true of the eastern end of the Popovo polje and of the Korana area near Bihac [317]. Work in the Imotski polje and other poljes has shown that there too local platforms occur on the limestones. Widespread surfaces of erosion are also evident in other parts of Jugoslavia such as in the platforms along the Dalmatian coast, near Šibenik for example. In a detailed study of Kupreš polje and of the Una and Korana areas, Roglič has demonstrated that it is possible for these surfaces to have been formed by corrosion or solution planation. He envisages corrosion of the limestones by water in contact with the rock but covered with thin overlying sands or clays or waterlogged alluvium; such corrosion surfaces develop particularly along the contact between limestones and non-limestone rocks, especially those which yield alluvium and sand. Roglič calls this rim corrosion and his scheme of the evolution of corrosion plains is given in Fig. 90. He is also of the opinion that such corrosion levels could only be formed under a rather warm climate with a great deal of alluvium and also vegetation to give rise to abundant CO_2 in the waters; this view is corroborated by the work of Terzaghi [318], Kayser [319] and O. Lehmann [214], particularly in tropical karst areas. This idea of a warm climate origin has recently been challenged by Gams; he is of the opinion that solution of limestone in polje basins could well have taken place beneath the glacial sands and muds laid down in the Quaternary period [275]. Poljes on this hypothesis are still enlarging today (i.e. they are not fossil landforms) and are areas of accelerated corrosion [280]. Gams also notes that four areas of the karst particularly important for polje development (the Notranjsko, eastern Bosnia, Hercegovina and western Montenegro) are areas of high annual precipitation at the present time. All these points illustrate one of the fundamental characteristics of poljes, that of horizontal and surface dissolution; this should be compared with the vertical dissolution which characterises dolines.

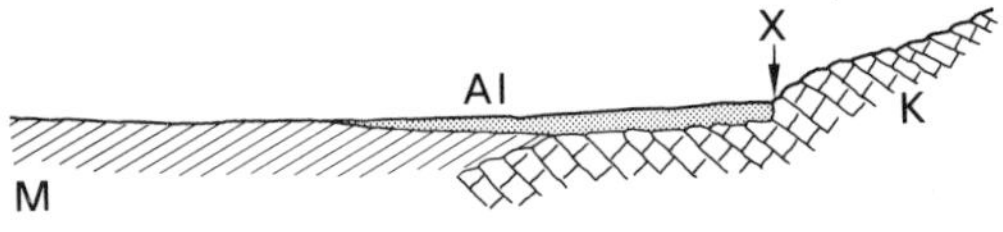

Recent tectonic movements have enlarged and redefined the karst poljes. Ancient lake terraces occur in most of them and were regarded by Cvijič as being once connected with vast lakes which formed in them during the Tertiary and the Quaternary. He attempted to correlate over wide areas some of the terrace and lake features. However, it has been shown that these terraces and lakes cannot be correlated from one polje to another. By a detailed study of the Duvno polje and its terrace levels, Roglič has shown that selective erosion followed the uplift of the polje area, and that the lacustrine deposits have been warped and dislocated. Recent deepening of the polje basin by tectonic movement can be proved [315]. In Imotski polje moreover the effects of recent earthquakes (1942 and 1946) are shown to have affected the water movements and underground cavities of the area; thus the movements are still continuing. Roglič says of the Duvno polje: 'Das Becken des Duvanjsko Polje ist also tektonisch angelegt und durch Erosions-

K = limestone
M = impermeable rocks
A1 = alluvial cover
X = the line of greatest corrosion

Fig. 90 Scheme of the evolution of corrosion plains (from Roglič 1951 [317])

prozesse in der Nachseephase, und zwar im mittleren und oberen Pliocän und im unteren Quartar ausgebildet worden' (loc. cit., p. 26). Workers in the Dinaric karst have shown since Cvijič that polje basins have not been formed as he believed by the progressive unification of several independent basins; instead the poljes themselves are being decomposed into numerous separate basins and uvalas [316].

The mode of formation is thus believed to be as follows. Polje depressions tend to originate by differential erosion where the limestones are in contact with less permeable rocks, such as the dolomites (which disintegrate into sands and are softer than the karst limestones) and the Neogene flysch. The deposition of this material is guided by the tectonic lines and by relatively young tectonic movements, which can be proved by the deformation of late Tertiary deposits. As a result of the differential erosion, a series of basins and valleys was formed into which the debris collected. If, as is supposed, the late Tertiary climate was warmer and wetter than it is now, it is imagined that shallow lakes and standing water collected around these deposits of impermeable material. Water lying on the alluviated limestones, together with abundant vegetation, is believed to be one of the main reasons for the formation of karst corrosion plains. The mountain fronts were pushed back by corrosion pedimentation and the polje basins widened. The drainage of the polje lakes depended upon the development of ponors; where the material coming into the basins was coarse and gravelly the ponors would not have the capacity to absorb so much water as where the material coming into the polje was of fine alluvium. Furthermore, water coming off impermeable rocks and dolomites (as those waters of the dolomites of Orjen to Popovo polje) would under certain circumstances block up the ponors. During the climatic changes of the Pleistocene period, erosion both of the limestones and the non-limestone rocks would be great and vast quantities of fluvial, fluvio-glacial and occasionally glacial material were poured into these basins. It is these deposits, particularly where they are of river gravels and alluvium, that form the flat floors of the poljes today. This material clogs the ponors so much that the poljes are subject to periodic inundations the moment the waters rise after heavy rain or snow. The deposition was particularly intense in the high mountain poljes, like Dugo and Nikšić. In the lower poljes the Quaternary deposition was finer and the ponors able to absorb more of the material; accumulation was less and mainly local, as in Kupreš and Glamoč poljes, or as in the Duvno polje, where there is only a sheet of alluvium. The intensity of the accumulation was therefore proportional to the mass of the material and inversely proportional to the capacity of the ponors. At the present time, however, the amount of material coming into the polje basins is less than that being carried away through the ponors. The capacity of the ponors is increasing and the intensity of the flooding has therefore diminished. As early as 1894 von Groller had calculated that 18,480 m³ of material disappeared through the ponors of Popovo polje per year [320]; the alluvium of that polje is slowly disappearing and the bare rock floor, planed by the former corrosion, is reappearing. The most recent processes are therefore reactivating the drainage channels.

The biggest and most important ponors develop in the massive and purest limestones; the most typical poljes develop in association with these ponors, because they can absorb the coarser debris, leaving the finer alluvial material to form the perfectly flat floors, as for example in Livanjskjo polje. Because the poljes are largely the result of fluvial and slope-washing processes, processes not truly karstic, yet found in an area surrounded by deep karst, Roglič prefers to refer to them not as karst poljes, but as 'strange features in the karst' [218].

Certain conclusions therefore emerge from this consideration of the poljes of the Classical and Dinaric Karsts. (1) They are always (perhaps 99 per cent) guided by tectonic lines, faults or folds of the area. (2) They are always associated with the appearance of impermeable strata in the limestone area. In the Karst this strata may be impermeable Eocene flysch, as it is at Livno and in many of the poljes in lower Hercegovina and Bosnia. In the higher Dinaric poljes the impermeable strata may be glacial or fluvio-glacial drift; in the lower Dinaric poljes the gravels, sand and varved clays are also of Quaternary age, some deposited in temporary lakes. (3) Poljes always lie in basins formed by differential erosion. (4) The water accumulates in the poljes today because the ponors and underground conduits are not sufficiently developed for all the water coming into them to be absorbed. (5) The terraces, both erosional and depositional, of every polje must be studied in their local context, and no overall correlation can be attempted. (6) Poljes are not related to an overall hydrographical scheme. (7) They do not form part of the series of landforms, doline-uvala–polje. (8) Poljes can only be explained in terms of climatic morphology and climatic change. They therefore result from the inter-relationships of several different conditions. In the Dinaric Karst these conditions of lithology, structure, recent tectonic movements and sequence of climatic phases have all combined to produce the poljes of that area. In other areas of similar environment, as in Provence, the combination of circumstances has produced poljes, but not as distinctive

as those of the Dinaric Karst. For a discussion of the poljes of the Karst compared with those of Provence see Nicod [517].

3. POLJES IN AREAS OUTSIDE THE KARST

Poljes occur in the limestone areas of other parts of the Mediterranean region, and in the years since 1945 there have been many studies on poljes in the Apennines of Italy, in Asia Minor, in Provence and other areas [321, 322]. In Provence, a good study has been made by Nicod of the polje of Cuges, near Marseilles [323]. This polje is 5 km by 2 km and has all the characteristics of those in the Classical Karst. It has been formed by differential erosion along a fault, is drained by ponors, is covered by up to 40 m of detrital material (remblaiement détritique), much of which is of Wurmian age, and it has been in the past subject to inundations, before it was drained in 1472–5. Part of another Provence example, the Canjuers polje, is shown in Photo 40(b). Poljes in Italy are known as *Piani*, and those in the Abruzzi have been studied by Demangeot [518].

In S.E. Europe, the Parnassos–Ghiona area of Greece on the north side of the Gulf of Corinth was examined by the writer for F.A.O. in connection with a development programme. This is an area of massive limestones similar to the Dinaric karst, alternating with flysch deposits. The geological structure of the Parnassos region consists of a series of southerly dipping nappes or chevauchements, rather different from the isoclinal and overfolded limestones of the Dinaric area. As a result, the strongly oriented poljes characteristic of the Dinaric karst do not form, and they are not elongated but circular in shape, as at Tritaia,

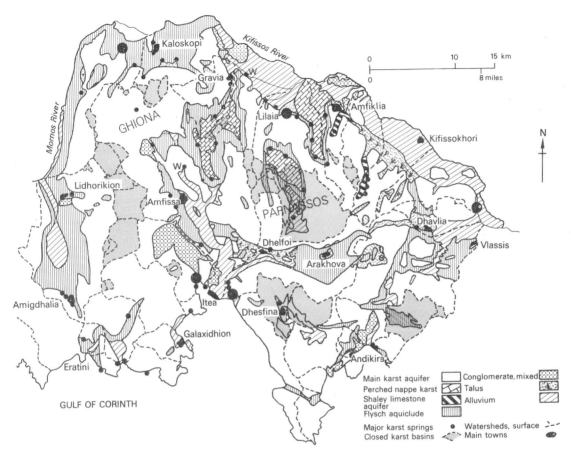

Fig. 91 Map of the Parnassos-Ghiona area showing closed basins (from Burdon [351])

near Delphi. On the high slopes of Parnassos, which rises to over 2,400 m, signs of activity by frost and streams in the Pleistocene are extremely abundant. The floors of the closed polje depressions also show corrosion surfaces on the limestones. A map of the closed basins of the Parnassos–Ghiona area is given in Fig. 91. The Tritaia polje is at 381 m above sea level and the Kalivia polje nearby is at about 1,100 m, yet Kalivia, because of differences in the hydrology, suffers the greater inundations [132].

As a result of his work in the Apennines, Lehmann has been able to differentiate the following types of polje:

(1) Poljes on high erosion surfaces (Hochflächenpoljen), poljes formed without a preceding valley system.

(2) Valley poljes (Talpoljen), poljes formed in a former valley system.

(3) Semi-poljes. These are differentiated from types (1) and (2) because they are developed 'on one side in impermeable rocks not liable to karstification'. The main type of semi-polje is the randpolje (marginal polje), which he describes as occurring 'on the boundary between . . . non-karstified and karstified rock complexes' [322].

Marginal poljes occurring in the Gordon limestones (Ordovician) in the Mole Creek area of northern Tasmania were examined by Jennings and the writer in 1959. This is an area of folded limestones and quartzites. After heavy rains, drainage from the quartzites spreads on to the limestones and the capacity of the swallow holes to absorb the water is reached. A series of temporary lakes is formed on the limestones at their junction with the quartzites and solution planation becomes important. Large amounts of alluvium have collected in these lake basins, which are separated from each other by ridges of quartzites [324]. In the Mole Creek region, the conditions of the Classical Karst have to some extent been reversed, the non-limestone rocks forming the ridges between the limestone basins.

In 1956, H. Louis maintained that the formation of poljes was a peculiarity of the periodically dry sub-tropics but not the humid tropics [321]. In the humid tropics, karst plains form more usually in relation to the level of the surface streams. At the Symposium of the I.G.U. Karst Commission held in 1954 there was much discussion of the term *vorfluter*, a term introduced to define the local levels of flooding in a karst region [325], where drainage is impeded. The vorfluter act as a locus for water accumulation and for alluvium in a karst area. At this level, corrosion of the limestone could take place, conditions in warmer areas being particularly favoured by luxuriant vegetational growth and in glacial areas by large quantities of melt-waters and snow melt enriched with CO_2.

In Jamaica, for instance, it has been shown that, wherever the geological conditions permit water to remain on the limestones, surface lateral planation and corrosion of the limestones takes place [134]. This is assisted by the deposition of alluvium in the neighbourhood of springs, deposition from them being more important in tropical than in temperate areas. Along the northern side of the Cockpit Country in Jamaica, for instance, highly permeable crystalline White Limestones are replaced along a well-defined fault belt by the less permeable chalky Montpellier Beds. Water, which has been absorbed into the crystalline White Limestones, is thrown out as springs at the junction of these limestones with the Montpellier Beds, which are much less highly fissured. Alluvium and flood water have accumulated here. Lateral planation and corrosion have taken place in the Montpellier Beds and elongated closed depressions have been formed along its zone of contact with the crystalline White Limestones. These depressions are a type of polje [134] (Fig. 92). The best examples occur south of Falmouth at Duanvale and Sherwood Content. The Duanvale polje is about 4 miles (6·4 km) long from east to west and about 1 mile (1·6 km) wide. It is an enclosed basin with a fairly flat and alluviated floor, with a line of springs along its faulted southern edge. Under conditions of heavy rainfall it is flooded by these strong springs, such as that at Fontabelle. The largest of these poljes (or interior valleys as they are known in Jamaica) is the Queen of Spain's valley, south-west of Falmouth, which is about 6 miles by 8 miles (9·7 by 12·9 km) in extent; the Queen of Spain's valley is, however, partially drained by the Martha Brae river and is therefore an open polje [326].

Further evidence of polje formation and lateral corrosion in the tropics is also seen at Lluidas Vale in central Jamaica. This has some characteristics of a randpolje, being close to the borders of the White Limestones with the non-permeable rocks of the Central Inlier of Jamaica. It is also fault-guided, being situated at the foot of an eastward-dipping fault block. During the dry season, water entering Lluidas Vale is

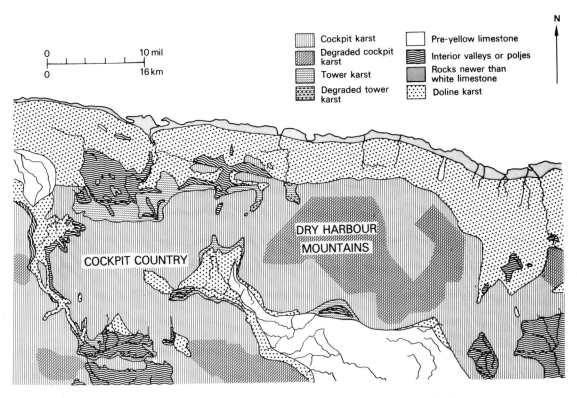

Fig. 92 Karst landforms, north central Jamaica (from Sweeting [134])

absorbed by ponors in the centre and on the east side; but in the rainy season the ponors cannot absorb all the incoming drainage and the lower part of it is flooded. The effects of these flood waters upon the limestones can be seen where the alluvial cover is thin, and where it overspills into the surrounding limestone cockpits. Standing water and small lakes occur frequently at the contact of the limestone with the alluvium – the alluvial cover sloping downwards into the limestone. Solution of the rock keeps the limestone hills steep and *foot caves* are common at the foot of these (Fusshöhle) [17]. Solution of the limestone at this zone of contact is particularly rapid.

Similar observations have been seen by Lehmann in Cuba who says: 'Jusqu'ici [in Cuba], le polje tropical semble confirmer la théorie de la corrosion appliquée au polje dinarique. Mais il manque au karst dinarique les versants verticaux et le phénomène des corniches caussées par la corrosion creusant des excavations au pied des versants' [17].

These observations seem to confirm that corrosion of limestones is particularly important in tropical conditions and that the flood level, or vorfluter, is highly significant. This does not, however, prove that the corrosion plains of the Dinaric karst are necessarily of tropical origin. The reason for this statement is that closed polje basins are much more rare, particularly in humid tropics, than might be expected, as already indicated by Louis; extensive areas of alluviated limestone occur but they tend to be drained by through-flowing rivers [321]. Such alluviated plains occur particularly along the contact of the limestones with

41 Malham Tarn area, N.W. Yorkshire; accelerated corrosion along the zone of contact of the Carboniferous Limestone with Silurian slates

other rock types; they have been called *karstrandebenen* (literally, karst border or margin plains), and were first described by Kayser [327]. Large quantities of alluvial material are poured out by karst springs on to the limestone surface and under this solution of the rock takes place. Moreover, the presence of thick alluvium also enables surface rivers to maintain their courses and closed basins are formed less frequently. Thus in humid tropical areas open poljes and karst margin plains occur more often than the closed poljes of the Mediterranean region. Such karst corrosion plains are a further example of the extension of these processes along the margins of a karst area and of accelerated corrosion [275]. Examples of karst border plains occur in the Sibun river area near Belize in British Honduras, in many parts of south-east Asia, and in Australia in the Fitzroy area at the contact of the Devonian Limestones with the Pre-Cambrian [31].

In north-west Europe the difference between the high and low water-levels in limestone areas is much less than in the Mediterranean regions; the swallow holes and caves are often adjusted to the volume of water coming into them, and the underground fissures can usually take all the water flow. However, local impeding of karst drainage does take place. Littondale, a valley in west Yorkshire, for instance, is floored by the Carboniferous Limestone.

Throughout most of the year in this valley swallow holes can absorb all the water reaching them, but after spells of heavy rain the amount of water reaching the valley is greater than can be absorbed and lakes are formed. Water rises under pressure through the swallow holes and alluvium is deposited on the limestone valley floor. The extent to which solution takes place under such alluvium is not known, but the valley is widened and solution is probably considerable. In the same district at Malham Tarn is one of the few depressions in Britain formed by differential erosion or accelerated corrosion along the zone of contact of the Carboniferous Limestone and a non-limestone rock, Photo 41. Drainage at Malham Tarn is impeded on the Silurian slates exposed along the North Craven Fault, at their contact with the limestones. Glacial erosion and deposition have modified the depression [126]. Both Littondale and the Malham Tarn areas have some aspects of their formation in common with poljes in the Classical and Dinaric karsts.

Such impeded drainage is also common in western Ireland, where intermittent flooding is frequent. After heavy rains more water reaches the limestone surface than can be absorbed underground and intermittent lakes are formed. One of the biggest of these occurs in the Carran depression which was described by the

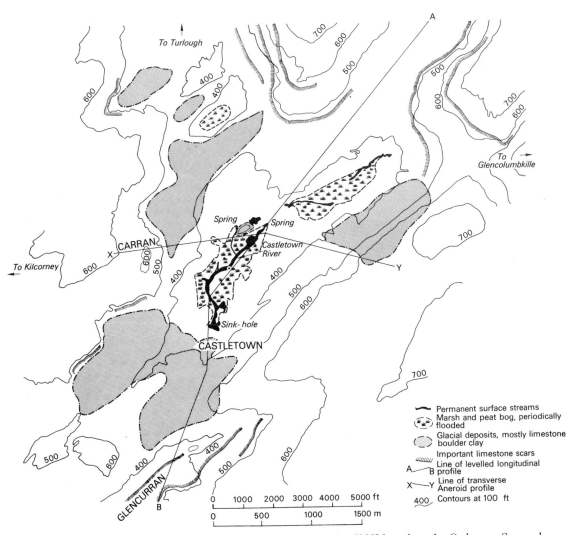

Fig. 93 Physical map of the Carran depression (from Sweeting [328] based on the Ordnance Survey by permission of the Minister for Finance, Eire)

Some very fine lake karren are frequently associated with these fluctuating lakes (see Williams [533])

writer in 1953 and a map of which is shown in Fig. 93 [328]. The Carran depression is about 2 miles long by 1 mile wide (3·2 by 1·6 km), and is related to the structure of the Carboniferous Limestones in its alignment from NE. to SW. It has been much modified by both glacial erosion and deposition but it is essentially of preglacial age. All interglacial sediments seem to have

been removed by glacial scour, but postglacial sediments have been found. Williams records peat, shell marl and grey clay up to 12 ft (4 m) deep [95]. Flooding in the Carran depression is caused by the rapid run-off from the surrounding glacial deposits and by the smallness of the underground channels. Such intermittent lakes are known in Ireland as *turloughs* (from Tuar Loch meaning a dry lake) [329] and may extend over many acres. The level of water in them may fluctuate considerably. In the Clare–Galway lowland, there are many such turloughs which are in general relatively shallow with gently sloping sides; some solution planation can be shown to take place along the lake shores [95]. Lough Bunny for instance is over 40 ft (13 m) deep in parts. Deposition of calcium carbonate in the form of tufa is also important along its shores [330]. Observations of other turloughs show that, while they flood after heavy rain from water brought in by surface streams developed on impermeable beds or glacial drift, yet their main fluctuations in the lake levels are due to a rising or lowering of a water level. This can be demonstrated by the falling of the lake water-levels in the summer, when the turloughs 'more or less dry up. It seems that the seasonal fall in water-table level generally more than accommodates flood water brought in by a few storms' (loc. cit., p. 264). Williams gives Newtown turlough near Gort as an example. Similar features can be seen in the low-lying Karst of Florida, especially in the Everglades area. Some aspects of the geomorphology of Florida are discussed by W. A. White [519].

Finally, in arid or semi-arid regions, where run-off is rapid and evaporation intense, planation of the limestone surface is largely brought about by pedimentation; there is little opportunity for alluviation to occur and for water to be retained on the limestone. Planed and pedimented rock surfaces are abundant, as in the Fitzroy River district of north-west Australia, particularly where limestones are in contact with other rocks. But poljes caused by the impeding of drainage in the limestones are relatively rare. Jennings and the writer described a possible example of a polje in the Limestone Ranges of the Fitzroy

district [31]. This is a closed depression, about one mile long and only 200 yards wide (1·6 km by 0·2 km); the central parts have a loam-covered, fairly flat floor and dry stream beds show that drainage, both from the east and west, comes into the depression during the wet season and disappears into ponors in the floor. Although described as a polje, it is in many ways more reminiscent of an uvala; but it may owe some of its features to processes of erosion which are now no longer operative.

The impeding of drainage in karst regions and the flooding which gives rise to solution planation occurs as a result of two main causes. First, by rapid surface drainage and the inadequacy of the swallow holes. Secondly, by the rising of the level of water in the underground channels and water issuing from fissures in the rock. Because many workers in the karst consider that there is no water-table in limestones, they attribute polje formation to the first cause [218]. However, it is quite clear that fluctuations in the water-level also cause flooding in limestones and solution planation. It is probable that flooding in many karst areas can be attributed to both mechanisms, to increased surface run-off and to rising underground water-levels; moreover polje formation in one area may be due to the first process and in another area to the second process. In the last few years studies in the hydrological phenomena of poljes have been undertaken and these will be discussed in the chapter on karst hydrology. The idea of poljes being associated with water-level fluctuations dates from Cvijič's paper in 1918 when he tried to relate them to three district hydrological zones; an upper zone in which poljes were never inundated; an intermediate zone, in which they were intermittently flooded; and a lower zone in which they were always inundated. It has been shown as a result of modern studies on the hydrology that each polje and indeed each part of a polje has its own hydrological regime, so that any exact correlation with water-levels is not tenable. Roglič moreover claims that areas in the karst which are flooded by water-level movements should not be classed as poljes at all.

Sensu stricto, poljes are plains of accumulation within depressions in karst regions, and introduce a foreign or non-karstic element into the karst. In the Classical and Dinaric karsts much of the accumulation was introduced during the Quaternary; in the sub-humid and humid tropics the accumulation is the result of alluviation during both the Quaternary and the modern periods. Strongly seasonal rainfall regimes in these areas assist the function of locally developed flood-levels or vorfluter; such local flooding gives rise to solution planation and rim corrosion, examples of accelerated corrosion particularly at the surface. Hence polje-type depressions develop horizontally instead of vertically as in doline development; this is a further reason for regarding poljes as basically non-karstic, since by definition karst drainage is vertical and underground.

The most significant classification of poljes is as follows:

(*a*) Poljes completely surrounded by limestones, impermeable beds (clays, moraines, alluvium, etc.) being on the polje floor.

(*b*) Border (or rand-) poljes at the contact of the limestones with impermeable rocks, and formed by differential corrosion.

The first type are frequently (though not always) closed poljes; the second quite often open poljes.

11 Karst Springs

SO FAR we have considered landforms largely related to the superficial aspects of karst, as seen in the explored caves in the shallow part of the karst. In discussing springs we begin to deal with the deeper aspects. As seen in the section on karst hydrology, one of the remarkable facts is the way in which water that disappears in many swallow holes and ponors does not come out at several resurgences but in a relatively small number of them. Thus for instance on Leck Fell on the Yorkshire–Lancashire border there are at least twenty inlet streams, but all the water going into the limestone in this area of 10 km² issues at one major spring head, Leck Beck Head, Fig. 94. The same can be repeated in every karst area. In Moravia, the Punkva river receives a number of watercourses 'flowing down into the limestones of the Moravian karst from the neighbouring non-carbonate areas. As soon as they reach the margin of the limestones they penetrate underground, join together and flow out on the surface on the opposite side of the limestone massif.' The total area drained by the rising of the Punkva river in this way includes 130 km² of non-calcareous rocks and 25 km² of the calcareous rocks, about 155 km² being drained by one major spring head [342].

Thus large springs or risings are characteristic of karst regions. Much could be written about the legends and lore that surround the conspicuous springs of karst regions. Frequently, as at Delphi in Greece, cult worship has grown up around them, partly perhaps because of the spectacular terrain. As with other types of karst landforms, local names have been given to the large springs; in the north of England they are known as *kelds*, in the Causse of Gramat as *fonts* or *doux*, and as *blue holes* in Jamaica (the name *Jamaica* means 'springs').

Karst springs are among the largest in the world. In Florida the average flow of some of each of seventeen of the largest karst springs is more than 100 ft³/sec – 1,000 gal/min. Silver Springs, the largest in Florida, has an average of 808 second ft per day (1 second ft = 646,000 gallons), which is an average daily discharge of approximately 500 million gallons. In Jamaica, Versey and Zans have recorded up to 800,000 gallons/day/ft. In Europe, two of the most famous springs occur in the karst area; one is the Timavo, which is the outlet for the river Reka in the Classical Karst and has a discharge into the Adriatic, near Trieste, of 2,300,000 m³ every twenty-four hours; the other is the Ombla river spring in the Dinaric karst near Dubrovnik, where the discharge varies from 4 to 140 m³/sec. The spring at Ombla is formed at the contact of Liassic limestones with Eocene flysch, along a fault trending NE.–SW. The immediate catchment area amounts to 450 km² but it receives water in part from a much bigger catchment area of approximately 2,100 km². The greater part of the Ombla water comes from the swallow holes on the Trebinjčica river, this being 40 km long and one of the biggest rivers to sink into limestones in the world. The river itself begins in a large spring, regarded by Petrovič and Prelevič as 'no doubt the biggest spring discharge known' [5], draining an area of 900 km². Its average temperature is 9·1°C (varying from 6·7°C to 11·0°C) [131].

The northern part of the Classical Karst

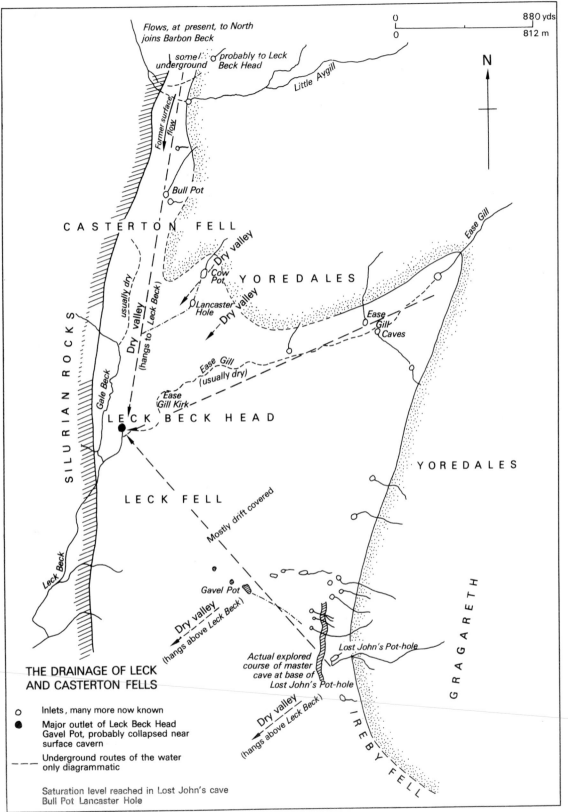

Fig. 94 The drainage of Leck and Casterton Fells (As a result of work by A. C. Waltham many more caves are known in this area [514])

is drained by the Ljubljanica Springs. These are situated at 291 m altitude, near to Vrhnika at the southern end of the Ljubljana Marsh (Ljubljansko Barje). There are two series of springs which rise from the foot of limestone walls at the end of two sack-like valleys. The highest water occurs in November, when the average flow is $52 \cdot 2 \, \text{m}^3/\text{sec}$. The average temperature is $10°C-11°C$. The temperatures of the springs vary, the springs in winter being warmer in the west and colder in the east, but in summer warmer in the east and cooler in the west.

There are two main types of karst spring: those where the water issues at the surface by means of free flow (Spaltenquellen) and those where water issues at the surface under forced or artesian flow (true Karst-quellen). The second type are often known as Vauclusian springs after the Fontaine de Vaucluse where the Sorgues river, 30 km west of Avignon, rises at the bottom of a

'vallée close'. The inclined tube-like cave from which this spring rises is over 100 m deep. The Fontaine is the biggest spring in France and has an average flow of $26 \, \text{m}^3/\text{sec}$, but has been known to be as low as $4 \, \text{m}^3/\text{sec}$ and as high as $150 \, \text{m}^3/\text{sec}$, a figure which is as high as the Seine at Paris at its mean level. A recent study of the variations of the Fontaine de Vaucluse has been made by Paloc [331].

Springs which emerge from the limestone under *free flow* are similar to normal springs as found in association with other rock types, though they are probably much larger in discharge than springs found in most other rocks, Photo 42. Frequently such springs emerge from caves which can be explored. A good example in this country is the rising of Clapham Beck at Ingleborough Cave, and in the Classical Karst, the Planina river cave. However, free-flowing springs are not always associated with penetrable caves, as for instance the rising of the Aire at Malham Cove, or the Greta river at God's Bridge in Chapel-le-Dale, Yorkshire.

Springs are often thrown out by perched water-tables in limestones caused by shale or less permeable bands; this is quite common in the Yorkshire area where ferruginous mudstone and shale bands give rise to well-defined perched spring lines; this is seen in the development of a well-marked shale band just below the *Crytina septosa* band both on Thieves Moss on the slopes of Ingleborough and also on the west side of Littondale, where a series of springs comes out along the west side of the valley in association with a well-developed shale horizon. In the limestones of the Burren in western Ireland shale bands are less common, but perched water-tables do occur and there are examples of perched karst springs such as the Seven Springs of Teeskagh, near Carran. The same type of phenomenon is to be seen in the Grands Causses of

France. The French call these risings 'sources d'affleurements'. As might be expected, these springs have a highly variable discharge and in some areas are truly intermittent, only flowing during wet seasons. The springs associated with perched shale bands in particular are frequently intermittent. Normal risings of this type are also often associated with fault lines or changes in the rock type. They arise from local underground reservoirs. In Jamaica an example is the spring at Deeside, on the south side of the Queen of Spain's Valley, which has a normal wet season flow of about 30 ft^3/sec, dropping to a very small yield in the dry season, Fig. 58.

Vauclusian springs occur where the underground water issues from the limestone or cover rock under hydrostatic pressure and *forced flow*. They arise from large underground reservoirs. The channel in the rock through which the water is being forced comes up from below and many Vauclusian spring channels are steeply inclined. Two varieties of Vauclusian spring can be discerned. The first occurs where the spring water issues from a tube cut into the rock, as at La Vaucluse; here the steeply inclined rock tube up which the water has been forced can be seen, particularly at low water. The openings of many of the artesian springs in Florida are tube-like; thus Bugg Spring at Okahumpka emerges from a nearly vertical walled opening which has a depth of 176 ft (54 m) [332].

The second type of Vauclusian spring, possibly the more usual occurrence, is where the water wells up through its rock tube or cavern but issues at the surface through alluvium or drift, although under pressure. In northern England, Turn Dub, through which issues the water from Alum Pothole, is of this type, and also the big spring in Lathkilldale in Derbyshire. The well known Löne spring at Urspring in the Swabian Jura is another good example; the Löne spring is one of the feeders of the Danube, is 4·20 m deep and is on the watershed between the Rhine and the Danube [333]. This kind of spring also occurs in areas where there is much alluvium and vegetation, as in tropical humid climates, and they are important in Florida and in the limestone regions of the Caribbean. In Jamaica, Zans distinguished between 'boiling springs' and 'blue holes'. Both are Vauclusian in character, but the boiling springs literally 'boil up' or are fountain-like, whereas blue holes are much quieter upwellings through deep pipes [326]. The discharge of boiling springs is quite variable, but they rarely dry up.* Blue holes on the other hand show much less variation in volume. In Jamaica, water rising in the blue holes is of a blue-green colour, possibly due to the presence of calcareous algae; two of the best known occur along the north coast of Jamaica – one the Dornoch River Head and the other near Brown's Town. Blue holes of this kind are among the most impressive karst phenomena in the world, Fig. 58. In temperate areas large karst springs are also of a blue colour, due to the clarity and depth of the issuing water. In Europe, such springs occur at Blautopfe, near Stuttgart and at the Source de St. Georges, near Montvalent in the Dordogne. The Source de St. George illustrates a common phenomenon associated with karst springs, that of issuing from two separate outlets, a few metres apart, as is also seen in the Ashwick Springs in the Mendips.

In the karst of Indiana, Malott and Powell describe artesian 'rise pits', where springs of considerable size and depth occur; thus the great Harrison Spring is

*Fontabelle spring near Windsor, Jamaica, has a maximum discharge of 100 ft^3/sec (see Zans [326]).

80 ft (25 m) wide, 110 ft (35 m) long and over 35 ft (10 m) deep [196, 334]. These are alluviated Vauclusian springs – springs that have been buried by accumulations of alluvial sediment in a previously deeper valley. A low rim or levée consisting of clays and silts surrounds the spring on all sides except the outlet. The minimum flow of Harrison Spring in 1960 was 27·5 ft^3/sec, measured when the water was clear. The rising of the Lost river, also in Indiana, occurs in a flat part of an alluviated valley; no bedrock is exposed either at the rise or in close proximity to it. The caverns, from which the water is issuing, lie 30–50 ft (10–15 m) below the top of the present valley fill. In Indiana outwash and deposits of Illinoian and Wisconsin glacial age have choked the former caves. Powell argues that the Harrison Spring 'may have originated suddenly as hydrostatic pressure forced trapped subterranean waters to ascend through the sediments that impounded the former cave spring'. It is also possible 'that the water welling up from the cavern prevented deposition within the area above the cave spring while alluvial or lacustrine deposits were filling the rest of the valley. Sediment settling within the mouth of the submerged cave spring was carried upward by the ascending water and was deposited at the margin of the opening where the current slackened, in somewhat the same way as a natural levée is formed. Natural levées are formed around some rise pits, especially those situated well within flood plains' [334]. Harrison spring is also an excellent example of a spring formed on the downstream side of a meander [334].

As we have seen, Vauclusian springs can vary in their discharge; like all karst springs they are normally characterised by very clear water, yet after heavy rain they can be muddy and turbid. In recent years karst springs of different types have been explored by cave divers: in England, at Wookey Hole in Somerset, where a normal spring is connected with an extensive series of underwater caverns; and in France, at the Fontaine de Vaucluse, where the Groupe de Recherche Sous-Marine, led by Cousteau, have explored the submerged pipe to over 100 m [120], Fig. 95(a).

In France and Germany karst morphologists distinguish between resurgences and exsurgences. A resurgence is literally a re-emergence to the outside air of a stream which began originally on the surface but was absorbed into the limestone through fissures, and is now resuming its surface course at the rising. The term resurgence was used in this sense by Martel in 1887; in German it is called *Wiederausfluss*. An exsurgence is a rising which largely or

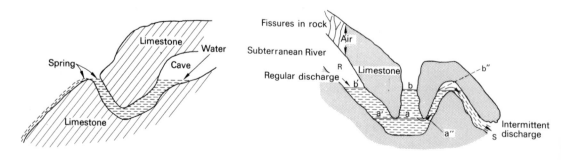

Fig. 95(a) Vauclusian spring (from Trombe [57])

Fig. 95(b) Intermittent spring (from Trombe [57])

almost entirely contains water which has come from that falling on to the limestone itself, and has been within the limestone mass all the time; the water is made up of percolation into the limestone, and also of internal condensation, and it is endogenous. The term was first used by Fournier, the great expert on the caves of the Jura; in German it is an *Austrittsstelle* (or even a *Karstquelle*), as this type of spring is strictly a karst water spring. In England, because our karst regions are so small, true exsurgences are rarer, and many of our springs are resurgences. The springs at the foot of Cow Close and Great Close Hill near to Malham Tarn in Yorkshire are percolation springs, as they are derived from water which has percolated and infiltrated into the limestones of High Mark to the north. Exsurgences usually have high calcium carbonate content as they have in the Cow Close springs (over 200 ppm). The importance of the distinction between resurgences and exsurgences has been made by Gèze and by Trombe, who both point out that an exsurgence is less likely to be contaminated with surface pollution than a resurgence, and thus an exsurgence is likely to give the better potable water supply [335].

A further type of spring which is peculiar to karst lands is the intermittent spring or ebbing and flowing well. Such springs are the result of the presence of irregular passages and siphons within the limestone behind the springs. The usual explanation is the one given in Trombe, see Fig. 95(*b*). The level of the waters in Fig. 95(*b*) oscillates from aa' to bb'; when the level is at bb', the siphon flows, and the spring at S flows with a discharge greater than it is fed by the underground river R. The level of the reservoir therefore falls to the level aa'. At the moment the siphon ceases, the flow of the spring at S ceases, until such time as the level of the reservoir has risen again to

bb'. This is a description of a truly intermittent or periodic spring where the flow runs dry in between the flows. The example given by Trombe is that of the Gouffre de Poudak, source of the Arize in the Hautes Pyrénées. The water at the base of this source rises periodically by about 4 m. This phenomenon was investigated by Rudaux and Jeannel in 1907, when they gave the following figures [57]:

Regular rising of the water	15 min
High level stage	3 min
Descent of water, 1 min rapid	40 min
3 min slow	
Total duration of each pulsation	58 min

The other nearby source of the Arize, which is in communication with the Gouffre de Poudak source, also has a periodicity, with a time of 29 min, exactly half that of the Poudak oscillation; there are two oscillations for one at Poudak. Trombe explains the phenomenon as due to the succession of two systems of siphons [57].

As is obvious, many types of combination of siphons and cavities are possible and there are records of other intermittent springs. One quoted in France is the Pontestorbes in the Ariège. In Britain the best known is the Ebbing and Flowing Well at Giggleswick near Settle in Yorkshire. This well is more truly a reciprocating spring, that is, one which does not dry up between the flows but runs continuously with irregular volumes of delivery. This difference between intermittent and reciprocating springs was in fact noticed by the elder Pliny (*Hist. Nat. Lib.* II, Cap. CIII). All observers of the well at Giggleswick have commented upon its irregular flow, and the article by G. Stevens in 1963 collects together some of the information about the well [336]. Thus John Swainson wrote in April 1796, 'Settled 11 inches in about four minutes; it flowed to the same height in two minutes. Next time it did not go so low by two inches. When at low ebb it begins to rise immediately. There seemed no interval between its low ebb and rising, nor betwixt its being full and beginning to ebb again' [337]. The writer once observed the rise and fall of the Giggleswick well with the following results:

> Rise to maximum height
> Fall by 4 in. in 3 min
> Rise by 3 in. in 2 min
> Fall by 3 in. in 5 min
>   (April 1947)

The well at Giggleswick now only ebbs and flows during periods of moderate rainfall. In dry weather it flows without interruption and after heavy rain it floods like others in the same area. The irregularity could therefore be due to the presence of air bubbles being associated with the ebb and flow. With the lapse of time the passages will be enlarged and an increasingly large flow will be needed to start up the ebb and flow action. Alternatively, the passage will be adjusted to take the flow at all times [338]. The Giggleswick well is certainly less active than it was in the past. The Tideswell in Derbyshire is named after an ebbing and flowing spring, which is now a normal spring. Thus in time all ebbing and flowing springs become normal karst springs.

Intermittent springs of a different kind are also associated with the karst. These are usually known as estavelles, and are, according to the season, swallow holes or springs. As we have seen, they are particularly connected with poljes (see Chapter 10). The term estavelle was first used in the Jura but is now used fairly widely for a hole which is at one time of the year a swallow hole and at another time a spring. Holes in alluvium, which are normally swallow holes, but which after much rain become artesian springs, occur in Littondale, Yorkshire. In the Dinaric karst, the Obod spring in the Fatnica Polje is often quoted [5]. As indicated earlier, such estavelles discharge water much more rapidly than they absorb it.

There are also submarine springs along the coasts of karst areas. Such springs are usually recognised by the presence of smoother, less 'choppy' water off-shore, and by water movements (often turbulent) different from those of ordinary sea waves. Submarine springs are numerous along the Adriatic coast, particularly along the steep coast of the Velebit mountains, where they are known as vrelo or vruljas; these are shown on the map by Baucič [5]. Also south of Dubrovnik they are particularly large, and are said to result from the continuous sagging of the Dalmatian coast, whereby old channels of karst water are now found below sea level. Along the coasts of southern Greece submarine springs are abundant; some of the best known are off the coast of the Peloponnese but there are many in the Gulf of Corinth near to Itea. Those off the island of Kephallonia are well known. In Florida, water of several artesian systems discharges on the sea bed many miles off-shore. A typical freshwater 'boil' exists about 3 miles (4·8 km) off-shore from Crescent Beach near St Augustine [332]. Stringfield asserts that discharge to the ocean occurs where the artesian head of the submarine outcrop is greater than the pressure of the sea water [339]. Springs are also well known along the coasts of Jamaica, of Yucatán and the coasts of the limestone areas in Thailand and Vietnam.

In western Ireland there are many off-shore risings associated with the drainage of the Clare-Galway plain; some of the best known are those near Kinvarra which are derived from the river Gort. There are three risings close to each other, situated between high and low tidemarks, about one-third mile (0·5 km) east of Kinvarra. 'At high tide these resurgences are not noticeable, but at low tide, large volumes of brackish water stream from beneath piles of large limestone boulders. . . . In the neighbourhood of Kinvarra water levels in the Caherglassaun Lough and in other depressions oscillate with the rise and fall of the tide . . . when the river Gort is in flood the effect of the tide is negligible but if the river is low the tidal range is several feet. At low tide the Caherglassaun Lough is completely drained, but it is a lake at high tide' [95].

At Argostoli on the island of Kephallonia certain of the submarine springs become under some circumstances changed into submerged swallow holes and the submarine channels absorb the sea water. These have been known from classical times. The swallow holes absorb the salt water and the current caused by the water being swallowed is so swift that it is used to drive two mills. During wet periods, the channels no longer absorb the sea water but emit fresh water. This phenomenon was discussed by O. Lehmann [214] in 1933 and more recently by Jenko [340] and by Zötl and Maurin [341]. It is caused by an unusual hydrostatic balance existing between water from the inland karst and the sea water, partly as a result of the tide. The water absorbed passes eastwards under the island of Kephallonia, and emerges in springs at the coast 15 km away [341] (Fig. 96).

The main relief forms associated with the karst springs on the surface are steep heads or sack-valleys (reculées or spring-head alcoves). Since large volumes of water are involved, big caverns may be found and frequently there is collapse of the limestone surrounding the spring head; thus spring-head sapping usually takes place. This is

seen at the Ombla spring, at Malham Cove in Yorkshire and at the head of the Loue and other valleys in the Jura. The extent of backward sapping is partly related to the volume of water and the type of limestone involved but also to the age of the spring, the oldest springs having had the longest time to cause the backward sapping. Hence the deeply recessed reculées of Arbois in the Jura are probably relatively old landforms. In the Garrigues of the Montpellier–Nîmes district, the source of the Lez and the source of the Lirou form a contrast of an 'old' and a 'young' spring head – the Lez being a much older spring head than the scarcely recessed Lirou. On this criterion, the reculée of Malham Cove is an old landform – but the present source of the Aire at its foot is much

Fig. 96 Argostoli (from Zötl & Maurin 1967 [341])

more recent; it is possible that glacial deposition has obstructed the spring head which gave rise to Malham Cove. Where a karst spring comes up through alluvium only a silt levée may mark its position.

Uplift of an area or the lowering of water-levels may cause springs to become drained and to dry up. Their former presence can usually be detected by the steep-walled recesses which we have just described. Examples of these can be seen in north-west Yorkshire. In areas of low relief and where the underground water is to some extent integrated into a connected water-table, former springs may appear as rounded ponds or 'sinks', which now no longer over-flow, the water not reaching to the lip of the tube-like passageways. This may be the explanation of the so-called 'sink holes' in Florida, which are steep-sided rounded features containing lakes about 100 ft (30 m) deep [332]. The same explanation may be given also for some of the cenotes of Yucatán which are rounded hollows with standing water in them. The conventional explanation of a simple collapse cavern origin for the cenotes does not seem entirely convincing, since their distribution and frequency are not entirely characteristic of collapse phenomena.

Karst springs are the subject of much work on variations in calcium and mag-nesium hardness and on variations in water temperature. In Britain systematic measure-ments of hardness and temperature have been carried out for some years in the Mendips, in South Wales and in north-west Yorkshire. As we have seen in Chapter 3, many of the springs show only small variations in calcium content, despite con-siderable fluctuations in discharge. As would be expected, springs associated with water which flows relatively rapidly through the limestones shows more variation than water which has been in longer and deeper

contact with the rock. The Fosse Spring in Littondale illustrates this well, water passing from inlet to outlet quickly and the varia-tions in calcium content being from about 60 ppm to over 180 ppm throughout the year. In the Clare–Galway lowland in western Ireland, work by Williams has shown that shallow water emerging from the Coole river cave has a hardness of 80 ppm, yet nearby wells yield a hardness of 300 ppm [95]. A study has been made of the chemical and physical properties of the waters in the Moravian karst [342]. There it has been found that the maximum con-centration of calcium carbonate was during rather dry months in both winter and in summer when, owing to the lowering of the underground karst water, the water move-ment is slow and when the planes of contact between water and limestone are numerous. Calcium content is less at maximum water stages when the water mass passes through the underground areas very rapidly.

Both in Moravia and in Jugoslavia work has been done on temperature variations in karst springs. These vary more in Jugo-slavia than they do in Britain; this is partly due to climatic factors, but also because of the large catchment areas in Jugoslavia. In Britain spring temperatures in the karst areas are almost constant – for example Rickford rising at about 10°C. But in the Trebinjčica springs the average yearly temperature is 9·1°C, the minimum is 6·7°C and the maximum is 11°C. The Ombla spring varies in temperature from 12°C to 16°C. In Moravia it was noticed that the difference of the water temperature regime between the swallow holes and the springs was quite striking. In the swallow holes, the water is influenced by the daily surface variations in temperature and there-fore the lowest temperature of the waters occurs in the coldest months, December, January and February, and the highest in

July and August. In the springs, the water temperature is influenced by the water discharge and the air temperature in the caverns. The springs have in general a steady well-balanced temperature curve. Extreme temperatures occur at the higher water stages when the excess surface waters are carried as it were on the bulk of the deeper water below. In these springs, the temperatures are lowest in March at the time of the spring thaw; the highest temperature occurs in the summer months with the highest discharge, in Moravia in June. The amplitude of temperature variation is also much less in the spring than in the swallow-hole water, for instance [342]:

Mean variation for the
  Sloupsky Brook
  swallow hole   25·4°C⎫ Swallow
Rudiče swallow hole   21·1°C⎭ holes
Tunnel spring   8·0°C⎫
Maly Vytok spring   6·0°C⎭ Springs

Kanaet has compared the temperatures of springs in limestones with those in dolomites and other rocks [343]. His results are interesting. He shows that the temperatures of springs from pure limestones are lower than those where the limestones are less pure. Temperatures are higher in clastic rocks and also in dolomites. Where the temperatures of volcanic rocks have been taken and where these rocks were fissured, then the temperatures were similar to those of fissured limestones. The following figures give the mean values of a number of observations from springs in different rock types but in similar topographical situations and in the same area of Jugoslavia:

Limestones	7·51°C
Dolomites	9·94°C
Eruptive rocks	10·74°C
Schists	10·61°C
Screes	9·22°C
Conglomerates	11·12°C

In Britain, in the Oxford region, Paterson's results indicate that the springs in the Berkshire Downs (chalk) have a temperature of 10°C, while those of the limestones in the Cotswold Hills vary from 11–12°C [520].

It can also be shown that karst springs have a less oscillating discharge than the surface watercourses from which the spring water is in part derived. For example, in Moravia the ratio of maximum to minimum discharge for the surface streams is approximately 1:137, whereas for the springs it is 1:42. More recently Nicod has made a study of the regime of various karst springs in Provence. By so doing he is able to deduce some of the characteristics of the reservoirs feeding the springs [521].

Karst spring water is therefore characterised first by well-balanced discharges due to the retardation ability of the karstified limestones; secondly, by water temperature compensation; thirdly, by the quite different curve of water temperatures depending upon the volume of the discharge and the cave water temperatures; and fourthly, the waters are transparent, colourless or only slightly light grey, when turbid, and contain little mud at low water stages.

12 Karst Water and Karst Water Tracing

1. KARST WATER

The chemical composition of a water is usually characteristic of the limestone and the limestone environment which it is draining. The difference between karst and non-karst waters is clearly shown in the work of Richardson on the waters of the Yoredales and Millstone Grit in north-west Yorkshire, compared with the waters of the Carboniferous Limestone in the same area [344]. Table XIV is from Richardson's work. Hence water draining from karst areas is identifiable, and moreover the calcium carbonate dissolved in the different limestone waters will usually show distinctive patterns. The dissolution of limestone leaves little insoluble residue; 'the real karst is almost without any erosional displacement of the material and karstic waters have almost no alluvium' [340]. Thus water issuing from karst springs has definite qualities from the point of view of temperature, calcium hardness, colour and transparency and other physical properties. This water is now known as *karst water*. As defined by Pitty, karst water 'describes surface or ground water with a chemical quality which reflects its activity in dissolving carbonates during its passage over or through a mass or outcrop of massive limestone' [79]. Karst water is clearly of two kinds. First, swallet water or *allogenic water* which has gathered partly on non-calcareous catchments and has entered the limestones through swallow holes, and, secondly, karst spring water or *autochthonous water*; this is derived from precipita-tion which has fallen only on the limestone surface, without any major additions from an allogenic source. Autochthonous water includes *percolation* water which is defined as 'that proportion of run-off following precipitation in a limestone area, which does not enter the channel of a surface stream, either by direct run-off or through flow' [345]. The terms allogenic and autochthonous water reflect the distinction already made between resurgences and exsurgences (p. 212). The term *groundwater* is also used to describe water which has long been in contact with the limestone – of whatever origin. Karst water derived from allogenic streams will contain more non-calcareous mineral matter and also more organic matter than water derived from karst spring water which has percolated through the limestone mass. Another type of water is sometimes recognised; this is *condensation* water. This is produced whenever the rock temperature within a cave is below the dew point of the atmosphere and when air drawn into the underground passages deposits some of its moisture. This is regarded by some people as an important contributor to karst water, particularly in tropical caves in the dry seasons [346]. However, both in Britain and in the Classical Karst, condensation water is probably not significant [340].

The study of karst water is still in its infancy, but is the subject of constantly growing interest. 'In contrast to the scale of interest in problems of solution, the study of the disposition and movement of the karst water underground has perhaps

TABLE XIV

CHARACTERISTICS OF CARBONIFEROUS LIMESTONE AND MILLSTONE GRIT WATERS

| | Carboniferous Limestone | | Millstone Grit |
	Fast-flowing	Slow-flowing	Fast- and slow-flowing
Total hardness	Low. Less than 70. Remains almost constant.	High. Increases with distance travelled; can be up to 250.	Very low, 0–10
Alkaline hardness	Low. Less than 70. Remains almost constant.	High. Increases with distance travelled; can be up to 250.	Very low, often zero
Non-alkaline hardness	Low. Remains almost constant.	Low. Remains almost constant.	Often equal to total hardness
Calcium	Low. Remains almost constant.	High. Increases with distance travelled; can be over 200.	Very low
Magnesium	Low. Remains almost constant.	Low. Remains almost constant.	Very low
Free carbon dioxide	0 to less than 10. More often 0.	Varies considerably, 0–100	Varies, can be considerable
Acidity to methyl orange	0	0	Can be considerable
pH	7·0–7·6, often constant.	7·4–8·5	3·0–7·0
Colour	Usually slightly coloured	Colourless	Often highly coloured

Hardness figures quoted in mg $CaCO_3$ per 1,000 ml
(From Richardson [344].)

received less attention amongst geomorphologists in recent years' [79]. Long-term observations reveal not only accidental variations in the composition of karst waters but also more systematic fluctuations. As already indicated, high calcium values are often associated with relatively low discharge rates and vice versa, but discharge values are only one of the variables to be considered. Various studies of the karst waters of the British Isles have been made, in particular of their fluctuations in calcium carbonate content, but less attention has been paid to variations in other qualities, such as temperature, colour, turbidity, etc. Some of the factors which affect the quality of karst waters will now be considered, Fig. 97(a).

Groom and V. Williams made a thorough study of the Mellte valley in South Wales where the Mellte river traverses the Carboniferous Limestone belt of the north out-crop of the South Wales Coalfield. The river Mellte flows as a surface stream for part of the year, and in 1960–1 it flowed for 213 days on the surface and for 152 days disappeared underground and was an underground stream. Analyses were made of the water of the Mellte during its surface and underground conditions, Fig. 97(b) [80]. Groundwater conditions occur generally during the summer when the water-table is quite low and also during long dry periods at other times of the year. Under these conditions the rate of solution of the limestone appears to be fairly constant in the underground stream and the amount of calcium carbonate in the water is generally constant, though the amount is higher in summer than in winter; values of 79 and 82 ppm in March had increased to 88 and 90 ppm in July. Under run-off conditions, however, there is a very wide variation of the calcium content of the

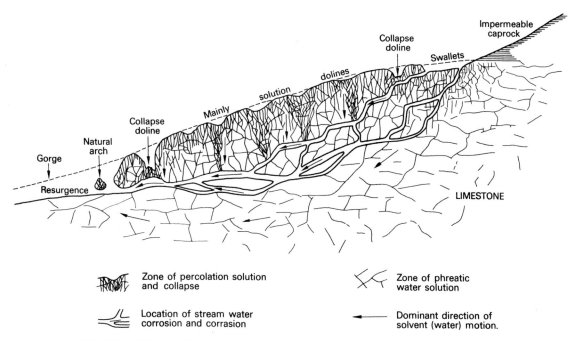

Fig. 97(a) The distribution of solution through a limestone mass (from Williams [533])

stream waters; this varied from as low as 14 ppm under conditions of severe flooding to about 50 ppm. Under flood conditions, the waters always contained less than 25 ppm; thus normal conditions gave a hardness of between 25 and 50 ppm.

Williams has investigated the condi-

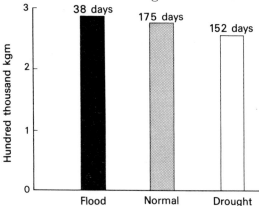

Fig. 97(b) Solution transport of CaCO₃ – R. Mellte 1960–1961 (from Groom & Williams [80])

tions of ground and flood water in western Ireland (Gort and Fergus basins). He also was able to show that the greater the rainfall the lower the total hardness concentration. The exact effect a storm of rain has on the flow of the Gort and Fergus rivers depends upon three main factors: first, the evapotranspiration rate; secondly, the state of the soil moisture; and thirdly, the proportion which run-off represents as a percentage of the total volume of the rivers. The most noticeable changes in hardness are produced under low-water conditions in winter. In that season evaporation rates are very low, the soil is saturated and a heavy storm results in a great increase in the rivers' volume. Hence a large reduction in the rivers' hardness follows [95]. Williams also examined other factors which might have influenced the water hardness but concluded that, although temperature was influential, in western Ireland the annual variation in temperature was not such that it was likely to be a big factor in determining river hardness. Flow of waters in western Ireland is at a maximum in winter (October to February) and at a minimum in summer; hardness is higher in summer than in winter, and in this area no factor other than flow is important enough to reverse this trend. Over the period 1962–3 the mean total hardness for the river Fergus was about 150 ppm in spring and summer and about 130 ppm for the rest of the year. Regular measurements were also taken on the Gort river. The increase in water hardness downstream of the river Gort is approximately 3·6 ppm per mile (or 2·3 ppm per km).

Water does not always show a general increase in hardness as more limestone is crossed; in the Fergus, downstream increase in hardness is attributed to the confluence of hard-water tributaries and not to direct solution. Over the 15 miles from the outlet of Lough Inchquin to Ennis the Fergus gains little in hardness and sometimes it is actually reduced. This is due to the dilution of its waters by run-off from tributaries which rise on non-calcareous rocks. Thus the river Claureen joins the Fergus near Ennis, and when the Claureen is in spate the drop in the water hardness of the Fergus is very marked indeed [95]. Because the Claureen's water is always aggressive, the place where it flows on to the limestone is one of accelerated corrosion, where the solution of the limestone is above the mean for the neighbourhood [280].

The Gort and the Fergus are also in parts supersaturated and much of the decrease in calcium hardness that takes place in these rivers is due to the deposition of tufa and other forms of calcium carbonate. Thus the total hardness decreases from over 260 ppm to under 180 ppm in one context. The deposition of tufa can be seen on the rocks

and shores of many of the lakes – Lough Bunny is an example – and many calcareous algae are found growing in them. The same phenomena can be seen in Malham Tarn in Yorkshire, where in the summer months the water coming into the Tarn has a hardness of about 160 ppm, but at the outlet of the Tarn the hardness has been reduced to 140–130 ppm. This again is due to the extraction of calcium carbonate from the water by calcareous plants and its subsequent deposition as tufa [76] (Fig. 12). Further comments on tufa deposition and hardness variations in waters in north-west Yorkshire are made by Pitty [522].

Groundwater in the Gort lowland reaches to even more than 300 ppm – its mean is about 340 ppm calcium carbonate. The average for samples of groundwater taken in summer was 352 ppm and for samples taken from the same points in winter 348 ppm, a result similar in kind to that given by Groom and V. Williams for the groundwater of the Mellte. In the Coole river cave measurements of percolation samples showed that water which had percolated through only 25 ft of the limestone forming the roof of the cave had a total hardness of about 300 ppm, confirming what has already been inferred, that the greater part of the solution of limestone takes place in the top 10 m of the rock [280]. Since the total hardness of the groundwater averages about 340 ppm, then about 88 per cent of the total corrosion has been accomplished by the infiltrating water in the top 10 m.*

We have already shown that the total amount of calcium carbonate dissolved in any water is largely dependent upon the CO_2 concentration (Chapter 3). The work of Pitty in the central and northern Pennines has suggested that the seasonal fluctuations in the solute concentration of

*Work by S. Letts in Devon indicates that cycles of corrosion and deposition take place.

many karst waters 'are in a close but lagged relation to the seasonal change of carbon dioxide output in the soil' [79]. He has also shown, for some waters at least, that there is a relationship between estimated length of flow-through time and their mean calcium carbonate content 'regardless of locality' [347]. The main factor controlling the fluctuations in calcium hardness in Poole's Cavern (Derbyshire) is the air temperature about three months prior to each sampling day [348]. Thus the time during which the karst waters are in intimate contact with the limestone and its fissures is a further factor affecting the quality of some karst waters.

Analyses of waters in Jamaica have received attention from Brown [210]. Samples were taken inside the Cave River Cave to see if there was any increase in the hardness downstream from the entrance point. The results are as follows [210]:

Points from entrance	Ca and Mg ppm	Ca ppm	Mg ppm
No. 1	124	102	22
2	130	100	30
3	128	100	28
4	132	102	30
5	130	104	26
6	130	102	28
Inlet 7	212	148	66
8	128	102	26

Apart from the inlet at point No. 7 there was no substantial difference in these water measurements; no distance is given for the measurements but, according to Brown, point No. 1 is three hours distant (caving time) from point No. 8. In the Cave river the hardness of the river at its inlet into the White Limestones is about half its hardness at the rising at Dornock Head (124 ppm against 224 ppm), which implies that, though much solution takes place at the surface, the underground solution is still

considerable; Dornock Head rising is some kilometres away from the cave.

In Jamaica, the deep Vauclusian springs such as Dornock Head have very constant discharges (about 250 ft^3/s) and only dropping 1–2 in. (2·5–5·0 cm) per week in the dry season. Dornock Head and Fontabelle, the springs which have the greatest catchments, also have the highest concentrations of calcium and magnesium, viz.:

Dornock Head	224 Ca and Mg	Ca 190	Mg 28
Fontabelle	210 Ca and Mg	Ca 192	Mg 20

Other swallow holes and risings were tested, and in them the water had travelled less distance, i.e. had passed through less limestone and tended to contain less calcium carbonate.

Different kinds of limestone also have different karst water patterns. In the limestone areas in the eastern Alps, the network of underground channels is much more extensive and larger in the pure limestone than in dolomites. Dolomites have a larger number of small springs dependent upon a larger number of fractures. Water in dolomites tends to be more slowly percolating and less well aerated, which may account for the point made below that dolomite waters always have a high degree of hardness. Zötl also found in the Dachstein area that the temperatures of the waters in dolomites are 1 °C higher than those in pure limestones, in addition to being as much as 100 ppm more in hardness [349].

In the Parnassos–Ghiona area of Greece, a study has been made of the groundwater of the area by Burdon and Dounas [350, 351]. As a result of this study, groundwaters characteristic of different aquifers could be distinguished; moreover the extent to which the underground waters have been contaminated by sea water has been deduced. Other examples of the influence of the type of limestone upon the karst

TABLE XV

CALCIUM AND MAGNESIUM CONTENT OF WATERS FROM VARIOUS SITES IN THE YORKSHIRE DALES

	N.G.R. SD	Calcium as CaCO$_3$	Magnesium as CaCO$_3$
RIBBLEHEAD			
Capnot Cave Well	790797	37·0	3·0
Great Bank Cave Sink	768798	8·0	2·0
Conduit Sink	770796	28·0	5·0
WHARFEDALE			
Black Keld Rising	974701	86·0	15·0
Braithe Gill Rising	995643	167·0	10·0
Robin Hoods Well	979658	168·0	6·0
BUCKDEN AREA			
Spring on Dale Head Scar	953804	121·0	46·0
Chow Close Gill	954794	79·0	38·0
Crook Gill	934785	103·0	27·0
Inlet inside Buckden Gavel Mine	955782	69·0	50·0
LITTONDALE			
Hesleden Beck	888746	137·0	71·0
Springs Cave	941710	137·0	68·0

mg CaCO$_3$ per 1,000 ml ± 1·0 mg CaCO$_3$ per 1,000 ml

(From Richardson [344].)

water can be given. Richardson gives an interesting series of analyses from north-west Yorkshire, Table XV [344]. He deduces from these figures that the higher values of magnesium in the Buckden area of Upper Wharfedale mean that the Carboniferous Limestone in that area shows some dolomitisation. Richardson's analyses also tend to support the writer's views that the limestones in the western part of north-west Yorkshire (Ribblehead, Clapham, etc.) are less soluble than those in the eastern part [37].

The effects of magnesium upon the solution of calcium carbonate have already been discussed (Chapter 3). The maximum value of the Ca:Mg ratio in waters from pure dolomites should be 1:1. The Ca:Mg ratio of waters from mixed limestone-dolomite rocks may be anything less than unity – and the lower the Mg content the more highly calcitic is the rock. A rough

division may be made at the point where the ratio is 1:0·3. From 1:1 to 1:0·3, the aquifer is a dolomite or dolomitic limestone. Below the ratio 1:0·3 the aquifer is a limestone. The writer concluded in 1965 that the ratio of magnesium to calcium in limestone waters was partly related to the length of time the waters were in contact with the rock. Shortly after the dissolution of the rock, the Mg:Ca ratio may be 1:0·3; but after many hours or days the proportion of calcium seems to rise and 'the longer the time the waters are in contact with the limestone, calcium becomes more important' [352]. The ratio of Mg:Ca becomes something more like 1:0·1 to 1:0·05 (or the ratio of Ca:Mg becomes 1:10 or 1:30).

It is noticeable also that water derived from pure dolomites has a very high hardness, both of magnesium and of calcium. Thus waters from the Permian limestones in northern England may con-

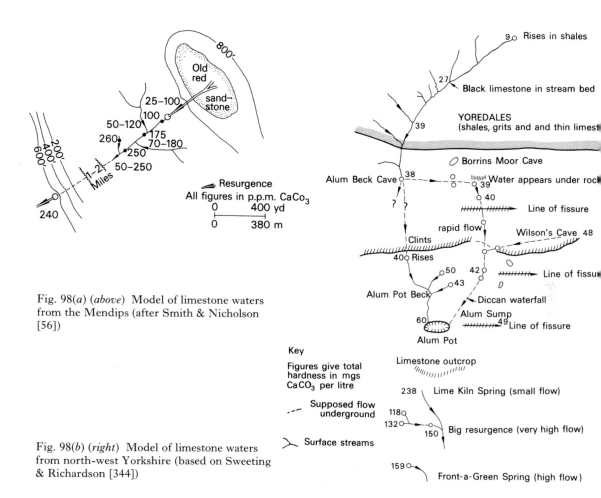

Fig. 98(a) (above) Model of limestone waters from the Mendips (after Smith & Nicholson [56])

Key

Figures give total hardness in mgs $CaCO_3$ per litre

--- Supposed flow underground

⟩ Surface streams

Fig. 98(b) (right) Model of limestone waters from north-west Yorkshire (based on Sweeting & Richardson [344])

tain as much as 400–500 ppm of calcium and magnesium hardness (compared with about 140–180 ppm for waters from the Carboniferous Limestones in north-west Yorkshire). Gams [302] and Gerstenhauer [62] also comment on this fact.

As a result of the studies on karst waters in the British Isles it is possible to construct models for waters passing through the different limestone areas, Fig. 98(a) and (b). The work of the University of Bristol Speleological Society has enabled models to be made for the Mendips and for the Burren of County Clare; the model for north-west Yorkshire is based on the work

of Richardson and of the writer [344]. However, more studies of this kind are needed because Ford has shown that the solution pattern may differ markedly in adjacent cave systems. Thus the pattern of karst water solution for the G.B. Cave is quite different from that for the nearby Swildon's Hole, Fig. 99 [226]; and it is likely that the pattern of solution for Clapham Cave in the western part of north-west Yorkshire is different from that of the Malham Tarn–Gordale system in the eastern part.

Nonetheless, within certain limitations it is possible to deduce water flow from

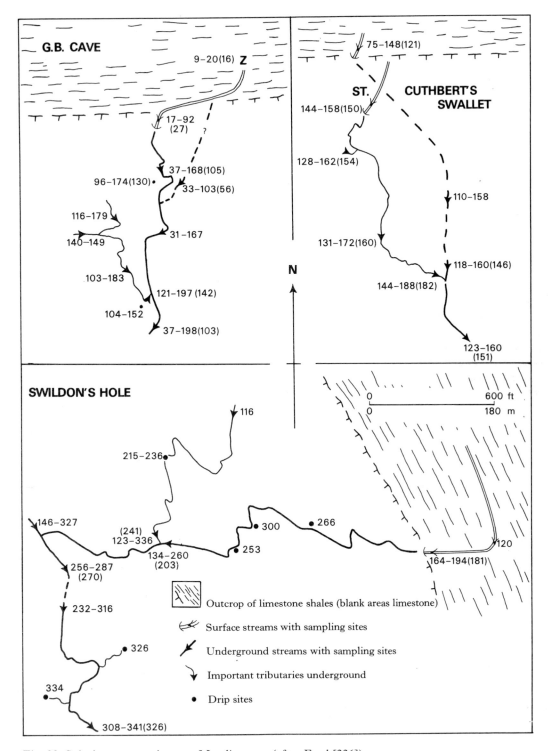

Fig. 99 Solution patterns in some Mendip caves (after Ford [226])

comparison of the qualities of karst waters. So far in Britain this has been done for hardness only. If the patterns of two karst waters show similar fluctuation, then either (a) the waters have had a similar history in the limestone, or (b) they are substantially the same flow of water. Pitty has calculated the correlation coefficient for carbonate measurements in the waters of the Malham

[342]. During the high water stages the karst waters contained about two-thirds of the soluble mineral content and a multiple extent of organic contamination. Alkalinity also decreased and there was a rise in non-carbonate hardness. Much more mud is contained in the karst waters during times of high water. As in many other areas, the maximum concentration of calcium carbo-

TABLE XVI

CORRELATION MATRIX OF CALCIUM CARBONATE OBSERVATIONS AT SIX
SAMPLING STATIONS IN THE MALHAM AREA

	(1)	(2)	(3)	(4)	(5)
(1) Smelt Mill Sink					
(2) Malham Tarn Outlet	−0·36				
(3) Goredale Beck (1)	0·43	−0·01			
(4) R. Aire at Malham Cove	0·62	−0·13	0·80		
(5) Airehead Springs	0·13	0·60	−0·04	0·25	
(6) Goredale Beck (2)	0·41	0·03	0·84	0·77	0·36

(After Pitty [348].)

Tarn area, Table XVI [348]. By means of these he has shown how the pattern of water at the Smelt Mill Sink resembles that of the Aire at its rising at Malham Cove, and how the water at the outlet of Malham Tarn resembles that of the Aire Head springs – both underground connections proved by water tracing in 1900 [353]. So far no pattern has emerged of the smaller-scale fluctuations, in both hardness and pH, which are known to affect some karst waters, throughout the day and night.

Karst water studies have been done in Moravia. Here samples of water were taken at ten localities and tests for twenty-four different properties, both physical and chemical, were made. Some of the physical properties have already been discussed in Chapter 11. The authors of this work state that at low and average water stages the karst waters showed 'a slight alkaline reaction, a mean high total concentration of soluble mineral salts and a rather low to very low total content of organic material'

nate occurs when the underground karst water movement is very slow and when the planes of contact between the water and the limestone are most numerous; minimum concentrations occur at the maximum water stages, especially at the periods of major floods when the water mass passes through the underground passages very rapidly and the chemical composition also varies considerably.   .

One important conclusion from the experiments in Moravia is that there is more carbonic acid in the waters which are circulating vertically than in those which are circulating horizontally. This is due to the greater percolation of such water through soil and humus and clays resting in joints, and vertically descending water acquires more biological CO_2. The authors claim that the erosion rate in the vertical solution zone is about ten times higher than that in the horizontal circulation zone as a result of the more rapid vertical denudation; much soil and sheet wash is drained into the

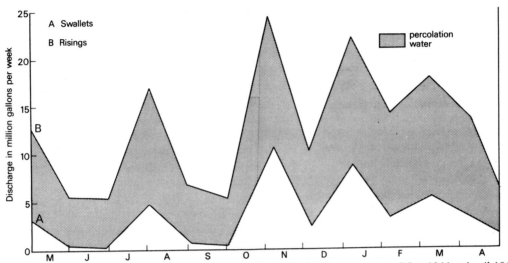

Fig. 100 Output discharge and percolation water for Ashwick Lower spring, May 1966 – April 1967 (after Drew [70])

widening joints. This is a possible explanation of the dominance of widened vertical fissures (kluftkarren or grikes) in many karst landscapes.

Part of the autochthonous water consists of percolation water. Drew has said that the 'contribution of percolation water to the total outflow at any karst resurgence may be approximately defined once the swallet feeders to the rising are known'. This is done by subtracting the inflow at the swallet feeders from the total outflow at the rising. In the eastern Mendips, Drew claims that percolation water is responsible for a relatively high percentage of the total outflow at the risings examined. At St Dunstan's Well, 74 per cent of the rising was calculated to be percolation water; at the two Ashwick Grove risings, the higher rising had values of 85–88 per cent and the lower 82 per cent percolation water, Fig. 100 [345]. However, much of the water called by Drew percolation water may coalesce a short distance below the surface into streamlets which then have physical characteristics similar to those of swallet waters [345]. The division of autochthonous

waters into part percolation water is therefore rather arbitrary.

Thus the properties of karst water depend upon the types of limestone, the climate, vegetation and soil cover, in addition to the hydrologically different streams which bring together waters of different chemical composition. As a result of the flow through the underground channels the water becomes of a definable quality, both physical and chemical. Hydrological work now makes use of these properties. In Syria, Burdon and Mazloum have mapped the occurrence of limestone waters and shown how the definite chemical qualities may be used in groundwater studies [354].

2. KARST WATER TRACING

Any discussion of karst water involves knowledge of its routes underground. Since the channels cannot all be followed by man, methods of karst water tracing have been developed. This section will only give an outline of what is a complex and well-developed field of study. Water tracing has taken place from the very earliest times, but it is only in recent years that the methods have become sophisticated. Formerly colouring of the water by a dye was almost the only method. In many ways colouring is still the simplest and cheapest and many workers think the most certain method of all. Many methods have been developed, some chemical, others depending upon physical changes in volume or temperature. However, the most significant water-tracing experiments have been done by the introduction of a substance into the water at its inlet into the limestone, which can be later recognised at the rising.

Such a substance must have certain qualities such as being (a) soluble in both acid and alkaline solutions of water, (b) not adsorbed on to calcium carbonate, (c) non-poisonous to both animals and man, (d) not objectionable, (e) absolutely certain to be determined, (f) detectable in very low concentrations, (g) not apt to cause soils or clays to coagulate, and (h) cheap and readily available.

In the pioneer water-tracing experiments in this country in 1900 and 1904 the Yorkshire Geological Society, in their experiments at Malham and Ingleborough, used a variety of chemical compounds, including ammonium sulphate and common salt; they also used fluorescein, an organic compound which when in solution is of a green colour and fluorescent in the light. By means of its strong fluorescence it may be detected at a dilution of one part in 40 million of water, and under favourable circumstances even down to one in 100 million [353]. Fluorescein is still used to a very large extent in water-tracing experiments. A large proportion of the recent water tracings done in Bosnia and Hercegovina by Energoinvest of Sarajevo used the compound sodium-fluorescein (uranin) [5]. Water has been traced by uranin up to more than 20 km in distance when more than 33 kg of the compound was used. The amount of fluorescein needed is calculated by a knowledge of the volume of water at the suspected rising; Jenko suggests that from 2 to 5 kg are needed for 1 m^3/sec of water in the rising. (If the volume at the swallow hole is used, about 24 kg for every m^3/sec of flow.) Fluorescein can be detected in much higher dilutions by the use of activated charcoal, the granules of the charcoal being suspended in a wire box at the rising in such a position as to be washed by the stream. The dye is obtained later from the charcoal by washing it with hot aqueous basic methanol. Other workers have used a fluorometer – an apparatus that detects fluorescein in varying amounts of dilution.

One of the great drawbacks to using fluorescein without charcoal detectors is that it involves a watch being kept on all possible risings over a long period of time. In Tasmania the writer took part in a study of water tracing from Honeycomb Cave to the rising at Mole Creek, Fig. 101, a distance of about 1 mile [356]. To do this water tracing, many people were necessary, as a watch had to be kept on all possible risings through two and a half days and nights. In this experiment the water travelled fairly rapidly (nearly 56 hours), but consider the case of Padirac in France where the dye was put into the cave on 22 July 1947, and did not reappear until 4 November 1947, at a spring $6\frac{1}{2}$ miles (10·4 km) away. Although fluorescein can be detected under great dilutions, in areas where the underground rivers are subject to great fluctuations the dilution caused by flooding may mean that the fluorescein goes undetected; this is one of the problems of using fluorescein in Jamaica. Furthermore in tropical areas with much vegetation, the presence of organic material may discolour the dye and so make its detection difficult. Peaty soils also attack it and render it colourless.

Other substances have also been introduced into the swallets, particularly those which can be detected by means of detectors installed at risings. One of these is *rhodamine B,* a dyestuff related to fluorescein. However, there is some doubt about its effect on wild life [357]. In his percolation-water experiments, Drew has used the fluorescent dye Pyranine Conc. [345]. This can be adsorbed from aqueous solution on to granular activated charcoal, similarly to fluorescein. Pyranine has been used with success both in the Mendips and in Jamaica where no decolorisation of the dye occurred. In the Canadian Rockies, in the Maligne Basin area Brown and Ford used *Rhodamine WT* with some success. They regard *Rhodamine WT* as the most economically efficient tracer available today. Even though more completely recoverable tracers are available, their secondary inefficient qualities often make them inappropriate [523, 524].

It will be obvious that water tracing is an ideal medium for the use of isotopes and radio-active tracers and these methods are being used increasingly. A discussion of these and some of the literature is given by Buchtela and others in *Die Wasserwirtschaft,* 1964 [358]. In the F.A.O. programme in Greece, neutron activation analysis was used. Radio-isotopes are also in use in both the U.S.A. and the U.S.S.R. So far in Britain there has been objection to the use of radio-active tracers in detecting underground water flow because of the possible contamination of drinking-water resources. Tritium (hydrogen^3) compounded with oxygen to form tritium water has also been used. Chemically tritium water is similar to ordinary H_2O, but there are several physical properties which are different, notably the

radio-activity. If tritium is used as a water tracer, it is detected by radio-active means. Electrical conductivity methods, using ammonium chloride, have also been developed in the U.S.A. – by Slichter as early as 1902.

One of the most successful methods of water tracing has been devised by Zötl and Maurin in the limestone areas of the northeastern Alps in the Graz area. These two authors pioneered the use of *Lycopodium* spores in tracing waters, and this method has been used with much success. The spores of *Lycopodium clavatum* are the most widely used, and the advantage of these is that they can be dyed different colours. Thus different coloured spores can be introduced into different swallow holes and as many experiments as there are coloured spores can be carried on at the same time. This is clearly an advantage over water tracings using fluorescein. *Lycopodium*

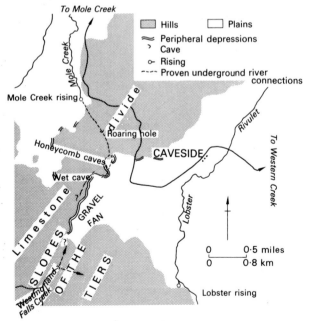

Fig. 101 Map of the vicinity of Caveside, showing underground river crossing of the divide between Mole Creek and Lobster Rivulet valleys (from Jennings & Sweeting [356])

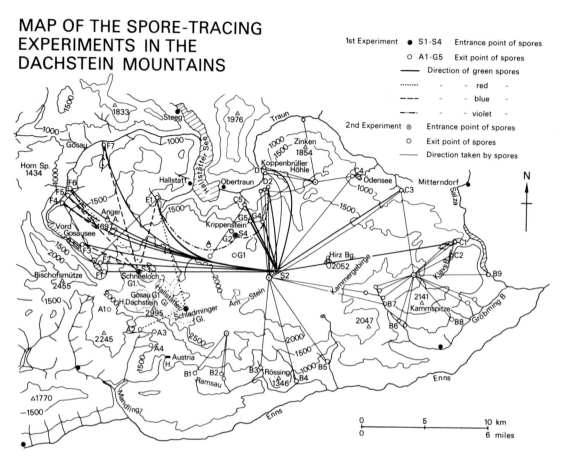

Fig. 102 Results of *Lycopodium* spore tests in the Dachsteingebiet (from Zötl & Maurin [359])

spores travel at approximately the same speed as water, which is faster than either fluorescein or rhodamine B [70]. The spores are very small, about 30 micron, and large quantities are needed – over 70 lb (32 kg) being used to investigate the Cave River swallow hole in Jamaica. One colour per swallow hole can be used. The spores are collected at the risings by means of plankton nets built of fine silk, which is placed in a protector. Analysis of the samples must be done in a laboratory and the numbers of each coloured spore are then counted for each sample. The spores are easily recognisable and one advantage is that they are quite unmistakable, there being no naturally occurring coloured spores of the shape produced by *Lycopodium*. The collection is simultaneous and does not need continuous watching. The main disadvantages are (1) the smallness of the spores (they can be filtered by sand), (2) the expense (they are about four times the cost of fluorescein), and (3) the time and equipment needed for the preparation, collection and analysis. The method of use of the *Lycopodium* spores is dealt with in detail by Maurin and Zötl in their paper in 1959 and is also discussed by M. C. Brown in his report of the Karst Hydrology Expedition to Jamaica in

1966. Fig. 102 is taken from Zötl and Maurin's paper and shows the results of tests using spores in the Dachsteingebiet, where it will be seen that green, red, blue and violet-coloured spores were used [359].

In water-tracing experiments involving the introduction of chemicals or spores it is essential to have a good idea of the hydrology of the area before embarking upon the investigation, so that the likely resurgences, etc., can be watched; this is partly because of the time and expense involved. Ideally, medium-volume waters are the most suitable for the introduction of any dye or spores, flood or very low waters being much less suitable. However, since underground water may take different paths during flood times, it is sometimes worth while to incur the expense and trouble to carry out the investigation then. The speed of travel of the underground water can be established from the distance of the swallow hole to the spring, and by comparing the mean of the time when the substance was placed in the swallow hole with the mean of the time when the substance appears in the spring. Jenko says that it is best to multiply these figures by 1·5 on an average, to account for the windings of the underground passages. The relation between the amount of the substance put in at the swallow hole and the intensity of its reappearance at the spring may give information about other properties of the underground passages, as for instance in Glennie's study of Ogof Ffynnon Ddu [360]. It is important also to undertake more than one test of any particular inlet-outlet system. As pointed out by Brown & Ford in their study of the Maligne Basin each of three tests 'yielded a different flow-through time and a possibly different pattern of dye dispersion. This suggests that reliable quantitative analysis by the dye method must be based on repeated testing' [523].

In addition to the methods which introduce substances into karst water, water tracing using the chemical and physical qualities of the waters themselves is growing in importance. As we have shown, karst water is often identifiable and waters from different kinds of limestone environments tend to have distinctive properties. In particular, the calcium hardness of karst waters has been shown to be a useful indicator; the example given by Pitty in his discussion of the Malham area has already been cited, p. 226. The method is not as positive as the visual ones, and needs detailed and systematic observations, but because of its simplicity and inexpensiveness it has much to recommend it. 'No artificial element is introduced into the natural system. This not only avoids contamination, but also the problem of deciding whether an artificial element in the water is moving at the same speed as the water. Finally, the technique does not necessarily depend on the aid of several assistants' [348].

The qualities of karst water are also used in flood-pulse techniques which are now being developed for the investigation of underground water flow. A 'flood pulse' is a sudden increase in the volume of water passing a given point, which is usually followed by a more gradual decrease. Such a flood pulse may be caused by natural means (by heavy showers) or artificially by releasing water from dams. Though the flood-pulse idea has been used in many older experiments, it is only in recent years that serious consideration has been given to it as a method of investigation of underground watercourses. It was first used in Hungary on the Kolmos resurgence, but it has been developed in Britain by Ashton in particular [346].

The theory behind the flood-pulse technique assumes that the water enters a cave from non-karstic rocks, and that the cave is a model consisting of a swallow hole, vadose passages, a master cave, a flooded zone (phreas), and a resurgence. A flood pulse is a flood wave which enters the system when it rains (or when a dam or barrier is released). It is possible to construct idealised graphs to illustrate the changes in qualities of the water as the flood pulse goes through the cave. It is assumed that each part of the cave, swallow hole, vadose passage, master cave, etc., is characterised by its own distinctive water, in terms of flow, total and calcium hardness and pH, and that these are altered by the flood water as the flood pulse goes through. The changes that are assumed to occur are shown in graph form in Fig.

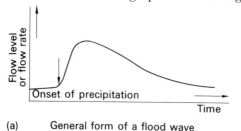

(a)   General form of a flood wave

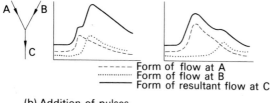

(b) Addition of pulses

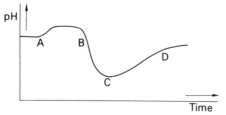

(c)   Basic pattern of a pH curve

Fig. 103 Flood pulse characteristics (from Ashton [346])

103 [346]. For example, at the swallow hole, at the beginning of the flood pulse, it is assumed that the total hardness and pH will decrease, since the volume of water coming off the non-karstic rocks will have increased; but at the resurgence the total hardness and the pH will be expected first to increase because of the pushing out of very hard groundwater from the phreatic zone by the flood, but later to decrease as the flood pulse arrives, Fig. 103. The length of time taken for these events to occur and the time of arrival of the flood pulse at the resurgence will give some indication about the size and shape of the underground passages. It will be seen that, in this flood-pulse theory, the cave system is treated as a 'black box', with the swallow hole being the 'input' and the resurgence the 'output'. The interior of the black box is a model of the cave system. In practice, a cave system does not normally consist of one main passage, but is complicated by many inlet passages, all of which produce more than one pulse from a single flood pulse [361].

Certain other properties may be observed, such as turbidity, organic content and temperature. The recording of all these properties, including hardness and pH, needs sensitive equipment, as pH values must be accurate to 0·05 and temperature to 0·02°C. Also observations must be more or less continuous or taken at intervals of not less than 15 minutes. Weather conditions should also be stable. Despite these considerations, flood-pulse techniques can be used without the need of chemicals or dyestuffs, and many of the measurements can be taken with recording meters. The analysis of the number of pulses received at the resurgence makes the problem an ideal one for application to computers. A discussion on the application of flood-pulse analysis of karst waters using computers is given in Wilcock [361].

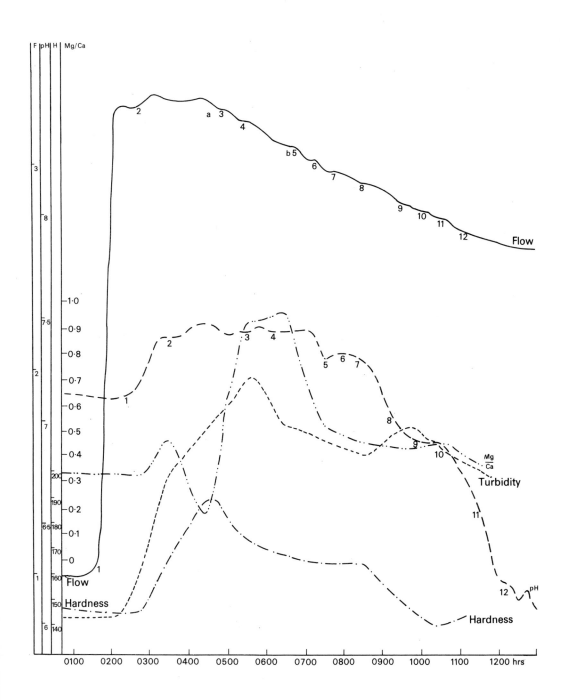

Fig. 104 Flood pulse experiment on the Black River, St Catherine's, Jamaica, 9.9.63 (from Ashton [363])

It is of interest to note that the form of a cave in Kingsdale, north-west Yorkshire, was deduced by the use of a flood-pulse experiment [361]. However, it is probable that tropical areas with their sharp heavy showers and flash-flooding are ideal for the investigation of underground water flow by flood-pulse techniques. Some experiments of this type were made by the Leeds University Hydrological Survey Expedition to Jamaica in 1963 [362]. The Black River in St Catherine's, Jamaica, was one cave where a flood-pulse survey was conducted;

useful deductions were made concerning the relationship between swallow holes and the rising, and these were of value, as previous tests with dyes had not yielded any results, Fig. 104 [362, 363]. An idea of the hydrology of the polje of Lluidas Vale was also obtained from these experiments.

From this consideration of the qualities of karst waters and the attempts that have been made to trace them, we can now turn to ideas and developments in karst hydrology.

13 Karst Hydrology

1. INTRODUCTION

In this chapter, some aspects of the hydrology and groundwater and water flow in karst areas will be considered. In many ways, karst hydrology is one of the most important aspects of the study of karst landforms. Many problems exist concerning underground water and there are many controversial issues. They concern the movement of the water and the main focus of cavern formation, the depth to which groundwater penetrates, and whether there is a water-table in karst limestones. All of these are problems associated with karst hydrology. For a long time it was argued, for instance, that caves were formed by corrasion and erosion and that solution was of minor importance. Moreover, as a result of the solution of the limestone, the passages through which the water flows are continually being enlarged and changed so that the type and nature of the water flow is changing continually. Is the zone of maximum removal (i.e. the cave) related to any definite zone of water movement within the limestone? Or is the seeking to relate cavern formation to phreatic, vadose and water-table conditions irrelevant, since each cave may be developed as a special consequence of a specific flow pattern [223]?

The main controversies centre around the question of the existence of a water-table, however approximate and irregular. As recently as 1965, Roglič could write: 'In compact limestones, no ground water-table can be formed and the dissolution of this pure rock leaves few insoluble remnants' [218].

The earliest workers in karst areas believed that most erosion underground was brought about by subterranean streams flowing freely and that corrasion, i.e. mechanical erosion, was the most effective agent. Solution of the limestone was regarded as of minor importance. It is now known from all the chemical work that has been done on the waters of the karst that solution by underground water is a very important factor in the development of karst hydrology [13]. This does not mean that mechanical erosion is unimportant as Newsom has recently shown [525, 526].

Modern ideas about the flow of water in karst areas date from the beginning of the century as our knowledge of the Classical Karst areas became established. At that time two, unnecessarily opposed, views of karst water conditions were developed. These were the views of Grund and Katzer. It can be said that to some extent today our thinking still revolves around the ideas that these workers put forward. Both worked in the Dinaric karst, though Grund was also probably equally aware of conditions in western Europe. The idea of groundwater in the karst goes back to Pilar in 1874, so that Grund was not entirely new in his conception of groundwater. Grund imagined that waters sinking into the karst fissures circulated within the karst until they settled at a groundwater level, which was interconnected throughout all fissures, but not necessarily immobile. The groundwater (*Grundwasser*) resembled in many ways groundwater conditions in non-karstic rocks, and it extended down to the level of the impermeable bed beneath the lime-

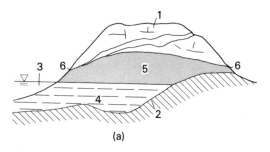
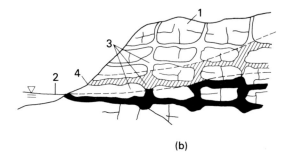

(a) Grund's theory
1. Permeable karst mass
2. Impermeable basis
3. Sea
4. Groundwater
5. Karst water
6. Karst springs

(b) Katzer's theory
1. Permeable karst mass
2. Sea
3. Caves and connecting corrosion channels
4. Karst springs

Fig. 105 Theories of karst waters (after Jenko [340])

stones. 'From the sea-level landwards, there is a rising surface, below which all joints are filled with stagnant water. At this surface, the downward movement of water ceases and begins the movement in a horizontal direction towards the sea. The surface of the stagnant water is not horizontal, but is inclined and in equilibrium with the sea-level' [182]. The groundwater was supposed to form the level of erosion in the interior of a karst area. Above the groundwater there was an integrated but more mobile body of water which fluctuated seasonally and moved laterally and which Grund called the *karst water*. Above the karst water was the atmospheric water circulating in the limestone. The seasonal movements of the karst water gave rise to the different types of the springs and Grund attempted to explain the various phenomena of the poljes with this hypothesis. Fig. 105(a) gives a simplified view of Grund's ideas.

It is clear to anyone who has worked in caves and in karst poljes that the idea of an interconnected body of groundwater is not a true picture of the underground water. The existence of siphons, and of distinct and discrete networks of underground water, all serve to contest the idea of an integrated network of groundwater. Both Katzer and Martel believed that subterranean watercourses were mainly separate and independent because great cave chambers alternate with narrow siphonic connections in many cave systems. Water circulates underground through permeable fissures and is under hydrostatic pressure which activates the siphons and makes the water move upwards. Much evidence therefore points to the existence of fissures throughout the whole limestone mass down to the impermeable base and that the water flows to the level of the impermeable rock regardless of the sea level. As evidence in support of this, Katzer quotes the existence of a submarine spring at 700 m below sea level at Cap St-Marin [364]. Other examples have also been cited; thus P. Fénelon quotes the example of fissure circulation of water at Rochefort, 800 m below sea level [365]. Katzer's ideas are shown in Fig. 105(b).

Jenko has pointed out that Grund's theory contained a hydraulic error because it maintained that water in the permeable karst does not move below the height of the erosional base of the sea level, and for this reason did not recognise deep underground streams in the groundwater. Katzer's theory is also regarded as hydraulically insufficient because it associates the independent karstic rivers too closely with tectonics without connecting them, at least during low water levels, with the erosional base; for this reason Katzer did not recognise the existence of groundwater or of deep underground streams associated with groundwater. Jenko goes on to say: 'As a consequence of all this there have been unfortunate results both in the field of [water] economy as well as in the scientific research. Since it has been considered that there were no water passages below the heights of the erosional bases, the karstic rivers were wrongly dammed; since it has been considered that the groundwaters and the deep underground streams do not exist, so the search for the water was frequently unsuccessful' [340].

Partly because of this groundwater controversy, Cvijič produced his idea of three hydrographical zones in his classic paper in 1918 [272]. While neither accepting the hypothesis of the existence of groundwater and the water-table, nor that of the existence of independent karst streams, Cvijič proposed that there existed within the karst (1) an upper 'dry' zone in which the water circulated freely; (2) a lower permanently saturated zone, where the water was under hydrostatic pressure and frequently ascended, (3) an intermediate zone, which was intermittently saturated but at other times dry. The oscillations of the lowest zone were not dependent upon the oscillations of the sea level but upon the level of the basal impermeable bed. The zones were not immovable but graded into one another, and as the karst areas were denuded, so the upper dry zone moved downwards and displaced the lower ones. As will be realised, Cvijič's ideas on the existence of dry, intermittently flooded and permanently flooded poljes fitted neatly though not correctly into this concept of underground water. Later he introduced the effects of sea level upon the development of groundwater, probably as a result of his acquaintance with W. M. Davis and the hypothesis of the cycle of erosion [366].

Investigations into the origin of cave systems have assisted in our knowledge of karst hydrology. W. M. Davis based his ideas on cave development on the concepts of groundwater of Hubert King, who believed that groundwater movements could be traced in accurate paths to great depths below sea level [367]. In putting forward his two-cycle theory of cavern development, Davis envisaged solution to be caused by slow-moving deep groundwater, which he called phreatic solution; solutional forms caused by groundwater were later modified after uplift by freely circulating vadose water. Davis did not differentiate between any part of the phreatic zone as being more susceptible towards speed of water movement and solution than any other, and in fact thought that solution and cave development would occur at great depths in the groundwater zone [215]. However, there has been a tendency, particularly in America, to believe that the upper part of the groundwater zone is characterised by widespread lateral movement of water – this being the zone of maximum solution and hence of cave formation [224]. The patterns of groundwater flow in limestones as discussed by various workers in the U.S.A. are given in Fig. 106. Swinnerton in particular maintained that the water at A will divide itself into proportions directly related to the ease of movement in the three directions. The largest amount of water will take route 1, and the smallest amount route 3. He said, 'the more opened joints near the surface will result in increased capacity for circulation and in diminished frictional resistance near the surface' [249]. He argued that, as the movement of water along the zone just below the water-table becomes more efficient, less water will move along routes 2 and 3. Swinnerton's ideas were further developed by Rhoades and Sinacori when they proposed the concentration of underground water flow near to the resurgences which they regarded as at the level of the water-table; these resurgences in their view are connected to master conduits, similar to the master caves described by Simpson and also the writer in north-west Yorkshire [50].

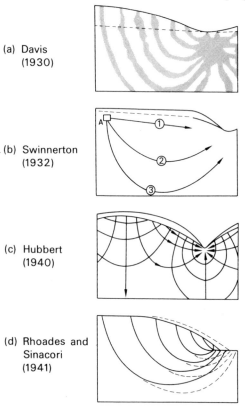

(a) Davis (1930)

(b) Swinnerton (1932)

(c) Hubbert (1940)

(d) Rhoades and Sinacori (1941)

Fig. 106 Patterns of groundwater flow in limestone (from Thrailkill [224])

Meanwhile, in Europe, work has been on entirely different lines. O. Lehmann (1932) proposed that karst water movement was complex, comparable to the movement of water through a series of communicating vessels; it was not envisaged to be a movement of torrential vadose water, nor of water moving as a uniform groundwater, or the separate movement of water through individual galleries as had been proposed by Katzer. Lehmann distinguished three types of water-flow: (1) a system of currents under pressure in the cavities filled with water, (2) a system of free currents analogous to a surface watercourse, found in the upper parts of the karst, and (3) an intermediate system with basins which retained water, sometimes free, sometimes under pressure, but which always escaped under pressure [214]. The first type of water flow was always found in the most profound parts of the karst; the second type in caves near the surface; and the alternating system became more normal as the first zone approached the surface. After heavy rains, when water is abundant, the currents with water under pressure rise. Lehmann's views are similar to those of Cvijič in that, as denudation of the limestone area proceeds, the three systems of water currents migrate downwards, currents under pressure being replaced by free-flowing currents in the passage of time. Because of this, a circular or elliptical cave section caused by flow under pressure becomes replaced by a cylindrical or corridor section, formed under free (or vadose) flow. One of the most important parts of Lehmann's work is concerned with a study of the hydrology of the Livno polje, one of the most remarkable of the Dinaric karst. As we have seen, Fig. 87, this polje has three separate basins, each of which has a distinct hydrological regime; Lehmann was able to show that there are many different hydrological 'circuits' in the vicinity of the polje, and only some of these are intersected by it [214]. He maintains that poljes remain dry and uninundated when they do not intersect the system of karstic fissures; because of this the smaller poljes tend to be less inundated since there is less chance of their intersecting the fissures. Large areas of the limestone remain completely dry, other areas contain water and are traversed by well-defined hydrological networks; dry cavities exist alongside periodic and perennial springs. Cavern formation is thus not restricted to any particular zone within the karst, and no integrated network of groundwater is recognised.*

In many ways these two major lines of thought have dominated subsequent work, the ideas of groundwater being more persistent in America and to some extent in Britain, the ideas of siphonic and independent networks being more characteristic of work both in Jugoslavia and in France; both sets of ideas have been prominent in the Alps. As would be expected, the divergence in ideas is due partly to the differences in the areas in which the morphologists are working. Thus American work has been based upon areas of flat-lying limestones; in Europe, particularly in Alpine areas and in the Karst, the limestones are steeply dipping and much fractured and folded. Ford in particular has pointed out the undue influence the Mammoth Cave-Flint Ridge Systems have had upon American hydrological thinking. In addition both these caves have developed beneath the caprock of the Big Clifty Sandstone, which has had the effect of elongating the bedding-plane passages, a phenomenon also seen in South Wales [511]. Reference will now be made to recent work on karst hydrology.

*O. Lehmann's work was much influenced by P. Ballif [539].

2. RECENT WORK IN KARST HYDROLOGY

Both Milojević [368] and Roglič [218] have applied the ideas of O. Lehmann to the circulation of underground water in the karst, and particularly the Dinaric karst. Roglič especially is of the opinion that much erosion and corrosion happens at depth in the karst. 'At deep levels, waters of different hardness mix (mixture corrosion), which revives their aggressiveness.... Thus everything points to the probability that the lowest levels of fissures offer more favourable conditions for mechanical erosion, the dissolution of the rock and the consequent widening of the fissures' [218, 313]. The development of karst cavities also reaches to the same depth as does the karstifying rock. In the highly mountainous coastal areas of the Dinaric karst, the mountains of Prenj and Snjeznik are both over 2,000 m and Velebit, Dinaria, Biokovo, Orjen and Lovčen are all over 1,700 m; they are all foci of heavy rainfall, in some cases over 5,000 mm a year, yet these enormous quantities of water disappear rapidly underground and reach great depths independent of sea level. There are no springs at the foot of Orjen, one of the most rainy mountains of Europe, and only a few intermittent submarine springs are visible. Hence, according to Roglič, the water circulation and the development of karst cavities reach depths independent of sea level. 'From the hydrological point of view such mountains are large absorbing basins' [313]. The greater part of these mountains manifest an inversion in water drainage. Since these quantities of water disappear, it leads to the conclusion that the deep karst underground must contain large caverns – caverns which it will be extremely difficult to explore and will need special techniques to do so. Such development of deep subterranean karst caverns in the Dinaric karst has taken place in the relatively narrow Adriatic belt which is dominated by the compact Cretaceous limestones which possess well-developed fissures to enable the circulation of water. The directions of the underground drainage differ from those of the surface; much water flows eastwards beneath the NW.-SE.-trending mountain ranges to the deep valleys of the Danubian river system.

Some of these points have been demonstrated by tests of dyes introduced into the swallow holes of the Dinaric mountains [5]. The underground connections of the main swallow holes and springs of Hercegovina and Bosnia and parts of Dalmatia have been discussed by Petrovič and Prelevič. The tests were made both by the use of fluorescein and by the introduction of spores, and were part of an extensive survey made by Energoinvest (Sarajevo) in order to harness the waters of the karst. It was shown that the underground waters either follow the direction of the Dinaric folding or are perpendicular to that folding, and follow tectonic fissures. The impermeable sediments of the polje floors represent barriers to water discharge from the higher to the lower ground and so cause the appearance of springs at the east and north-east of the poljes and of the swallow holes (ponors) on the south and south-west edges. In some poljes like Kupres and Glamoč, the waters drain from them in two completely opposite directions; in fact these poljes are on the watershed between the Adriatic and the Black Sea drainage; this is known as bifurcation. The underground waters of the Hercegovenian karst run mainly in concentrated flows; where several channels converge, there are areas of big springs and the underground water has a general level or local water-table. However, sometimes water disappearing into the same ponor drains in different directions. In Croatia,

Baucič says that the results of the repeated dyeings of the same ponor show that it is extremely rare for the waters from one ponor always to appear in the same spring. Each underground connection only corresponds to the conditions obtaining at the time of the investigations – any future investigations are quite likely to give a different result. Mostly these changes are small, but occasionally the underground streams may flow off into a different catchment area. Since we do not know the real length of the underground streams, we cannot properly investigate the speed of flow, though the greatest speeds seem to be in the largest underground channels. In Croatia, taking the surface distances between the ponors and the springs, velocities in this part of the karst vary from 0·95 cm/sec to 16 cm/sec. As a result of his investigations Baucič says that it is impossible to generalise about the behaviour of the underground streams, and that each one must be observed separately under its different hydrological conditions [369].

The deep and fissured nature of the Dinaric karst may explain why the most typical part of it is characterised by deep holes, jamas, developed vertically, and why horizontal caves are relatively poorly represented. This fact strikes any visitor to the Dinaric karst (though not the Slovenian karst). Roglič explains that there is no native name in Serbo-Croat for cave [218]. The Serbo-Croats use the word *spilja* from the classical Latin (*spelunca*) for cave. In Serbo-Croat *jama* is a hollow developed in a vertical sense, while in Slovene *jama* is also used for cave, as in Postojnska Jama. For a deep hole, the Slovenes use the term *brezno*, a chasm (loc. cit., p. 31). The jama is the surface reflection of a deep ramified fissure system in the deep karst. Caves, as we have already seen, are more typical of areas where the limestones are thinner, where shallow connecting channels have developed and where more abundant waste and alluvium have prevented the water from sinking into greater depths. It is only in recent years that any attention has been given to these deeper systems of the karst; in the earlier stages of research, the more accessible caves were the focus of attention. Hence jamas are associated with deep karst, while caves are typical of shallow karst.

Occasionally such jamas as are regarded as typical of the deep karst are seen. One example is the Crveno Jezero (the Red Lake) on the east side of Imotski polje, in the Adriatic littoral [218]. It is formed in Upper Cretaceous compact limestones lying on dolomites. The dolomites were more easily eroded than the limestones and collapses have taken place at the contact of the limestones and dolomites (Roglič, 1938). Crveno Jezero is an immense collapsed abyss with its highest rim at over 520 m above sea level; its diameter is about 400 m; at its deepest measured part the bottom is only 4·1 m above sea level, and so it has a relative depth of at least 500 m from the highest part of its rim. A cross-section is shown in Fig. 107. The bottom is uneven and formed of collapsed rock and it is probable that it is even deeper. The lower part of Crveno Jezero is filled with water, which periodically changes its level. The varying levels of this water bear *no* relationship to the water levels in the polje floor of Imotski which is only a few metres away. The existence of this feature which is now over 500 m deep may mean that the original cavity into which the collapse has taken place was more than 1,000 m deep. The existence of chasms as large as this must mean that very large caverns exist in the deep karst [218].

Conditions are rather different in the Classical Karst area of Slovenia, and some interesting and significant work has been done by Jenko. He has been interested in the speed of flow of the underground water, and he refers to the 'hydraulic paradox'. Thus the speed of flow of underground water is lowest when the water level is at a minimum, and also when it is high; the speed of flow is greatest at medium water-levels. On an average, the speeds of the low and high waters are about one-tenth of those in streams in non-karstified areas. Jenko's main interest has been in the regime of the poljes of the Ljubljanica area. In a series of diagrams, one of which is given in Fig. 108, he gives an indication of the length of inundation of the poljes and the measured quantities of water flowing into them from the springs, and the efflux of water through the ponors. From these investigations he maintains that once the ponors begin to function their rate of efflux is constant. Jenko says, as a result of recent work in the Slovenian karst, that the water is really composed of three components that are united into one whole: (1) the groundwaters, (2) normal rivers which flow partly on the surface and partly underground, and (3) deep underground currents. The deep underground currents are the basic effluxes from the karst with piezometric levels at the low-water levels dependent upon the lowest outlets of the lowest erosional bases. Jenko's views are rather different from those of workers in the Dinaric karst, and he recognises the existence of 'undulating water-tables, fractionised horizontally and

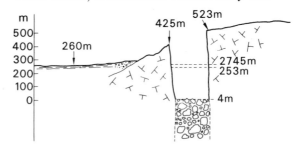

Fig. 107 Profile through the rim of Imotsko polje and Crveno Jezero (from Roglič [218])

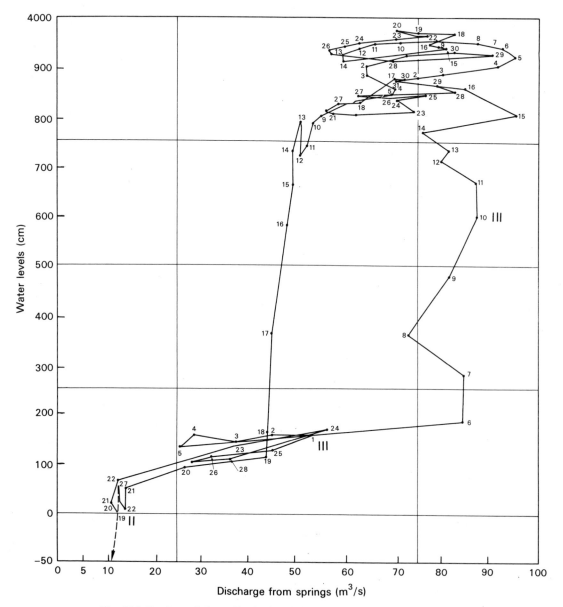

Fig. 108 Regime of the poljes in the Ljubljanica area (from Jenko [340])

vertically at various depths down to the base erosion level' [370]. In all probability these views of the Classical Karst approximate to conditions occurring in many other areas, the conditions for the Dinaric karst being almost unique. Further data on the springs of the Slovene Karst are provided by Gams who has given a detailed survey of the Cerknica and Planina area [527].

Jenko also contends that the evidence for the great amounts of surface solution which can be proved in the karst areas means that the water will be over-saturated at the great depths, and that the main erosion underground deep in the karst is by corrasion (mechanical) work and not corrosion [370]. This view has also been expressed by recent French cave explorers, notably Chevalier [237], and has revived the older ideas of Martel [13].

In Britain, the study of the underground waters of the Malham and Ingleborough areas made by the Yorkshire Geological Society in 1900 and 1904 was of significance not only from the point of view of water tracing, but also from the point of view of the hydrology. It indicated that:

(1) All the underground waters drained radially outward from the higher ground and in no case was the drainage controlled entirely by the dip of the strata (here to the north).

(2) The flow of underground water was much slower than was expected at the time; for instance, water took twelve days to travel $1\frac{1}{2}$ miles (2·3 km) from Alum Pot Hole to the resurgence at Turn Dub; ten days to travel from Long Kin East Cave to Austwick Beck Head, a distance of about 1 mile (1·6 km); and times varying from five days in April to ten to fourteen days in June to travel the one mile from Gaping Gill Hole to Clapham Beck Head. The times of travel of the water were more under dry conditions and less when the weather was wet.

(3) The experiments showed great control upon the direction of flow of the underground water by the master joints and fissures of the region; the relief in the underlying impermeable floor with its ridges and valleys also affected the direction of flow of the underground streams; this is an indication that the Carboniferous Limestone of the Ingleborough district is highly fissured and karstified throughout its entire thickness of 600 ft.

(4) The underground streams crossed each other during their subterranean passage, a point which is well illustrated by the drainage in the neighbourhood of Malham. Underground streams also pass beneath those on the surface of the ground, as for example in the waters from Alum Pot passing below the surface water of the river Ribble.

(5) Streams could disappear into a swallow hole in one river basin but reappear through a rising in another; the drainage of Nick Pot Sike (stream), for instance, if continued on the surface, would flow to the Ribble, but its underground course takes it to Austwick Beck Head, which is in the Lune drainage area.

(6) It was noticed, in connection with the Smelt Mill swallow hole and its connection with the rising at Malham Cove, that the Smelt Mill stream contributes only about one-twentieth of the water issuing from the cove, the remaining 19/20 consisting of water absorbed from the west and from rain water absorbed by the limestone pavements, i.e. the proportion of autochthonous and percolation water was high. Tratman, in a study of the Langford and Rickford Springs in the Mendips, calculated that autochthonous water comprised about 90 per cent of the total volume at these risings, i.e. only 10 per cent is derived from the swallow holes [206].

North-west Yorkshire has been one area in Britain where attempts have been made to connect the idea of corrosion and erosion in an underground water zone with the locus of formation of major cave passages. The correlation shown in Fig. 48 was made by the writer in 1950; although, as we have indicated, the results of the underground water tests show the Carboniferous Limestone to be highly fissured, there is enough evidence to suggest that an irregular watertable exists at least in parts of this area. The distribution of the known caves suggested that the water-table zone was of importance in their formation. The evidence for this is best seen in the Gaping Gill area, but it has also been recently re-examined in the Lost John's Cave area on Leck Fell, by Eyre [371]; here, although it is suggested that the development of the cave is very recent, the various levels may be related to a series of descending water-levels. Warwick has furthermore discussed the behaviour of the river Greta in the neighbourhood of Chapel-le-Dale, which is best explained if an irregular water-table is assumed [204]. However, a water-table in the conventional sense does not exist in the Carboniferous Limestones in north-west Yorkshire, for if a well or borehole is sunk into these rocks, it is by no means certain that water will be found at a predictable depth. Thus, in Littondale, three boreholes were sunk at approximately the same height and within 100 m of each other, yet only one of them yielded water (at 28 m depth); the others went down to the base of the limestones (at over 120 m), but were almost dry. This indicates that water in these limestones flows through fissures and is not in a unified body of groundwater. In many cases also the water is perched, particularly when the limestone sequence contains shale bands, as in north-west Yorkshire. Water then concentrates along the bedding planes rather than in vertical fissures, and bedding planes become important in determining the routes of underground water [372]. Further work suggests more structural and less water-table control of the caves. This view has been confirmed by Waltham's ideas on the caves of north-west Yorkshire – ideas which at first sight contradict any existence of a water-table zone. However, the age and origin of the north-west Yorkshire cave passages still present many problems [514].

Further evidence in support of fissure control of water in British limestones is discussed by Pitty [79]. In a study of the seepage rates in a small area surrounding Poole's Cavern in Derbyshire, he has calculated that water seeping into the cave from precipitation takes about eighty-four days to reach its outlet point. There is a lag of two days before there is any increase in water flow following precipitation, even though the water has only to percolate through about 30 m of rock. Marked contrasts also exist in the chemical quality of adjacent waters. Thus it seems that the karst water exists in discrete systems of fissures with little lateral integration. Pitty remarks that these results are in keeping with the views of Otto Lehmann, who said that in some areas water might take years to flow through a karst mass. (We now know from experiments using radio-isotopes that waters issuing from karst massifs can be some years old, as in the Fontaine de Vaucluse and also in the Berkshire Downs [373].) Thus isolated networks of karst water are a more accurate description of the conditions in the Poole's Cavern area; the fissure systems are independent and not an integrated lattice.

Work from the Mendips also suggests a combination of an irregular water-table with fissure control of water in well-defined flow lines. In his study of the Mendip caves, Ford [375] makes the point that 'within considerable limitations it may be said that the large caves are accordant to particular water-tables. . . . But the latter do not precede them in the cave zone. Each cave (or principal flow path) determines its own water-table gradient' (loc. cit., p. 127). Moreover, Ford remarks that 'while the cave defines the water-table, its passages need not be developed along it for more than a small part of the course from sink to rising' (loc. cit., p. 128). Fig. 109(a), showing a model of the Mendip caves, indicates the predominance of sub-water-table loops in the flow path and not all loops ascend to the water-table. Such variation more nearly agrees with Warwick's definition of a water-table, as 'a theoretical surface formed by joining up the levels of standing water in voids in the rock' [204], not an entirely satisfactory definition. More recently, the water-tracing studies of Drew have indicated the existence of completely separate water-flow lines from the different sinks and to the risings [374]. Drew has concluded that his work shows that a water-table, if it does exist in such fissured rocks, is very different from ordinary conventional ideas (Fig. 109(b)).

In western Ireland, Williams has demonstrated the influence of geological and physiographical factors upon groundwater movement. Thus bedding planes, joints and synclines, in that order, are the most frequent routes for underground water. Widened joints in the areas of limestone pavements absorb the rainwater so that swallow holes and dolines do not exist.

Water which enters the rock along the joints soon reaches an enlarged bedding plane and then follows the direction of maximum dip. This gives rise to bedding-plane conduits, as in the Burren, where such cave passages are aligned from north to south in the direction of the dip [95].

A comparison of the water conditions in the Burren uplands with those in the Gort

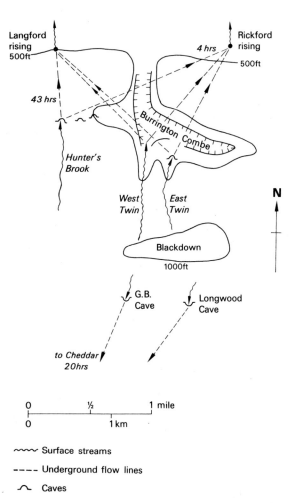

Fig. 109(a) Mendip hydrology. Diagrammatic section to illustrate the proposed Mendip Model drawn for two successive water-tables (from Ford [375])

Fig. 109(b) Limestone hydrology, Blackdown, Mendips, (from Tratman [206])

lowlands has also been made. On the upland (ranging in height from 200 to 300 m), records of boreholes and wells show that the groundwater levels are very varied and that most borings for water on the Burren have been unsuccessful. The Carboniferous Limestones of the Burren do not yield water nor do they transmit it. Flood water is rapidly absorbed into the joints and bedding-plane caves, but these are quickly filled; the flood water backs up the cave passages and does not pass into the limestone mass. The underground conduits are not yet sufficiently developed to deal with high-water conditions. The springs respond very rapidly to an increase in precipitation, which indicates a percolation and rain water, not groundwater, origin, since springs from groundwater origins have a more even discharge; they also show wide variations in hardness. Good examples are seen at St Brendan's and at Killeaney on the eastern slopes of Slieve Elva. Hence Williams concludes there is no well-integrated system of channels within the Burren limestones; the caves for the most part act as discrete water conduits. Flood water rises to different levels in neighbouring caves according to the capacity of each cave system and the balance between inflow and outflow. Because of the lack of connections, vertical fluctuations of water levels are quite considerable. The groundwater is therefore not integrated and the concept of a regional water-table is untenable, though locally developed watertables may be shown to exist.

On the Gort lowland, however, east of the Burren uplands, there is evidence of the existence of an integrated network of groundwater. This area stretches from Ennis to Kinvarra on the south side of Galway Bay, and its altitude ranges from sea-level to about 250 ft (80 m). There is sufficient data from boreholes and levels of water in lakes and rivers to enable a contoured water-table surface to be drawn, which Williams regards as accurate to within 10 ft (3 m). Where the water channels have not been obstructed by glacial drift the annual water-level fluctuations in the turloughs (which we have already discussed on p. 205) is between 1–4 ft ($\frac{1}{2}$–1 m). Furthermore, changes in the water balance in the lowland are transmitted through rock fissures to affect all the water bodies in the district. This is reflected partly by the connection of some of the turloughs with the sea; for instance, Hawkill Lough over five miles inland and having no surface connection with the sea is reported to be tidal. The permeability of the Carboniferous Limestones of the Gort lowland, however, is by no means perfect. The yield of water from pumps may be as low as 100 gallons an hour and evidence from the chemical qualities of the groundwater also indicates that the underground connections are only moderately developed; large differences in the hardness of the groundwater can be shown to exist which would presumably not occur if the mixing of ground with surface water was more complete. The groundwater network of the Gort lowland is therefore only moderately well developed.

Williams attributes the fact that a groundwater network exists beneath the Gort lowland, but not beneath the Burren upland, to the length of time the limestone has been exposed in the two districts. The lowland has been exposed to corrosion since the Tertiary period, which has given sufficient time for hundreds of feet of limestone to be removed and for the water to circulate underground for perhaps millions of years. Moreover, the Gort lowland has been the reception basin for the drainage and aggressive waters from the sandstones of Slieve Aughty and the Namurian shales and flagstone uplands of west Clare; innumerable underground conduits have been developed. In the Burren, by contrast, erosion has only recently exposed the limestones from their impermeable shale cover. Stripping probably started at the end of the Tertiary period, but there is no doubt that the Glacial period was responsible for removing a large amount of shale cover from the Burren. Thus the Burren has had very little time to develop a groundwater network. This corresponds to north-west Yorkshire, which is rather similar.

It has been pointed out that under western European conditions only two zones of groundwater are present; these can be said to approximate to the first and third zones of Cvijič, the intervening central zone of alternating water fill and free air being omitted. This is because the cave passages in western European limestones are adapted to carry away the flood water with only a small rise in the head. Like our river channels, the caves are adjusted to high-water conditions. Fluctuations in the discharge of the underground channels in a western oceanic climate are also infinitely smaller than those in a Mediterranean climate [87, 375].

The compromise views suggested by the British work is to some extent endorsed by studies from the north-eastern limestone Alps by Zötl [376]. The University of Graz has over a period of years studied the underground waters of the mountains of the Totes Gebirge in the Dachstein group and other limestone massifs. One would have expected the geological considerations to predispose the results in favour of the ideas of Otto Lehmann. Detailed experiments in water tracing using *Lycopodium* spores have been conducted. These have indicated among other conclusions that the underground drainage is directly related to base level. Zötl is of the opinion that, 'while fully appreciat-

ing the pursuits of O. Lehmann which greatly further karst researches, the principal conclusions in his *Karsthydrographie*, 1932, have turned out to be wrong in respect of the north-eastern Limestone Alps' [376].

Again in his work on Hölloch in central Switzerland, Bögli accepts the existence of a karst water surface (Karstwasserfläche), which he says 'behaves according to hydro-mechanical laws and is thus more aptly called a piezometric surface. Its location is largely determined by the main drainage [377]. The Hölloch Cave possesses cave levels 'or subterranean karst levels'. Three main levels can be recognised and these can be related to phases in the formation of the main valley. Bögli's diagram resembles that given by Ford for his model of a Mendip cave related to a series of different water levels. Ford himself comments 'The similarity to the example from Swildon's Hole is quite evident though the scale is much larger' [511].

In the U.S.A. hydrological thinking has been much more concerned with assuming the existence of groundwater and of a water-table than in Europe or even in Britain. This is probably not only due to the ideas of W. M. Davis, but also to the less complicated hydrology of much of the interior of the United States. Karst morphologists there have been much interested in underground water flow and its relation to the locus of cavern formation [224]. This work has followed that laid down by Davis, Bretz and Swinnerton, and has been concentrated in the relatively flat-lying limestones of Indiana, Kentucky, Tennessee, and also Florida.

At a Symposium of the National Speleological Society in 1959, it was shown that most of the known caves of the U.S.A. have a horizontal pattern; in the folded limestones of the Appalachians many caves are developed in a series of horizontal levels, indicating a repetition of a rigid hydrological control. Such caves are quite unlike the vertical jamas discussed by Roglič from the Dinaric karst. This evidence from the vertical distribution of the caves shows that solution within the mass of limestone is not random; if cave formation were random throughout the limestone mass, there would be one vast chamber or numerous small passages along all joints and fractures. This is not the condition observed, where only small non-integrated tubes occur between the main cave levels [258]. Davies showed from the evidence in the caves in the Appalachians that the cave passages become larger in size as the major valleys are approached. This enlargement reflects an increasing flow through the developing passages [68]. The most rapid flow in groundwater is at or just below the piezometric surface. In accord with the observations of Kaye, 1957, solution would be most rapid in this zone; at greater depths below the piezometric surface, where there is much less movement of groundwater, solutional activity is reduced. Thus Davies's conclusions were as follows: (1) that from his study of the caves in plan, profile and section, the greatest solution occurs when a zone of maximum solvent flow in the watertable is nearly horizontal; (2) the passages were integrated and enlarged in a narrow zone near the top of the groundwater; and (3) the slope of the passages shows a gentle gradient of the piezometric surface towards the major surface valleys. This zone of preferred region for cave excavation has been called by Thrailkill the *shallow-phreatic zone* [224].

Thus American work has until now accepted almost without question the concept of a water-table in karst regions. Moore [378], and more recently Thrailkill [224], are much more concerned with the apparent localisation of solution and greater water flow in the vicinity of the water-table or the shallow-phreatic zone. Thrailkill has reviewed the factors which influence the location of this greater solution and considers the different kinds of water flow and the effects of temperature and mixture corrosion upon the hardness of the water as being conducive to increased flow and solution in this zone. 'It may eventually be convenient to separate the shallow-phreatic zone from the rest of the aquifer. In any case, it seems best to consider the upper limit of the shallow-phreatic zone as an "average, steady-state, flood-water table"' (loc. cit., p. 43). This kind of statement is completely different from that made about the Dinaric karst.

It is useful also to discuss the hydrological conditions in a tropical humid region. The hydrology of the White Limestone areas of Jamaica were first discussed by Zans [326]. He believed that underground water in the crystalline White Limestones circulated through large relatively independent channels, and referred to the underground water circulation beneath the Cockpit Country as resembling that of a 'canalisation system beneath a city. . . . The underground water flow is in conduits of the labyrinthine fissure system and is comparatively rapid. One can hardly speak of definite water-tables in such areas' [326]. In the less permeable Montpelier Beds along the north coast, poljes have been formed, as has already been indicated, and a water-table can be inferred.

Although many streams disappear into the White Limestones in the central area of Jamaica, the greater part of the underground water in the White Limestones is autochthonous, derived from the relatively heavy rainfalls over the White Limestone areas. The direction of the underground water flow is controlled, first, by the directions of the dip, jointing and faulting within the limestones; secondly, by the changes in the lithology of the White Limestones; and thirdly, by the height and relief of the karst basis which is formed by the middle and upper beds of the Yellow Limestones [134]. Versey has recently brought forward evidence for believing that the groundwater in the White Limestones behaves as if a water-table does exist, but he is also of the opinion that some of the major cave systems form water conduits which are perched above the main groundwater-table; this can be demonstrated in Lluidas Vale, where flooding occurs in the local caves before the water-table present under the vale itself rises. Versey was also inclined to believe that the depths of the cockpits were partly related to the depth of the groundwater circulation, the cockpits themselves being deepened as a result of flood-water circulation at no great depth [143].

In 1958 the writer made the point that, to anyone familiar with British and western European karstlands, the pattern of groundwater circulation in the White Limestone areas of Jamaica seemed relatively free and unconfined, and that the actual flow of the water underground was very rapid. In recent years two hydrological expeditions have been able to engage in some water tracing in parts of these areas. The results of the Karst Hydrology Expedition, 1966, are of interest in this respect [210]. Brown says the following conclusions may be drawn. The rivers flow in fairly discrete channels and at a velocity of about 1 mile (1·6 km) a day (2½ miles – 4 km – in 42 hours). This is faster than in more temperate climates, but he quotes an example of a test done in New Guinea by Brongersma in 1959 in which an underground river was traced for ten miles in four hours [210]. Very fast underground flow patterns have now been recorded by water-tracing experiments in the Rocky Mountains by D. C. Ford, in Canada (personal communication). Brown notes a point also made by the writer that pebbles and debris of relatively large size are transported throughout the caves in Jamaica and for long distances (up to 13 miles (21 km), for instance, in the Cave River-Dornock Head system). Pebbles (up to 2–5 cm diameter) derived from the rocks of the Central Inlier occur in the springs and outlet caves along the northern edge of the Cockpit Country and the Dry Harbour Mountains. This indicates, says Brown, that the aquifer 'has no lengthy sand filters in it, and that the flow is not through a tightly connected anastomastic network'.

Elsewhere in Jamaica in the Pedro Plains, in the south-west, exploratory drilling and testing has indicated 'that the water movement is confined to the top 20–30 ft (6–9 m) of the saturated zone' [379]. Wozab and Williams have recently shown in the Pedro Plains area that 'contrary to that of a normal coastal plain, the water table does not conform to the topography'. The Plains slope in general to the west and north, whereas the unconfined water-table, though essentially flat, slopes north and south-west [380].

These examples illustrate some of the problems in karst hydrology.

3. CONCLUSIONS

While the characteristic of openings in karst limestones is the ability of their surfaces to react with the bicarbonate anion of the water which passes through them, and such enlargement of the openings is typical, the reprecipitation of the dissolved bicarbonate leads also to the filling and sealing of the openings. An essential feature of karst hydrology is the presence of both a diffuse and a concentrated circulation. Direct infiltration of the rainfall favours diffuse groundwater circulation and the general enlargement of joints over a wide area. Surface run-off water and surface concentration leads to concentrated groundwater circulation and the concentrated waters will infiltrate most rapidly into the most fissured zone or point; such localised infiltrations form zones of accelerated corrosion and lead to the formation of swallow holes.

High infiltration and low run-off also characterise the hydrology of karstlands. In Greece, for instance, in the Parnassos-Ghiona area, the infiltration into the limestone aquifer has been calculated to be 45·2 per cent, while surface run-off is only 3·6 per cent [350].

Furthermore there exist differences not only between one karst area and another, but between parts of the same karst region. Pitty's work in Poole's Cavern stressed a slow seepage rate and a discrete network of underground channels, but elsewhere in the Peak District, only a few kilometres away, there are much more fissured limestones where the seepage rates are much greater. Thus each sector of the karst must be looked at separately. The permeability of limestones normally increases with time as the underground conduits are enlarged; as a consequence of the increasing water-holding capacity of the underground passageways, the higher conduits become dry as the lower ones develop. If the permeability of the limestone mass becomes widely and uniformly developed, the transmissibility is high and an irregular level of saturation or irregular water-table will be formed. If the transmissibility is low then the underground drainage is through more or less independent systems. The depth of flooding in the independent conduits varies accord-

ing to the relative discharge of the influent and effluent streams. Deeper flooding occurs in drainage systems made up of discrete channels than in an integrated network with a high transmissibility. But since the permeability of limestones is achieved through the fissures, bedding planes, and the interconnecting voids, with the vast mass of the limestone normally impermeable, a water-table in karst limestones, such as occurs in porous rocks like a chalk or a sandstone, does not exist. Methods of groundwater hydrology developed for non-fissured rocks will only give misleading results when applied to karst limestones. The intricate relationships and complexes between cave systems can only be explained on this assumption. In areas of thick and compact limestones like those in the Dinaric karst the circulation is deep and the caves, which tend to be vertical, are only developed at depth. In areas of thinner horizontal limestones and shallower karst, there seems no doubt that the most important zone of water movement, and hence of solution and locus for cave development, lies in the upper part of the saturated limestone.

Though there is still dispute 'about the merits of the water-table and channel-flow theories of the nature of karst water' [370], four vertical hydrodynamic zones of karst water can be distinguished. These are:

(a) The zone of aeration, in which the downward movement of infiltration and inflow water prevails. This includes 'suspended' or perched water.

(b) The zone of seasonal fluctuation of karst water. This zone is transitional; when the water-level falls, it becomes part of the zone of aeration; when the water-level rises, it merges with the zone of full saturation.

(c) The zone of full saturation where drainage is governed by the local drainage network. In this zone karst waters move all the year round.

(*d*) The zone of deep circulation, where the groundwaters are not influenced by any local drainage network. This zone is characterised by slow water exchange.

Each area develops in its own peculiar way [381].

The distinctive nature of karst hydrology was recognised in the Dubrovnik Symposium, 1965, held to discuss the Hydrology of Fractured Rocks (Hydrologie des roches fissurées), under the auspices of the United Nations Organisation.

14 Types of Karst

1. INTRODUCTION: ATTEMPTS TO CLASSIFY KARSTLANDS

From the beginning of karst studies there have been attempts to distinguish different types of karstland. It was realised that they were not all like the Classical or Dinaric areas. Cvijič divided karstlands into the *holokarst,* the *merokarst* and the *transitional karst.* In his original *Das Karstphänomen* he only dealt with the distribution of karst phenomena in geological time; but in his essay 'Types Morphologiques des Terrains Calcaires' [382] and in his book *La Géographie des Terrains Calcaires* [148], he makes the distinctions that are now well known. Both in *Das Karstphänomen* and the later works, Cvijič at no time considers the differentiation of karst types solely on a climatic basis, lithology always being taken into account. Though Cvijič is often regarded as the originator of the ideas of holokarst and merokarst (partial karst), Roglič has pointed out that Grund had already made the distinction in 1914 in his paper 'Das Geographische Zyklus im Karst', when he used the terms *karst* and *halbkarst* (half or semi-karst) [2].

The *holokarst,* in Cvijič's definition, is the most perfectly developed karst, both from the point of view of the landforms and also of the subterranean hydrology. The possibilities of development are regarded as almost unlimited both in the horizontal and in the vertical sense. The holokarst is constituted of such massive and pure limestones dissected by vertical fissures that its evolution is unhindered from the crest of its mountains to the impermeable bed which forms the karst basis, and evolution can go on below sea-level. The lack of river valleys gives rise to extensive surfaces, characteristic of the karst. Impermeable beds within the limestones are regarded as insignificant. It is only in the holokarst that 'les vrais poljes karstiques avec leur phénomènes hydrographiques spéciaux ont pu se développer complètement' [148]. Cvijič regarded the best examples of the holokarst to be in the Dinaric karst, in parts of Greece, particularly in the Peloponnese. He also cites parts of Asia Minor, notably Lycia, and the karst in Jamaica.

The *merokarst* is an imperfect or partial karst, with certain traits of karstic relief. Merokarst occurs in relatively thin or less pure limestone, and particularly where the limestones alternate with marly bands. The depth of development is not as great as in holokarst and the evolution of the relief is more rapid. Mechanical erosion is more important and normal valleys are developed. The merokarst is generally covered with soil, and Cvijič thought that free karren are absent and dolines only sparingly developed; there are no poljes. Swallow holes and caves are common. The hydrology is less complex than in the holokarst, it being possible to follow the underground river courses, and deduce the resurgences with certainty. Underground drainage is more obstructed by impermeable material. Examples of merokarst were to be found in the Franconian Jura, the Carboniferous Limestone areas of Britain and Ireland, the karst of Galicia in Poland and the Devonian limestone karst of Moravia; he also included the chalk lands of southern England and northern France.

The *transitional karst,* of which Cvijič's

major example is the Causses of France, 'approaches the holokarst more than the merokarst', and is developed in a great thickness of limestone permitting of deep karstic forms. However, the karst basis formed by the impermeable bed is not so deep as in the holokarst and therefore the karstic evolution is more rapid; normal valleys are much more frequent than in the holokarst, and hence the Causses are divided up into more numerous and less extensive 'compartments' than the true karst. Poljes are almost completely lacking. The other transitional type that Cvijič mentions is the Jura type, based on the karstic phenomena of the Jura mountains, where the karst forms are less developed and even more divided into compartments than in the Causses. The Causses type is represented by limestone plateaux separated by gorge-like valleys; the surfaces between are extensive and were considered by him to have been planed by river erosion before their karstification. In the same category as the Causses, Cvijič includes the plateaux of the eastern Alps, such as the Dachstein, and karst plateaux of the eastern Balkans. The Jura transitional type is characterised by alternations of thick-bedded limestones with substantial marly beds; karst phenomena are more dispersed and sporadic than in the Causses type and are more often attacked by retrogressive erosion. On the surfaces between the main valleys, dolines and gouffres (potholes) are frequent, but the only larger type of depression to occur is the uvala. Included in the Jura type are the Vercours and the Chartreuse massifs of the French pre-Alps.

There were other classifications. Sawicki, in 1909, distinguished between the bare (nackter) karst of the Dinaric area, and soil-covered (bedeckter) karst more typical of central and western Europe [383]. In differentiating Mediterranean-type karst from Middle European karst, Sawicki thought climatic factors (rainfall and temperature) as important as the limestones themselves, and thus he was one of the first to classify karst areas on a climatic basis. Albrecht Penck also distinguished between bare and soil-covered karst. In his essay in 1924 on 'Unterirdische Karst', he introduces a third type, that of subsurface (or unterirdische) karst, which he refers to karst forms developed beneath a cover of other rocks [127]. The influence of W. M. Davis and the ideas of the cycle of erosion also affected attempts to classify karst landforms. As will be seen later, karst studies have been less influenced by cyclic thinking than other branches of geomorphology. Baulig, Chabot and Clozier working in France all attempted to differentiate karst landforms from the point of view of the cycle of erosion, and came to the conclusion that the 'expression de cycle fluvio-karstique répond mieux à la réalité des faits' [117], and that the real distinction in karst areas was between holokarst and fluviokarst.

Between 1920 and 1940 climatic geomorphology developed rapidly in Europe and the importance of previous climatic phases in the evolution of karst landforms began to be realised. Furthermore other karst areas in the world were being studied and the classification of karst on a climatic basis began to be an obvious method. This was linked with the development of cycles of landform development associated with different climatic types, put forward by Peltier [384] in 1950 and developed by Birot [77] and others in the last few years. In many ways H. Lehmann may be regarded as a pioneer in the study of the climatic differentiation of karst landforms, with his work on the Goenoeng Sewoe, a tropical karst in Java, published in 1936 [385]. In the Karst Symposium held in Frankfurt in 1953 it was stated that each climate had its own 'clima-specific' karst development. The characteristics of each clima-specific were discussed and the main landforms of each were described [325].

The main climatic zones in which karst landforms are considered to be distinctive on the grounds of climate are as follows: the periglacial and polar zones; the high Alpine zones; the cool oceanic west European-type zone; the Mediterranean zone; the dry desert zone; and the humid tropical zone. It was also noted, at the meeting of the Karst Commission of the I.G.U. in Rio de Janeiro in 1956, that in view of the dependence of karst upon climatic conditions it was unfortunate that 'the classical karst research started with the karst regions of the middle latitudes. The landforms of the karst are complex in this zone . . . because they were exposed to changing climatological conditions during their development' [386]. In the humid tropical areas, in the periglacial regions of the Arctic and in the interior of the great deserts it was possible that conditions during the Quaternary and the Tertiary had not changed enough to affect the development of karst landforms in those areas. One problem, to which we shall return, concerns the extent to which the landforms developed in these climatic zones, where the conditions have been relatively unchanging, are typical of the landforms developed in the continuously changing zones of the middle latitudes. H. Lehmann, for instance, claims that the landforms developed in the tropical humid karstlands are 'specific for the hot climate and cannot be transferred to other climates', i.e. that the tropical limestone landforms are unique to the tropics [387].

Whilst it is undeniable that climate is a major determinant in the differentiation of karst landforms, it is by no means the only one, and it could be said that to a certain

extent modern German and French karst morphologists have been obsessed with this one factor. Morphologists working in the Classical Karst, while recognising the importance of climate, are also aware of the importance of the thickness and fissurisation of the limestones and the lithological type. Jenko says in 1959, 'Decisive for the karstification is the structure of the rocks. The climate does not form the karst, it only gives to it certain characteristics, otherwise we could explain the existence of the karst in all regions from the Arctic down to the tropics' [340].

However, Jenko goes on to distinguish High Mountain karst, Polar and Tropical karsts, so that he too is using a partial climatic classification [340]. The writer herself has shown how, in Jamaica, lithology is an important determinant in karst landforms, the crystalline White Limestones, the Montpelier Beds and the Yellow Limestone all being characterised by different kinds of landforms [134]. Monroe stresses the same point in Puerto Rico [388].

The U.S.S.R. has many types of karst both in European Russia and in Siberia. A recent classification by Gvozdeckij distinguishes the following [389]:

(1) *Bare karst,* more or less equivalent to the Mediterranean Dinaric karst (holokarst).

(2) *Covered karst,* a karst where the limestones are covered with sediments that are unrelated to the limestone mass, i.e. limestones covered with fluvioglacial material, alluvium, or with a cover rock such as a sandstone.

(3) *Soil-covered or 'soddy' karst,* a karst where the limestones are covered with soil or terra rossa derived from the limestones themselves.

(4) *Buried karst,* a karst landscape which has been completely buried by later rocks so as to be no part of the contemporary

landscape and only detectable in borings and wells.

| (5) *Tropical or cone karst* | Both distinguished on a climatic basis, |
| (6) *Permafrost karst* | as in Jenko's classification. |

Gvozdeckij also recognises karst in other rocks besides karst limestones, and gives as his types: limestone karst; dolomite karst; chalky karst; gypsum karst; and rock-salt karst. Gvozdeckij says that if we combine both the morphological and the lithological classification we have 'a more or less complete list of the main types of karst in the U.S.S.R.'. He says furthermore that the types can be divided into mountain and lowland karst, since the high-altitude phenomena of the mountains, and also often their tectonic structure, separate them from the lowland karst.

In a paper presented to the American Association for the Advancement of Science in 1966, Quinlan outlines a classification of karst types on similar lines to that of Gvozdeckij. He uses the following six criteria: (1) Type of cover (bare, covered, soil, etc.), (2) type of lithology, (3) type of climate, (4) geological structure, (5) physiography (i.e. mountain or plain, etc.), (6) modification during or after karstification (i.e. buried or rejuvenated, etc.) [390]. It will be seen therefore that, in areas away from western and central Europe, climatic classifications alone are not felt to be completely satisfactory and that more complex classifications of karst types are used.

In 1965, Roglič differentiated between the Dinaric karst proper and fluviokarst; this is similar to the difference between deep and shallow karst [218]. Roglič's map of the morphological types of the Dinaric karst is given in Fig. 110. Fluviokarstic relief, or shallow karst, is characterised by some form of slope washing and alluvial cover; river valleys cut through the limestone beds and

horizontal caves develop. The deep karst occurs where the deep water circulation is not reflected in the surface landforms; it is characterised by jamas which are connected with ramified systems of deep fissures; and it is poor in caves. As an example of fluviokarstic relief, Roglič mentions the Swabian and Franconian Jura [179]. It will be seen that Roglič is restating in modern terms the holokarst and merokarst of Cvijič, and says in 1964: 'We consider the term fluviokarst . . . indicates the combination of the two morphogenetic processes' [179]. It seems to the author that such a classification, based on a combination of climate and process, is the most valuable at the present time. However, the landforms of temperate latitudes have been affected by recent climatic changes, so that it is difficult to assess the extent to which they are the result of present or of past climatic conditions. This is particularly true of areas in central Europe where Tertiary and Quaternary climatic changes were many. Panoš has shown how the karst areas of Czechoslovakia possess examples of landforms brought about by conditions in different climatic periods which are now relict or fossil forms [391]. He remarks 'in the author's opinion the climate morphogenetic typification recently undertaken in some papers and based only on the main climatic types of the world is not convincing'. But even he speaks of a 'central European karst', dividing it into the central European karst of the Old Block Mountains, and the central European karst of the Young Fold Mountains, indicating a structural/climatic classification (loc. cit., p. 21).

Thus the perfect classification does not exist. Cavaillé has said, in a study of the Causses de Quercy, that the static morphological and spatial outlook should be replaced by one which is both more dynamic and chronological. In his view the

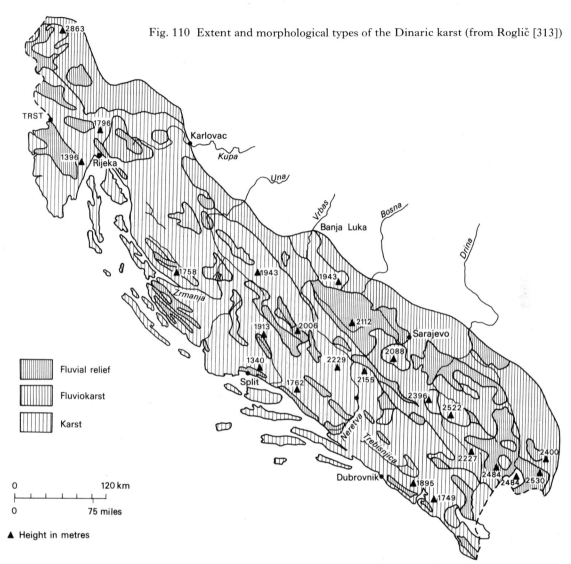

Fig. 110 Extent and morphological types of the Dinaric karst (from Roglič [313])

karst forms of the Causses de Quercy have been 'classified' for far too long. The karst in Quercy is, in his words, 'ni petit, ni grand, ni complet, ni incomplet, ni holo, ni méro. Il est complexe, formé de karsts superposés, de moins en moins évolués à mesure qu'ils sont plus récents' [290, 392].

However, though each karst area is unique, some typification must be made and because of this some discussion of karst types is now given.

2. THE CHIEF TYPES OF KARSTLANDS

Since karstland forms owe their origin to the predominance of the process of solution, a classification based on both climate and process is proposed, since almost no karst is the result of only one process or set of climatic conditions. According to the dominant process or climatic regime which has fashioned the landscapes, karsts are:

43 Dinaric holokarst, near Karlobag, Jugoslavia

(1) *True karst* (holokarst). Landforms produced dominantly by the karst processes – solutional.

(2) *Fluviokarst*.

(3) *Glacio-(Nival)karst,* including Permafrost (High Arctic) karst.

(4) *Tropical karst*.

(5) *Arid and semi-arid karst*.

Clearly each of these main types is divisible on a structural basis into high mountains, usually contorted limestone, karst, and lowland, often flat-lying limestone, karst. Other types, such as buried, sub-surface (inter-stratal), relict or fossil and pseudo-karsts occur, but are not as widespread; they will be discussed in Chapter 16. The classification given above is based on our present knowledge. As more is known, particularly of tropical karsts, especially in south-east Asia, this classification will undoubtedly be modified. In this chapter, true (holokarst), fluviokarst and glacio- and nivalkarst will be considered. Tropical and semi-arid karst will be dealt with in Chapter 15.

(A) TRUE KARST (HOLOKARST)

The world's best-known true karst is the Dinaric karst, Photo 43, though as more knowledge is accumulated it may no longer remain the type area for karst landforms.

We have already indicated that the karst-lands of Jugoslavia include the so-called 'Classical' karst in Slovenia, and the Dinaric karst which extends along the coast of the Adriatic as far as Albania. Cvijič regarded both regions as holokarst, but Roglič thinks that the Classical Karst is of a more transitional and even fluviokarstic nature [5].

The Dinaric karst stretches from Rijeka to the Albanian border, a distance of over 600 km, extending inland for about 100 km. It shows, of course, much regional differentiation, but its chief characteristic is its pitted nature or 'wannenlandschaft'. Thus, in Montenegro, over 64 per cent of the total country consists of dolines, which is probably the most karstic part of Europe. The landscape consists of one hollow after another, a succession of funnel-like dolines separated by cone-shaped hills with slopes varying from 20° to 30°. The dolines vary in depth from a few metres to over 100 m. The limestones are over 4,000 m thick, the Dinaric mountains over 2,000 m high, and in parts the rainfall is over 2,500 m per year, yet no streams run down the mountain slopes and dry valleys and river-formed features are absent. The water is concealed in the cavities of the karst and the water circulation is very deep and does not bear any relation to the landforms at the surface.

Caverns and jamas exist probably at great depth, but may never be discovered; subterranean collapse of their roofs will reveal some of the deeper circulation. Horizontal caves are not typical. The fissures extend deeply into the rock, the karst basis being provided by the impermeable layers at depth. Corbel's figures illustrate the number of caves per 100 km^2; in Montenegro it is 3, whereas in the Classical Karst it is 50 per km^2 [393]. Thus strictly all true karst should be doline karst, with the emphasis on vertical dissolution. In the purist sense, all non-doline type landforms are deviants.

Where any impermeable rocks occur on the surface, slope-wash and fluvial erosion take place. Differential erosion occurs at the contact of the limestones and the impermeable beds and debris from them is washed into fissures in the limestones, to disappear into the deep circulation. This process has formed the poljes, the depressions formed in impermeable layers and surrounded by limestones. Roglič explains the principal allogenic valleys which cross the Dinaric karst as having been formed by the joining-up of widened poljes, developed in the impermeable beds, by canyons in the limestones. Unlike the poljes in the Classical Karst, poljes in the Dinaric karst are drained by vertical ponors and not by large horizontal cave passages. Corbel claims that the poljes in the Dinaric karst are drained more slowly than those in the Postojna area, where they are drained by big caves [393].

The Cretaceous limestones are the most pure and compact in the Dinaric karst; they are also the least fissured. In these are the deepest cavities and on them the largest corrosion plains occur – both features being related to the purity of the limestones. Because of the small amount of residual material, such pure limestones tend to have less soil cover; and, as a result of recent soil erosion, they are now mostly bare karst, on which rillen- and rinnenkarren are well developed. Near-surface collapse features are infrequent.

The Jurassic limestones on the other hand tend to be less pure and more fissured, and less compact. As a result of the greater number of fissures, the limestone blocks are smaller, collapse of the surface strata is more frequent and the subterranean cavities are smaller. Because the rock is rather less pure, there is more rock waste and more soil cover and vegetation. The dolines are therefore rather wider and there is more surface dissolution.

The coast of the Dinaric karst was the subject of an excellent essay by Milojevic [178], who points out the influence of the compact limestones and the intercalations of Eocene flysch upon the coastal landforms. Because of the predominance of limestones, sandy coasts are rare, and the beaches consist of limestone pebbles. The coastal parts of the Dinaric karst have less vegetation because of the strong winds of the Bora. Large submarine springs occur along the entire coast.

Complete karst such as the Dinaric karst occurs in parts of central and southern Greece; in the Parnassus area, for instance, there are over 4,000 m of virtually uninterrupted limestone sequence. Other regions of the world where thick uninterrupted deposits of limestones occur are in the West Indies and in south-east Asia; in these areas tropical karst has developed and this will be considered separately in Chapter 16.

The 'Classical' karstland, between the Ljubljana Marsh and the head of the Adriatic, like that of the Dinaric karst is made up of limestones of Secondary age with interruptions of Eocene flysch, and folded in a NW.–SE. direction. But because the impermeable flysch beds are thicker and more extensive, there are large areas of the Classical Karst which are subject to normal fluvial drainage. Thus streams rising on the flysch sink into caves on reaching the limestones; large river-formed caves, many miles long, are therefore typical of the Classical Karst, of which the Postojna Cave and the Škocjan Cave, into which the Pivka and Reka rivers disappear, are two well-known examples. We have already given the figures for comparing the number of caves per 100 km² of limestone for the Classical Karst (50 for the Classical Karst as against 3 per 100 km² for Montenegro and 10 for the coastal part of the Dinaric karst). The limestones in the Classical Karst are much fissured and jointed; as a result large near-surface collapse landforms are common, like the Rakov Škocjan, where collapse dolines and natural bridges occur. As in the Dinaric karst, poljes form on the impermeable beds; they are drained by through caves rather than by vertical ponors. Because of the slightly cooler climate and more continental rainfall regime, the Classical Karst is well wooded. Rillen- and rinnenkarren develop on bare rock surfaces, and rundkarren occur beneath the soil cover.

Both the Dinaric and 'Classical' karsts are in an area affected by the climatic changes of the Pleistocene; it is therefore important to differentiate between the effects on the landforms caused by non-climatic and by climatic factors.

(B) FLUVIOKARST

Fluviokarst is formed by the combined action of fluvial and karst processes. It will be realised that many of the karstlands described in western and central Europe are fluviokarstic. Because of the importance of rivers in fluviokarsts, such areas are cut through by allogenic rivers and are much more 'compartmented' than true karst. The extent of the limestones is much less, both horizontally and vertically; there is also much less opportunity for the development of a deep circulation irrespective of the base-level. The basal karst is less controlled by the extent of and thickness of the limestone beds, local water-levels being more important in providing a karst basis for the development of the landforms. Springs develop both at the level of the impermeable layers beneath the limestones, and also at the local water-tables; regressive erosion is also important. Normal river valleys and gorges are common, like the Tarn, the Lesse and the Dove; dry valleys also occur. Landforms associated with the disappearance and reappearance of water are frequent, in particular blind valleys and swallow holes of all types. Fluviokarst areas are also the most important for caves; caves are formed at the junction of the limestones with impermeable beds by the allogenic drainage and are associated with the development of the rivers through the limestones. Thus the caves are frequently arranged in a series of levels related to fluvial erosion stages [391]; they are often of considerable size, and collapse features due to near-surface cavern collapse are common, as at the Macocha in Moravia.

Between the main allogenic valleys, the karst processes are much more unhindered and the landforms are much more truly karstic. Vertical drainage and solutional processes become important. Thus dolines and potholes (gouffres) are often very numerous on the karst plateaux; where the limestones are thick, uvalas may form, as in the Jura, or polje-type depressions as the Plaine de Chanet in the Causse Méjean in Gévaudan. Marginal poljes occur where the aggressive water from the non-permeable

44 Fluviokarst, West Virginia

strata flows on to the limestones; local planation surfaces are found at these localities (*Ausraumbecken*) [315].

Limestone surfaces in fluviokarstic areas tend to be more soil-covered due to the presence of slope washing and debris, caused by the fluvial processes; the karst is therefore more often covered than bare. Bare karst surfaces may, however, occur if the area has suffered deforestation or soil erosion. Rundkarren develop under the soil cover, though occasionally free karren will form. As more work has been done on fluvio-karstic terrains it is becoming clear that many of these areas have experienced climatic changes in the Quaternary period. Thus in western and northern Europe, a warmer period in the Pliocene when karstification and underground drainage developed, was followed by glacial and periglacial periods when water flowed on the surface and the valleys were formed. The fluvio-karst areas of Europe about to be discussed are therefore partly the result of recent climatic change and to some extent possess relict landforms.

Many regions closely studied by geomorphologists in Europe and in North America are fluviokarstic, Photo 44. Hence many of the disputes about the relationship of the caves to former erosion levels and to

river terraces, etc., arise from the fact that fluviokarst landforms are developed differently and have had a different history from true karst forms. Some examples of fluviokarstic relief are: in Britain, the Mendips and the Peak District; in Europe, the Causses of France, the N.E. Bavaria (Fig. 111), the Moravian karst near Brno in

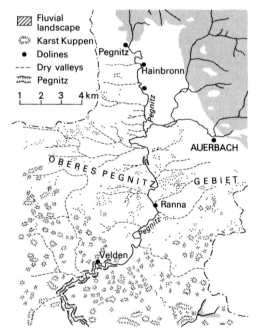

Fig. 111 Fluviokarst, Kuppen Alb, Franconian Jura (from Dongus [452])

Czechoslovakia, the Lesse area of Belgium; in Australia, the Buchan Caves district, the Bungonia and Jenolan Caves areas, and to a certain extent the Mole Creek area in Tasmania; in North America, the karst areas in the Appalachians in Virginia and West Virginia, where the karst is developed in folded limestones, and in Kentucky, Indiana and Tennessee where the fluviokarst is in gently dipping limestones. Fluviokarst is also important in the eastern part of the Dinaric karst, as shown in Roglič's map, Fig. 110, p. 256 [313].

Despite Cavaillé's assertion (see above), the Causses of Quercy in central France show many features characteristic of fluvial karst. These include the meandering valleys of the Lot and the Dordogne, together with many dry valleys, blind valleys and swallow holes. Thus Cvijič said of the Causses: 'Dans aucun terrain karstique je n'ai observé d'anciennes vallées sèches aussi bien développées que dans les Causses.' This is further confirmed by the presence on the plateaux of the Causses of alluvial deposits of gravels, etc., derived from the surrounding impermeable rocks and transported on to the Causses by fluvial action when the main allogenic and dry valleys were at the same height as the limestone plateaux [115, 117]. As has been indicated, these fluvial landforms in the Causses are considered to be largely of Pleistocene (particularly Riss and Würm) age.

In Britain the Peak District is probably the best example of a predominantly fluviokarstic type. Since this area suffered less severe glaciation, but much periglaciation, during the last Glacial phase, it has remained largely fluviokarstic, whereas the Ingleborough district in north-west Yorkshire was transformed into a glacial karst. Warwick's map in 1964 gives some idea of the network of the dry valleys on the Carboniferous Limestones of the Peak District, Fig. 53(a) [199]. The Peak District limestones are surrounded on almost all sides by sandstones and shales of the Millstone Grit series, which form a barrier to the escape of water from the limestones; the Peak District is an example of a *karst barré*, and because of this it contains much water [394].

The heart of this area is formed by the limestone plateau at a height of 280–340 m above Ordnance Survey Datum. The main allogenic valleys, the Wye, the Dove and Manifold, have cut down as much as 150 m below the general surface of the plateau. Such rivers cut across the geological structures in the limestones. Warwick regards the dry valleys as having been formed in response to the cutting down through the limestones of the major valleys, as a result of multiple rejuvenation and lowering of the local water-table and also as a result of captures. T. D. Ford, however, is of the opinion that the dry valleys have resulted from periglacial conditions [395]. The upper parts of the valleys are gently graded and often 'consist of a wide "bowle", oval or circular in shape'. The 'bowles' are poljelike extensions of planed limestones caused by accelerated corrosion from acidic water coming from the surrounding shales, and are *Ausraumbecken*, e.g., Wardlow Mires.

Blind valleys are numerous, and inlet caves are associated with the disappearing streams, as at Perry Foot and Giant's Hole. These are also areas of accelerated corrosion. Caves tend to be distributed either around the edge of the limestone massif or in association with the valleys, Fig. 53(a). This is what one would expect in a fluviokarst – those caves around the edge of the limestone mass being connected with the disappearance and resurgence of the underground water, and those in association with the valleys being formed as the rivers have been cut down through the limestone.

Definite cave-levels, however, have not been recognised. One or two caves are found some distance from the limestone shale edge, as for example Eldon Hole; Warwick suggests that this was formed before the shale edge was eroded to its present limit when it was nearer Eldon Hole. Caves are numerous in the Reef facies of the limestones, especially in Dovedale. Because the Peak District limestones are surrounded by impermeable rocks, the water-levels tend to be controlled by levels in these beds; hence there are local groundwater-levels in parts of the area. Resurgences of this groundwater are common and there are some big springs, notably the rising of the river Lathkill and at Russet Well. Warwick maintains that the caves associated with the spring heads are larger than those associated with the swallow hole-inlet caves [27].

Between the valleys, the plateau-like surface of the Peak District shows some karst features. The surface is in general soil-covered; this is believed by Pigott to have been better preserved on the Derbyshire limestone because the region escaped the most recent glaciation [396]. However, beneath the soil cover, in some parts of the area, solution-enlarged fissures can be shown to be present and shallow dolines occur. Solutional lowering of the limestone surface after the stripping of the overlying shales is believed by Pitty to explain the existence of platforms of different height; such solutional lowering is diversified by the presence of volcanic rocks within the limestones [397].

The plateau is also diversified by shallow conical hills, called 'lows', which rise above the general level of its surface. They are particularly important along the watershed between the Wye–Derwent drainage and the Dove drainage. An example is End Low which is 1,283 ft (400 m) high and about 200 ft (65 m) above the main plateau. These conical lows appear in many ways to be the most karstified landforms of the Peak District, resembling in a subdued way the conical hills of the Classical Karst. In support of an earlier karstification there is the evidence of deep holes (possible collapsed caverns) now filled with Triassic sands; associated with these holes are caverns which are quite different from those related to the river valleys, Fig. 81 [398]. Some people have regarded the deep holes filled with sand as relics of a former, possibly warmer karst [399]. Thus the centre part of the limestone plateau in the Peak District has been partly formed during an earlier, probably Tertiary, period of karstification and possesses relict landforms. Even earlier phases of karstification (i.e. Permian) may be represented [395]. Thus the Peak District resembles in this way the Causses of Quercy, in that it illustrates more than one phase of karstification, despite being essentially a fluviokarst. T. Ford's work on the Peak District has been highly elucidating, and has shown that the sand pockets contain both Triassic and Tertiary material. The control in their location is the occurrence of dolomitised Carboniferous Limestone. Ford indicates that solution collapse, often under a sand cover, has been an important process in the evolution of these landforms. From these important conclusions it may be postulated that the Derbyshire 'lows' developed largely under a sand cover in a warmer Pliocene climate [528, 529].

The Jurassic limestone and the Chalk areas of Britain are also fluviokarstic, but are more fluvial than karstic. These rocks are not strong enough to support karst features, such as caves and swallow holes, on any well-developed scale. Solution, however, can be shown to be important in the denudation of these rocks, as witness the very high figures for the calcium and magnesium content of their spring waters. It can be shown that the average calcium and magnesium content of spring waters from the Jurassic limestones and the Chalk are as follows:

Jurassic limestones: 230 ppm $CaCO_3$, 40 ppm $MgCO_3$.

Chalk springs: 260 ppm $CaCO_3$, 20 ppm $MgCO_3$.

Dry valleys, diffuse underground drainage and large springs are all important. Thus the limestones of the English scarplands illustrate the features of a fluvial landscape with some karstic landforms, Fig. 53(b), and merit more attention than has so far been paid to them. They are also nival-karstic because of the susceptibility of soft limestones to peri-glacial processes; hence much of the valley and slope formation in the limestone of the English Scarplands has been caused by snow and frost action and melt-water during the Quaternary.

In the U.S.A. the great areas of karst in Tennessee, Indiana and Kentucky are all regions of fluvial karst. Evidence of fluvial action is well described by Malott in all his accounts [121, 196, 208, 261]. The caves of this karst region tend to occur in levels, which have been suggested to be related to the stages in the down-cutting of the major rivers, and this is particularly well shown in the series of levels in Mammoth Cave. The meandering valleys which cut through the Indiana karst show all the features expected of a fluvial karst, with subterranean cut-offs, underground stream piracy, large river caves and springs associated with the rivers. Similarly in the folded Appalachians in Virginia, Palaeozoic limestones gave rise to areas of fluviokarst, one of which is in the neighbourhood of the 'Natural Bridge' [188]. The recent work on these doline and fluvial karsts of the Central

U.S.A. has already been cited [500, 501].

The fluviokarst of the Buchan Caves area in Victoria, Australia, was described by the writer in 1960 [183]. Fluviokarst is very widespread and is the most commonly occurring type of karstland in south-east Australia and many other parts of the world.

(c) GLACIOKARST AND NIVAL KARST

In the same way that fluviokarst is a combination of fluvial karst processes acting upon a limestone mass, so glaciokarst results from the action predominantly of glaciation and glacial processes upon a limestone area. As in the regions of fluvio-karst, the glacial action is not the only action by non-karstic agencies that the area has suffered, but glaciation has been predominant. Nival karst (snowy karst) is formed by the action of snow upon limestones, frequently in glacial or periglacial environments.

Glaciokarst occurs in limestone areas at present being glaciated or in limestone areas which have recently been glaciated. It is thus characteristic of the high calcareous massifs of the Alps. The landforms depend upon the type of glacial action which has affected the limestones, in addition to their structural characteristics. Glaciokarst is typified by features of glacial scour and glacial erosion and by features of glacial deposition, and meltwater. Karst which has suffered glacial erosion usually consists of ice-scoured surfaces; Bögli divides this kind of karst into two main types: the first is *schichttreppenkarst* or *karst en banquettes structurales* and the second is *rundhocker-karst* or *karst en roches moutonnées*, Photo 45 [400].

Glaciokarst caused by erosion consists of ice-scoured surfaces, frequently in the form of limestone pavements, and it is usually a bare karst. Glacial erosion on limestones is

particularly selective; the weaker and shaley
layers are scoured away by leaving the
stronger and more massive layers. In this
way alternating ledges and cliffs may be
formed. If the limestones are well jointed,
great blocks are torn away by the ice and
steep cliffs formed. The actual profiles
formed on the limestones depend partly
upon the nature of the bedding; where there
is much difference in strength between the
limestone beds a more stepped profile will
be formed; where there is less difference
between the beds a smoothed or even a
curved outline is more likely. This contrast
is noticeable in the effects of glacial erosion
upon the limestones in north-west Yorkshire and in the Burren of County Clare,
the more variable vertical limestone
sequence of north-west Yorkshire having
a much more stepped outline. Where there
has been intense ice pressure on limestone,
'boiler plated' or exfoliating surfaces are
formed, as can be seen on the north side of
the Burren. Unless protected, striae usually
disappear quickly from limestones as a

result of solution – an experiment on a
glaciated limestone pavement on the
southern slopes of Ingleborough showed
that striae disappeared after about ten
years [76]. The nature of the glacially
scoured surfaces depends upon the nature
of the limestone, dense and compact
limestone forming the most extensive and
undissected pavements [162]. After their
formation the pavements are corroded by
solution caused by atmospheric CO_2 or
from vegetation; remnants of the original
pavement surface are left as tables. These
are called in the Alps *Karrentische* or *tables
de corrosion* [401]; Corbel refers to them as
pseudo-erratics. Such pseudo-erratics together with true erratics are essential
elements in certain types of glacial karst
[87]. True erratics in limestone areas are
often perched – as at Norber in north-west
Yorkshire [76, 402].

Schichttreppenkarst as described by
Bögli is stepped karst caused by the
differential glacial erosion on beds of varying strength [400]. Much of the Ingleborough and Malham areas of north-west
Yorkshire is thus a schichttreppenkarst,
though somewhat subdued now as a result
of postglacial weathering, Fig. 112. Bögli
also distinguishes between a schichttreppen-
and a schichttrippenkarst, the distinction
being essentially caused by the dip of the
limestone, the treppenkarst being formed
in more or less horizontal rocks, and the
trippenkarst when the rock is dipping [400].
Rundhöcherkarst is rounded, glacially
eroded limestone relief; it is seen in the
Durmitor region of Montenegro and in the
northern part of the Burren where ice
pressures were very great; otherwise most
of the Burren is schichttreppenkarst. Where
soft rocks, like shales, overlie limestones, the
amount of glacial scour can be considerable;
on Ingleborough hill, the shale/limestone
boundary receded by as much as 150 yds

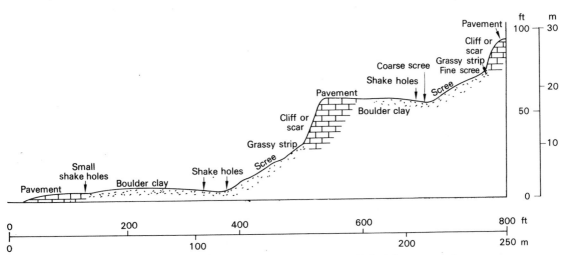

Fig. 112 Schichttreppenkarst. Diagram of the main features in the relief of the scars and pavements, Ingleborough area, north-west Yorkshire (from Sweeting [76])

(150 m) as a result of glacial scour during the last glaciation. Considerable amounts of shale were removed from the Burren limestones, too [95].

Since most glaciated areas are also snowy regions, there are many landforms in glaciokarst areas that have been formed by snow-patch erosion. These include the *kotlici* we have already described (from the Julian Alps) and shallow snow dolines (dolines nivales) (see p. 51).

Meltwater from both glacial and snow patches form conspicuous features in glaciokarstic terrains. Enlarged bedding planes occur in the form of near-surface caves and enlarged joint planes (forming 'potholes'). Thus caves and vertical chasms are characteristic of glaciokarst. These are added to by streams draining from boulder-clay deposits; Corbel's index of the number of caves per 100 km^2 for the glaciokarst of the Julian Alps is 100 [393]. Caves are related both to meltwater streams and to the distribution of morainic deposits. Under these circumstances the caves, unless under the ice, tend to contain few stalactites, and poorly developed thin stalagmites. Meltwater flowing on to the surface from both glaciers and dead ice gives rise to conspicuous meltwater gorges, which are also typical of glaciokarsts; some good examples can be seen today in Switzerland in those areas where the limestones are still covered by ice. In northern Norway, adjacent to the Svartisen ice cap, glaciokarst is being formed today; meltwater streams flow from the ice cap on to the folded Silurian limestones. Similarly in the Julian Alps, in the neighbourhood of Triglav, the Triglav glacier rests upon Triassic limestones, and its meltwater penetrates the limestones to form the well-known Triglav pothole (or gouffre), Fig. 113. Both the Svartisen and the Triglav areas are important for caves, those in the Svartisen district having been described by St Pierre [246]. As in most meltwater caves, the Svartisen caves have long and winding vadose passages, undecorated with stalactite deposits.

In Britain, it is perhaps unfortunate that our most discussed karstland, Ingleborough in north-west Yorkshire, is a glaciokarst, as it possesses few features of a classical karst. Both the Ingleborough district and

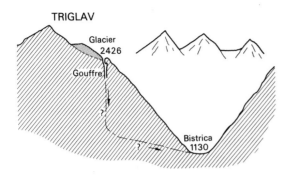

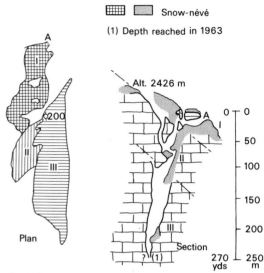

Fig. 113 (*above and right*) The Triglav Pothole, Slovenian Alps (from Corbel, after Gams [393])

the Burren of north Clare are glaciokarsts formed by glacial action on Carboniferous Limestones during the Quaternary period; they are to some extent now relict karsts, being subjected to weathering and solution in the present oceanic climatic conditions. In addition to limestone pavements and erratics, and landforms of glacial scour, the Ingleborough district in particular possesses many features due to meltwater. These include gorges like Ease Gill Kirk (Leck Fell) and the upper part of Trow Gill, both probably formed by meltwaters from stationary ice, Fig. 54. In addition, long near-surface 'corridor' caves are common on the slopes of Ingleborough, as for example on the north-east in the neighbourhood of Alum Pot Hole, and on the west side near the foot of Park Fell. Joint planes have also been enlarged to form potholes, and these are related to the distribution of the boulder-clay cover and possibly to former ice fronts, both in the neighbourhood of Gaping Gill Hole and on Leck Fell. On the Allotment on the south-eastern slopes of Ingleborough, there are at least twenty potholes (widened and deepened faults and joints) more than 300 ft (100 m) deep in an area of about 4 km^2; this kind of relief is typical of a glaciokarst (Fig. 23).

Glacial scour removes much of the pre-glacial relief. Pre-glacial dolines and other hollows are scoured away so glaciokarst has normally few and only small dolines; those that occur are often collapse dolines caused possibly by meltwater, as at Gavel Pot Hole on Leck Fell and at Hull Pot Hole on the slopes of Pen-y-Ghent, or Poulavallan in the Burren. Since the end of the last glaciation small dolines have been formed and are an indication of the extent of the postglacial solutional rate. Bauer in his work on the Austrian Alps gives some idea of the dolines and other solutional forms which have developed during the postglacial [152]. Both in north-west Yorkshire and the Burren in Clare, there is relatively little solutional doline development, except in selected areas where it is probable that the glacial scour was less intense (as in the area north of Malham Tarn), or where the enclosed hollows were sufficiently large not to be removed [171].

Furthermore in both north-west Yorkshire and the Burren the relict nature of the glaciokarstic landforms can be demonstrated. If the limestone pavements are removed by quarrying, they do not form again [76]. Solution and wastage of the limestone surface under western oceanic weathering conditions has caused the lowering of the pavements by 49 cm in northwest Yorkshire, and up to 20 cm in the Burren [404]. This reduction of the surface has been accentuated by solution caused by acid peaty waters draining from the deposits of boulder clay [76].

Glacially scoured hollows become dammed by glacial drift; such hollows are also partly karstic in origin. In the Gort lowland and in the central plain of Ireland, many of the lakes are of glaciokarstic origin. Hull thought that the lakes of the Irish plain were all formed essentially by solution; but many of the lake hollows are ice-scoured hollows or hollows dammed by drift, solution of the limestones having partly contributed to their formation [405, 95]. Newtown Turlough near Gort is such an example and is a gently sloping basin in thin glacial drift [95]. In the Julian Alps in the Triglav area, the celebrated seven lakes of Triglav occur in a glaciated limestone valley, and are dammed by valley and lateral moraines [108]. Where there is considerable glacial and periglacial accumulation, underground drainage may be so impeded as to give true polje forms, as in the Dinaric karst [316]. Gams thinks that small poljes have been formed by the accumulation of glacial drift and alluvium in the Triglav region [406].

The karst areas of the High Alps and the Pyrenees are perhaps the type areas for the development of glaciokarst.* They exhibit all types of glaciated limestone pavements (lapiaz, lapiés champs, etc.) and the diversity of the surface features on the limestone is probably greater than in the Dinaric karst itself, which shows only a few glaciokarstic features (on the higher parts of the Velebit mountains Roglič has described some

*To this must be added the Mt. Castleguard area of the Canadian Rockies [540].

glacial landforms [218]). Snow dolines are abundant, as many as 900 dolines per km^2 being recorded from one area of the Alps [152]. Meltwaters from former and from modern glaciers have formed gorges, caves and vertical potholes. One of the longest caves so far explored in the world (over 70 km), Hölloch, in Muotatal, central Switzerland, has been formed by meltwaters flowing under intense pressure, during the glacial and interglacial periods. Caves containing ice and snow are also characteristic of a glaciokarst, as in the Eisriesenwelt (which is over 30 km long) and the Riesenhöhle. Long and ramifying caves are typical. In the high Pyrenees, many of the highest areas have been dissected by a cirque glaciation, the most notable cirque formed in the limestones being the Cirque de Gavarnie. Recently Barrère has discussed the interaction of glacial and karstic action in the Pyrenees [407]. Glacial cirques have been transformed by solution into closed depressions, and are called cirque-dolines. Solution takes place in the limestones around local glaciers and particularly at the base of cirque glaciers; cirques tend to be more rounded and less armchair-shaped than cirques in other rock types. They are often flat-bottomed and filled with alluvial deposits in which alluvial dolines form, giving rise to features sometimes known as cirque-plats. These phenomena are well seen in the Picos de Europa area, and recent studies of some of the karst features of the Picos de Europa have been made by Barrère and Miötke [407].

In addition to the abrasion of ice and the solutional effects of meltwater and snow, glaciokarsts are subject to frost action. Whereas ice and snow tend to give rise to smoothed surfaces, frost shatters limestones along bedding planes and joints, and produces an irregular stone-covered surface.

46 'Frost Pot', Periglacial karst, Castleguard, Alberta. The doline is at 2490 m altitude (*Photo by D. C. Ford*)

Corbel has named this kind of stony surface on limestones, *clapier* [87]. In the north of England such stony limestone ground is known as scales or 'scriddlings'. Frost also causes scree formation and this is important in most glaciokarsts; screes are well developed on Twisleton Scars near Ingleton, in Yorkshire [76]. As mentioned by the writer in 1965, screes in limestones are more stable than in other rocks, because they tend to become cemented by the deposition of tufa between the blocks. Where frost action is more important than snow, ice or meltwater, solutional features are less developed. Fossil screes (grèzes litées) are an important element in the landscape of many areas in Europe which were subject to cold periods in the Quaternary. Such screes are particularly noticeable in parts of the Causses.

In regions of permafrost, meltwater and snow are unable to penetrate the permafrost layer. They flow over the surface and canyons and gullies are formed. Where the permafrost is continuous caves cannot be formed, but where the permafrost is discontinuous caves are formed in the warmer part of the year; such caves are usually less than 300 m long and often only about 100 m; they normally contain only a few straw stalactites, and occasional thin deposits of stalagmite. Micro-solutional features (vermiculations or micro-karren) can be important and finely chisel the surface blocks of limestone; they vary from about one or two centimetres wide and up to about 20–30 cm long, Photo 46. Nicod has described cryo-karstic phenomena in Montenegro [530].

Corbel has written most fully on periglacial and permafrost karsts, which occur in high polar regions or in the centre of continents where there is much frost and snow in winter [87]. Corbel distinguishes two types of karst in the Arctic. The first, that of complete permafrost, where there is no underground circulation and no caves; this is found in the northern Canadian islands, such as Somerset Island, in northern Greenland, in the Tamyr peninsula of Siberia, and in central Vestspitsbergen. This kind of karstland is essentially a karst of gelivation and is made up of frost-shattered limestone fragments, which lie on the surface and are fretted with micro-karren. Occasional gullies form, as in Bünsow Land, central Vestspitsbergen. Secondly, regions where the permafrost is discontinuous or where it is now fossil or relict karst; in this type there is some underground circulation and a few caves. This kind of karst occurs in southern Greenland, Iceland, northern Norway and Lapland. In both types of Arctic karst, frost-shattered scree slopes are important features of the landscape. In central Vestspitsbergen, in Bünsow Land, for example, the Permian limestones have disintegrated into scree slopes at about 40°–50°, which are very loose and unstable; the landscape is made up almost entirely of these slopes and the cliffs of limestone that have given rise to the screes. Dolines and enclosed hollows are extremely rare or occur only where snow patches can form. In northern Norway and Lapland, towards the margin of the permafrost areas and in a district of heavy precipitation, caves become increasingly important, until the area grades into the glaciokarst of Svartisen. Canyons formed by meltwaters are more common in the second type of Arctic karst.

A continental type of sub-Arctic karst can be seen on the island of Gotland in the Baltic. In this island lies the much described cave of Lummelunda, the subject of patient researches by Tell [267, 408]; this cave is about 100 m long, and has only a small development of stalactites and stalagmites. Despite a great thickness of Silurian limestones in Gotland, dolines and other true karst hollows are rare. Recently, however, more caves have been explored [267].

In Britain, the only regions which approach the characteristics of a nival and permafrost karst are those of the Durness Limestones areas of Scotland, around the village of Durness, and near Inchnadamph, and those of Pre-Cambrian limestones on the island of Lismore in Loch Linnhe. These are areas of relict permafrost karst since they are no longer subject to permafrost conditions today. They possess frost-shattered rocks which are now becoming smoothed by solution in a more oceanic climate; micro-karren are being transformed. Dolines formed by snow-patch erosion occur along fault and thrust planes in the limestones; vadose caves occur, as in the Traligill area near Inchnadamph and to the south, but they are in general short and undeveloped [409]. One of the biggest caves is the well known Smoo Cave, near Durness, which may have been formed during a period of heavy precipitation at the end of the Glacial period [87]. Corbel maintains that the limestone areas on the island of Lismore resemble the limestone areas of Bear Island (Byörnöya) [87]. Ben Bulben, western Ireland, is also a nival karst.

15 Tropical Karst

THE STUDY of tropical karstlands is reaching the stage when it could profitably have a book to itself. In this chapter some of the main problems and ideas will be discussed. The processes at work are similar, but often quite different in degree from those in temperate latitudes. The most important differences are caused by the intensity of the rainfall in tropical latitudes, and by the intensity of the evaporation. The intensity of rainfall means that flash floods occur on the limestones and that sheet-wash and gulleying by short surface streams is common; this makes the hollows in limestone in a tropical climate much less regular and rounded than in temperate climates. In Indonesia, for instance, the 'rainfall maxima of 18 stations (the highest amount of precipitation measured during 24 hours) yielded an average figure of 124 mm, which is considerably higher than the results obtained in the temperate belt. . . . In studying the records of the gauging stations 6 additional rainy days were found on which from 600 to 700 mm of rain had fallen; values of 500 to 600 mm could be found for another ten days. I think it needs no commentary how enormous devastation may result from the precipitation of this colossal amount of water on a karsted surface' [410].

The intensity of evaporation gives rise to secondary deposition of calcium carbonate (often hard and stalagmitic) which is often regarded as the cause of the much steeper slopes in tropical limestone areas.

In his discussion of types of karst Cvijič included the karstlands of Jamaica as an example of his holokarst. Using the descriptions of the Jamaican areas as given by Sawkins, Hill and Daneš, Cvijič discusses the Cockpit Country, and assumes that the cockpits and glades of Jamaica are similar to dolines and uvalas of the Dinaric karst [148]. As a result of this transference of the terminology of the Dinaric and Classical Karst areas to those of the humid tropics, many misconceptions arose. It was mainly because of the accounts given by the Czech geographer Daneš [411], that Grund was able to put forward his scheme of evolution of karst areas in 1914 [2]. Grund believed that the doline karst of the temperate areas evolved towards the type of karst seen in Jamaica, and that the 'classical' was an earlier stage of development.

Of all types of karst it can be said that tropical karst forms are the most distinctive. It is still arguable to what extent the karst features found in tropical areas are unique to the tropics, but it is undeniable that in general the karstlands appear to show different landforms from those in extra-tropical areas; landforms that occur in temperate areas do occur in the tropics, but the reverse is so far not known. The work, in particular, of H. Lehmann in his *Morphologische Studien auf Java* in 1936 [385] laid the foundations of tropical karst geomorphology. In this, the work of von Wissmann in south-east Asia was also important, since south-east Asian karst is a highly important and significant area in karst studies [412].

The immediate reaction to a map or description of a tropical karst area is to observe that the depressions and the intervening areas have become reversed, Fig. 114(*a*) and (*b*) and Photo 47. Dolines are normally hollows with more or less rounded convex contours; in the tropics the depres-

47(*a*) Jamaican Cockpit Country
from the air

sions tend to be irregular, sometimes sinuous, with concave contours. In the temperate karstlands, the intervening higher lands tend to be irregular; in the tropics, the hills between the irregular hollows are usually rounded and regular. We have already noted Lehmann's comment on karst country in the tropics: '... nous donne donc l'impression du paysage karstique à dolines classique, mais inversé; au lieu des dolines rondes qui caractérisent le karst des zones tempérées, ce sont les cones, les pitons calcaires arrondis, qui attirent notre atten-

tion dans le karst tropical' [413]. Lehmann goes on to say that it is the hills at all stages of their development that dominate the tropical karst relief; according to him there is no temperate equivalent to the 'rounded pitons calcaires', not even in the karst of Montenegro which is the most evolved of the Dinaric karsts. 'The temperate-belt karst plateaux are characterised by broad, dishlike depressions – dolines, uvalas and poljes; the positive forms such as pinnacles and cones being subordinate. . . . The tropical karst plateaux . . . are characterised,

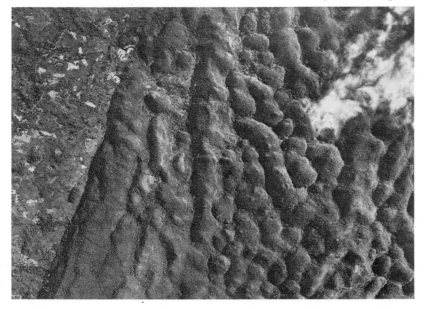

47(*b*) Crofts Mountain area, Jamaica, from the air (*Jamaican Geological Survey*)

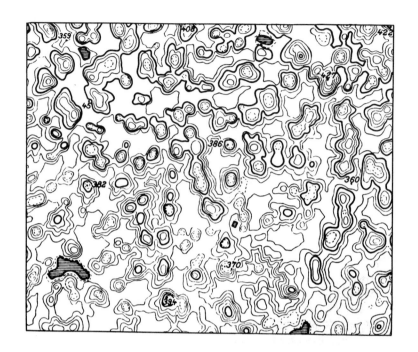

Fig. 114(*a*) (*left*) Tropical karst, Goenoeng Sewoe, south of Giritontro (from H. Lehmann [385])

Fig. 114(*b*) (*below*) Delimitation of temperate and tropical closed depressions (from Williams [533])

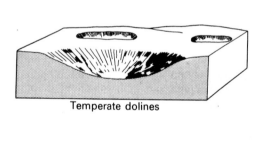

Temperate dolines

Tropical cockpits

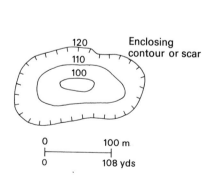

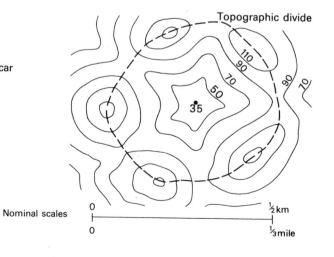

on the contrary, by the predominance of the emergent or positive forms, the multitude of karst hills and cones, while depressions, if any, are insignificant' [410]. In a doline karst all portions of the upland surface are connected and it possesses a continuous upper surface. In the cone karst of the tropics there is no continuous upper surface, the relief consisting of isolated cone hills whose top surfaces may be concordant, but are discontinuous. P. W. Williams has endeavoured to focus our attention upon the depressions in the tropical karstlands. Such relief is so spectacular that perhaps many workers have inevitably concentrated their attention upon the hills. By looking at the nature of tropical karst depressions and finding that the basins are crudely polygonal in shape, Williams refers to the cone karst in the Darai Hills in New Guinea, as *polygonal karst* [505].

Tropical karstlands are usually divided into two main types:

(1) *Kegelkarst* (cone karst or karst à pitons) or, as Flathe and Pfeiffer prefer to call it, *sinoid karst* [414].

(2) *Turmkarst* (tower karst or karst à tourelles) or, as Balázs would call it, *pinnacle karst* [409]. In time more work may suggest other ways of dealing with tropical karst and a form of classification based on the nature of the depressions may emerge. This is not possible yet.

Not all karstlands in the tropics belong to these two types, but they are dominant. There has, however, been some confusion about the terminology. This is because H. Lehmann and others have at times used kugel- and also kuppenkarst. Kugel means cupola or bowl in German and in some of the tropical karst areas the hills tend to be hemispherical or bowl-shaped in form. This is apparent in Lehmann's first work in 1936, where in Fig. 4, in his scheme of the evolution of the kegelkarst of the Goenoeng

Sewoe in Java, the hills are distinctly rounded. Kuppen means a top or point of a head, and the karst hills are frequently referred to in German karst literature as Karstkuppen, particularly when the karst hills tend to be pointed [385]. All three types, however, are usually regarded as variations of kegelkarst, and many workers now tend to reject the established terms. French work on tropical karst has been less involved in terminology [461].

1. KEGELKARST (CONE KARST)

Kegelkarst is characterised by numerous cone-like hills or buttes rising one after another in quick succession, and is illustrated by the maps, Fig. 34 (p. 70) and Fig. 114. The name was originally given by Handel-Mazettis and O. Lehmann (1927), from travels in China [415]. Kegelkarst occurs in the East and West Indies, in Malaya, in other parts of south-east Asia (including Vietnam and southern China) and in many regions of central America, notably in Tabasco and Chiapas in Mexico, and in parts of British Honduras. There are now many accounts of the kegalkarst in these areas. The writer described the kegelkarst from Jamaica in 1958. The conical hills vary in height from 300 to 400 ft (100–130 m) and they may be as much as 3,000 ft (about 1 km) in diameter. The traverse across the Cockpit Country in north-central Jamaica, shown in Fig. 34, gives an idea of the alternation of kegel (cone) hills with the cockpit depressions. The slopes of the hills consist of cliffs and precipices as well as screes, the general impression of even slopes as seen in the air photographs being due to the thick forest cover. A detailed survey by Aub of two cone hills is given in Fig. 35 (p. 71).

In eastern Yunnan and in Kweichow, Silar describes the cone hills as reaching to a relative height of about 300 ft (approximately 100 m), and having a diameter of 300–600 ft (approximately 100–180 m) at their foot, the sides sloping at 40°–60°. In places, lower and smaller hills with gentler slopes are found and at the boundary of Yunnan with Szechuan the low hills rise to about 150 ft (50 m) [416]. In Java, H. Lehmann describes the hills of the Goenoeng Sewoe as rising for about 75 m and that in one area '30 Kuppen auf den Quadratkilometer kommen' [385]. Goenoeng Sewoe (Gunung Sewu) means 'thousand peaks', and consists of thousands of conical hills (about 40,000 is estimated) in an area of 1,300 km² (85 km by 15 km) [409]. A superb example of kegelkarst in the Philippines is shown in Voss [531].

It was the intervening depressions which originally attracted the attention of the first European workers in the tropical karst regions; Daneš and Grund were both impressed by the *cockpits*, the name the depressions are given in Jamaica where they are said to resemble the arenas once used for cockfighting. This was why the Jamaican karst was named *Cockpitlandschaft*. This early work was quite rightly focused upon the depressions, and it could be said that we must still focus our attention upon these in order to understand the tropical karstlands. As can be seen from Fig. 114, they appear to form remains around the cones, with a connecting series of corridors between them. These sinuous corridors are interrupted by shallow passes or thresholds which are much lower in height than the main divides between one corridor and the next. The sinuous corridors are made up of coalescent cockpits and are rather like uvalas, as shown in the map by Gerstenhauer [62]. The cockpits frequently occur in lines following faulting or jointing;

this is well shown in the aerial photograph of the cockpit country in Jamaica, Photo 47(a). Such directed lines of cockpits and depressions were called by Lehmann *gerichteter karst* (karst orienté) [385]. Directed karst is possibly more common in the tropics than in temperate areas [51]. Gerstenhauer has also examined the main lines of the kegel karst in the Sierra Madre of the Chiapas in Mexico and has given a rose diagram for their chief directions [62].

However, as Aub has shown on the ground, there is often no apparent fault or joint to guide the cockpits [111]. Wilford and Wall also found in the Bau region of Sarawak that, while many depressions are fault-controlled, others are irregular or circular and do not appear to follow any detectable structural feature [154]. Aub studied an area of cockpit karst near the Pedro river in central Jamaica, and came to the conclusion that generalisations about the nature of the conical hills and the cockpits were in many ways unfounded, since he found the slopes of the cones and depressions very variable; it is certainly important not to generalise too quickly on the nature of the kegelkarst. One important aspect of Aub's work was his detailed rainfall readings within his area. He found that an analysis of over 3,000 readings taken over a period of fifteen months showed that the depressions receive significantly more throughfall (i.e. rainfall plus the throughfall from the thick tree cover) than the hill summits; the difference was of the order of 14 per cent. This suggests that solution by this throughfall is likely to be greater in the depressions; it also suggests that the depressions are to some extent self-perpetuating, and might be 'able to survive long after the processes responsible for the formation of the original depression have ceased to operate' [417].

Compared with our work on temperate

karst our knowledge of the origin of the kegelkarst is still rudimentary. Detailed and statistical work such as has been done by Williams on the kegelkarst, with its hills and depressions, is just being begun. Lehmann feels that it is not correct to use the term doline for the sinuous corridor and star-like depressions, though he is prepared to say that the cockpit is the tropical form of the doline. In his work in 1936 Lehmann gives a diagram, Fig. 115, and also his views on the formation of the Goenoeng Sewoe kegelkarst. It is obvious that at that time he imagined the kegelkarst to have been developed from a series of ravines and gullies, upon the limestones, following the structural lines. As these streams became dismembered by the development of swallow holes and enlargement of the fissures, so the cupola hills formed, with irregular depressions left in between. This implies a preceding phase of ravine erosion, before karstification, and this concept is due to the influence of A. Penck [179]. As pointed out by Roglič, this first view of Lehmann's of the development of such a karst area is

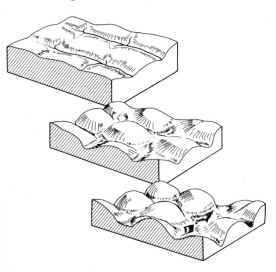

Fig. 115 Formation of the Goenoeng Sewoe kegelkarst (from Lehmann [140])

possibly an incorrect one and, as suggested by the writer in 1958 in considering the Cockpit Country in Jamaica, probably only very slight surface erosion has ever taken place [134].

Nonetheless, because of the much more intensive precipitation, sheetwash and surface run-off is much greater than in temperate latitudes; tropical streams form torrents between the limestone blocks, resulting in the formation of limestone 'islands'. Such gulleying gives rise to the corridor hollows which are the beginning of the cockpits. Surface water flow is stressed by P. W. Williams in his study of 'polygonal karst' in New Guinea. Williams's morphometrical work lays much more emphasis on the closed basins than other tropical studies. (Paper presented to 5th Int. Congress in Speleology, Stuttgart, 1969.) We have already noted that in areas where surface run-off is very rapid (as in semi-arid regions), dolines and enclosed hollows are rare and are replaced by valleys adapted to flood conditions. 'On the other hand, the slow rains typical of the temperate belt are favourable for the formation of shallow depressions produced by the dissolving effect of the infiltrating rainwater' [410], and dolines form as a result of relatively slow diffused solution into limestone fissures.

These opinions are corroborated by the detailed studies of Aub in Jamaica. He shows how the surface channels lead to central swallow holes in the cockpits from the surrounding passes, and he goes on to say 'This surface drainage is purely temporary. During short periods of light rain there is no run-off at all and the water disappears immediately among the joint openings, rubble and soil. But the greater part of the total rainfall comes in torrential afternoon showers, or continuous, heavy "October rains".' Therefore a substantial part of the drainage water from the depression runs off, 'finding its way into swallow holes, but not percolating directly into the rock' [111]. He recognises six types of hill-slope associated with the cockpits:

(*a*) *Staircase slopes* made up of ledges and vertical steps. The steps are up to 2–3 m high and bedding planes are conspicuous.

(*b*) *Broken cliffs*, with higher steps and less uniform ledges. The steps are intersected by widened joints.

(*c*) *Steep even slopes*. The honeycombed limestone is covered with loose limestone fragments and large blocks.

(*d*) *Major cliffs* undercut by horizontal notches to a depth of 2–3 m and often associated with springs.

(*e*) *Cliffs* without any undercutting.

(*f*) *Scree slopes*, covered by small broken material.

Versey noted that there is some correlation between the depth of the cockpits and where underground water movement is fairly close to the surface, the deepest cockpits tending to occur where the water movement is nearest the surface. In fact Versey goes so far as to say 'it is doubtful whether the rainfall into a particular cockpit is sufficient to excavate it to such a magnitude'. . . . 'It is much more plausible that the perpetuation of the physiographic character of the Cockpit Country is due to the hydraulic and abrasive action of flood waters in the underground drainage system' [143]. In his view the confined flow of flood waters can accomplish much mechanical and solutional erosion and this action is responsible for the enlargement of the cockpits; collapse and mechanical abrasion must be added to solution in their formation. This opinion is similar to that held by Meyerhoff on the Sumideros of Puerto Rico [418].

Aub considered this problem and came to the conclusion that there was little evidence in support of any widespread collapse or mechanical action in an area of cockpit country that he investigated and that the cockpits are surface solution features. He also states that in the area investigated by him, there was no noticeable correlation of cockpit shape or size with height above the underground drainage. Erosion by vertically or horizontally moving groundwater is therefore not an important factor, and the processes of cockpit formation must be acting mainly at the surface [417]. Aub's most interesting contribution to the cockpit problem is his consideration of the degraded cockpit karst discussed by the writer in 1955. He shows that there is a connection between this degraded cockpit karst and the occurrence of bauxite and alluvial soil formation. He points out that the formation of the shallower cockpits in Jamaica tends to be associated with those parts of the Central Inlier which were breached first, where it is possible that more alluvial material derived from the Central Inlier might have been deposited. In such circumstances, the so-called degraded cockpits are not a development from 'normal' cockpits, but have a different history [417].

There is considerable variety in kegelkarst, and much of this is due to variations in the lithology of the rock (porosity and texture). The relative ages of the limestones cannot, however, be of any great significance in this respect. In the areas already discussed, the limestones are of varying ages. In Yunnan, for example, limestones are more than 9,000 ft thick (3,000 m), representing over 60 per cent of the entire known thickness of the strata, and range in age from the Proterozoic to the Quaternary; kegelkarst to some extent is developed on all these limestones. Furthermore kegelkarst can be shown to exist in Central America and the West Indies upon limestones of varying ages from the late Jurassic

48(*a*) Dolines in Aguada limestone, SSE of Manati, Puerto Rico. Aerial view towards NE (*Photo by W. H. Monroe*)

through to the late Tertiary. Verstappen has also shown that, in the Malayan archipelago, older reef limestones of Quaternary age are characterised by 'beautiful conical karst development' [419]. Hence the age of the limestones is not an important factor.

In Jamaica the restriction of kegelkarst to the areas of the hard, highly fissured White Limestones has already been noted [134]. Cockpits do not appear on the more chalky and less fissured Montpelier beds, nor on those White Limestones which are associated with bauxitic deposits, as in the Manchester Plateau area surrounding Mandeville. These districts possess normal funnel-shaped dolines like those in the Classical Karst. However, in New Guinea the restriction of dolines to impure calcareous beds does not occur [420].

Verstappen has suggested from his experiments with karst limestones that porosity is one of the essential factors in the development of kegelkarst [421]. This was also the opinion of Wilford and Wall in their survey of karst landforms in Sarawak; in this area there is little kegelkarst, and they suggest that 'The low primary porosity of most Sarawak limestones may account for the lack of conical karst development' which is common in parts of the Malayan archipelago [154].

In Puerto Rico, Monroe maintains that the lithological variety of the limestones is decisive in the development of the karst types. 'Each lithologic type gives rise to a specific group of solution phenomena, and few karst features seem to be common to all lithological types' [388]. . . . 'Each of the limestone units has its own distinctive suite of solution phenomena. Some of the phenomena appear to be restricted to the Tropics; others are common to both the tropical and temperate zones' (loc. cit., p. 2).

48(*b*) Lares limestone karst, Barrio Hato Viejo, 4 miles east of Ciales, Puerto Rico (*Photo by W. H. Monroe*)

In Puerto Rico, the limestone formations are of Oligocene and Miocene age and dip gently northwards in a broad belt about 18 km by 120 km long stretching along much of the northern coast of the island. Monroe says that on the Aguada limestone a type of relief develops with sink holes (cockpits) separated from one another by only narrow ridges, Photo 48(*a*) and (*b*). The Aguada is a Miocene limestone which consists of alternating layers of hard crystalline limestone and soft chalky limestones and marl. 'Many of the sinks are 50 m deep, with discontinuous rims that in places rise as much as 50 m still higher. . . . Some of the sinks are so close to each other that only a knife edge separates one from the next. The sinks do not appear to follow any definite pattern of alignment, although for short distances several will be more or less in line with a low rim separating one from the next' [285]. However, on the Aymamón and Lares limestones, also of Oligo-Miocene age, the kegelkarst is more pinnacled and the slopes are steeper [285]. This interpretation of the Puerto Rican karst has been questioned by Thrailkill who believes that the various karst types in northern Puerto Rico result from stages in the degradation of a limestone upland, and believes that the lithological details of the limestones are of secondary importance [135].

Lithological and structural characters of the limestones are also believed to be an important factor in the differentiation of the karst types in Cuba [422]. Panoš is of the opinion that climatic components influence the intensity and speed of processes that act upon the landscape, but that the limestones themselves give rise to basic fundamental forms [422]. On inclined beds conical hills tend to be higher and steeper than they are on horizontally bedded limestones [421].

The effects of altitudinal variations upon the development of kegelkarst within the tropics has been looked at, though not studied in any real detail. The area most often quoted is New Guinea, which has been studied by Verstappen [421] and Jennings and Bik [420] and more recently by Williams [505]. Verstappen found that temperature was one factor which limited the distribution of kegelkarst in New Guinea and that above 1,500–2,000 m it lost its typical character and was replaced by a (sink hole) doline plain. He also thought that there was a precipitation limit, and that at least 1,500 mm per year is about the minimum needed for the development of conical karst; he was of the opinion that the length of the dry season is also of importance, a rather long dry season being less favourable to the development of kegelkarst. Jennings and Bik found, in Australian New Guinea, that at low levels at about 200 m in the lower Kikori area normal kegelkarst is developed, but that at higher levels, above about 1,500 m, both a doline karst and a pyramid and doline karst are found. At low levels in New Guinea normal kegelkarst occurs, but at higher levels the karst resembles the picture conceived by Grund in his attempt to put tropical and temperate forms into one evolutionary sequence in 'his theoretical block diagram sketching hollow-chested, hornlike peaks rising between inosculating, flat-floored dolines' [420]. Thus the altitudinal zonation of karst in New Guinea is not simple and will be considered again later.

In many areas the cone hills are more or less symmetrical. In certain areas, such as Cuba, the symmetry can be shown to be structural – related to the dip or to faults in the limestones which have led to the development of an asymmetric profile [422]. The presence of asymmetric cones (or mogotes) in the northern part of Puerto Rico was first mentioned by Hubbard [423], and later by Thorp in 1934 who saw that there

49(a) Asymmetric kegelkarst, Puerto Rico (*Photo by W. H. Monroe*)

was some relationship with the direction of the trade winds [424]. In Puerto Rico the cone hills are more gentle in their easterly and northerly facing sides and steeper on the westerly and southerly facing sides. When viewed from the north-east or north-west the hills show a saw-tooth profile – the windward sides being gentle with few slopes more than 45°, the leeward sides being steep and often overhanging, Photo 49(a). Where the hills are protected from the trade winds no asymmetry can be observed. Thorp believed that solution was more extensive on the eastern or windward side because of the greater rainfall which would fall on that side. Recent work has been done by Monroe [425]. He has noticed that the karst cones (mogotes) in Puerto Rico are covered with a very hard caprock, generally 5–10 m thick; below the indurated strata the limestone is much softer and in parts of Puerto Rico is quite powdery and chalky, and in many mogotes the soft interior has been partially removed, leaving the capping as a shell, Photo 49(b). As a result of the investigation of several sections cut through the mogotes, Monroe has shown that the hard caprock is due to secondary deposition of calcium carbonate in the form of a stalagmite layer on the surface of the softer powdery limestone. In humid tropical areas like Puerto Rico, rainstorms consist of torrential showers which may last only a few minutes; these storms are followed by brilliant sunshine and consequent rapid evaporation. The caprock is formed by the thorough soaking of the upper beds with the slightly acidulated rainwater, followed almost immediately by almost complete evaporation. The production of such a caprock is common to all limestone areas in the tropics and is known as *case-hardening*. In Puerto Rico, the indurated layer forms a rim rock or overhang, protecting the softer strata. Cliffs form by collapse of the caprock once the softer rock has been removed.

49(b) Solution holes in Aymamón Limestone, side of Highway 2, 30 km west of San Juan, Puerto Rico, showing chalky nature of the rock before case hardening (*Photo by W. H. Monroe*)

Thus Monroe has shown that on the eastern (windward) sides of the karst hills in Puerto Rico, there is a greater cementation and a thicker caprock that extends farther into the heart of the hills, whereas their western sides have a less well-developed caprock; according to him, on the west the hills have vertical cliffs caused by the thinner caprock and a steeper and more extensive outcrop of the softer strata [425] – an explanation that is not entirely convincing.

These caprocks have been called 'calcareous weathering crusts' by Panoš and Štelcl and have been described from Cuba. They can also be seen in the limestones of Yucatán and British Honduras in Central America. Such case-hardening of lime-stones in tropical climates is the reason for the strong rocks in such areas, which form the outstanding relief [426, 94]. 'Due to this fact, the bare limestone surface preserves its morphology for a long time' [426].

The slopes of the conical hills become undermined; they collapse and retreat slowly.

The cockpit depressions enlarge and give rise to elongated depressions, known in Jamaica as *glades* [134]. They are the tropical equivalent of uvalas, but are more sinuous and tend to have concave and angular contours and steep sides. A plan of a tropical uvala from Chiapas, Mexico, is shown in Fig. 36 from Gerstenhauer [62], and a section of surveyed glade in Jamaica from work by Aub in Fig. 116. In a cockpit the lowest point is normally near the centre, but the floors of glades consist of a series of shallow basins separated by low divides. The solid rock floor is visible in only a few glades, the floor being covered with limestone rubble and soil. In the cockpits the drainage openings tend to be towards the centre, but in glades the drainage from sharply incised channels is frequently by means of caves or swallow holes at the sides; however, the whole terrain in a tropical karstland is riddled with holes and drainage may disappear anywhere, even on the top of the hills. The lower slopes of the cockpits are

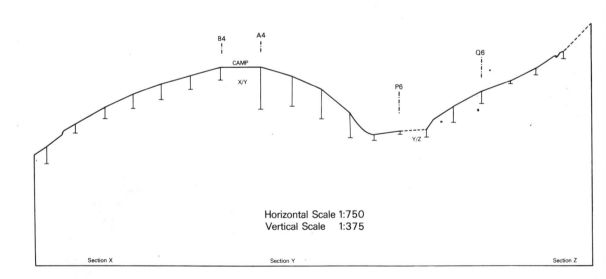

Fig. 116 Longitudinal section of a glade (surveyed and drawn by C. F. Aub)

50 Mogote on south side of Highway 2, 30 km west of San Juan, Puerto Rico, looking east (*Photo by W. H. Monroe*)

slightly concave, becoming convex above the fissure-like potholes which frequently are associated with them. In the larger glades there is a marked break of slope at the foot, i.e. there is a definite floor quite distinct from the surrounding slopes. The swallow holes often lead into vertical caves formed in solid limestone, evidence which further convinced Aub that solution from the surface downwards was more important than collapse from below upwards [417].

Kegelkarst often occurs in the form of winding sinuous chains or ridges separated by long sinuous glades; this is seen in the Crofts Mountain area of Jamaica, and in Puerto Rico in the Florida district. The Puerto Rican name for the long ridges is *pepino hills* (from the Spanish word for cucumber). The ridges may be fault- or joint-controlled. The summits are usually highly dissected along joints and fissures and the rock is everywhere pitted and etched by solution beneath the vegetation cover. Enlarged joints up to 3 m wide and obscured by matted vegetation make traversing of

this type of terrain difficult. Pinnacles and tower-like castles rise from the summits and may be up to 6 m high. Occasionally the summits are crossed by linear depressions and narrow trenches, about 100 m long, like the *zanjones*, which were discussed in Chapter 5.

2. TURMKARST OR TOWER KARST (KARST À TOURELLES)

This is the second main form of tropical karstland. It is sometimes called pinnacle karst and, by Lehmann, the Mogoten type, Photo 50 [385]. It consists essentially of steep-sided hills usually occurring in groups, each hill or group of hills often being surrounded by a river or alluvial plain. In the Bai Dahlong in Vietnam, the limestone towers rise from the sea, which has covered the former alluvial plain. In tower karst the hills are normally steep, 70°–90°, and may be up to 200 m – 300 m

51 Karst with mogotes, Puerto Rico, from the air (*Photo by W. H. Monroe*)

high. Typical tower karst may develop where lateral solution is caused by a temporary or permanent water-level, either in lakes or where allogenic rivers cross the limestone outcrop and alluviation takes place. In tropical areas the rivers bring down much debris and mud and there is a tendency for the regions cut through by rivers to become alluviated relatively rapidly. Tower karst is, therefore, as has been said by Verstappen, cone karst developed under special hydrological conditions [419]; or as Balázs says, 'The formation of the karstic cones and [towers] pinnacles represents an instantaneous state of one and the same process . . . so there are numerous forms of transition and differences between the two leading types' [410] (Fig. 114, p. 272).

The interrelations of tower and cone karst are well seen in parts of Puerto Rico and in Jamaica. In the Manati quadrangle of northern Puerto Rico, the Aguada limestones form cockpit karst, not far from the impermeable non-limestone rocks of the areas to the south. In the region of the lake of El Salto, the Quebrada el Salto and other northerly flowing streams coming from the less permeable strata have brought quantities of alluvium into the Aguada cockpits

which have become filled up. The thresholds between adjacent cockpits have become submerged, and sinuous strips of alluvium now wind in valleys between the conical hills which become steepened and tower-like. In Jamaica, this can also be seen on the western side of the polje of Lluidas Vale. Alluvium brought into the vale by streams flowing off the impermeable rocks of the Central Inlier has overlapped on to the surrounding cockpit karst; the thresholds are covered by alluvium, the limestone slopes steepened and winding alluviated glades up to a mile long have been formed. However, tower karst can be formed without lateral undercutting or alluviation.

There are two main types of tower karst. The first is where the towers are the visible remnants of outliers of a planed limestone area and rise out of the limestone through a cover of sands and alluvium; this is the case in northern Puerto Rico, Photo 51. The second type occurs where the limestone towers form residuals upon a plain of non-limestone rocks; this type is found in parts of central Jamaica where the crystalline White Limestone residuals rest upon a floor of the much less pure Yellow Limestones, and in British Honduras, where in the Mountain Pine Ridge area isolated towers of the Mesozoic Limestones rest upon a granitic base [134, 94]. The distribution and extent of the towers is frequently controlled by lines of faulting and jointing, well exemplified by the tower karst of the Bau region in Sarawak, Fig. 117(a) [154].

The towers vary in extent from small pinnacles to blocks some square kilometres in area. Their surfaces are usually irregular, broken by numerous depressions and linear corridors, sometimes up to 150 m deep. Oval or rounded hollows, probably collapse caverns, also occur. Corridors 1–2 m wide and 2–6 m deep, like bogaz, are common [154].

The contact between the alluvium and the towers is a locus of spring sapping and cave formation. This is brought about by solution caused by water flow in the alluvium and springs which issue at the foot of the towers. The alluvium forms in fact a local vorfluter. Because of the solution and spring sapping, the slopes of the conical hills become steepened (corrosional underwash, or Lösungsunterschneidung) [385, 427], and may be nearly vertical. Small lakes often occur at the contact of the alluvium and the limestone, and acid waters also cause much solution. Hence, as already indicated, the foot of the towers is a locality for foot caves (Fusshöhlen or niches de

sapement) [17, 18]. Swamp and stream waters also cut grooves into the rock, and have been described by Paton in the limestone hills of Malaya near Ipoh and at the base of the Gunong Rapat [428]. In Sarawak, horizontal grooves some hundreds of metres long are a common feature at the base of karst towers; they may be as much as 6 m high and overhang by 20 m. Other towers are grooved by swamp undercuts or slots, which average a few centimetres to about a metre deep and about 50 cm high. They are numerous and over thirty have been found in one cliff section 16 m high in the Subis area [154]. The foot caves and the grooves contain solutional rock pendants (deckenkarren), described by Lehmann from Cuba [142]. Both the caves and the walls of the towers become encrusted with thick deposits of stalagmite and stalactite, caused by the rapid evaporation and the loss of CO_2; they are sometimes known as *aussenstalaktiten* and *aussenstalagmiten* [142, 410, 427]. (Figs. 117(b) and 118.)

Cliff-foot caves were also discussed by Jennings and the writer from the rather drier tower karst region of the Limestone Ranges of the Fitzroy area of north-west Australia [31], where they may be relict landforms from a formerly more pluvial climate. A good group of such caves is cut

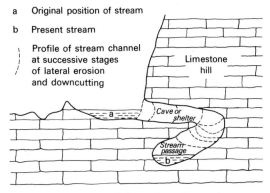

a   Original position of stream

b   Present stream

Profile of stream channel at successive stages of lateral erosion and downcutting

Limestone hill

Cave or shelter

Stream passage

Fig. 117(b) Suggested formation of caves by stream erosion (after Wilford & Wall [154])

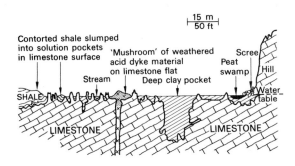

Fig. 117(a) Towers and "flats" in Sarawak

into an algal reef limestone facies north-east of Barnet Spring in the northern Napier Range and is shown in Fig. 119. These caves are from 5 to 10 m deep; there were also rock benches 2–3 m above the floor of the plain, indicating a higher relict level of corrosion of the cliff, Photo 52.

Where such basal sapping is still active, the towers remain steep, particularly if the conditions are swampy and much solution is accomplished; under these conditions any loose limestone boulders and scree falling from the towers are soon dissolved away. But where the alluvium dries out or the water level falls, scree may accumulate and the steep angle of the foot of the tower may change. Excellent examples of this can be seen along the coastal plain of British Honduras, south of Belize, where isolated towers of Mesozoic limestone rise out of an

alluvial and swamp plain; as activity at the foot of the tower karst hills has ceased, so scree has accumulated, giving rise to fairly stable and forest-covered slopes of up to 40°–45° at the foot of the vertical cliffs. Frequently, there is a depression at the foot of the scree slope where it rests upon the alluvium of the plain (like a bergfuss-niederung); this is formed where water issues from the foot of the towers beneath the scree as at one locality in British Honduras, near Gales Point. In Tabasco, Mexico, Gerstenhauer gives an evolutionary scheme for the degradation of the tower karst [62].

Solution planation of the limestone at the foot of the towers takes place by corrosion from the swampy alluvial waters and by sheet floods from the intense rain showers. Pinnacles of limestone often project through

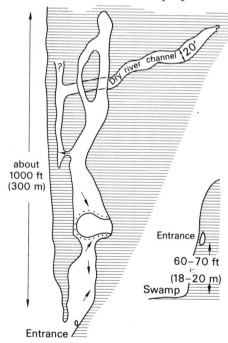

Fig. 118(a) Cliff-foot caves, Gunong Benarat Melinau area (nos. indicate caves)

Fig. 118(b) Cliff-foot cave, plan and section, Gunong Benarat, Melinau area

(from Wilford & Wall [154])

52 Foot caves, near Barnet Spring, Limestone Ranges, Fitzroy area, north-west Australia (*Photo by J. N. Jennings*)

the alluvium and deep cavities penetrate into the rock. A section through one of these planed surfaces is given by Wilford and Wall, Fig. 117(a) [154]. Fine pedimented surfaces on limestones were also described by Jennings and the writer from the Fitzroy area in north-west Australia, Fig. 120 and Photo 53 [31]. Analyses of the swamp and stream waters at the foot of the towers show that they are extremely aggressive, water in peat overlying limestone having a pH value of between 3 and 4·5; in Malaya they are as low as 3·5 [154]. As noted by Paton, there is a great contrast in the nature of the trickling rain water in the fissures of the rock with a fairly high pH and the highly

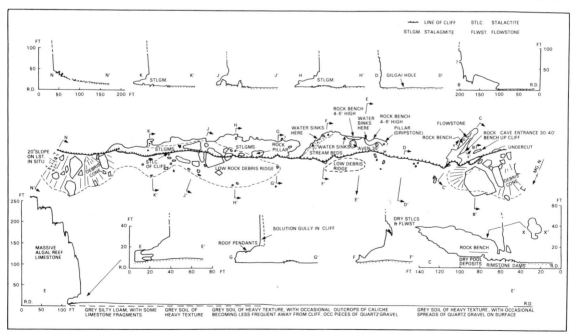

Fig. 119 Cliff-foot caves, near Barnet-Spring, West Kimberley, Western Australia (from Jennings & Sweeting [31])

53 Pediment surface on Limestones, Limestone Ranges, Fitzroy area, north-west Australia

aggressive swamp and river water in the plains below [428]. Furthermore, on the towers, redeposition of calcium carbonate as hard stalagmite serves as a protection against their solution. Thus, though there is some solution on the hills themselves, it is very much less than that occurring at their foot at the level of the alluvial plains. This is another example of accelerated corrosion [198]. The difference in the rates of solution is so great that, once formed, tower karst is perpetuated, the highest rates of erosion taking place at the lowest levels. Hence, such limestone relief is 'typified by vertical cliffs rising from flat benches. The mechanical strength of the limestone also supports overhanging cliffs which, on other rocks, would collapse' [428]. Monroe also says that in Puerto Rico, erosion on the limestone hills (mogotes) 'has almost ceased. In contrast the valleys covered with thick deposits of soil apparently are being rapidly deepened by solution under the soil, so that the relative relief is growing. The only limits to this growth are the base-level of the water – presumably mean sea-level – and the competence of the denuded hills to maintain their height against gravitational force' [429]. The solution of the actual hills is therefore very slow [430, 431, 432, 433].

Tower karst relief occurs even where the outcrops of limestone are relatively re- stricted. Where planation of limestones occurs on a large scale, a *karstrandebene* (karst border plain) is formed (see p. 204). The occurrence of extensive corrosion plains in temperate latitudes is frequently regarded as evidence of warmer climatic conditions, as was discussed in connection with the origin of the poljes. Frequently, the karstrandebenen are cut across the adjoining rocks in addition to the limestones, forming features similar to rand- poljen (marginal poljes). Descriptions of some excellent karst border plains are given by Lehmann from Celebes (Sulawesi), where in the Maros and Bantimurung areas are steep, almost vertical, hills overlooking a flat alluvial corrosion plain. Other karst border plains are described by Gersten- hauer from the Tabasco region of Mexico [62].

Tower karst in Jamaica was originally described by the writer in areas where alluvium and lateral solution planation of the White Limestones occurs. It is particularly well developed where waters from the rocks of the Central Inlier flow on to the White Limestones, as in the marginal poljes of Cave river and of Hectors river. The formation of steep towers is assisted in these two areas, where the basal beds of the White Limestone are involved, by the outcrop of the strongly jointed Troy limestones.

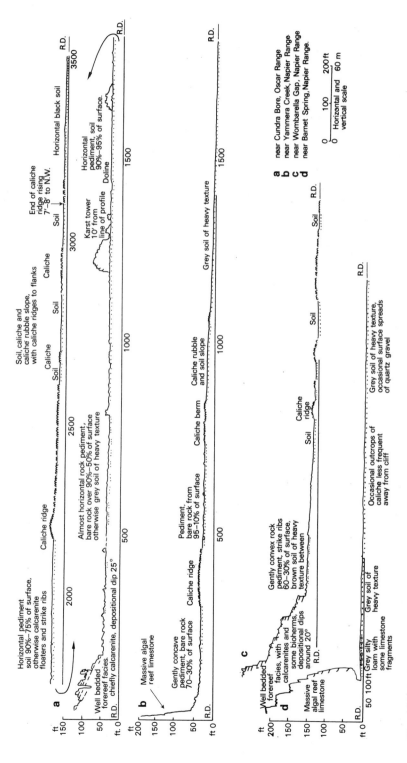

Fig. 120 Pediment profiles, Limestone Ranges, Fitzroy Basin, West Kimberley, Western Australia (from Jennings & Sweeting [31])

In Puerto Rico, tower karst is important and according to Thrailkill occurs in two zones on either side of a belt of kegelkarst [135]. Along the north coast of Puerto Rico west of San Juan, isolated groups of limestone towers are conspicuous features in the landscape; they rise out of a sandy clay plain covered both with fluvial material and also with marine sediments of Quaternary age [429, 434]. The towers are from 50 to 150 m high. Monroe is of the opinion that the tower karst of Puerto Rico develops on dense and medium-dense limestones, and that the formation of case-hardened caprock is important. Monroe also believes that some of the tower karst has developed *beneath* the cover of sands. As the sands have been removed, case hardening of the exposed limestones has taken place; once exposed the limestones become relatively resistant while further solution takes place under the cover of the sands. In Puerto Rico, these towers are called *mogotes* (Spanish: a hill or stack), and tower karst is often considered to be the same as mogotenkarst – the name given to it by Lehmann [17]. This nomenclature is not accepted by all workers [422].

Compared with Jamaica there is much more tower karst in Puerto Rico. The denudation of the limestone is more advanced in Puerto Rico and rivers cut through the karst; the result is that more alluvium is brought into the karst areas there than in Jamaica. The kegelkarst has become submerged by alluvium and greater mechanical erosion has taken place. In his work on the caves of the Rio Camuy, Thrailkill notes that the evidence suggests that a good deal of the erosion by the underground river is mechanical and not solutional [135].

The influence of structural and lithological controls on the development of the tower karst in Cuba has recently been made by Panoš and Štelcl, who show that many different tropical karst landforms exist there [422].

Dissected tower karst is found in parts of British Honduras, where the isolated hills of Mesozoic limestones rest upon granites. Large rivers draining from the granite areas cut through the towers in large caves formed at the level of the unconformity between the granite and the limestones; an example is the Rio Frio Cave near Augustine [94].

Undoubtedly the most spectacular and interesting area of tower karst in the world is in the monsoon area of south-east Asia. The kegelkarst of the Yunnan is replaced eastwards in central Kweichow and in Kwangsi province by a vast area of tower karst, which extends into Vietnam. Cone and tower karst are also important in the

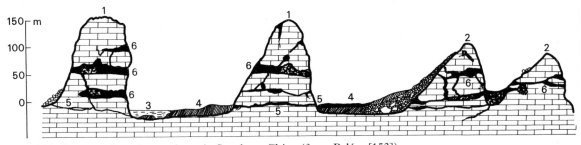

Fig. 121 Cross-section of tower karst in Southern China (from Balázs [153])

1. Tower karst hills trimmed by lateral fluvial erosion
2. Typical kegelkarst hills
3. River
4. Karst border plain
5. Active foot cave
6. Inactive (fossil) foot cave

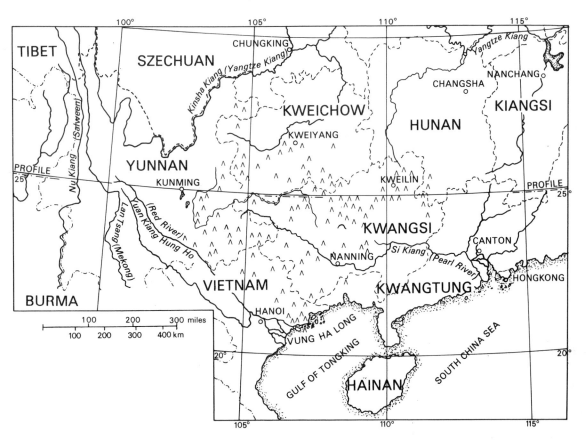

Fig. 122 Distribution of tower karst in southern China and North Vietman (from Silar [416]) (The areas with tower karst are marked by ∧)

Malayan archipelago and in Indonesia [153, 410]. The total limestone area in the provinces of Yunnan, Kweichow and Kwangsi is about 600,000 km² and it is therefore the largest karst region of the world. As already indicated, the western part forms a kegelkarst highland, but the eastern part, largely in Kwangsi, forms a classical tower karst. The towers are from 100 to 200 m high, with steeply inclined slopes at 80°–90°, see Fig. 121. The areas where the kegel- and tower karst occur are shown in the map, Fig. 122; and in the cross-section, Fig. 121, which is taken from Balázs [153]. The magnificent towers in the neighbourhood of Kweilin (valley of

the Jang) have often been photographed, so too have those in the Bai d'Along (Vung da Lhong) near Hanoi. Cotton in his book *Landscape* in 1948 briefly reflected upon the influence this tower-karst relief has had upon Chinese art [435]. Much of this karst in south-east Asia was first studied by the French in Indo-China. Both Blondel [436] and Cuisinier [439] worked here in the 1920s; von Wissmann wrote on the area in 1954 [412]. More recently our knowledge of this karstland is due to Hungarian and Czech geographers, particularly D. Balázs [153] and J. Silar [416]. Much of what follows about south-east Asia is derived from their explanations.

The limestones occupy over 60 per cent of the total known strata in Yunnan, and over 73 per cent in Kwangsi. They are very strongly jointed, which has influenced the development of the vertically sided towers. The general level of the land also rises from Kwangsi, westwards to the Yunnan–Kweichow plateau and further into Tibet. The karst development has been assisted by tectonic uplift, associated with the uplift of the Himalayas, occurring in several phases. Each uplift has rejuvenated the karst relief, with the result that several stages of karst development can be recognised. The tower karst probably originated in the early Tertiary or at the boundary between the Cretaceous and the Tertiary, during the tectonic rest which followed the Yenshan folding and before the beginning of the Himalayan movements in the Miocene. Cressey explained the differentiation between the western Yunnan kegelkarst and the eastern tower karst as due to the gradual dissection of the Yunnan–Kweichow plateau towards the east [438]. Recent work, however, shows that this is too simplified an explanation and that several phases of tower karst formation and deep valley cutting have occurred in both Yunnan and in Kwangsi [416].

Both Silar and Balázs consider that the south Chinese karstlands are influenced by climate. Thus on the high plateau of Yunnan, as at Kunming, the landforms of a temperate karst occur, with dolines and gouffres (potholes), etc. But at Kweilin, there is cone and tower karst. The figures for these two localities are as follows:

Height above sea-level	Temp. mean annual	Rainfall per year
KUNMING:		
1,893 m	15·9°C	1,039 mm
KWEILIN:		
154 m	19·5°C	1,914 mm
	(max. 28°C)	(max. per year)

Balázs thinks that 1,200 mm per year rainfall and 18°C average temperature are the minimum figures for the formation of kegel- and tower karst. Von Wissmann considers the tower karst in China to occur as far north as 30°N (though here at low altitudes) [412]. Added to the high average temperatures and rainfall in this part of south-east Asia, is the great intensity of heat and rainfall coinciding with the monsoon period.

In the karst of the high Yunnan plateau there is an extensive hydrological network and long active caves, many of which were formed in the Quaternary. At lower levels in the tower karst, the caves are the dissected remnants of once former extensive systems; Balázs gives two examples, the Partie House Cave and the cave of Pilientung, both in the Jangso area in Kwangsi province [153]. The caves in the tower and kegelkarst are old, dating probably from the late Tertiary, and are largely river caves, related to the stages in the down-cutting. The dry caves in the tower karst areas are those which have been used for centuries by the Chinese for both homes and workshops.

Kegelkarst occurs today outside the tropical zone in China in northern Kwangsi; this is accounted for by the fact that the Tertiary climate in this part of China is considered to have been warmer then than it is today.

In the last few years studies of karst areas in the East Indian islands have been made. In the British parts of Borneo, the Geological Survey has produced a detailed and enlightened volume on the caves of Sarawak by Wilford and Wall, who have also contributed various articles on the karst areas of Sarawak [430, 431, 432, 433]. More recently, Balázs has issued a survey of the karst regions of Indonesia [410]. The work in all these areas confirms the views already expressed about the two main types of karst and their suggested origins. Unlike

Williams, Balázs distinguishes karst types in S.E. Asia, using a morpho-genetic index applied to the hills. The diameter at the base of the hills and their altitude is known – then d/a is the morpho-genetical index. On this basis Balázs recognises four types in S.E. Asia and China; these are the Yangshuo, the Organos (after Cuba), the Goenoeng Sewu and the Tual types [532].

3. OTHER TYPES OF TROPICAL KARST

Tropical climates are very diverse, particularly from the point of view of rainfall amounts and periodicity. This variation, combined with the great geological variety to be found within tropical karstlands, means that not all the landforms fit neatly into the categories of cone and tower karst. However, most other types of tropical karst are variations to some extent on this theme. In Guadeloupe, Lasserre has described the karst forms in an area of relatively low relief. The 'mornes' of Guadeloupe are similar to the karst towers (mogotes) of the other West Indian islands, but are on a more subdued and smaller scale. He also describes a karst with dolines in Guadeloupe, but makes the point that this occurs where the surfaces are horizontal and where run-off is trapped. Lasserre states that a karst with dolines never develops into a cone karst [541].

From the work of Jennings and Bik and of Verstappen in New Guinea it seems that the character of the cone and tower karst changes with altitude within the tropics. All these writers stress the intense vigour and complexity of the karsts at high levels in New Guinea, the arête and doline karst of Jennings and Bik [420] and the labyrinth-ine karst of Verstappen [421] being some of the most complex and spectacular yet described. The deeply dissected arête with doline karst in New Guinea is possibly of Pleistocene age and is therefore a young karst. Jennings makes the point: 'The possibility needs to be considered therefore whether, at certain levels, high tropical mountains may not provide the optimal conditions for karst evolution combining as they do lower temperatures . . . with a fairly high and an effective precipitation and with the prolific vegetation growth of mossy montane forest throughout the year' [420]. The arête and doline (or as Williams prefers to call it, the arête and pinnacle karst) is developed at 9,500 ft (2,900 m). Crevice karst is also described by Jennings and Bik; this consists of an irregular, widened joint-network system. Widened joints up to 6 m across and 20 m deep isolate blocks of limestone. Since both blocks and crevices are completely overgrown by thick rain forest and are not visible from the air, it is country which is almost impossible to cross. It is found at about 1,000 m in the Darai Hills in New Guinea and on both chalky and dense limestone. Jennings and Bik were of the opinion that crevice karst occurred along major valleys on flat surfaces that may once have been alluviated [420].

In the semi-arid tropics the surface run-off from intense rain showers is even more rapid than in the humid tropics, and closed depressions are less well developed or non-existent. The Limestone Ranges of the Fitzroy area in north-west Australia have a semi-arid monsoon climate with heavy rain showers falling in a short period of the year. In this area there is a type of tower karst, produced by the growth and extension of 'karst corridors', which resembles enormous bogaz (or karstgassen) of the Dinaric karst [31, 122]. The corridors have developed

54 Box-like development of tower karst, Limestone Ranges, near Geikie Gorge, north-west Australia

along joints and join together to form integrated valley systems of box-like cross-section, Fig. 123. The box valleys have a rectangular, joint-controlled branching pattern. They contain the dry silty beds of the wet-season streams and form confluent valley systems, Photo 54. Elsewhere the flat valley floors bear evidence of sheet-flood flow only. The box valleys are more continuous and confluent than the stream courses within them; the streams sink into small clay or silt-filled hollows. But the downward gradients of the valleys are uninterrupted and the longitudinal profiles are only very slightly reversed. Deposition of secondary calcium carbonate (travertine) in tongues along the stream beds, during the periods of declining flow at the end of the wet season, also helps to seal the valley floor by preventing the water from sinking underground, and also assists the widening of the valleys, Photo 55 [31]. The extension of the box-like valleys breaks down the limestone into a scattered field of towers, pinnacles and ridges. The towers are only about 50 m high, because of the limiting available relief, and rise abruptly from the surrounding planed limestone surface. Such a karst is tropical in style, resembling southeast Asia rather than the Dinaric karst.

A factor in the formation of this tower karst is the introduction of alluvium and debris from the surrounding non-limestone

areas on to the limestone surface. This alluvium prevents water from percolating into the rock, and in areas of tropical downpours encourages lateral planation by sheet-flood flow. Thus in the Limestone Ranges the most advanced tower karst occurs in the part near the Oscar Ranges where its formation has been helped by run-off from the Proterozoic rocks of the Oscar Ranges which has deposited quartz sands on the limestone surface. Mechanical abrasion therefore has been important in addition to the solutional breakdown of the karst limestones. However, the introduction of non-limestone debris 'is not a necessary element

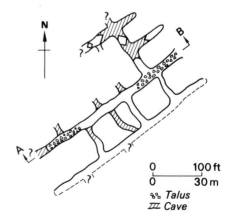

Fig. 123 Joint-controlled karst development, Geikie Gorge, Fitzroy area, north-west Australia

in the production of tower karst, because it develops in other situations' (loc. cit., p. 29). But the more one sees of tower karst, the more it seems to be associated not only with a local vorfluter, but also with non-limestone debris or alluvium. Moreover, in the semi-arid climate of north-west Australia the process of pediment formation has assisted the development of the tower karst, the perfectly planed rock floor contrasting sharply with the vertical walls of the towers. In the relatively unbedded and massively bedded reef or algal facies of the limestones, the combination of structure and of erosional processes has produced striking tower karst. Pediments occur in other rocks in this part of Australia, but they are much more perfectly developed on the limestones. Pedimentation has been accentuated by the formation of calcrete ridges, the result of strong evaporation during the dry season. These ridges pond back-water and retain it on the pediment, causing increased solution of the limestones [439].

In tropical and sub-tropical desert areas, closed hollows are again unusual. In the Carlsbad area of New Mexico, it has already been shown that dolines have been replaced by gulleys adapted to the rapid run-off (see p. 57). As would be expected, in the truly arid regions limestones show few surface solution features and only an occasional enclosed hollow. The development of calcrete (caliche) is particularly important in tropical arid and semi-arid limestone areas. Strong evaporation after sudden rainstorms gives rise to the precipitation of calcium carbonate at the surface or just below, and gives a hard protective skin of secondary calcium carbonate. Calcrete thus occurs in the desert of the Hadramaut, Arabia, discussed by von Wissmann in 1957, and in the dry areas of the limestone of northern Kenya [263]. Calcrete crusts are also

55 Tufa barrier, Barnet Spring Valley, Fitzroy area, north-west Australia

important in northern Yucatán [94]. Few studies of karsts in the arid zones of the tropics have so far been made. One of the problems in examining such areas is to decide the extent to which landforms have been subject to climatic change; since karst landforms are particularly susceptible to changes in climate, the examination of desert karst could be of great significance.

In areas of the tropics where the run-off is slower, dolines tend to develop. At Katherine, also in the monsoonal region of northern Australia at latitude 14°S, a doline karst has formed on limestones of Palaeozoic age. The rainfall at Katherine is higher than in the Limestone Ranges, but the most significant fact seems to be that the limestones have only recently become exposed and there is much residual impermeable material resting on them; because of this, water remains on the surface for a longer time and run-off is delayed and this has encouraged doline formation [31].

Areas, just inside or marginal to the tropics with reasonable rainfalls, tend also to have doline rather than cone or tower karst. This is exemplified by the Barkly Tableland in Queensland, in latitude 20°S. This karstland formed in Cambrian dolomites is characterised by shallow collapse dolines, and was the subject of a paper by the Czech geographer Daneš in 1915 [411]. In a similarly situated area in the Transvaal in South Africa, in about latitude 24°–25°S, the Transvaal dolomites also give rise to a shallow doline karst; in parts, as in the eastern Transvaal in the region of the Blyde canyon, a form of cone karst has developed. In both these regions transitional landforms, temperate/tropical, occur, in addition to features associated with dolomites, such as the strongly developed joints [509].

Finally, though not strictly tropical, there are the karsts on the temperate margins of the sub-tropical deserts. Examples occur in the Nullarbor Plain in South Australia, and in the northern part of Libya. Karst in these areas usually has shallow dolines [284]. Like the karsts on the sub-tropical margins of the deserts, these have also been subject to many climatic changes, which are reflected in enormous tufa and stalagmite deposits, both in the dry valleys and in the caves. In Libya cone-like hills occur, the relics probably of a wetter climate.

4. CONCLUSIONS

Because of the rapid evaporation in tropical climates, corrosion is restricted particularly to the surface layers of the limestones and the solution that occurs in the deeper zones in cooler regions may not always take place. Cuisinier made this point when discussing the karst of Indo-China in 1929 and described the innumerable pitons and needles up to 12 m high which occur on the surface. He also said, 'C'est le karst développé,

poussé jusqu'à l'absurde' [437]. 'Ferociously' jagged surfaces of corrosion, with solution furrows 10 m deep, are common in tropical karsts. Despite this fierce superficial corrosion, corrosion at depth is less spectacular and deep caves are rarely found in tropical areas. The long caves found in such regions are almost always associated with the allogenic rivers, though much more exploration and study of tropical caves is needed to substantiate this opinion. It does seem, however, that the main corrosive action in tropical karsts is at the surface.

Renault in particular has taken up this point. He stresses how limestones in tropical zones suffer 'applanissement' at the soil level, showing the importance of biochemical and biological activity in dissolving the rock. Micro-organisms are important in the dissolution of $CaCO_3$ in tropical caves, where the temperatures are often over 71°F (21°C). Moon milk (Mondmilch), for example, regarded as of biochemical origin, is particularly important in many tropical caves. The figures for calcium carbonate content of stagnant water in pools and lakes is high in tropical areas, and can reach as much as 500–600 ppm $CaCO_3$; whereas the calcium figures for cave water and stream waters are frequently very low, from 12 to 40 ppm. Solution is assisted in tropical regions, according to Renault and Corbel, by the presence of nitrous dioxide in the atmosphere which by the addition of water gives rise to nitric acid, thereby making the rainwater of tropical regions more acidic at the moment of impact on the rock, and adding to the intensity of the surface solution. Douglas feels there is not evidence to prove this point, however [75]. Moreover, Ford is of the opinion that differences of climate do not influence the development of tropical caves [511].

It is usual to divide karsts in temperate zones into three vertical zones. These are:

(a) Zone of superficial dissolution, karren, dolines, etc. – sometimes known as the croute karstique.

(b) Neutral zone where the solutional enlargement of the cracks is at a minimum.

(c) Zone of deep dissolution where water becomes aggressive again and deep cavities are formed.

In temperate karst there is a dissociation between the surface and the deeper solution, which does not exist in a tropical climate. This dissociation between surface and deep underground gave rise to the concept of *karstic immunity* discussed by Clozier [117] and Baulig [440]. By this is implied that temperate karst regions are more resistant to erosion than non-karst areas, generally an erroneous conclusion. In tropical regions where the seasonal variation of temperature is much less, the thermal variations within the limestone are also less. The dissociation between the top layers and the deep zone is reduced or non-existent, and solution is entirely concentrated at the surface.

Thus certain generalisations about karst development in tropical zones can now be made:

(1) Tropical waters dissolve the limestones rapidly but are quickly saturated. The solutions soon become supersaturated and calcium carbonate is redeposited. We have already noted that large concretionary stalagmite and stalactite deposits are a feature of tropical caves. In general the deposits of stalactite in tropical caves are formed of aragonite, compared with calcite in temperate caves. The case-hardening of limestones in the tropics is also the result of the rapid solution and equally rapid redeposition.

(2) Because of the rapid solution and evaporation and the great variations in the amounts of calcium carbonate dissolved, the pH of the waters is very unstable and changes quickly both in time and place. Thus, for instance, at the Wire Spring in the Limestone Ranges, the pH of the water changed from 6·8 to 8·7 in a few seconds [31]. Corbel also compares variations in waters from Yucatán and Miami with those in Alaska [136]:

.Yucatán	pH varies between		6·0 and 9·0
Miami	pH	,, ,,	4·3 and 9·0
Alaska	pH	,, ,,	7·1 and 7·3

(3) Since most of the solution takes place at the surface, lateral corrosion is the predominant form of erosion. Solution is controlled by bacteria and other micro-organisms and tends to take place in swamps, lakes and the bases of the cockpits. These are the foci of accelerated corrosion in the tropics. Because of the importance of vegetation and soil, rivers tend to flow on the surface of alluvium, and fluvial erosion and corrosion is more important in tropical karst regions than in temperate regions. All these processes tend to dissect the limestones into isolated towers or pinnacles so that the final landscape is a field of scattered towers or 'inselbergs' between which are swamps or slow-flowing rivers; this is the landscape of much of the tower karst landscape of south-east Asia.

(4) Because of the great surface solution and the redeposition of calcium carbonate, caves are generally small, and tend to be a network of small tunnels, 'un réseau de grottes tunnels' [222]. The redeposition of calcium carbonate seals the joints and cracks, making it difficult for the water to sink further into the ground. Large caves in tropical areas, like those in Jamaica and Puerto Rico, are due essentially to erosion by through-flowing rivers.

There has been much controversy, which was referred to in Chapter 3, about the effectiveness of water in tropical latitudes to dissolve calcium carbonate. Corbel and others maintain that, because it can be shown that cold water and snow melt dissolve relatively large quantities of $CaCO_3$ whereas water at higher temperatures dissolves much less (for instance, Renault's figures are temperature $21°C$, equilibrium $CaCO_3$ 90 ppm; temperature $13°C$, equilibrium $CaCO_3$ 150 ppm) the total rate of dissolution of the limestones is much more rapid in the colder areas than in the warmer. Corbel considers that the development of the tower karst in south-east Asia and in the West Indies is much slower than the evolution of karst areas in colder climates. His evidence is based largely upon analyses of waters in the areas concerned [136]. However, the evidence of the analyses by themselves is conflicting, as the writer and Jennings pointed out in 1963 [31].

Gerstenhauer's analyses also give the reverse conclusion to that of Corbel [62]. Tropical limestone landforms are resistant, not because of the slowness of solution, but because of the reprecipitation and the formation of the hard caprock which, as we have seen, form 'strong' landscapes in the tropics.

Though there are many kinds of tropical karst, it seems that cone and tower karst and their variations form a continuously varying species. But Verstappen has said that 'it is too much of a simplification to distinguish any normal (temperate) and tropical karst' [421], since there are numerous interacting causes in the differentiation of karst areas – lithology, structure, regional geomorphological history, present climate, past climatic changes, etc. Thus any one of these may override the influence of a tropical climate and give rise to a type of karst very different from what might be expected on a climatic basis.

16 Other Types of Karst

AS WE have indicated on p. 257, other types of karst have been recognised. The literature on most of these is sporadic and scattered, even though some of these karst types occupy relatively large areas of the earth's surface. The most important include those known as covered and interstratal karsts, and also fossil karst. Reference to other karst types will also be given.

1. COVERED (UNTERIRDISCHE) KARSTS

In our classification of karst types given on p. 254, the distinction was made between *bare karst* (nackter karst) and *covered karst* (bedeckter karst). In the literature, covered karst can refer either to limestones covered simply with soil and vegetation, or to limestones covered with alluvium or other sediments. On the basis of Sawicki's original paper in 1909, Mediterranean karsts were the true bare karsts, central and north-west European were covered karsts. Bare karst occurs where the rock is exposed at the surface and is cut up by fissures and crevices, as in Montenegro and in some Alpine glaciokarsts.

However, much of the bare karst particularly in the Classical and Dinaric karst areas is due to historical causes. Periods of intensive transhumant livestock breeding caused deforestation of the extensive mountain plateaux, despite the fact that forests could grow on them easily [313, 318]. Roglič says that during the last 150 years, when the population has become more sedentary and has also grown greatly, there has been a great increase in winter grazing. This, together with the summer droughts, the sudden autumn rains, the prevalence of the strong winds of the Bora in certain districts, and the spread of goat breeding, has caused the great deforestation that is typical of parts of the Dinaric karst. However, in more recent years, as a result of rural depopulation and reduced pressure on the soil, and the banning of the goat, there has been a regeneration of the forest in many parts. This illustrates the 'sensitivity of the karst to agricultural and sociological influences' [313]. Along some of the coastal parts of the Dinaric area, particularly along the steep slopes of the Velebit mountains, which are exposed to strong sun and to the violent winds of the Bora, the karst has probably always been bare. Many authorities hold the Venetians responsible for the deforestation of the karst; though this is to a certain extent true, there are other factors which brought about deforestation and the formation of a bare karst.

In Britain, the limestone pavements of Ingleborough may be regarded as bare karst. This is also almost certainly the result of grazing sheep and cattle, who eat the young shoots of the trees and prevent regeneration. When the pavements are fenced, and sheep and cattle kept off, scrub, and later woodland trees, become established. This has been demonstrated at Warton Crag, near Morecambe Bay, a nature reserve, and also near Malham Tarn House, in a controlled experiment. The same is probably true of the bare limestone pavements of the Burren of County Clare, which have also been over-grazed by sheep, cattle and goats. Thus in western Europe almost all the karst is soil-covered, and there is relatively little naturally true bare karst. In the tropics, except for the steepest slopes, the karst is covered with vegetation.

In the U.S.A. the karsts of Kentucky, Virginia and Indiana are excellent examples of soil covered (or green) karsts.

In a soil-covered karst, the corrosion of the rock is more evenly distributed and is also greatly increased. This was demonstrated by Terzaghi in the Dinaric karst in 1913 [318], and more recently by Gams from Slovenia [243]. It is also possibly supported by the calcium content analyses of waters in the karst areas of the British Isles, those draining from the Mendips and the Peak District limestones containing much more calcium bicarbonate than waters draining from the barer karsts of Ingleborough or of the Burren [76]. In the Alps, doline formation is particularly important below the tree line. Soil-covered karst occurs particularly where limestones are in contact with other rock types and with alluvium. Sawicki thought that the more gentle rains of western and central Europe would not wash the soil cover so rapidly into cracks in the limestones as in the Mediterranean karsts. Soil-covered karst areas also have shallower and wider (more bowl-shaped) dolines caused by the washing-in of soil by trickling water; the clogging-up of the fissures prevents the deepening of the dolines. We have also seen that a soil cover produces rounded and smoothed surfaces; moreover, in the bauxite-covered areas in Jamaica, the cover of bauxite soil on the White Limestones produces a smoothed surface.

In a soil-covered (or soddy) karst the surface forms are normal forms modified by the cover of detritus or soil.* Corbel has written on the *karst couvert* in the Lesse Valley in Belgium and sums up the differences between soil-covered karst and bare karst as follows [87,542].

*Limestones covered by peri-glacial deposits (pergelisol) have been called 'karsts cutanés' (cutaneous karsts) [544].

Bare karst	Covered karst
(1) Numerous lapiés (karren).	(1) Lapiés rare.
(2) A predominance of vertical avens over horizontal forms.	(2) A predominance of horizontally cut forms.
(3) Little infilling (remblayage) of caves.	(3) Cave infilling important, particularly by clays.
(4) Collapse forms frequent.	(4) Collapse forms rare.

There is, however, another type of covered karst, which gives rise to somewhat different phenomena and develops in limestones covered by a thick deposit of non-limestone rocks, a non-autochthonous cover. This can develop under recent thick moraine or alluvium but also under another lithified stratigraphical unit such as a clay or a sandstone. This kind of karst was first discussed by Katzer in 1905 who called it the *unterirdische Karstphänomen* [364], which literally means subterranean or subsurface karst. A. Penck wrote a long essay on 'Unterirdischer Karst' in 1924 in a volume of essays presented to J. Cvijič [127]. In this essay Penck used the term to include both soil-covered karst and karst developed in limestones covered by thick clays or sandstones, since he gives as an example that formed beneath the lower Bunter Sandstone in the southern Harz mountains [127]. This kind of karst is called by the French *karst sous-jacent*. Quinlan proposes the term *interstratal karst* to distinguish it from that developed beneath a soil cover. It is proposed to use this term in this chapter.

In his essay in 1924 Penck deals with the morphological effects of the solution of Triassic salt beds in the Harz which underlie the lower Bunter Sandstone. Collapse hollows (Erdfallen) are common, caused by the settling and adjustment of the cover beds to the effects of solution in the beds below, i.e. by the process known as suffosion. He also discussed examples from the Franken Jura where the dolomite of the White Jura is overlain by the Cretaceous Veldensteiner Sandstone.

Stratigraphical series, including gypsum and salt beds in addition to limestones and dolomites, also give rise to interstratal karst. Subsidence landforms, formed either rapidly or slowly, are the most common. In Britain, such subsidence landforms are associated with the salt beds of the Trias in Cheshire and with the gypsum beds, also of the Trias, in Cumberland. This kind of interstratal karst and its associated landforms will not be discussed here.

In Britain there are forms of interstratal karst connected with the Carboniferous Limestones. On the eastern slopes of Ingleborough, for instance, the limestones are covered by up to 30–40 ft (10–13 m) of sandy glacial ground moraine. As a result of the solution of the limestones beneath this cover, the ground moraine slowly subsides into cracks in the limestone and crater-like hollows (the shake-holes) are formed on the surface. Such hollows are up to 50 ft (17 m) deep. In the eastern Mendips, the limestones are covered by Liassic rocks; solution in the limestones has taken place and subsidence of the Liassic rocks has given rise to some of the largest hollows in the Mendip area (an example being Wurts Pit). The best example in Britain of interstratal karst is probably that in South Wales, where the Carboniferous Limestones are overlain by up to 100 m of Pennant Grit; solution of the limestones at depth has been so great that solution subsidences occur in the Grits up to 100 ft (30 m) deep [128]. As in many areas of interstratal karst, the number of enclosed hollows on the Grits is greater than the number occurring on the limestones themselves.

One of the most interesting interstratal karsts in North America is to be found in the Santa Rosa area of New Mexico in the Pecos River valley. In this region the Santa Rosa Sandstone of Triassic age overlies limestones and gypsum of Permian age. The sandstone is about 300 ft (100 m) thick and dips gently eastwards. Solution of the limestone and gypsum takes place chiefly by groundwater which is derived from the mountains to the west and which moves slowly within the rocks. Solution of the rocks is more important near the Pecos river because groundwater is more abundant. The largest collapse hollows associated with solution beneath the Santa Rosa Sandstones are found nearest the river. The hollows are steep-sided and often filled with alluvium. Cracks and fissures occur in the Sandstones as a result of the subsidence. The hollows are frequently the sites of powerful springs (as at Santa Rosa) which emerge from the Sandstones. Away from the Pecos river solution of the underlying beds is less obvious, and the hollows are less steep-sided and become degraded; cracks and fissures in the sandstones become less important. Recession of the sides takes place by parallel retreat and the hollows evolve into shallow, flat-floored, dish-like depressions. In the area between Colonias and Santa Rosa, at least three stages in the development of these hollows can be recognised, which are related to former water-levels and to the terraces in the development of the river Pecos. Nearest the river, the hollows are still developing, and are of relatively small diameter (about 100 m and less); on the middle level the hollows are still recognisable as having originated by collapse, but they have now become alluviated and the sides have slumped in; on the highest levels the hollows are shallow and flat, much more irregular and may be as much as 200–300 m long. They still occur in the sandstones. In some parts, particularly at the middle and upper levels, the collapse material has been removed sufficiently to reveal the underlying rocks and in places the deep cracks and caves which exist in the limestones.

To the south, also in the Pecos River valley, Quinlan has discussed the interstratal karst of Roswell, where sandstones overlie thick gypsum deposits. Solution of the gypsum by the groundwaters has been extensive and collapse hollows in the upper beds have been formed. These hollows are at the water-level and form deep lakes, known as the 'Bottomless Lakes' [441], and they form a series in the Pecos valley at Roswell.

Interstratal karst is widespread in the U.S.S.R., and it is discussed by Gvozdeckij [389]. According to him it is 'widely spread in many regions of the Russian Plain where karstifying limestone is covered either with moraine or fluvio-glacial or alluvial sediments'. A classical example of covered mountain karst occurs in the 'section south and south-west of Kislovodsk in the North Caucasus where karst forms are developed on structural terraces and flat gully bottoms formed by the Valanginian limestone, covered with loose insoluble Hauterivian sediments' [442].

There are many varieties of covered and interstratal karsts and they would repay more attention.

2. RELICT AND FOSSIL KARST FORMS

Implicit in any discussion of karst landforms is the assumption that their formation reflects the conditions of climate prevailing at the time, and that their survival or lack of erosion enables the periods of former climates to be reconstructed. It is quite obvious that many (or most) of the landforms in the karst regions of the world were formed under different climatic conditions from those now prevailing. As we have already indicated, only the regions of the humid tropics, the interior of the great deserts, and high Arctic did not suffer repeated changes during the Quaternary. Going back beyond the Quaternary into the Tertiary, it is probable that even these regions were not immune from climatic change, so that in all karst areas, except where the landforms are of very recent origin, there are fossil or relict karst forms. Certain climatic phases have hindered karstification, while in other phases karst landforms developed rapidly. Thus most limestone areas show evidence of many phases of karstification.

Fossil karst landforms are of two main kinds. First, those formed in earlier geological periods and never covered by later rocks; these may be called relict landforms. And secondly, those formed in earlier geological periods, subsequently covered by non-limestone rocks and later re-exhumed; these are exhumed or resurrected landforms.

Both types occur in Britain, though relict karst is more common because of the relative newness of our karst areas. In north-west Yorkshire, as we have shown, the relief is essentially the result of the phases of the last glaciation. The pavements, the screes, and many of the potholes and caves are the result of former glacial and periglacial conditions. In the Peak District many of the uniform valley slopes are fossil scree slopes of Quaternary age. In the Mendips many of the screes, gulleys and dry valleys are of periglacial origin, and are relict landforms.

But in addition to these relict landforms of cold periods, there may also be those of former warmer periods, possibly Tertiary in age. In the Mendips, Frey considers that the relief of parts of the western area is the result of the resurrection of former Triassic valleys cut into the Carboniferous Limestones during the formation of the Dolomitic Conglomerate and buried by Mesozoic rocks; the valleys are now being exhumed. Corbel regards the Winscombe area of the Mendips as part of a former tropical karst, the hills surrounding the Winscombe depression, such as Crook's Peak, being isolated limestone buttes or relict kegelkarst hills. He claims that in the western part of the Mendips there are few caves and that there is no development of a deep karst, and that this is indicative of warm climate conditions; he contrasts the relief of the Mendips east and west of Blackdown Hill, the fossil tropical (but possibly exhumed) karst being characteristic of the western part and a periglacial relict karst of much of the eastern [443, 87].

Furthermore in many British karst areas at least two or three phrases of karstification are common. The Carboniferous Limestones in the region surrounding Morecambe Bay in north-west England is an area of isolated limestone hills resting on a planed floor of Silurian slates, and includes the well-known hills of Whitbarrow Scar, Arnside Knott, Hampsfell, Warton Crag, and those around Ulverston and Millom. These hills have large deposits of scree alongside them, as for example on the east slope of Whitbarrow Scar where they are being quarried and the east side of Arnside Knott. The screes are layered and are probably of periglacial or glacial age. If the limestone slopes beneath these screes are examined they are found to be much smoothed and potholed and weathered by solution, and associated with a reddish soil or clay. The formation of this red clay and the smoothed limestone walls may represent an earlier, warmer phase of karstification in this area. Such an opinion has long been held by Corbel, who has regarded the hills of the Morecambe Bay area as a relict tropical karst [87], resting upon a planed rock floor. A section through the limestone hills of this area illustrates his point. Corbel has said, 'Le grand nombre de ces buttes, leur allure évoque immédiatement des kegels, les collines calcaires de ces karsts tropicaux. La ressemblance des formes est poussée jusque dans le détail. Le dessin contourné de Cartmel Fell par exemple peut trouver aisément son équivalent dans le delta du Tonkin' (loc. cit., p. 289). This comment is made without any reference to the geological structure of the isolated hills (dips, faults, etc.), but many detailed aspects of the hills of the Morecambe Bay area suggest that one phase of warm climate has occurred. The Morecambe Bay karst area also abounds in melt-water features, relicts of a wet phase during the glaciations. In this respect the hills and flat-lying polje-type floors of the Morecambe Bay area resemble the Mole Creek area of Tasmania examined by the writer and Jennings [324].

In north-west Yorkshire, though most of the karst is of recent (Glacial) origin, there are parts which are older and were developed under warmer conditions. These include the parts of the region north of Malham Tarn and in the neighbourhood of the Craven Faults between Malham and Austwick. These are the only districts in which well-developed dolines or uvalas occur [171], and their general relief is quite different from the newly stripped glacial karsts immediately surrounding Ingleborough and Whernside [444].

The most complex karst in Britain is that of the Peak District, which has suffered several phases of karstification. The first was probably a warm phase and is now represented by the cone-like hills or 'lows' which occur along the highest watershed of the Peak District. Deep limestone hollows, in which there are Triassic sand deposits, also occur in the central and southern parts of the Peak District. These hollows were erroneously regarded by both Corbel and H. Lehmann as cockpits formed under tropical conditions, and filled with residual Triassic sands; they could, however, equally have been formed by solution *in situ* below a cover of the Trias and have originated as an interstratal karst. The second phase in the Peak District was the production of the fluvial karst which is now dominant in the region. This began in the Miocene, and is reflected in the downcutting of the rivers, the gorges and the valley side-benches, and the formation of the caves associated with the downcutting. The third phase was a period of cold and glaciation during which the periglacial valleys, screes and 'aiguilles', like Tissington Spires, were formed by frost action [395].

The karst of Ireland similarly shows many phases. As we have seen, recent glacial karst occurs in the Burren in County Clare, and in the Marble Arch area on the border between the Republic and Northern Ireland; periglacial karst is seen in Ben Bulben. But the Irish Plain is partly a karst plain, with a long history, and many of the landforms associated with it are fossil or relict forms. Corbel has already noted the existence of isolated limestone buttes standing above the corroded limestones in the Irish Plain. Some of these buttes are formed of reef limestones and owe their existence partly to structural causes. Others are reminiscent of a kegelkarst: 'L'origine de tous ces karsts anciens à buttes en pains de sucre que l'on trouve dans toute la plaine centrale et jusqu'au sud de Sligo parait bien liée comme nous l'avons montré autour de Dublin à une érosion sous un climat tropical du type Sud-Chinois' [87]. It is

possible that the tropical kegelkarst was formed in the Eocene and Oligocene when there is sufficient evidence for the warmer climate; for instance there is the evidence of the flora of the Lough Neagh region [445]. The conical hills rest on a planed surface which has later been cut into by gorges, the result of the Pliocene (and Miocene) uplifts, in the period which followed the tropical weathering. The Quaternary glaciation which deposited moraine and fluvio-gravels upon the Irish Plain has occupied so much of our attention that the problems of the Tertiary have been neglected. South of Sligo, in the isolated hill of Keshcorran, there are over seventeen caves in one small hill – typical of the kinds of small cavities one would expect from a tropical karst. Owens Cave and other caves in the Michelstown area of Tipperary contain stalagmites 'en assiettes' and big concretionary dripstone forms – also regarded as more typical of a warmer karst than is forming in Ireland today.

In south-west Ireland similar relict karsts may be found. In the Blackwater and the Suir valleys isolated knolls like the residual cones or hums of the Mediterranean occur. Corbel is quite definite in his remarks: 'Il s'agit incontestablement là d'une forme fossile absolument analogue aux "cockpits" de la Jamaique, à la Baie d'Along, à tous les kegelkarsts nés sous un climat tropical humide' [87]. In the south-west, in the valley of Kenmare river, the Carboniferous Limestone forms low planed ground with isolated knolls between ridges of Old Red Sandstone; Corbel ascribes the karstic phenomena of this part of south-west Ireland to the prodigious speed of dissolution of limestones in the humid periglacial conditions experienced by this area during the Quaternary period. Hence Corbel seemingly chooses his climate to provide an explanation for the landforms (see also [536]).

One of the most completely studied areas which shows several phases of karstification is the Causses of Quercy – namely, one phase at least in the Eogene and three in the Quaternary. The Causses of Quercy contain numerous pockets of phosphorites which occupy old karst hollows; these pockets were shown by Clozier and later by Gèze to be the remains of a fossil karst now filled with an assemblage of deposits of varied origin – detrital, chemical and organic. The ages of these deposits were dated by normal stratigraphical means, and the age of the fossil karst shown to be Eogene [117, 120]. The Quaternary phases distinguished by Cavaillé correspond to phases in accord with the incision of the main valleys. Each phase began with a periglacial period, and the lowering of the valleys took place during the following interglacial; deposition of clay and also of concretions in the caves took place during the interglacial. During the following cold period the new karst system was formed at a lower level and corresponded to the river terraces. After each periglacial period, as the rivers became incised, so the upper part of the valleys became dry and was the locus for doline formation once the valley was dry. The last phase was during the Wurmian glaciation, when the third karstic system was constituted, many valleys dried up and a new phase of doline formation took place. At the end of the Wurmian there was much solifluction, taking the form of solifluction pebbles, etc. Under conditions today, little except solution is happening to the landscape, and it is nearly fixed (or figé) [290]. Between the Eogene karstification and the Quaternary phases, fewer traces are discernible. The present hydrographical network originated in the Pliocene. The Eogene karst is to a certain extent an exhumed karst, the Quaternary karsts are relict. Just north of the Causses of Quercy,

near Souillac, traces of a warmer Pliocene phase may occur. At Carsac, tropical cone-like hills are found and are the subject of work by Fénelon. Parts of the Causse of Sauveterre may also preserve elements of relief formed in a warmer pre-Glacial climate.

In other areas in Europe where karst limestones were exposed during the Tertiary, evidence of warmer or tropical erosion can be found. We have already seen that the solution planation of some of the polje floors in Jugoslavia is regarded by Roglič to be of Tertiary age [218]. In Poland, several periods of karst development since the Permian are recognised. Gilewska gives a table showing the different periods of karst phenomena together with the type of karst formation (type of caves, sink holes, towers, bare rock surfaces, etc.). She makes the point that karst always develops under the humid conditions (either warm or cool) in the periods which follow phases of earth movements. This is because phases of tectonic activity produce, in addition to a high relative relief, a well-developed jointing system enabling the karst processes to take place. During the phases of great heat and moisture, as in the Tertiary, the formation of large karst depressions took place. In the Pleistocene cave formation was most important, and surface karst landforms were of minor importance. In the limestones of Silesian Uplands present-day karstification is taking place with the formation of small dolines up to 10 m in diameter and 4 m deep, alongside the partial revival of old karst depressions [446]. Phases of high humidity (whether tropical or temperate) strengthen karst development; in phases of arid climate (whether warm or cold) mechanical weathering (scree formation) dominates over chemical weathering.

North of Krakow, a formerly warm or

56 Fossil karst near Krakow, Poland; limestone tower being exhumed from more recent sediments

sub-tropical karst is illustrated by the presence of towers (or mogotes) which rise above the lower Tertiary, Karstverebnungs-fläche, at 450 m above sea-level [447]. The towers are now being exhumed and are separated by wide depressions. The bottoms of these depressions have numerous pinnacles, pipes and deep clefts which have been widened by solution and buried under a mantle of impermeable preglacial red residual clays-with-flints, up to 10 m thick. Caves associated with the towers, often of the cliff-foot type, can be shown to be of at least Pliocene or early Pleistocene age by reason of their deposits of bones. (Fig. 124 and Photo 56.)

Relict and exhumed tropical karst is important in other parts of central and southern Europe. A relict semi-arid tropical karst is believed to be present in Ithaka in the Ionian Islands. Zötl [448] describes a landscape which resembles that which the writer and Jennings [449] found in north-west Australia, and which he regards as a semi-arid tropical karst of upper Pliocene age. A somewhat similar relict karst can be found in the Gulf of Corinth area of southern Greece, near Galaxihidion, west of Delphi. One of the most interesting fossil karsts of central Europe is believed to occur in the Franconian Jura, where the Kuppen Alb is considered by many people to be a relict cone karst of Upper Pliocene age, formed under a tropical or sub-tropical climate. It

1. Reef limestones
2. Bedded limestones

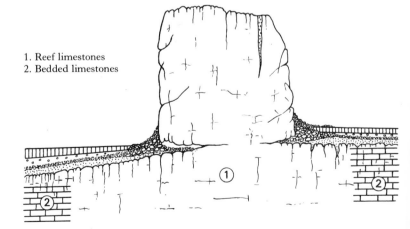

Fig. 124 Residual tower, north of Krakow (from Gilewska [447] after J. Pokorny)

was discussed by Budel [450] in 1951, but has been the subject of other works since then, particularly those by Spöcker [451] and Dongus [452].

The Kuppen Alb may be defined as partly an exhumed karst and partly a relict erosional karst. In the exhumed karst area, the tops of the cone hills are submerged beneath a cover mainly of quartz sands and loams. As the cover is removed, so the old kuppen or cone hills are being uncovered. Spöcker gives some idea of the stages of the resurrection of this type of relief in his work in 1952 [451]; he also shows how the distribution of the present-day cover rocks and of the karstified limestones suggests the former groupings of tropical karst hollows. Cramer said in 1933 that it was a covered cockpit landscape, and this view has been to some extent substantiated by the recent work of the climatic morphologists. Examples of the distribution of the kuppen-type hills and the nature of the exhumation are given in Fig. 111. Some of the best examples occur in the Pegnitz country north-east of Nuremberg. One of the important facts about the distribution of the cone hills of the Kuppen Alb is their relationship to the famous cliff-line of Heldenfingen, the limit of the Molasse Sea, of late Miocene age.

Exhumed tropical karst has been discussed in Bohemia by Panoš [453], and in Hungary by Szabó [454]. In many areas, exhumed tropical karst is associated with bauxite deposits. Though the actual origin of bauxite is still disputed and the literature on its origin is extremely large, bauxite deposits are frequently connected with the weathering, especially under tropical conditions, of limestones [326]. In Hungary, in the areas discussed by Szabó, a tower karst occurs with the bauxite and is partly covered by it. In southern France (Les Baux and the Var district of Provence), in Montenegro,

and in central Greece, all the bauxite deposits are connected with fossil tropical karst landscapes [326].

In other parts of the world, late Tertiary and Quaternary climatic phases are not so well distinguished, and it is more difficult to identify fossil karst. It is likely, however, that in the karst regions of the Appalachians and of the Rockies, the cold phases of the Quaternary will have left many marks upon the limestones and that relict karst caused by periglacial and permafrost conditions is abundant [455]. In the southern continents, where the phases of climatic change are even less recognised, the identification of relict karst landscapes can scarcely begin. But in both Australia and in South Africa (in the Transvaal), the writer has seen many karst landforms which in Europe would undoubtedly be regarded as relict or fossil karst [509].

While not all karst landforms can be explained on a climatic or palaeoclimatic basis, yet of almost all rock types limestones are the most sensitive to climatic changes. Because also of their strength and hardness the effects of those changes are preserved upon the limestones, unlike for instance the effects of similar changes wrought upon a clay slope. As the main erosive agent is solution, limestones do not adjust so rapidly to the prevailing conditions as more friable rocks; it was this property that (partly) gave rise to the idea of the 'immunité karstique', as karst landscapes bear a bigger proportion of older relict landforms than landscapes in other rock types. As a result of this, karst landforms are probably the most useful in the reconstruction of the evidence for climatic change. They are a palimpsest of the changes which have taken place in the climate of a region.

This further illustrates the difficulties of classifying karst landscapes, since unless they are of very recent origin they are all made up of landforms developed in the many different types of climate experienced in Tertiary and Quaternary times. Because of the climatic changes which have affected the Classical and Dinaric karsts, many workers would no longer regard these as the type karsts, but rather those in equatorial and tropical humid areas. 'The sensitive karst country differs in space and changes with time and makes it impossible to divide it into types linked to space and stable in time' [313].

rapidly develop karst landforms. Verstappen also gives examples of well-formed karst features on recently emerged coral reefs in New Guinea [421]. The formation of beach rock in warm seas is a problem in the formation of limestones; the solution and wearing away of the beach rock is partly a karst problem in so far as it concerns the solution of a carbonate rock. The literature on beach rock is extensive, and is summarised in Stoddart, but will not be discussed here [177].

3. SYNGENETIC KARST

Jennings used this term at the International Geographical Congress in 1964 to describe karst landforms which are developed at the same time as the consolidation and compaction of the limestones themselves. The example he used was of the aeolianite sands of the coastal dunes of South Australia, which are largely made up of calcarenite. This calcarenite is being cemented by the formation of a caprock and is becoming hardened at the present time. The caprock formation is similar to the case-hardening of limestones in tropical areas. Alongside its formation various karst features are developing at the same time in the aeolianite. These include solutional dolines (30 m across and 6 m deep); collapse dolines (up to 65 m diameter and with vertical walls of 25 m); caves formed by the activity of streams flowing within the aeolianite; and solution pipes. These have recently been described by Jennings [456].

Syngenetic karst is important in coastal areas where coral or carbonate sand is being consolidated and where there is sufficient rainfall to cause solution as well. Thus in Puerto Rico and other islands of the Caribbean, cemented coral and coral sand

4. PSEUDO-KARST

It is difficult to know to what extent pseudo-karst can be considered karst. Pseudo-karst is the name given to phenomena developed on non-limestone rocks, but which resemble karstic forms. Normally, such features have resulted from solutional processes acting upon the rock and they are therefore in that sense karstic. Many people would include such landforms as part of karst [457]. It seems to the author, however, that to include such forms is to make the definition of karst too wide and thus to lose much precision.

Pseudo-karst phenomena have been defined as karst-like features in non-carbonate and non-evaporite rocks which have the morphology (though rarely the hydrological flow pattern) of karst features produced in carbonate rocks. In general, such pseudo-karstic features are restricted to the superficial and smaller landforms.

Grooves resembling karren have been described in many kinds of rocks, and are formed by a solutional process similar to that which occurs in carbonate rocks, though it is possible that mechanical erosion is also quite important. Wilford and Wall describe karren which have formed on microgranodiorites in Sarawak. These are flutes which form on relatively stable boulders and are as much as 6 m long, and have widths of 2 to 100 cm, but average about 30 cm. They are both V-shaped and U-shaped and may be up to 90 cm deep. The ribs between may vary from sharp to smoothly rounded. It is noticeable that the better-developed flutes are found on outcrops of the microgranodiorite that are open to the atmosphere or are covered by secondary forest. The flutes on the nearby limestones are much more ubiquitous and occur on almost all slopes; they tend to be smaller than those on the microgranodiorite. Fine ripple marks with a wave-length and amplitude of up to 3 mm occur on both the types of rock on overhanging rocks, and are of about the same size in both limestones and in microgranodiorites. In both rocks, the formation of the flutes is largely the work of solution, the rainwater being relatively acid (pH 4·9–6·0), and corrasion by particles in the formation of the flutes in the microgranodiorites is regarded as unlikely. The ripple marks are also thought to be the result of rainwater solution in both cases; funnelled seepage of water from above moves down the overhanging slope where the opposing effects of surface tension and gravity induce pulsating flow which produces the ripple pattern [458].

Similar grooves resembling rundkarren were observed by the writer in granites near Mbabane in Swaziland. In this example it seems as if the rundkarren are formed under atmospheric conditions, and not under forest as they would be in a limestone area. They average about 20–30 cm wide and deep, and are from 0·5 m to over 2 m long; they occur on upstanding and isolated outcrops of the granite.

Runnels which resemble rinnenkarren and rundkarren also occur on the Millstone Grits in northern England, and have been described by Cunningham [459]. They have

also been observed by the writer on gritstone boulders and tors in the neighbourhood of the Brimham rocks near Harrogate, on the east side of the Pennines. Other solutional phenomena on the Millstone Grits, such as solution pits, have been observed by Clayton [126] on Fountains Fell near Malham, and by the writer on Swarth Fell, overlooking the Rawthey valley in Westmorland. It is normally assumed that these groovings and pittings are the result of solutional activity attacking the cement or the quartz in the Millstone Grit. One point in favour of this view is that the rock pools on the Millstone Grit surfaces have a very low pH, as low as

57 Dolines formed in loess overlying sandstones, North Bohemia; an example of pseudo-karst.

2·0–3·0 – much lower than any of the pH values obtained on the limestones, in fact.

Small doline hollows are quite usual in pseudo-karstic relief. In the area of pseudo-karst on the granites in Swaziland, just referred to, dolines occur particularly at the intersection of the joints and are aligned along the joints forming lines. They are quite small, from 1 to 3 m deep and about 2–6 m in diameter.

In northern Bohemia, there is an area of pseudo-karst at Miškovice, near Kutna Hora. This is formed on loess which overlies both limestones and sandstones. Loess usually has a carbonate cement and frequently gives rise to pseudo-karst. Dolines up to 13 m deep and 40–50 m diameter have been described by Kunsky from Miškovice [460]. Small caves can also occur in pseudo-karst and have been described from sandstones, Photo 57.

Caves are common in volcanic rocks, but are usually syngenetic cavities formed while the lava was cooling. Such syngenetic cavities have been discussed by Ollier in the lavas of the western part of Victoria, in Australia [543]. Lava caves also occur in the basalts in western New Mexico. Epigenetic caves in volcanic rocks are formed by the weathering of the fissures in the rocks. In northern Bohemia, at Lysa Hora, one cave in a phonolite is 29 m long. Corbel also has recorded pseudo-karst features in Iceland where many caves have been formed in the basalts, and collapse of the cave roofs has given rise to collapse dolines. Corbel uses the term *sub-karstic* for these features [87].

However, though pseudo-karstic phenomena may be quite common, there is no connection between the surface and underground as in true karst phenomena, and pseudo-karstic features are usually near-surface ones. Thus, as has been said by

Fénelon, '. . . ces reliefs semblables à ceux des massifs calcaires, ne sauraient être assimilés aux reliefs karstiques sous peine de confusion. On peut noter les analogies sans pousser jusqu'à la coincidence, car dans la composition chimique et physique des roches, comme dans les aggressivités respectives des processus d'érosion, existent trop de différences qu'il ne faut pas négliger. Le karst classique, celui de Cvijič et de de Martonne, reste exclusivement lié aux calcaires riches en $CaCO_3$' [461].

5. THERMAL KARST

The term thermal karst is correctly used to denote karst phenomena which are affected by thermal mineralisation during the development of karst landforms. The most usual example given is that of the Zbrašov area, in Moravia, where mineralised and gaseous waters have welled up through limestones [299]. Since limestones are not normally found in highly mineralised zones, thermal karst is rare. However, carbonatites, volcanic rocks made up of calcium carbonate, found in volcanic regions show some interesting karst features. These have been described in carbonatites in the Rift Valley in East Africa [462].

Thermal karst should be distinguished from thermokarst which is a term used to describe the phenomena caused by the melting of ice in the subsoil. Melting of ice in the subsoil gives rise to a collapse of the soil, forming landforms resembling collapse dolines. Though such thermokarstic landforms are the result of the removal (or shrinkage) of material from beneath the soil (in this case ice), this is probably the only analogy with true karst that exists.

17 The Effect of the Cyclic Concept upon the Knowledge of Karst Landforms

SOME MISUNDERSTANDING of the mode of development of karst landforms was introduced by the use of the cyclic concept. This was developed by W. M. Davis and first applied to landforms on impermeable rocks, and was later so pervasive as to penetrate the thinking of all the karst morphologists. Davis himself visited the karst area in 1909, and published an essay on an 'Excursion in Bosnia, Hercegovina and Dalmatia' [463]. Davis's cycle ideas influenced the thought of Cvijič, A. Penck and Grund and many others. In *Das Karstphänomen*, Cvijič's thought is free from ideas of the erosion cycle and he discusses the factors of karstification, the landforms themselves, and the main areas of karst development [3]. However, he does imply some genetic relationship between dolines and poljes, there being a series of stages from the evolution of a doline to that of a polje. Grund in a paper on 'Karsthydrographie' in 1903 [182], in which he discusses his ideas of *grundwasser* and *karstwasser*, sees the strong connection between structure and the impermeable beds with poljes, and is less certain of there invariably being an evolution from dolines, through uvalas, to poljes. Grund noticed that poljes do not occur everywhere in limestone areas and that the poljes were not a necessary part of the karst. On the other hand, in the same paper, Grund talks of the poljes being morphological end-products or

morphological termini, which might indicate that he had absorbed the ideas of cyclic evolution. Richter was one of the first to propose the application of the cycle idea to karst landforms [464]. An early attempt to discuss a karst cycle was that by Sawicki in 1909 [383], whose paper was in many ways very perceptive. He differentiated between the evolution and the development of the individual karst landforms, i.e. karren, dolines, etc., and the evolution of the landscape as a whole. Where the limestones are pure the development of the individual landforms is continuous, but where the limestones are impure, or where there is much residual terra rossa, then the dolines and ponors become clogged and surface drainage reappears. As a result of the reappearance of the surface drainage, the rivers remove the clogging material from their valleys, the limestone is re-exposed and the karst cycle starts all over again. Sawicki thought that continuous development took place in Mediterranean-type karst, where there is little clogging of the fissures due to the heavy and torrential rainfall and lack of vegetation; in these areas drainage is rapid. The discontinuous development was characteristic of the central and western European karsts, where the abundant soil and vegetation cover and the more gentle rainfall regime meant that the drainage was impeded and the fissures became clogged. Sawicki, along with others,

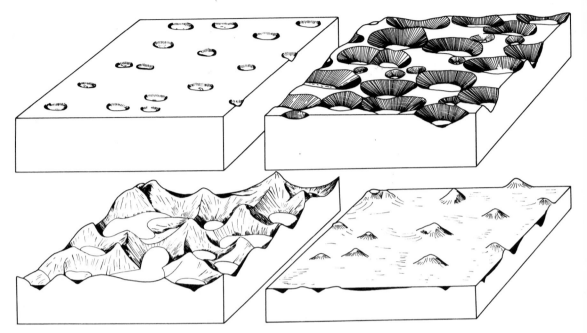

(*upper left*) 'Young' karst with extensive flat surfaces between dolines, much of the original surface remaining.
(*upper right*) 'Adolescent' karst, with larger dolines and many coalescing.
(*lower left*) 'Mature' karst (*Cockpitlandschaft*): the original surface has disappeared; large dolines and uvalas lie between the *Cockpithügeln*.
(*lower right*) 'Old' karst. Only isolated hills remain upon the residual plain.

Fig. 125 Karst cycle (from Grund [2])

contended that karst development is preceded by a stage in which there is surface
drainage.

This contention that karst development
followed a period of river erosion on limestones was largely due to the work of A.
Penck. Penck probably taught almost all the
morphologists who worked on the karst at
this period, including Cvijič himself. Thus
Penck's paper in 1900, on his 'Studies in
Hercegovina' (as Roglič has said), 'excellently propagated the antecedence of river
erosion in the development of landforms in
limestone terrain' [179]. This scheme of
Penck's was later adopted into the cyclic
pattern, and the stage of river erosion on
limestone areas became the first in their

cycle of evolution. Since in many ways it
is misleading to assume that river valleys
form in limestone country at all, the cycle
idea started its first stage using an erroneous
assumption, and one which Roglič says was
'without any justification' (loc. cit., p. 114).

In 1914 Grund produced his geographical
cycle in the karst, the diagram for which is
given in Fig. 125. As a piece of theoretical
thinking this was extremely valuable, but
at this stage the difference between doline
karst in temperate areas and cockpit karst
in the tropics had not been fully accounted
for. As a result Grund believed that the
dolines of the Classical Karst area were an
early stage in the development of the cockpit karst of the humid tropics. As we have

shown, it is unlikely that dolines evolve to become cockpits. However, Jennings and Bik, in their studies in New Guinea, have described a karst which contains elements of both the temperate and the tropical karst. Thus they say 'the relief resembles most closely, not tropical kegelkarst as described . . . by modern workers, but the false picture Alfred Grund conceived of it in his attempt to put tropical and temperate forms into one evolutionary sequence. His theoretical block diagram (Fig. 125) sketches hollow-chested, horn-like peaks rising between inosculating, flat-floored dolines. These imagined residual projections correspond in large measure with the pyramidal hills of much of the karst of New Guinea. . . . The Davisian deductive approach has been adversely criticised recently, but certain virtues may be demonstrated in that something very close to Grund's nature karst, which was at least as much the product of his theoretical deduction as of Daneš's observations, occurs in New Guinea' [420].

Cvijič's paper in 1918 on 'Hydrographie Souterraine et Evolution Morphologique du Karst' was a synthesis of the main ideas on karst development at that time. The chief contribution was the concept of three hydrographical zones within the karst, which was an attempt at a compromise between the views of Grund and those of Martel and Katzer, who believed that the concept of groundwater in the karst did not apply. Cvijič begins his ideas on the development of his three hydrographical zones by assuming that the initiation of karst relief is by means of a series of normal valleys upon the surface. This phase is relatively rapid, and the surface valleys are quickly disintegrated. At this stage there is only one hydrographic zone. As the surface drainage is absorbed the upper part of the limestone mass becomes dry, and there are now two hydrographic zones, an upper dry zone and

a lower saturated one. As a result of the continuous enlargement of fissures in the limestones, both these zones become progressively displaced to lower levels. Three zones are eventually recognised (a lowest zone which is permanently saturated, an intermediate one which is intermittently saturated, and the uppermost dry zone which only rarely has flowing water). The full development of these hydrographic zones was considered by Cvijič to represent the mature karst development, and this was only stopped by the impermeable bed at the base of the limestones (not the sea-level). The final development, as the limestone mass was worn away, was the gradual elimination of these zones, and their replacement by one zone only.

Cvijič discussed the evolution of karst landforms in relation to the development and vertical displacement of these hydrographic zones. The first stage in his scheme occurs at the critical moment in the evolution of the limestone terrain when karstic erosion is 'substituted for normal', i.e. the essential fact of karst development is the 'enfouissement des eaux'. The correspondence of landforms with the different phases according to Cvijič was as follows:

1st phase. This corresponds to the existence of one hydrographic zone. The fissures in the rock are small, the largest ones being uppermost. On the surface, there are still normal valleys and the dolines are small; poljes and uvalas are undeveloped.

2nd phase. This is the mature phase and is considered to have developed when the three hydrographical zones have become established. This gives rise to the most advanced karst landforms. Dolines and uvalas are well developed and poljes have been formed by karst planation in the middle hydrographical zone.

3rd phase. This is the phase of the gradual disintegration of the limestone landforms.

The impermeable beds at the base of the limestone mass begin to appear and regressive erosion may give rise to the reappearance of normal valleys.

4th phase. In this phase the limestone mass has almost completely disappeared, leaving only isolated limestone residuals or hums on the impermeable beds. Normal drainage has been re-established.

By correlating the landforms with the stages in the development of the relief, Cvijič made the same kind of error which befogged all Davisian thinking. In the vertical displacement of the hydrographical zones, it is assumed that the evolution of the surface karst forms is intimately connected with the development of the caves; in the stage of youth the upper caves will be more developed than the lower ones because the fissures and cracks have been more opened out in the upper part of the limestone mass. This is essentially the reverse of what Davis himself said later in his paper in 1930 on the origin of caves. Erosion platforms are a conspicuous element in the relief of the Dinaric karst. Cvijič believed that many of these were of the same age but of different altitudes and explained them as having formed one extensive plain that had been later dislocated [272]. Krebs later showed this to be erroneous [465]. Cvijič was equivocal on the origin of the poljes, realising that they were essentially controlled by structural and lithological factors, yet at the same time saying that it was karstic planation which gave them their definite form (i.e. the periodic inundations were the cause of the poljes rather than a consequence). Although he thought that elongated dolines might evolve to form uvalas and eventually poljes, he could also see that poljes might develop separately.*

A short synopsis of part of Cvijič's 1918

*Beede in America independently thought out a similar cycle [490].

paper was given by Sanders in the *Geographical Review* for 1921 [466]. This article has been for many English-speaking people the subsequent and only source of Cvijič's ideas. It omitted many points and concentrated particularly on the application of the ideas to the cycle of erosion.

Cvijič modified his ideas somewhat in his later work and abandoned many of the cyclic ideas in *Geomorfologija*, his last book published in 1926. The work that was published posthumously, however, *La Géographie des Terrains Calcaires* (1960), is still influenced by the cyclic ideas, and by the notion of holokarst [148] Cvijič had endeavoured to subdivide the Dinaric karst into regions (the karst of Trieste, the karst of Carniola, the karst of Karlovac and Lika, the littoral karst and the most developed karst of Jugoslavia, that of Hercegovina and Montenegro). Yet all of these are so different that, as Roglič says, 'they cannot severally be reduced to the simple and identifying notion of the holokarst' [313].

The cyclic idea was therefore much used in the years between the two world wars. Many papers like Cvijič's in the *Geographical Review*, 1924, were concerned with the cyclic development of one set of landforms; in this paper Cvijič deals with the evolution of lapiés and claims that a series of stages in their development can be recognised [148]. Other studies, particularly in France, were concerned with the philosophical problems of the cycle concept. In a long discussion on the distribution of dolines, Clozier remarks that 'in the family of karstic forms the dolines are the last to manifest themselves' [117], showing that the dolines have not yet disorganised dry valleys formed in the Quaternary; this conclusion is the opposite from what Cvijič supposed in his cycle of karst development. Both Clozier [117] and Baulig [440] come to the conclusion that the karst cycle is only a local episode in the normal cycle, and that the term 'fluviokarst cycle' fits the facts better.

Dicken discussed the Kentucky karst landscapes entirely in terms of the cyclic concept, asking no questions as to the real origin of the landforms or the processes at work [129]. He recognised four main stages in the development of this karst, each stage according to him being characterised by a distinctive landform. These stages are:

The initial landscape, in which swallow holes (ponors) and small dolines appear but in which the landscape is still dominated by the pre-karst rivers and valley.

The doline karst, which is characterised by the development of dolines and is the characteristic Kentucky karst.

The basin karst. In this phase the dolines become choked with sediment, and the convex profile of the dolines becomes changed to the concave profile of the shallow basins. The dolines have become widened into the basins, and this occurs when the karst processes are retarded.

The streams and basin karst. This is the last phase and represents the disintegration of the karst. It is caused by the infilling of the basins with sediment and the formation of streams within the basins. Such streams begin to integrate the drainage and the karst decays. Rejuvenation is caused by the entrenchment of the major streams.

As we have seen, W. M. Davis himself attempted to relate types of cave passages to a two-cycle development of the limestone mass, i.e. phreatic passages are deduced to be formed early in the cycle, vadose passages to occur after uplift. However, Davis indicated that the kind of cave is controlled by the type of water flow and that there is no necessary correlation between the nature, size or abundance of the cave passages with any specific group of surface landforms. Consequently, although

Davis's views were based on the cyclic concept, they advanced rather than hindered work on karst landforms especially caves.

The ideas of a series of stages in a karst area, based on the progressive development of the size of the caves, was discussed by Coleman and Balchin in 1959 [113]. Their article shows the difficulties that can be got into if cyclic concepts are closely adhered to.

Thus the cyclic ideas have died hard, particularly in Britain and America. In the U.S.A., even as recently as Thornbury's *Regional Geomorphology of the United States* [332], some indications of the correlation of specific landforms with definite stages in the erosion of limestone terrain can be detected (loc. cit., p. 195). For example, in the discussion of the karst plain immediately up-dip from the Dripping Springs–Chester escarpment, Thornbury says that it is in a 'mature state of karst development', where sink holes (dolines) exist by the tens of thousands, and surface streams are practically lacking.

The new directions of research inspired by the developments in hydrology, speleology and climatic geomorphology led to criticism of the cyclic concept as applied to the development of karst landforms. As a result of these new directions multiple karstifications in many areas have been proved by stratigraphical means; each karstification is a process which takes place only once, and 'no stages in the development can be observed' [340]. The basic forms in the karst are the swallow holes and the dolines, and it can be shown that these depend upon the density of the fissures and openings on the karstic surface, the one not being developed from the other. All kinds of transitional landforms exist from the doline to the uvala and the polje, but the one is not necessarily the initial stage of the other. In the Dinaric karst no stages of development have been observed; all the landforms exist together and this, according to Jenko, 'proves their independent origin' (loc. cit., p. 230).

Hence each karst area and landform must be judged on its own merits and looked at in the light of its own development. Neither caves nor dolines nor poljes occur at any particular stage in the development of a karst landscape but only when the conditions which favour their development exist. Karsts can exist without dolines, they can also exist without caves; poljes are features often formed by river or other extraneous erosion. Karsts are also particularly sensitive to climatic and vegetational changes. There is therefore no cycle of landforms as described by Cvijič or by Dicken. The principles of karst morphology rest upon the principles of the chemistry of calcium carbonate and those of karst hydrology, in addition to chronology.

This does not mean to suggest that developmental sequences of landforms do not occur or that studies of developmental sequences are of no value. However, each sequence is self-contained and refers to one set of landforms only. Thus Williams, in his discussion of limestone pavements in western Ireland, suggests a scheme of evolution. By this he means that the pavements have undergone or will undergo the series of stages described, and that the different pavement types belong to one of the stages [162]. Other developmental sequences have been discussed, for example the formation of tower karst in the Limestone Ranges as given by the writer and Jennings in 1963 [31] or that discussed by

Paton on the origin of the limestone hills of Malaya [428]. Paton attempts to show that the development of the hills in the limestones differs from the development of hills in other rock types, because of the different nature of the erosion. In broad outline the manner of the levelling of the terrain in a karst area is distinguishable from the manner of levelling in other rock types, but there is no correlation of phase with specific landform. Though Jenko states [340] that 'the geomorphological cycle of the levelling of the terrain takes place in karst only on the surface – it is due mainly to corrosion and is therefore much slower' (loc. cit., p. 231), the speed of erosion of the karst depends upon climate, vegetation cover, and the lithology. Thus in snowy or recently glaciated areas, the karst landforms are relatively young and development rapid, whereas in arid and semi-arid regions they are much older than in other rock types. Because of case-hardening, they are also slower in development in the tropics.

All sciences need generalisations, and developmental sequences of landforms provide these; they form the stimulus to further observation and experimental research. They later form the objects of criticism from which new generalisations emerge. The very success of the cyclic idea meant that it survived its usefulness for a much longer period of time than less successful theories would have done. The study of the development of karst landforms has probably been hindered less by the dominance of cyclic ideas than by the lack of contact of workers in the different karst regions.

18 The Aims and Applications of Karst Landform Study

1. THE MAIN PROBLEMS IN KARST LANDFORMS

We can now discuss the trends of further research in karst landforms. Since karst erosion is concerned with descending and subterranean waters, the most important work in the future will be in the development of karst hydrology. With this goes hand in hand an increase in knowledge of the varying physical and chemical properties of karst waters and the differential solubilities of the many kinds of limestone that have been discussed by modern sedimentologists. The main problems may be divided into the following four groups: landform description and analysis; the study of the limestones from the point of view of porosity and differential solubility; the study of the chemical quality of the water; and the study of caves and of karst hydrology.

(A) LANDFORM DESCRIPTION AND ANALYSIS

Although we now know much about individual karst landforms, much careful work is still needed, particularly in tropical areas. Apart from Aub's work [417] and now P. Williams, there is no detailed study of tropical cockpits. Ordinary descriptions both from ground field work and from aerial photographs are still useful. We do not yet know all the possible variations of karst phenomena over the earth, and many karst areas need to be described in modern terms. Even in well-known areas in western and southern Europe the phenomena of distribution have not had the attention they deserve, and new laws of distribution may be discovered. This is indicated in the lines of approach of Matschinski, who is applying more sophisticated statistical techniques to the phenomena of doline distribution [123]. Williams recently has attempted to apply to karst landforms some of the morphometric techniques used in the study of fluvial landforms. He used these on a part of the Ingleborough district and his work suggests that the well-known relationships that exist in fluvial morphometry also apply to certain karst landforms. From this data, Williams concludes that:

(1) When swallow holes are examined and plotted against the log. of number, it suggests that the number of the swallow holes of different orders in a given area tend to approximate to an inverse geometric series, Fig. 126.

(2) Swallow-hole order plotted against log. of the mean area of swallow-hole catchments suggests that their mean basin areas in each order tend to approximate to a direct geometric series.

(3) Swallow holes plotted against the log. of mean distance to the nearest swallow hole of the same order suggest that the mean distance between swallow holes of the same order also approximates to a direct geometric series.

These similarities to the relationships of fluvial morphometry serve to illustrate Roglič's assertion that swallow holes and blind valleys are really fluvial and not true karst landforms. So far the only and not

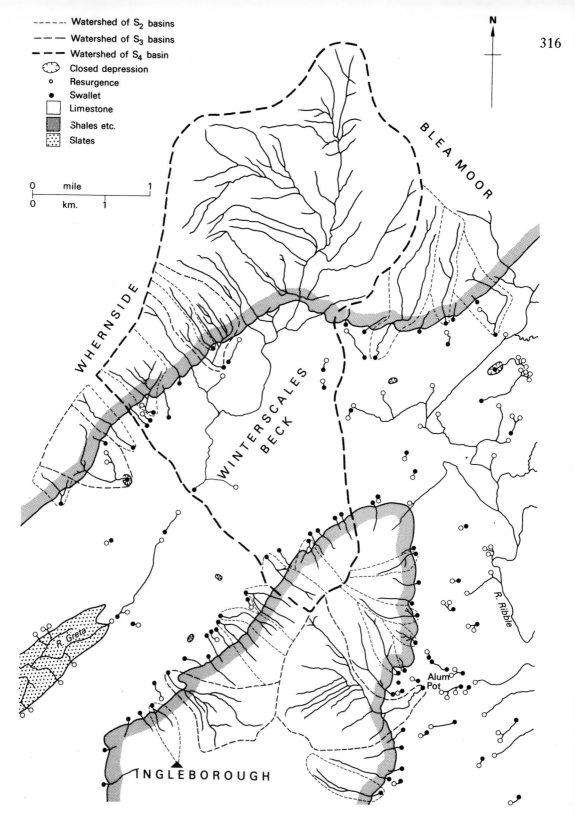

Fig. 126(a) Some karst features in the Ingleborough district (from Williams [260])

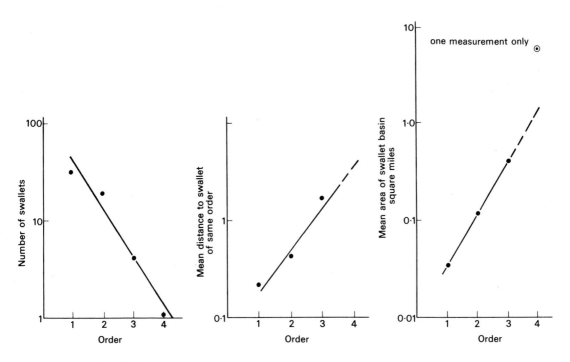

Fig. 126(*b*) Swallet relationships in the Ingleborough district (from Williams [260])

very successful morphometric study of dolines is that by Lavalle [125]. Morphometry should be particularly well suited to studies of cone karst, as is being demonstrated by P. Williams. In his studies in New Guinea Williams has treated the irregular cockpit hollows as small drainage basins. By this means he is able to recognise a series of basins of order 0, 1, 2, 3. The largest hollows in the New Guinea karsts are of order 3 and the evolution of the karsts is effected by the elimination of the lower order basins. This particularly perceptive study of an area of polygonal karst completely pitted with depressions demonstrates the degree of organisation of tropical karsts [505]. Statistical methods are only just beginning to be applied to underground landforms [260].

The study of non-calcareous deposits associated with surface and underground landforms needs more attention; Pigott has shown for instance what can be made of a study of limestone soils [396]. In addition, the study of the calcareous deposits, both on the surface and underground, is beginning to yield results of interest [489].

(B) THE STUDY OF THE LIMESTONES

The study of the limestones has up till now been largely in the hands of the oil geologists. But it is becoming increasingly obvious that the type and nature of karst limestones 'is not a negligible factor' in the development of limestone landforms. The structure and texture of the limestones, the amount of pore space and extent to which water can permeate the rock, all influence its differential permeability and solubility. The

factors which affect the nature of the jointing and fractures in the limestones are also
important [46]. These properties of the rock
will determine its reactions to different
climatic conditions, such as frost, heat, and
prolonged rain. In Britain we still do not
know precisely why the Chalk and the
Cotswold Jurassic Limestones are more
soluble than the true karst limestones. Thus
detailed lithological studies are needed to
be done alongside the description and
analysis of the landforms. Studies such as
these are being undertaken in Jamaica by
Robinson, where the effects of varying
lithologies upon the landforms are more
than usually obvious [467].

(C) THE CHEMICAL, PHYSICAL AND BIOLOGICAL STUDY OF KARST WATERS

Though there is now a good deal of literature on the chemistry of karst waters, much
of the work has not been done systematically.
Isolated estimations of the chemical content
of limestone waters are a useful guide to the
intensity of solution in an area, but it will be
seen that in any run of observations there
is great variation; hence for estimations
of the solutional activity of the waters, runs
of several readings are absolutely essential.
This is even more necessary if the readings
are to be treated to some form of multi-
variate analysis. And not only are long runs
of readings needed for just one locality in
one region, they are needed for several
different localities in the same area; this has
been recently indicated by both D. C. Ford
and by Pitty, who show that widely different
values are obtained from waters occurring
near together [79]. We need the values not
only for calcium and magnesium but also
for the other constituents of the waters
associated with calcium carbonate. Such
variations in the chemistry of the karst

waters are of interest not only to the
morphologist but also to the large-scale,
particularly industrial, user of the water.
The International Speleological Union now
has a special Commission which hopes to
standardise methods and results of karst
water analysis. Some progress was made in
the Brno (Czechoslovakia) Symposium in
1968 and at Stuttgart in 1969 [493].

The physical qualities of karst waters
have only recently been investigated. The
temperatures of springs, the degree of
clearness or opacity, their varying load and
speed of flow are all characteristics which
may throw light upon the deeper problems
of karst hydrology once we know more
about them. Hence again we need many
more straightforward series of observations
on these phenomena. From such observations more will become known about the
behaviour of the water underground. This
is needed in many ways, more perhaps than
for the study of surface rivers, since so much
of the karst water will never be seen in its
travels through the limestone. In their work
for F.A.O., both in Syria and in Greece,
Burdon and others have indicated the kind
of data that is useful [354].

The biological study of underground
water is not strictly relevant to a study of the
landforms. However, the biological and
organic quality of the water is of importance
to the user and may affect the utilisation of
the spring or karst water.

(D) KARST HYDROLOGY

The new methods in water tracing will
enable us to deduce more easily the underground paths of karst water. It is for
instance only in the last year or so that the
origin of the spring water at Cheddar and at
Wookey Hole in the Mendips has been
correctly ascertained by the use of the
Lycopodium spore method [70]; previously

it was not known where this spring water came from. Similarly in north-west Yorkshire, though the main water paths are known, there are many aspects of the underground water which are quite unknown. In Littondale, the origin of water reaching the main river and the conduits through which it travels are not by any means known even today. The speed of descent of the underground water, its pathways through the limestone, its method of enlarging the cracks in the rock, all give scope for new investigations and methods in dealing with the problems of underground water. More underground exploration will clearly be important and give opportunities for the sporting exploration of the caves. In the sphere of the application of the study of karst landforms, the study of karst hydrology is clearly the most important. Hydrology for its own ends and the study of water as an intellectual discipline is becoming much more important and significant, and karst hydrology will play its part in this development.

2. APPLICATIONS OF THE STUDY OF KARST LANDFORMS

The basic problems of the karstlands concern water. There may occasionally be too much water on the land during temporary flooding of poljes and blind valleys, but karstland surfaces are normally dry. Until the 1950s little had been done to tackle any of these problems. Settlements in karstlands were restricted to the vicinity of the karst springs, and as these became congested with the normal growth in population, chronic over-population has resulted. This development is part of much of the human geography of the Dinaric karst and Greece, where greatly increased modern populations are clustered around the classical springs which once provided adequate water for small populations but are grossly inadequate for today. Thus in places like Khrison, near Delphi, villages were relying, until recently, upon springs which had not been developed significantly since classical times. It is always assumed that limestone lands are barren and that it is impossible to find water, and this despite these areas having some of the highest rainfall figures in Europe. The Slovenian karst has nearly 2,000 mm of rain per year, whilst the coastlands of the Montenegrin karst have over 5,000 mm. Karst water has often travelled long distances in the rock and is usually of good quality, with few impurities and relatively little sediment. Thus it is highly suitable for domestic, industrial and hydro-electric use.

There has arisen a great interest in the development of karst waters from the economic point of view, based on the new-found laws of karst hydrology and of fissured rocks. Since 1945 great progress has been made in collecting data from many karst areas. Springs have been observed, rivers gauged, the rainfall and evaporation figures obtained, and fluorescein and other water-tracing tests devised. These data are now providing some of the essential information needed for harnessing the limestone waters for man's use. Much more progress has been made now that each karst area is treated on its own and with its own problems, and is not subject to the conclusion of generalised theories. At present there are no satisfactory geophysical methods of locating the underground water conduits; according to Jenko, such methods have been able to locate dry caves down to depths of about 60 m with an accuracy of only about 10 m in 100 mm^2, so the precise location of the underground water still has to be made by some form of borehole or shaft [340].

Certain karst water projects in different areas will now be discussed.

In Austria, Zötl and Maurin were interested in the exact delimitation of hydrological basins in the limestone masses of the Dachstein, Totes Gebirge and other areas of the north-eastern Alps. One of the reasons for this investigation was to ascertain the extent to which the large karst springs which were being used for domestic water supply in large urban areas in Austria (Salzburg and Innsbruck in particular) were being contaminated. It was found that much of the spring water which permeated through the limestone mass was not effectively filtered, partly due to the rapidity with which the water travels through the rock; it was concluded that if *Lycopodium* spores could get through the limestones, then the typhoid bacillus, which is much smaller, could also. It was therefore necessary to know the exact delimitations of the catchment basins feeding the springs which are used for the domestic water supply of the large urban areas, and to take any measure to prevent access to such basins. In the determination of these watersheds Zötl and Maurin elaborated their methods of water tracing by the means of coloured *Lycopodium* spores [349].

The Food and Agriculture Organisation's groundwater programmes have formed part of the UNESCO attempts to assist underdeveloped countries. This groundwater programme has been particularly active in many karst areas, as for example in Syria, Greece and Jamaica. In both Syria and Greece, particular attention has been paid to the greater utilisation and development of the major karst springs. The idea behind these developments is to control the discharge and outflow of the springs so as to make their water more useful and to prevent

waste. In Syria the spring known as Ain Senn was controlled by the raising of the outflow level [468]. In Greece investigations showed that there was abundant groundwater issuing as springs, but that much of this water was wasted since it was discharged very quickly after the rain and at a season when the water was useless for the irrigation of the crops, i.e. the springs in such a Mediterranean climate are at their highest in February, March and April, and at their lowest from June to September when the water is most needed for agriculture. It is therefore necessary to alter the temporal distribution, reducing the spring yields in winter and early spring, and increasing them in summer and in early autumn. As in other karstified limestone areas, it is difficult to locate the position of high-yielding boreholes, because of the absence of a watertable.

The spring chosen for the investigation by the UNESCO groundwater project in 1961 was the Lilaia spring group [468]. This group lies on the NNW. side of the Parnassos mountain massif. The mountains are composed almost entirely of limestones with some dolomites; many closed basins contribute to the Lilaia spring waters, Fig. 127(*a*), (*b*) and (*c*). The spring group discharges where the limestone aquifers meet the relatively impermeable alluvium of the Kifissos river plain. In winter some of the water is used but most of it goes unused into the main Kifissos river which flows into the Copias lake; in summer almost all the water from the springs is used and loss to the river and the lake is negligible. The spring group consists of five main springs, of which the Aghia Eleousa with the highest discharge was regarded as the most suitable to develop. The area drained by the springs has comparatively heavy rainfall, the average for the groundwater basin draining towards the springs being of the order of 1,400 mm, of

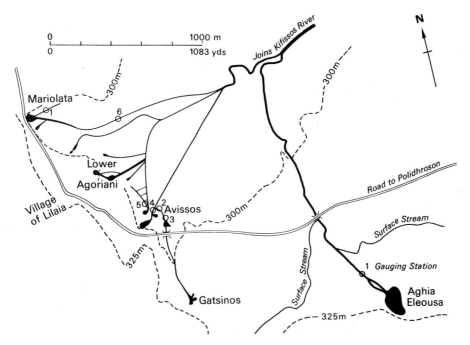

Fig. 127(a) Lilaia spring group (UNESCO)

which 74 per cent comes in the winter, from October to March, with a maximum in December. The region has high temperatures in the summer, but there is a cold winter and much of the precipitation falls as snow. The Aghia Eleousa issues from solid limestone, which affords a good foundation for the pumping installations.

The investigators remark that the determination of the exact limits of the basin which feeds the groundwater to the spring proved one of their most difficult tasks [469]. As far as could be deduced, there were 95 km² feeding the groundwater to the Lilaia spring group. The limestones forming the aquifer constitute a great mass of autochthonous strata ranging in age from the Triassic to the Palaeocene; these limestones have been thrust southwards and the thrusting has taken place on the flysch beds [469]. There are strong reasons for suspecting that the limestones have been subject to

karst development at two earlier periods.

There is a close relationship between the average monthly rainfall and the average monthly spring discharge, Fig. 127(b). The precipitation peak is generally in December and this produces peak discharge in the two smallest springs of the group, and finally in April the greatest of the springs, the Aghia Eleousa. The larger the basin feeding the spring, the longer it takes for the greater proportion of the infiltrating precipitation to reach the spring, the time-lag in this case being four months. In general the average rate of movement of the groundwater through the limestone is about 100 m per day. Minimal rainfall occurs in August and the minimum yield for all the springs is in September. The effects of even a small recharge is most noticeable when the springs are at their lowest. From the calculations it is shown by the authors that none of the aquifers feeding the springs contains a large reserve of water to be carried forward from one meteorological year to the next; a meteorological year of high precipitation will produce a year of high spring discharge, and a low precipitation will pro-

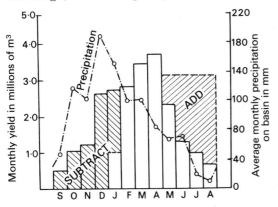

Fig. 127(b) Proposed controlled discharge from Aghia Eleousa spring (UNESCO)

duce a year of low spring discharge. The object of the development of the Aghia Eleousa spring is to determine how much additional water could be obtained from the spring during the irrigation months of May, June, July and August and thereby reduce the unused flow of October to April to nil or to negligible amounts. The proposed controlled discharge of the spring is shown in Fig. 127(b). It will be seen that 9·3 million cubic metres of water above the normal yield was to be extracted during the four months May to August, to make a total extraction of 16 million cubic metres. The success of this proposal depends upon the assumption of the existence of a ground-water reservoir in the limestones to a depth of some 5 m below the normal spring level. If a porosity of 2 per cent is assigned to the karstified limestone mass, then some 9·0

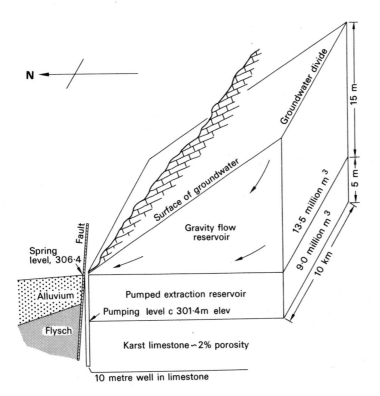

Fig. 127(c) Diagrammatic presentation of gravity flow and pumped extraction groundwater reservoirs supplying Aghia Eleousa (UNESCO)

million cubic metres of groundwater could be stored in the limestone extending over some 90 km^2 of area (the approximate area of the basin feeding the springs) with a thickness of 5 m and a porosity of 2 per cent. This forms the extraction reservoir. Many assumptions have been made in connection with this scheme. If successful it can be seen that the extraction of extra water during the warm summer months will enable farmers to grow much more remunerative crops, such as cotton and alfalfa, and so increase their annual income.

In the Slovenian and Dinaric karsts many new schemes have been started since 1955. The older economic measures in the karst were not very successful. Swallow holes and caves were widened and enlarged to facilitate drainage, but such measures did not always prove useful. The Romans and others built long aqueducts to convey water over the karst; today methods must be devised to obtain water from deep underground streams. The Jugoslavs have been most concerned with the poljes. This is because not only do the polje areas receive a high rainfall (from 1,500 mm to over 5,000 mm a year in some places), but they also form the richest land for cultivation in the whole of the karst. Yet, as we have already indicated, they are inundated for part of the year and are dry for much of the summer; thus during the part of the year when the sun and heat are strongest, the water is at its lowest. As a result both of the inundations of the polje floors and the summer drought, only a small percentage of the total cultivable area of the poljes is in fact cultivated. It was in order to make more use of the rich alluvial polje lands that work was started in the karst after the end of the war in 1945. The ascertaining of the directions of the underground water flows was essential. Water tracing was conducted by Energoinvest (Sarajevo) for the rivers Trebinjčica,

Neretva, Rama and Pliva; and for the Cetina river by the Hydrometeorological Institutes in Sarajevo and Zagreb. As will be seen from the results published in *Naše Jame*, the water-tracing methods mostly used Na-fluorescein and *Lycopodium* spores [5]. The experiments were performed mainly to determine the confluence area of the individual springs, the discharge of the springs and surface rivers; watersheds between the different river basins were established and the direction of main underground water flows determined, Fig. 89, p. 195.

The most modern method of dealing with the waters in the Dinaric karst is to cement up the swallow holes and control the emptying of the poljes. In this way, certain parts of the polje areas can be kept permanently inundated to form permanent lakes and reservoirs, while other parts can be properly drained and cultivated throughout the year. The methods include the use of large-scale grouting curtains; thus in the Grančarevo dam on the Trebinjčica river the total length of the grouting is 23,000 m. Several schemes using these methods have now been initiated in the Karst and are now nearing completion. Alongside the creation of dams and drainage areas in the poljes are proposals to build dams on the major rivers, such as the Cetina and Neretva, and to improve the head of water, so diverting the water in the reservoirs for use in hydro-electric plants. One of these storage reservoirs is the Peruča reservoir, which is located on the upper course of the Cetina river. The volume of this dam is 550 million m^3 and the total potential head to the sea-level represents an energy potential of 360 million kWh. Some basic problems that had to be solved in the design of the Peruča reservoir include: (1) the water-tightness of the watershed on the lower side (south) of the reservoir; (2) the sealing of the permeable and karstified area of the dam site and its wings. The dam site was sealed with a large injection curtain, 2 km long and 200 m deep, one of the largest that has so far been made in Jugoslavia. The seepage control curtain on the dam site has a surface area of 240,000 m^2; it was constructed with an average consumption of 216 kg of dry material per m^2 of curtain. The grouting mixture consisted of 65–70 per cent clay, 5 per cent bentonite and 25–30 per cent cement, and was very thixotropic. The efficiency of the grouting was checked during 1959 and 1960 and the total seepage loss was about 0·75 per cent of the average discharge of the Cetina at the dam; this is considered less than the loss allowed for in the design of this type of reservoir. A record is kept of the underground water-level to watch the changes in the water-tightness of the reservoir. The most suitable material for tightening the swallow holes is a layer of loam or loam and stones placed above a filter of larger stones. Above the layer of loam is placed one of sand and, above that, larger scree material. Not only must the holes in the limestone be sealed, but the limestones must be bound to the impermeable rocks.

Other work is proposed on the Trebinjčica which when completed will prevent the flooding of the large Popovo polje and create possibilities for its irrigation in the dry season. The Grančarevo dam, which is located about 17 km upstream from Trebinje, is the first stage and will be constructed as a high-pressure hydroelectric development at the dam site. In addition to the grouting for seepage control, consolidation grouting has been planned to improve the physical and engineering properties of the rock. The Dubrovnik hydroelectric plant is the second stage in the Trebinjčica scheme. The machine hall for this system is located near the seashore, underground in a cave.

After the erection of the hydroelectric power-plant system on the Trebinjčica river, the regime of the famous Ombla spring near Dubrovnik will be changed; high and mean water-levels will be diminished and the spring regime will become more uniform. It is hoped also that this scheme will solve the drainage of the Popovo polje by draining the waters of the Trebinjčica river direct to the sea and by lowering the water level to prevent activity of overflow springs in the wet season. Water retained in the reservoirs for the hydroelectric plant will be let out when necessary for the irrigation of the polje floor.

In Slovenia, a large scheme has been proposed to deal with the whole of the waters of the Ljubljanica system from the headwaters above the Cerknica polje to the springs on the Ljubljana moor [340]. One of the consequences of this scheme will be to dam up part of the lake waters in the Cerknica polje and not allow the waters to drain away during part of the year as they do now; in this way it is hoped to provide a permanent lake suitable for recreation. Water from poljes usually needs purification for domestic use. The best drinking water flows in the deep underground streams, but these are much more difficult to locate precisely [340].

A method used in the Karst to estimate lengths of boreholes needed is to calculate the total permeability of the mass of the rock and compare this with the permeability of the borings deduced from the loss from the borings; from this may be calculated the length of shafts necessary for the quantity of water required. In the Karst the most frequently occurring permeability is $k = 10^{-5}$ to $k = 10^{-7}$ m/s. It is theoretically possible to achieve an average influx from the karst water of 50 litres per second in a length of shaft of 120 m. This water is good for domestic purposes.

Schemes are in progress in other parts of the Jugoslav karst, notably at the polje of Nikšić in Montenegro [470]. Along the coastal areas of the Adriatic karst one of the main problems is the loss of water into the sea from the submarine springs. Various methods have been tried to recover this water, but the fresh water mixes with the sea water beneath the coast. Hence the only way to capture the fresh water is to sink boreholes and shafts some distance back into the hinterland of the coast where the mixing of the fresh with the sea water has not taken place. Recently water mains (pipes) have been designed to connect the island of Brač with the mainland at Omis and to transport water by pipeline from the mainland to this dry Adriatic island. Some of the schemes which hope to transform the economic life of the Dinaric karst and the Adriatic coastlands are discussed in a series of essays, published in 1969 [535].

In Jamaica, in the limestone districts, until quite recently much of the water supply of the rural areas was collected by tanks and concrete catchments and the groundwater resources had not been developed. Since 1951 increasing attention has been given to the groundwater resources of the White Limestones, partly as a result of the stimulating activity of Zans [326]. Versey has also written on the hydrological character of the White Limestones of Jamaica [143]. He states that the limestones in Jamaica, as elsewhere, 'fall into two broad categories with respect to their influence on the occurrence of groundwater. There are those limestones which are massive and compact and in which the water moves along only fissures and conduits; in these there is no primary permeability. Other limestones, while of variable lithology, have as a common feature, primary permeability. Included in this category are chalks, soft marly limestones, and rubbly, nodular limestones' (loc. cit., p. 59). The nodular limestones form the best part of the White Limestones as far as its function as an aquifer is concerned, and wells with yields of 2,000 gal/min are not uncommon. Confined conduit flow is characteristic of the cockpit areas. The location of these conduits has been the object of resistivity and other surveys in Jamaica (loc. cit., p. 67). Preliminary resistivity surveys in limestone areas have indicated that in general a three-layer case is involved – the high resistivity zone of aeration, the low resistivity saturated rock head, and the high resistivity of the compact limestone. Each of these, and the depth to the water-table, can be determined quite accurately and the optimum depth of a proposed well can be inferred. According to the first test made by the drillers for the F.A.O. project on the Pedro Plains area in south-west Jamaica, there are conspicuous conduits of water flowing within the top few feet of a calculated water-table. These results resemble Jenko's in Slovenia, but not those of Herak and others in the Dalmatian and Dinaric karst. The chalky Montpelier limestone facies in Jamaica have a much lower transmissibility and retain the water; the Queen of Spain's valley in northern Jamaica is such a groundwater reservoir [44].

Two university expeditions, Leeds [471] and Bristol [472], and the Karst Hydrology Expedition (1965–6) [473] have added greatly to our knowledge of the water movements in the Jamaican karst areas.

Enough has therefore been said to indicate the enormous importance of the study of karst landforms and of karst hydrology to the development of water supplies in karstlands. In addition to water, other resources are associated with the occurrence of karst landforms. This is because of the vertical and underground drainage. Water percolating through the karst is trapped within caves and hollows and the debris and sediment which it contains is deposited in the hollows. Thus products of weathering are frequently associated with karst landforms, and the most common is bauxite. The origin of bauxite is still disputed, but whether it originates as a weathering product of immense quantities of limestone, or whether it is derived from non-limestone material, it is believed that karst limestones act as a trap for suspended sediment. Water percolates through caves and cockpit hollows, and if it contains much debris rich in aluminium minerals, the sediment may become lodged within the cavities in the rock. In time such deposits may become a source of bauxite. Bauxite usually occurs in deep dolines and caves, and is irregularly distributed over weathered limestone surfaces. This is well shown in deposits in Jamaica and in Istria. Such deposits occur in pre-existing hollows and pipes (geological pipes) or in actively forming hollows; they have normally been subjected to a long period of weathering and the existence of bauxite usually indicates a previous period of karstification, probably under warm or tropical conditions. Erosion of the limestones reveals the karstified surface and the bauxite infills [474, 477].

Other weathering and sedimentary deposits also become lodged in fissures and caves in karst limestones. These include the phosphorites which occur in hollows in the Causses of Quercy [475]. Such phosphorites now occupy hollows formed during an earlier phase of karstification in the Eogene. In Derbyshire we have already noted the presence of silica sands now preserved in hollows in the Carboniferous Limestones; these sands are partly of Triassic origin and have been let down from the Triassic rocks which formerly covered the limestones. Modern deposits, as distinct from ancient sediments, include guano,

formed in caves by the numerous bats which inhabit them. The exploitation of bat guano in caves was one of the main reasons for the survey of Jamaican caves by the Geological Survey of Jamaica. The guano is used as a source of phosphate for fertiliser and many tons have been quarried from caves in the White Limestone areas of Jamaica.

Where metalliferous rocks are in contact with the limestones, alluvial deposits associated with the limestones are often important sources of minerals. In Malaya, granitic rocks bearing tin ores are closely connected with the karst limestones. Alluvium contained in streams draining from the granites passes into the limestones. Caves and fissures in the Malayan tower karst are important sources of alluvial deposits of the tin ore [476].

Thus karst limestones act as a trap for many kinds of sediments. They are also known for acting as country rocks for hydrothermal and other kinds of mineral deposits.

The use of limestone and its related deposits (tufa, travertine, etc.) for building, road metal, fertilisers, etc., is the subject for another book. Furthermore, the actual use of karst limestones does not strictly fall within the purview of karst landforms or karst hydrology. However, the need for the extraction of limestones for many industries is well known. In the Peak District in Derbyshire in England are some of the most productive limestone quarries in the world, and in most karst areas the quarrying of limestone is an important industry.

As is well known, the great areas of doline and kegelkarst form some of the most rugged and difficult areas of the world's surface. Road and railway building is difficult because of the lack of alluvium and level land in both temperate and tropical karst. The railway from Rijeka to Ogulin in the Dinaric karst is an example of the difficulty of building communications in such regions. Lack of transport is probably the second most important problem in the karstlands after the lack of water. Because of this, many areas of karst landforms are still relatively unknown and inaccessible, such as the Cockpit Country in Jamaica. They also form regions of refuge or hiding, again witnessed by the Cockpit Country, where the runaway slaves (the Maroons) have always lived relatively independently. The political and military history of Montenegro and Vietnam also illustrate this point.

It is incorrect, however, to assume that all areas of karstlands are regions of difficulty. From the agricultural point of view, in both temperate and tropical karsts, soils derived from limestones are always to be preferred to acidic ones derived from sandstones or granites. In northern England the limestone pastures of the Craven Uplands are much to be preferred to the more acidic wastes of the Millstone Grits. Similarly in France the causses soils (the terres chaudes) are more sought after than the soils on the damp schists and clays. The maize areas of Kentucky and Indiana, where the limestones are well covered with crops and vegetation, are quite unlike the traditional idea of bare limestone country.

However, in the modern world, the chief attractions of karstlands are the natural wonders which are now being developed and exploited. In particular this applies to the development of caves for their tourist and scientific attractions. As already pointed out, scientific interest in caves is relatively recent, and it is only in the past hundred years that they have been opened up for tourism. Caves have often served as hiding places both for men and for treasures in times of war and unrest; this has been true of the caves of the Classical Karst as well as the caves of Vietnam. One of the oldest show

caves in the Classical Karst is Vilenica Cave, near the village of Lipica. This cave was known in the eighteenth century, but has been overshadowed as regards the tourist trade by the development of the Škocjan Caves and by Postojna Cave. The cave tourist business in Slovenia is now concentrated in Postojna Cave which was opened to tourists in 1818. The galleries in Postojna are relatively horizontal and are over 10 m high. This enabled the 2 km railway line to be constructed in 1872, the only cave railway line in the world. The gradient of the gallery in which the railway is constructed is 4·5 per cent, while the gradient of the river Pivka in the 'wet' cave below is 5·8 per cent. About 5·2 km of the total length of the cave is shown to the public. A great increase in the number of visitors to Postojna took place after the construction of the railway line from Vienna to Trieste (the 'Southern Railway') in 1857. Today over half a million people a year visit the cave, of whom more than half are from outside Jugoslavia. The other caves of the Slovenian karst have a much smaller tourist trade.

In Britain our caves are small but not without scientific and general interest. Little has been done, however, to develop any real tourist interest in British caves. The most developed and well-known are those in the southern Mendips at Cheddar, and Kent's Cavern in the Devonian Limestones near Torquay. In both the Peak District and north-west Yorkshire, various caves are open to the public, and maintained by private bodies. One of the most interesting of these is Ingleborough or Clapham Cave on the southern slopes of Ingleborough, a river cave which can be followed for over half a mile by the ordinary tourist [253]. There has been very little publicity by the local and National Park authorities to make the features of British caves known. The general public is also relatively uneducated in the scientific study of caves, and visitors tend to be given a talk on the fanciful shapes of stalactites and stalagmites rather than a helpful discussion on the origin of caves and cave deposits. This is in contrast to many other countries where guides are normally much better informed and there is usually much literature on the caves available. In the past few years the William Pengelly Cave Studies Trust has been founded with the object of educating the British public in cave studies. This Trust has acquired a site at Buckfastleigh in south Devon where it has excavated caves and established a museum. Much more is made of both the tourist and educational possibilities of caves in many other countries of the world.

In Czechoslovakia, in particular, not only are the large caves, like the Punkva and Demänovska, extremely well run, but even the small caves have been developed, often into small museums of natural history. In France, as one would expect with her fine areas of karst, there are some notable tourist caves; all of these are integrated into the tourist attractions of the karst regions and are well advertised and described. The French caves include not only those like Lascaux, famous for Palaeolithic cave art, but also the well-known caves of Padirac, Aven Armand, and the Grotte de la Clamouse in the Hérault. In the U.S.A., many of the finest caves lie within the National Park system; these include both Mammoth Cave and Carlsbad Caverns. In these areas well-thought-out conducted tours are available and guides and maps have been prepared. Some criticisms have been levelled at the National Park authorities in that they are somewhat restrictive to the development of new research ideas, but as teaching institutions the National Parks in the U.S.A. are second to none.

There are other wonders of the karst in addition to caves. These include the great karst springs, gorges and chasms. Today many karst areas are becoming important recreational regions. This is illustrated by the fact that two of our own National Parks comprise in addition to other districts two of our chief karst areas, the Peak District and Yorkshire Dales National Parks. In France many of the most scenic districts lie in the karst regions, for example the Gorges du Tarn in central France and the Gorges du Verdon in the Alpes Maritimes. The Classical and Dinaric Karsts, both in the pre-war and in the post-war years, have also attracted increasing numbers of tourists. In the Soviet Union, the karst regions of the Crimea and of the Caucasus have become tourist assets.

The development of tourism on an increasing scale will therefore bring fresh problems to the karstlands. One of the main problems concerns the conservation of caves, cave deposits and cave fauna and flora. The enormous number of people who visit caves tends to destroy the original deposits and life of caves. Thus, as more tourist facilities are developed, certain safeguards become necessary to preserve the caves' original features. This has been recognised by the creation of a special section on cave 'development' and preservation in the International Congress of Speleology [19].

3. THE PRESENT STAGE IN THE STUDY OF KARST LANDFORMS

As has already been shown, the study of karst landforms started as a central and southern European occupation, because of the occurrence of the large karst areas in Mediterranean and Alpine Europe. In modern times the great influence of the University of Vienna dates from the days of the Austro-Hungarian Empire, when scholars from all over central Europe and the Balkans were drawn to it. Added to this was the influence of Albrecht and Walther Penck who both worked in Vienna, with the result that their work became known in all German-speaking lands. This explains the interest taken in karst studies in all south and central European countries, such as Hungary, Poland, Czechoslovakia and Roumania, in addition to the obvious interests in the Classical and Dinaric karsts. Many of these countries have State Karst Institutes.

In western Europe, large areas of France are formed of karstland, with the result that studies of 'le relief calcaire' have played an important part in French geographical thinking. Some of the best work in karst landforms has been done in France, and many of the controversies that have been discussed in connection with the Jugoslav karstlands have been reproduced in France. The French in particular have for a long time played a leading part in the development of speleology. This has been helped by the discovery in France of many caves of great prehistoric interest, but is also due to the fact that some of the greatest caves in the world are in France, including the world's deepest cave at present known, the Gouffre Grotte Berger. Many of the first studies of caves and underground waters in the modern sense were done by the French, such as E. A. Martel and E. Fournier. The French probably still lead in scientific speleology, and the first President of the International Speleological Union is Bernard Gèze from Paris. The Société de Spéléologie produces a periodical of much interest to speleologists and karst morphologists. There is a French National Committee for the study of karst phenomena,

which has recently published the *Vocabulaire Français des Phénomènes Karstiques* [18]. There was also set up in France in 1948, by the Centre National de Recherche Scientifique [477], an underground laboratory at Moulis in the Ariège, where experiments and observations in caves can be carried out. Textbooks on the practical and scientific aspects of speleology have been written by Trombe and Renault [478, 510]. The practical aspects of the karstlands were stressed in the early work of Martel, and were continued by Casteret in his work on the sources of the Garonne in Pyrenees, so well described in *Dix Ans sous Terre* [479].

Since 1918 many universities have been founded in areas which were once part of the Austro-Hungarian Empire. This has led to the formation of geological and geographical institutes with strong interests in the karst, some of the most notable in Jugoslavia being in the Universities of Ljubljana, Zagreb and Sarajevo. At Postojna, in the Classical Karst nearby, the world's first bio-speleological research station was established in 1924 and is housed in a side gallery of the main cave. Gams [275] has commented that this establishment has 'had extraordinary moment for speleology' (loc. cit., p. 119). There was also founded in 1928 at Postojna an Institute of Karst Research of the Slovene Academy of Sciences and Arts, renewed in 1951. One of the aims of this Institute is to survey and describe all karst hollows of definite speleological interest; in the Slovenian karst these total over 3,000.

The pupils of Albrecht Penck have likewise extended the study of the karst; these include Cvijič himself. They also include many German geographers and geologists who have become great travellers in karstlands. Herbert Lehmann, well known for his work on tropical karst, established a school of karst morphology at Frankfurt,

West Germany. In Austria, the areas of high Alpine karst have received much attention. At the University of Graz there is an institute for the study of hydrology, and there is also a state centre for the study of caves and karst phenomena in Vienna.

In Britain we have always had an interest in caves, though more particularly from the archaeological point of view. But our work on karst has tended to be somewhat peripheral and empirical. It has also developed separately from work on the Continent, partly for linguistic reasons. We are only beginning to see the possibilities of work and developments in karst morphology and hydrology. The formation of the Cave Research Group in 1947 speeded up the work on British caves. There are also numerous sporting caving clubs in Great Britain and these have been responsible for adding many miles of explored caves to our knowledge. University speleological societies are active in many of the karst areas, some of the most noteworthy work being done by the University of Bristol Speleological Society. In addition, groups of people interested in hydrology have been formed by geological and engineering societies, and this has focused attention upon the hydrological aspects of the karst areas.

Work in the U.S.A. and in the English-speaking countries of the Commonwealth seems even more separated from the developments on the Continent. In the U.S. work on the karst was dominated by the cyclic hypothesis for much longer than elsewhere. Furthermore most Americans are still reluctant to read the results of work being done in Europe. In consequence there has been much parallel writing on some of the main problems. Research on caves has been carried out by the National Speleological Society of America. More recently the Cave Research Foundation and the Cave Research Associates have been formed as

organisations with the avowed aim of pressing forward the scientific studies of caves.* Hydrology of karst terrains has always occupied the attention of geologists in the United States, but there has not everywhere been co-operation between the geologists and the speleologists. However at Penn. State University, W. B. White has always fostered limestone and cave studies from the geological, geographical and geochemical points of view. In Canada, karst studies form part of an energetic programme under the direction of Dr D. C. Ford at McMaster University, Hamilton, Ontario. In Australia, the geography department of the Australian National University in Canberra has focused much attention upon Australian karst regions, the work of J. N. Jennings being particularly vigorous. Moreover, each State has a caving society; in South Australia caves and karst have been explored in the difficult area of the Nullarbor Plain, and in Tasmania the caving club has explored and opened up some of the most beautiful caves in the world.

In the U.S.S.R. much good work is being done. Because of the similarity of all the Slav languages, Russian karst morphologists have always been in touch with developments in the Classical Karst. In 1954, Gvozdeckij produced a comprehensive work on *Karst*, illustrated by many maps and photographs of Soviet karst areas and a long bibliography of Russian literature on the subject. Gvozdeckij refers to work in the Classical and Dinaric karsts as well as to that on south-east Asia; he is also knowledgeable on French and German ideas, so that the Russian work, though isolated to some extent, is much more in touch with modern European work than that in America. More recently Gvozdeckij

*The C.R.F. has worked particularly in the Flint Ridge Cave.

has written on the different types of karst in the U.S.S.R. [389]. Soviet research is directed towards studies both in climatic morphology and in the structural and lithological differences between karst limestones. Much progress has been made on the study of karst areas in central Asia, such as around Lake Baikal, and also in work on interstratal and gypsum karsts. No doubt in China the interest in terrain extends to the caves and karstlands that are so extensive in the south and south west. Many of the caves have been used as human habitations for centuries. Reviews of Chinese karst studies occur from time to time in East European literature.

The Karst Commission of the International Geographical Union did much to help in the international collaboration of people interested in karst problems. It is to be hoped that this book, now only a beginning to the study of karst landforms, will give some idea of the kind of problems and the complexities involved. Both in Britain and in the world as a whole we are at the beginning of a new phase in the development of research into karst landforms. In addition to the purely academic study of the areal differentiation of karst landforms throughout the world and of the light this can throw on palaeoclimatology, there are the exciting developments to be made in karst hydrology; in this field the new techniques can help to dispel some of the older ideas about the barren and useless karstlands. For this we need international co-operation in the diffusion of the knowledge available.

Selected Glossary · Compiled by K. ADDISON

ACCELERATED CORROSION A localised concentration of solution intensity, produced by factors favouring greater aggressivity of the karst water in certain parts of the karstland, which creates differential solution rates and thereby a marked unevenness in the overall erosion of the karstland.

AGGRESSIVE WATER Karst water charged with dissolved CO_2 often at a greater pressure than free CO_2 and thus capable of actively dissolving calcium carbonate.

ALLOGENIC VALLEY A karst valley incised by a watercourse originating on impervious rock with a volume sufficient for it to traverse a limestone area on the surface. The valley is incised from the limestone contact and with the passage of time the river is increasingly likely to pass underground as the waters enlarge joints. Occasionally such a valley may represent the large-scale collapse of the cavern system along a subterranean stream or the enlarging of a series of karst windows.

ALLUVIAL CORROSION Greater intensity of solution, caused by the passage of water through unconsolidated deposits rich in CO_2, thus increasing aggressivity.

BLIND VALLEY A karst valley abruptly terminated by the passage underground of the watercourse which has hitherto resisted the karst processes and remained at the surface. An intermediate type, the *half-blind valley,* exists in which the valley form continues downstream from the sink-hole (q.v.) used under conditions of normal river flow. The watercourse only flows here intermittently and the valley may (except from its use as a flood conduit) be fossil in that it represents the section abandoned by the river as it sought progressively higher swallow holes.

BLUE HOLE An artesian spring with little turbulence or variation in discharge.

BOGAZ (STRUGA) Joint-corridor in a limestone surface, wider and deeper than kluftkarren and formed by solution and mechanical processes.

BOILING SPRING A variable-discharge artesian spring in which hydrostatic pressure is great enough to cause a turbulent or even fountain-like discharge.

CALCITE RAFT A veneer of reprecipitated calcite forming a sheet over all or part of the surface of a static cave pool in conditions favouring the release of CO_2.

CAVE CORAL Globular concretions of reprecipitated calcite located on cavern walls and formed by general seepage of karst water.

CAVE PEARL A concretionary nodule of carbonate formed in caves by reprecipitation around a solid nucleus under a source of dripping karst water.

CAVE SHIELD A semicircular plate of reprecipitated calcite located beneath joints in a cavern ceiling and believed to be formed by the seepage of hydrostatic water along the joint. Two shields form beneath one joint, descending from each side of the opening.

CAVERN BREAKDOWN The process of cave enlargement which depends upon the mechanical failure and eventual collapse of sections of the cavern walls and ceiling.

CLINT (DALLES) *See* LIMESTONE PAVEMENT.

COCKPIT KARST A tropical karstland type consisting of irregular solution hollows separated by residual, steep-sided conical hills.

CONDENSATION WATER Atmospheric moisture deposited inside caves when the surface temperature of the exposed rock falls below the dew point of circulating air.

COVERED KARST A fossil or currently developing karst in karst limestone which underlies superficial deposits or other rock, and which may produce landforms at the surface which reflect subsurface karstification.

CUTTER An enlarged limestone joint which developed beneath a soil cover; found in the Mid-West karstlands of the U.S.A.

DOLINE A small enclosed depression formed by the solutional enlargement of joints and consequent settling of the calcareous surface. The level floor is usually a jumble of small blocks dislocated by subsidence; sediment is washed into the doline, so accelerating the rate of solution (*see* ALLUVIAL CORROSION). Enlargement is either circular in plan, if there is one dominant vertical joint, or otherwise irregular if there are several, and can achieve dimensions of up to 1,000 m in diameter and 100 m deep. Where the karst limestone possesses a cover of superficial deposits, solutional enlargement permits the latter to subside into vertical fissures, creating *subsidence cones* or *alluvial dolines,* whose slopes are unstable because of the unconsolidated nature of the surface material. The limestone remains covered in the first instance. Dolines are also formed by the large-scale subsidence caused by roof-collapse of near-surface caverns; in this instance, the *collapse doline,* the sides are cliff-like and the floor composed of the irregular blocks from the fragmented roof. A doline which is largely dependent upon snow for solution-enlargement is known as a *kotlici* or *schneedoline.*

DRY VALLEY A valley form of fluvial or periglacial origin in which surface drainage is intermittent or totally absent. Fossil, usually with steep scree slopes, it is variously identifiable as a product of nival processes or higher water-tables subsequently lowered by allogenic valley (q.v.).

EXSURGENCE The re-emergence at the surface, as a stream, of meteoric water which has fallen entirely upon and percolated through a calcareous massif.

FLOWSTONE A smooth, concretionary deposit of carbonate reprecipitated from karst water as it flows across cavern walls or floors.

GRIKE A solutionally enlarged vertical or steeply inclined joint in the surface of a karstland, extending for up to a few metres into the limestone.

HELICTITE A stalactite (q.v.) formed by the seepage of hydrostatic water, which causes an eccentricity of form, often creating a spiral column.

HUM A residual low mound of karst limestone lying within a polje (q.v.).

INLET CAVE That cave developed beneath a swallow hole where a surface watercourse first passes underground in karst limestone.

INTERMITTENT SPRING A karst spring with a pulsating flow, caused by the presence within the rock of cavities and siphons fed by a subterranean water course. When the cavity is full the siphon is complete and causes a pulse of water to issue from the spring. This diminishes or empties the water supply in the cavity and no further water is discharged from the spring until the system is reactivated. The discharge is said to be a *reciprocating* spring when a reduced level of flow is maintained between pulses.

KAMENITZA A small depression (a few metres in diameter and several centimetres deep) in a level calcareous surface, enlarged by the solution effect of water collecting between slight undulations. It is developed vertically at first by stagnant water; the steep sides thus evolved then induce the flow of water which flutes the slope and so eventually widens the basin. Sediments and low orders of plant life frequently collect on the even floor, the latter aiding further solution by reactivating the pH of the water.

KARREN (pl.) Minor solution channels on a karst surface caused by meteoric or soil water before it permeates underground. The individual channel-form depends upon the nature and disposition of the rock and the solution process.

KARST A solution-controlled landform type, characterised by an exclusive surface morphology, subsurface drainage and collapse features, which is specifically developed in calcareous rock. These elements remain constant even though climate, structure and petrography generate greatly diverse surface features.

KARST WATER Water discharged from karst springs which possess characteristics, primarily that of calcium content, indicating solution during the passage of that water across and through karst limestone. That part of karst spring water which is derived from watercourses sinking into the rock (and therefore originates mainly on impermeable rock) is said to be *allogenic*; that which derives from precipitation over the karst area alone is said to be *autochthonous* – the distinction between resurgence and exsurgence waters.

KARST WINDOW A section of subterranean river exposed by roof collapse. Intermittent collapse leaves an intervening 'natural bridge' between windows.

KARSTIC Pertaining to karst landforms or processes.

KARSTIFICATION The processes of solution and underground infiltration whereby the surface features and subterranean drainage network of a karstland are developed. An area currently or formerly undergoing karstification, and thus characterised by karst landforms, is said to be *karstified.*

KARSTLAND An area of the earth's surface possessing karst landforms.

KELD *See* RISING.

LAPIÉS (pl.) *See* KARREN.

LIMESTONE PAVEMENT A glaciokarstic landform, produced on a glacially planed limestone surface which has subsequently become dissected into blocks (clints or dalles) by solution-enlargement of vertical joints.

MIXTURE CORROSION The increased aggressivity of karst water resulting from the mixing of two saturated waters of differing calcium carbonate concentrations. The new volume of water requires less CO_2 for equilibrium than do the individual waters, and so CO_2 is liberated – reactivating the solubility of the water.

OUTLET CAVE A cave developed at the point of re-emergence of an underground karst watercourse.

PERCHED KARST SPRING The emergence of underground water some way above the basement of a calcareous massif caused by the interbedding of an impermeable or less permeable stratum. This creates a permanent or intermittent *perched water-table* by restricting the vertical movement of water, which instead issues from the contact.

PERCOLATION WATER Autochthonous karst water which permeates directly through karst limestone without using a surface watercourse.

PHREATIC WATER That part of the underground water in a karst limestone which lies within the zone of permanently saturated rock – the phreatic zone. Caves formed within this zone are known as *phreatic caves*.

POCKET *See* SPONGEWORK.

POCKET VALLEY The reverse of a blind valley, extending headwards into the foot of a calcareous massif. The upstream end is terminated by a cliff, frequently lunate, from whose base emerges a subterranean karst stream meandering across a flat, steep-sided valley below the resurgence.

POLJE A depression in karst limestone, whose long axis is developed parallel to major structural trends and can reach tens of kilometres in length. On the floor accumulates superficial deposits, and it is drained either by surface water-courses (when the polje is said to be open) or by swallow holes (a 'closed' polje). Their development is encouraged by any impedance in the karst drainage.

PONOR *See* SWALLOW HOLE.

POTHOLE A steep-sided, usually vertical hole, into which water disappears. Locally used in northern England.

RECULÉE *See* POCKET VALLEY

RESURGENCE The re-emergence at the surface of a watercourse which originated as a surface stream on impermeable rock and then passed underground through fissures in intervening calcareous strata.

RIMSTONE POOL A pool sited on a cavern floor and enclosed by a rim of carbonate reprecipitated from the karst water in the pool at points locally favouring the release of CO_2.

RISE PIT An artesian spring rising up through alluvium accumulated in an earlier surface valley phase and often fringed, except on the outlet side, by a minor levee deposited as the force of the vertical discharge dissipates at the surface.

RISING The resurgence of an underground watercourse, usually at the base margin of the calcareous massif, although in the instance of a blind valley the rising has eroded headwards for some distance. Each rising accounts for the collective discharge of several sinks (q.v.) and in this way has a relatively high discharge as the sole drainage outlet for a large area. If the water issues freely, the rising is said to be *free-flowing*, but if it issues under pressure, the terms artesian, forced or *Vauclusian spring* are used (after the type-example of the resurgence of the Sorgue river at Vaucluse in France).

ROCK PENDANT An isolated protuberance of limestone in a cave ceiling, resembling a stalactite, and formed by the more rapid, differential solution of the surrounding rock.

SHAKE-HOLE The colloquial term for an alluvial doline (q.v.), used in the north of England.

SOLUTION SUBSIDENCE A crater-like doline in rock other than karst limestone, formed by surface subsidence above solutionally enlarged fissures in a sub-surface karst limestone stratum.

SPELEOLOGY The scientific study of the nature and origin of caves and cave life.

SPONGEWORK An arrangement of partitioned depressions found in cave ceilings and walls, and attributed to the differential solution of submerged karst limestones. Larger and more isolated hollows are known as 'pockets'.

SPRING HEAD ALCOVE The arcuate cliff surrounding many risings, formed by progressive headward sapping and cavern collapse. The rapidity of their formation is increased by the cliff-line which frequently exists already at the lower margin of the karst area.

STALACTITE A columnar concretion descending from a cave ceiling, formed by the reprecipitation of carbonate in calcite form from percolating karst water.

STALAGMITE The reverse of a stalactite (q.v.), being a column of reprecipitated carbonate *ascending* from a cavern floor and perpendicularly beneath a constant source of karst water percolating through the cavern roof or dripping off the lower extremity of a stalactite.

SUBTERRANEAN CUT-OFF The diversion underground of a surface watercourse beneath a surface meander neck, marked by a swallow hole on the upstream side and a spring on the downstream side.

SWALLET *See* SWALLOW HOLE.

SWALLOW HOLE The location in a karst limestone at which a surface stream wholly or partially commences an underground course (swallet). A swallow hole in a polje is often called a *ponor*.

TRAVERTINE Regular, laminated concretions of crystalline carbonate, of similar origin to, but harder than, tufa.

TUFA Soft, porous concretions of carbonate reprecipitated from saturated karst water, often around plants.

UVALA A coalescence of neighbouring dolines (q.v.) which have enlarged towards each other; the floor is irregular, being a combination of doline floors and the degraded slopes of the individual hollows.

VADOSE WATER That part of the underground water in a karst limestone which circulates freely under gravity above the level of saturation – the *vadose zone*. Caves formed by flowing water are said to be *vadose caves*.

VASQUE A large, shallow solution pan formed in the intetridal zone of warm seas by the action of brine and marine organisms.

VERTICAL CAVE A vertical passage within a cave system, formed along joints by which underground watercourses are transferred from a higher to a lower bedding plane.

ZANJON *See* BOGAZ (Central America).

References

C.R.G. = Cave Research Group of Great Britain

[1] DE MARTONNE, E. (1924) *Traité de Géographie Physique.*

[2] GRUND, A. (1914) 'Der geographische Zyklus im Karst', *Z.Ges.Erdkunde,* **52,** 621-40.

[3] CVIJIČ, J. (1893) 'Das Karstphänomen', *Geogr. Abhand.vonA.Penck* **5** (3), 215-319.

[4] PENCK, A. (1904) 'Über das Karstphänomen', *Vortr.Ver.Verbr.Naturwiss.Kenntn.,Wien.* **44** (1), 1-38.

[5] (1965) *Naše Jame,* Organe de la Société pour l'Exploration des Grottes de Slovénie (Ljubljana) **7,** 1-2.

[6] LORENZ, J. (1859) 'Geologische Recognoscirungen im Liburnischen Karst von den vorliegenden Quanerischen Inseln', *Jahrb.K.K.Geol. Reichsanst.* **10,** 332-45.

[7] PRESTWICH, J. (1854) 'Swallow holes on chalk hills, near Canterbury', *Q.J.Geol. Soc.* **10,** 222.

[8] BOYD-DAWKINS, W. (1874) *Cave Hunting: Researches on the Evidence of Caves, respecting the Early Inhabitants of Europe* (London, Macmillan).

[9] TIETZE, E. (1880) 'Zur Geologie der Karsterscheinung', *Jahrb.K.K.Geol.Reichsanst.* **30,** 728-56.

[10] MOJSISOVICS, E. VON (1880) 'Zur Geologie der Karsterscheinung', *Z.Deutsch.Österr.Alpenvereins* **11,** 111-16, 349-50.

[11] REYER, M. (1881) 'Studien über Karstrelief', *Mitt.K.K.Geogr.Ges.Wien,* N.F., **14,** 76-86, 101-7.

[12] SCHMIDL, A. (ed.) (1854) *Zur Höhlenkunde des Karstes: Die Grotten und Höhlen von Adelsberg, Planina und Lass* (Vienna).

[13] MARTEL, E. A. (1921) *Nouveau Traité des Eaux Souterraines* (Paris, Delagrave).

[14] MARTEL, E. A. (1894) *Les Abîmes* (Paris, Delagrave).

[15] MARTEL, E. A. (1897) *Irlande et Cavernes Anglaises* (Paris, Delagrave).

[16] FOURNIER, E. (1926) *Les Eaux Souterraines* (Besançon).

(1934) 'Les résurgences du réseau souterrain du plateau compris entre l'Hôpital du Gros-Bois, Mamirolle, Trépot et la vallée de la Loue', *Spél.,* 2 sér., **1** (5), 3-7.

[17] LEHMANN, H. (1960) 'La terminologie classique du karst sous l'aspect critique de la morphologie climatique moderne', *Rev.Géogr.Lyon* **35,** 1-6.

[18] (1965) *Vocabulaire Française des Phénomènes Karstiques* (Commission Française des Phénomènes Karstiques du Comité National de Géographie, Orléans).

[19] (1963) Third International Congress of Speleology, Vienna.

[20] ROGLIČ, J. (1965) 'The depth of the fissure circulation of water and the evolution of subterranean cavities in the Dinaric Karst', *Prob. Speleol.Res.,Proc.Int.Speleol.Conf.,Brno 1964,* 25-36 (Prague).

[21] HAM, W. E. (1962) *Classification of Carbonate Rocks: A Symposium* (American Association of Petroleum Geologists).

[22] SAWKINS, J., *et al.* (1869) 'Report on the geology of Jamaica', *Mem.Geol.Survey.*

[23] CLARKE, F. W. (1924) 'The data of geochemistry', *U.S.Geol.Surv.Bull.* 770, 84 pp.

[24] BATHURST, R. G. C. (1959) 'Diagenesis in Mississippi calcicutites and pseudo-breccias', *J.Sediment.Petrol.* **29,** 365-76.

[25] ROQUES, H. (1969) 'A review of present-day problems in the physical chemistry of carbonates in solution', *Trans.C.R.G.* **11** (3), 139-63.

[26] LOWENSTAM, H. A. (1954) 'Factors affecting the aragonite:calcite ratios in carbonate-secreting marine organisms', *J.Geol.* **62,** 284-322.

[27] WARWICK, G. T. (1962) in *British Caving: An Introduction to Speleology* (ed. C. H. D. Cullingford), pt 1, chap. 5, 120-217 (London, Routledge & Kegan Paul).

[28] PETTIJOHN, K. (1957) *Sedimentary Rocks,* 2nd ed. (New York, Harper).

[29] CHAVE, K. E. (1954) 'Aspects of the geochemistry of magnesium. 1: Calcareous marine organisms', *J.Geol.* **62,** 266-83.

[30] CUMINGS, E. R. (1932) 'Reefs or bioherms', *Bull.Geol.Soc.Amer.* **43,** 331-52.

& SHROCK, R. R. (1928) 'Niagaran coral reefs of Indiana and adjacent states and their stratigraphic relations', *ibid.* **39,** 579-620.

[31] JENNINGS, J. N., & SWEETING, M. M. (1963) 'The Limestone Ranges of the Fitzroy Basin, Western Australia: a tropical semi-arid karst', *Bonner Geogr.Abhand.* **32,** 1-60.

[32] ILLING, L. V. (1954) 'Bahaman calcareous sands', *Bull.Amer.Assoc.Petrol.Geol.* **38** (1), 1–92.

[33] WOOD, A. (1941) 'Algal dust and the finer-grained varieties of Carboniferous Limestone', *Geol.Mag.* **78**, 192–200.

[34] FOLK, R. L. (1959) 'Practical petrographic classification of limestones', *Bull.Amer.Assoc. Petrol.Geol.* **43** (1), 3.
(1965) *Some aspects of recrystallisation in Ancient Limestones,* Soc. Econ. Palaeontol. Mineral., Spec. Pub. 13, 14 (Tulsa, Oklahoma).

[35] CHILINGAR, G. V., BISSELL, H. J., & FAIRBRIDGE, R. W. (eds.) (1967) *Carbonate Rocks,* Developments in Sedimentology series 9A and 9B (Amsterdam, New York, London: Elsevier).

[36] SCHOELLER, H. (1950) 'Les variations de la teneur en gaz carbonique des eaux souterraines en fonction de l'altitude', *C.R.Acad.Sci.* **230**, 560–1.
(1962) *Les Eaux Souterraines* (Paris, Masson).

[37] SWEETING, M. M., & SWEETING, G. S. (1969) 'Some aspects of the Carboniferous Limestone in relation to its landforms', *Méditerranée*, no. 7, 201–9.

[38] POWERS, R. W. (1962) 'Arabian Upper Jurassic carbonate reservoir rocks', in *Classification of Carbonate Rocks* (ed. W. E. Ham), Amer. Assoc. Petrol. Geol., Mem. 1, 122–92.

[39] NEWELL, N. D., *et al.* (1953) *The Permian Reef Complex of the Guadalupe Mountains Region, Texas and New Mexico* (San Francisco, Freeman).

[40] SCHWARZACHER, W. (1958) 'Stratification of the Great Scar Limestone in the Settle district of Yorkshire', *Liverpool and Manchester Geol.J.* **2** (1), 124.

[41] WHITE, W. B. (1960) 'Termination of passages in Appalachian caves as evidence for a shallow phreatic origin', *Bull.Nat.Speleol.Soc.* **22**, 43–53.

[42] GINSBURG, R. N. (1957) 'Early diagenesis and lithification of shallow-water carbonate sediments in South Florida', in *Regional Aspects of Calcium Carbonate Deposition* (ed. R. J. Leblanc and J. G. Breeding), Soc. Econ. Palaeontol. Mineral., Spec. Pub. 5, 80–99 (Tulsa, Oklahoma).

[43] GEORGE, T. N. (1958) 'The Lower Carboniferous palaeogeography of the British Isles', *Proc.Yorks.Geol.Soc.* **31** (3), 227–318.

[44] SWEETING, M. M. (1972) 'The Karst of Great Britain', in *Karst: Important Karst Areas of the Northern Hemisphere* (ed. Herak

and Stringfield) (Amsterdam, New York, London: Elsevier).

[45] WAGER, L. R. (1931) 'Jointing in the Great Scar limestone of Craven and its relation to the tectonics of the area', *Q.J.Geol.Soc.* **87**, 392–420.

[46] DOUGHTY, P. S. (1968) 'Joint densities and their relation to the Great Scar Limestone', *Proc. Yorks.Geol.Soc.* **36** (4), 479–512.

[47] HANCOCK, P. L. (1968) 'Joints and faults: the morphological aspects of their origin', *Proc. Geol.Assoc.* **79** (2), 141–51.

[48] DWERRYHOUSE, A. R. (1904) 'Underground waters of north-west Yorkshire', pt 2 (pt 1, 1900), *Proc.Yorks.Geol.Soc.* **15**, 248–304.

[49] KENDALL, P. F., & WROOT, H. E. (1924) *The Geology of Yorkshire* (privately printed).

[50] SIMPSON, E. (1935) 'Notes on the formation of the Yorkshire caves and pot holes', *Proc.Univ. Bristol Speleol.Soc.* **4**, 224–32.

[51] PANNAKOEK, A. J. (1948) 'Enige Karstlerreinen in Indonesie', *Tijdschr.K.Ned.Aardrijksk. Genoot.* **65**, 209–13.

[52] HUTCHINSON, G. E. (1957) *A Treatise on Limnology* (New York and London, Wiley).

[53] PIA, J. (1952) 'Theorien über die Löslichkeit des hohlensauren Kalkes', *Mit.Geol.Ges.Wien* **25**, 1–93.

[54] KENDALL, J. (1912) 'The solubility of calcium carbonate in water', *Phil.Mag.* **23**, 958–76.

[55] ROQUES, H. (1961) 'Éléments pour une cinétique des phénomènes karstochimiques', *Ann. Spéléol.* **16**, 329–39.
(1965) *Ann.Spéléol.* **20**, 7.

[56] SMITH, D. I., & MEAD, D. G. (1962) 'The solution of limestone with special reference to Mendip', *Proc.Univ.Bristol Speleol.Soc.* **9** (3), 188–211.
See also:
SMITH, D. I. and NICHOLSON, F. H. (1964) 'A study of limestone solution in N.W. Co. Clare, Eire', *Proc.Univ. Bristol Speleol.Soc.* **10**(2), 119–38.

[57] TROMBE, F. (1952) *Traité de Spéléologie* (Paris, Payot).

[58] STENNER, R. D. (1969) 'The measurement of the aggressiveness of water towards calcium carbonate', *Trans.C.R.G.* **11** (3), 175–200.

[59] BÖGLI, A. (1960) 'Kalklösung und Karrenbildung', *Z.Geomorph.,* Supp. 2, *Internationale Beiträge zur Karstmorphologie,* 4–21.

[60] PICKNETT, R. G. (1964) 'A study of calcite solutions at 10°C', *Trans.C.R.G.* **7** (1), 39–62.

[61] CORBEL, J. (1959) 'Erosion en terrain calcaire: vitesse d'érosion et morphologie', *Ann.Geogr.*

68, 97–120.

[62] GERSTENHAUER, A. (1960) 'Der tropische Kegelkarst in Tabasco (Mexiko)', *Z.Geomorph.,* Supp. 2, *Internationale Beiträge zur Karstmorphologie,* 22–48.

(1966) 'Beiträge zur Geomorphologie des mittleren und nördlichen Chiapas (Mexiko) unter besonderer Berücksichtigung des Karstformenschatzes', *Frankf.Geogr.Hefte* **41.**

[63] GERSTENHAUER, A., & PFEIFFER, K. H. (1966) 'Beiträge zur Frage der Lösungsfreudigkeit von Kalkgesteinen', *Abhand.Karst- Höhlenkunde,* Reihe A: *Speläologie* (München) **2.**

[64] PREISNITZ, K. P. (1967) 'Zur Frage der Lösungsfreudigkeit von Kalkgesteinen in Abhängigkeit von der Lösungsfläche und ihren Gehalt an Magnesium-Karbonat', *Z.Geomorph.* **11** (4), 491–7.

[65] DOUGLAS, I. (1965) 'Calcium and magnesium in karst waters', *Helictite* **3** (2), 23–37.

[66] PRAY, L. C., & MURRAY, B. C. (eds.) *Dolomitization and Limestone Diagenesis,* Soc. Econ. Palaeontol. Mineral., Spec. Pub. 13.

[67] GARRELS, R. M., & CHRIST, C. L. (1965) *Solutions, Minerals and Equilibria* (New York, Harper & Row).

[68] KAYE, C. A. (1957) 'The effect of solvent motion on limestone solutions', *J.Geol.* **65,** 34–47.

[69] GUILCHER, A. (1952) 'Formes de décomposition chimique dans le zone des embruns et des marées sur les côtes britanniques et bretonnes', *Vol.Jubil.Cinquant.Anniv.Labor.Géogr.Rennes,* 167–81.

(1953) 'Essai sur la zonation et la distribution des formes littorales de dissolution du calcaire', *Ann.Géogr.* **62,** 161–79.

[70] DREW, D. P. (1967) 'Aspects of the limestone hydrology of the Mendip Hills, Somerset', unpublished Ph.D. thesis, University of Bristol.

[71] SCHWARZENBACH, G. (1957) *Complexometric Titrations,* trans. H. Irving (London, Methuen).

[72] SMITH, D. I., & MEAD, D. G. (1962) 'The solution of limestone with special reference to Mendip', *Proc.Univ.Bristol Speleol.Soc.* **9** (3), 188–211.

[73] DOUGLAS, I. (1969) *Technical Bulletin* no. 1, British Geomorph. Res. Group.

[74] DOUGLAS, I. (1962) 'An evaluation of some techniques used in the study of landforms with special reference to limestone areas', unpublished B.Litt. thesis, University of Oxford.

[75] DOUGLAS, I. (1968) 'Some hydrological factors in the denudation of limestone terrains', *Z. Geomorph.,* N.F., **12,** 241–55.

[76] SWEETING, M. M. (1966) 'The weathering of limestones, with particular reference to the Carboniferous Limestones of northern England', in *Essays in Geomorphology* (ed. G. H. Dury), 177–210 (London, Heinemann).

[77] BIROT, P. (1954) 'Problèmes de morphologie karstique', *Ann.Géogr.* **63,** 160–92.

[78] ADAMS, C., & SWINNERTON, A. (1937) 'The solubility of calcium carbonate', *Trans.Amer. Geophys.Union, 18th Annual Meeting,* **11** (2), 504–8.

[79] PITTY, A. F. (1966) *An Approach to the Study of Karst Water,* University of Hull Occasional Paper, Geography, no. 5.

[80] GROOM, G. E., & WILLIAMS, V. (1965) 'The solution of limestone in South Wales', *Geog.J.* **131,** 37–41.

[81] WHITE, W. B. & STELLMACK, J. A. (1968) 'Seasonal fluctuations in the chemistry of karst groundwater', *Proc.4th Int.Congr.Speleol., Ljubljana,1965,* **3,** 261–7.

[82] GAMS, I. (1968) 'Versuch einer Klassifikation der Tropfsteinformen in der Grotte von Postojna', *Proc.4th Int.Congr.Speleol.,Ljubljana 1965,* **3,** 117–26.

[83] FETZER, W. G. (1946) 'Humic acids and organic acids as solvents of minerals', *Econ. Geol.* **41,** 47–56.

[84] JONES, R. J. (1966) 'Aspects of the biological weathering of limestone pavement', *Proc.Geol. Assoc.London* **76,** 421–33.

[85] KONONOVA, N. N. (1961) *Soil Organic Matter, its Nature, its Role in Soil Formation and in Soil Fertility,* trans. T. Z. Nowakowski and G. A. Greenwood (Oxford, Pergamon).

[86] WILLIAMS, J. E. (1949) 'Chemical weathering at low temperatures', *Geogr.Rev.* **39,** 129–35.

[87] CORBEL, J. (1957) *Les Karsts du Nord-Ouest de l'Europe et de quelques Régions de Comparaison: Etude sur le Rôle du Climat dans l'Erosion des Calcaires,* Institut des Etudes Rhodaniennes de l'Université de Lyon, Mémoires et Documents 12.

[88] EK, C. (1964) 'Note sur les eaux de fonte des glaciers de la Haute-Maurienne, leur action sur les carbonates', *Rev.Belge Géogr.* **88,** 127–56.

[89] GAMS, I. (1961) 'Triglavsko Brezno', *Glasilo Drustva za Raziskovanje Jan Slovenije* **3,** 1–2.

[90] BÖGLI, A. (1964) 'Mischungskorrosion: ein Beitrag zum Verkarstungsproblem', *Erdkunde* **18** (2), 83–92.

[91] BÖGLI, A. (1956) 'Der Chemismus der Lösungsprozesse und der Einfluss der Gesteinsbeschaf-

fenheit auf Entwicklung des Karstes', *Int.Geogr. Union, Report of Commission on Karst Phenomena* (Rio de Janeiro) p. 7.

[92] KAYE, C. A. (1957) 'The effect of solvent motion on limestone solutions', *J.Geol.* **65**, 34–47.

[93] WEYL, P. K. (1958) 'The solution kinetics of calcite', *J.Geol.* **66**, 163.
(1961) 'The carbonate saturometer', *J.Geol.* **69**, 32–44.

[94] SWEETING, M. M. (1968) 'The University of Edinburgh British Honduras-Yucatán Expedition, Section C (Karst morphology)', *Geogr.J.* **134**, 49–54.

[95] WILLIAMS, P. W. (1964) 'Aspects of the limestone physiography of parts of Counties Clare and Galway, West Ireland', unpublished Ph.D. thesis, Cambridge University.

[96] GAMS, I. (1962) 'Measurements of corrosion intensity in Slovenia and their geomorphological significance', *Geogr.Vestnik Ljubljana* **34**, 3–20.

[97] CHILINGAR, G. V. (1956) 'Use of calcium: magnesium ratio in porosity studies', *Bull. Amer.Assoc.Petrol.Geol.* **40**, 2489–93.
(1956) 'Durov's classification of natural waters and chemical composition of atmospheric precipitation in the U.S.S.R.: a review', *Trans. Amer.Geophys.Union* **37**, 193–6.

[98] COSYNS, G. (1907) 'Essai d'interprétation chimique de l'altération des schistes et calcaires', *Bull.Soc.Belge Géol.Paléont.Hydrol.* **21**, 325–46.

[99] TERJESEN, S. G., ERGA, O., THORSEN, G., & VE, A. (1961) 'Phase boundary processes as rate detection steps in reactions between solids and liquids', *Chem.Eng.Sci.* **14**, 277–88.

[100] WILLIAMS, V. (1964) 'Studies in the Carboniferous Limestone of the North Crop of the South Wales Coalfields', unpublished thesis, University of Wales, Swansea.

[101] KILROE, J. R. (1907) 'The River Shannon: its present course and geological history', *Proc. Roy.Irish Acad.* **26B**, 74–96.

[102] EWING, A. (1885) 'Attempt to determine the amount and rate of chemical erosion taking place in the limestone valley of Center Co., Pennsylvania', *Amer.J.Sci.*, ser. 3, **29**, 29–31.

[103] WILLIAMS, P. W. (1963) 'An initial estimate of the speed of limestone solution in County Clare', *Irish Geogr.* **4** (6), 432–44. See also ref. [456].

[104] DOUGLAS, I. (1968) 'Some hydrological factors in the denudation of limestone terrains', *Z.Geomorph.*, N.F. **12**, 241–55.

[105] GAMS, I. (1962) 'Measurements of corrosion intensity in Slovenia and their geomorphological significance', *Geogr.Vestnik Ljubljana* **34**, 3–20.

[106] GAMS, I. (1965) 'Types of accelerated karst corrosion', *Prob.Speleol.Res.,Proc.Int.Speleol. Conf.,Brno 1964*, 133–9 (Prague).

[107] HACK, J. T. (1960) 'Relation of solution features to chemical character of water in the Shenandoah Valley, Virginia', *U.S.Geol.Surv. Prof.Paper* **400-B**, 387–90.

[108] KUNAVER, J. (1965) *Guide through the High-Mountainous Karst of the Julian Alps*, 4th International Congress of Speleology, Postojna-Ljubljana-Dubrovnik.

[109] GAMS, I. (1962) 'Contributions to the Discussion on Karst Terminology', Slovenian Geological and Geographical Society, *Geogr. Vestnik Ljubljana* **34**, 115–37.

[110] CRAMER, H. (1941) 'Die Systematik der Karstdolinen', *Neues Jahrbuch für Mineralogie, Geologie und Paläontologie*, **85B**, 293–382 (Stuttgart).

[111] AUB, C. F. T. (1964) 'Limestone scenery in Jamaica' (private communication).

[112] KUNSKY, J. (1958) *Karsts et Grottes*, French trans. (Paris, B.R.G.M.) of *Kras a Jeskyně* (Prague), 164 pp.

[113] COLEMAN, A., & BALCHIN, W. G. V. (1959) 'The origin and development of surface depressions in the Mendip Hills', *Proc.Geol. Assoc.* **70**, 291–309.

[114] FORD, D. C. (1963) 'Aspects of the geomorphology of the Mendip Hills', unpublished D.Phil. thesis, Oxford University, Bodleian Library.

[115] MARRES, P. (1933) *Les Grands Causses*, 2 vols (Tours, Arrault).

[116] CHABOT, G. (1927) *Les Plateaux du Jura Central: Etude Morphogénique,* Publications de la Faculté des Lettres de l'Université de Strasbourg, no. 41.

[117] CLOZIER, R. (1940) *Les Causses du Quency.* Paris, Librairie J.-B. Baillère et Fils, 183 pp.

[118] CORBEL, J. (1956) 'Le karst du Vercors', *Rev. Géogr.Lyon* **31**, 221–41.

[119] CORBEL, J. (1957) 'Karsts hauts-Alpins', *Rev.Géogr.Lyon* **32**, 135–58.

[120] GÈZE, B. (1965) *La Spéléologie Scientifique*, Collection Microcosme – Le Rayon de la Science No. 22 (Paris, Editions de Seuil).

[121] MALOTT, C. A. (1939) 'Karst valleys', *Bull. Geol.Soc.Amer.* **50**, 1984.

[122] MILOJEVIĆ, S. M. (1936) 'Les brachyclases et leur rôle dans les relations hydrographiques

et le relief du karst', *Posebna izdanja Srp.Kralj. Akad.*, 21 Dec.

(1938) 'Phénomènes et problèmes du karst. Études dans le karst dinarique et de Serbie orientale', *ibid.* **32.**

[123] MATCHINSKI, M. (1962) 'Sur le problème "d'alignement" de données apparemment dispersées., *C.R.Acad.Sci.* **254,** 8069.

(1968) 'Alignment of dolines north-west of Lake Constance, Germany', *Geol.Mag.* **105** (1), 56–61.

[124] MORAWETZ, S. (1965) 'Zur Frage der Dolinenverteilung und Dolinenbildung im Istrischen Karst', *Petermanns Geogr.Mitt.* **109,** 161–70.

[125] LAVALLE, P. (1967) 'Some aspects of linear karst depression development in south-central Kentucky', *Ann.Assoc.Amer.Geogr.* **57,** 49–71.

[126] CLAYTON, K. M. (1966) 'The origin of the landforms of the Malham area', *Field Studies* **2,** 359–84.

[127] PENCK, A. (1924) *Das Unterirdische Karstphänomen,* Receuil de Travaux offert à J. Cvijič (Belgrade).

[128] THOMAS, T. M. (1954) 'Swallow holes on the Millstone Grit and Carboniferous Limestone of the South Wales Coalfield', *Geogr.J.* **120,** 468–75.

[129] DICKEN, S. (1935) 'Kentucky karst landscapes', *J.Geol.* **43,** 708–28.

[130] BRINK, A. B. A., & PARTRIDGE, T. C. (1965) 'Transvaal karst: some considerations of development and morphology, with special reference to sinkholes and subsidence in the Far West Rand', *S.A.Geogr.J.* **47,** 11–34.

[131] *Guide-book of the Congress Excursion through the Dinaric Karst,* 4th International Congress of Speleology in Yugoslavia, Ljubljana, 1965.

[132] SWEETING, M. M. (1961) *The Karst Geomorphogeny of the Parnassus-Ghiona Region, Greece,* for F.A.O.–U.N.S.F. Groundwater Project Report.

[133] JENNINGS, J. N. (1963) 'Collapse doline, Australian landforms examples no. 1', *Austr. Geogr.* **9,** 120–1.

[134] SWEETING, M. M. (1958) 'The karstlands of Jamaica', *Geogr.J.* **124,** 184–99.

[135] THRAILKILL, J. V. (1964) 'Preliminary geological report, Rio Camuy area', *Report, Rio Camuy Expedition to Puerto Rico 1964,* 8–23.

[136] CORBEL, J. (1959) 'Les Karsts du Yucatan et de la Florida', *Bull.Assoc.Géogr.Fr., 282–3;* 2–14.

[137] SWEETING, M. M. (1950) 'Erosion cycles and limestone caverns in the Ingleborough district',

Geogr.J. **115,** 63–78.

[138] GARROD, D. A. E. (1962) Huxley Memorial Lecture, 'The Middle Palaeolithic of the Near East and the problem of Mount Carmel Man', *J.Roy.Anthrop.Inst.* **92** (2).

[139] WALL, G. P., *et al.* (1869) Mem. Geol. Survey: *Reports on the Geology of Jamaica,* or Part II of the West Indian Survey, 1–340 (London, H.M.S.O.).

[140] LEHMANN, H. (1936) 'Morphologische Studien auf Java', *Geogr.Abhand.* (Stuttgart) **3,** 9.

[141] LEHMANN, H. (1953) 'Der tropische Kegelkarst in Westindien', *Tagungsber.und wissens. Abhand.Deutsch.Geographentag, Essen.*

[142] LEHMANN, H., *et al.* (1954) 'Der tropische Kegelkarst der verschiedenen Klimazonen', *Erdkunde* **8,** 130–9.

(1956) 'Karstmorphologische, geologische und botanische Studien in der Sierra de los Organos auf Cuba', *Erdkunde* **10,** 185–203.

[143] VERSEY, H. R. (1959) 'The hydrological character of the White Limestone formation of Jamaica', *Trans. 2nd Caribbean Congr., Kingston,* 59–68.

[144] VERSTAPPEN, H. TH. (1960) 'Some observations on karst development in the Malay Archipelago', *J.Trop.Geogr.* **14,** 1–10.

[145] JENNINGS, J. N., & BIK, M. (1962) 'Karst morphology in Australian New Guinea', *Nature* **194,** 1036–8.

[146] KOSACK, H. P. (1952) 'Verbreitung der Karst- und Pseudokarsterscheinung über die Erde. Ein Beitrag zur Karstforschung und Hydrographie', *Petermanns Geogr.Mitt.* **96,** 16–21.

[147] HEIM, A. (1878) 'Uber die Karrenfelder', *Jahrb.Schweiz.Alpenclubs* **13,** 421–33.

[148] CVIJIČ, J. (1924) 'The evolution of lapiés: a study in karst physiography', *Geogr.J.* **14,** 26–49.

(1960) *La géographie des terrains calcaires',* Acad. Serbe des Sciences et des Arts, Monograph 241 (Belgrade).

[149] CHAIX, E. (1895) 'La topographie d'une partie du Désert de Platé', *Le Globe* **34,** 67–108.

[150] ECKERT, M. (1902) 'Das Gottesackerplateau, ein Karrenfeld im Allgäu', *Wissens.Ergänz., Z.Deutsch.Osterr.Alpenvereins* **33,** 3. See also:

(1900) 'Das Gottesackerplateau (ein Karrenfeld) in der Gebirgsgruppe des Hohen Ifen', *Z.Deutsch.Osterr.Alpenvereins* **31,** 52–60.

(1890) 'Die Karren oder Schatten', *Petermanns Mitt.* **44,** 69–71.

(1895) 'Das Karrenproblem: die Geschichte

seiner Lösung', *Z.Naturwiss.* (Leipzig) **5** (2), 321–432.

[151] LINDNER, H. (1930) 'Das Karrenphänomen', *Petermanns Mitt.Ergänz.* **208, 83**.

[152] BAUER, F. (1962) 'Nacheiszeitliche Karstformen in den Österreichischen Kalkhochalpen', *Proc. 2nd Int.Congr.Speleol., Bari-Lecce-Salerno 1958*, **1**, 299–329.

[153] BALÁZS, D. (1962) 'Beiträge zur Speläologie des südchinesischen Karstgebietes', *Karszt-és barlang-kutatás*, **2**, 3–82.

[154] WILFORD, G. E., & WALL, J. R. D. (1965) 'Karst topography in Sarawak., *J.Trop.Geogr.* **21**, 44–70.

[155] CURL, R. L. (1966) 'Caves as a measure of karst', *J.Geol.* **74** (5), no. 2, 798–829.

[156] GARWOOD, E. J., & GOODYEAR, E. (1924) 'The Lower Carboniferous succession in the Settle district and along the line of the Craven Faults', *Q.J.Geol.Soc.* **80**, 184–270.

[157] LAUDERMILK, J. D., & WOODFORD, A. O. (1932) 'Concerning Rillensteine', *Amer.J.Sci.*, ser. 5, **23**, 135–54.

[158] ZOTOV, V. D. (1941) 'Potholing of limestones by the development of solution cups', *J. Geomorph.* **4, 71**–3.

[159] UDDEN, J. A. (1925) *Etched Potholes*, University of Texas Bulletin No. 2509.

[160] SMITH, J. F., Jr, & ALBRITTON, C. C., Jr (1941) 'Solution effects as a function of slope', *Bull.Geol.Soc.Amer.* **52**, 61–78.

[161] (1897) Report, British Association.

[162] WILLIAMS, P. W. (1966) 'Limestone pavements with special reference to West Ireland', *Trans.Inst.Brit.Geogr.* **40**, 155–72.

[163] PIGOTT, C. D. (1965) 'The structure of limestone surfaces in Derbyshire', *Geogr.J.* **131**, 41–4.

[164] LATTMAN, L. H., & OLIVE, W. H. (1955) 'Solution-widened joints in Trans-Pecos, Texas', *Bull.Amer.Assoc.Petrol.Geol.* **39** (10), 2084–7.

[165] TRICART, J., & DA SILVA, T. (1960) 'Un exemple d'évolution karstique en milieu tropical sec: le morne de Bom Jesus da Lapa (Bahia, Brésil)', *Z.Geomorph.*, N.F., **4**, 29–42.

[166] MONROE, W. H. (1964) 'The zanjon, a solution feature of karst topography in Puerto Rico', *U.S.Geol.Surv.Prof.Paper* 501B, 126–9.

[167] HASERODT, K. (1965) 'Untersuchungen zur Höhen- und Altersgliederung der Karstformen in den nördlichen Kalkalpen', *München.Geogr.* **27**.

[168] SCRIVENOR, J. B., & JONES, W. R. (1921) 'Physical geography of the southern part of the Malay Peninsula', *Geogr.Rev.* **2, 251**.

[169] SMYK, B., & DRZAL, M. (1964) 'Untersuchungen über den Einfluss von Mikroorganismen auf das Phänomen der Karstbildung', *Erdkunde* **18**, 102–13.

[170] GOODCHILD, J. G. (1875) 'The glacial phenomena of the Eden Valley and the west part of the Yorkshire Dales district', *Q.J.Geol.Soc.* **31**, 55–99.

[171] MOISLEY, H. A. (1954) 'Some karstic features in the Malham district', *Ann.Rep.Council for the Promotion of Field Studies* **38**.

[172] SWEETING, M. M., & SWEETING, G. S. (1969) 'Réunion internationale de Karstologie, Languedoc-Provence 1968', *Méditerranée*, no. 7, 201–9.

[173] CLARKE, M. J., personal communication.

[174] ROGLIČ, J. (1931) 'Glacijalni tragovi na Biokovu (Les formes glaciaires sur le Biokovu)', *Posebna, Izdanja Geogr.Drust.Beograd* **10**.

[175] COMMON, R. (1955) 'Les formes littorales dans les calcaires en Northumberland septentrionale', *Ann.Géogr.* **64**, 126–8.

[176] LEWIS, J. R. (1964) *The Ecology of Rocky Shores* (London, English Universities Press) chap. 7, 71–114.

[177] STODDART, D. R., & CANN, J. R. (1965) 'Nature and origin of beach rock', *J.Sediment. Petrol.* **35**, 243–7.

[178] MILOJEVIĆ, B. Z. (1953) *Le Littoral et les Îles Dinariques*, Mem. Soc. Géogr., Belgrade.

[179] ROGLIČ, J. (1964) 'Karst valleys in the Dinaric Karst' (Symposium, Karst Commission of the I.G.U., Stuttgart, 1963), *Erdkunde* **18** (2), 113–6.

[180] CVIJIČ, J. (1900–1) 'Morphologische und glaciale Studien aus Bosnien, der Hercegovina und Montenegro. 1: Die Karstthäler. 2: Die Karst-Poljen', *Abhand.Geol.Ges.Wien* (1900) **6**, (1901) **2**.

[181] NICOD, J. (1968) 'Premières récherchés de morphologie karstique dans le Massif du Durmitor', *Méditerranée* **3**, 187–216.

[182] GRUND, A. (1903) 'Die Karsthydrographie, Studien aus Westbosnien', *Geogr.Abhand. von A.Penck* **7** (3), 103–200.

[183] SWEETING, M. M. (1960) 'The caves of the Buchan area, Victoria, Australia', *Z.Geomorph.*, Supp. 2, 81–9.

[184] HODGSON, A. (1950), unpublished thesis, Imperial College of Science and Technology, London.

[185] CORBEL, J. (1954) 'Les phénomènes karstiques

dans les Grands Causses', *Rev.Géogr.Lyon* **29** (4), 287–316.

[186] HUDSON, R. G. S., BISAT, W., *et al.* (1933) 'Geology of the Yorkshire Dales', *Proc.Geol. Assoc.* **44**, 228–69.

[187] WARWICK, G. T. (1958) 'Some observations on by-passed swallow-holes in the Meuse and Lesse valleys', *Mem.Colloq.Int.Spéléol.,Féd. Spéléol.de Belgique* (Brussels) 66–72.

[188] LOBECK, A. K. (1939) *Geomorphology: An Introduction to the Study of Landscapes* (New York and London, McGraw-Hill).

[189] SINKER, C. A. (1960) 'The vegetation of the Malham Tarn area', *Proc.(Sci.)Leeds Phil.Lit. Soc.* **8**, 139–74.

[190] GREGORY, J. W. (1911) 'Constructive waterfalls', *Scot.Geogr.Mag.* **27**, 537–46.

[191] PEVALEK, I. (1938) 'Biodinamika Plitvickih Jezera i njena zaštita', *Zastite Prirode* **1**; and 'Der Travertin und die Plitvice Seen', *Verhand. Int.Ver.Limnol.* (Belgrade) **7**, 165–81.

[192] ROGLIČ, J. (1939) 'Beitrag zur Kenntnis der Karstformen in den dinarischen Dolomiten', *Hrv.Geogr.Glasnik* (Zagreb).

[193] *Guide-book of the Congress Excursion through the Dinaric Karst,* 4th International Congress of Speleology, Ljubljana, 1965.

[194] WARWICK, G. T. (1965) 'Influent streams of the south and central Pennines', no. 5 of 'Denudation in Limestone regions: a symposium', *Geogr.J.* **131**, 49–51.

[195] JOHNSON, R. H. (1967) 'Some glacial, periglacial and karstic landforms found in the Sparrowpit–Dove Holes area of North Derbyshire', *East Midland Geographer* (Nottingham) **4** (4), no. 28, 224–38.

[196] MALOTT, C. A. (1945) 'Significant features of the Indiana karst', *Proc.Indiana Acad.Sci.* **54**, 8–24.

[197] KUNSKY, J. (1961) *Macocha a Morasky Kras (Macocha and Moravian Karst),* Československé Akademie Věd, Prague, 367 pp.

[198] GAMS, I. (1965) 'Types of accelerated corrosion', *Prob.Speleol.Res.,Proc.Int.Speleol. Conf., Brno 1964,* 133–9 (Prague).

[199] WARWICK, G. T. (1964) 'Dry valleys of the southern Pennines, England', *Erdkunde* **18**, 116–23.

[200] FAGG, C. C. (1923) 'The recession of the Chalk escarpment', *Proc.Croydon Nat.Hist.Sci.Soc.* **9**, 93–112.

[201] PINCHEMEL, P. (1954) *Les Plaines de Craie* (Paris, Armand Colin) 502 pp.

[202] STANTON, W. I., & FORD, D. C. (1968) 'The geomorphology of the south-central Mendip Hills', *Proc.Geol.Assoc.* **79** (4), 401–27.

[203] RAPP, A. (1960) 'Recent development of mountain slopes in Kärkevagge and surroundings, northern Scandinavia', *Geogr.Ann.* **42**, 65–200.

[204] WARWICK, G. T. (1960) 'The effect of knick-point recession on the water-table and associated features in Limestone regions, with special reference to England and Wales', *Z.Geomorph.,* Supp. 2, 92–9.

[205] WARWICK, G. T. (1950) 'The Reef Limestone caves of the Dove and Manifold valleys', *C.R.G.Newsletter* **31**, 2–6.

(1953) 'The geomorphology of the Dove-Manifold region., unpublished Ph.D. thesis, University of Birmingham.

(1955) 'Polycyclic swallow holes in the Manifold Valley, Staffordshire', *Proc.1st Int. Congr.Speleol.,Paris 1953,* **2**, 59–68.

[206] TRATMAN, E. K. (1963) 'The hydrology of the Burrington area, Somerset', *Proc.Univ.Bristol Speleol.Soc.* **10** (1), 22–57.

[207] (1962) 'Kraska terminologija (Karst terminology)', *Geogr.Vestnik Ljubljana* **34**, 115–37.

[208] MALOTT, C. A. (1932) 'Lost River at Wesley Chapel Gulf, Orange County, Indiana', *Proc. Indiana Acad.Sci.* **41**, 285–316.

[209] FORD, D. C. (1965) 'The origin of limestone caverns: a model from the central Mendip Hills, England', *Bull.Nat.Speleol.Soc.Amer.* **27**, 109–32.

[210] BROWN, M. C. (1966) *The 1965-6 Karst Hydrology Expedition to Jamaica. Full Report* (privately printed).

[211] TRATMAN, E. K., & OLLIER, C. D. (1956) 'The Geomorphology of the caves of N.W. Clare, Ireland', *Proc.Univ.Bristol Speleol.Soc.* **7**, 138–57.

[212] MARTEL, E. A. (1928, 1930) *La France Ignorée,* vols I and II (Paris, Delagrave) 600 pp.

[213] MARTEL, E. A. (1936) *Les Causses Majèurs* (Millau, Ed. Artières et Maury) 510 pp.

[214] LEHMANN, O. (1932) 'Die Hydrographie des Karstes', *Enzyklopädie der Erdkunde* (ed. O. Kende) (Leipzig and Vienna, Deuticke). See also:

(1922) 'Morphologische Beobachtungen in der Eisriesenwelt im Tennengebirge', *Speleol. Jahrb.* (Vienna) **3**, 52–121.

(1926) 'Eisriesenwelt im Tennengebirge. Morphologische Beobachtungen', *Speleol. Mon.* (Vienna) **6**.

(1927) 'Das Tote Gebirge als Hochkarst',

Mitt.Geogr.Ges.Wien **70**, 201–42.

(1931) 'Über die Karstdolinen', *Mitt.Geogr. Ethnogr.Ges.* (Zürich) **31**, 43–71.

(1931) 'Besprechung der Arbeit H. G. Lindner's *Das Karrenphänomen*', *Z.Geomorph.* (Leipzig) **6**, 31–5.

[215] DAVIS, W. M. (1930) 'Origin of limestone caverns', *Bull.Geol.Soc.Amer.* **41**, 475–628.

[216] BRETZ, J. H. (1942) 'Vadose and phreatic features of limestone caverns', *J.Geol.* **50**, 675–811.

[217] Bulletins of the National Speleological Society of America.

[218] ROGLIč, J. (1965) 'The depth of the fissure circulation of water and the evolution of subterranean cavities in the Dinaric Karst', *Prob.Speleol.Res.,Proc.Int.Speleol.Conf.Brno 1964*, 25–36 (Prague).

[219] BRETZ, J. H. (1956) 'Caves of Missouri', *Miss. Geol.Surv. and Water Resources*, ser. 2, **39**.

[220] CURL, R. L. (1964) 'On the definition of a cave', *Bull.Nat.Speleol.Soc.* **26** (1), 1–6.

[221] HOWARD, A. D. (1964) 'Processes of limestone cave development', *Int.J.Speleol.* **1** (1–2), 47–60.

[222] RENAULT, P. (1960) 'Role d'érosion et de la corrosion dans le creusement d'un réseau karstique', *Rev.Geomorph.Dynam.* 1–3.

(1967/68) 'Contributions à l'étude des actions mécaniques et sédimentologiques dans la spéléogenèse', *Ann.Spéléol.* **22** and **23**.

[223] WHITE, W. B., & LONGYEAR, J. (1962) 'Some limitations on speleogenetic speculation imposed by the hydraulics of groundwater flow in limestones': abstract in *Bull.Nat.Speleol. Soc.* **20** (8), pt 2; complete text in *Nittany Grotto Newsletter* **10** (9), 155–67.

[224] THRAILKILL, J. V. (1968) 'Chemical and hydrologic factors in the excavation of limestone caves', *Bull.Geol.Soc.Amer.* **79**, 19–46.

[225] GLENNIE, E. A. (1950) 'Further notes on Ogof Ffynnon Ddu', *Trans.C.R.G.* **1** (3), 1–47.

[226] FORD, D. C. (1966) 'Calcium carbonate solution in some central Mendip caves, Somerset', *Proc.Univ.Bristol Speleol.Soc.* **11** (1), 46–53.

[227] TRATMAN, E. K. (ed.) (1969) *Caves of North-West County Clare,* by Members of the University of Bristol Speleological Society (Newton Abbot, David & Charles).

[228] *Carlsbad Caverns, New Mexico,* map published by U.S. Geological Survey, 1957, Text by P. T. Hayes.

[229] GAMS, I. (1960) 'Prečni jamski profil in njegova odvisnost od lege skladov', *Naše Jame*, 47–54.

[230] GLENNIE, E. A. (1948) 'Some points relating to Ogof Ffynnon Ddu', *Trans.C.R.G.* **1** (1), 13–25.

[231] MYERS, J. O. (1955) 'Cavern formation in the northern Pennines', *Trans.C.R.G.* **4** (1), 31.

(1948) 'The formation of Yorkshire's caves and potholes', *ibid.* **1**, 26–9.

[232] GLENNIE, E. A. (1952) 'Evidence in caverns of deep freezing during the Ice Age', *C.R.G. Newsletter* **37**, 3–4.

[233] FORD, D. C. (1964) 'On the geomorphic history of G.B. Cave, Charterhouse-on-Mendip, Somerset', *Proc.Univ.Bristol Speleol.Soc.* **10** (2), 151.

[234] ARNBERGER, E. (1954) 'Neue Ergebnisse morphotektonischer Untersuchungen in der Dachstein Mammuthhöhle', *Mitt.Höhlenkommission für 1953* **1**, 68–79.

[235] SWEETING, M. M. (1950) 'Erosion cycles in limestone caverns in the Ingleborough district.', *Geogr.J.* **115**, 63–78.

[236] TRATMAN, E. K. (1957) 'Some problems of solution in caves under vadose conditions', *Trans.C.R.G.* **5** (1), 55–9.

[237] CHEVALIER, P. (1944) 'Distinction morphologique entre deux types d'érosion souterraine', *Rev.Géogr.Alpine* **32**, 475.

(1953) 'Erosion ou corrosion. Essai de contrôle du mode de creusement des réseaux souterrains', *Comm. 1er Congr.Int.Spéléol., Paris*, **2**, 33–9.

[238] BÖGLI, A. (1965) 'Scientific research in the Hölloch, the longest cave of the world', *Prob. Speleol.Res.,Proc.Int.Speleol.Conf.,Brno 1964*, 201–7 (Prague).

[239] GLENNIE, E. A. (1954) 'Artesian flow and cave formation', *Trans.C.R.G.* **3** (1), 55–71.

[240] CHEVALIER, P. (1951) *Subterranean Climbers,* trans. E. M. Hatt (London, Faber & Faber).

[241] CURL, R. L. (1966) 'Scallops and flutes', *Trans. C.R.G.* **7** (2), 121–60.

[242] LANGE, A. (1959) 'Introductory notes on the changing geometry of cave structure', *Cave Studies,* no. 11 (Cave Research Associates, California) 69–90.

[243] GAMS, I. (1962) 'Measurements of corrosion intensity in Slovenia and their geomorphic significance', *Geogr.Vest. Ljubljana*, **34**, 3–20.

[244] POHL, E. R. (1955) 'Vertical shafts in limestone caves', *Nat.Speleol.Soc.Amer., Occ. Paper 2*.

[245] COLEMAN, J. C., & DUNNINGTON, N. J. (1944) 'The Poulnagollum Cave, County Clare,' *Proc.Roy.IrishAcad.* **50B**, 105–32.

COLEMAN, J. C. (1965), *The Caves of Ireland* (Tralee, Anvil Books), 88 pp.

[246] PIERRE, D. ST (1966) 'The caves of Graatadalen, northern Norway', Report of the South-West Essex Technical College Caving Club Expedition, 1963-5, *Trans.C.R.G.* **8** (1).

[247] BLEAHU, M. (1965) 'Sur les confluences souterraines', *Int.J.Speleol.* (Weinheim) **1** (4), 441-59.

[248] POWELL, R. L. (1966) 'Groundwater movement and cavern development in the Chester Series in Indiana', *Proc.Indiana Acad.Sci.* **75**, 210-15.

[249] SWINNERTON, A. C. (1932) 'Origin of limestone caverns', *Bull.Geol.Soc.Amer.* **43**, 663-94.

[250] RHOADES, R., & SINACORI, M. N. (1941) 'The pattern of groundwater flow and solution', *J.Geol.* **49**, 785-94.

[251] GLENNIE, E. A. (1954) 'Artesian flow and cave formation', *Trans.C.R.G.* **3** (1), 55-71.

[252] FOLEY, I. (1936) 'Lost John's Cave', *Yorkshire Ramblers Club Journal* **6**, 44.

[253] FORD, T. D. (1967) *Ingleborough Cavern* (Dalesman Publishing Co., Clapham, Yorks.).

[254] DROPPA, A. (1966) *The Correlation of Some Horizontal Caves with River Terraces*, Studies in Speleology, Assoc. of the Pengelly Cave Research Centre, **1** (4), 186-92.

[255] JENNINGS, J. N. (1964) 'Bungonia Caves and rejuvenation', *Helictite* **3** (4), 79-84.

[256] EK, C. (1961) 'Les terrasses de l'Ourthe et de l'Amblève inférieures', *Ann.Soc.Geol.Belge* **80**, 333-53.

[257] WOLFE, T. E. (1962) *An Investigation of the Controls of Cavern Development in the Greenbrier Limestones of Southeastern West Virginia* Unpubl. Thesis (University of Pittsburgh).

[258] DAVIES, W. E. (1960) 'The origin of caves in folded limestones', *Bull.Nat.Speleol.Soc.* **22**, 15-18.

[259] MERRILL, G. K. (1960) 'Additional notes on vertical shafts in limestone caves', *Bull.Nat. Speleol.Soc.* **22** (2), 101-8.

[260] WILLIAMS, P. W. (1966) 'Morphometric analysis of temperate karst landforms', *Irish Speleol.* **1**, 23-31.

[261] MALOTT, C. A. (1921) 'A subterranean cut-off and other subterranean phenomena along Indian Creek, Laurence Co., Indiana', *Proc. Indiana Acad.Sci.* **31**, 203-10.

[262] MALOTT, C. A., & SHROCK, R. R. (1930) 'Origin and development of Natural Bridge, Virginia', *Amer.J.Sci.* **21** (9), 257-73.

[263] WISSMAN, H. VON (1957) 'Karsterscheinungen in Hadramaut', in *Geomorphologische Studien* by F. Machatschek, 259-68; *Petermanns Geogr. Mitt., Erg.* 262.

[264] JENNINGS, J. N. (1963) 'Some geomorphological problems of the Nullarbor Plain', *Trans.Roy.Soc.S.Australia* **87**, 41-62.

[265] FORD, D. C. (1963) 'Aspects of the geomorphology of the Mendip Hills', unpublished D.Phil. thesis.

[266] BUTZER, K. W. (1965) *Environment and Archaeology* (London, Methuen).

[267] TELL, L. (1962) 'Lummelunda: un endroit karstique encore actif dans les chaux siluriennes de l'île de Gotland', *Proc.2nd Int.Congr. Speleol., Bari-Lecce-Salerno 1958*, **1**, 106-27.

[268] TERZAGHI, K. (1913) 'Beitrag zur Hydrographie und Morphologie des Kroatischen Karstes', *Mitt.Jahrb.K.Ungar.Geol.Reichsanst.* 307-8.

[269] RENWICK, K. (1962) 'The age of caves by solution', *Cave Sci.* **32**, 338-49.

[270] HANNA, F. K. (1966) 'A technique for measuring the rate of erosion of cave passages', *Proc.Univ.Bristol Speleol. Soc.* **11**, 83-6.

[271] CAHOUX, J. (1957) *1000 Metres Down* (London, Allen & Unwin).

[272] CVIJIČ, J. (1918) 'Hydrographie souterraine et évolution morphologique du Karst', *Rec. Trav.Inst.Geogr.Alpine*, 375-426.

[273] THRAILKILL, J. V. (1965) 'Origin of cave popcorn', *Bull.Nat.Speleol.Soc.* **27** (2), 59.

[274] DEAL, D. E. (1962) 'Geology of Jewel Cave National Monument, Custer County, S. Dakota, with special reference to cavern formation in the Black Hills', Master's thesis, University of Wyoming.

[275] GAMS, I. (1965) 'La Grotte de Postojna' from *Guide-book of the Congress Excursion through the Dinaric Karst*, 4th Internat. Congr. Speleol.

[276] JENNINGS, J. N., & SWEETING, M. M. (1963) 'The Tunnel, a cave in the Napier Range, Fitzroy Basin, Western Australia', *Trans. C.R.G.* **6**, 53-68.

[277] GLENNIE, E. A. (1952) 'Vertical development in caverns', *Trans.C.R.G.* **2**, 75-93.

[278] GLENNIE, E. A. (1964) 'The Pohl cell: a unique cave system', *C.R.G.Newsletter* 90/91, 9-11.

[279] EYRE, J. (1966) 'Proventina', *C.R.G. Newsletter* 104, 10-3.

[280] GAMS, I. (1966) 'Faktorji in dinamika korozije na karbonatnih kemeninah slovenskega dinarskega krasa', *Geogr.Vestnik Ljubljana* **38**, 11-68.

[281] MISKOVSKY, J. C. (1966) 'Les principaux types de dépôts des grottes, et les problèmes que pose leur étude', *Rev.Géomorph.Dynam.* **16** (1), 1–11.

[282] DAVIES, W. E. (1951) 'Mechanics of cavern breakdown', *Bull.Nat.Speleol.Soc.* **13**, 36–42.

[283] SWEETING, M. M., unpublished manuscript on the Bezez Cave, Lebanon.

[284] JENNINGS, J. N. (1962) 'The limestone geomorphology of the Nullarbor Plain, Australia', *Proc.2nd Int.Congr.Speleol., Bari 1958*, 371–86.

[285] MONROE, W. H. (1962) 'Geology of the Manati Quadrangle, Puerto Rico', *U.S.Geol. Surv., Misc.Geol.Inv.* Map 1–334.

[286] SUTCLIFFE, A. J. (1957) 'Cave fauna and cave sediments', unpublished thesis, University of London.

[287] WHITE, W. B., & WHITE, E. L. (1964) 'Processes of cavern breakdown', *Bull.Nat. Speleol.Soc.* **26**.

[288] BRUCKER, R. W. (1966) 'Truncated cave passages and terminal breakdown in the Central Kentucky karst', *Bull.Nat.Speleol.Soc.* **28** (4), 171–8.

[289] WHITE, W. B. (1962), Symposium on Cave Mineralogy, *Bull.Nat.Speleol.Soc.* **24** (2), 53–106.

[290] CAVAILLÉ, A. (1963) 'L'age des Grottes du Quercy', *Proc.3rd Int.Congr.Speleol.Vienna*, 153–62.

[291] WARWICK, G. T. (1962) in *British Caving : An Introduction to Speleology* (ed. C. H. D. Cullingford), pt 1, chap. 4, 83–119 (London, Routledge & Kegan Paul).

[292] SIFFRE, M. (1959) 'Alluvions souterraines', *Stalactite* **4** (3), 55–62.

[293] BRAIN, C. K. (1958) *The Transvaal Ape-Men-Bearing Cave Deposits*, Transvaal Museum, Pretoria, Mem. 11.

[294] WARWICK, G. T. (1961) 'Cave deposits and palaeoclimatology', *Soc.Speleol.Ital.Mem.* **5** (1), 127–50, 182–6.

[295] MOORE, G. W., & NICHOLAS, G. (1964) *Speleology – The Study of Caves* (Boston, D. C. Heath).

[296] HOLLAND, H. D., KIRSION, T. V., HUEBNER, J. S., & OXBURGH, O. M. (1964) 'On some aspects of the chemical evolution of cave waters', *J.Geol.* **72** (1), 36–67.

[297] FRANKE, H. W. (1963) 'Formprinzipien des Tropfsteins', *Proc.3rd Int.Congr.Speleol., Vienna*, **2**, 63.
   (1965) 'The theory behind stalagmite shapes', *Stud.Speleol.London*, **1** (2–3), 89–95.

[298] MOORE, G. W. (1962) 'The growth of stalactites', *Bull.Nat.Spel.Soc.* **24** (2), 95–104.

[299] KUNSKY, J. (1957) 'Thermomineral karst and caves of Zbrašov, northern Moravia', *Zvlastni Otisk Sborn.Československ.Spol.Zeměpisné* (Prague) **62** (4), 306–51.

[300] WELLS, A. W. (1968) 'Stalactites', *C.R.G. Newsletter* 110.

[301] JENNINGS, J. N. & SWEETING, M. M. (1966) 'Old Napier Downs Cave, West Kimberley, West Australia', *Helictite* **4** (2), 25–32.

[302] GAMS, I. (1968) 'Versuch einer Klassifikation der Tropfsteinformen in der Grotte von Postojna', *Proc. 4th Int.Congr.Speleol., Ljubljana 1965*, **3**, 117–26.

[303] CZAJLIK, I. (1961) 'New results of the detailed hydrological study of the Vass Imre Cave' (in Hungarian: English summary), *Karszt-és Barlangkutatas*, **3**, 3–19.

[304] MALOTT, C. A., & SHROCK, R. R. (1933) 'Mud stalagmites', *Amer.J.Sci.*, ser. 5, **25**, 55–60.

[305] WARWICK, G. T. (1952) 'Rimstone pools and associated phenomena', *Trans.C.R.G.* **2** (2), 149–65.

[306] MOORE, G. W. (1954) *The Origin of Helictites*, Nat. Speleol. Soc. Occ. Paper 1.

[307] PRINZ, W. (1908) 'La cristallisation des grottes de Belgique', *Nouv.Mém.Soc.Belge Géol.* (Brussels), 1–90.

[308] GÈZE, B. (1957) *Les Cristallisations Excentriques de la Grotte de Moulis* (Paris, C.N.R.S.).

[309] MOORE, G. W. (1956) 'Aragonite speleotherms as indications of palaeotemperature', *Amer.J. Sci.* **254**, 746–53.

[310] GÈZE, B. (1955) 'À propos Mondmilch', *Bull. Comm.Nat.Spéléol.* **5** (3), 2–5.

[311] KING, L. C. (1951) 'The geology of the Makapan and other Transvaal caves', *Trans. Roy.Soc.S.A.* **33**, 121–51.

[312] CVIJIČ, J. (1901) 'Morphologische und glaciale Studien aus Bosnien, der Hercegovina und Montenegro: die Karst-Poljen', *Abhand.Geol. Ges.Wien* **2**.

[313] ROGLIČ, J. (1965) 'The delimitation and morphological types of the Dinaric Karst', *Naše Jame* **7** (1–2), 12–20.

[314] MELIK, A. (1935) 'Slovenija', *Slovenska Matrica* (Ljubljana) **1**, 1.

[315] ROGLIČ, J. (1940) *Geomorphologische Studie über Duvanjsko Polje (Polje von Duvno) in Bosnien* (Geographische Gesellschaft Wien).

[316] ROGLIČ, J. (1964) 'Les poljés du karst dinarique et les modifications climatiques du quaternaire', *Rev.Belge Géogr.* **88**, 105–25.

[317] ROGLIČ, J. (1939) 'Morphologie der Poljen von Kupres und Vukovsko', *Z.Ges.Erdkunde* (Berlin) **7/8**, 299–316.

(1951) 'Unsko-Koranska zaravan i Plitvicka Jezera, geomorfoloska promatranja (La surface de l'Una et de la Korana et les lacs de Plitvice, étude de géomorphologie), *Geogr.Glasnik* (Zagreb) **13**, 49–68 (C.R. 1953, *Geogr.Vestnik* **25**, by Sv. Ilesic).

[318] TERZAGHI, K. (1913) 'Beiträge zur Hydrographie und Morphologie des Kroatischen Karstes', *Mitt.Jahrb.K.Ung.Geol.Reichsanst.* (Budapest) **20**, 225–369.

[319] KAYSER, K. (1955) 'Karstrandebene und Poljeboden. Zur Frage der Entstehung der Einebnungsflächen im Karst', *Erdkunde* **9**, 60–4.

[320] GROLLER, M. VON (1897) 'Das Popovo polje in Hercegovina', *Mitt.K.K.Geogr.Ges.Wien.*

[321] LOUIS, H. (1956) 'Die Entstehung der Poljen und ihre Stellung in der Karstabtragung – auf Grund von Beobachtungen im Taurus', *Erdkunde* **10**, 33–53.

[322] LEHMANN, H. (1959) 'Studien über Poljen in den Venezianischen Voralpen und im Hochapennin', *Erdkunde* **13**, 258–89.

[323] NICOD, J. (1967) *Recherches morphologiques en Basse-Provence Calcaire* (Imprimerie Louis-Jean, Gap), 557 pp.

[324] JENNINGS, J. N., & MABOTT, J. D. (eds.) (1967) *Landform Studies in Australia* (Cambridge University Press).

[325] (1954) I.G.U. Karst Commission, Frankfurt.

[326] ZANS, V. A. (1951) 'On karst hydrology in Jamaica', *Un.Geod.Geophys.Int.Hydrol.Sc.Assemb.Gen., Bruxelles,* **2**, 267–79.

[327] KAYSER, K. (1934) 'Morphologische Studien in Westmontenegro: 11. Die Rumpftreppe von Cetinje und der Formenschatz der Karstabtragung', *Z.Ges.Erdkunde* (Berlin), 26–49, 81–102.

[328] SWEETING, M. M. (1953) 'The enclosed depression of Carran, Co. Clare', *Irish Geogr.* **2** (5), 218–24.

[329] FREEMAN, T. W. (1950) *Ireland* (London, Methuen).

[330] SWEETING, M. M. (1955) 'The landforms of N.W. County Clare, Ireland', *Trans.Inst.Brit. Geog.*, Publ. 21, 33–49.

[331] PALOC, H. (1970) 'Connaissances actuelles sur la Fontaine de Vaucluse', *Méditerranée,* **7**, 75–82.

[332] THORNBURY, W. D. (1965) *Regional Geomorphology of the United States* (New York and London, John Wiley) 45–50.

[333] BINDER, H. (1960) 'Die Wasserfühung der Lone', *Karst und Höhlenkunde* (Stuttgart) **7**, 211–48.

[334] POWELL, R. L. (1963) 'Alluviated cave springs of south-central Indiana', *Proc.Indiana Acad. Sci.* **72**, 182–9.

[335] GÈZE, B. (1962) 'Sur quelques caractères fondamentaux des circulations karstiques', *Proc.2nd Int.Congr.Speleol., Bari-Lecce-Salerno 1958,* **1**, 3–22.

[336] STEVENS, G. (1964) 'Intermittent springs', *Trans.C.R.G.* **7** (1), 3–9.

[337] HOUSMAN, J. (1800) *A Descriptive Tour and Guide to the Lakes, Caves, etc. of Cumberland, Westmorland and Parts of the West Riding of Yorkshire* (ref. to J. Swainston).

(1804) Paper, *Lit.Phil.Soc.Manchester.*

[338] MYERS, J. O. (1962) in *British Caving: An Introduction to Speleology* (ed. C. H. D. Cullingford), pt 1, chap. 7, 226–57 (London, Routledge & Kegan Paul).

[339] STRINGFIELD, V. T. (1964) 'Relation of surface-water hydrology to the principal artesian aquifer in Florida and southeastern Georgia', *U.S.Geol.Surv.Prof.Paper* 501-C, 164–9.

[340] JENKO, F. (1959) *Hidrologija in vodno gospodarstvo kras* (Ljubljana).

[341] MAURIN, V., & ZÖTL, J. (1960) 'Karsthydrologische Aufnahmen auf Kephallonia (Ionische Inseln)', *Steierische Beiträge zur Hydrogeologie* (Gtaz) **1**.

(1967) 'Salt-water encroachment in the low-altitude karst water horizons of the island of Kephallonia (Ionian Islands)', *Proc.Dubrovnik Symposium 1965* (Paris, A.I.H.S.-Unesco).

[342] CORBEL, J., *et al.* (1965) 'Chemical erosion in the Moravian karst', *Prob.Speleol.Res., Proc. Int.Speleol.Conf., Brno 1964*, 107–24 (Prague). See also:

RAUŠER, J., ŠTELCL, O. & VLČEK, V. (1965) 'Principal characteristics of karst water in the Central European area according to the results of research from the Moravian karst', *Prob. Speleol.Res., Proc.Int.Speleol.Conf.Brno 1964*, 85–105 (Prague).

[343] KANAET, T. (1963) 'Température des sources par rapport a la structure petrographique', *Geogr.Pregled.Sarajevo,* **7**.

[344] RICHARDSON, D. T. (1968) 'The use of chemical analysis of cave waters as a method of water tracing and indicator of type of strata traversed', *Trans.C.R.G.* **10** (2), 61–72.

[345] DREW, D. P. (1968) 'Tracing percolation

waters in karst areas', from 'Symposium on cave hydrology and water-tracing', *Trans. C.R.G.* **10** (2), 107–14.

[346] ASHTON, K. (1966) 'The analysis of flow data from karst drainage systems', *Trans.C.R.G.* **7** (2), 163–203.

[347] PITTY, A. F. (1968) 'Calcium carbonate content of karst water in relation to flow-through time', *Nature* **217**, 939–40.

[348] PITTY, A. F. (1968) 'Some notes on the use of calcium hardness measurements in studies of cave hydrology', *Trans.C.R.G.* **10** (2), 115–20.

[349] ZÖTL, J., & MAURIN, V. (1965) 'Tasks and results of karst hydrology', *Prob.Speleol.Res., Proc.Int.Speleol.Conf., Brno 1964*, 141–5 (Prague).

[350] BURDON, D. J., & DOUNAS, A. (1961) 'Hydrochemistry of the Parnassos–Ghiana aquifers, and problems of sea-water contamination in Greece', paper on Groundwater Resources, Unesco.

[351] BURDON, D. J. (1967) 'Hydrogeology of some karstic areas of Greece', *Proc.Dubrovnik Symposium 1965*, 308–17 (Paris, A.I.H.S.-Unesco).

[352] SWEETING, M. M. (1968) 'Some variations in the types of limestone and their relations to cave formation', *Proc.4th Int.Congr.Speleol., Ljubljana 1965*, **3**, 227–32.

[353] (1902) 'The underground waters of north-west Yorkshire, Part 1', *Proc.Yorks.Geol.Soc.* **14**, 1–48.

(1905) 'The underground waters of north-west Yorkshire, Part 2', ibid. **15**, 248–92.

[354] BURDON, D. J., & MAZLOUM, S. (1959) 'Some chemical types of ground-water from Syria', *Salinity Problems in the Arid Zones*, F.A.O. (Unesco).

[355] CULLINGFORD, C. H. D. (ed.) (1962) *British Caving – An Introduction to Speleology* (London, Routledge & Kegan Paul).

[356] JENNINGS, J, N, and SWEETING, M. M. (1959) 'Underground branch of a divide at Mole Creek, Tasmania', *Austral.J.Sci.* **21**, 261–2.

[357] MARSTON, T. K., et al. (1962) Articles on 'Rhodamine B', *C.R.G. Newsletter* 84,. 4–19.

[358] BUCHTELA, K., et al. (1968) 'Comparative investigations into recent methods of tracing subterranean waters', *Nat.Speleol.Soc.Bull.* (U.S.A.) **30** (3), 55–74.

(1964) 'Comparative investigations into new methods for the observation of subterranean waters' (in German), *Die Wasserwirtschaft* (Stuttgart).

[359] ZÖTL, J. (1958) 'Beitrag zu den Problemen der Karsthydrographie mit besonderer Berücksichtigung der Frage des Erosionsniveaus', *Mitt. Geogr. Ges. Wien, Festschr. H. Spreitzer* **100**, 1 and 2.

& MAURIN, V. (1959) 'Die Untersuchung der Zusammenhänge unterirdischer Wässer mit besonderer Berücksichtigung der Karstverhältnisse', *Steierische Beiträge zur Hydrogeologie* (Graz), 184 pp.

[360] GLENNIE, E. A. (1952) 'Ogof Ffynnon Ddu', *C.R.G. Newsletter* 4, 2.

[361] WILCOCK, J. D. (1968) 'Some developments in the pulse-train analysis', *Trans.C.R.G.* **10** (2), 73–98.

[362] ASHTON, K. (1968) 'Hydrological analysis applied to tropical karst', *Proc.4th Int.Congr. Speleol., Ljubljana 1965*, **3**, 13–16.

[363] ASHTON, K. (1967) 'Report of the 1963 expedition of the University of Leeds to Jamaica', *Trans.C.R.G.* **9**, 1.

[364] KATZER, F. (1909) *Karst und Karsthydrographie*, Zur Kunde der Balkanhalbinsel, no. 8 (Sarajevo).

[365] FÉNELON, P. (1954) 'Le relief karstique', *Norois* **1**, 51–77.

[366] ROGLIČ, J. (1961) 'Razvoj Cvijičeve misli o krsu' (The development of Cvijič's concept of the Karst), *Geogr.Glasnik* (Zagreb) **23**, 37–53.

[367] KING, F. H. (1899) 'Principles and conditions of the movements of ground-water', *U.S.Geol. Surv., 19th Ann.Rep.* **2**, 59–294.

[368] MILOJEVIĆ, B. Z. (1922) *Quelques Remarques au Sujet de l'Erosion Karstique*, Spomenica pedesetgodisnjice professorskog rada S. M. Lozanica, priredili prijatelji i postovanci (Beograd) 123–6.

[369] BAUCIČ, I. (1965) 'Hydrological characteristics of the Dinaric karst in Croatia with special regard to the underground water connection', *Naše Jame* **7** (1–2), 61–72.

[370] JENKO, F. (1967) 'L'hydrographie du Karst', *Proc.Dubrovnik Symposium 1965, Hydrology of Fractured Rocks* **1**, 172–82 (Paris, A.I.H.S.-Unesco).

[371] EYRE, J., & ASHMEAD, P. (1967) 'Lancaster Hole and Ease Gill Caverns, Westmorland', *Trans.C.R.G.* **9** (2), 65–123.

[372] GLENNIE, E. A. (1954) 'Artesian flow and cave formation', *Trans.C.R.G.* **3** (1), 55–71.

[373] Personal communication.

[374] DREW, D. P. (1966) 'The water-table concept in limestones', *Proc.Brit.Spel.Assoc.* **4**, 57–67.

[375] FORD, D. C. (1965) 'The origin of limestone caverns: a model from the central Mendip Hills, England', *Bull.Nat.Speleol.Soc.Amer.* **27**, 109–32.

[376] ZÖTL, J. (1961) 'Die Hydrographie des nordostalpinen Karstes', *Steierische Beitr.Hydrogeol.* (Graz) 1960–1, **2**, 54–183.

[377] BÖGLI, A. (1966) 'Karstwasserfläche und unterindische Karstaiveaus', *Erdkunde* **20**, 11–19.

[378] MOORE, G. M. (1960) 'The origin of limestone caves', *Bull.Nat.Speleol.Soc.* **22** (1), 3–4.

[379] Personal communication.

[380] WOZAB, D. H., & WILLIAMS, J. B. (1967) 'Flow problems in limestone plains, Jamaica, W.I. – a progress report', *Proc.Dubrovnik Symposium 1965, Hydrology of Fractured Rocks* **1**, 407 (Paris, A.I.H.S.-Unesco).

[381] SOKOLOV, D. S. (1967) 'Hydrodynamic zoning of karst water', *Proc.Dubrovnik Symposium 1965, Hydrology of Fractured Rocks* **1**, 204 (Paris, A.I.H.S.-Unesco).

[382] CVIJIČ, J. (1924) 'Types morphologiques de terrains calcaires', *Glasnik Geogr.Društva* (Beograd) **10**, 1–7.

[383] SAWICKI, L. S. (1909) 'Ein Beitrag zum geographischen Zyklos im Karst', *Geogr.Z.* (Vienna) **15**, 185–204, 259–81.

[384] PELTIER, L. (1950) 'The geographic cycle in periglacial regions as it is related to climatic geomorphology', *Ann.Assoc.Amer.Geogr.* **40**, 214–36.

[385] LEHMANN, H. (1936) 'Morphologische Studien auf Java', *Geogr.Abhand.* (Stuttgart) **3**, 9.

[386] (1956) I.G.U. Karst Commission Report, Rio de Janeiro, 3.

[387] LEHMANN, H. (1956) 'Der Einfluss des Klimas auf die morphologische Entwicklung des Karstes', in *I.G.U. Report of the Commission on Karst Phenomena*, 3–7.

[388] MONROE, W. H. (1964) *Lithological Control in the Development of a Tropical Karst Topography* (U.S. Geol. Surv. in co-operation with Puerto Rico Econ. Devel. Admin.).

[389] GVOZDECKIJ, N. A. (1965) 'Types of Karst in the U.S.S.R.', *Separatum, Prob.Speleol.Res.* (Prague) 47–54.

[390] QUINLAN, J. F. (1966) 'Classification of karst and pseudokarst types: a review and synthesis emphasising the North American literature, 1941-1966', *Paper, 123rd Meeting of Amer. Assoc.Adv.Sci., Symposium on 25 Years of American Speleology.*

[391] PANOŠ, V. (1965) 'Genetic features of a specific type of the Karst in the Central European Climate morphogenetic area', *Prob.Speleol. Res., Proc.Int.Speleol.Conf., Brno 1964*, 11–23 (Prague).

[392] CAVAILLÉ, A. (1953) 'L'érosion actuelle en Quercy', *Rev.Géomorph.Dynam.* **4**, 45–8.

[393] CORBEL, J. (1965) 'Karstes de Yougoslavie et notes sur le karst tchèque et polonais', *Rev.Géogr. de l'Est* **5** (3), 245–94.

[394] BLANC, A. (1958) 'Répertoire bibliographique critique des études de relief karstique en Yougoslavie depuis Jovan Cvijič', *Mém.Cent. Doc.Cart.Géogr.* **7**, 135–227.

[395] BRADLEY, P. S., & FORD, T. D. (ed.) (1968) *Geology of East Midlands* (University of Leicester Press).

[396] PIGOTT, C. D. (1962) 'Soil formation and development on the Carboniferous Limestones of Derbyshire: parent materials', *J.Ecol.* **50**, 145–56.

[397] PITTY, A. F. (1968) 'The scale and significance of solutional loss from the limestone tract of the Southern Pennines', *Proc.Geol.Assoc.* **79** (2), 153–74.

[398] FORD, T. D., & KING, R. J. (1966) 'The Golconda Caverns, Brassington, Derbyshire', *Trans.C.R.G.* **7**, 91–114.

[399] YORK, C. (1961) *The Pocket Deposits of Derbyshire* (Birkenhead, privately printed).

[400] BÖGLI, A. (1964) 'Un exemple de complexe glacio-karstique: le Schichttreppenkarst', *Rev. Belge Géogr.*, Ed. Soc. Roy. Belg. Géogr. Special Publ., *Karst et Climats Froids* **88** (1–2), 63–82.

[401] BÖGLI, A. (1961) 'Karrentische, ein Beitrag zur Karst morphologie', *Z.Geomorph.* **3**, 185–93.

[402] EMBLETON, C., & KING, C. A. M. (1968) *Glacial and Peri-Glacial Geomorphology* (London, Arnold).

[403] PULINA, M. (1960) 'Wroclavska wyprava speleologicana w kras wysokogorski Alp Julijskich (Jugoslavia)', *Czas.Geogr.* **31**, 3.

[404] SWEETING, M. M. (1955) 'The Landforms of North West County Clare, Ireland', *Trans. and Papers, Inst.Brit.Geogr.*, Publ. 21, 33–49.

[405] HULL, E. (1878) *Physical Geography and Geology of Ireland* (London, Stanford).

[406] GAMS, I. (1961) 'Triglavsko Brezno', *Glasilv Društva za Raziskovanije Jan Slovenije* **3**, 1–2.

[407] BARRÈRE, P. (1964) 'Le relief karstique dans l'ouest des Pyrénées centrales', *Rev.Belge Géogr.*, Ed. Soc. Roy. Belge Géogr. Special Publ., *Karst et Climats Froids* **88** (1–2), 9–62.

[408] TELL, L. (1961) 'Erosionsförloppet med särskild hänsyn till Lummelundagrottorna', *Ark. Svensk Grottforsk.* no. 1 (Norrköping, Sweden).

[409] FORD, T. D. (1959) 'The Sutherland caves', *Trans.C.R.G.* **5** (2), 139–89.

[410] BALÁZS, D. (1968) 'Karst regions in Indonesia', *Karszt- és Barlangkutatas* (Budapest) **5**.

[411] DANEŠ, J. V. (1917) 'Karststudien in Australien', *Sitzungsb.K.Böhm.Ges.Wiss.1916*, no. 6, 1–75.

[412] WISSMANN, H. VON (1954) 'Der Karst der humiden heissen und sommerheissen Gebiete Ost-Asiens', *Erdkunde* **8**, 122–30.

[413] LEHMANN, H. (1960) 'La terminologie classique du Karst sous l'aspect critique de la morphologie climatique moderne', *Extr., Rev. Géogr.Lyon* **35**, 1.

[414] FLATHE, H., & PFEIFFER, D. (1965) 'Grundzüge der Morphologie, Geologie und Hydrogeologie im Karstgebiet Gunung Sewu (Java, Indonesien)', *Geol.Jahrb., Hannover* **83**, 533–62.

[415] LEHMANN, O. (1925) 'Die geographischen Ergebnisse der Reise durch Guidschon, Expedition Dr Handel Mazzettis 1914–1918', *Denkschr. Akad.Wiss.Wien,Math.-Nat.Kl.* **100**.

[416] SILAR, J. (1965) 'Development of tower karst of China and North Vietnam', *Bull.Nat. Speleol.Soc.* **27** (2), 35–46.

[417] AUB, C. F. T. (1964) 'The Cockpits of Jamaica', unpublished paper to Karst Symposium of the I.G.U., Seattle.

[418] MEYERHOFF, H. A. (1933) *Geology of Puerto Rico*, Puerto Rico Univ. Monograph, ser. B, no. 1.

[419] VERSTAPPEN, H. T. L. (1960) 'Some observations on karst development in the Malay Archipelago', *J.Trop.Geogr.* **14**, 1–10.

[420] JENNINGS, J. N., & BIK, M. (1962) 'Karst morphology in Australian New Guinea', *Nature* **194**, 1036–8.

[421] VERSTAPPEN, H. T. L. (1964) 'Karst morphology of the Star Mountains (central New Guinea) and its relation to lithology and climate', *Z.Geomorph.* **8** (1), 40–9.

[422] PANOŠ, V., & STELCL, O. (1968) 'Problems of the conical karst in Cuba', *4th Int.Congr. Speleol., Ljubljana 1965*, **3**, 533–55.

[423] HUBBARD, B. (1923) 'The geology of the Lares district, Puerto Rico', *N.Y.Acad.Sci., Scientific Survey of Puerto Rico and the Virgin Islands* **2** (1), 115.

[424] THORP, J. (1934) 'The asymmetry of the "Pepino hills" of Puerto Rico in relation to the trade winds', *J.Geol.* **42**, 537–45.

[425] MONROE, W. H. (1964) 'Origin and interior structure of mogotes of northern Puerto Rico', *20th Int.Geogr.Congr., London*.
(1966) 'Formation of tropical karst topography by limestone solution and reprecipitation', *Caribb.J.Sci.* **6** (1–2), 1–7.

[426] PANOŠ, V., & ŠTELCL, O. (1968) 'Physiographic and geologic control in development of Cuban mogotes', *Z.Geomorph.*, N.F., **12** (2), 117–63.

[427] BALÁZS, D. (1962) 'Beiträge zur Speläologie des südchinesischen Karstgebietes', *Karszt- és Barlangkutatas* (Budapest) **2**, 3–82.

[428] PATON, J. R. (1963) 'The origin of the limestone hills of Malaya', *J.Trop.Geogr.* 134–47.

[429] MONROE, W. H. (1964) *Origin of the Mogotes of Puerto Rico* (London, I.G.U.).
(1964) *Lithological Control in the Formation of the Towers of Puerto Rico* (London, I.G.U.).

[430] WILFORD, G. E. (1964) *The Geology of Sarawak and Sabah Caves,* Borneo Reg. Malaysia Geol. Survey Bull. 6.

[431] WILFORD, G. E. (1965) *Penrissen Area, West Sarawak, Malaysia, Explanation of Sheets 0–110–2, 1–110–13 and 1–110–14*, Borneo Reg. Malaysia Geol. Survey Rep. 2.

[432] WILFORD, G. E., & WALL, J. R. D. (1965) 'Karst topography in Sarawak', *J.Trop.Geogr.* **21**, 44–70.

[433] WILFORD, G. E., & WALL, J. R. D. (1966) 'Two small-scale solution features of limestone outcrops in Sarawak, Malaysia', *Z.Geomorph.*, N.F., **10**, 90–4.

[434] Personal communication.

[435] COTTON, C. A. (1948) *Landscape as Developed by the Process of Normal Erosion*, 2nd ed. (Cambridge).

[436] BLONDEL, F. (1929) *Les Phénomènes Karstiques en Indochine Française*, Bull. Service Géologique de l'Indochine, Hanoi.

[437] CUISINIER, L. (1929) 'Régions calcaires de l'Indochine', *Ann.Géogr.* **38**, 266–73.

[438] CRESSEY, G. B. (1955) *Land of the 500 Million : A Geography of China*, 223–5 (New York, McGraw-Hill).

[439] SWEETING, M. M., & JENNINGS, J. N. (1961) 'Caliche pseudo-anticlines in the Fitzroy Basin, Western Australia', *Amer.J.Sci.* **259**, 635–9.

[440] BAULIG, H. (1928) *Le Plateau Central de la France et sa Bordure Méditerranéenne* (Paris, Colin).

[441] QUINLAN, J. F., private publication.

[442] GVOZDECKIJ, N. A. (1965) 'Types of Karst in the U.S.S.R.', chapter in *Types of Karst of*

Northern Caucasus, 47–54 (Moscow).
(1954) *Karst* (Moscow).
(1959) *Speleology and Studies in Karst,* Proc. Conference on Speleology and Karst, 1958 (Moscow).

[443] FREY, M. (1967) 'Excursion to the Mendips', I.B.G., Bristol (unpublished).

[444] FÉNELON, P. (1965) 'Evolution des versants calcaires dans les Cravens (Yorkshire)', *Bull. Assoc.Géogr.Française*, no. 33–333, 2–14.

[445] CHARLESWORTH, J. K. (1955) *The Geology of Ireland : An Introduction* (Edinburgh, Oliver & Boyd).

[446] GILEWSKA, S. (1965) 'The evolution of karst phenomena in the southern part of the Silesian Upland', *Prob.Speleol.Res., Proc.Int.Speleol. Conf., Brno 1964*, 37–45 (Prague).

[447] GILEWSKA, S. (1964) 'Fossil karst in Poland', *Erdkunde* **18,** 124–35.

[448] ZÖTL, J. (1966) 'Ein fossiler semi-arider tropischer Karst auf Ithaka', *Erdkunde* **20** (3), 204–8.

[449] JENNINGS, J. N., & SWEETING, M. M. (1966) 'Old Napier Downs Cave, West Kimberley, Western Australia', *Helictite* **4** (2), 25–31.

[450] BUDEL, J. (1951) 'Fossiler Tropenkarst in dem Schwäbischen Alb und den Ostalpen', *Erdkunde* **5,** 168–70.

[451] SPÖCKER, R. G. (1952) *Zur Landschaftsentwicklung im Karst des oberen und mittleren Pegnitz-Gebietes* (Remagen, Verlag des Amtes für Landeskunde).

[452] DONGUS, H. (1962) 'Alte Landuberflächen der Ostalb', *Forschungen zur Deutschen Landeskunde,* **134** (Bad Godesberg) 71 pp.

[453] PANOŠ, V. (1964) 'Der Urkarst im Ostflügel der Böhmischen Masse', *Z.Geomorph.*, N.F., **8** (2), 105–62.

[454] SZABÓ, P. Z. (1960) 'Karstic Landscape Forms in Hungary in the Light of Climate Studies in Hungary', *Geogr.Sci.* (Budapest).

[455] Personal communication.

[456] JENNINGS, J. N. (1968) 'Syngenetic Karst in Australia', in *Contributions to the Study of Karst,* 41–110 (University of Canberra Press).

[457] MANDEL, S. (1967) 'A conceptual model of karstic erosion by groundwater', in *Proc. Dubrovnik Symposium, Hydrology of Fractured Rocks* **2,** 662–4 (Paris, A.I.H.S.-Unesco).

[458] WALL, J. R. D., & WILFORD, G. E. (1966) 'A comparison of small-scale solution features on micro-granodiorite and limestone in West Sarawak, Malaysia', *Z. Geomorph.*, NF **10,** 462–8.

[459] CUNNINGHAM, F. F. (1965) 'Tor theories in the light of South Pennine evidence', *East Midland Geogr.* **3** (8), no. 24, 424–33.

[460] KUNSKY, J. (1957) 'Types of pseudokarst phenomena in Czechoslovakia', *Czechoslovensky Kras,* **10** (3), 111–25.

[461] FÉNELON, P. (1964) *Commission des Phénomènes Karstiques – Rapport Quadriennal 1960–4* (Com. Nat. Géogr.).

[462] SMITH, W. C. (1956) 'A review of some problems of African carbonatites', *Q.J.Geol. Soc.* **112** (2), 189–219.

[463] DAVIS, W. M. (1909) 'Excursion in Bosnia', *Proc.Acad.Philadelphia.*

[464] RICHTER, E. (1907) 'Beiträge zur Landeskunde Bosniens und Herzegovina', *Wiss.Mitt. aus Bosnien und Herzegovina* (Vienna).

[465] KREBS, N. (1929) 'Inselberge und Ebenheiten im Karst', *Z.Ges.Erdkunde* (Berlin) **67,** 87–94.

[466] SANDERS, E. M. (1921) 'The cycle of erosion in a karst region (after Cvijič)', *Amer.Geogr. Rev.,* 593–604.

[467] Personal communication.

[468] ARONIS, G., BURDON, D. J., & ZERIS, K. (1961) *Development of a Karst Limestone Spring in Greece*, Report for Unesco, Groundwater Resources, Athens.

[469] PAPAKIS, N., & SWEETING, M. M. (1961) *Methods of Investigating the Groundwater Resources of the Parnassos-Ghiona Limestones,* Unesco Groundwater Resources, Athens.

[470] (1965) *Guide-book of the Congress Excursion through the Dinaric Karst,* 4th International Congress of Speleology in Yugoslavia, Ljubljana 1965.

[471] FINCHAM, A., & ASHTON, K. (1967) 'The University of Leeds Hydrological Survey Expedition to Jamaica, 1963', *Trans.C.R.G.* **9,** 1–60.

[472] SMITH, D. I. (ed.) (1969) 'Limestone geomorphology in Jamaica: University of Bristol Karst Hydrology Expedition to Jamaica 1967', *J.Brit.Speleol.Assoc. Cave Science* **6** (3–4).

[473] BROWN, M. C. (1966) *Karst Hydrology Expedition to Jamaica, 1965–6* (privately published).

[474] ZANS, V. A. (1956) 'The origin of the bauxite deposits of Jamaica', *20th Int.Geol.Congr., Mexico, 1956, Res.Trab.Present.,* 108.

[475] CLOZIER, R. (1931) 'Les surfaces d'aplanissement des Causses du Quercy', *C.R.Congr.Geol. Paris* **2,** 461–7.

[476] SCRIVENOR, J. B. (1913) 'The geology and mining industries of the Kinta District', *Perak, F.M.S., Geol.Surv.Mem.,* old series.

[477] FÉNELON, P. (1968) Publication of the Centre National de la Recherche Scientifique, Mémoires et Documents, *Phénomènes Karstiques,* **4,** 9–68.

[478] TROMBE, F. (1952) *Traité de Spéléologie* (Paris, Payot).

[479] CASTERET, N. (1939) *Ten Years under the Earth* (London, Dent).

[480] MONROE, W. H. (1970) 'A Glossary of Karst Terminology', *U.S.Geol.Survey Water Supply Paper* 1899 – K, 26 pp.

[481] BATHURST, R. G. C. (1970) 'The lithification of carbonate muds', *Proc.Geol.Assoc.* **81,** 429–440.

[482] FORD, D. C. (1971) 'Research methods in karst geomorphology', *Research Papers in Geomorphology, 1st Guelph Symposium 1969* (Sci. Res.Assoc., Canada), 23–47.

[483] PLUHAR, A., & FORD, D. C. (1970) 'Dolomitic karren of the Niagara escarpment, Ontario, Canada, *Z. Geomorph.* **14,** 392–410.

[484] ROQUES, H. (1969) 'A review of present-day problems in the physical chemistry of carbonates in solution', *Trans.C.R.G.* **11,** 139–163.

[485] EK, C., DELECOUR, F., & WEISSEN, F. (1968) 'Teneur en CO_2 de l'air de quelques grottes Belges', *Ann.Spéléol.* **23,** 243–257.

[486] EK, C., GILEWSKA, S. *et al.* (1969) 'Some analyses of the CO_2 content of the air in five Polish caves', *Z.Geomorph.* **13,** 267–286.

[487] BRAY, L. G. (1969) 'Some notes on the chemical investigation of cave waters', *Trans. C.R.G.* **11,** 165–174.

[488] DREW, D. P., NEWSOM, M. D. & SMITH, D. I. (1968), Mendip Karst Hydrology Research Project, Phase 3, Wessex Cave Club.

[489] FORD, D. C., FULLER, P. G., & DRAKE, J. J. (1970) 'Calcite precipitates at the soles of temperate glaciers', *Nature* **226,** 441–442.

[490] BEEDE, J. W. (1911) 'The cycle of subterranean drainage as illustrated in the Bloomington Quadrangle (Indiana)', *Proc. Indiana Acad. Sci.* **20,** 81–111.

[491] RAUCH, H. W., & WHITE, W. B. (1970) 'Lithologic controls on the development of solution porosity in carbonate aquifers', *Inst. Res.Land and Water Resources, Pennsylvania,* reprint series No. 13, **6** (4), 1175–1192.

[492] THRAILKILL, J. (1970) *Solution Geochemistry of the Water of Limestone Terrains,* Univ. Kentucky Water Resources Inst., Lexington, Kentucky, 125 pp.

[493] STELCL, O. (ed.) (1969) *Problems of Karst Denudation,* published for the International Speleological Congress by Inst. Geogr. Brno, Czechoslovakia.

[494] GAMS, I. (1969) 'Some morphological characteristics of the Dinaric karst', *Geogr.J.* **135** (4), 563–572.

[495] ENJALBERT, H. (1968) 'La genèse des reliefs karstiques dans les pays tempérés et dans les pays tropicaux', in *Phénomènes Karstiques,* ed. Fénelon, P., C.N.R.S., **4,** 295–327.

[496] MORAWETZ, S. (1970) 'Zur Frage der Dolinenerstehung', *Z.Geomorph.* **14** (3), 318–328.

[497] NICOD, J. (1967) *Recherches Morphologiques en Basse-Provence Calcaire,* Thesis (Gap, Imprimerie Louis-Jean), 559 pp.

[498] WEYDERT, P. (1970) 'Le Karst des Monts de Vaucluse', Actes de la Réunion Internationale de Karstologie, 1968, *Méditerranée* **7,** 85–91.

[499] MORAWETZ, S. (1968) 'Dolinen auf Pleistozänen Schottenterrassen an der Save', *Z.Geomorph.* **12** (2), 224–230.

[500] QUINLAN, J. F. (1970) 'Central Kentucky Karst', Actes de la Réunion Internationale de Karstologie, *Méditerranée* **7,** 235–253.

[501] WHITE, W. B. *et al.* (1970) 'The Central Kentucky Karst', *Geogr.Rev.* **60** (1), 88–115.

[502] TRATMAN, E. K. (ed.) (1969) *The Caves of North-west Clare, Ireland* (Newton Abbot: David & Charles), 256 pp.

[503] MIÖTKE, F. D. (1968) 'Karstmorphologische Studien in der glazial-überformten Hohenstufe der "Picos de Europa", Nordspanien', *Jahrb.Geogr.Ges.Hannover,* Sonderheft 4, 1–161.

[504] BIROT, P., CORBEL, J., & MUXAIT, R. (1968) 'Morphologie des régions calcaires à la Jamaique et à Porto Rico', in *Phénomènes Karstiques,* C.N.R.S., **4,** 335–392.

[505] WILLIAMS, P. W. (1971) 'Illustrating morphometric analyses of karst with examples from New Guinea', *Z. Geomorph.* **15** (1), 40–61.

[506] THOMAS, T. M. (1970) 'The limestone pavements of the north crop of the South Wales coalfield', *Trans.Inst.Brit.Geogr.* no. 50, 87–105.

[507] DE VAUMAS, E. (1970) 'Formes de relief des grès littoraux du Quaternaire de la Méditerranée Orientale', *Méditerranée* **7,** 151–188.

[508] MOUSSA, M. T. (1969) 'Quebrada de los Cedros, southwestern Puerto Rico, and its bearing on some aspects of karst development',

[509] MARKER, M. E. (1971) *Karst Landforms of the North-east Transvaal,* unpublished thesis, University of Witwatersrand.

[510] RENAULT, P. (1970) *La Formation des Cavernes* (Paris: Presses Universitaires de France), p. 95.

[511] FORD, D. C. (1971) 'Geological structure and a new explanation of limestone cavern genesis', *Trans.C.R.G.* **13** (2), 81–94.

[512] Symposium held in June 1971 on Origin and Development of Caves, *Trans.C.R.G.* **13** (2).

[513] GOODCHILD, M. F., & FORD, D. C. (1971) 'Analysis of scallop patterns by simulation under controlled conditions', *J.Geol.* **79**, 52–62.

[514] WALTHAM, A. C. (1970) 'Cave development in the limestone of the Ingleborough district', *Geogr.J.* **136** (4), 574–585.

[515] WHITE, E. L., & WHITE, W. B. (1968) 'Dynamics of sediment transport in limestone caves', *Nat.Speleol.Soc.Bull.* no. 30(4), 115–129.

[516] WIGLEY, T. M. L., & BROWN, M. C. (1971) 'Geophysical applications of heat and mass transfer in turbulent pipe flow', *Boundary-layer Meteorology* **1**, 300–320.

[517] NICOD, J. (1969) 'Poljes karstiques de Provence, comparaison avec les poljes dinariques', *Méditerranée* **8**, 53–75.

[518] DEMANGEOT, J. (1965) 'Géomorphologie des Abruzzes Adriatiques', *Mém. et Doc. C.N.R.S.*

[519] WHITE, W. A. (1970) 'The geomorphology of the Florida Peninsula', *State of Florida Geol. Bull.* no. 51 (Tallahassee, Florida) 164 pp.

[520] PATERSON, K. (1970) *Some Aspects of the Oxford Region*, unpublished thesis D.Phil. Oxford.

[521] NICOD, J. (1969) 'Sur le régime de quelques sources karstiques de Basse-Provence la problème des réservoirs karstiques', *Bull. Section de Géographie* **80**, 257–320.

[522] PITTY, A. F. (1971) 'Observations of tufa deposition', *Area* Pub. by Inst.Brit.Geogr. **3** (3), 185–189.

[523] BROWN, M. C., & FORD, D. C. (1971) 'Quantitàtive tracer methods for investigation of karst hydrologic systems', *Trans.C.R.G.* **13** (1), 37–51.

[524] DREW, D. P., & SMITH, D. I. (1968) 'Techniques for the tracing of subterranean drainage', *Brit.Geomorph.Res.Group Tech.Pub.*, series A, 36 pp.

[525] NEWSON, M. D. (1969) 'Erosion in the limestone stream system – some recent results and observations', *Brit. Speleol.Assoc.Proc.* **7**, 17–25.

[526] NEWSON, M. D. (1971) 'The role of abrasion in cavern development', *Trans. C.R.G.* **13** (2), 101–107.

[527] GAMS, I. (1970) 'Maximisation of the karstic underground water flow' in 'Examples of the area among the karst poljes of Čerknica and Planina' (in Slovenian – English summary), *Slovenian Acad.Arts and Science, Inst.Karst. Res.* **5** (4), 173–187.

[528] FORD, T. D., & KING, R. J. (1969) 'The origin of the silica sand pockets in the Derbyshire limestone', *The Mercian Geologist* **3** (1), 51–69.

[529] FORD, T. D. *et al.* (1971) 'The Brassington Formation', *Nature, Phys.Sci.,* **231** (23), 134–6.

[530] NICOD, J. (1968) 'Premières recherches de morphologie karstique dans le massif du Durmitor', *Méditerranée* **3**, 187–216.

[531] VOSS, F. (1970) 'Typische Oberflächenformen des tropischen Kegelkarstes auf den Philippinen', *Geogr.Z.*, Wiesbaden **59** (3), 214–227.

[532] BALÁZS, D. (1971) 'Relief types of tropical karst areas', Symposium on Karst Morphogenesis, I.G.U., Hungary.

[533] WILLIAMS, P. W. (1969) 'The geomorphic effects of ground water' in *Water, Earth and Man,* ed. R. J. Chorley.

[534] BATHURST, R. G. C. (1972) *Carbonate Sediments and Their Diagenesis* (Amsterdam, Elsevier), 620 pp.

[535] PETRIK, M. & HERAK, M. (ed.) (1969) *Krš Jugoslavije* **6**, 622 pp. (Zagreb).

[536] WILLIAMS, P. W. (1970) 'Limestone morphology in Ireland' in *Irish Geographical Studies*, ed. N. Stephens and R. E. Glasscock, published by Dept. of Geography, The Queen's University, Belfast, 105–24.

[537] GROOM, G. E. and COLEMAN, A. (1958) 'The Geomorphology and Speleogenesis of the Dachstein Caves', *C.R.G. Occasional Publications* **2**, 1–22.

[538] STRINGFIELD, V. T. and LE GRAND, H. E. (1966) 'Hydrology of limestone terrains in the coastal plain of the S.E. United States', *Geol.Soc.Amer.Spec.Papers* **93**, 46 pp.

[539] BALLIF, P. (1896) *Wasserbauten in Bosnien und Herzegovina* (Vienna).

[540] FORD, D. C. (1971) 'Alpine karst in the Mt. Castleguard area', *Arctic and Alpine Research* **3**, 239 and 252.

[541] LASSERRE, G. (1961) *La Guadeloupe, Étude Geographique*, 2 vols. (Bordeaux).

[542] CORBEL, J. (1947) 'Observations sur le karst couvert en Belgique', *Bull.Soc.Belge Études Géogr.* **17** (1/2), 95–105.

[543] OLLIER, C. D., & BROWN, M. C. (1965) 'Lava caves of Victoria', *Bull.Volcan.* **28**, 215–30.

[544] CIRY, R. (1959), *Ann.Spéléol.* **14**, 23–30.

Index of Authors

Adams, C. 32
Albritton, C. C. 84
Arnberger, E. 138
Ashton, K. 231
Atkinson, T. 132
Aub, C. F. T. 34, 71-2, 127 273-6, 280, 315

Balázs, D. 77, 273, 282, 289, 290
Balchin, W. G. V. 47, 66, 158, 313
Ballif, P. 239
Barrère, P. 267
Bathurst, R. G. C. 10, 13
Baucič, I. 240
Bauer, F. 74, 90-1, 266
Baulig, H. 253, 295, 312
Beede, J. W. 312
Bik, M. 278, 291, 311
Bingelli, V. 42
Birot, P. 32, 253
Bleahu, M. 147
Blondel, F. 289
Bögli, A. 26-7, 35, 42-3, 74, 81-2, 86-7, 100, 131-2, 142, 247, 263-4
Boyd-Dawkins, W. 96, 129, 189
Brain, C. K. 176, 191
Bray, L. G. 31
Bretz, J. H. 129-30, 137, 142-3, 174, 186, 189, 190
Brink, A. B. A. 63, 67
Brongersma, 249
Brown, M. C. 175, 222, 229-31, 249
Drucker, R. W. 172
Buchtela, K. 229
Budel, J. 305
Burdon, D. 4, 222, 227, 318
Burke, J. 168

Casteret, N. 329
Cavaillé, A. 255, 261
Chabot, G. 48, 51, 253
Chaix, E. 74, 92, 100
Chevalier, P. 140, 144, 243

Chilingar, G. V. 11, 12, 28, 38-9
Christ, C. L. 30
Ciry, R. 298
Clarke, F. W. 11
Clarke, M. J. 100
Clayton, K. M. 60, 307
Clozier, R. 48, 50, 59, 115, 117-18, 122-3, 253, 295, 303, 312
Coleman, A. 47, 66, 313
Coleman, J. C. 158
Common, R. 100
Corbel, J. 28, 35, 40, 41, 51, 82, 106, 125, 258, 265, 268-9, 294-5, 298, 301-2, 308
Cosyns, G. 39
Cotton, C. A. 289
Cousteau, J. 212
Cramer, H. 45, 52, 305
Cressey, G. B. 290
Cuisinier, L. 289, 294
Cumings, E. R. 15
Cunningham, F. F. 307
Curl, R. L. 130, 144, 158
Cvijič, J. 1, 3, 44, 46, 52-3, 57, 59, 62, 64-5, 74, 88, 103, 106-7, 110, 120-2, 124, 128-9, 158, 192, 198, 206, 237, 252, 257, 261, 270, 309, 311-12, 314, 329
Czajlik, I. 181

Dakyns, J. R. 96
Daneš, J. V. 70, 270, 274, 294
Davies, W. E. 151, 170, 174, 248, 258
Davis, W. M. 129, 140, 158, 165, 174, 237, 247, 309, 313
Deal, D. E. 161, 190
Demangeot, J. 200
Dicken, S. 63, 313-14
Dongus, H. 305
Doughty, P. S. 22, 100
Douglas, I. 30-2, 40, 42, 294
Dounas, A. 222
Drew, D. P. 30, 229, 245
Drzal, M. 95

Eckert, M. 74, 77, 87, 100
Ek, C. 26, 35
Enjalbert, H. 50, 183
Ewing, A. 40
Eyre, J. 168, 244

Fagg, C. C. 121
Fellows 87
Fénelon, P. 236, 303, 308
Fetzer, W. G. 34
Flathe, H. 273
Foley, I. 151
Folk, R. L. 15-16
Foot, F. J. 96
Ford, D. C. 47, 78, 127, 133-4, 141-2, 145, 149-51, 156, 184, 190-1, 224, 229, 231, 244, 247, 249, 267, 294, 318, 330
Ford, T. D. 261-2
Fournier, E. 3, 213, 329
Franke, H. W. 182
Frey, M. 301

Gams, I. 31, 34-5, 38, 42-3, 113, 135, 139, 145, 154, 162-3, 181, 183, 198, 224, 242, 267, 329
Garrels, R. M. 30
Garwood, E. J. 78
Gerstenhauer, A. 28-9, 40, 224, 274, 280, 284, 286, 296
Gèze, B. 170-1, 184, 186, 188, 190, 213, 303, 329
Gilewska, S. 303
Glennie, E. A. 133, 135-7, 142-3, 151, 168, 231
Goodchild, J. G. 40, 97
Goodchild, M. F. 145
Goodyear, E. 78
Gregory, J. W. 109
Groom, G. E. 32, 35, 219
Grund, A. 1, 70, 104, 192, 235, 252, 270, 274, 278, 309-11
Guilcher, A. 30, 102
Gvozdeckij, N. A. 254, 300, 330

Haserodt, K. 91
Heim, A. 74
Hodgson, A. 105
Holland, H. D. 177
Howard, A. D. 130, 149, 150–1
Hubbard, B. 278
Hull, E. 267
Hutchinson, G. E. 24–5, 31

Jeannel, G. 213, cf. Trombe ref. 57
Jenko, F. 215, 231, 236, 241, 254, 313–4, 319
Jennings, J. N. 15, 26, 66, 77, 84, 93, 161, 165, 171, 180, 186, 202, 206, 278, 283, 285, 291, 296, 301, 304, 306, 311, 314, 330
Jones, R. J. 34, 86–7, 92, 95, 97
Jones, W. R. 93

Kanaet, T. 217
Katzer, F. 235–6, 298, 311
Kaye, C. A. 30, 248
Kayser, K. 198, 204
Kendall, P. F. 23
Kilroe, J. R. 40
King, F. H. 237
King, L. C. 191
Kosack, H. P. 73
Krebs, N. 312
Kunaver, J. 82, 101
Kunsky, J. 46, 113, 180, 184, 308

Lange, A. 144
Lasserre, G. 291
Laudermilk, J. D. 80
Lavalle, P. 54, 68, 317
Lehmann, H. 3, 23, 69–70, 201, 203, 253–4, 270, 273–5, 281, 283, 286, 302, 329
Lehmann, O. 129–30, 140, 198, 215, 238, 244, 247, 273
Letts, S. 221
Lindner, H. 74
Livesey, A. 165
Lobeck, A. K. 108
Longyear, J. 133
Louis, H. 202
Lowenstam, H. A. 12
Lund, 191

McGrain, P. 165
Malott, C. A. 52, 112–13, 123, 155, 165, 184, 211, 263

Marker, M. A. 110
Marres, P. 48, 50
Martel, E. A. 3, 21, 23, 128–9, 137, 186, 212, 236, 243, 311, 329
Martonne, E. de 62
Matchinski, M. 53, 315
Maurin, V. 215, 229–30, 320
Mazloum, S. 227
Mazzetti, H. 273
Mead, D. G. 26, 30, 32, 38
Melik, A. 196
Merrill, G. K. 154
Meyerhoff, H. A. 276
Miall, L. C. 96, 124
Milojević, B. Z. 102, 239, 258
Milojević, S. M. 53
Miötke, F. D. 74, 77, 267
Miskovsky, J. C. 170, 174
Moisley, H. A. 97
Mojsisovics, E. von 3
Monroe, W. H. 89, 171, 254, 277, 279, 286, 288
Moore, G. W. 181, 188, 248
Morawetz, S. 50, 53
Moussa, M. T. 108

Newson, M. D. 235
Nicod, J. 50, 104, 200, 217, 268

Ollier, C. D. 156, 308

Paloc, H. 210
Pannakoek, A. J. 23
Panoš, V. 255, 278, 280, 288, 305
Papakis, N. 321
Partridge, T. C. 63, 67
Paterson, K. 217
Paton, J. R. 283, 285, 314
Peltier, L. 253
Penck, A. 1, 3, 117, 253, 275, 298, 310, 329
Perrin, H. 42
Petrović, J. 240
Pettijohn, K. 14, 15
Pevalek, I. 109
Pfeffer, K. H. 29, 40
Pfeiffer, D. 273
Pia, J. 24
Pickn'ett, R. G. 18, 28, 38
Pigott, C. D. 42, 87, 262, 317
Pilar, J. F. 235
Pinchemel, P. 121
Pitty, A. F. 32, 38, 42, 181, 218, 221, 226, 231, 244, 262, 318

Pluhar, A. 19, 78
Pohl, E. R. 148, 154, 168
Powell, R. L. 148, 211
Powers, R. W. 20
Preisnitz, K. P. 29, 40
Prelević, V. 240
Prestwich, J. 47
Prinz, W. 188

Quinlan, J. F. 52, 166, 255, 298, 300

Railton, C. L. 142
Renault, P. 132, 172, 294, 296, 329
Renwick, K. 157
Reyer, M. 3
Rhoades, R. 151, 238
Richardson, D. T. 218, 223–4
Richter, E. 309
Robinson, E. 318
Roglič, J. 4, 103, 109–10, 115, 117, 130, 192, 197–8, 207, 235, 239, 241, 252, 255, 257–8, 261, 267, 275, 297, 303, 310, 312, 315
Roques, H. 25, 27, 30
Rudaux, 213

St Pierre, D. 146, 265
Sanders, E. M. 312
Sawicki, L. S. 253, 297–8, 309
Sawkins, J. 8, 70
Schmidl, A. 3, 65, 129
Schoeller, H. 24, 28, 32
Schwarzacher, W. 100
Schwarzenbach, G. 30
Scrivenor, J. B. 93
Shaw, T. 158
Shrock, R. R. 15, 184
Siffre, M. 174
Silar, J. 274, 289
Silva, T. da 88
Simpson, E. 23, 137, 151, 238
Sinacori, M. N. 151, 238
Sinker, C. A. 108
Slichter, J. 229
Smith, D. I. 26, 30, 32, 38
Smith, J. F. 84
Smyk, B. 95
Spöcker, R. G. 305
Štelcl, O. 280, 288
Stellmack, J. A. 32
Stevens, G. 213
Stoddart, D. R. 306
Stringfield, V. T. 214
Swainson, J. 213

Sweeting, M. M. 15, 26, 40, 42, 67, 70, 77, 87, 93, 100, 105-6, 108, 143, 161, 165, 180, 186, 200, 202, 206, 214, 224, 228, 238, 249, 254, 268, 273, 275, 283, 285-6, 293, 296, 301, 304, 307, 314, 321
Swinnerton, A. C. 32, 151, 237
Szabó, P. Z. 305

Talent, J. A. 183
Tell, L. 269
Terjesen, S. G. 39
Terzaghi, K. 157, 198, 298
Thomas, T. M. 62, 97
Thornbury, W. D. 313
Thorp, J. 278
Thrailkill, J. V. 133, 140, 159, 189, 248, 278, 288
Tietze, E. 3, 65
Tratman, E. K. 120, 137, 156
Tricart, J. 88

Trombe, F. 18, 26-7, 129, 213, 329
Udden, J. A. 84

Vaumas, E. de 102
Versey, H. R. 42, 72, 276, 325
Verstappen, H. T. L. 39, 277-8, 282, 296, 306
Voss, F. 274

Wager, L. R. 22
Wall, J. R. D. 77, 80, 85, 88, 274, 277, 285, 290, 306
Waltham, A. C. 151
Warwick, G. T. 12, 108, 117, 120-2, 174, 176, 182, 184, 186, 188, 245, 261-2
Wells, A. W. 180
West, T. 61, 96
Weyl, P. K. 35, 85, 130
White, E. L. 172
White, W. A. 206

White, W. B. 21, 32, 40, 52, 133, 135-6, 172, 330
Wigley, T. M. L. 175
Wilcock, J. D. 232
Wilford, G. E. 77, 80, 85, 88, 274, 277, 285, 290, 306
Williams, J. B. 249
Williams, J. E. 35
Williams, P. W. 40, 42, 44, 66, 73, 85-7, 92, 96-8, 100, 155, 205, 216, 220, 245, 273, 275, 278, 291, 314-15, 317
Williams, V. 32, 38, 42, 219
Wissman, H. von 270, 289-90, 293
Woodford, A. O. 80
Wozab, D. H. 249
Wroot, H. E. 23

Zans, V. A. 211, 248, 325
Zötl, J. 215, 229-30, 247, 304, 320
Zotov, V. D. 83

Index

Where a page number is in italics the reference is to an illustration; 'm' indicates a map

Abîme de Rabaoul, Lot 125
Africa, karst in 8
Agen Allwedd, S. Wales 157, 174
Aggressivity, of water 26
Agriculture, and karst 297
Aigoual, Mt., S. France 112
Alberta. *See* Rocky Mts
Algae, and pH 85, 105
Alluvium, and tower karst 292
Alps, karst morphology 8
— snow and dolines 51, 76
— karren 74, 79, 82
— karrenröhren 87
— triassic age in 77
— pavements 100
— potholes 125
— cave types in 140
— ice caves 175
— Julian 101
Alum Pot Hole, Yorks. 90, *106*, 211, 242
Americas, karst in 8, 9, 247
— *see also individual States*
Anastomoses, in caves 142
Anemolites, in caves 187
Anthodites, in caves 187
Appalachian Mts, caves 151, 155, 172, 247
Arabian deserts 293
Aragonite 12, 176, 188
Arctic, karst in 8, 268
— *see also* Vestspitzbergen
Ardennes Mts, Bel. 7, 39
Ariège R., Pyrenees 188
Arize R., S. France 213
Arizona 80
Arnside Knott Weald 100
Asia, tower karst in S.E. 8, 288, *289*, 294
Atiyo shi dai, doline, Japan *48*
Australia, karst in 6, 8, 22, 26
— *see also individual States*
Austrittsstellen 213
Aven Armand, S. France 125, 183
Aven de la Bresse, S. France 64
Axe R., Som. 115

Beach rock 102
Belgium, 7, 39, 104, 108, 151
Bezez el Mugharet, Lebanon 146
Bienne R., Jura 104
Bihač, Bosnia 198
Biomicrites 16, *17*
Black Hills, S. Dakota 189
Blättersteppige (relief) 1
Blocks, deposits of, in caves 176
Blue holes 211
Bogaz *88*, 283
Bohemia, relict and pseudo-karst 305, *307*
Boiling springs 211
Bonheur R., Cevennes 112, 121
Bore passages, in caves 144
Bouts du monde 114
Boxwork, cave forms 190
Bramabiau, Cévennes 121
Brazil 88
Breccias, cave 176
Bristol Univ., Speleological Socy 129, 157
— — Jamaica expd. 325
British Honduras 104, 154–5
— — cockpits *69*
— — limestones 19
— — tower karst 282, 284
British Isles, karst in 7
British Speleological Assn. 129
Buckfastleigh, Devon, caves 157, 174, 189
Burrens, Co. Clare: limestones 19, 21, 34
— trittkarren 81, *82*
— pavements 97
— swallows and caves 120, 146
— perched springs 210
— hydrology 245
— glaciokarst 266

Calcite 12, 176
— cave rafts 189
Calcrete (caliche) 293
California 80, 181

Canada, karst in 8, *78*, 267
— *see also* Rocky Mts
Caprocks, in tropics 280
Carbon dioxide, pressure 32, 34, 35
— — and solution pans 84
Carlsbad Caverns, New Mex. 15, 20, 135, 157–*160*
— cave forms 182, 184, 189
Carran depression, Co. Clare 204–5
Case-hardening, of tropical limestone 279–80
Castleguard, Mt., Alta, Can. *78*, *178*, *264*, 267 *268*
Causse de Camprieu 112
— de Gramat *111*, 123, 208
— de Martel *111*
— de Quercy 50, 123, 125, 303
— Méjean 19, 57, 259
Causses, les, S. France:
— character 48–50, 49, 80, *111*
— limestone 19
— dolines 57
— valley types 104–5, *111*, 115, 118
— swallow holes 122, 125
— poljes 259
— karst phases 303
Cave City Cave, Cal. 181
Cave River Cave, Jamaica 123, 165, 222
Caves 129–191
— terminology 130, 240
— main types 158
— largest known 157–8
— and swallow-holes 123
— and valleys 112, 155
— corridor 146
— vertical 166–*169*, 240
— without entrances 147
— formation, factors in 133–157
— — limestone structure 134–140, *136* 259
— — water flow 140–147, *141*
— — physiography 147–155

Caves, formation, climate 155-7
— and earth movements 170
— air in 131
— collapse *136*, 170 *172*
— springs in 219
— water, studies 26, 31
— — condensation 218
— solution forms, cavities 140ff,
  145, *147*, 243
— — crystals 175
— — dams 186
— deposits 173-191
— — clays, etc. 173
— — ice 174, *175*
— — stalagtites, stalagmites
  177-185
— — rimstones 185-7
— — seepage 187-9
— tropical 283
— dry, in China 290
— in volcanic rock 308
— research on 129, 190
— flow pulse study 232
Cazelle R., S. France 112
Cenotes, Yucatan 216
Čerknica polje 194, *195*, 196
Cetina R., Dalm. 103, 323
Cetinje, Montenegro 192
Chalk, Gt Britain, as karst type 6,
  14, 262
— as limestone 15, 42
— drainage 47, *117*m, 217, 244
Chapel-le-dale, Yorks. *106*m,
  210
Cheddar Gorge 67, 118, 329
— swallow holes 121
China, tower karst in S.E. 288,
  289
Clapham Cave, Yorks. *54*m,
  106-7m, 174, 184, 187, 329
Clapier (limestone surface) 268
Clare Co., limestones 86
— pavements 96
— caves 134-*137*, 146, 149, 157,
  166
— *see also* Burrens; Fergus; Gort
Clay, in caves 173
Climate, and karst 155-7, 188, 270
Clints, limestone blocks *96*, *97*, 98
Cloups (dolines), Quercy 50
Clowders (scales) 97, 59
Coasts, limestone solution on
  102
Cockles, in caves 144

Cockpit country, Jamaica 19,
  69-72, *71*, *271-2*, 276
— caves and water 148, 202, 248
Coloured waters, in karst 110,
  211
Cone karst (Kegelkarst) 69,
  273-80
Coole R., W. Ireland 221
Coral, and karst 8, 12, 20
Corniche, des Causses 114
Corrasion 242
Corrosion landscape 1, 42
Corrosion, mixture 132
Couronne, des Causses 114
Cousteau, Commandant J. 212
Craven faults, Yorks. *106*-7m
Crveno Jezero, Dalm. *241*
Cuba 283
Cutters, *see* Grikes

Dachstein Mts, caves 138, 171
— water tracing in *230*
—*see also* Mammuth Höhle
Dalles (clints) 100
Demänová Caves, Slovakia
  151-*154*
Dams, in js 323
Dan yr Ogof, S. Wales 157
Deckenkarren *94*
Dee R., N.W. Yorks. 105
Denudation, of karst 43, 157, 297
Depressions, factors affecting
  55-6
Derbyshire 32, 42, 43, 108
— caves 181, 262
— dolines 47
— pavements 98
— valleys 104, 112, *116*m, 119,
  121
— *see also* Peak District
Derwent R., Derbys. 108, *116m*
Désert de Platé, Savoy 92, 100
Devon, caves in 102, 176
— *see also* Buckfastleigh
Dinant, Belgium 7
Dobsina ice cave, Slovakia 175
Doe R., Yorks. *106*m
Dolines 44-73, *46-49*, *51*, *54*,
  60-67
— areas notable for 59
— formation and types 49, 55, 62,
  69
— in tropics *67-70*, 69, 293
— flora of 65

Dolines and caves 64, 67
— Einstürz- 64
— d'effondrement 64
Dolomite rock 12, 20
Dome pits 184, 166
Dordogne R., 104, *111*
Dove R., Derbyshire 104, *116*
Dowkabottom, N.W. Yorks. 59
Drips, cave 180
Dry valleys 115,
— in tropics 119
— Derbyshire *116*m
Dubrovnik 214, 324
Dugo, polje 197, 199
Durmitor, Mt., 104
Durness area, Scotland 269
Durognost, indicator 31
Duvno polje 192, 198

Ease Gill Caves, Lancs/Westl'd
  105, 176, *209*m
Eastwater Swallet, Mendips 112
Eccentrics (cave forms) 187
Eisriesenwelt cave, nr Salzburg
  82, 138, 157, 175
Eldon Hole, Derbys. 125
Energoinvest, Jugoslavia 240
Erratic blocks *99*, 264
Estavelles 127, 214

Fatničke polje 194
Faults, and caves 137
Feizor Nick, N.W. Yorks. *114*
Fergus R., W. Ireland, water
  study 220-1
Flachkarren 97
Flint Ridge, *see* Mammoth Caves
Flood pulse system, in tracing
  232-4
Flooding, of poljes 193-4, 203,
  206
Florida 6, 89
— sink holes 216
— springs 208, 211, 214
Flowstone, in caves 185
Flutes, in caves 144
Fluviokarst 259-261, *260*
Fontaine de Vaucluse 141, 212
Fossil karst 300-306
France, karst in 7, 200
— *see also* Causses, les; Jura Mts
Frost and limestones 171
Funnel-karren 81
Fusshöhle (foot-caves) 203

Gacko polje 127, 192
Galway, Co., limestones 86
Gaping Gill cave 166, *167*, 174
Garrigues, S. France 215
Gavel Pot, N.E. Lancs. *209*m
G. B. Cave, Mendips 38, 88,
   *245*m
Gibraltar, cave-shields 188
Giggleswick well, N.W. Yorks.
   213
Glacial erosion, of limestones 264
Glaciokarst 263
Glades, Jamaica 72, *280*
Glamoč polje 199
Glattalp, Switzerland 74, 81, 87
Goenoeng Sewoe, Java *275*
Golconda Caverns, Derbys. 172
Gordale Beck, N.W. Yorks.
   106-7m, 108
Gorges, limestone 104
Gort R., Co. Clare, depressions *66*
— limestones 86, 97
— swallow holes 128
— offshore risings 214
— hydrology 220, 245
Gotland, Sweden 7, 156, 269
Gouffre Grotte Berger, Drôme
   138, 158, *170*
— du Roc de Corne, Lot 112, 125
— de la Pierre St-Martin, Basses
   Pyrénées 158
— de Padirac, Lot 65, *111*m
— de Poudak, Hautes Pyrénées
   213
Gough's Cave, Mendips 185
Gours, rimstone pools 186
Gower peninsula, S. Wales 102
Grassington, Yorks. *107*m
Greece 9, 101
— dolines 59
— poljes 200
— submarine springs 214
— *see also* Ionian Is, Lilaia,
   Parnassus, Proventina
Greta R., N.W. Yorks. *106*m, *119*,
   120, 210, *316*m
Grikes 86, *87*, 227
— relation to runnels *92*
Grotta Gigante, Trieste 157
Grotte de la Cigalère, Ariège 189
— de la Clamouse, Hérault 178
— de la Glacière, Jura 175
— de Pèche-Merle, Lot
Groundwater 218, 235, 247

Guadalupe 20
Guiers Vif cave, Savoy 136, 139
Gurgling Hole, Westl'd *113*
Gypsum, and caves 172, 176, *62*

Harrison Spring, Indiana 211
Heldenfingen, cliff-line of 305
Helictites 187-8
Helks, or clints 97
Hohlkarren *93*
Hollows, *see* Dolines, Cockpits
Hölloch, cave, Switz. 131, 142,
   147, 157, 247, 267
Holokarst 302
Honeycombing, in caves 142
Horton-in-Ribblesdale, Yorks.
   107
How Gorge, Yorks. 105
Hum, village and feature 193, 197
Human activities, and karst 297
Hungary, caves 181
— water tracing 231
— relict karst 305
Hutton Roof Crag, Westl'd *83*, 99
Hydrology, karst 235-251, 319,
   323
— — in Gt Britain 243

Ice, cave 174, *175*
Igue de Gavel, Lot 138
Imotski polje 198, 241
Indiana, dolines *52*
— limestone 87
— swallows 113, 128, 155, 211
— caves 147-8
Indonesia, karst in 290
Ingleborough dist, N.W. Yorks.
   106-7m
— karst features *54*m, 91-101,
   *316*m
— pavements 264-6, *265*, 297
— caves 137, 140, 154, 158, 210
Ionian Is, relict karst 304
Ireland, karst in 6, 7, 302
— limestones 19, 20, 22, 40, 86
— lakes, origin 267
— *see also* Clare Co.
Istria blind valleys 112
— karst 52-3, 208
Impeded drainage, in karst 206
Isotopes, in tracing 229, 244
Italy, poljes in 200, 201

Jamaica 19, 42, 66, 94, *202*m, 271
— drainage features *128*m
— springs 211, 214
— valleys 104, 112, 115
— caves 123, 127-8, *190*
— water 272
— flood pulse technique 234
— karst expedition 325
— *see also* Cockpit country
Jamas, potholes 124, 130
Japan 47, *48*, 59
Java 70, 253, *275*
Jewel Cave, S. Dakota 161, 190
Jointing, in limestone 22, *23*, *105*
Judaea hills 9
Jugoslavia, karst areas *2*m, *256*m
Julian Alps 101
Jura mts, France 48, 51, 52, 115,
   127, 253
Jura, Swabian 211
   Franconian *260*, 304

Kalkklamm 104
Kamenitzas 75, 83
Karren 74-102, *79-99*, *101*
— table of types 75
Karrenfussnäpfe *91*
Karrenrohren 86
Karrentische 264
Karst, world *2*m, *7*m, *256*m
— conferences 3, 253-4
— cyclic theory of 309
— folklore 9, 208
— mineral wealth 326
— non-limestone 255
— studies 2, 315-31
— terminology 1, 3, 44, 65, 122,
   176, 212, 252, 270, 273
— transport, tourism 327
— water projects 320-24
— windows 106
— world research 329-31
— *see also* Tropical karst
Karst en banquettes 263
— en roches moutonnés 263
Karstgassen 291
Karstkuppen 273
Karstrandebenen 204
Kegelkarst 69, 273-80
Kelds (risings) 208
Kentucky 6, 52, 54, 63, 147, 155
— *see also* Mammoth Cave
Kephallonia, Greece 215
Kingsdale, cave, Yorks. 151

Kinvarra, Co. Clare 214
Kluftkarren 75, *86*, *87*, 227
Korana R., Bosnia
Korrosion landschaft 1
Kossovo polje, Serbia 192
Kotlici, dolines *51*
Krakow, Poland *304*
Krka R., Dalm., 103, *104*, *110*
Kupreš, polje 199
Kuppen Alb, Franconia *260*, 305

Lake District, England 83
Lapiés, see Karren 74–102
Lapland 82
Lasko polje 194
Lathkill R., Derbys. 108, *116*m,
  211
Lebanon 52, 69, 101–2, 171
Leck Fell, N.E. Lancs. *209*
Leeds Univ., Jamaica expdn. 325
Lesse R., Belgium 104, 108
Libya 294
Lichens, and limestone solution
  95
Lika R., Dalm. 192
Lilaia Springs, Greece *320–322*
Lily-pads 190
Limestone, karst 10–43
— textures 19, 162
— jointing *22, 23, 105*
— in G.B., as type 263
— in caves 134, 140
— tropical *88*, 270–296
— solution of 24–43
— factors in 31, 161, 223–7
— rates of 42
— by mixture corrosion 131
— underground 131, 161, 168,
  225
— marine 101
— and organisms 85, 88, 105
— see also Vegetation
Litany R., Lebanon 104
Littondale, N.W. Yorks., springs
  214
Livno polje, Bosnia 127, *193*, 196,
  238
Ljubljanica R., Slovenia 115, *195*,
  210
— hydrology 241, *242*
— control 324
Lluidas Vale, Jamaica 202, 282
Lokva R., Slovenia 163
Löne spring, Swabian Jura 211

Long Churn, Pen y Ghent 158
Long Kin potholes, Yorks. 125,
  *54*m, *96*
Lost John's Pot-hole, N.E. Lancs.
  151, 176, *209*m
Lost R., Indiana *52*, 113, 212
Lows, Derbyshire 262
Lug, limestone beds, js 197
Lummelunda Grotte, Gotland
  156
Lune R., N. Lancs./Westl'd 243
Lycopodium, in tracing 229

Macocha doline, Moravia 64
Malaya 93, 104, 277, 285, 289
Malham area, N.W. Yorks 57,
  *58*m, *106–7*m, 204
— — valleys 113, 114, 118
— — waters 32, 108, 226
— — drainage 122, 204, 213, 221,
  243
Mammoth–Flint Ridge caves,
  Kentucky 157, *165*
— — solution features 21, 144–6,
  154
— — cave flowers 189
— — sediments 174, 176
— — breakdown 172
— — hydrology 239
Mammuth Höhle, Dachstn.
  138–9
Manifold R., Derbs. 104, 108,
  121, 122, 135, 155
Marboré ice cave, Pyrenees 175
Marine organisms 14
Master caves 151
Matlock, Derbs. 108
Meanderkarren 75
Mediterranean region 76, 80, 102
— — poljes 220
Mellte R., S. Wales 32, 35, 108,
  169
— — water study 219
Meltwater 265
Mendip Hills, Som., risings 35,
  36–38
— — swallows 123
— — valleys 112, 118, 120
— — dolines 47–9
— — grikes 87
— — depressions 67, 299
— — caves 141–156, *141*, 150,
  156, 176, 190, 264
— — hydrology 224–5, 243–5

Merokarst 252
Meuse R., Ardennes 104, 108
Mexico, caves *73*, 158, 171, 284
— springs 214, 216
— limestones 276
Micrites 16
Micro-organisms, and cave depo-
  sits 190
Mineral deposits 173, 326
Millbridge Cave, Can. Rockies
  135–7, *142–3*
Missouri, State 87, 94, 143, 189
Mixture corrosion 131, *132*
Moking Hurth, Teesdale 137
Montenegro, 47, *48*, 59, 103, 257,
  268
Montpellier-le-Vieux 104
Monuments, weathering of 40
Moon milk 190, 294
Moraines 91
Mogotes, Puerto Rico 278, *281–2*,
  288
Moravia, čs 7, 46, 64, 112, 113,
  184
— — water study 226
Morecambe Bay area, Lancs. 301
Morocco 51, 102
Moss, effect on limestones 95
Moulis cave, Ariège 188

Napier Ra., see W. Australia
Natural arches 108
Neff's Canyon Cave, Utah 158
Neretva R., Hercegovina 103
Nevada, cave shields 188
Newbiggin Crags, Westl'd 98, *23*,
  95
New Guinea 40, 73, 170, 249, 277,
  291
New Mexico 15, 51, 57, 63, 110,
  119, 299
New South Wales, Bungonia 80,
  115, 151
— — — Wee Jasper Caves 26, 66,
  180
New Zealand 83, *91*, 93
Niagaran dolomites 19
Nival karst 263
Nikšić, Montenegro 192, 199, 325
Norway 82, 100, 127, 147, 157
— glaciokarst 265
Notranjska R., Slovenia 65, 112

Obod spring, Dalm. 214

Ogof Clogwyn, S. Wales 137
Ogof Ffynnon Ddu, S. Wales
  135-6, 142-3
— — — cave forms 188-9
— — — water tracing 231
Ombla R., Dalm. 9, 208, 324
Ontario 86
Oolites 15
Organisms, rock-building 12, 14
Orgues, France 47
Otok, doline, Slovenia 65
Ourthe R., Belgium 151

Pacific region 8, 102
Padirac, Lot, caves *111*, 125, 186,
— — tracing 228
Palintest, indicator 31
Parnassos-Itea area, Greece 9, 66,
  200, *201*m, 222, 258, 320, *321*m
Pas de Souey, Tarn 106, 108
Pavements, limestone 91, *95-9*
— types 100, *101*
— and grazing 297
Pazinski Potok, Istria 112
Peak District 33, 261, 301
—*see also* Derbyshire
Peat, and solution 84
Pebbles, as indicators 105, 108,
  174, 249
Pembrokeshire 189
Pen-y-Ghent, N.W. Yorks. 123,
  157, *106-7*
Pendants, in caves 143
Pennsylvania 40, 87
Pepino hills, Puerto Rico 281
Perched water-tables 210
Permafrost karst 255, 268-9
Permeability, of karst 324
Petrifying springs 108
Piani, poljes, Italy 200
Pitches, cave 166
Piva R., Montenegro 103
Pivka R., Slovenia 123, 162
Planinsko polje, Slovenia *195, 196*
Plitvice lakes, Bosnia *109*m
Pocket valleys 113
Pohl cells (cavities) 168
Poland *304*
Poljes 192-207
— principal examples 196-8
— characteristics 199, 200
— main types 207
— inundations 193-4, 206
— tropical 202

Ponors 123, 194, 127
Poole's Cavern, Derbyshire 181
— — water in 222, 244
Popcorn, cave forms 188-9
Popovo polje, Bosnia 193, 197,
  324
Postojna caves, Slovenia 121, 139,
  161
— — as type 158
— — stalactites 181-2
Potholes 124-6, *58*m, *106-7*m,
  *209*m
— *see* individual names
Predjama caves, Slovenia 121,
  162, 163
Proventina cave, Greece 168
Pseudo-karst 306
Puerto Rico, limestone 89, 94, 104
— — collapse doline 67-8
— — caves 155, 171
— — tower karst *277-282*, 288
Punkva R., Moravia 104
Pyrénées, France 74, 125
— cirques 267
— ice caves 175

Quercy, *see* Causse de Q.
Queen of Spain's valley, Jamaica
  202, 211
Queensland, dolines in 294

Rainfall, effects of 6, 239, 298
Rak R., Slovenia 65, 107
Reed's Cavern, *see* Buckfastleigh
Reka R., Istria 208
Relief, in karst areas 6
Resurgences, and groundwater
  169
— terminology of 212
Ribble R., Lancs. 104, *106-7*, 242
Rillenkarren 75, *78-81*
Rimstone 186
—*see also* Flowstone
Rinnenkarren 75, 82, *83*
Rocamadour, Lot, area *111*
Roches peignées 82
Rock milk 190
Rocky Mts, Canada 34, 170
  See also Castleguard Mt, Mill-
  bridge Cave
Rundhockerharst 263-4
Rundkarren 75, 89, *90, 91*, 93
Russia, karst studies 330

Sacktäler 113
St Dunstan's Well, Mendips *29*
Salisbury, Wilts., region 117
Sapping, at spring heads 215
Sarawak, 80, 82, 83, *88*, 94
— tower karst 277, *283*
Saut de la Pucelle, Quercy 123
Scales (dowders) 97
Scallops, in caves 144, *145*
Schichttreppenkarst 100, 263,
  264, 265
Schichttreppenkarst 264
Schneedolinen 52
Schratten 74
Schrattenkalk 77
Scotland, beaches 102
— permafrost karst 269
Scree, in glaciokarst 268
Seekarren 101
Serbia 59, 107, 109
Settle dist, Yorks. *106-7*, 213
Shake-holes, N.W. Yorks. 59, *60*,
  61
Šibenik, Dalm. 110, 198
Silver Springs, Fla 208
Sink-holes, U.S. 52, 216
Sistema della Piaggia Bella, Piedm
  158
Skadar, Lake 194
Skirfare R., N.W. Yorks. *105,
  106-7*m, 108, 174
Škotsjan, Slovenia, doline *65*
— — caves 139, 163, 186
— — valley 107, 112
Skraplje (rinnenkarren) 82
Slovakia, caves *153*, 175
Snow, in potholes 127
— and stalagmites 183
— dolines *51*
Solution basins 83, *84-5*, 86
Solution subsidence *62, 63, 64*
Sorgues R., Vaucluse 210
Sotana de los Golondrinas, Mex.
  158
Sotchs, S. Cent. France 48, 49
South Dakota 189
Sparites 16
Sparry limestones *16, 17*, 21
Speleology, Congresses 130, 275
— Nat. Society, U.S. 247
— studies 329
Speleothems 176
Spitzkarren 75, *84*
Spodmol, cave type 130

Spongework, in caves 142
Springs, karst 210, 208–17
— largest 208
— and relief 215
— Vauclusian 210–*12*
— intermittent *212*–14
— submarine 214–*15*, 325
— water props. 216–17
Stalactites and stalagmites
   176–85, *175*, *177–9*, *182*
— growth of 179–82
— drips 180
— and climate 183
— dating 184
Stalagmites, mud 180
Strugas (bogaz) 88
Sumn, limestone beds, JS
Stylolites 18
Sulphate minerals, and cave collapse 172
Swallow-holes 47, 121, 122–8,
   123, *124*, *126*
— tropical 127, *128*
— control of 323
Swildon's Cave, Mendips 123,
   *245*m
Syngenetic karst 306
Syria, water studies 227

Tallandschaft 1
Tara R., Montenegro 103
Tarn R., S. France 104, 106
Tasmania 19, 93, 127
— poljes 202
— dry valley *118*
— cave pools 186
— tracing in 228, *229*
Teesdale, England 137
Texas 84, 87
Thailand 214
Thermal karst 308
Timavo spring, Slovenia 208
Tissington Spires, Derbs. 105
Tower karst 281–90
— formation of 286, *288*
Transvaal 63, *64*, 81, 110, *94*, 294
Travertine deposits 108
Trebič, type of pothole 124
Trebinjčica R., Slovenia 208, 197,
   323
Tres Pueblos Sink, Puerto Rico *67*
Trichterkarren 81
Triglav area, Slovenia 101, 170,
   265, *266*, 267

Trittkarren 75, *81*, 82
Tropical karst *67*, *69*, 77, 102,
   254, 270–296
— cave features 132, 183–5
— springs 211
— hydrology 248
— climatic aspects 275, 278–9, 294
— *see also* Tower karst
Trou du Glaz, Savoy 144
Trow Gill, Yorks. *118*
Tufa deposits 108–*10*
Tunnel Cave, N.W. Aust. *164*–5
Turloughs, Ireland 205
Twain, Mark 165
Twisleton Scars, N.W. Yorks. *90*,
   92, *96–9*, 268

Underground karst 168
Urspring, Swab. Jura 211
Utah 158
Uvalas *57–59*, *73*

Vah R., Slovakia 154
Vallées reculées 113
Valleys, karst *103–21*
— — allogenic *104*, *105*
— — blind 101, *111*, 112
— — pocket 113, *114*
— — dry 115, *118*, *119*
— — disorganized 120
Vaucluse, Fontaine de 210, *212*
Vegetation, and dolines *52*
— in depressions 72, 84–5
— and karren 79, 94
— and tracing 229
— *see also* Limestones, solution of
Vercors massif, Savoy 51, 138
Verdon R., Provence 104
Vestspitsbergen, Norw. 19, 80,
   84, 119
Victoria, Australia: Buchan–
   Murrindal area *126*m
— limestone texture 19
— river terraces 105
— caves 135, *136*, 138, 151, 155
— stalactites 183
Victoria Cave, N.W. Yorks. 157,
   174
Viet-nam, tower karst in 214, 288,
   289
Virginia 32, 43, 108, 155, 181
Vorfluter 202, 283
Vreli, submarine springs 214
Vrtace, dolines 45

Wales, karst in 62, *63*, 97, 299
— *see also* Agen Allwedd, Dan yr
   Ogof, Mellte R.
Water, quality 30–4, 227
— of karst springs 216–234
— cave 26, 31, 218, 222
— flow, and caves 140, 145
— flow underground 222, 242
— percolation 227
— colour 110, 211
— table 210, 235
— projects, JS 323
— *see also* Hydrology, Limestone,
   solution of
Water tracing 227–233, *230*
— detectors for 228–9
— hydrology and 231
— flood pulse technique *231–3*
Wannenlandschaft 1
Weathering, of limestone 74–102
— of soil 94
— *see also* Karren
Wee Jasper Caves, N.S.W. 26, 66,
   180
Wells, ebbing and flowing 213
West Australia: N.W. limestone
   area
— reef facies 15, 19, *21*
— drainage features 57, *119*
— Brooking Spring *115*
— dry valleys 110, *119*
— solution pans 84
— karren types 80, 82, 88, 93
— pediments 287
— tower karst 291–3, *292*
— caves 135, 283, *284–6*
— Tunnel Cave, Napier Range
   164–5
— Old Napier Downs Cave *186*
— — rimstone dams in 186–7
West Australia: Nullarbor Plains
   66, 84, 294
Westmoreland 98, *23*, *83*, *95*, *113*
West Virginia 112, *94*, 151, *123*,
   210, 260
Wharfe R., Yorks. 104, 105, *106–7*
Whernside Mt., Yorks. *316*,
   *106–7*m
Wiederausflusse 212
Wiltshire, dry valleys *117*
Wookey Hole, Somerset 9, 116,
   212
Wyandotte Cave, Indiana 147
Wye R., Derbyshire *116*

Yorkshire: karst area *54*m, *58*m,
      *106-7*m, *209*m, *316*m
— karst phases 301
— limestones 15-*22 passim*, 124
— soln. factors *18*, 29, 32-9
      passim, 223
— karren types 80, 81, *85*, *86-90*
— pavements *96-7*, *99*, *265*
— swallow-holes 122, *124*

Yorkshire potholes 124-5, 128
— dolines *54*m, 57-8, 61, 65, 67
— valleys 104, *106-7*m, 112, 119
— caves 129-72 *passim*, *134*, *165*
— water studies 218-24
— hydrology 243
— glaciokarst 266-8
— screes 268
— Geological Socy. 243

Zagreb 192
Zanjones, Puerto Rico *89*, 281
Zlebiči (rinnenkarren) 82
Zrmanja R., Dalm. 103
Zugspitz, Bavaria 34
Zvekara (potholes) 124